RETHINKING GLOBAL SECURITY

MEDIA, POPULAR CULTURE, AND THE "WAR ON TERROR"

EDITED BY

ANDREW MARTIN AND **PATRICE PETRO**

RUTGERS UNIVERSITY PRESS

New Brunswick, New Jersey, and London

LIBRARY OF CONGRESS CATALOGING-IN-PUBLICATION DATA

Rethinking global security : media, popular culture, and the "War on terror" / edited by Andrew Martin and Patrice Petro.
     p.   cm. — (New directions in international studies)
  ISBN-13: 978-0-8135-3829-7 (hardcover : alk. paper)
  ISBN-13: 978-0-8135-3830-3 (pbk. : alk. paper)
  I. Security, International. 2. Terrorism and mass media. 3. Popular
culture. I. Martin, Andrew, 1946– II. Petro, Patrice, 1957– III. Series.

JZ5588.R48 2006
973.931—dc22

                    2005024638

A British Cataloging-in-Publication record for this book is available from the British Library

Manufactured in the United States of America

RETHINKING
GLOBAL SECURITY

WITHDRAWN

NEW DIRECTIONS IN INTERNATIONAL STUDIES

PATRICE PETRO, SERIES EDITOR

New Directions in International Studies expands cross-disciplinary dialogue about the nature of internationalism and globalization. The series highlights innovative new approaches to the study of the local and the global as well as multiple forms of identity and difference. It focuses on transculturalism, technology, media, and representation and features the work of scholars who explore various components and consequences of globalization, such as the increasing flow of peoples, ideas, images, information, and capital across borders.

Under the direction of Patrice Petro, the series is sponsored by the Center for International Education at the University of Wisconsin–Milwaukee. The Center seeks to foster interdisciplinary and collaborative approaches to international education by transcending traditional professional and geographic boundaries and by bringing together international and Milwaukee-based scholars, artists, practitioners, and educators. The Center's book series originates from annual scholarly conferences that probe the political, economic, artistic, and social processes and practices of our time—especially those defining internationalism, cultural identity, and globalization.

MARK PHILIP BRADLEY AND PATRICE PETRO, eds.
Truth Claims: Representation and Human Rights

LINDA KRAUSE AND PATRICE PETRO, eds.
Global Cities: Cinema, Architecture, and Urbanism in a Digital Age

ANDREW MARTIN AND PATRICE PETRO, eds.
Rethinking Global Security: Media, Popular Culture, and the "War on Terror"

TASHA G. OREN AND PATRICE PETRO, eds.
Global Currents: Media and Technology Now

FOR SOPHIE AND NATASHA

CONTENTS

ACKNOWLEDGMENTS

Despite the timeliness of its subject matter, this volume was several years in the making. The original impetus for the essays gathered here was an international conference organized by faculty and staff at the Center for International Education at the University of Wisconsin–Milwaukee in the spring of 2003. This conference, entitled "Rethinking Global Security," aimed to expand security studies beyond its traditional emphases on the international system and the nation-state and its military capacities. Interdisciplinary in scope and by design, the conference addressed such issues as global health, the environment, human rights, and peace-building efforts, as well as media, popular culture, and technology. We would like to thank Bob Beck, Terry Miller, Rob Ricigliano, and Kris Ruggiero, our co-organizers of this conference, for helping us bring together such an impressive array of speakers on such a range of issues. We wish we could have included every presentation in this volume.

But in shaping this collection for publication, we chose to emphasize the aspects of security that have been shaped by media and popular culture in the current war on terror. In this regard, we want to express our gratitude to James Castonguay and Tony Grajeda for helping us secure the participation of several scholars who did not attend the conference but whose work we believe is so crucial to "rethinking global security" that it belongs in this collection.

We would like to express our deep appreciation of the College of Letters and Science at the University of Wisconsin–Milwaukee, and especially of Dean Richard Meadows. His ongoing support of the Center for International Education and our efforts to broaden international, interdisciplinary, and intellectual linkages on campus have made this volume possible. We offer our heartfelt thanks to Amy Kuether, who has worked tirelessly on this and other volumes in this series, New Directions in International Studies. We thank Robin Leephaibul, who helped us in the final stages of putting this volume together. And once again, we are indebted to Bobbe Needham for her outstanding copyediting work. Finally, we are deeply grateful to Leslie Mitchner, editor at Rutgers University Press, for her consistently invaluable support, guidance, and assistance.

RETHINKING GLOBAL SECURITY

INTRODUCTION

PATRICE PETRO AND ANDREW MARTIN

This volume brings together ten essays that address multiple constructions of global security, the "war on terror," and subsequent notions of fear, insecurity, and danger in contemporary U.S. media and popular culture.

Why a focus on media and popular culture when thinking about global security? Such a focus might surprise scholars of international studies and international relations.[1] Even the decades-old field of security studies, while recognizing the influence of technology on cultural politics and practices, has not seen the media or popular culture as central to explorations of national or global security.[2] Nevertheless, the proliferation of digital technologies has transformed our experience of near and distant events, including that of war and suffering. In the twenty-first century, the politics of war, terrorism, and security can hardly be separated from the practices and processes of mediation, which continue to expand and intensify. Hence, whether their focus is television, radio, or film, the PATRIOT Act, satellite imaging, or the Internet, all the authors in this volume examine the profound impact of media and popular culture on our political, cultural, and social life. In so doing, they show how both fictional and fact-based threats to U.S. and global security have helped to create and sustain a culture of fear, with far-reaching effects.

Doug Davis's timely consideration of "strategic fictions" in U.S. policy and popular film opens this collection and frames the issues taken up in the essays that follow. Davis explains how U.S. national security analysts routinely invoke narrative fictions from the past and project them into an imaginary future to buttress current security strategies and policies. These "strategic fictions" fill our airwaves and our television, film, and computer screens. Davis contends that they likewise "represent unprecedented future realities that national security strategists themselves must also imagine." To be sure, strategic fictions and future-war planning are not unique to the twenty-first century, as contributors to this volume point out. Nearly half a century ago, cold-war doctrines of deterrence and containment were similarly created and sustained through tales of catastrophic future wars whose scenarios both citizens and defense planners treated as legitimate historical facts. Today, however, we are faced with subtle and not-so-subtle variations on these cold-war narratives of security, insecurity, and imminent danger. Only now, as Davis points out, fears of mass destruction are met not by fantasies of technological wizardry or programs for strategic weapon design but by a revitalized national security policy based on a permanent war strategy.

To illustrate this point, Davis considers President George W. Bush's 2003 State of the Union Address, which made the case for the second Iraq war as part of the larger war on terror. Davis explains that Bush framed his argument for war "not on the strategic fact of an attack that had happened or definitely would happen, but on the strategic fiction of an attack that might have happened on September 11." As Bush famously claimed: "Before September the 11th, many in the world believed that Saddam Hussein could be contained. But chemical agents, lethal viruses and shadowy terrorist networks are not easily contained. Imagine those nineteen hijackers with other weapons and other plans—this time armed by Saddam Hussein. It would take one vial, one canister, one crate slipped into this country to bring a day of horror like none we have ever known." In his analysis of this speech in the context of the history and generic conventions of strategic fiction making, Davis concludes: "A techno-thriller imaginary organizes U.S. global policy in the twenty-first century. Strategic fictions have returned from the cold war, and the United States has once again started a grand fight against its own worst enemy—its future." Indeed, Bush's strategic fiction about Hussein and weapons of mass destruction, extrapolated from the first Iraq war and read through the attacks of 9/11, creates the conditions for a war on terror without end in the twenty-first century.

And yet, while strategic fictions have supplied the rationale for waging war, they have simultaneously provided alternative visions, insights, and ideals. Such is the case with many of the texts analyzed here, whether they emerge from popular culture, satellite imaging, radio, or the Internet, or from the act of critical analysis itself. Indeed, given that fact-based fictions and fictionalized facts have organized so much of our media culture and so many of our national security priorities, critical analysis—the careful attention to media content, form, structure, temporality, and historical context—remains among the most strategic activities that students, scholars, and citizens can engage in today. This volume is dedicated to providing such strategic thinking by exploring the complex relationships among media, popular culture, and global security, and by doing so across a wide variety of interrelated texts and forms: security documents and policies, film, television, satellite images, radio, and photography.

Taking up the challenge to think critically about security, several of the authors begin by examining the rhetoric, grammar, and motives of key terms and concepts, notably "security," "terror," "danger," and "war." For Mary Layoun, this involves careful review of such terms' history and meaning to demonstrate how current policies (such as the USA PATRIOT Act) and practices (Israel's "security wall") are predicated on a deeply problematic logic. "Security," she explains, literally means to be safe or free from danger (in the Latin sense of "without care"). But it also carries with it an alternative and equally familiar definition of "something given, deposited, or pledged to make certain the fulfillment of an obligation." "Terror," too, she contends, is a complicated term. The word first entered French in the eighteenth century as a term for "state terrorism" or "government by intimidation as directed and carried out by the party in power." However, it quickly came to signify actual and rhetorical threats—both real experiences and projected fears. Layoun writes: "Terrorism is a violently and for some often mortally performative act that seeks to produce an effect, not only on those who bear the brunt of the physical attack but, more crucially, on a larger audience who witnesses the event." "Security" and "terror" are thus bound up with notions of freedom and obligation, physical coercion, and performative display. Although rooted in earlier times and traditions, they are tailor-made for the information age. Layoun examines their circulation and meaning in current security policy and military practice and concludes by arguing that there can be no security without freedom, and no freedom without obligation. This is an obligation, moreover, whose contours are beginning to emerge in works of fiction and criticism that explore new ways of imagining and speaking about "security" not simply as the absence of fear, but as "a pledge of human responsibility in the name of social justice."

Marcus Bullock expands on these observations in an essay that examines the role of Western intellectuals in providing a rationale and a motive for the irresistible appeal of danger in the modern age. Bullock explains how the emergence of new military technologies in the nineteenth century transfixed a generation of thinkers such as Friedrich Nietzsche, Ernst Jünger, and Walter Benjamin. The technological transformation of the visible world—through warfare, as well as through such media as photography and film—fascinated many intellectuals, who were compelled to write and theorize about images of destruction and danger as a preeminent value. Indeed, danger as a value became an ideal that thrived in modern entertainment forms because it offered the promise of an intensity of experience at once entirely artificial and intensely lived.

Bullock relates this philosophical tradition to our current confusion about terrorism in the United States: "That we should feel materially disquieted at the thought of attacks by terrorists is not irrational. That we should have permitted ourselves to launch our entire society into the national obsession with homeland security, with the shifting colors of alerts, with encroachments on civil liberties, certainly amounts to an irrational exaggeration." To compare the attack on the World Trade Center to the attack on Pearl Harbor, he argues, "reveals a comparable apocalyptic component, insofar as each event contained the idea of a hostile manifestation from an alien realm, mysterious, impenetrable, and Eastern." But the attack on Pearl Harbor came from an organized imperial state with a huge modern navy and superior air power, whereas the attack on the World Trade Center was led by a "semi-organized group of murderous eccentrics." So how do we account for the exaggeration of the dangers now facing us, or the palpable sense of fear in the war on terror today? Bullock answers: "Security is a value to us, but the sense of danger is a value as well. . . . We are always traveling toward a future we do not yet know. We have to imagine ourselves changed, and continuing to change, until we disappear from our own clear sight. This is the character of modernity. To think about ourselves, therefore, cannot be accomplished without entertaining images of our own destruction."

Of course, the future orientation of our own modernity, with its long-standing investment in entertaining images of security as well as danger, has now encountered itself in a new catastrophic narrative that imagines an endless war that must be waged and won against "a world of terror and missiles and madmen." In a prepared speech given at the Citadel on 23 September 1999, President George W. Bush painted a dire picture of the world. It is "a world of terror and missiles and madmen," he said. He added, "We see the contagious spread of missile technology and weapons of mass destruction." "This era of American pre-eminence," he elaborated, "is also an era of car bombers and plutonium merchants and cyber terrorists and drug cartels and unbalanced dictators." This is the starting point for Robert Ricigliano and Mike Allen's essay, which reconsiders notions of terror and terrorism as deployed by the Bush administration in policies that reproduce many of the terms and ambitions of the cold war. The authors argue that just as cold-war rhetoric simplified U.S. national security policy nearly fifty years ago, the current war on terror is misguided in its identification of the enemy and its own mission and goals. Ricigliano and Allen point out that while the Bush administration is quite deliberate in using the word "war" in its approach to dealing with terrorist threats, its strategy for ending terrorism "capture by capture, cell by cell, and victory by victory" creates numerous problems, not just for the global order but for U.S. security as well.

This is because terrorism is a tactic and not an enemy or adversary; it can never be completely eliminated, only managed and controlled. The preemptive use of military force against adversaries who are stateless and elusive, moreover, strains international relationships, violates international treaties and statutes, and weakens the very infrastructure required to respond to global threats. The revival of cold-war thinking in the twenty-first century makes it impossible to identify and counter the complexity of security threats in a globalized world: AIDS, SARS, and other public health threats, armed conflicts outside of Iraq, humanitarian crises and natural catastrophes worldwide. Ricigliano and Allen argue that there has never been only one threat to U.S. national security, either today or in the recent past. "Terrorism will always be with us," they conclude, "just as weak and ineffective states will always exist. . . . Millions of dollars are spent each year on flood control, not in an effort to stop the rain from falling but to control its destructive effects. Likewise, international mechanisms need to be developed that will work toward the prevention of state failure, the rebuilding of failed states, and postconflict reconstruction." Only in this way will the United States and the international community begin to address the multiple and complex threats to global security today.

This point has not been lost on the professional field of security studies, which understands that the challenge is no longer how to manage an arms race or superpower competition, but how to deal with health and environmental crises, as well as ethnic, nationalist, and other forms of conflict. In his contribution to this collection, Andrew Martin looks critically at the work of one such national security expert, Anthony Cordesman, chair of the Center for Strategic and International Studies. Curiously, as Martin points out, Cordesman frames his argument about the unpredictability and uncertainty of international relations and global security today by referencing a long-running television series, *Buffy the Vampire Slayer*. "The seemingly nonmainstream implication of Cordesman's argument," Martin writes, "is that a popular TV show based on the horror film and its subgenre of vampirism has much, if not more, to tell us about national security than have those who are actually responsible for planning and implementing security policies: our elected officials, administrative experts, and policy analysts." While Martin agrees with Cordesman that popular culture often provides more complex worldviews than does current security policy, he expands on Cordesman's example of *Buffy the Vampire Slayer* to make a larger argument about the role of popular culture in contemporary conceptions of global threats and notions of national security.

Indeed, given that most of our shared cultural signs and signifiers are embedded in texts of popular culture, Martin argues that it is not surprising that popular cultural references permeate multiple and often disparate discourses and practices, from print journalism to broadcast news to security studies. And as media scholars have often remarked, while journalism and network news are constrained from showing the horrific effects of war, torture, and death, the representation of such graphic detail is the stock-in-trade of popular fiction. Like Cordesman, Martin contends that *Buffy the Vampire Slayer* is "unique in U.S. popular culture in that it at once registers the changed reality of post-cold-war thinking (constant threats in a borderless world) and proposes a collaborative, group effort to examine, research, debate, and dispel these threats." But unlike Cordesman, Martin shows how the TV series is built on several overlapping and preexisting narratives (which are generically conventional and self-referential) and thus how it allows a wider mediation on danger and security than Cordesman imagines. *Buffy the Vampire Slayer*, in other words, is not simply a TV show that illustrates or reflects current global threats and uncertainties. It is rather both a complex cultural text and an example of how popular fictions become so embedded in our culture (just as reporters are embedded in military units) that their references seem obvious, ubiquitous, and invisible—like popular culture itself.

Patricia Mellencamp also recognizes the pervasive impact and complexity of popular culture and remarks briefly upon the importance of popular narratives in film and television today. She focuses her essay, however, on official stories about security and danger in a distinctive argument about the aftereffects of television news coverage of the first and second Gulf Wars. Drawing on Freudian theories of obsession, compulsion, and revision, Mellencamp argues that contemporary war and catastrophe coverage is remarkable for the ways it severs causal connections through repetition and paradoxically removes news events from their context and setting. The 1991 Gulf War, she points out, was viewed from the air, where the effects of bombs on the ground could not be seen. The 2003 Gulf War coverage, by contrast, showed us little beyond an empty parking lot, shot by a stationary surveillance camera that recorded only flashes of the bombing in the distance. "By banishing bodies, by eliminating shots of the people on the ground, and in the cool demeanor of third-person reporter-speak, TV withdrew affect," Mellencamp argues. The result has been a mode of reception at once fearful, distracted, and detached, produced through relentless talk and a repetitive focus on granular, nearly indecipherable images.

While popular narratives provide compelling stories about war and combat and affective terror, Mellencamp argues, television news has dispensed with all of this and refigured the vaunted status of the image and the assumed veracity of sight. Simply put, seeing on TV is not believing, since TV news coverage exists only to create anxiety (through obsessive thought) that requires more TV viewing (in the manner of a compulsion), which raises the level of fear in a repetitive loop: anxiety triggers viewing, viewing triggers anxiety, and all we see are repetitive images—the same image of the same parking lot, different day and time of day, viewed endlessly from the same vantage point, buried in words and finally discounted altogether. Mellencamp concludes: "The sheer number of sights on TV—of locales, of hundreds of reporters reacting, of twenty-four-hour coverage—ultimately conceals the paucity of meaningful visual information."

Lisa Parks draws on Mellencamp's insights to make a similar argument about vision, remoteness, and abstraction in the war on terror in her consideration of satellite imaging and its deployment as visual evidence for policy making and persuasion. Satellite images, Parks explains, are typically aligned with official forms of knowledge that draw on the authority of meteorology, photography, cartography, and state intelligence to produce their reality and truth effects. Historically, the United States has used satellite images to isolate and contain threats to national security and to rationalize U.S. interventions around the world. Unlike television news, which presumes to render information within a visual and aural field, satellite images appear to most people as sites of abstraction that must be infused with meaning in order to signify anything other than their own orbital perspective. "The satellite's gaze is trained on particular places for particular reasons," Parks points out, but a satellite also "randomly acquires information about all kinds of places for no apparent reason at all." It can thus be mobilized either as a representation of state authority or as a completely abstract and uncertain point of view.

Parks underlines this contradictory status of satellite imaging through an analysis of Secretary of State Colin Powell's 2003 presentation to the UN Security Council in which he used declassified satellite images of alleged weapons facilities to provide "undeniable proof" of Iraqi treaty violations. Powell's presentation preempted regularly scheduled programming on the major U.S. networks, and he spoke uninterrupted for more than an hour to Security Council members and the U.S. television public. For Parks, more remarkable still was Powell's stately use of the terms of close analysis and his decoding of eleven satellite images in an interpretation that strained credulity and ultimately revealed these images as sites of contestation and insecure meaning rather than as fields of objective, official truth. The point of Parks's own analysis is not simply to unmask Powell's inconsistent and arbitrary use of forms of evidence. She reviews the rationales for rendering, viewing, and publicizing satellite images—and exposes these to scrutiny and debate: "We need to infuse military satellite images with public debates, countervisions, and situated knowledges precisely because they appear so far removed from spheres of civic and public life." Witnessing in the information age, Parks concludes, involves being responsible for what one sees, recognizing horrific acts that are not meant to be seen, and questioning interpretations that might not be part of the visual field.

Of course, information in our information age is as much aural as it is visual and image based. As James Castonguay argues in his essay, media scholars have generally neglected the role of radio in their analyses of security and the war on terror, even though, since 9/11, radio has experienced the most radical and undemocratic of transformations in the United States, and despite Americans using radio as their primary source of information in the weeks following the World Trade Center and Pentagon attacks. Castonguay traces the increasing concentration of ownership in the radio, television, print media, and Internet industries and explores the consequences for U.S. political and popular culture. These include radio talk shows dominated by conservative, pro-Republican political viewpoints, the collusion between the Bush administration and executives of all major media outlets, and the censorship of those who, like Howard Stern, would criticize the Bush administration's policies or tactics in the war on terror.

Castonguay emphasizes that contemporary developments in radio cannot be separated from more disturbing trends of media conglomeration, which are as much industrial as textual, with a reach that is local and global. In a November 2001 meeting with presidential advisor Karl Rove and executives from major media industries, Motion Picture Association of America president Jack Valenti reminded those present of the global scope of U.S. media imperialism: "We are not limited to domestic measures," he said. "The American entertainment industry has a unique capacity to reach audiences worldwide with important messages." Castonguay recognizes that despite its imperial reach and ambition, the media does provide forums for new forms of dialogue, discussion, and distribution, often circulating otherwise censored audio texts and video images. But rather than celebrate oppositional readings of these new interpretative communities, Castonguay remains skeptical about the creative or political potential of media outlets, given the unprecedented structural complicities he outlines in his essay: "Under current conditions, . . . the complicity between U.S. media conglomerates, the government, and the military create a context of reception with limited possibilities for oppositional or politically progressive readings. In the end, the 'war on terror text,' like the Bush administration's policy toward Iraq, remains both constrained and managed, offering little room for negotiation."

There can be no question that the war on terror creates a myriad of challenges for critical analysis, especially for analysis of media and popular culture. When news comes to us sanitized and prepackaged, and when media institutions are themselves deeply implicated in state censorship, policy making, and war promotion, it would indeed appear that the "danger market" is thriving while dissent has become virtually impossible. As many of the contributors to this volume suggest, the quest for an elusive security against an equally elusive threat in a culture driven by fear and suspicion makes it hard to escape feeling a deep sense of distrust—of images, stories, reports, and policy decisions—that accrues from the powerful and far-reaching institutions of government and media alike.

Yet the final two essays in this collection argue otherwise. Wendy Kozol and Rebecca DeCola explore complex meanings of citizenship in photographs produced and published by mainstream and progressive news media following the U.S. bombing in Afghanistan. The authors suggest that gendered and racial conventions produce an ideal of citizenship that conforms to U.S. foreign policies. And yet these conventions are often destabilized and reconfigured in acts of viewing and reception. Even the infamous Abu Ghraib photographs resist a unified meaning and gaze. For example: "what does it mean for Americans in different historical locations, such as African Americans or Arab Americans, to look at the pictures of [Lynndie] England holding an Iraqi prisoner by a leash? Surely spectators' multiple and differential social positions shape the historical resonances of this image." Presented in these photographs without faces, names, or life histories, the Abu Ghraib prisoners appear to be simply victims; but if we look elsewhere, as Kozol and DeCola do in this essay, it becomes possible—indeed, critically important—to understand how images circulate within more complicated spaces that challenge simplistic binaries of East and West, first and third world, and colonizer and colonized.

In the final essay, Tony Grajeda similarly challenges unexamined assumptions about viewer passivity and government manipulation in today's media environment. Taking the 1999 film *Three Kings* and the photographs of torture and abuse that emerged from the Abu Ghraib detention facility as his primary examples, he contends that popular culture has contributed to a critique of the war on terror in unflinching and visceral ways. One of the few films to date about the first Gulf War, *Three Kings* narrates the role of mainstream media in war and foregrounds its own status as mediated text. As one character in the film puts it, "This is a media war," although, in this instance, not without bodies in pain and scenes of torture and interrogation.

As Grajeda explains, *Three Kings* returns to our field of vision the casualties of war lost in mainstream coverage with the film's "unblinking shots of death and dying, of bodies in distress, of corpses scorched beyond recognition." The film discusses what CNN failed to report or show, such as Iraqi soldiers being burned alive. It contains scenes of Iraqi soldiers relaxing in a bunker, watching the Rodney King video. It includes "anatomy lessons" that demonstrate what happens when a bullet pierces flesh, illustrated by a shot zooming much like a bullet itself through a body. Finally, there is a brutal interrogation sequence in which a U.S. soldier is tortured not for information but for reeducation. When compared with the Abu Ghraib photographs, the brutality of this sequence suggests the difference between forcing a body under duress to surrender meaning for purposes of information and forcing a body to serve as proof of a brutal display of power and domination. In Grajeda's view, works of narrative fiction like *Three Kings* are thus uniquely able to disrupt the seemingly closed circuit of highly managed media representation. Not all texts, and not all images, are created equal, he explains, and by restoring historical memory to the first Gulf War, *Three Kings* challenges "the unacknowledged media amnesia accruing around the latest conflict and thereby potentially returns us to the ground of history itself."

This effort is part of the larger ambition of this collection: to restore historical memory to our understanding of past and present wars, to challenge the amnesia surrounding official media coverage, and to rethink notions of global security that posit a single response to danger and terrorist threat: permanent war. As Marcus Bullock puts it, "That we should feel ourselves embroiled in a war for the very survival of civilization manifests an apocalyptic idea pure and simple—although apocalyptic ideas themselves are seldom pure and never simple." The essays gathered here aim to complicate ideas that are today routinely represented as equally pure, simple, and apocalyptic, and thus to inspire further thinking and debate about global security as it is imagined in the media, popular culture, and the war on terror.

NOTES

1 Indeed, the role of media and popular culture remains unexplored in much international studies scholarship. In a recent essay, for example, James H. Mittelman argues for a "critical" approach to global issues: "At a minimum, a critical approach is suspicious, troubling, and open-ended in its search for knowledge. ... Critical intellectuals attempt to sharpen the tensions, gain leverage from them, and go against means established by such institutions as the mass media, incorporated into culture goods, and apparent in imaginary realms (e.g., films, television, and magazines). *These products can diminish the capacity to think independently and make individuals more susceptible to the language of competitive market relations*" (220, our emphasis). On the next page, Mittelman writes: "Cognizant of the dimension of hierarchical power relations, time, and space, intellectuals embarking on reconstructing knowledge face the difficult challenge of constructing *grounded utopias*. I use the term grounded utopia to mean an imagined alternative that never existed; yet, a future, or futures, rooted in real historical tendencies and embodied practices" (221). For media and humanities scholars, Mittelman's condemnation of popular culture and simultaneous call for "grounded utopias" rooted in real historical tendencies

and embodied practices misses the point entirely. Media and popular culture offer precisely the grounded utopias Mittelman calls for but fails to recognize or explore. See James H. Mittelman, "What Is Critical Globalization Studies?" *International Studies Perspectives* 5 (2004): 219–230.

2 Two books that offer insight into national security and cultural politics are Jutta Weldes, ed., *Cultures of Insecurity: States, Communities, and the Production of Danger* (Minneapolis: University of Minnesota Press, 1999), and Peter Katzenstein, *The Culture of National Security* (New York: Columbia University Press, 1996). These works explore how notions of security were challenged and evacuated of meaning with the end of the cold war and wrestle with inherited models in security studies.

FUTURE-WAR STORYTELLING

NATIONAL SECURITY AND POPULAR FILM

DOUG DAVIS

Popcorn and Politics

A specter is haunting America—the specter of destruction. "In the aftermath of Osama bin Laden's 9/11 assault, which awakened the world to the reality of global terrorism, it is incumbent upon serious national security analysts to think again about the unthinkable," write Graham Allison and Andrei Kokoshin in the fall 2002 issue of the *National Interest*. A decade after the end of the cold war, and following a brief respite when "the threat of nuclear weapons catastrophe faded away from most minds," the United States along with Russia once again faces the threat of nuclear attack. "Consider this hypothetical," Allison and Kokoshin continue: "A crude nuclear weapon constructed from stolen materials explodes in Red Square. A fifteen kiloton blast would instantaneously destroy the Kremlin, Saint Basil's Cathedral, the ministries of foreign affairs and defense, the Tretyakov Gallery, and tens of thousands of individual lives. In Washington, an equivalent explosion near the White House would completely destroy that building, the Old Executive Office Building and everything within a one-mile radius, including the Departments of State, Treasury, the Federal Reserve and all of their occupants—as well as damaging the Potomac-facing side of the Pentagon."[1]

As veteran U.S. and Russian security specialists respectively, Allison and Kokoshin admit that this scenario is an "unprecedented event."[2] Much as a global nuclear war fought with tens of thousands of strategic weapons has no precedent in military history, no act of terrorism anywhere near as technically complex or physically destructive as an act of nuclear terrorism exists in the historical record. Unfortunately, the parallels between nuclear war and nuclear terrorism only begin here. As was the case with global nuclear war in the cold war, that an act of nuclear terrorism hasn't happened hardly means it can't happen. Quite the opposite. In the national security planner's world, that nuclear power technology, terrorists, and hostile nation-states exist at all means that it surely can.

Allison and Kokoshin employ the vintage language and verve of RAND strategist Herman Kahn's 1962 hair-raiser about how to fight a nuclear war, *Thinking about the Unthinkable*, to drive home their point that the prospect of nuclear terrorism, like that of nuclear war before it, is all too thinkable and must therefore be meticulously analyzed and planned for. It is a difficult and often thankless job to chart the course of catastrophic attacks and imagine responses to them. Yet the job has been done numerous times, long before 9/11, for the entertainment of millions of readers and filmgoers who have witnessed in hundreds of books and films the kinds of catastrophes that serious national security analysts are now called upon to prevent.[3] As with the threat of nuclear war, today's nuclear terrorism was yesterday's fiction.

Allison and Kokoshin invoke the precedent of narrative fiction to emphasize the strategic fact of their nuclear terrorism scenario. Analogous events have happened, albeit between the covers of techno-thrillers as dense as the global networks and military systems they portray. "Psychologically," the authors write, "such a hypothetical is as difficult to internalize as are the plot lines of a writer like Tom Clancy (whose novel *Debt of Honor* [1994] ends with terrorists crashing a jumbo jet into the U.S. Capitol on Inauguration Day, and whose *The Sum of All Fears* [1991] contemplates the very scenario we discuss—the detonation of a nuclear device in a major American metropolis by terrorists). That these kinds of scenarios are physically possible, however, is an undeniable, brute fact."[4]

That national security analysts invoke narrative fictions set in the near future to buttress today's strategic facts underscores the centrality of future-oriented and narrative ways of thinking in what historians and security specialists are already calling the second nuclear age.[5] It also presents metaphysical and ethical quandaries that once haunted the cold-war arms race: Do these threats really exist? Dare defense planners think otherwise? The United States may or may not be threatened by real weapons of mass destruction in the hands of terrorists, either at this very moment or in the future. (If the history of surprise attacks upon U.S. soil offers us any guidance here, we may know the truth of such claims only tragically after the fact.) However, the country certainly is threatened by *stories* of mass destruction. So far, such attacks have occurred only in expert scenarios and narrative fictions set in the future, the realm of the imaginary. Yet the mere possibility of their existence in the future, regardless of their verified reality, now determines the national security strategy of the United States, which since 9/11 has sanctioned the waging of two wars.

The nuclear terrorism scenario that Allison and Kokoshin cite from Tom Clancy's *Sum of All Fears* reached new heights of cultural prominence when Paramount released a film based on the book in May 2002. Combined with an aggressive promotional campaign—movie trailers and television commercials featuring the conspicuous nuclear destruction of a city, special premieres for U.S. senators and Bush administration officials in Washington—the timing guaranteed the film's topicality and notoriety.[6]

Production on *The Sum of All Fears* began well before 9/11.[7] It was supposed to be a mildly cautionary but mostly escapist thriller with a deliberately irrelevant plot: CIA analyst Jack Ryan is pitted against a global cabal of neo-Nazis who conspire to kill the president of the United States with a long-lost nuclear weapon. The weapon is smuggled into the United States and detonated at a Baltimore football game to set in motion a chain of events that leads to a total nuclear war between the United States and Russia, from whose ruins a new Third Reich will emerge, maybe even a Fourth Reich. That unlikely story experienced a sea change when released seven months after 9/11. "A year ago, you'd have said, 'great popcorn film,'" the film's director, Phil Alden Robinson, told CNN. "Today you say, 'that's about the world I live in.'" Bush administration officials were quick to agree. "It was genuinely scary," Deputy Secretary of Defense Paul Wolfowitz told *Variety* following the Washington premiere. "Arguably, in the real world we are dealing with this every day."[8]

In this essay I argue that the national security strategy of the United States is predicated upon just such future-war storytelling, which occurs most visibly in Hollywood film, where the "Bush revolution" in foreign and domestic policy is writ large for a mass audience. An analysis of two films about nuclear terrorism that straddle the attacks of 9/11—Robinson's *Sum of All Fears* (Paramount Picture's most profitable film of 2002) and Mimi Leder's *Peacemaker* (released to much fanfare in 1997 as the first film from Steven Spielberg's new DreamWorks studio)—shows how fictions of nuclear terrorism help build its political reality by representing in dramatic, technologically systematic detail those catastrophic events that the new *National Security Strategy of the United States of America* (the *NSS*) promises to prevent.

Strategic Fiction and the History of the Future

Fictions of nuclear terrorism have become part of a privileged class of story-telling that represents the strategic facts of U.S. national security. Straddling fact and fiction, they are "strategic fictions," tales of catastrophic future wars whose scenarios everyday citizens and defense planners alike treat as seriously as historical fact. Strategic fictions became an intrinsic part of U.S. national security strategy during the cold war with the formulation of a policy of nuclear defense built on an imagined catastrophic future war. Imagined nuclear terrorism and other kinds of indefensible catastrophic attacks now occupy the central place in the imaginary of national defense once held by the vision of nuclear war. The events described by these stories and scenarios are not real, but they could be. For national defense planners, that is reality enough. The catastrophic near-future worlds these imaginary narratives build are, in a dramatic way, the future of our world. The threats they represent are a license to act, to arm, and to war.

To understand the technological world of threat and response that strategic fictions of nuclear terrorism help build, it is helpful to understand the storytelling tradition they come from. The high-tech storytelling in *The Sum of All Fears* and *The Peacemaker* stems from a popular literary genre that critics in the 1980s identified as the "techno-thriller" (both films are based on books: the first on Clancy's book of the same name and the second on Andrew Cockburn and Leslie Cockburn's 1997 new-journalistic exposé on "loose nukes," *One Point Safe*). The heroes of both films pit advanced technology against advanced technology. To see these fictional professionals at work is to witness acts of cybernetic wizardry. In *The Sum of All Fears*, members of the CIA and the Department of Energy's Nuclear Emergency Search Team defuse World War III in the nick of time by using radiological analysis to identify the U.S. components of a lost Israeli bomb rebuilt in a secret Russian lab and then exploded in Baltimore. In *The Peacemaker*, the National Security Council's Nuclear Smuggling Group teams up with Army Special Forces to stop a nuclear bomb from blowing up the UN building in New York City, calling upon the combined forces of satellite imaging, airborne radiation sniffing, and the mastery of the physics of nuclear detonators to help them do so.

The techno-thriller, a specific U.S. kind of storytelling about fighting high-tech war, became a literary phenomenon during the Reagan administration with the publication of books such as Tom Clancy's *Hunt for Red October* (1984) and *Red Storm Rising* (1986).[9] Expressions of the Reagan administration's view of the world, according to historian Walter Hixson, techno-thrillers reasserted U.S. military and social power along with traditional values of male identity in the post-Vietnam, postfeminist era.[10] They are heroic war-fighting fantasies for an era not of heroic wars, but of nuclear brinksmanship and heroic diplomacy. Part ideology and part propaganda, they reassert the value of conventional weapons systems and conventional people by showing how both would be essential in the next grand conflict, assuming there ever was one.[11]

Techno-thriller authors during the cold war sold fantasies about fighting a nonnuclear war against the Soviet Union. Soon after the cold war they shifted to telling stories that pitted cold-war military and intelligence institutions against terrorists.[12] Changing enemies did not change the genre. The thrillers retained their technical bent and futurological vantage, telling war-on-terror stories before there was a war on terror.

The techno-thriller is a versatile reinvention of the tale of future-war fiction, a genre that was first popularized in Europe in the late nineteenth century as a response to the century's sweeping technological and scientific developments.[13] With narratives putting heavy emphasis on new weapons and tactics, the future-war tale constituted, as I. F. Clarke describes, "a new type of purposive fiction in which the whole aim was either to terrify the reader by a clear and merciless demonstration of the consequences to be expected from a country's shortcomings, or to prove the rightness of national policy by describing the course of a victorious war in the near future." In the nineteenth and early twentieth centuries, hundreds of such tales were written by military officers, journalists, and fiction writers. A regular feature of newspapers, monthly periodicals, and serial magazines, each dramatized and opined upon "a major anxiety of the moment" felt by the West's great powers. Tales of future war were often written as propaganda for or against a specific course of action (don't build a tunnel under the English channel, invest in blimps).[14] Transported to the United States, the tale of future war sold "prophecies of doom" to the nation, first by dramatizing the weakness of the U.S. Navy and going on to perpetuate what H. Bruce Franklin calls the U.S. "cult of the superweapon" by presenting Edison-like feats of technological wizardry that either save the nation at war or change the course of world history.[15]

Once a goad to a course of national strategy, one kind of cautionary future-war storytelling became a literal expression of national strategy after World War II: nuclear war storytelling. Nuclear war stories had been written well before the invention of the atomic bomb, most notably by H. G. Wells, whose novel *The World Set Free* (1914) depicts an atomic war. Several nuclear war stories appeared during World War II in science-fiction magazines such as *Astounding*. Yet no matter how prescient, during World War II these stories were still simply stories. They were not expressive of that war effort until the technology was invented that realized their forecasts. The bombing of Hiroshima and Nagasaki, in turn, made this kind of future-war storytelling took less like fiction and more like prophecy.[16]

As nuclear weapons replaced troops on the front lines of the cold war in the 1950s, nuclear war fictions acquired the epistemological status of strategic fact. They became a hybrid literary form specific to the cold war: strategic fictions. Strategic fiction is a special case of a future-war fiction that represents the unprecedented future realities that national security strategists themselves must also imagine. These fictional future-war scenarios become even more purposive and propagandistic, serving as instantiations of national security strategy itself. As such, they became especially powerful at building the political reality of the nuclear threat, because the catastrophic future war they once fantasized not only was now possible, but also had become central to the strategic imaginary of the nation's defense planners. Under the policy of deterrence, with its evolving promises of massive retaliation and mutually assured destruction, the threat of nuclear war had become the nation's defense against another world war. Yet that threat referred to a "non-event," a kind of war that had never been fought but could only be imagined.[17] The only places global nuclear war ever was fought were in the expert scenarios of pro- and antinuclear propagandists;[18] the theoretical models and war games of nuclear strategists;[19] and the film, art, and literature of the nuclear age.[20] With every telling of a nuclear war story in each of these specialized areas, global nuclear warfare was in a sense proven and the narrative world of nuclear defense strategy was built anew.

As antinuclear activist Jonathan Schell observes in *The Fate of the Earth*, without much real-life experience to draw upon, cold-war subjects were "forced in this one case to become the historians of the future—to chronicle and commit to memory an event that we have never experienced and must never experience." Hayden White reminds us that all historians consider historical events to be "stories waiting to be told"; history as we know it is delivered to us wrapped up in a closed-plot structure.[21] The history of the future is no exception. The historical closure presented by global nuclear warfare contained a great deal of meaning for cold-war subjects, but that meaning was divisive, because the story of nuclear war necessarily represented not the success of nuclear defense policy, but its failure to prevent a nuclear war in the first place. Whether one reads about it, is threatened with it, or sees it in a movie, the future history of nuclear war as delivered in strategic fiction conveys a sense of urgency. It represents not simply a possible future but the meaning of nuclear defense policy itself. Like future war tales before it, the story of nuclear war is an admonition, an inherent lesson to its beholders on what to do in the present. Yet the meaning of its future remains intensely contradictory. First, there is the imperative meaning of nuclear deterrence itself: A nuclear war must not be fought. Antinuclear advocates and reasonable cold warriors could generally agree on this meaning, as well as on the premise behind it: This unprecedented kind of high-tech war certainly could be fought. Second, there is the ethical meaning, which presents a greater problem: What should we do now to ensure that a nuclear war is never fought? The solution to that problem depended on what kind of faith the leaders of the world's nuclear powers placed in their military technologies and in each other.[22]

Strategic fictions put a human face on an abstract act, dramatically fleshing out what the historian Thomas Hughes calls a "technological system," the "people and organizations" who work alongside the "hardware, devices, machines and processes, and the transportation, communication, and information networks that interconnect them" that together comprise the practice of nuclear warfare.[23] Thus films that let us look into the top-secret world of nuclear defense are strategic fictions, much as are films that represent World War III. Yet strategic fiction is also a representation of a machine that if used would produce a historical world catastrophe. For this reason, we find a great deal of fanfare and controversy attached to films, novels, and tracts about nuclear war. Their fictional visions can change what people think about the real-world policy of nuclear defense. Early in the cold war, the U.S. Air Force saw cinematic strategic fictions as public relations tools that could work, much as had the air-power films of World War II, to build confidence in nuclear defense. At one star-studded premiere, Jimmy Stewart was given a citation of honor by the Air Force Association for flying a B-36 nuclear bomber in *Strategic Air Command*, Anthony Mann's lavish 1955 celebration of the U.S. Air Force's nuclear defense fleet.[24] Air Force chief of staff General Curtis LeMay personally bucked a mid-cold-war congressional ban on military-Hollywood collusion to rush Sy Bartlett's B-52-studded spectacle, *A Gathering of Eagles* (1963), to the screen ahead of Stanley Kubrick's *Dr. Strangelove* (1964), even allowing Rock Hudson to perform in the Strategic Air Command's underground command center.[25] But Kubrick's fictional underground war room looked better, and his Strategic Air Command worked better too, a war machine so deadly that, once launched, it couldn't be stopped, even when run by buffoons. *Dr. Strangelove* was released in 1964 along with two other films adapted from best-selling novels about the threat of accidental nuclear war, *Fail-Safe* and *Seven Days in May*. All three were made without any support from the Pentagon, mainly because they demonstrated how this kind of fiction could change what people thought about the real world of nuclear defense. Their insider looks at the technological system of nuclear warmaking not only exposed a basic inhumanity (or excess of humanity) behind the policy, but also prompted the U.S. Air Force to sponsor films such as *A Gathering of Eagles* and to publicly address the potential dangers of nuclear defense.

While the public accepted the technological certainty of nuclear war, its faith in nuclear defense was insecure. The tenuousness of that faith increased over the next decades until in 1982 all the Ground Zero Group had to ask on the cover of its book *Nuclear War: What's in It for You?* was, "Why do you feel scared with 10,000 nuclear weapons protecting you?" to enlist readers to the cause of antinuclear activism.[26] A trio of films produced for television in the early 1980s—PBS's *Testament* (1983), ABC's *The Day After* (1983), and BBC's *Threads* (1984)—inspired many viewers to join the million-member antinuclear movement simply by depicting nuclear war, which in the ABC and BBC films is fought justly against a maniacal Soviet Union that sends its troops marching suicidally across Western Europe.[27] Nevertheless, the critical reception of these demonstrations of U.S. nuclear might was mixed. "Why is ABC doing Yuri Andropov's job?" the *New York Post* asked in an editorial review of the film. William F. Buckley, writing in the *National Review*, called *The Day After*'s haunting depiction of the nation's nuclear defenses in action "a massive deception." After almost forty years of cold war, the history of the future just wasn't what it used to be.[28]

The conclusion of the cold war turned future-nuclear-war storytelling back into fiction, at least temporarily. In retrospect, all strategic fictions of nuclear war can be seen to have constituted a grand U.S. narrative of strategic defense that accompanied the nation's grand strategy of containment through deterrence, a tale of future war whose telling united Americans as cold-war subjects whether they liked it or not.[29] The U.S. narrative of strategic defense seemed to vanish after the formal dissolution of the Soviet Union in 1991, a surprise ending few had foreseen. The threat of nuclear war diminished to such a point that Jonathan Schell was now complaining to the *New York Times* that "the post–cold war generation knows less about nuclear danger than any generation." He was horrified to find that the young were even enjoying movies about nuclear weapons that saved humanity, such as Disney's *Armageddon* (1998), which features a nuclear weapon that destroys an asteroid before it can demolish planet Earth.[30] The strategic fact of nuclear weaponry remained, but strategic fictions seemed hopelessly dated.

The Way of the Worlds

Strategic fictions of nuclear attack would soon be back in the revised form of the techno-thriller. Knowing the literary and cinematic tradition of the new strategic fiction helps us understand how tales of nuclear terrorism can shape the political consciousness of national security strategy. Yet just as strategic fictions originally helped shape the consciousness of nuclear defense strategy, nuclear defense strategy also shaped the narratives of strategic fictions. Like their cold-war predecessors, strategic fictions of nuclear terrorism express a sense of national catastrophism, a certainty of impending national doom that originates in the national security strategy of the cold war.[31] Defense planners have revised that cold-war sense of national catastrophism for the war on terror. In doing so, they have once again placed the literature and film of catastrophic attack on the cultural front of a global conflict.

In the decade after the cold war, stories of nuclear war no longer spoke for grand strategy. Nevertheless, the threat of nuclear war had not gone away. The United States was in no rush to disarm; the U.S. Senate even voted against the Comprehensive Test Ban Treaty in 1999 to keep the door open for building more nuclear weapons. Other nations were seeking to develop nuclear arms, much as Pakistan had when it successfully tested a nuclear device in 1998. Yet while strategic nuclear weapons remained in the world's arsenals, the narrative of strategic defense that defined their use in the cold war—as engines of defense from themselves—was no longer as culturally or politically prominent as it once had been. Who was there left to fight a nuclear war with? The Clinton administration for its part had backed away from grand U.S. strategizing, emphasizing "progress toward political self-determination and economic integration" through international coopera-tion, arms-control treaties, and limited, multilateral military engagements conducted under the banner of peacekeeping.[32]

The character of the world had changed since the cold war. But so had the way of describing the character of the world, and especially the characters in it. A new narrative world order was emerging from the right wing of U.S. politics. While campaigning in 2000, George W. Bush began warning of a new kind of catastrophic threat, "the contagious spread of missile technology and weapons of mass destruction." Our world is not a world at peace or in need of peacekeepers, he claimed. It is "a world of terror and missiles and mad-men." The threats of the future will come not from the world's great powers, but from "car bombers and plutonium merchants and cyber terrorists and drug cartels and unbalanced dictators."[33] The attacks of 9/11 gave credence to candidate Bush's dangerous visions. Afterward, the threat of nuclear attack was rewritten into the new U.S. grand strategy, crafted for a world once again at war. In the Bush administration's 2002 report on that strategy, *The National Security Strategy of the United States of America* (the *NSS*), nuclear attack figures as the worst of all possible threats in a world full of malicious characters, lawless states, and weapons of mass destruction. It is precisely this world that we see in such high-profile strategic fictions as Robinson's *Sum of All Fears* and Leder's *Peacemaker*.

In the new world of national security, nuclear weapons no longer serve as engines of defense from nuclear attack. In mass culture, tales of nuclear terrorism have accordingly replaced tales of nuclear war as popular expres-sions of the nation's new grand narrative of national security, one not of strategic defense but of strategic defenselessness, that now accompanies the Bush administration's grand strategy of unilateral preemptive war and homeland defense. It is a tale of future catastrophic attack whose mass tell-ing unites Americans as terrorized subjects in a war on terror. Much like its predecessor, it is a lesson to its beholders on what to do in the present: Ensure that these catastrophic attacks never happen in the future.

The future-historical threat of nuclear terrorism retains much in common with its cold-war predecessor, the story of global nuclear war. The revolution in foreign policy ascribed to the Bush doctrine proves to be more a literary revision of the cold-war narrative of strategic defense than a revolutionary departure from it. National security strategy in both eras—as exemplified by key policy documents such as National Security Council document 68 (NSC 68), *United States Objectives and Programs for National Security* (1950), the blueprint for the cold war; and the *NSS*, the blueprint for the war on terror—can be analyzed as a literary process of building a world and imagining its future: peopled with characters described by metaphor, plotted to express certain grand themes, and, above all, riven by conflict. Taken side-by-side we can see much that is similar in the world written then and the world written today. Only the characters have changed, but that revision has been enough to change the relationship of the United States to the world.

After the Soviet Union acquired nuclear weapons in 1949, President Truman asked the National Security Council (NSC) to codify the nation's global security plans, resulting in the production of the top-secret document NSC 68, the blueprint for the grand strategy of Soviet containment. "The issues that face us are momentous," NSC 68's introduction reads, "involving the fulfillment or destruction not only of this Republic but of civilization itself." Describing the Soviet Union as a "slave state" bent on conquering the United States, the NSC urged the "rapid build-up of political, economic, and military strength in the free world." In five years the Soviet Union would be ready to launch a crippling "surprise atomic attack" unless the United States "substantially increased general air, ground, and sea strength, atomic capabilities, and air and civilian defenses to deter war."[34] Following the outbreak of war in North Korea in 1950, Truman turned the advice offered in NSC 68 into a master plan for fighting the cold war.[35]

President Eisenhower made this grand strategy catastrophic. NSC 68's outline for containing the Soviet Union ship for ship and man for man was simply too expensive for him. As an economizing measure during wartime, the new president cut Truman's military budget and shifted most of the burden of Soviet containment to nuclear weapons.[36] Early in his first term, Eisenhower sent Secretary of State John Foster Dulles to the Council on Foreign Relations headquarters in New York City to announce the administration's new strategy of "massive retaliation." Dulles informed those present that the new administration intended to build "a maximum deterrent at a bearable cost" by reinforcing "local defenses ... [with] the further deterrent of massive retaliatory power." From now on, the nation would "respond vigorously at places and with means of its own choosing" to any Soviet aggression.[37] Eisenhower's new look for U.S. military power resulted in a huge increase in the number of nuclear weapons in the U.S. arsenal, from one thousand in 1953 to eighteen thousand in 1961.[38] As the Soviet Union replied to these threats by building its own atomic arsenal in the following decade, U.S. defense planners in the Johnson administration reformulated the policy of massive retaliation as a policy of assured destruction. Global nuclear catastrophism thus became one of the pillars of cold-war U.S. grand strategy.

It is important to note that the United States was the pioneer in nuclear weapons development in the first decades of the cold war. Long before any enemy nation had the bomb, the United States was arming itself with nuclear weapons against them. The United States remained committed to nuclear weapons after World War II because of its defense planners' basic assumptions about the way of the world, which we can loosely recognize as part of a "realist" view of international relations. The philosophy of international realism was articulated in the 1940s by political theorists such as Hans Morgenthau and soon applied to nuclear weapons policy by military strategists such as Bernard Brodie.[39] The realist worldview represents the world of nations as in essence a hostile place. As Morgenthau describes it in *Politics among Nations*, ours is "inherently a world of opposing interests." Defining interest "in terms of power," a realist analysis seeks to divine the rational core within all political action and thus conceives of international relations as naturally favoring behavior that "minimizes risks and maximizes benefits." One upshot of this worldview is that its adherents remain agnostic about ideology and questions of character and good- or bad will.[40] State actors will generally act in their own best interest, no matter who they are or what they think; that is the way of the world. Power, therefore, must be balanced between states if peace is to be achieved.

The U.S. decision after victory in World War II to continue building nuclear weapons as defensive weapons was the only rational course of action in a world conceived in threatening terms. U.S. defense planners extrapolated from the military successes of the recent past to imagine the threats the nation would face in the future. The German blitzkrieg and the Japanese surprise attack on Pearl Harbor served as the most plausible models available for how nuclear weapons, which won World War II, would be used against the United States: in a swift, crippling surprise attack, most likely against U.S. cities, much as the United States had used them in Japan.[41] "So much the more reason, therefore," the pioneer nuclear strategist Bernard Brodie urged, "to take all possible steps to assure that multilateral possession of the bomb, should that prove inevitable, be attended by arrangements to make as nearly certain as possible that the aggressor who uses the bomb will have it used against him."[42] In the realist world of nuclear weapons and rational actors, only a careful balance of nations' power to unleash nuclear catastrophe can keep the world at peace. Thus the leaders of the Soviet slave state, no matter how pernicious, could be trusted—once they acquired nuclear weapons—to think rationally and be deterred by the power of the U.S. nuclear arsenal.

The national security strategy produced by the Bush National Security Council reproduces many of the grand themes first articulated in NSC 68, foremost among them the sense that the world is comprised of forces opposed to the United States that are intent upon using against it nuclear and other weapons of mass destruction. Bush introduced the themes that would guide his new national security strategy in his 2002 commencement address at the U.S. Military Academy. While casting his new strategy as a departure from the past, Bush pitted the fate of the nation once more against "a threat with no precedent," telling the graduates that

> enemies in the past needed great armies and great industrial capa-
> bilities to endanger the American people and our nation. The attacks
> of September 11 required a few hundred thousand dollars in the hands
> of a few dozen evil and deluded men. All of the chaos and suffering
> they caused came at much less than the cost of a single tank. . . . The
> gravest danger to freedom lies at the perilous crossroads of radical-
> ism and technology. When the spread of chemical and biological and
> nuclear weapons, along with ballistic missile technology, when that
> occurs even weak states and small groups could attain a catastrophic
> power to strike great nations.

Like the bombing of Pearl Harbor before it, the terrorist attacks of 9/11 dem-onstrated not just how vulnerable the nation was but also how vulnerable it would remain in the future:

For much of the last century America's defense relied on the cold-war doctrine of deterrence and containment. In some cases those strategies still apply. But new threats require new thinking. Deterrence, the promise of massive retaliation against nations, means nothing against shadowy terrorist networks with no nation or citizens to defend. Containment is not possible when unbalanced dictators with weapons of mass destruction can deliver those weapons on missiles or secretly provide them to terrorist allies. We cannot defend America and our friends by hoping for the best. . . . If we wait for threats to fully materialize we will have waited for too long.[43]

The Bush doctrine retains a fundamentally oppositional and catastrophically threatening view of the world reminiscent of the cold war. However, the character of the forces opposing the nation has changed greatly. The text of the *NSS* delivered to Congress in 2002 presents a revision of the threatening world of NSC 68. The rational superpowers of the cold war have been replaced by new kinds of international characters: irrational "rogue states" and "shadowy networks of individuals."[44] With its redefined enemy, the *NSS* betrays the influence of another philosophy of international relations, a "neoconservative" worldview. As first articulated by political theorists such as Leo Strauss and Allan Bloom and as applied to international affairs by public intellectuals (e.g., Irving Kristol and Francis Fukuyama) and Bush administration members (e.g., Paul Wolfowitz, Richard Cheney, and Zalmay Khalilzad), the neoconservative philosophy of world affairs views the free-market mode of U.S. Judeo-Christian democratic culture as the pinnacle of civilization.[45] President Bush and his advisors reduce world affairs to terms of character and intent, good and evil, and use those terms to assess the course of global policy. In the neoconservative world of the *NSS*, things such as character, ideology, and the consequent exercise of good- and bad will are far greater determining factors in international relations than is the balance of national power.

The rogue states and terrorist networks described in the *NSS* are prototypically neoconservative bad characters. They "reject basic human values and hate the United States and everything for which it stands." Unlike the United States, rogue states "brutalize their own people and squander their national resources for the personal gain of the rulers"; "display no regard for international law, threaten their neighbors, and callously violate international treaties to which they are party"; and are "determined to acquire weapons of mass destruction, along with other advanced military technology, to be used as threats or offensively to achieve the aggressive designs of these regimes."[46]

The introduction of the concepts of irrational rogue states and terrorist networks radically changes the meaning of the nuclear weapons inherited from the cold war, turning them into technological threats against which there is no defense. The basic narrative operation of national security strategizing, on the other hand, remains the same from the cold war to the war on terror. Nuclear defense strategy in both eras is extrapolative: An attack from the past, coupled with massively destructive weapons technology and strategy, is set in a threatening world full of enemies to create a new, worse scenario set in the future. The scenarios divined through that process of extrapolation then serve as guides for U.S. global policy. In the cold war, the scenarios of nuclear war extrapolated from the experience of World War II guided the nation through permutations on the policy of nuclear defense. No more. The scenarios of catastrophic terrorism extrapolated from the attacks of 9/11 cannot be used to support any policy of nuclear defense against actors who, we are told, do not care about minimizing risks and maximizing benefits.

President Bush first announced a war on terror in a speech to a joint session of Congress on 20 September 2001. The new narrative order of the *NSS* was presaged by his rhetoric of a new world that the attacks had wrought. "Americans have known surprise attacks," he reminded the Congress, "but never before on thousands of civilians. All of this was brought upon us in a single day—and night fell on a different world, a world where freedom itself is under attack."[47] In the revised national security strategy for a war on terror, the imagination of that catastrophic attack leaves open no defensive course but that of war.

Mantra for the Second Nuclear Age

Strategic fiction adopts the extrapolative narrative form of national security strategy in both the first and second nuclear ages. Its authors and filmmakers look to the history of catastrophic threats and attacks to imagine future catastrophes the nation may face. In the strategic fiction of the cold war, the catastrophes of World War II served as models for the catastrophe of a third world war in tales about waging and surviving the final total war. In the strategic fiction of the war on terror, the surprise attacks of 9/11 serve as the model for scenarios of catastrophic attack in techno-thriller tales about terrorism. Strategic fictions of nuclear terrorism released both before and after 9/11 are transitional films that bridge two strategic eras and two world-views, moving viewers from the cold-war past to a new world of terror, and from a realist worldview to a neoconservative worldview. Strategic fictions of nuclear terrorism are thus primers for daily life as lived in the U.S. narrative of strategic defenselessness, a new world order where fears of nuclear attack must be met by the technological wizardry not of strategic nuclear weapons design, but of a revitalized national security apparatus.

Consider this hypothetical: A corrupt Russian general working for the Russian mafia hijacks a train carrying a decommissioned SS-18 nuclear missile, planning to sell its ten warheads on the black market. To cover up the theft, the general detonates one warhead in the Ural Mountains, destroying the train and all traces of his crime and killing more than a thousand people in the process. But his ruse doesn't work. U.S. military intelligence officers, privy to spy-satellite images of the blast, see through the deceit. Combining gutsy fieldwork with more satellite surveillance, they track the general's movements, discovering that he is transporting the warheads in a truck through Azerbaijan to the Iranian border. Green Berets intercept the general's truck and recover eight warheads. However, Serbian terrorists and a freelancing Pakistani nuclear physicist working with the general have already absconded with the plutonium detonator from the ninth warhead, turning it into a bomb small enough to fit into a backpack. The bomb is smuggled into New York in a diplomatic pouch from the failed state of Bosnia, where the Serbian terrorists plan to use it to blow up the United Nations in revenge for NATO's peacekeeping operations in the former Yugoslavia. The U.S. security apparatus is ready. The Department of Energy, the Federal Bureau of Investigation, the New York Police Department, U.S. Customs, the National Guard, the Federal Emergency Management Agency, Army Special Forces, and the National Security Council's Nuclear Smuggling Group combine forces and, working in coordination from a command center full of computer screens and glass maps of Manhattan, sniff out the radioactive bomb with airborne radiation detectors, plant snipers up and down the East Side, comb the streets, catch the terrorist, and defuse the nuclear bomb.

This scenario never happened, but according to the investigative journalists Leslie Cockburn and Alexander Cockburn, it certainly could. The Cockburns pitched this scenario to producers at DreamWorks studio, which turned it into a script for the new studio's debut feature, *The Peacemaker*. The Cockburns had developed their plot while researching their book *One Point Safe*, a work of new journalism that popularized the threat of "loose nukes"—the prospect that NATO or more likely Russian nuclear weapons could easily be stolen or accidentally launched in the post-cold-war world. The idea of loose nukes became the basis not only of a Hollywood film in 1997 but also of two episodes of *60 Minutes*, all of which the Cockburns helped produce.[48] *The Peacemaker*, accordingly, is serious stuff. "The more I read, the more frightening it became," director Mimi Leder says of her motivation for the project. "I thought it was a very timely issue. There are a lot of loose nukes on the black market. We are a vulnerable world and we need to protect ourselves."[49] The Cockburns didn't say that there were any loose nukes on the black market in *One Point Safe*, but they recount several real-world examples of attempted nuclear thefts, lost Russian suitcase bombs, radical Islamic nuclear ambitions, and lax security at nuclear installations around the world.

As a dramatization of several of the real actors and events represented in *One Point Safe*, *The Peacemaker* is about our world. But it wasn't strategic fiction. In 1997 *The Peacemaker* still looked more like fiction than fact, and not particularly relevant fiction at that. U.S. audiences were not overly interested in it (total domestic ticket sales failed to cover the $50 million cost of the picture);[50] nor was the Pentagon. The U.S. Army refused to lend the filmmakers the three helicopters they requested for filming in Slovakia and Macedonia (although the Russian Army did rent them one hundred uniforms).[51] The White House staffers invited to the premiere laughed at it. "Not boring old nukes again," one reviewer quipped. Whether positive or negative, the reviews of 1997 are telling—but especially the negative ones—emphasizing the film's generic qualities over its political meaning. "The cineplex equivalent of the airport paperback novel," the film "resurrects an old standby—a stolen nuclear device—" and remains beholden to "nuclear-thriller clichés."[52] In 1997 a film about nuclear terrorism was still judged not by its relevance to the world but by its adherence to the formula of the techno-thriller.[53]

Preventing nuclear catastrophe was not a central national security issue in the 1990s. The job of containing the threat of loose nukes was left to small government and private operations such as the Nunn-Lugar Cooperative

Threat Reduction Program begun in 1991, in which the U.S. and Soviet (and later Russian) governments worked together to secure and dismantle old Soviet missiles, and the "megatons to megawatts" nonproliferation agreement entered into by the United States and Russia in 1993, for which the private company USEC Inc. contracted to purchase uranium from dismantled Russian and U.S. nuclear weapons as fuel for U.S. reactors.[54] U.S. nuclear policy in the post-cold-war decade was mostly concerned with dismantling the old nuclear war machine, not with building a new one. In 1992 President George H. Bush oversaw the standdown of the Strategic Air Command and the signing of the first Strategic Arms Reduction Treaty (START). Bill Clinton later cancelled the top-secret "contingency of government" program started by Ronald Reagan to preserve a small nucleus of leadership in case of a surprise nuclear attack and, after the cold war, a nuclear terrorist attack.[55] Terrorism in general before 9/11 was not a focus of national security strategy. As the Senate commission on the attacks noted in its final report: "The United States did not, before September 11, adopt as a clear strategic objective the elimination of al Qaeda"—or of any other terrorist network, for that matter.[56]

The threat of nuclear terrorism was as real then as it is now. The only thing different about that threat before 2001 is that it had not attained the status of strategic fiction. It had certainly been the stuff of fiction. From Terence Young's James Bond film *Thunderball* (1965) to James Cameron's *True Lies* (1995) to John Woo's *Broken Arrow* (1996) to *The Peacemaker*, nuclear terrorism had become an almost yearly target for Hollywood. In 2002, three films were released that had a nuclear terrorist plot or subplot: Barry Sonnenfeld's *Big Trouble*, Joel Schumacher's *Bad Company*, and Robinson's *Sum of All Fears*. Robinson's film is even obliquely based upon another filmic terrorist thriller, John Frankenheimer's *Black Sunday* (1977), in which Palestinian terrorists plot to blow up the Super Bowl with an arcane dart bomb that can kill as many people as a small atomic bomb can (in Clancy's book *The Sum of All Fears*, the terrorists are repeatedly amused by the idea that their plot to blow up the Super Bowl was first a movie).

Watching terrorists hijack nuclear weapons and, in more recent films, blow them up used to be a lot of fun, no matter who the terrorists were. Yet at the turn of the century, this scenario started to be taken more seriously than in past film seasons, which is why, when producer Mace Neufeld decided to turn Tom Clancy's book about nuclear terrorism into a movie, he made several changes to the story to make the scenario *less* representative of world affairs. The nuclear terrorists in Clancy's book are Arabs, Native Americans, *and* Communists. Responding to a plea from the Council on American-Islamic Relations not to perpetuate any more negative stereotypes, Neufeld and director Robinson turned the terrorists into neo-Nazis.[57] The National Football League, which let a blimp crash into two of its pro teams in 1976 for the filming of *Black Sunday*, refused to sanction even a mention of the Super Bowl or the NFL in the Paramount film;[58] Robinson had to rent two Canadian Football League teams in Montreal and blow them up instead.[59] The one thing the filmmakers didn't change was the hinge of Clancy's original plot, which by 2002 had become an anachronism: Russia's relationship (still the Soviet Union, in Clancy's text) with the United States would continue to be determined by a residual cold-war competitiveness and hair-trigger suspicion (thus when terrorists try to kill the president at Clancy's Super Bowl most of his advisors think it is a Soviet sneak attack, which is precisely what the terrorists hope for).

Despite these changes and anachronisms, the film has a very authentic look to match the increasingly real threat posed by its scenario. The filmmakers used cold-war locations for their primarily Canadian shoot, setting scenes supposed to take place in the president's real-life Mount Weather Command Center, for instance, in Canada's old governmental bomb shelter, the Diefenbunker.[60] More fortunately for the producers, the armed and intelligence services all saw the film as an excellent venue for product placement and eagerly used it to sell defense—or at least the need for defense—in the new millennium. The Pentagon rented Paramount a small military force—"two B-2 bombers, two F-16 fighter jets and the National Airborne Operations Center; . . . three Marine Corps CH-53E helicopters, a UH-60 Army helicopter, four ground vehicles and more than 50 marines and Army troops; . . . [and] an aircraft carrier, too: the John Stennis, a 97,000-ton, nuclear-powered floating city with more than 80 aircraft and a crew of 5,000"—all for the price of the fuel used during filming. The Central Intelligence Agency threw its doors open to welcome a film that represented the agency as both central to U.S. defense and as intelligent, assigning a special Hollywood agent to help the film's star, Ben Affleck, practice manning a desk inside CIA headquarters. Paramount architects and landscapers toured and measured the top-secret building so as to accurately recreate it on set. Producer Mace Neufeld contracted the security company RSA to provide his actors with real "RSA SecurID® two-factor authentication device[s]" while shooting in the ersatz CIA.

The PCs in the national security apparatus and the terrorist network all run on Microsoft Windows. The film's locations are established with shots taken by the IKONOS satellite, an ultra-high-resolution imaging platform once available only to government intelligence services. According to the CIA's Hollywood agent, the results of Robinson's and Neufeld's efforts at security-state authenticity are nothing less than "extraordinarily realistic."[61]

When *The Sum of All Fears* premiering after 9/11, its realistic depiction of a nuclear terrorist attack conveyed the contradictory assurance reserved for works of strategic fiction: the certainty that such an attack can happen. Viewers started treating the film as having the power to change how people thought about national defense. Paramount promoted viewing its picture as an act of patriotism, organizing two premieres in Washington, D.C.—one for the national press corps, hosted by arms-control advocate Senator Richard G. Lugar of Nunn-Lugar fame; and the other for an audience of senators, Bush cabinet members, and Pentagon brass. Senator John Kerry praised the film on *Late Night with Conan O'Brien*: "It's a provocative film that makes you ask a lot of tough questions."[62] Matt Drudge reported that President Bush hated the film and quoted "one senior Bush official" as complaining that "after what we've all been through the past year, how can Hollywood so casually roll out a movie which shows Marines pulling a bleeding president from his motorcade? . . . I mean, I was watching CNN the other day, they actually jumped from a news story on increased security around our nuclear power plants to later showing a clip from this movie which had windows being blown out by a nuclear blast. Really, how is this positive?"[63] U.S. Customs Service officials felt equally threatened, even though Robinson prescreened the movie for them to get their thoughts on it.[64] U.S. Customs Service Commissioner Robert Bonner described the detonation of a nuclear bomb in a port as "truly the sum of all fears" but told journalists that his agency was ready for that future. His brusque assurances read like dialogue from a techno-thriller: "We have equipment and technology that we did not have when Mr. Clancy wrote that book. . . . Any kind of nuclear weapon is going to stand out like a sore thumb."[65]

Robinson's film is a showcase for much of that technology, dramatizing in detail the networks of nuclear terror and the national security technological system arrayed against them. The film straddles two worlds, the old world of nuclear defense and the new world of nuclear terror, representing each in its own story line throughout much of the film before finally subordinating the new world to the old. Robinson's security state is in an uneasy transition in which the shift to a new narrative of national security plays out as a clash of generations. Each generation is committed to its own mode of security production, the young to the systems of intelligence and intervention favored by the CIA and the old to the systems of power politics and massive retaliation favored by the National Security Council and the U.S. Air Force.

Robinson's CIA has been rejuvenated for the twenty-first century, as has Clancy's hero Jack Ryan (Ben Affleck), whose character has been revised from his earlier cinematic roles as a senior officer in the CIA to that of a freshman Russian analyst. Cast with attractive actors in their late twenties and early thirties, the agency is comprised of members of a new boyish generation who banter in casual tones about the sexual antics of the Soviet high command on display in their CIA spy monitors, sport hip beards and dreadlocks, and have commitment issues with their girlfriends. The only woman in the group, the motherly Mary Pat Foley (Lee Garlington), is heavily pregnant and ready to give birth to the new generation of national security agents. In contrast, Robinson cast the president, his cabinet, and everyone in Congress with veteran male actors at least a generation older than their CIA counterparts, all sporting gray hair, craggy features, reddening faces, and quick tempers, qualities found in abundance in the character of President Bob Fowler (James Cromwell).

The bridge between these two generations is the director of Central Intelligence, Bill Cabot (Morgan Freeman), the only member of the president's inner circle who understands that the way of the world is changing and national defense strategy must change with it. The CIA has responded to that change. It is a networked agency that works with other agencies such as the National Security Agency not to win wars, but to keep the peace. As Cabot tells Ryan: "We keep the back channels open in hopes of staving off disaster." The CIA is serious about safety, sending senior agents to Russia to verify that nation's compliance with START. The U.S. enemies have changed too; they use e-mail. "The world has changed," the Nazi Dressler (Alan Bates) says. "Global communications, cable TV, the Internet. Today the world is smaller." Any small group can use the new technologies to effect great change in the world, even neo-Nazis.

The film opens with a description of the new strategic situation of the post-cold-war world, showing how a nuclear weapon can be lost in the fog of war in a foreign land (in this case, the Arab-Israeli War of 1973), only to return years later to threaten the United States. As the CIA tracks the steps of three missing Russian nuclear scientists who happen to be working on that bomb, Ryan describes the defense of the United States as a process now more akin to riddle solving than to war fighting: "What's a South African doing in the Ukraine with three Russian scientists and a crate from Israel?" Only by tracing the network laid out by these clues does the CIA realize that a nuclear attack is imminent; all responses to that attack by the president and his senior staff serve only to lead the nation closer to nuclear war.

The old national security generation represented by President Fowler is unaware that the nation faces any new threats. Following a nuclear war game held in the underground command center at Mt. Weather, Fowler confides to Cabot how outdated he feels that preparing for nuclear war is:

FOWLER: We gotta update these fire drills, Billy. I mean if the shit ever hits the fan, I'm not goin' underground. The place is a goddamn tomb down there.

CABOT: We also have to choose someone to face off against beside the Russians all the time.

FOWLER: Really? Let's see. Who else has twenty-seven thousand nukes for us to worry about?

CABOT: It's the guy with one I'm worried about.

Cabot's riposte is the mantra for the second nuclear age, but the old guard of the federal branch won't hear it. The CIA is treated hostilely by the graying members of Congress, all of whom think their old political horse sense is better than the CIA's careful character analysis of Russian leaders. For the young Jack Ryan, character matters more than do the old ways of power; he even wrote a character analysis of the new Russian president. In the film's climactic scene, as the two superpowers are less than a minute away from launching their nuclear missiles after wrongly blaming each other for the terrorist attacks against them, Ryan breaks into the hotline communication between the presidents and saves the world by telling the Russian president simply, "Sir, I know you."

Character may save the day and Cabot may be correct about the new way of the world, but *The Sum of All Fears* ultimately retains a cold-war worldview. The CIA almost catches up with the bomb, but halfway through the film the bomb explodes and the film's strategic fiction of nuclear terrorism comes to an end. The film then splits into two story lines, one following Ryan's attempts to identify the source of the bomb and the other following Fowler's escalating path to nuclear war. Ryan's search retains the cybernetic plotting of a techno-thriller: We watch a NEST robot dig into the radioactive debris of Baltimore to identify the source of the bomb's plutonium (one conversation at this point goes: "Wow, check out that gadolinium reading." "Yeah, the mass fraction is huge"); CIA agents sitting in chairs in Langley break into the computers of an arms dealer in Damascus and identify the terrorist mastermind Dressler; Ryan saves the world by having someone type words into the hotline. Yet this new kind of warfare is set against a cold-war plot of superpower posturing that remains intact almost line for line from Clancy's 1991 text (Fowler on the Russians: "Can't afford for them to see us as weak. They've gotta know we have the guts to take it to the next level"). The film concludes as a realist story of superpower politics, ending with a treaty signing in Moscow intercut with some cold-war-style assassinations that restabilizes not a new but an old bipolar world order. In the end the CIA stands more or less an agency alone, not a party to much interagency cooperation or integrative national defense planning at all.

But despite its narrative failings to come to terms with the new world of the national security strategy of the United States, *The Sum of All Fears* did not fail to build the political reality of nuclear terrorism. It is an instantiation of the U.S. narrative of strategic defenselessness. Stripped of its narrative particulars, the film still provides a future-historical scenario of electronic networks and security apparatus into which one may plug any kind of shadowy actor to imagine a story of a United States under threat. For instance, remove a few minor variations that deliberately distanced the film from our world, and *The Sum of All Fears* plays like an almost exact remake of *The Peacemaker*.

In *The Peacemaker*, we find the U.S. narrative of strategic defenselessness expressed in its clearest, most humanized form, for the Cockburns have deliberately scripted it as a piece of post-cold-war agitprop. *The Peacemaker*'s nuclear terrorist, Dusan Gavrich (Marcel Iures), is a self-described enemy everyman of the post-cold-war United States. "I am a Serb. I'm a Croat. I'm a Muslim," he tells the world in a taped message. "I'm just like you, whether you like it or not." Dusan Gavrich is a truly bad character, a broken man driven by a sense of third-world injustice and a desire for revenge against the powers that have waged war in the Balkans. Leder and the Cockburns deploy the same network of spy satellites and the same cybernetic plotting as does Robinson to represent national defense as a techno-thriller. The action in the film moves at the speed of technology: the time it takes for facial recognition software to identify someone, the time it takes to download a file, the time it takes a satellite to move across the sky, the time it takes to receive e-mail.

The film represents as intricate and high-tech both the international networks of nuclear smuggling and hatred, and the new U.S. institutions that protect the nation from them, especially the real-world Nuclear Smuggling Group of the Clinton White House that the film is based on. Watching the Group in action, audiences see a fantasy prototype of the Department of Homeland Defense: youthful and energetic whiz kids with stylish glasses, wavy hair, a networked office without walls, and their own airborne command post. They do not work alone but distill intelligence from other agencies and provide intelligence to Army Special Forces and any other national security agency that requires it. The group is headed by Dr. Julia Kelly (Nicole Kidman), who works alongside a Special Forces liaison, Colonel Thomas Devoe (George Clooney). They are an odd couple, but the friction between them is philosophical, not institutional or personal. They see the world differently, and they discuss those differences calmly in the time they have between gunfights and car chases.

While headed to Vienna to follow up on some intelligence, Kelly and Devoe have a telling debate over how to understand the threat of nuclear terrorism as embodied by the bad Russian general, Kodoroff, who stole the weapons. The scene is written as an argument between two Hollywood types, the brainy novice theoretical analyst Kelly and the brawny veteran field officer Devoe, but it is also a debate over how the national security apparatus should view the world: in Devoe's realist terms of power and interest, or in Kelly's neoconservative terms of character and will. The debate begins as a contest between equals over the character of the Russian general, the shot-countershot editing giving each position its fair turn.

KELLY: Would you call Langley [CIA headquarters]? We're still waiting on the psych profile on Kodoroff.

DEVOE: He's an asshole. I'll save you a trip.

KELLY: Thanks. I'll settle for the official version.

DEVOE: Okay. Officially, he's an asshole. He'll do anything for money, which is the good news 'cause it makes him fairly predictable.

KELLY: Really? I'd say he's been anything but predictable.

DEVOE: He took an order for an expensive, hard-to-find product and he intends to make good on delivery. Supply and demand. . . .

KELLY: So, it's really that simple?

DEVOE: It is to me that simple. . . . Doctor, you can run your charts and your theories all you want. In the field, this is how it works. The good guys—that's us—we chase the bad guys, and they don't wear black hats. They are, however, all alike. They demand power and respect, and they're willing to pay top dollar to get it. And that is our highly motivated buyer.

KELLY: What about other motivations?

DEVOE: Not important to me.

KELLY: Whether it's important to you or not, there are people out there who don't care about money and don't give a damn about respect, people who believe the killing of innocent men and women is justified.

At this point the rhythm of the shot-countershot editing changes to privilege Kelly's position over Devoe's. While Kelly is talking, we cut briefly to a reaction shot of Devoe, now shifting uncomfortably in his seat and not looking Kelly in the eye, before cutting back to Kelly. She is no longer speaking to Devoe but directly to the audience. The change in editing rhythm changes the way of the world.

KELLY: For them it is about rage, frustration, hatred. They feel pain and they are determined to share it with the world.

When Devoe responds, he is no longer looking at Kelly but down at his belly.

DEVOE: That does me no good. Now let's deal with the facts at hand. Twenty-three hours ago, General Aleksander Kodoroff stole ten nuclear warheads.

KELLY: He's just a delivery boy.

Devoe is silent in a reaction shot. Kelly seizes the opportunity to introduce the mantra for the second nuclear age.

KELLY: I'm not afraid of the man who wants ten nuclear weapons, Colonel. I'm terrified of the man who only wants one.

Kelly's neoconservative worldview proves to be the correct one in *The Peacemaker*'s post-cold-war world, and she soon wins Devoe over to it. Later, Devoe teaches the security expert the tactics of preemptive action as he leads a small fleet of Special Forces helicopters illegally over the Russian border to secure the loose nukes before they disappear from the sight of a spy satellite, thus effecting the union of idealism and action that would become the basis of the new national security strategy of the United States.

The Peacemaker concludes with a fantasy that the Bush revolution in foreign and domestic policy has yet to realize: the smooth integration of the institutions of the national security state in a continual, limited, flexible war against terror at home and abroad. In the world of strategic fiction, it takes the strategic fact of a terrorist headed for the United States with a nuclear weapon to achieve that result. In the real world, all we have are strategic fictions to organize the nation's national security priorities, and the results have been anything but limited. The nation has not been able to muster a flexible, precision response to match the techno-thriller threats it foresees.

The U.S. government's calls to war in Afghanistan and Iraq conform to the narrative structure of the 2002 *NSS*. When read within the new U.S. narrative of strategic defenselessness, the signs of Iraqi armament, denial, and deceit cited by Bush throughout 2002 and 2003 translated into an imminent catastrophe. Congress's joint resolution authorizing the war against Iraq waxed strategically fictional when it listed primary justifications for war: "Iraq's demonstrated capability and willingness to use weapons of mass destruction, the risk that the current Iraqi regime will either employ those weapons to launch a surprise attack against the United States or its Armed Forces or provide them to international terrorists who would do so, and the extreme magnitude of harm that would result to the United States and its citizens from such an attack, combine to justify action by the United States to defend itself."[66] In his 2003 State of the Union address, President Bush based his case for the Iraq war not on the strategic fact of an attack that had happened or definitely would happen, but on the strategic fiction of an attack that might have happened on 9/11. "Before September the 11th, many in the world believed that Saddam Hussein could be contained," he reminded the nation before shifting its attention to the new world order of the U.S. narrative of strategic defenselessness. "But chemical agents, lethal viruses and shadowy terrorist networks are not easily contained. Imagine those nineteen hijackers with other weapons and other plans—this time armed by Saddam

Hussein. It would take one vial, one canister, one crate slipped into this country to bring a day of horror like none we have ever known."[67] A techno-thriller imaginary organizes U.S. global policy in the twenty-first century. Strategic fictions have returned from the cold war, and the United States has once again started a grand fight against its own worst enemy—its future.

NOTES

1 Graham Allison and Andrei Kokoshin, "The New Containment: An Alliance against Nuclear Terrorism," *National Interest* 69 (fall 2002): 35.

2 Ibid., 36.

3 Herman Kahn, *Thinking about the Unthinkable* (New York: Horizon Press, 1962). As Mick Broderick shows in *Nuclear Movies: A Critical Analysis and Filmography of International Feature Length Films Dealing with Experimentation, Aliens, Terrorism, Holocaust, and Other Disaster Scenarios, 1914–1989* (Jefferson, N.C.: McFarland, 1991), the theme of nuclear terrorism has been a part of cinematic storytelling since the 1920s; variations on the scenario are as common as tales of nuclear war. See also Timothy L. Sanz's two survey articles, "Nuclear Terrorism: Selected Research Materials," *Low Intensity Conflict and Enforcement* 1, 3 (winter 1992): 337–345, and "Nuclear Terrorism: Published Literature since 1992," *Military Review* 77 (July/August 1997): 139–148, for a comprehensive listing of how national security specialists treated the scenario of nuclear terrorism prior to the 9/11 attacks.

4 Allison and Kokoshin, "The New Containment," 35.

5 While published in 1991, Tom Clancy's *Sum of All Fears* is set "a few . . . years" before the millennium (*Three Complete Novels* [New York: G. P. Putnam's Sons, 1994], 1010); its successor in the series, *Debt of Honor*, opens two years later. Soon after the cold war ended, historians and security analysts began a serious dis-cussion of how nuclear and other kinds of weapons of mass destruction would pose new threats. For a sense of such discussions, see Paul Bracken, *Fire in the East: The Rise of Asian Military Power in the Second Nuclear Age* (New York: Harper-Collins, 1999); Keith B. Payne, *Deterrence in the Second Nuclear Age* (Lexington: University Press of Kentucky, 1996); Colin S. Gray, *The Second Nuclear Age* (Boul-der, Colo.: Lynne Rienner, 1999); Graham Allison, Owen R. Coté, Jr., Richard A. Falkenrath, and Steven E. Miller, *Avoiding Nuclear Anarchy: Containing the Threat of Loose Russian Nuclear Weapons and Fissile Material* (Cambridge: MIT Press, 1996); Andrew Cockburn and Leslie Cockburn, *One Point Safe* (New York: Anchor Books, 1997); and Fred Charles Iklé, "The Second Coming of the Nuclear Age," *Foreign Affairs* 75 (January/February 1996): 119–128.

6 Christian Toto, "'All Fears' Limited to Film Screen," *Washington Times*, 27 May 2002; Dana Calvo and Robert W. Welkos, "Hollywood Shakes Off Fear of Terror Images," *LA Times on the Web*, 20 May 2002, www.latimes.com/news/nationworld/world/la-052002fears.story (accessed 10 August 2004); Anita Chabria, "Holly-wood Calls on Military Ties as It Releases Disaster-Themed Films," *PR Week*, 3 June 2002, 7.

7 Leo Rice-Barker, "Taurus 7 Produces Musical MOWs for VH1, MTV," *Playback*, 19 December 2000, 18.

8 Robinson quoted in Paula Zahn, Mike Galanos, and Gail O'Neill, "Profiles of Mike Tyson, Jewel, Morgan Freeman," *CNN People in the News*, 1 June 2002,

LexisNexis Academic (accessed 10 August 2004). Wolfowitz quoted in Bill Higgins and Pamela McClintock, "'Fears' Factor," *Variety*, 3–9 June 2002, 55.

9 J. William Gibson, "Redeeming Vietnam: Techno-Thriller Novels of the 1980s," *Cultural Critique* 19 (fall 1991): 180.

10 Walter L. Hixson, "Red Storm Rising: Tom Clancy Novels and the Cult of National Security," *Diplomatic History* 17 (fall 1993): 605; Gibson, "Redeeming Vietnam," 182–183.

11 Gibson, "Redeeming Vietnam," 188. Some politicians took techno-thrillers seriously in the 1980s. Senator Dan Quayle once displayed a copy of Clancy's *Red Storm Rising* to the Senate while arguing his case for the government to fund an antisatellite (ASAT) system. "Have you read this book?" he asked his assembled colleagues. "ASAT technology is what wins the war!" Quoted in Hixson, "*Red Storm Rising*," 613.

12 William F. Ryan, "The Genesis of the Techno-Thriller," *Virginia Quarterly Review* 68 (winter 1993): 34.

13 On the genre as reinvention, Gibson, "Redeeming Vietnam," 185; on its nineteenth-century popularization, I. F. Clarke, *Voices Prophesying War: Future Wars, 1763–3749* (New York: Oxford University Press, 1992), 3, 40; H. Bruce Franklin, *War Stars: The Superweapon and the American Imagination* (New York: Oxford University Press, 1988), 19.

14 Clarke, *Voices*, 33, 58, 98.

15 Franklin, *War Stars*, 21, 22, 48.

16 Albert Berger, "The Triumph of Prophecy: Science Fiction and Nuclear Power in the Post-Hiroshima Period," *Science Fiction Studies* 3 (1976): 143–150.

17 Jacques Derrida, "No Apocalypse, Not Now," *Diacritics* 14 (summer 1984): 23.

18 The step-by-step description of a nuclear attack is a familiar literary tactic in cold-war propaganda. Dubbed "the bombing run" by the Physicians for Social Responsibility (Hugh Gusterson, *Nuclear Rites: A Weapons Laboratory at the End of the Cold War* [Los Angeles: University of California Press, 1996], 199), it is a prominent feature of antinuclear literature such as John Hersey, *Hiroshima*, rev. ed. (New York: Knopf, 1985), 3–23; Helen Caldicott, *Missile Envy: The Arms Race and Nuclear War*, rev. ed. (New York: Bantam Books, 1986), 9; and Jonathan Schell, *The Fate of the Earth* (New York: Knopf, 1982), 132. It is also a prominent feature of civil defense literature and patriotic mass-distribution magazines from earlier in the cold war, as in *Collier's* special issue, "Preview of the War We Do Not Want," 27 October 1951, a future-historical chronicle of U.S. resolve to fight and win a nuclear war, written by many of the leading lights of the U.S. press. As we have seen, the bombing run has been revised for the war on terror to raise consciousness about the threat of nuclear terrorism. Once again the vivid depiction of nuclear attack can be mustered to support the interests of global disarmament advocates (David Krieger, "Preventing a Terrorist Mushroom Cloud," *Humanist* 62 [January/February 2002]: 4) and of hawks eager to wage preemptive war against "demented and venomous regime[s]" such as those of North Korea and Iran before they lay waste to U.S. cities (Gabriel Schoenfeld, "The Terror Ahead," *Commentary* 116 [November 2003]: 21).

19 The history of nuclear strategy and war gaming is reviewed in Fred Kaplan, *The Wizards of Armageddon* (New York: Simon and Schuster, 1983), and Gregg Herken, *Counsels of War* (New York: Knopf, 1985).

20 Comprehensive surveys of nuclear war storytelling across genres and media include Broderick, *Nuclear Fear*, 56–191; Spencer R. Weart, *Nuclear Fear: A History of Images* (Cambridge: Harvard University Press, 1988); Martha A. Bartter, *The Way to Ground Zero: The Atomic Bomb in American Science Fiction* (New York: Greenwood, 1988); and Paul Boyer, *By the Bomb's Early Light: American Thought and Culture at the Dawn of the Atomic Age* (Chapel Hill: University of North Carolina Press, 1994).

21 Schell, *Fate of the Earth*, 21; Hayden White, "The Value of Narrativity in the Representation of Reality," *Critical Inquiry* 7 (fall 1980): 10, 24.

22 No world power has disarmed after building a nuclear arsenal, and South Africa is the only nation that has voluntarily dismantled its nuclear weapons after acquiring the means to build them on its own. Ukraine, Kazakhstan, and Belarus acquired Soviet weapons after the cold war but returned them to Russia in 1991. See "Nuclear Weapons: Who Has What at a Glance," Arms Control Association, www.armscontrol.org/factsheets/Nuclearweaponswhohaswhat.asp (accessed 10 August 2004).

23 Thomas Hughes, *American Genesis: A Century of Invention and Technological Enthusiasm* (New York: Penguin, 1989), 3.

24 Bosley Crowther, review of *Strategic Air Command*, *New York Times*, 21 April 1955.

25 Lawrence H. Suid, *Guts and Glory: Great American War Movies* (New York: Addison-Wesley, 1979), 170.

26 Ground Zero Group, *Nuclear War: What's in It for You?* (New York: Pocket Books, 1982).

27 Gusterson, *Nuclear Rites*, 201.

28 Quoted in James W. Harper, "Images of Armageddon: Nuclear War in Three Mass Audience Films," in Ulrich Roebel and Otto Nelson, eds., *War and Peace: Perspectives in the Nuclear Age* (Lubbock: Texas Tech University Press, 1988), 31.

29 In identifying nuclear defense policy as a narrative formation reproduced across culture, I am extending a method of analysis begun in U.S. studies of cold-war culture. In *American Fiction in the Cold War* (Madison: University of Wisconsin Press, 1991), Thomas Hill Schaub identifies a liberal narrative of cold-war leftist disenchantment that structured many great works of postwar literature. Alan Nadel identifies an even more wide-ranging narrative formation in his collection of essays *Containment Culture: American Narratives, Postmodernism, and the Atomic Age* (Durham, N.C.: Duke University Press, 1995), which equates such cultural themes as domesticity, sexuality, and industrialization with the politics of communist containment. The anthropologist Hugh Gusterson reads the cold-war conflict in toto as a postmodern narrative. Describing the "cold-war worldview" as a particularly self-referential kind of narrativizing, Gusterson argues that, given "its penchant for simulation . . . the postmodern character of the American cold-war narrative may enable it to survive the death of its villain in a way that would be difficult for a more 'realist' narrative" ("Endless Escalation: The Cold War as Postmodern Narrative," *Tikkun* 6 [September/October 1991]: 44–45). Gusterson's provocative insight proved to be more correct than he could know, for the cold-war narrative of national security has indeed been revised in a way that pits cold-war institutions against a new postmodern kind of villain, the terrorist network.

30 Schell quoted in Christina del Sesto, "Champion of Human Survival Tries to Awaken Academics to a Nuclear Menace," *New York Times*, 18 November 2000.

31 Before the cold war, the term "catastrophism" was primarily associated with scientific theories of geological catastrophism long-discarded by geologists. In the latter years of the cold war, however, the threat of nuclear war made the idea of global catastrophe plausible again. Geologists consequently imported the idea of catastrophism back into their discipline, using nuclear explosions and the threat of nuclear war as metaphors to explain how catastrophic impacts could cause both large geological features and mass extinctions, in the process launching a new catastrophist paradigm of planetary science. For a detailed study of the institutional and theoretical ties between nuclear and geological catastrophism, see Doug Davis, "'One Hundred Million Hydrogen Bombs': Total War in the Fossil Record," *Configurations* 9 (2001): 461–508.

32 The quote is from John Lewis Gaddis, *Surprise, Security, and the American Experience* (Cambridge: Harvard University Press, 2004), 77; see also Ivo H. Daalder and James M. Lindsay, *America Unbound: The Bush Revolution in Foreign Policy* (Washington, D.C.: Brookings Institution Press, 2003), 12–14.

33 Bush quoted in Jonathan Schell, "The Unthinkable," *The Nation*, 8 November 1999, 7.

34 Quoted in Ernest R. May, ed., *American Cold War Strategy: Interpreting NSC 68* (New York: Bedford Books, 1993), 26, 61, 76.

35 Ibid., 16.

36 Walter LaFeber, *The American Age: U.S. Foreign Policy at Home and Abroad since 1896*, vol. 2. of *The American Age: U.S. Foreign Policy at Home and Abroad*, 2nd ed. (New York: Norton, 1994), 541.

37 John Foster Dulles, "The Evolution of Foreign Policy," *Department of State Bulletin*, 25 January 1954, 108.

38 David Alan Rosenberg, "The Origins of Overkill: Nuclear Weapons and American Strategy, 1945–1960," *International Security* 7 (spring 1983): 133.

39 Gusterson, *Nuclear Rites*, 252.

40 Hans J. Morgenthau, *Politics among Nations: The Struggle for Power and Peace*, 3rd ed. (New York: Knopf, 1960), 4, 6, 8, 10.

41 Lawrence Freedman, *The Evolution of Nuclear Strategy*, 2nd ed. (New York: St. Martin's Press, 1989), 34.

42 Bernard Brodie, "Bernard Brodie on the Absolute Weapon, 1946," in Philip L. Cantelon, Richard G. Hewlett, and Robert C. Williams, eds., *The American Atom: A Documentary History of Nuclear Policies from the Discovery of Fission to the Present*, 2nd ed. (Philadelphia: University of Pennsylvania Press, 1991), 197.

43 George W. Bush, "West Point Commencement Address," 1 June 2002, www.whitehouse.gov/news/releases/2002/06/20020601-3.html (accessed 10 August 2004).

44 National Security Council, *The National Security Strategy of the United States*, 17 September 2002, www.whitehouse.gov/nsc/nssall.html, 13, preface (accessed 9 August 2004).

45 James Mann, *Rise of the Vulcans: The History of Bush's War Cabinet* (New York: Viking, 2004), 27–28.

46 National Security Council, *The National Security Strategy*, 13–14.

47 George W. Bush, "Address to a Joint Session of Congress and the American People," 20 September 2001, www.whitehouse.gov/news/releases/2001/09/20010920-8.html (accessed 10 August 2004).

48 Bruce G. Blair, "Loose Cannon," *National Interest* 52 (summer 1998): 92.

49 "George Clooney/The Peacemaker," *Hollywood Reporter*, 24 September 1997, Lexis-Nexis Academic (accessed 10 August 2004).

50 Nick Madigan, "Frosh Dream Team Finds Film Legs," *Variety*, 12 January 1997, 33.

51 Tom Friend, "When an Unofficial Military Presence Is Welcome," *New York Times*, 21 September 1997.

52 Jeffrey Smith, "A Woman with Throw-Weight," *Washington Post*, 27 September 1997; Tom Shone, "Let's All Make a Bomb," *Sunday Times* (UK), 26 October 1997; Duane Byrge, review of *The Peacemaker*, *Hollywood Reporter*, 25 September 1997, 5; Dolores Barclay, "At the Movies: *The Peacemaker*," Associated Press, 25 September 1997, LexisNexis Academic (accessed 10 August 2004); Desson Howe, "*Peacemaker*: Bombs Away," *Washington Post*, 26 September 1997.

53 One review that demonstrates how much the meaning of the fictional scenario of nuclear terrorism has changed over the past decade describes Leder's nuclear destruction of two square miles of Manhattan in a way few would dare in the years since the 9/11 attacks: "I like the smallness of the conceit. They're not 'saving the world' or even the United States. They're not even saving the city, only a couple of its better delis and coffee shops, including the one where Jerry, Elaine and George hang out. The weapon is one of those little bitty bomblets, part of a larger package originally designed to deploy from space from among a nesting of nine more of its brothers and do specific hard-target damage. It would melt, say, most of midtown and part of Queens but probably leave the Bronx intact. Long Island? No problemo. You'd be safe out there, and you'd pick up a really fine tan without having to spend much time at the beach. Stephen Hunter, "*The Peacemaker*: Right on Target," *Washington Post*, 26 September 1997.

54 See www.usec.com (accessed 10 August 2004).

55 Mann, *Rise of the Vulcans*, 144.

56 National Commission on Terrorist Attacks upon the United States, *The 9/11 Commission Report* (Washington, D.C.: Government Printing Office, 2004), 108.

57 Jonathan V. Last, "War? What War? Hollywood Ignores Today's Biggest Story Line," *Wall Street Journal*, 10 October 2003; "Paramount Film's Super Bowl Villains Changed to Neo-Nazis; Islamic Group CAIR Had Concerns about Stereotyping in *The Sum of All Fears*," *PR Newswire*, 26 January 2001, LexisNexis Academic (accessed 10 August 2004).

58 John McClain, "League Cool to Cinematic Super Bowl Blast," *Houston Chronicle*, 26 May 2002.

59 Tom FitzGerald, "Action Didn't Make the Cut," *San Francisco Chronicle*, 22 May 2002.

60 S.D., "Captain America Returns—but without the Geritol," *Maclean's*, 10 June 2002, 62.

61 On the rented military force, Katherine Q. Seelye, "When Hollywood's Big Guns Come Right from the Source," *New York Times*, 10 June 2002; on the CIA building, Paul Bedard, Suzi Parker, David E. Kaplan, and Linda Fasulo, "CIA Says Clancy Spun It Right in *Sum of All Fears*," *U.S. News and World Report*, 13 May 2002, 4; on RSA, "RSA Security Featured in *The Sum of All Fears;* Company Consults with Paramount Pictures on Authentication Technologies for Fourth Tom Clancy Film," RSA Security Press Release Archive, 30 May 2002, www.rsasecurity.com/press_release.asp?doc_id=1308 (accessed 10 August 2004); on satellite imaging,

"The Sum of All Fears Uses High-Resolution IKONOS Satellite Imagery to Create Hollywood Magic; Space Imaging Product Provides Realism to Key Movie Scenes," *PR Newswire*, 31 May 2002, LexisNexis Academic (accessed 10 August 2004); on security-state authenticity, Bedard et al., "CIA Says," 4.

62 On Lugar, see Calvo and Welkos, "Hollywood Shakes Off Fear"; on the high-level decision makers, Chabria, "Hollywood Calls on Military Ties," 7; on Kerry, see Toto, "'All Fears' Limited."

63 Matt Drudge, "Bush Official Questions Release of Paramount's Nuke-Scare 'Fears,'" *Drudge Report*, 26 May 2002, www.drudgereport.com/mattsf.htm (accessed 10 August 2004).

64 Donna Leinwand, "Officials Try to Ease 'Sum' Fears," *U.S.A Today*, 3 June 2002.

65 First Bonner quote in Susan Reda, "Container Security: The Sum of All Fears," *Stores: The Bulletin of the N.R.D.G.A.* 84 (October 2002): 30; second Bonner quote in Julia Malone, "Customs Chief: Have No 'Fears'; Unlike Movie, Today's Gear Would Detect Nuclear Bomb," *Atlanta Journal-Constitution*, 4 June 2002.

66 *Joint Resolution to Authorize the Use of United States Armed Forces against Iraq*, Public Law 107–243, 107th Cong., 2nd sess., 2 October 2002, www.whitehouse. gov/news/releases/2002/10/20021002-2.html (accessed 10 August 2004).

67 George W. Bush, "The State of the Union," 28 January 2003, www.whitehouse. gov/news/releases/2003/01/20030128-19.html (accessed 10 August 2004).

VISIONS OF SECURITY

IMPERMEABLE BORDERS, IMPASSABLE WALLS, IMPOSSIBLE HOME/LANDS?

MARY N. LAYOUN

In his acceptance speech for the Peace Prize of the German Publishers and Booksellers Association in mid-October 2001, entitled "Faith and Knowledge—An Opening," Jürgen Habermas cautions that when "current events become so overwhelming that they rip the choice of topic out of our own hands, so to speak, the John Waynes among us intellectuals are of course greatly tempted to compete instead as to who can be the quickest to shoot from the hip." Habermas heeds his own caution with a sustained and almost poignant reflection on "the still-unresolved dialectic inherent in our own western process of secularization" between "religion and secular society," or the "faith and knowledge" of his title, insisting on a "hope for a return of the political in another form ... as a world-wide, civilizing power of formation."[1]

Habermas's specific reference to overwhelming current events is, of course, a reference to what we elliptically refer as 9/11. In this essay, I, too, address a succession of events in the months and years since 11 September 2001.[2] Yet given my disciplinary predilection for comparative languages, literatures, and cultures, I focus on two terms ("terrorism" and "security"), two terribly instructive instances that deploy those terms (the USA PATRIOT Act and Israel's "security wall"), and two literary texts that offer a perspective on those terms and on their deployment.[3]

There is a model of sorts for this comparative configuration in the example of reading nationalisms.[4] If the rhetoric and the grammar of national formations are in fraught and sometimes productive tension with one another, what cannot be articulated in language is suggested in and by that very tension. Rhetoric calls out and persuades its audiences with visions of likely possibility. Grammar enacts a correct or orderly placement and use of its constituent elements. Attentiveness to both in a given historical and cultural instance can allow recognition of that which is effaced or excised, as well as that which escapes or refuses incorporation.

In this regard, it is instructive to recall that the first definition of terrorism is "state terrorism," most particularly the Reign of Terror (1793–1794) of the postrevolutionary French regime. In fact, the word "terrorism" enters French in 1795 as a term for "government by intimidation as directed and carried out by the party in power." Minimally, terrorism is action or threat that instills terror or dread. Some three centuries after the historical moment that inspired the term's entry into European languages, terrorism is an evermore complex knot of shadow fears and actual dangers. The threat and the practice of terrorism are seized by diverse actors across states and within states in the attempt to inflame fear, to secure compliance, or to enunciate a claim or grievance. The primary audience for terrorism is not simply the usually noncombatant recipients of terrorist violence. It is the far larger audience who witnesses and draws conclusion from that violence. Inherently then, terrorism is a violently and often mortally performative act that seeks to produce an effect—not only on those who bear the brunt of the physical attack but also, more crucially, on a larger audience who witnesses the event(s).[5] It is a theatrical act to draw attention and evoke a response in those who witness the violence.[6]

The distinctions are many between state terrorism and that of smaller groups operating within and across—and often in recent decades, virtually regardless of—states and their boundaries.[7] In fact, it is to this discrepancy that Habermas refers in the essay cited earlier when he suggestively characterizes terrorism as that which "express[ed] also—and I emphasize the word 'also'—the ominously silent collision of worlds that must find a common language beyond the mute violence of terrorism against military might." Before the almost poignant moral imperative to "a common language beyond the mute violence," terrorism, then, is also a fearful and violent call, a mute rejoinder to military (and economic and cultural) domination. I would like to keep both senses of "terrorism" in the forefront—that is, terrorism as inspiring terror or dread through action or threat, and terrorism as deadly and unequal relations in a shouting match of the mute. If the former is performative or theatrical in the sense in which we just defined it, the latter may well shade that theatrical performance as a kind of postmodern tragedy.

"Security," the second term which I would recall, is the absence of terror or dread. Literally, "security" is to be *se*—the privative "without"—*cura* or "care." In late Latin, then, *secura* is to be safe or free from danger. That sense of security as safety or freedom from danger remains in the present moment. So, in the United States, the Department of Homeland Security is established in response to the "terrorist" (as opposed to criminal) acts of 9/11, putatively to create a "secure homeland safe and free from danger." But there is also an alternative and equally familiar meaning of "security" as "something given, deposited, or pledged to make certain the fulfillment of an obligation." I would like to keep both senses of "security," too, in the forefront—that is, security as safety, as the absence of care or fear, and security as a pledge in fulfillment of an obligation.

These, then, are our two terms. The first of two efforts at rethinking security to which I would point—both of which revolve around the name and concept of "terrorism" and of "security"—is the USA PATRIOT Act of 2001 and its immediate offspring, the draft of the Domestic Security Enhancement Act of 2003 and, most recently, numerous smaller bills introduced in Congress.[8] It is worth remembering—in spite of the ostensible meaning of the USA PATRIOT Act's title—that it is a clumsily clever acronym for Uniting and Strengthening America by Providing Appropriate Tools Required to Intercept and Obstruct Terrorism. Submitted just four days after 9/11, hurriedly and uncritically passed by Congress, and signed into law by President George W. Bush on 26 October 2001, the USA PATRIOT Act is divided into ten separate titles with nearly 150 sections.[9] It radically and broadly extends the powers of the president and of U.S. intelligence-gathering bodies, limits the oversight and jurisdictional authority of Congress and of the court system, and, no less significantly, radically redefines the terms of security and terrorism and thereby of civil rights and citizenship. In spite of claims to the contrary, most of its provisions are permanent unless the act is revoked. Recent fervent discussion of the 2005 sunset clause for some of the act's provisions neatly sidesteps the fact that most of the USA PATRIOT Act's provisions are not affected by a sunset clause of any sort.

Although there are a number of noteworthy historical precedents for the curtailment of constitutional rights in the twentieth-century United States, one of the more immediate antecedents of the USA PATRIOT Act of 2001 is the Foreign Intelligence Surveillance Act (FISA) of 1978.[10] The PATRIOT Act predicates itself on extensive reformulation of FISA. But, most starkly, the (already uneasy) distinction in FISA between foreign intelligence gathering and domestic investigation, between intelligence and law enforcement, is collapsed in the USA PATRIOT Act in its submission of domestic criminal investigation to the same (lowered) standards as those for foreign intelligence surveillance.[11] The distinction between the citizenry of a country and its noncitizen residents and visitors, on the one hand, and "agents of a foreign government," on the other, is at least a familiar and arguably necessary one. The ability of state agencies to investigate potential threats to the state and those residing within it by citizens and noncitizens alike is just as necessary. What is, however, equally and simultaneously necessary to a democratic state and an open and democratic society is the protection of citizen and noncitizen alike by the rule of law and by judiciary procedures rigorously subject to a system of checks and balances. It is this necessity that is so drastically compromised—in the name of security against terror—by the USA PATRIOT Act and its offspring. And in this drastic compromise—hastily approved by Congress in response to the perhaps startling realization that the United States is vulnerable to attack—the possibility of any meaningful security *beyond* terror for society is gravely jeopardized.

The USA PATRIOT Act bristles with stipulations that take aim at a safe and open society, its members, and, ultimately, the state in which they live. The insistence on the need for secrecy, for widespread surveillance, for draconian response to all that is characterized as the appearance of terrorist intent is striking. In fact, in one remarkable passage, the USA PATRIOT Act defines domestic terrorism (in a parallel to its definition of international terrorism) as:

activities that—

(A) involve acts dangerous to human life that are a violation of the criminal laws of the United States or of any State;

(B) *appear to be intended*—

    (i) to intimidate or coerce a civilian population;

    (ii) to influence the policy of a government by intimidation or coercion; or

    (iii) to affect the conduct of a government by mass destruction, assassination, or kidnapping [*sic*]; and

(C) occur primarily within the territorial jurisdiction of the United
States [emphasis added].[12]

The phrase "appear to be intended"—one that recurs throughout the
PATRIOT Act—is a striking formulation. If intention is ascribed to appearance, then the distinction rests on the interpretive abilities of whoever
decides what intention is indicated by what appearance. As critics of the
PATRIOT Act have increasingly noted, the capacious definitions of terrorist activity allowed by the act could be used to characterize a wide range of
public conduct, including legitimate and peaceful protest. Those definitions
could be (and have been) used to characterize a disturbingly wide range of
appearance—those who appear, for example, to be Muslim or Arab. And most
particularly, characterizing intention on the basis of appearance at least
implicitly offers a chilling invitation to potentially virulent discrimination
against any outsiders, strangers, and foreigners whose appearance is notable.
The interpretive ability of agents of the state—or, by extension, of citizens
and residents of the state who notify state agents—to discern intent based on
their assessment of appearance is legitimated and given fearful weight by the
USA PATRIOT Act's radical lowering of standards for domestic investigation
to a level previously maintained only for the investigation and collection of
evidence concerning suspected agents of foreign governments in the United
States. What was previously an (only arguably) acceptable lower evidentiary,
investigatory, and civil liberties threshold for suspected foreign intelligence
operatives in the United States is now extended to U.S. residents and citizens—the potential enemy within the homeland. One of the three essential
components of identifying that domestic terrorist enemy is the "appearance
of intent" as interpreted not only by state officials but also by ordinary citizens and residents—who interpret intent through appearances and act on
that interpretation. Yet what does appearance indicate about intent? And
who interprets that appearance? Based on what signs? The abusive potential
of this guideline for defining terrorism to ensure security is abundant.

In the battle against terror, in the name of security, there is a further and
now often-noted provision of the USA PATRIOT Act that conflates what FISA
defined as criminal law enforcement, as distinct from foreign intelligence
gathering—legal protection afforded citizens and residents and even illegal
residents suspected of criminal activity, as opposed to those suspected of
being agents of a foreign government. Section 213 of the USA PATRIOT Act

abrogates the concept of a lawful police search of a home, apartment, or office. Amending section 3103a of Title 18 of the U.S. Code, section 213 allows the FBI to secretly enter an apartment or house while the residents are asleep or away; to take, alter, or copy things; and not to inform the residents of their entry for days, weeks, or even months. This radical expansion of the purview of intelligence-gathering agencies applies not just to residents, aliens, or citizens suspected in terrorism cases, however dubiously "terrorism" is defined. Remarkably, it applies to drug violations, tax fraud, falsified student-loan applications, or any other federal crime.[13] And it is not subject to the sunset provision under which a limited number of the new law's strictures were to expire after four years (in 2005) unless renewed by Congress.[14] In this way, the emergency atmosphere generated by the 9/11 attacks and their aftermath was used to make permanent, fundamental changes in law-enforcement and intelligence-gathering procedures, many of which are of questionable efficacy in preventing terrorism. Their efficacy in promoting security is even more questionable.

In 2003, the Domestic Security Enhancement Act Amendments ("Patriot II"), drafted by Attorney General John Ashcroft's office and presented as essential to the war on terror, sought to extend what were claimed to be the restrictive limitations of the USA PATRIOT Act of 2001. Leaked in draft form in early 2003, Patriot II became the object of considerable public discussion and debate. Since then apportioned into other legislative efforts to expand the powers of Patriot I, two aspects of the draft of Patriot II are noteworthy in the context of intentions derived from appearance and the conflation of foreign intelligence gathering and domestic law enforcement. Section 402 of that document, "Providing Material Support to Terrorism," amends the definition of international terrorism "to make it clear that it covers acts which *by their nature appear to be intended* for the stated purposes" (emphasis added). The "stated purposes" are, of course, engaging in "international terrorism." The section continues: "Hence there would be no requirement to show that the defendants actually had such an intent." And, no less strikingly, Ashcroft's 2003 proposed amendments reiterate the conflation of domestic law enforcement and foreign surveillance already noted in the USA PATRIOT Act of 2001: "(There is a conforming amendment to the definition of 'domestic terrorism' to maintain the existing parallel between the two definitions.)"[15]

Terrorism, then, both rhetorically and literally in this definition, derives from within as well as from without the homeland. And the effort to procure homeland security in the face of that (definition of) terrorism must necessarily exert terror (instill fear and dread)—in the name of security—against those who appear to possess an intent to commit terrorism themselves. Included in the expanded definition of terrorist activity in Patriot II is material support provided to a designated "terrorist organization"—whether or not those providing such support intended to support "terrorism." Such intent does not have to be proven by the prosecuting authorities. It can simply be inferred from appearances.

Although further promotion of Patriot II was suspended, at least as a single massive bill, some of its most egregious expansions of already egregiously expanded security, surveillance, and intelligence powers were redirected to other bills and efforts at Patriot I revision and expansion. Those reformulated segments of Patriot II introduced into the 108th Congress included:

- H.R. 3037, The Antiterrorism Tools Enhancement Act of 2003, allowing the government to seize records and compel testimony in terrorism cases without prior review by a court or grand jury.

- H.R. 3040 and S. 1606, The Pretrial Detention and Lifetime Supervision of Terrorists Act of 2003, allowing the government to deny bail without proving danger or flight risk for a list of federal crimes said to be terrorism related. (Under current law, pretrial detention is available for all federal crimes, but a presumption of detention applies to terrorism crimes only if they are "acts of terrorism transcending national boundaries.")

- H.R. 2934 and S. 1604, the Terrorist Penalties Enhancement Act of 2003, establishing a new death penalty for "domestic terrorism" as defined by the Patriot Act—a definition that applies not only to specific crimes of terrorism but also to any violation of federal or state law if it involves a dangerous act and is intended to influence government policy.

Most of these bills were referred to—and never emerged from—House or Senate subcommittees. But various provisions of these bills continue to work their way through new and differently titled bills. Or provisions are attached to bills which bear no obvious connection to these outgrowths from the USA PATRIOT Act. That act and the federal and state bills that have proliferated in its wake are stunning legislative examples of policy predicated on deeply problematic notions of terror and security. In the rhetorical fabric of its legislation, as in the social grammar which that rhetoric would impose, the USA PATRIOT Act is a fearful assault on the very security it purports to protect. This U.S. example of "rethinking global security" run frighteningly awry—of the ill-conceived effort for security against terror creating its own terror in turn—is thrown into even starker relief by another more harshly

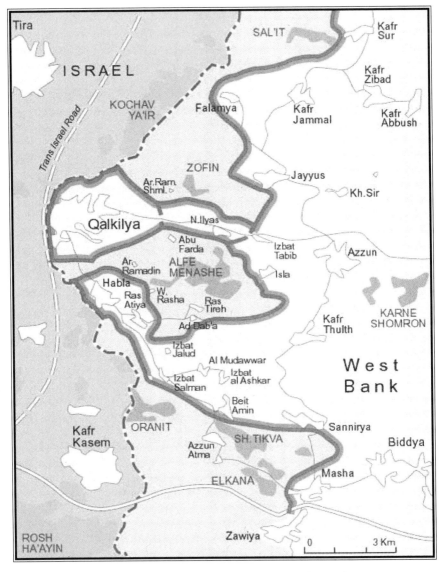

1. Segment of the Israeli wall in the Qalqiliya region.
The double gray line is the wall; the dot and
dash line is the Green Line, February 2003. (JTF-NAD)

graphic and visceral but no less egregious instance of the effort to construct a bulwark of security against terrorism.

If terrorism can presumably be located in the appearance of intent for the USA PATRIOT Act as that which must be discerned, interpreted, contained, and eliminated, in the quite literal and material construction of Israel's "security wall" around the West Bank and Jerusalem (with a second wall proposed to the east around the Jordan Valley), the very possibility of "appearance" of any sort is rather fiercely eradicated (see figure 1). At a cost assessed at two million dollars per kilometer and an estimated length of some 670 kilometers (420 miles) when completed—three times as long and twice as high as the former Berlin Wall—the already existing wall of almost 150 miles cuts deep into Palestinian territory, either razing or incorporating into Israel Palestinian water resources, businesses, stores and schools, farmland, grazing fields, and olive groves (see figures 2–4). The territorial basis for a potential Palestinian state and the boundaries of land seized and occupied by Israel in the 1967 war (the Green Line) are violated and seized once again—now by the construction of the wall.[16] If the Berlin Wall was built

2. Segment of the fence with razor wire and trench in Jayyous, Qalqiliya district. (PENGON/Anti-Apartheid Wall Campaign)

to keep residents of East Berlin in, Israel's wall is built to keep Palestinians out. Not coincidentally, in the name of security, it also serves to keep out not just the appearance of Palestinians, but any interaction between Palestinians and Israelis at all.

Citing an increasing frequency of Palestinian suicide attacks on Israelis, the Israeli government of Prime Minister Ariel Sharon in May 2002 adopted a plan to begin building a "fence" between Israel and the West Bank. In June 2002, fields were plowed under, houses demolished, and land confiscated in preparation for the first segment of the wall between Qalqiliya and Jenin. Construction began near the village of Salem west of Jenin and extended in stages to split up and enclose Qalqiliya, Tulkarem, Jenin, Jerusalem, and Bethlehem areas. An intrusive network of electronic fences, concrete walls, trenches, and surveillance towers, the wall itself comprises either a wire-and-mesh "fence" or twenty-five-foot-high concrete walls. Rolls of razor wire and a four-meter deep ditch mark one side of it. On the other is a road for Israeli

3. Five-hundred-year-old olive trees uprooted to build the security wall in the Qalqiliya district, June 2003. (PENGON/Anti-Apartheid Wall Campaign)

military vehicles. In addition, the structure is fitted with electronic sensors and has an earth-covered "trace road" beside it that reveals the footprints of anyone attempting to cross the wall. Qalqiliya City is now virtually enclosed by an eight-meter-high concrete wall punctuated by massive watchtowers (see figure 5). It is justified by the Israeli government as a "sniper wall" to prevent gun attacks against Israeli motorists on the nearby Trans-Israel Highway.

On 31 July 2003, the Israeli Ministry of Defense announced the completion of the first phase of the wall. Its route covers 145 kilometers: 125 kilometers from Sallem, which lies within the Green Line, in the north to the Elqana settlement in the south. Another 20 kilometers that run along the northern and southern boundaries of the Jerusalem Municipality are part of what the Israeli government calls the "Jerusalem envelope." In addition to the main barrier, Israel is planning subsidiary barriers—referred to as "depth barriers"—in three areas along the route of the first phase. In some of the areas in

4. The wall enclosing Bethlehem.
(PENGON/Anti-Apartheid Wall Campaign)

which depth barriers are planned, Israel has seized control of private Palestinian land, but construction has not yet begun.

The second phase of the security wall extends forty-five kilometers from Sallem to Teysar, bordering the Jordan Valley. Israel's Ministry of Defense announced completion of this phase in 2004. And, even before the second phase of the wall's construction was completed, the fiercely debated path of the third phase of the wall—intruding nearly fifteen miles into West Bank territory to include the Jewish settlement of Ariel—was announced by the Israeli government in early October 2003.

A far more visceral and graphically apparent intervention in the debates and policy formulations on security and terror than the USA PATRIOT Act in the United States, Israel's wall against the Palestinians was asserted to be a necessary self-defense measure. On 14 August 2002, Raanan Gissin, an aide to Prime Minister Sharon, told Reuters News: "This is a security border intended to meet the immediate threat that we are facing, which is unprecedented, as

5. The wall coils some five kilometers around Qalqiliya City, making an enclave of its forty-two thousand residents; there is a single armed Israeli checkpoint for entrance to or exit from the city. (PENGON/Anti-Apartheid Wall Campaign)

wave after wave of suicide bombers penetrate our heartland. This is not a political border." A little more than a year later, with the third and ever-more-invasive phase of the security wall approved, a UN Commission on Human Rights report authored by the South African lawyer John Dugard unequivocally characterized the barrier as effectively annexing Palestinian land.[17] In an earlier if less official op-ed article in the *International Herald Tribune*, Dugard had noted that "the time has come to condemn the wall as an act of unlawful annexation in the language of Security Council Resolutions 478 and 497. . . . Israel's claim that the wall is designed as a security measure with no ulterior motive is simply not supported by the facts."[18] Sara Roy, an authority on the economy of the West Bank and Gaza, pointed even more explicitly to the effect of that annexation in reference to a World Bank Report on Israel's security wall: "The World Bank projects that when completed, the wall could isolate as many as 250,000–300,000 Palestinians, mostly residents of East Jerusalem, which equals approximately 12–14 percent of the population of the West Bank. Furthermore, the wall could annex as much as 10 percent of the West Bank to Israel. The resulting context is one of oppression, desperation and suffocation, and one in which extremists thrive."[19] If Israel's wall makes a rhetorical claim to provide security, its grammar—its order on the ground—is anything but security for Palestinians. And it is, finally, anything but security for Israelis. In fact, the wall—and the extremes of misery and deprivation it has caused for Palestinians—may have exacerbated the potential for attacks.[20]

But if we return to that alternative and simultaneous meaning of "security" not only as freedom from care or worry or fear but also as that which is "given, deposited, or pledged to make certain the fulfillment of an obligation," we might see a different vision of security in the struggle against terror. That vision, suggested by the continuing actions of Palestinian farmers from the village of Jayyous in the Qalqiliya district, is of security as a pledge in fulfillment of an obligation—a shared obligation of social justice and human rights. Sharif Omar, a farmer and community leader from Jayyous and a member of the Land Defense Committee for the Qalqiliya district, has a different response to Israeli state terror and violent Palestinian response to that terror. From a detailed account of what the Israeli security wall means for Palestinians in Jayyous, Omar moves to an alternative—and, it must be said, fragile and endangered—practice of security against terror.

With the wall, Israel is taking 75 percent of Jayyous' most fertile land, including all of our irrigated farmland, seven wells, and 12,000 olive trees. Jayyous' 3000 residents depend almost entirely on agricultural income. So this means a loss of our livelihoods, dreams, hopes, future, and heritage. . . . The wall is cutting through Palestinian villages all across our fertile Qalqiliya region and causing destruction in dozens of West Bank villages. . . . Israeli officials have justified the wall's construction as necessary for security. However if it were for security it would follow the Green Line. Building it four miles inside the Green Line means only one thing: the Israelis are confiscating more Palestinian land and water. . . . The wall is an unwritten order for emigration from Palestine, because people who have no income will have no choice but to leave. To avoid this, I and many other farmers began building sheds and tents so we can live on our farmland. I've planted 150 citrus trees since they started building the wall to show other farmers we don't have to yield. Jayyous farmers, with the assistance of international and Israeli activists, have held many peaceful protests during which they face the bulldozers destroying their fields as well as armed Israeli soldiers and guards. . . . I've chosen peaceful resistance to the wall because . . . I hope peaceful protests will leave a positive impact on Israeli soldiers and strengthen our partnership with Israeli peace groups; . . . the wall is wrong. It will never lead to a just and real peace . . . [but to] preventing the development of understanding between our cultures. It is so important for us to find one language—for peace.[21]

Sharif Omar's eloquent statement suggests a response to threat and fear other than violent repression, separation, and retaliation. If the farmers of Jayyous can envision another response to danger and a vision of security, surely philosophers and political theorists—perhaps even political leaders— might do so as well. Or they might at least note Omar's words and actions in the face of imminent and quite material threat.

And on the other side of the sea, in our contemporary age (reign?) of terror, it is not only Jürgen Habermas who questions the character of responses to terror in the name of security. Habermas's well-known interlocutor Richard Rorty states bluntly that "our military prowess can do little to lessen the danger that our cities will be subject to unpredictable and unpreventable attacks by small non-governmental organizations like al-Qaeda."[22] Elsewhere on the spectrum of political thought and analysis, Richard Perle, the former chair of the Pentagon's Defense Policy Board, opens his commentary in the 21 March 2003 London *Guardian* with the pronouncement: "What will die [with "Saddam Hussein's reign of terror"] is the fantasy of the UN as the foundation of a new world order, . . . the liberal conceit of safety through international law administered by international institutions." Yet even Perle concludes his querulous essay with the observation that "there can never be a purely military solution to a problem with deep political roots."[23] And in this configuration of call and response across the Atlantic, Rorty poses a question to Perle's concluding observation: "[So] how can democratic institutions be strengthened so as to survive in a time when governments can no longer guarantee what President Bush likes to call homeland security?" In the concluding lines of his essay, Rorty offers a conditional answer to his own question. Democratic institutions can be strengthened "if the voters of the democracies stop their governments from putting their countries on a permanent war footing—from creating a situation in which neither the judges nor the newspapers can restrain organizations like the FBI from doing whatever they please, and in which the military absorbs most of the nation's resources."[24]

There are precautions; there are prudent attention and national and international legal (and armed) responses to the world around us. But there is no security. Or there is only a provisional security, that is, if—as the example of Sharif Omar suggests—we are willing to pledge that second sense of security in the name of a local and global obligation. It is an obligation that has no name in the twenty-first century. It is not quite the nationalist internationalism of the twentieth century. It is not quite the state-fixated structure of the United Nations and its affiliated bodies and organizations—as important as their work is and although the United Nations is the best and only organization we have. But there is a small but powerful suggestion—a faint outline—of how we might think and act on that obligation (to a redefined sense of community and connection to the land) in Sharif Omar's response to terror.

There is another small but powerful suggestion of connection to land and community in the collaborative struggle of Palestinian and Israeli peace coalitions—even in the face of the desperation and brutality of recent weeks and months (and years). The British sociologist Cynthia Cockburn concludes

her carefully specific account of just such coalitions across fearful divides—
of the necessity and difficulty of maintaining women's alliances in Northern
Ireland, Israel and Palestine, and Bosnia-Herzegovina—in *The Space between
Us* with this observation:

> In trying to create sustainable democratic politics, then, the three
> women's projects are . . . resisting the temptation to erase things and
> people who (like a lesbian aunt left out of the family tree) do not con-
> form to the dream. They are withstanding the allure of tidy closures
> and conclusions. . . . Because it is only possible for partners in an alli-
> ance to hold on in there, to survive the compromise and the anger,
> if they believe that new times will come (can be brought about) in
> which the outline of future justice is discernible . . . when the conflict
> has shapeshifted and no longer seems impossible to resolve.[25]

Cockburn's study of an earlier moment ends with the implicit hope of a
common language—or at least a shared perception of the outline of a future
justice, as there is no common language between officials of Palestine and
Israel, no matter the shared languages of coalitions of individual Palestinians
and Israelis. Nor is there a common language between the U.S. government
and those who oppose its unquestionably fearsome military (and economic)
might. In the deadly equation based on a shouting match of the mute, then,
terrorism—as experience and as fear—is used to justify the deafening silence
in which we tell a mortally brutal story of the right to security in the face of
terrorism—for Palestinians, a fearful grammar of loss, uprooting, injury, and
death. It is this grammar that cohabits with the rhetorical formulation of
"security." And if it is a violent and oppressive one for Palestinians, the Palestinian suicide bombers utter an awful cry, in despair of any other language
in which they can speak and be heard. Their Israeli victims, too, are forced
to "listen" to bitter injury and death.

An eerie prefiguration of this shouting match of the mute—of a war on
terrorism in the name of security, be it a security wall or a USA PATRIOT
Act—appears in a novel from the mid-1970s by the Palestinian-Israeli journalist and author Imil Habiby. Habiby's novel of Saeed, "the ill-fated pessoptimist," finds the arguably wise fool of the title, having returned to his
homeland (now Israel) across the border from Lebanon in 1948, riding in the
jeep of the Israeli military governor on the way to Acre. The military governor
spies a woman and child hiding in a field and, after threatening the small

child, orders both mother and child at gunpoint "anywhere you like to the east"—that is, out of Israel.

> "If I ever see you again on this road, I'll show you no mercy."
>
> The woman stood up and, gripping her child by the hand, set off toward the east, not once looking back. Her child walked beside her and he too never looked back.
>
> . . . The further the woman and child went from where we were, the governor standing and I in the jeep, the taller they grew. By the time they merged with their own shadow in the sinking sun they had become bigger than the plain of Acre itself. The military governor still stood there awaiting their final disappearance. . . . Finally he asked in amazement, "Will they never disappear?"[26]

The answer to the military governor's not simply rhetorical question is, of course, no. They will never disappear. Desperately, deadly, without a common language, in defiance of what we know to be the natural law that departing figures grow smaller, these figures remain, grow larger, and cover the face of not just the plain of Acre but of Israel itself—to the absolute *in*security of Israelis and their lethal ethnic cleansing of Palestinians, and to the sometimes suicidal desperation and indescribable misery of the Palestinians.

In a manner as utopian as the texts just cited, Habermas, too, calls for "worlds that must find a common language." Let me conclude, then, with a poetic text written in the aftermath of that now more than two-decades-old event that the current situation on the West Bank and in Gaza initially called to mind, the 1982 Israeli invasion of Lebanon and the siege of Beirut. The text, echoing Habermas's sentiment perhaps, is Mahmoud Darwish's poem "We Travel Like Other People." It begins: "We travel like other people but we return to nowhere." It concludes: "We have a country of words. Speak, speak so I can put my road on the stone of a stone. / We have a country of words. Speak, speak so we may know the end of this travel."[27]

If the time has come to speak, it has come not only for we who have a country made of words. It has also come for we who have countries made of fearsome military might and also—at least sometimes—of rhetorical goals of social justice and democratic freedom.[28] The tension between rhetoric and grammar of this latter country—the United States—is fierce. Can we rethink global security and threats to security while we simultaneously speak

6. Build trust not walls.
(PENGON/Anti-Apartheid Wall Campaign)

in our various languages against the fearsome violations of citizens and
noncitizens in the United States? Against the fearsome violation of citizens
and noncitizens in other countries? Can we imagine and speak for security
as not just the absence of fear—though that's a laudable if most likely impossible goal—but also as a pledge of human responsibility in the name of social
justice? Darwish's poetic injunction to speak—and to listen—is a first step
in an effort to "find a common language" beyond "mute violence" against
military might, beyond "the ominously silent collision of worlds." For, finally,
security might well not be the absence of fear or of threat. There may be
no such security, though certainly danger can be mitigated through wise
foreign and domestic policy, through clear and unwavering commitment to
the struggle for—if not the discovery or creation of—a "common language."
Perhaps security against terror hovers not in an "unending war on terror"
but in the alternative sense of security as something offered to make certain—or, at least, more likely—the fulfillment of an obligation. "Speak so we
may know the end of this travel" and begin to know—to discern the outline
of—a future social and economic justice that may well be our only security
against terror.

NOTES

1 Jürgen Habermas, "Faith and Knowledge—An Opening," speech accepting the Peace Price of the German Publishers and Booksellers Association, Paulskirche, Frankfurt, 14 October 2001; *Süddeutsche Zeitung*, 15 October 2001 (trans. Kermit Snelson).

2 I am grateful to Elyse Crystall for the invitation to participate in the lecture series she organized on the aftermath of 9/11 and the then-impending war in Iraq in spring 2002 and for her commitment and encouragement, and to the lively and engaged communities at the University of North Carolina and Duke University.

3 Not surprisingly, the appellation for the mammoth Israeli edifice depends on location and perspective. As Ahmed Bouzid and Mazin Qumsiyeh point out in their article "Speaking with One Voice" (*Jordan Times*, 15 January 2004), the "barrier" or "wall" is variously modified by "colonisation" or "expansionist" or "apartheid" or "West Bank" in the language of Palestinian official documents and organizations. The Israeli government uses the term "security fence" consistently. The U.S. media echoes this terminology, sometimes substituting "security barrier" for "security fence." The reference of human rights groups ranges more widely, though few appear to use the official Israeli government designation of "security fence."

4 See Mary N. Layoun, *Wedded to the Land?* (Durham, N.C.: Duke University Press, 2001), for a more detailed discussion of this configuration.

5 Mary Kaldor locates an important aspect of "audience response" to contemporary terrorism in her observation that "both symbolic and strategic violence" can also serve "as a form of political mobilisation for extremist groups. In Yugoslavia, killings and displacement in conflict generated the very ideologies supposed to have been the cause of the conflict" ("Terrorism as Regressive Globalization," 25 September 2003, www.opendemocracy.net/debates/article-3-77-1501.jsp#).

6 As Brian Michael Jenkins, a senior advisor on terrorism to the Rand Corporation, notes: "Terrorists ... aim their violence at the people watching. This distinction between actual victims and a target audience is the hallmark of terrorism and separates it from other modes of armed conflict. Terrorism is theater" (*Inside Terrorism* [New York: Columbia University Press, 1998], 132).

7 See for example, Kaldor's characterization of this difference as residing "in their goals (anti-modernist religious and national rather than left or right); in the forms of violence mainly directed against civilians and symbolic targets rather than state or high value economic targets; in their forms of organisation, which tend to be transnational networks rather than hierarchical command structures; in their use of the new media and internet; and in their forms of funding, which tend to be transnational and criminal. Above all, these groups share a commitment to the idea of violent struggle, of war between good and evil" ("Terrorism as Regressive Globalization").

8 The so-called Patriot II Act or "Son of Patriot" was obtained and made public by the Center for Public Integrity in February 2003, just prior to the launching of the U.S. and British invasion of Iraq. Evoking far more public debate and concern than did its predecessor, Patriot II was consequently quietly dropped by the Bush administration. Its provisions were disassembled and reassembled, however,

into other legislation introduced in—and, in a number of instances already passed by—Congress. In November 2003, for example, legislation that funded all intelligence activities of the federal government (the Intelligence Authorization Act for Fiscal Year 2004) included a simple yet pernicious redefinition of "financial institutions." Unfettered and unrestricted federal access—with no judicial or legislative oversight—to the records of "financial institutions" (which previously referred to banks) was already available to federal intelligence agencies. In the new expanded definition, access to the records of "financial institutions" includes those of stockbrokers, car dealerships, casinos, credit-card companies, insurance agencies, jewelers, airlines, the U.S. Post Office, and any other business "whose cash transactions have a high degree of usefulness in criminal, tax, or regulatory matters."

9 The bill passed the House with a vote of 357 to 66. In the Senate, only Wisconsin's Russ Feingold voted against passage. The final bill is H.R. 3162, the result of negotiations to resolve differences between the House and Senate antiterrorism bills H.R. 2975 and S. 1510.

10 See C. William Michaels, *No Greater Threat*, Part I, "Some Notable Historical Attacks on Civil Liberties," for a succinct survey of the precedents. *No Greater Threat* is also a systematic and informed review of the USA PATRIOT Act and its (substantial) contribution to what Michaels analyzes as the "rise of a national security state" (New York: Algora, 2002).

11 The protections outlined in FISA were incurred at least in part by public and state recognition of the domestic intelligence abuses before the mid-1970s and of the necessity for a distinction between law-enforcement and intelligence-gathering agencies in order to protect civil liberties in the United States. See Kate Martin, "Intelligence, Terrorism, and Civil Liberties," for a succinct account of this distinction (www.abanet.org/irr/hr/winter02/martin.html). Anthony D. Romero, executive director of the American Civil Liberties Union, characterizes their collapsed distinction in the PATRIOT Act as an "evisceration of the wall between foreign surveillance and domestic criminal investigation" ("In Defense of Liberty at a Time of National Emergency," www.abanet.org/irr/hr/winter02/romero.html).

12 Title VII: Increased Information Sharing for Critical Infrastructure Protection, sec. 802, "Definition of Domestic Terrorism."

13 It is this construction of a presumable link between drug crime and terrorism on which Senator Orrin Hatch's Vital Interdiction of Criminal Terrorist Organizations (or "Victory") Act of 2003 depends. Its full title is "A Bill to combat narco-terrorism, to dismantle narco-terrorist criminal enterprises, to disrupt narco-terrorist financing and money laundering schemes, to enact national drug sentencing reform, to prevent drug trafficking to children, to deter drug-related violence, to provide law enforcement with the tools needed to win the war against narco-terrorists and major drug traffickers, and for other purposes."

14 In July of 2005, both Houses of Congress approved proposals to reauthorize USA PATRIOT Act sections that had been scheduled to expire at the end of 2005. The House passed H.R. 3199 on 21 July 2005, the Senate, S. 1389 on 29 July 2005. Though not identical, both bills make permanent all but two of the temporary USA PATRIOT Act sections. Expiration of those two sections—having to do with FISA roving wiretaps and authority to seize library or business records—has been postponed, though some provisions of those sections have

been modified. There is a capable comparison of the two bills by the Congressional Research Service, a branch of the Library of Congress, available at: fpc.state.gov/documents/organization/51133.pdf.

15 Domestic Security Enhancement Act Amendments, Title IV: Enhancing Prosecution and Prevention of Terrorist Crimes, Subtitle A: Increased Penalties and Protections against Terrorist Acts, sec. 402, 21. The dispensation for prosecuting authorities from the legal requirement to prove intent—or to demonstrate knowledge of "terrorist" organizations on the part of those charged with supporting terrorism—is reiterated in one of the four provisions of the Victory Act that echoes the Domestic Security Enhancement Act (Victory Act, Title I: Combating Narco-Terrorists Who Aid and Support Terrorists or Terrorist Organizations, sec. 101 Prohibition of Narco-Terrorism, [e] "Proof Requirements," 9).

16 The Green Line, originally the 1949 Armistice Line, is the 190-mile internationally recognized border between Israel and the West Bank.

17 Greg Myre, "Israel Seen as Likely to Approve Barrier," *New York Times*, 1 October 2003.

18 John Dugard, "Tear Down Israel's Wall: An Illegal Annexation," *International Herald Tribune*, 2 August 2003.

19 Sara Roy, "How to Stop Hamas: First End the Occupation," *Beirut Daily Star*, 10 June 2003.

20 In spite of its relentless advance, in midsummer of 2004, Israel's wall was declared illegal by the International Court of Justice, and the wall's construction was indicted as the cause of human rights violations. Though its 9 July 2004 ruling in response to a query from the UN General Assembly was only advisory, the finding of the International Court of Justice was nonetheless an important legal landmark against the wall. Only days earlier, Israel's Supreme Court itself—in response to a petition brought to it by residents of several villages northwest of Jerusalem and an Israeli NGO—found the path of the wall an illegal encroachment into Palestinian territory. After the decision of the high court, Prime Minister Ariel Sharon directed the defense establishment to review the entire route of the wall. The new route, proposed by the Ministry of Defense in September 2004, was approved by the cabinet on 20 February 2005.

21 Sharif Omar, "Israel's Wall Hems in Livelihoods—and Dreams," *USA Today*, op-ed, 17 August 2003. It must be noted that there are active, astute, and articulate women's organizations throughout the area also protesting the wall and demanding basic human rights—the Jayyous Women's Charitable Society, for one, in precisely this area. Mainstream-media accounts of Palestinian community activism, however, are striking in their ignoring of women's groups and women activists. For an update on the continuing violence and destruction wrought by the Israeli wall in Jayyous, see www.stopthewall.org/latestnews/832.shtml.

22 Richard Rorty, "Fighting Terrorism with Democracy," *The Nation*, 21 October 2002, 13.

23 Richard Perle, "Thank God for the Death of the UN: Its Abject Failure Gave Us Only Anarchy. The World Needs Order," *The Guardian* (London), 21 March 2003.

24 Rorty, "Fighting Terrorism with Democracy," 13.

25 Cynthia Cockburn, *The Space between Us: Negotiating Gender and National Identities in Conflict* (London: Zed Books, 1998), 229–230.

26 Imil Habiby, *The Strange Events in the Disappearance of Saeed the Ill-Fated Pessoptimist (Waqa'i al-gharibah fi ikhtifa' Sa'id Abi al'nahs al-mutasha'il)* (Tunis: Dar al-Janub lil-Nashr, 1982); translated by Salma K. Jayyusi and Trevor LeGassick as *The Secret Life of Saeed the Pessoptimist* (Brooklyn, N.Y.: Interlink Press, 2002), 15–16.

27 Mahmud Darwish, "Nas~faru ka'l'n~s" / "We travel like other people," *Victims of a Map*, ed. and trans. Abdullah al-Udhari (London: al-Saqi Books, 1984), 30–31.

28 In the aftermath of 9/11 and George W. Bush's war on terrorism, much media attention was paid to U.S. aid for the reconstruction of Afghanistan. Less notice was given to the massively increased military aid provided to countries that surround Afghanistan. In the name of "security assistance" for the war on terrorism, the emergency supplemental appropriations bill of October 2001 gave $20 billion each to the administration and to Congress to distribute. On 19 December 2001, a foreign appropriations bill was passed increasing the funds for "security." Israel's already phenomenal aid was increased by $2.4 billion for foreign military financing, $720 million for an economic support fund (both passed by Congress in December 2001), and $200 million in additional foreign military assistance to set up a U.S.-based production line for Arrow missiles (approved by the Senate Foreign Relations Committee, November 2001). Armenia, Azerbaijan, Egypt, India, Jordan, Kazakhstan, Krygyzstan, Pakistan, Tajikistan, Turkey, Turkmenistan, Tunisia, and Uzbekistan were all also recipients of "security assistance." (The inclusion of India and Pakistan for "security assistance" is noteworthy, since neither had received military aid previously and their new military funding totaled a substantial $50 million. And in the case of Pakistan, until 9/11, there were nuclear test–related sanctions and, because of the 1998 military coup in that country, arms-sales restrictions imposed on that country.) Military appropriations and aid to U.S. allies in the wake of the U.S. invasion of Iraq have, of course, expanded exponentially. This is the context of "military might" against which Habermas's "mute violence of terrorism" speaks.

THE ORIGINS
OF THE DANGER MARKET

MARCUS BULLOCK

Friedrich Nietzsche looked closely at the form human existence had taken in his time and offered the world this succinct recommendation: "Live dangerously!"[1] His phrase has the classic quality of formulas that move from the realm of philosophical ideas to the popular canon. If we restrict ourselves to a single enthusiastic glance, we understand exactly what it says. But the longer we look at it, the vaguer its meaning becomes. The element that stirs our immediate reaction is its uncompromising eagerness. We embrace it by identifying, not by thinking. This is all about impatience, especially impatience with thinking.

The process, indeed, looks more like making a sale than expounding a philosophy. We feel drawn to identify with that bold, imprudent injunction, to see ourselves in the intense simplification of the subjective moment, and want nothing from the complexities of prudence.

Everyone understands the thrill of a present danger. How would we describe it? Are we crossing a precarious footbridge that might break beneath us at each step? Suddenly our senses focus with exclusive intensity in every movement we make. Our feet quiver under us; all our senses sharpen. Wakened and alert for the first hint of something giving way, we listen for the slightest warning crack, ready to react instantaneously.

Fear tells us to get out of a precarious situation, but we resent the power of fear as though it were an alien imposition. We feel the lure of going on, as though persisting against all that holds us back will reveal us to ourselves at last in our bold Nietzschean image, beyond all half measures and postponements. If we go back and end the fear by giving way to it, we give up the bodily immediacy of our enthralled senses. We resume an existence diffused in vaguer anxieties, defined only in equivocations, in care, in measurement, amid the complicated world of plans with a purpose and of relationships that map our interests and obligations. These all feel foreign and distant and constricting to us.

From the perspective of careful concern, that thrill seeking seems like a crazy self-indulgence. To a physiologist, it could be accounted for by the intoxicating flood of adrenaline and endorphins and all manner of other secretions. Certainly, as described here, it could appear just an individual oddity, natural enough to a person who feels it but an aberration or miscalculation to a person who is immune to the lure. For Nietzsche, however, it raises a vast question of social organization, of culture and history, as these larger realms serve the obscure interests of life. The pursuit of security that had become such an attractive feature to many of his contemporaries as the nineteenth century achieved its great advances in power over material conditions produces in him, and not only in him, an impulse to resist and to reject that value. He assumes his intellectual responsibility toward his own time by contradicting its movement toward calculable advantages. The spirit of that calculus could be summed up in the term "progress." Its exponents, those who pursue freedom in that movement toward increasing certainties in everything, may be loosely termed "the bourgeoisie." And yet we can hardly imagine a voice like Nietzsche's coming from anywhere but a bourgeois origin, addressing a bourgeois audience.

This should not surprise us. The ideology of progress presupposes a class in debate with itself, always considering the next step in constant change. The bourgeois critique of progress figures as a variant and a dramatic intensification of that same debate. The thesis by which we might explain a philosophy of danger requires a setting in which individual predilection enjoys an indispensable privilege. It would be quite unhistorical simply to reduce it to another version of some chivalric code that demands courage in the service of an established social value. Even though Nietzsche himself may on occasion hark back to models of heroic honor in aristocratic codes, he cannot revert to nostalgic dreams of the past if he wants to sustain the real force of his vision. Nor could that force have produced so much response in the philosophical reverberations of the twentieth century. To be blunt and disrespectful, the appeal he makes addresses a person who is out on the intellectual equivalent of a shopping spree. The passage in which Nietzsche's famous call to live dangerously occurs does not neglect the appropriate inducement:

"Believe me, if you want to realize the greatest fecundity and joy in your existence, then follow this one precept: live dangerously!" Despite its radical proposal, the formula contains the essential maneuver of the shopkeeper. If you want these good things, fecundity and joy—and I know you do (because I'm just like that myself)—then you should accept this commodity I offer you. The price? The price is small: All you have to do is believe me, be my creditor, and acknowledge my position in the profession of intellectual authority.

Putting it in these terms does not deny the attraction of the commodity in question. To have described it through this figure of speech, however, reminds us that, to the extent that danger does circulate in our society as an object of fascination and desire, it does so because we choose it. This does not unmask such danger as necessarily unreal, or only self-imposed. The dangers that offer the greatest challenge and the greatest thrill in meeting that challenge are the ones imposed on us. At the same time, much of what we experience as danger or encounter through dangerous influences in our existence establishes a characteristic sway over us in relationships that are of our own making, our own choosing, and in response to desires that find fecundity and joy in those dangers, just as Nietzsche so expertly understood.

Before we look more closely at his manner of presenting this desire in the form of philosophy, we should add one small element from his original context: "Build your cities on the slopes of Vesuvius!" The image of a city, the manifestation of a civilization, that courts danger indicates how insistently Nietzsche wants to extend the experience of danger from a personal thrill to a collective principle. Human labor establishes a city as the expression of social order. Its solidity and expansion shape the lives it contains according to the greatest manifestations of permanence and of security we can construct. The story of Pompeii persists across the ages as a cautionary tale. Watch for the signs, heed the warnings, choose your places wisely, that story tells us. But at the same time, the extraordinary nature of that event also offers us its own security. The day on which a whole city was consumed by fire and smothered in ash may have burned itself into the memory of Western civilization, but once the first shock wore off, its very clarity and the uniqueness of its image emerged to reassure an attentive world. This was an exception that spoke with great precision. The lesson for many centuries continued in its certain and permanent validity that if we learn from history and from the study of natural causes where dangers lie, we can avoid them.

Unfortunately for us, however, the option of paying prudent heed no longer remains in force. Ever since the historical destruction of Guernica from the air, or the Japanese bombardments of Nanking and Shanghai in 1937, every city stands threatened by eruptions of fire, smoke, and poison gases just as in Pompeii. Nietzsche wrote his call to embrace danger in 1873, two years after his service in the Franco-Prussian War as an artilleryman. The use of Prussian artillery against Paris had presented the world with its first spectacle of modern technology applied as a means of terror in the devastation of civilian lives. The presence and form of danger in modern existence had changed at this quite literal level, as it has continued to change from his time up till our own, but that fact alone does nothing to explain his point.

The way Nietzsche's call to live dangerously has entered popular usage, it sounds as though he is appealing to individual decision and offering insights into the richness of a fully realized personal experience. Much of his rhetoric addresses the reader in that vein. He often speaks like an existentialist, addressing those who are roused by the idea of standing before an indeterminate future, readying themselves to remake life according to a radical commitment. And in that vein, Nietzsche rises here to the benchmark set for all philosophy that aspires to compete with Socrates: He gets a shot at corrupting youth. One has to grow quite old to feel entirely impervious to this call. "Live dangerously?" Of course, one says to oneself. I shall start today.

Though the formula rings so well with the popular appeal that has given it widespread currency in the world at large, that passage in *The Joyful Science* rises to the level of philosophy because it asserts itself in a context that has already rewritten the fundamental mood, tempo, and rhythm of historical knowledge.

Thus, what Nietzsche offers us out of the benefit of his experience does not simply promise a pleasurable exploration of danger as something we can adopt if we believe his high recommendation. He finds us already casting about for a new way of forming our relationship to dangers already incurred—dangers from which we were never secure, but with which we are now constrained to contend according to the instabilities of bourgeois history itself. In a world that has accepted the need to change continuously, we can rise and fall with equal freedom according to the law of competition. In its invitation to all comers to try their luck or their skill according to that law, the bourgeoisie can claim to be the universal class. The only thing that retains the aura of eternity is the disorder that this law creates.

To understand how Nietzsche is thinking here, we need to bear in mind the interplay between the insights into new hazards on the material plane and the psychological grasp of danger as a perpetual fascination for our private sensations. Nietzsche understands nostalgia for the eternal.

The language that Nietzsche developed through his new representation of history separated the spirit and the experience of different epochs more than anyone had done before. The same assertiveness enters philosophy in a conscious undoing of a security established in the past. This turmoil of ideas divided between the backward glance at an outmoded past and the shock of transitions encountered in the present corresponds, quite evidently, to the condition of modernity.

For Nietzsche, the concept "Man," standing as it does for the universality of experience and the continuity between epochs of past time, also stands at the endangered forefront of history, threatened by the decline into modernity. The concept and the image of "Man" so shifts and melts away in the process of modernity that we lose the quality of eternity by which the present once derived its shape and its orderliness from the past. Without that stability and power in the present, we lose the continuity in our history that lets us look back on the monuments of the past for reassurance through their lasting power. What Nietzsche calls monumental history in his essay "On the Uses and Disadvantages of History for Life" (Vom Nutzen und Nachteil der Historie für das Leben) constitutes itself in the principle by which we might look forward into a future that reflects the same monumental and permanent ideas: "That which once had the capacity to unfurl the concept 'Man' and fill it out in greater beauty, that must remain eternally available to us in order to preserve that capacity eternally."[2] Yet, as Nietzsche makes quite clear, the eternal is mortal. Even in the context where he shows the benefits of this idea for the "greater beauty" of life, he acknowledges all the forces that threaten it. In fact, according to a yet more famous slogan of his than the call to live dangerously, the traditional conception of eternity is now dead.

If we can speculate that the experience of a new military technology played a part in clarifying the urgency in Nietzsche's sense of the present, there can be no doubt that the 1914–1918 war overwhelmed the minds of a new generation and carried them yet farther in that direction. While some did, of course, react with pure revulsion to the spectacle of human lives consumed in organized mass destruction, many derived a revolutionary lesson from it. They embraced a renovated conception of life derived from that irresistible ruination and built up philosophical interpretations of the event that swept them onward to new intensities in the elevation of danger. We also need to acknowledge as an extraordinary aspect of this development that it crosses what otherwise look like sharp ideological differences. It does not surprise us that a shared opposition to the bourgeois tradition should produce similar negative evaluations of continuity and stability on both the revolutionary Left and the reactionary Right. Voices on both sides agree in their contempt for any surviving desires to restore the conditions of the pre-war social order. Yet perhaps it should still surprise us to find such a similar affirmation of danger so deeply embedded in concepts of history, experience, and true perception of what are otherwise opposing worldviews, and opposing views of the war itself.

We can illustrate this through two figures, Ernst Jünger and Walter Benjamin, who supply, as nearly as this can be imagined, decisive identities on the Right and Left in the turmoil of German cultural politics from the end of the first world war to the beginning of the second.

Ernst Jünger had volunteered with the greatest enthusiasm for service on the front and had found the intoxications of violence there exceeded his highest fantasies. His writings through the Weimar period and beyond reiterate the same conviction that this apotheosis of conflict provides a model for all modern social relations. "In this sense," he writes in an essay entitled "On Danger," "the world war appears as the great, red balance line under the bourgeois era." The event that in his mind shattered all validity in everything that went before should not be taken simply as a breakdown, a decay, or a disillusionment. Its destructive work has generated a new and distinctive era. The war drew its force from a demonstration of what Jünger thought of as "elemental" and as permanent, but it did so in a way that was entirely characteristic of this time and no other. Jünger arrives at a new idea of what is permanent, and asserts a new conception of order on that basis. "What especially characterizes the era in which we find ourselves, into which we enter more deeply with every passing day, is the close relationship that exists between danger and order. It may be expressed this way: danger appears merely as the other side of our order."[3]

The specific quality of order in this world of struggle carried on by modern means comes from the part played by technology and technical organization. The total mobilization of human effort according to the demands of a total war has taught humanity a lesson about its true potential and its true nature together. Under the sign of this ever more powerful model of orderliness and mechanization of effort, all relations fall into place according to a new set of criteria. In our era, the shock of conflict does not merely revert to the empty instinctual relations of undeveloped nature. "People have always found themselves in passionate struggle with things, animals, or other people, as is the case today," Jünger remarks, but this present case now includes a new factor: "The particular characteristic of our era . . . is precisely that all this transpires in the presence of the most acute consciousness." He set himself the task of portraying this consciousness in his first book, *In Storms of Steel,* a first-person account of the enthralled awe he discovered through the effects of modern weaponry in the shock of battle after battle on the western front. The transforming vision mediated by that awe revealed conflict as almost completely freed from the political engagements of bourgeois national interests. To Jünger it offered instead a revelation of the dawning era of danger that was displacing that of security: "This was a war that not only nations but two epochs conducted against each other. As a consequence, both victors and vanquished exist here in Germany. Victors are like those who, like salamanders, have gone through the school of danger. Only these will hold their own in a time when not security but danger will determine the order of life."[4]

Walter Benjamin regarded the war with ever increasing abhorrence as he observed its effects. He managed to avoid military service by feigning illness, but he experienced it as a direct catastrophe through two shattering personal losses. The first of these came with the death of a close friend, Friedrich Heinle, who made a suicide pact with his girlfriend rather than undergo the separation of joining the army. The second occurred when the radical youth leader Gustav Wyneken, whom Benjamin had until then followed as an ardent disciple, abandoned the spirit of independence in which he had stood firmly against state authorities and made the national cause his own. Unlike Jünger, Benjamin saw the war in political terms all the way through. His disillusionment with the postwar order would take a similarly political turn.

In a short essay written in 1933, "Experience and Poverty," Benjamin describes the collapse of security after the war as a complete disappearance of value in anything that could have been couched as a communicable experience and thus hold together the fabric of generations. "For never has experience been contradicted more thoroughly: strategic experience has been contravened by trench warfare; economic experience by inflation; bodily experience by hunger; moral experience by those in power." All this change is proper to those who had grown up during the years 1914 to 1918, when "a generation that had gone to school in horse-drawn streetcars now stood under the sky in a landscape where only the clouds had not changed, and in the midst of a force field of destructive currents and explosions there stood the tiny, fragile human body."[5] In a later essay, "The Storyteller," Benjamin quotes these same images as a way of introducing a realm of language that reaches back to an age preceding the bourgeois era, that of handcrafts and the oral tale. Here, however, he uses this shocked consciousness of vulnerability to suggest a solution to be found in a different direction. Having lost all that constituted the old comforts of humanity and stripped of human experience altogether, we are obliged to see ourselves as barbarians, and to accept a "new, positive conception of barbarism."[6]

Just as Jünger sees this new postbourgeois epoch as "simultaneously civilized and barbaric" in that we now combine the conscious application of technological power in a world devoid of humanity, Benjamin envisages a form of life with similar depletions. "Where does poverty of experience bring the barbarian?" he asks. "It brings him to the point where he must start again; to start from this new situation; to get by with little; to build up from little and to look neither to the left nor to the right."[7] At all points in Benjamin's writing after the Great War, he emphasizes the cognitive processes and the productive effects of shock, shattering, stripping away of all continuity in our grasp of these times and the potential they contain for a revolutionary transformation. In *One Way Street*, the collection of short observations about the postwar inflation and social collapse that he published in 1928, Benjamin closes with a statement that offers the largest possible perspective on technology as the basis of a new relationship with nature. This technical transformation has shifted the foundations of human identity. "The paroxysm of genuine cosmic experience is not tied to that tiny fragment of nature that we are accustomed to call 'Nature.' In the nights of annihilation of the last war, the frame of mankind was shaken by a feeling that resembled the bliss of the epileptic. And the revolts that followed it were the first attempt of mankind to bring the new body under its control."[8]

Like the futurists just before the war who were so fascinated by the airplane and the automobile, Benjamin has learned a lesson from the new modes of conveyance unknown to that generation which went to school in horse-drawn vehicles: "One need only recall the experience of velocities by

virtue of which mankind is now preparing to embark on incalculable jour-
neys into the interior of time."[9] This sounds a note that Jünger also hears
in the music of modernity. Jünger observes that the great potential in the
new combination of civilization and barbarism "finds expression above all
in the circumstance that in all of these conflicts the most powerful servant
of consciousness, the machine, is always present." In his time, as in ours,
this is modeled by the forms of conflict: "Thus does the battle appear as a
process during which the armored engine moves fighting men through the
sea, over land, or into the air." And as we would clearly expect, a concept
of the machine, and of movement, burned into our imagination by modern
warfare, does not see this servant of consciousness as working toward the
interests of safety and convenience anywhere. That would mean sustaining
the continuities formed by past generations in their pursuit of progress and
material interest. In the "interior of time" reached by this violent motion,
we can expect to find nothing but the disruption and fragmentation that
the human qualities of experience encounter in all circumstances where a
mechanical order outstrips the power of human values to contain it. Jünger
goes on: "Thus does the daily accident itself, with which our newspapers are
filled, appear nearly exclusively as a catastrophe of a technological type."[10]

For both Benjamin and Jünger, the realm of technology provides not only
the material substance through which forms of experience will undergo
change but also the medium through which technology communicates itself
as a new language. Walter Benjamin has achieved a unique fame in essays
like "The Work of Art in the Age of Mechanical Reproduction" for his insights
into the connection between the new technologies of representation and the
forms of experience that develop in tandem with them. Film and photography have transformed our consciousness of a transformed objective realm.
For Benjamin, the camera contains the same force of shock and terror that
has entered the once-human domain through military technology. The camera image conveys the city in its transient appearance, as a fleeting remnant
of the briefest moment, and subordinate to that very mechanism which
captures it in this aspect. The brevity of the time that it takes to create the
image recalls all too clearly the violent speed with which any structure can
be shattered and thrown down from its oppressive dignity: "Our taverns and
our metropolitan streets, our offices and furnished rooms, our railroad stations and our factories appeared to have us locked up hopelessly. Then came
the film and burst this prison-world asunder by the dynamite of the tenth of

a second, so that now, in the midst of its far-flung ruins and debris, we calmly and adventurously go traveling."[11]

Benjamin agrees precisely with Nietzsche here. Such vulnerability in the once-secure scenes of history and culture turns the balance of power decisively to our advantage. We, the inhabitants of those endangered places, acquire a new boldness in our discoveries of time appropriate to a new, positive dispensation of barbarism. The camera has simply replaced Vesuvius.

Benjamin will later on in his essay argue that this transformation implies a clearing away of obstacles toward the emancipation of proletarian revolutionary power. In this passage, however, one must understand him as addressing another situation or another consciousness. The calm and adventurousness of freed movement does not belong to the revolutionary masses, but to a narrower group that he identifies as "we." These are people like himself, for who else reads an essay couched in this extraordinary elegance of intellectual style? Who else enters into this sudden sense of freedom in the imaginative revelation that links a new mode of representation in the world with its vulnerability to destruction? Who else experiences this kind of exhilaration amid structures and spaces whose hold on history and permanence are stripped away? Though Benjamin invokes proletarian class politics, the actual point within society that registers the seismic activity of change touches him through a different kind of mediation, something that ties him to a counterpart across the full range of political opposition. We do, certainly, have to envisage an utterly distinct entity from Benjamin's notion of class-historical transformation when Jünger announces that "a wholly different society has already long since established itself beneath the surface of bourgeois society."[12] Yet what separates them at the level of political analysis clearly joins them quite closely in a broader coloring of those moods or imaginings that attract them, and this seems to define what we might call the ideology of intellectualism. The intellect, under conditions of dissolving and fading identities, may hypertrophy into a source of identity itself by realizing a realm of activity sharply divided against any other way of apprehending the world. It inevitably finds itself reflected in locations among the new disruptive powers into which it can project aspects of its own image-making activity. That will include tactical moments of identifying with technical processes.

Jünger writes a great deal over a long period to develop the notion of the camera delivering a violent impact to the object it captures, shattering it, diminishing its sacrosanct aura, tearing it from the context and dignity of its tradition. This carries with it the barbarous quality of civilization that he invokes when he identifies the "we" whom he addresses in the essay "On Danger." He therefore addresses something quite akin in a contemporary identity when he writes: "Already today there is hardly an event of human significance toward which the artificial eye of civilization, the photographic lens, is not directed. The result is often pictures of demoniacal precision through which humanity's new relation to danger becomes visible in an exceptional fashion."[13] But he goes on to emphasize that it is a "style" that we encounter here, not just the immediate consequence of these "new tools." And through the notion of style, a whole range of shared antecedents and common rhetorical elements invites us to tighten the weave of interconnections that includes these two men. Through Baudelaire and the aestheticism of the nineteenth century, to name just one such common element, we see a large array of parallels that link Benjamin and Jünger in the exploration of decadence, of drugs and intoxication, of gambling, and the posture of the flaneur.

In his essay "Work of Art in the Age of Mechanical Reproduction," Benjamin makes no bones about placing what he calls "the richest historical energies" in the realm of artistic style or the play of ideas in and among intellectual groups rather than in material conditions of a revolutionary class outside the bourgeois sphere. The example that produces this assertion of special value lies in "the extravagances and crudities" of "so-called decadent epochs" that he finds in the "barbarisms" of Dada. And just as Jünger explicitly connects the optics of the camera with the telescopic sights that bring a new destructive level to firepower, so Benjamin can assert that the art of the Dadaists "became an instrument of ballistics. It hit the spectator like a bullet." And this impact on the class of visitors to art galleries, in turn, marked the Dada experience as a precursor that "promoted a demand for the film" in other sectors of society.[14]

The purpose of this comparison in their imagery and rhetoric should in no way suggest that the political differences between Benjamin and Jünger can be discounted, but rather draw us back to the attraction of danger itself. More specifically, it should draw us back to the idea of danger as identifying an appeal to something beyond the bourgeois realm. We could expand and nuance the opposition and correspondence of ideas across the two bodies of writing that these two men have produced, but to do so would merely postpone the larger hypothesis suggested by the somewhat surprising observation of common language that we have now established. If the attraction of danger runs across this ideological opposition, why do we assume that it cannot also run across the opposition between these bourgeois critics of the bourgeois realm and the bourgeois domain itself? Nothing could be more self-evident, of course, than that it does. On a personal and individual level, everyone knows the lure of risk that at times grips and fascinates them. As a general observation of social phenomena, everyone knows that an uncountable number of popular entertainments involve spectacles of danger or representations of actual catastrophes. Furthermore, there is no limit to the pastimes that involve real dangers in which great numbers of ordinary people engage for their own amusement.

Law enforcement in bourgeois society almost certainly spends more time and effort in imposing safety regulations than in protecting property from theft. Armies of officials will stop you from cluttering fire escapes, driving too fast or without a seatbelt, canoeing without a lifejacket, or swimming off the wrong beach. While all these measures express the bourgeois concern with safety and security, they also indicate the impulse among bourgeois citizens to enjoy insecurity unless constrained from another level.

The mere fact that bourgeois individuals do something of any particular nature has nothing whatever to do with explaining the nature of bourgeois society. Most of what people do, whoever they are, simply indicates what is human, not what is bourgeois, or anti- or unbourgeois for that matter. To fit any such behavior into a social or historical model requires that we examine it as a matter of style or language. Thus the first part of any test to establish social definitions as they pertain to modes of life that can run so wide and deep across social boundaries requires that we identify how they fit into the institutions that give or deny value. One way to deal with the realm of dangerous activities that have social identity would be to consider them as industries, and examine how particular aspects of the danger they entail circulate as commodities or as attributes of commodities. Similarly, we could look at the institutions that control, license, or otherwise regulate danger or security as matters of law and administration. In this particular case, however, we need to consider Friedrich Nietzsche, Walter Benjamin, and Ernst Jünger themselves as institutions.

Certainly, any effort that undertakes to critique the bourgeoisie can attack that realm only in terms it will register. Only an individual educated within that domain, and conscious of the values that circulate there, can find a line of criticism that penetrates its sensibility. Moreover, insofar as anything written requires a market, a readership through which it can circulate, that too implies entry into the bourgeois sphere. In short, no one who undertakes to engage bourgeois society in that process of differentiating himself or herself from its values can stand outside those values. The essence of bourgeois society consists in processes of expansion. It flourishes in all stages of its history by adding to its numbers from any adjoining community. This happens by class mobility in both directions, upward as the proletariat acquires education and accumulates property, or downward as the nobility collapses in its competition with active business. This expansion also happens internationally and globally, as modern knowledge and techniques spread into new regions. In other words, the bourgeois world is always in a process of criticism directed against its own boundaries, and thus its identity. The process of expansion in its most radical point of movement can easily be felt and seen as dangerous, since it will permit an outside element to pass through what had been understood as a defensive line.

When Oswald Spengler trembles with fear for the declining West, the yellow peril that seems to him to be rising up in the East can reach across the globe only by virtue of its becoming bourgeois. Only by acquiring the means to compete through trade and technology, which means by adopting the education and organization characteristic of Western modernity, can the East signify as a global reality. The Islamic fundamentalism that threatens us today can reach us only because its active arm consists of trained engineers, supported by adroit international financiers, accountants, businesspeople. The Arab nationalism against which we find ourselves at war is built on a concept of nation that derives from bourgeois history. The same thing that applies to the global process of extension also applies to the unfolding process of ideas in the bourgeois homeland. The very things that look like dangers on the level of ideas are in reality only playing an extreme role in an expansion of self-understanding and the powers of renewed inclusion. The passage "Preparatory human beings" in which Nietzsche exclaims that we should build our cities under Vesuvius also calls on us to set sail into uncharted waters and extend our realms as conquerors. For the world of actual powers, as these have emerged among us, this can mean only that the energies of unbridled production embolden us to take any risk, and inspire us to charge forward into monumental development with reckless disregard of any possible loss. In the closing words of Benjamin's *One Way Street*: "Living substance conquers the frenzy of destruction only in the ecstasy of procreation."[15] Capitalism has emerged in our history as just such a frenzy, uniquely capable of just such a conquest. No matter how it turns on others or on itself, or surges from crisis to crisis, it always grows by that same process of extension.

The institutional place of figures like Nietzsche, Jünger, and Benjamin expresses itself in the modality of an intellectualism dedicated to dialectically negating the limitations of the bourgeois intellect, but in that process also to unfolding new space and energies for that form of life. Thus Jünger is entirely correct, where he claims that those who "like salamanders have gone through the school of danger" can never know defeat, to identify his own position as an intellectual within this process. "Nor can the inclination to danger be overlooked in intellectual endeavors," he insists, "and it is unmistakable that new forms of the volcanic spirit are at work"[16] The specific mode of intellectual endeavor that defines this order of intellectualism depends on its apocalyptic urge. The essential quality of the danger that these intellectuals invoke appears exactly where its visible quality disappears. It is volcanic in the sense that it lies concealed in the earth's crust; it is demonic, as Jünger says of the camera's precision; and it is messianic, as Benjamin claims for the promise of a proletarian revolution. The technological transformation of the visible world fascinates both Jünger and Benjamin in equal and comparable measure because both of them look to the camera as a means by which the presence of the invisible communicates itself. The world others see as the immediate appearance of reality manifests itself to them as the beginning point for a process of intellectual divination.

Jünger's practitioners of the volcanic spirit cannot be defeated, because they identify with the hidden forces. When this hidden realm manifests itself as cosmic or elemental danger, the event confirms such experience as their essential substance. The danger confers on them, just as Nietzsche promised, "the greatest fecundity and joy" in their existence. The intellectualism of that experience also excluded Jünger from any involvement in the political movement with which he seemed to share so much rhetoric in his militarism and the cult of violence and sacrifice. His writing frequently sounds so much like the language of German National Socialism that many critics simply cite his work as the prime example of fascist literary aesthetics in German. Indeed, Walter Benjamin, reviewing a collection of essays edited by Jünger in 1930, made exactly that point himself.[17] The facts of Jünger's life, however, show him maintaining a scrupulous distance from the crude realities of Nazi power.

The same incapacity to identify directly with any actual political organization also separates Benjamin's revolutionary theory from direct practice. Benjamin had no respect for a socialism that pursues visible and tangible goals within the rationally discernible possibilities of progress. Labor socialism, or social democracy, promised him nothing but palliatives that continue in the conformism of an all too evident tradition. That is, bourgeois history. The messianic apocalypticism in his work reaches its peak in his "Theses on the Philosophy of History." In this collection of enigmatic brief statements written in the wake of the Hitler-Stalin Pact of 1939, Benjamin abandons support even for the material organization of a soviet revolution. He once again takes up an idea of divine violence much like that developed in his essay of 1920, "Critique of Violence." In response to this final separation from any visible manifestation of political organization, he falls back entirely on an image of himself as an isolated subject registering impulses inaccessible to the rationalized continuities of historicism. The apparent meanings of events in the constant unfolding of reason and progress obscure what he picks up by the closer proximity to a seismic epicenter: "Historical materialism wishes to retain the image of a past which unexpectedly appears to a man singled out by history at a moment of danger."[18]

Now, if we return to the idea of such figures as institutions within that tradition, we begin to see how the quest for security might always be accompanied by the attraction of danger. We may be quite wrong to read these intellectuals as positioned at the outer margin of bourgeois culture, much less as having labored beyond its limits. What they have accomplished in their thinking indicates rather the form of an island of extraordinary intensity within the realm that they critique. And that critique, which looks like the prophetic proclamation of a rapidly approaching demise, can also represent a point of intensified growth. To remake Nietzsche's metaphor of the volcano through a literal aspect of volcanism, we could remind ourselves that there is no part of the continents we walk on that did not emerge originally as an outpouring of lava from the magma layer hidden below or was not thrown up in cataclysmic tectonic events. This permits us to offer the hypothesis that bourgeois thinking cannot proceed at all without images of its own destruction.

Danger is the form in which we apprehend any power that lies outside our own realm of knowledge. The approach that we feel it making to us, which we would characterize as its threat, also corresponds to our own approach toward it when we are impelled to incorporate it into our realm of knowledge. Thus, quite obviously, we need to distinguish between two very different components of any danger. On the one hand, in the realm of what we know, there may be visible and objectively describable sources of potential damage to us. These are the rational objects of efforts to exert control, and they constitute the elements that we may endeavor to secure by explicit and pragmatic measures. But on the other hand, there are dangers that exist solely as manifestations of a cognitive process. To pursue practical measures, to take material action in the pursuit of security against a material risk, makes perfectly good sense. To pursue practical measures to secure ourselves against the subjective jeopardy when we are caught up in a moment of shifting knowledge does not. The problem embroils us in our worst errors, naturally, whenever the two forms of danger arrive in a single phenomenon.

This is the source of confusion we are going through in the struggle against international terrorism, especially in the United States. That we should feel materially disquieted at the thought of attacks by terrorists is not irrational. That we should have permitted ourselves to launch our entire society into the national obsession with homeland security, with the shifting colors of alerts, with encroachments on civil liberties, certainly amounts to an irrational exaggeration. That the destruction of the World Trade Center should prompt the United States to take measures against the repetition of such an event is a prudent step. That we should feel ourselves embroiled in a war for the very survival of civilization manifests an apocalyptic idea pure and simple—although apocalyptic ideas themselves are seldom pure and never simple. To set the attack on the World Trade Center beside Pearl Harbor, for example, reveals a comparable apocalyptic component, insofar as each event contained the idea of a hostile manifestation from an alien realm, mysterious, impenetrable, and Eastern. We also see a vast difference in the material threat of Pearl Harbor in that there the attacker was a highly organized imperial state armed with a huge modern navy and superior air power. The opening of that war did embroil us with a global axis of truly threatening military might. Defeat was certainly a possibility, and the final destruction of the United States as a nation could enter the realm of imagination.

Today, we are an invincible superpower threatened, for the moment at least, by a semi-organized group of murderous eccentrics. We might compare our situation with that of Israel, to put this in perspective. We are a nation of 290 million, protected by two oceans and with neighbors who have no interest in antagonizing us. Israel is so small that a tank division moving at the speed of the U.S. advance into Iraq would fragment it in about half an hour, and overrun it in half a day. The United States exists within borders that no one disputes. Israel stands on no ground that is recognized as its own by all its neighbors. We have enjoyed periods of years previously without incident, and have suffered no losses in the homeland since the destruction of the World Trade Center. Israel, no matter how far it goes in trying to prevent attacks, can lose the struggle to weekly, and sometimes daily, outrages. We can afford to confront an enemy anywhere on the planet, with or without support from allies. Israel cannot survive without the assistance of the United States. Yet we are talking about living in a state of war as though our survival were at stake. This is not meant to judge anything one way or the other that the nation has actually done. The issue lies in the way we have been speaking and thinking, the way we have been developing within our institutions and social attitudes, whether this be in the sudden inflorescence of flags across the country or the incidents of violence against people who look vaguely, and often only very vaguely, like an enemy.

The eagerness, one might almost say frenzied appetite, we have shown for the danger we imagine we are in reveals something about the security we have every reason to establish. Security is a value to us, but the sense of danger is a value as well. We have seized on the heightened state of alarm because this intensity of experience offers us a state of consciousness in which we can encounter ourselves in a heightened mode. The state of crisis manifests something that both attracts us and repels us. It figures as an internal part of our appointment with destiny. It is the first light of our sense that we must take up that burden to meet with and transform something that as yet exists for us only in the all too distant, all too unimaginable realm of an exotic tradition. We are always traveling toward a future we do not yet know. We have to imagine ourselves changed, and continuing to change, until we disappear from our own clear sight. This is the character of modernity. To think about ourselves, therefore, cannot be accomplished without entertaining images of our own destruction. When a new force or influence enters the scene, and the pressure of change takes on a further accentuation, the vividness of those images becomes too intense for us to sustain in one identity, and we slip into another. The only way in which we then recognize ourselves is in the role of "the man singled out by history at a moment of danger." In that role, it is we who threaten to grow truly dangerous.

NOTES

1 Friedrich Nietzsche, *The Gay Science*, trans. Walter Kaufmann (New York: Random House, 1974), sec. 283, "Preparatory human beings," 228 (translation slightly modified).

2 Ibid., *Untimely Meditations*, ed. Daniel Breazeale, trans. R. J. Hollingdale (Cambridge: Cambridge University Press), 68 (translation modified).

3 Ernst Jünger, "On Danger," trans. Donald Reneau, *New German Critique* 59 (summer 1993): 29, 30.

4 Ibid., 31, 30.

5 Walter Benjamin, "Experience and Poverty," *Selected Writings*, vol. 2, *1927–1934*, ed. Michael W. Jennings, Howard Eiland, and Gary Smith; trans. Rodney Livingstone, Michael Jennings, Edmund Jephcott, and Harry Zohn (Cambridge: Harvard University Press, 1999), 732 (translation modified).

6 Ibid.

7 Ibid.

8 Walter Benjamin, "One Way Street," *Reflections: Memories, Dreams, Aphorisms*, ed. Peter Demetz, trans. Edmund Jephcott (New York: Schocken, 1986), 94.

9 Ibid., 93

10 Jünger, "On Danger," 31.

11 Walter Benjamin, "The Work of Art in the Age of Mechanical Reproduction," *Illuminations*, ed. Hannah Arendt, trans. Harry Zohn (New York: Harcourt, Brace and World, 1969), 236.

12 Jünger, "On Danger," 32.

13 Ibid.

14 Benjamin, "The Work of Art," 237, 238.

15 Ibid., "One Way Street" 94.

16 Jünger, "On Danger," 30.

17 Walter Benjamin, "Theories of German Fascism," trans. Jerrold Wickoff, *New German Critique* 17 (spring 1979): 120.

18 Walter Benjamin, "Theses on the Philosophy of History," *Illuminations*, 255.

COLD WAR REDUX

ROBERT RICIGLIANO AND MIKE ALLEN

The current the war on terrorism, as elaborated in the 2002 U.S. *National Security Strategy* and in security policies evident in the PATRIOT Act, the treatment of detainees in Cuba, and the war in Iraq, bears a striking resemblance to the ideology that underpinned the cold war between the United States and the Soviet Union. The parallels are understandable, given that many of the actors in the George W. Bush administration (Dick Cheney, Donald Rumsfeld, John Ashcroft, etc.) were participants in that struggle. Fears of global annihilation spread with the traumatic dawning of the nuclear age, and they spawned a cold-war ideology that provided what seemed to be a clear picture of the threat to the United States: the Soviet Union, weapons of mass destruction, and the spread of Communism. The threat was not just to the physical safety of the United States (the threat of nuclear attack), but to the ideals upon which the United States was built—freedom, democracy, and free enterprise.

Countering the Soviet threat became the preeminent goal of the United States and led to a clear set of policy responses. The U.S. position was that the Soviet Union should be contained (the containment doctrine was elaborated in 1947 by George F. Kennan in the "X" article in *Foreign Affairs*) and that any expansion of Soviet influence should be countered aggressively to reduce Soviet expansion (e.g., conflicts in Korea, Vietnam, Afghanistan, Cuba, El Salvador, Nicaragua, Eastern Europe, etc.).[1] The origination and continuation of various organizations (e.g., North Atlantic Treaty Organization, South East Asian Treaty Organization) were predicated on the United States' developing counterorganizations to contain the Soviet threat. The main question about a foreign relationship was whether such a policy worked to promote U.S. interests in stopping Communism. In response to regional conflicts or threats to the peace, the critical questions were whether the destabilization was Communist inspired and, if so, how it should be stopped. Even if the Communist threat was not immediately identified, the conflict was analyzed in terms of what the conflict meant for East/West relations.

The cold-war mindset is important, because once it was established that one side was Communist or received support from the Soviet Union, the U.S. reaction was clear. The thinking generated a litmus test; you were either with the United States in opposition to this global threat or you were against it. Allies were seen as allies when they supported U.S. actions, as dupes when they did not, and as pinkos when they opposed U.S. actions, even within the United States itself. Given the cold-war worldview—mortal threat to core U.S. values—almost any action could be and was justified, from war in Vietnam to a covert operation to overthrow the socialist government in Chile to selling arms to Iran to support freedom fighters in Nicaragua. And, especially in the 1950s, the framing of the threat against the United States left very little space for critical public dialogue and even created conditions for the McCarthy era witch hunts against Communist sympathizers.

The development of the Bush administration's *National Security Strategy* and its centerpiece—the war on terrorism—has closely followed the cold-war mindset since the traumatic events in the fall of 2001. The war on terrorism was an immediate response to the events of 9/11; the war in Afghanistan was a first move in the war on terrorism; the 2002 *National Security Strategy* was a codification and expansion of the strategy that produced Afghanistan and other post-9/11 policies; the attack on Iraq was mandated by the 2002 *National Security Strategy.* The question of who's next for the policy is answered by identifying perceived threats to the United States. Given that no weapons of mass destruction have yet been found in Iraq, the standards for what constitutes a threat and necessary evidence for proving that the threat exists are quite lax. Like the cold-war ideology, the war on terrorism paints a world where there is one preeminent and obvious threat comprised of three elements—terrorists, rogue states, and weapons of mass destruction (WMDs). In his 2003 State of the Union address, President Bush tied these three elements together: "The gravest danger facing America and the world, is outlaw regimes that seek and possess nuclear, chemical, and biological weapons. These regimes could use such weapons for blackmail, terror, and mass murder. They could also give or sell those weapons to terrorist allies, who would use them without the least hesitation." The president went on to make direct reference to the war on terrorism as a successor to the great ideological crusades of the twentieth century: "Now, in this century, the ideology of power and domination has appeared again, and seeks to gain the ultimate weapons of terror. Once again, this nation and all our friends are all that stand between a world at peace, and a world of chaos and constant alarm. Once again, we are called to defend the safety of our people, and the hopes of all mankind. And we accept this responsibility."[2] As in the fight against Communism, the war on terrorism is about protecting not only the physical safety of the United States but also fundamental U.S. values. President Bush has declared: "In the war against global terror, we will never forget that we are ultimately fighting for our democratic values and way of life."[3]

The response to this mortal threat is also seemingly obvious—a war on terrorism that "must be fought on many fronts, against a particularly elusive enemy over a protracted period of time."[4] As in the cold war, extreme measures (e.g., the PATRIOT Act, detainees in Cuba, war in Iraq) are justified and U.S. policy is dominated by absolutist thinking. States are with us or against us. They support terrorism or they fight it. As President Bush stated: "Nations that enjoy freedom, must actively fight terror."[5] To be a nation that fails to actively fight terror is to be a nation that permits terrorists to use its territory as a safe haven, tacitly supports terrorists, or simply does not understand the severity of the threat. As in the early days of the cold war, there is little room for public dissent or debate about actions taken in the name of the war on terrorism. In the rapid pace of events, and paranoia stoked by disclosures of new threats, dissenting views are dismissed as soft on terrorism, unpatriotic, or disloyal to the memory of those who died on 9/II.

Problems with the War on Terrorism as Cold War Redux

The similarities between the cold-war mindset and the war on terrorism may make the latter seem a familiar, even an expected, form of foreign policy response. The cold war simplified the goal and the means to attain U.S. national security and justified taking extreme measures in pursuit of the policy objective. However, the current incarnation of the cold-war ideology in the form of the war on terrorism should make us pause to consider whether a policy conceived more than fifty-six years ago is adequate for the radically changed international environment of today. The cold-war mindset provided an easily identifiable and potentially defeatable adversary (the Soviet Union, aka the "Evil Empire"), a moral mission (defend freedom), and a preeminent goal (stop the spread of Communism), all of which served to simplify the policy calculus and responses (wars of containment, nuclear deterrence, covert operations, economic sanctions, political confrontation, etc.). The war on terrorism has tried to force the twenty-first-century world into the cold-war mold. Terrorism is cast as the adversary to be defeated, the moral cause is the defense of freedom and democracy, and the preeminent goal is to end terrorism by "catching all the terrorists."

But the cold-war mindset does not work as the basis for today's U.S. security policy, for two basic reasons. First, war as a strategy for stopping terrorists is fatally flawed. The war strategy produces a nested series of problems, from the need for preemptive action to doctrines of U.S. exceptionalism that undermine, rather than promote, U.S. national security. Second, terrorism is a tactic, not a foe to be defeated. Focusing on the tactic of terrorism masks the need to focus on the underlying conditions that spawn and facilitate the operations of terrorist groups.

The Fatal Flaws of War as a Strategy for Stopping Terrorism

The Bush administration has been quite deliberate in its use of the word "war" in a literal sense—an attempt to defeat an opponent through physical force—to describe its approach to dealing with the threat of terrorism. War has traditionally meant an armed conflict between states that focused on boundaries and control of territory. Hence, war would seem to be an odd policy choice for countering actors that are stateless and know no national boundaries. However, the administration position is that the war on terrorism is unlike previous wars, as it has to be waged "capture by capture, cell by cell, and victory by victory."[6] In this war, defeating terrorists does not mean conquering territory. Rather, victory in the war on terrorism means capturing all terrorists.

The administration's choice of the word "war" leads to several deeply problematic policy implications. In choosing to wage war as the approach to dealing with terrorists, the administration has set the bar of success impossibly high. Terrorism is a tactic and can never be eliminated. Nor is it possible to teach all terrorists, "one by one," the meaning of "American justice," as President Bush has pronounced.[7] More importantly, as one critic has explained, declaring that a nation is at war "arouses an immediate expectation, and demand, for spectacular military action against some easily identifiable adversary, preferably a hostile state—action leading to decisive results."[8] This quite accurately explains the shift in U.S. policy from targeting the elusive Osama bin Laden and the shadowy and borderless al Qaeda terrorist network to launching an attack on Iraq and Saddam Hussein.

It also begs the question of how to exert "spectacular and decisive" military force against secretive and decentralized terrorists. Terrorism can occur anywhere and can be carried out by anyone, regardless of nationality, race, or ethnicity. Persons using the tactics of terror can be U.S. citizens with no foreign connections (e.g., the Unabomber, attackers of abortion clinics) or nationalists uninterested in the United States (e.g., Basque separatists). The potential targets of terrorists include places where people gather, such as streets or buildings, as well as critical infrastructures, such as power plants or other structures involved in industrial, military, or recreational applications. Most terrorists work to keep their actions secret. Military force used in a passive and preventive way to physically protect all potential terrorist targets is neither workable nor spectacular. A reactionary use of force in response to terrorist attacks is not likely to be effective or decisive.

Thus, if terrorists are to be physically prevented from attacking and military force is to be used in a "spectacular and decisive" way, then a policy of the preemptive use of military force is required. The Bush administration has declared that "the United States can no longer solely rely on a reactive posture as we have in the past."[9] However, the preemptive use of military force against adversaries that are stateless, elusive, and difficult to identify requires a substantial revision of traditional doctrines of international law that require preemptive force to be used only if absolutely necessary and in the face of an imminent threat.[10] Hence, the Bush administration has decided to do away with immanency as a necessary condition for preemption. As Deputy Secretary of Defense Paul Wolfowitz explained: "Anyone who believes that we can wait until we have certain knowledge that attacks are imminent has failed to connect the dots that led to September 11."[11] The paucity of evidence that Iraq posed a threat to the United States, let alone an imminent threat, demonstrates how radically the Bush administration has lowered the threshold for what justifies the preemptive use of force.

One might argue that weapons of mass destruction and well-financed terrorist networks pose new challenges and hence require new concepts of international law. However, the unilateral way in which the United States dispensed with the requirement of immanency, especially in the case of Iraq, creates numerous problems not just for the international order, but for U.S.

national security itself. If concepts of immanency and self-defense need to be revised, the critical questions are, How should this question be decided? And by whom? In response to these questions, the United States has adopted an unequivocal policy of exceptionalism. The Bush administration has made it clear that its highest obligation is to protect the security of U.S. citizens, which in turn justifies a policy that the United States "will not hesitate to act alone, if necessary, to exercise our right of self-defense by acting preemptively against such terrorists."[12] So it is for the United States to decide when a threat is sufficiently imminent to warrant an attack, and this is a right the United States reserves for itself. This form of U.S. exceptionalism is rooted in the neoconservative belief that the United States needs to "accept responsibility for America's unique role in preserving and extending an international order friendly to our security, our prosperity, and our principles."[13]

The doctrine of U.S. exceptionalism, however, poses several problems for global and U.S. national security. It is difficult, if not impossible, to reserve to the United States alone the justifiable use of unilateral military force against a self-defined threat. For example, Israel can use the U.S. precedent to justify incursions in the West Bank, the building of an internationally condemned security barrier, and the use of force to assassinate persons it deemed were terrorists. Similarly, states such as India (in relation to Pakistan), Rwanda (in relation to the Democratic Republic of Congo), or Uganda (in relation to Sudan) could use the U.S. precedent to justify incursions into other countries. Regimes that are prone to abusing the human rights of their own populations can cite the need to combat terrorists to further justify their actions.[14]

Moreover, U.S. exceptionalism, especially in the case of Iraq, undermines the legitimacy of the United Nations and strains key bilateral relationships with European and other allies. In addition to weakening the very infrastructure of rules needed to combat terrorists, the policy of U.S. exceptionalism weakens international cooperation and provides the conditions for allies and others to avoid cost-sharing arrangements. A war policy, as opposed to other forms of international cooperation to combat terrorism, is expensive and requires not only resources for war fighting, but also resources for occupation and reconstruction. As a result, the United States has had to shoulder a disproportionate share of the cost of the Iraq conflict. Further, there are the additional costs of the war on terrorism outside Iraq, such as the global pursuit of terrorists (hunting them down one at a time), the war in Afghanistan, and military actions in the Philippines, Georgia, and elsewhere. Many policy analysts have pointed out how the war on terrorism has stretched the U.S. military way beyond its limits and contributed to record U.S. budget deficits.[15] Overcommitting the U.S. military and weakening the U.S. economy significantly diminish the ability of the United States to respond to other imminent threats that may arise. Further, as a recent report from the International Monetary Fund points out, large U.S. budget deficits pose "significant risks" to global economic stability.[16]

The investment, over two years (March 2003–March 2005), of over $160 billion in Iraq means that resources have been diverted from pressing foreign policy objectives in Africa, Latin American, Eastern Europe, and Asia. The 2004 budget of $18 billion for reconstruction in Iraq alone was five times the total 2003 budget for the U.S. Agency for International Development ($3.6 billion), and the $85 billion earmarked for Iraq in 2004 was sixty-five times the 2002 budget for Foreign Assistance Programs ($1.3 billion).[17]

In congressional hearings regarding the funding of the war in Iraq, members of Congress pressed for and received assurances from the Bush administration that funds that were being reallocated from programs in other parts of the world to fund the war would be restored. Subsequently, the administration has reneged on its pledge, leading many officials to complain privately about the lack of funds for other key foreign policy priorities. The implication of a war on terror is that such a policy eventually becomes the sole focus of U.S. foreign policy, as resources must be given to fight and win a war. The key to any policy is to provide criteria for setting priorities to guide the use of limited resources. However, such criteria are missing from the 2002 *National Security Strategy*.[18] This overconcentration of resources in one area, and the lack of criteria for priority setting, makes it impossible to adequately address the terrorist threat, let alone counter other threats to U.S. security—such as AIDS, SARS, and other public health threats; armed conflict outside Iraq; threats to international trade; humanitarian crises, and so on. In short, a war strategy for dealing with terrorists means less, not more, security for the United States and the world.

Terrorism: A Tactic

Although the Bush administration has boasted that it is hunting down the terrorists "one at a time," it is hard to see how such a strategy is going to end the use of terrorism. To declare war on a tactic is to set about an unachievable task. Terrorism is a means to an end, driven by certain motivations fueled by certain root causes. A law-abiding citizen today could be a suicide bomber tomorrow. The real threat is not the tactic, but the conditions that motivate terrorists in the first place and that facilitate their operations. Focusing on the tactic of terrorism leads to two key policy failings of the war on terrorism. The first critical shortcoming is the failure to distinguish terrorists who are targeting the United States, its interests, and its allies from those who have other motivations. A second critical flaw is the failure to target the root causes that motivate terrorists and facilitate their operations. Both these shortcomings lead to a diffusion of effort and resources and to unintended negative consequences for U.S. national security.

To not distinguish on the basis of the type of motivation for the group is to create a reaction system that will fail, in much the same way a cold-war politics failed to distinguish between Communists motivated by nationalistic agendas versus those motivated by other ideologies. Not all Communists wanted to be affiliated with the Soviet Union, but the U.S. policy made no such distinction. Similarly, the current U.S. policy makes no distinction between terrorists targeting the United States and terrorists with other agendas. Terrorists generally fall into three categories: those who are nationalist driven; those who are resource driven; or those who are ideologically driven. This argument is not to say that groups do not combine interests that go across the three categories or that only particular types should be considered. However, there are fundamental distinctions between these groups that are important for constructing a security strategy.

The nationalist-driven terrorists either are associated with targeting a particular government and wanting to replace it or constitute separatist movements that seek to gain power or independence from a central government. Typically, these organizations target only those who seek to prop up the current government; they have little desire to project power outside a particular nation. Generally, these terrorists are not interested in the internal workings of the other government and oppose a U.S. presence only in a particular location. Many of these groups would welcome normal relationships with the United States after they gain control of the area. Terrorism is simply a tactic to undermine and subvert the existing government. This type of terrorist seeks to free the country from some government or occupation and generally is satisfied when the country is "free." While such groups may adopt or reflect a particular ideological viewpoint, that view is not something that requires extension beyond the borders of the country.

Resource-driven groups use terror as a means to gain and retain control over a resource.[19] A drug cartel has no interest in power or ideology apart from how these might affect the cartel's ability to conduct its business profitably. The warlords in Somalia or the drug cartels in South America do not constitute a direct threat to the United States so long as it does not threaten their operations. The actions taken by those groups against U.S. nationals or interests reflect the perception of a threat to their interests. This is not to say that these groups should not be targeted for attention by the U.S. government, only that the justification for such attention should not stem from the fear of a 9/11 type of attack. These groups do contribute to the formation of weakened centralized governmental states, as in Afghanistan, and provide the possible conditions for hostile ideological groups to seize control. Some ideological groups (such as al Qaeda) may seek to finance part of their operation through control of a resource. However, resource-driven groups intend to corrupt and create fear in an existing national government rather than to replace the existing civil structure. Organized-crime groups generally do not want to run schools, build sewers, or regulate general commerce. Generally, other than targeting Drug Enforcement Agency or other local operations, these groups want to operate beneath the radar and seek to avoid the attention of the United States. Terrorist attacks from these groups alone represent no fundamental threat to vital U.S. interests.

The terrorist groups that represent the fundamental threat to the United States are ideologically motivated. The first two kinds of groups will attack U.S. interests only so far as the interests of a group conflict with those of the United States. Ideological groups attack the United States because the United States personifies all that they oppose. The political, social, or religious ideology (religious extremist, Red Brigade communist, radical environmentalist) seeks some fundamental change in social institutions. These conditions are usually not limited to national boundaries. The groups identify actors who must be held responsible for a problem and target those actors. The Unabomber targeted various officials he believed responsible for the world's problems. Osama bin Laden targeted persons he believed responsible for the desecration of his holy land.

There have been many analyses of the root causes of the fanatical Islamic terrorist movements like al Qaeda, such as totalitarian rule in Saudi Arabia,

U.S. support for Israel, the spread of a radical version of Islam (e.g., Wahabism), economic and political disparities, and the deep sense of powerlessness felt by most of the nonelite population of the Muslim world. The United States is seen as the symbol of the source of this powerlessness and grievance. Potential targets for the ideological terrorist are sites in the United States, U.S. businesses and government entities abroad, and U.S. allies.

If the goal of the war on terrorism is to safeguard the United States and its democratic way of life, ideological groups, not nationalistic or resource groups, clearly pose the central threat to U.S. national security. Paradoxically, as the United States takes the lead role in the global crusade against terrorism, the nation increases its visibility as a target for ideologically motivated terrorists. The U.S. policy reinforces the very conditions that drive this form of terrorism. The more the United States acts unilaterally to hunt down and find terrorists (Iraqis already call U.S. raids "deliberate humiliation" and degrading to women by inappropriate touching), the greater the motivation to engage in terrorism.[20]

A key to countering ideological terrorists is to target the conditions that motivate them and facilitate their operations. To be effective on the world stage, ideological terrorists require a place to train, plan, and gather resources sufficient for them to project their power outside their immediate base of operations. This, in turn, requires a number of factors. The most important is a weak nation-state (e.g., Afghanistan) with a government that is sympathetic to, tolerant of, or powerless to oppose the existence or operations of a terrorist group. The danger posed by these groups is magnified significantly when they are able to operate safely in some existing state. The weakness of a central government to control or challenge the strength of these groups creates the necessary safe haven for them to form, plan, and organize. The attacks of al-Qaeda represent as much the success of the organization as they do the inability or unwillingness of the Taliban to interfere or regulate the actions of an organization present in Afghanistan.

The policy prescription is not to end all possible motivations for terrorism (such as poverty or injustice), just as it is not to catch all the terrorists. The real threat to the United States is the existence of weak, failing, and failed states. Failed states provide territory for terrorists to plan, access to resources (e.g., drugs or commodities such as conflict diamonds or conflict timber), porous borders, and safe havens, and they contribute to the disaffection and hopelessness that aid recruitment. President Bush himself has articulated this connection, saying that "persistent poverty can lead to hope-lessness and despair. And when governments fail to meet the basic needs of their people, these failed states can become havens for terror."[21]

However, the administration has sought to target the symptom of the disease, terrorism, as opposed to one of the main root causes of the disease, failed states. The roots of this decision lie in a very conscious move by the Bush team, pre-9/11 (including the 2000 presidential campaign), to eschew anything that looked like Clinton-style nation building.[22] Yet the danger to the United States posed by failed states has been documented for years.[23] In April 2001, Rachel Stohl of the Center for Defense Information and Michael Stohl of Purdue University accurately predicted that the Bush administration's disinterest in the issue of failed states "will be tested in short order and found wanting."[24] Months later, terrorists operating out of a failed state struck New York and Washington, D.C., and the war on terrorism was launched with the U.S.-led war in Afghanistan.

To the extent that the Bush administration policy does address the problem of creating stable, democratic countries in place of rogue states that sponsor terrorism, its strategies are inadequate, even counterproductive. For example, in the 2002 U.S. *National Security Strategy*, the Bush administration boldly asserted that there is "a single sustainable model for national success: free-dom, democracy, and free enterprise." Further, the administration proclaimed that "free trade and free markets have proven their ability to lift whole societies out of poverty."[25] The war in Iraq is held out as an example of how forced regime change, through military conquest, would lead to the building of a free-market democracy and end the terrorist threat posed by Iraq.

However, evidence suggests that building liberal market democracies in many of the war-torn, unstable countries in the world has actually made conflicts worse and had a destabilizing effect—quite the opposite of the Bush administration claim.[26] The experience in Iraq as of the summer of 2005 is a prime example of this phenomenon. Moreover, the U.S. track record of build-ing democracies through forced regime change is not good. In the twentieth century, only five of the eighteen forcible regime changes led by the United States succeeded. When regime change came about as a result of unilateral military action by the United States, only one country, Panama, succeeded in building a more democratic state.[27]

In addition to the policy of forced regime change, the problem with the Bush position is the emphasis on a single model for building stable societies.

The administration is reluctant to accept variants on the democratic model that might include a prominent role for groups that want to see variants on the U.S. approach, such as an Islamic democracy or theocratic state in Iraq. Many experts on building democratic institutions argue that democracy cannot be imported but has to take root from within. Democratic institutions, to be successful, have to be sensitive to local values, conditions, and culture. Rather than a single model, as democracies spread to more and more parts of the world and encounter a greater diversity of cultures, there are more and more variants on the basic democratic model. Rather than a single model of success, a diversity of models will emerge.

An Alternative Approach: Promoting Sustainable Peace

Although the war on terrorism is riddled with problems, no critique of it is complete without at least the outlines of an alternative policy. As with the cold-war mindset, if one accepts the threat definition and operating assumptions of war on terrorism, then arguing against actions taken to implement the war on terrorism is seen as irrational. In the case of the cold war, arguing against the war in Vietnam was seen as the same as promoting the spread of Communism. Arguing against the war in Iraq is seen as acquiescing to the terrorist threat and putting U.S. ideals and lives at risk. If the threat is as extreme as the Bush administration says it is, then only the most extreme measures will counter it. To argue for a partial or muddled response in Iraq is to be soft, leaving the United States vulnerable for the sake of esoteric values like international unity. Without presenting an alternative frame, any critique of the war on terrorism runs the risk of showing that the policy, while problematic, is a necessary evil.

An alternative security strategy needs to start with a different definition of the threats facing the United States. The cold-war mindset targeted the spread of Communism as the core threat facing the United States. The war on terrorism focuses on a combination of terrorism, rogue states, and weapons of mass destruction as the "next big threat" facing the United States after the fall of the Communist bloc. In creating an alternative vision, the first step is to realize that there is not a single "big threat" to U.S. national security analogous to the Soviet Union during the cold war.[28] Rather, threats to U.S. security, including many that are not traditionally thought of as security threats, are diverse and interconnected. This lesson has been learned in postconflict peace-building operations. Major General William Nash, who served in peace-building operations in Bosnia and Kosovo, has said that the main lesson he learned in those experiences was that "everything is related to everything, and it is all political."[29] Nash explains that while he was in charge of security issues, issues of economics (lack of jobs for former combatants), rule of law (management of local disputes), development of local governance (to address local problems), and provision of basic services (to provide for people's basic needs) all affected the security situation.

This nexus among diverse issues can be transferred to the macrolevel of international security. As noted earlier, it is no coincidence that terrorist groups tend to flourish in environments where there are failures of core state functions such as respect for human rights, participatory and accountable governance, sustainable environmental policies, the rule of law, sustainable economics, and the management of conflict through nonviolent means.[30] Moreover, these elements of state failure are threats in and of themselves, not simply because they may fuel the creation of terrorist groups or facilitate their operation. For example, a study by the National Intelligence Council concludes that new and emerging infectious diseases "will endanger U.S. citizens at home and abroad, threaten U.S. armed forces deployed overseas, and exacerbate social and political instability in key countries and regions in which the United States has significant interests."[31] According to a report by the Council on Foreign Relations: "Research shows that low or declining average health status correlates over time with a decline in state capacity, leading to instability and unrest."[32] This instability, in turn, contributes to other security threats, such as the thriving drug trade in Latin America, or the debilitating conflicts in the Democratic Republic of Congo and in other African countries.

To direct the application of scarce resources against these diverse threats, U.S. national security strategy ought to focus on combating state failure. Failed and failing states provide a nexus for addressing diverse threats (e.g., health risks, environmental damage, conflict), as well as for countering terrorism and weapons of mass destruction. Chester Crocker, a former assistant secretary of state in the Reagan administration and currently a professor of political science, argues that the Bush administration and its war on terrorism "overlooks the failed-state crucible in which many threats to U.S. interests are forged."[33] The phenomenon of state failure has been called the "ultimate disintegrative force" on the global stage and as such should be at the center of U.S. foreign policy.[34] Jeffrey Record, professor at the Sam Nunn

School of International Affairs, has proclaimed the "emergence of weak and failed states as the primary threat to U.S. security."[35] In combating state failure, the United States would be addressing root and proximate causes of terrorism, as well a range of other threats. Hence, as Crocker argues, U.S. foreign policy should be centered on a "comprehensive failed-state strategy."[36]

What would it mean to have a foreign policy that focused on countering state failure as opposed to waging war on terrorism? As noted earlier, the "failed state foreign policy paradigm" would give up on the notion of finding a single, all-consuming threat and see instead the complexity and enormity of the causes of state failure. Coming to grips with the enormity of the failed-state challenge leads to several important implications. First, threats to U.S. security, whether they emanate from shadowy groups of terrorists or from failed states, are problems to be managed, not defeated. Terrorism will always be with us, just as weak and ineffective states will always exist. Success is not ending the problem, but creating structures and processes for managing threats and minimizing their damage to the United States and the international system. Millions of dollars are spent each year on flood control, not to stop the rain from falling but to control its destructive effects. Likewise, international mechanisms need to be developed that will work toward the prevention of state failure, the rebuilding of failed states, and postconflict reconstruction.[37] The United States and the international community need to coordinate on criteria for which areas are most threatening to global stability.

The enormity of countering the causes of state failure and working to rebuild weak states also leads to the necessity of making a true commitment to multilateralism. No single state, including the United States (or the United States and a limited number of "willing" partners), can tackle the failed-state problem. Building systems to manage the impact of state failure, or to prevent state failure in the first place, requires a strong multilateral coalition for monitoring and intervention. In combating failed states, British foreign minister Jack Straw argues that "collective international engagement matters above all else."[38] Given the sheer enormity of the problem of addressing potential causes of state failure—everything from AIDS to economic development to protracted conflict—multilateral cooperation and burden sharing are a necessity.

In addition to burden sharing, multilateralism offers several advantages when dealing with failed states. Different states and international organizations bring important nonmonetary assets to the table. States like Norway are known as trusted third parties, as evidenced by the Oslo Channel of 1994 and several other low-key diplomatic efforts Norway has sponsored. Regional groupings of states provide access and resources that can be critical to successful intervention, like the Economic Community of West African States and their sending peacekeeping troops to Liberia. In addition, when military intervention is necessary, true multilateral support, including sanction by the United Nations, will increase both the legitimacy of military intervention and the effectiveness of postconflict peace building.

A true commitment to multilateralism, as part of a comprehensive strategy to counter state failure, will also require consistency of approach. It is not sufficient to choose a multilateral approach when the occasion fits U.S. self-interest and a unilateral approach when it does not. This is a sharp contrast with the Bush administration's attitude toward multilateralism, best summed up by John Bolton, currently undersecretary of state for arms control and international security and formerly undersecretary of state for international organizations in the first Bush administration (1989–1993): "There is an international community that occasionally can be led by the real power left in the world, and that is the United States, when it suits our interests. . . . When it suits our interests to do so, we will do so. When it does not suit our interests we will not."[39]

A true multilateral policy requires that the United States not always be permitted to implement a policy, undertake an action, or exempt itself from the rules of the game based simply on its own self-interest. It cannot work counter to international cooperation (e.g., opposition to international agreements such as the Kyoto Protocol or the International Criminal Court) or undermine the United Nations and international law (e.g., the decision to go to war with Iraq) and then expect the full endorsement and cooperation of the same countries it spurned on these other issues. A true multilateral approach requires an agreement to respect international rules, even if it means that the United States must practice restraint, as well as lose some political battles.

Finally, a strategy for dealing with failed states will require an investment in values over the political expediency of alliances that further the war on terrorism. Kurt Campbell and Michelle Flournoy of the Center for International and Strategic Studies argue that the United States cannot forgo respect for fundamental values such as democratic governance and respect for human rights in prosecuting the war on terrorism: "If the United States prevails in its quest to make attitudes toward international terrorism a defining litmus test in international politics, then the practices of buying off extremists, suffocating legitimate voices of opposition, and seeking to export the violence outside national borders must cease."[40] A strategy that focuses on combating state failure would see the denial of these basic values—human security, good governance, justice, and sustainable economics—as the threat to U.S. national security, not as an acceptable tradeoff for short-term cooperation by potential allies. As one critic has pointed out, denial of these basic "public goods" is the defining factor for failed and failing states.[41]

Some may consider a policy that centers on combating state failure and forging a new multilateralism a naïve hope or a lofty but unrealistic mission. Certainly this approach will be difficult. But is it more difficult than embarking on the impossible and counterproductive task of trying to "catch all the terrorists" or waging war on a tactic like terrorism? Some, like John Bolton, would argue that we put our safety at risk if we try to work though international organizations like the United Nations. But are we safer now after several years of the war on terrorism? In Iraq alone, more than 1,341 U.S. soldiers had died as of 5 January 2005, with more than ten thousand U.S. casualties (more than five thousand of these wounded have not been able to return to battle).[42] According to data from the Oklahoma City National Memorial Institute for the Prevention of Terrorism, in the two years after the start of the war on terrorism (1 January 2002 to 1 January 2004), there was a 59 percent increase in the annual number of terrorist incidents worldwide as compared to the five years previous to the war on terrorism (1 January 1998 to 1 January 2002).[43] In that same two-year period, the annual number of injuries from terror attacks was up 31 percent and deaths were up almost 4 percent. If the extraordinary death toll from the three attacks on 9/11 is taken out, the number of annual fatalities has increased by 70 percent since the war on terrorism.

Fear of terrorism and the trauma of 9/11 are powerful forces, just as fear of Communism was to the formation of cold-war policies. President Truman was reportedly convinced that if he could "scare the hell out of the country," he could win approval for a critical aid package before Congress. According to Warren Goldstein, historian at the University of Hartford, Truman then announced the Truman Doctrine as "recasting world affairs into a potentially endless global struggle between 'freedom' and 'tyranny.'"[44] The Bush administration is trying to cast its war on terrorism as the successor to the cold war. Given the inherent flaws of war on terrorism, the dangers it poses, and the counterproductive impact of the policy, our response to the threat of terrorism should not be an ill-advised war based on a strategy that is more than half a century old. Instead, enlightened self-interest should occasion a bold new strategy responsive to the dynamics of the early twenty-first century that centers on a truly multilateral approach to addressing failed and failing states.

NOTES

1 George F. Kennan, "The Sources of Soviet Conduct," *Foreign Affairs*, July 1947, 566–582.

2 George W. Bush, "2003 State of the Union Address," 28 January 2003, www.whitehouse.gov.

3 Ibid., *The National Security Strategy of the United States*, 19 September 2002, 7, www.whitehouse.gov.

4 Ibid., 5.

5 Ibid., 17.

6 "President Bush Addresses Nation on the Capture of Saddam Hussein," 12 December 2003, www.whitehouse.gov.

7 Bush, "2003 State of the Union."

8 Michael Howard, "What's in a Name? How to Fight Terrorism," *Foreign Affairs*, January/February 2002, 9.

9 Bush, *National Security Strategy*, 15.

10 See Anthony Clark Arend, "International Law and the Preemptive Use of Military Force," *Washington Quarterly* 26, 2:89–103.

11 Paul Wolfowitz, speech before the International Institute for Strategic Studies, Arundel House, London, 2 December 2002, www.dod.mil/speeches/2002.

12 Bush, *National Security Strategy*, 6.

13 Project for a New American Century, *Statement of Principles*, 3 June 1997, www.newamericancentury.org. See also Tom Barry and Jim Lobe, "U.S. Foreign Policy—Attention, Right Face, Forward March," *Foreign Policy Prospectus*, April 2002.

14 See Kurt Campbell and Michelle Flournoy, *To Prevail: An American Strategy for the Campaign against Terrorism* (Washington, D.C.: Center for Strategic and International Studies, 2001), 308.

15 Paul Krugman, "Fistful of Dollars," *New York Times*, 29 August 2003.

16 Elizabeth Becker and Edmund L. Andrews, "I.M.F. Says Rise in U.S. Debts Is Threat to World's Economy," *New York Times*, 8 January 2004.

17 Office of Management and Budget, *Budget of the United States Government, Fiscal Year 2004* (Washington, D.C.: U.S. Government Printing Office, 2003), 223.

18 Charles Knight, "Essential Elements Missing in the National Security Strategy of 2002" (Cambridge, Mass.: Commonwealth Institute Project on Defense Alternatives Commentary, November 2002), 4, www.comw.org/qdr/0210knight.html.

19 Paul Collier, *Breaking the Conflict Trap: Civil War and Development Policy* (Oxford: Oxford University Press, 2003).

20 Steven R. Weisman, "U.S. Must Counteract Image in Muslim World, Panel Says," *New York Times*, 1 October 2003.

21 George W. Bush, "Speech to the Inter-American Development Bank," 14 March 2002, www.iadb.org/NEWS/DISPLAY/SpeechView.cfm?Speech_Num=03.14.02_1&Language=English.

22 Rachel Stohl and Michael Stohl, "The Failed and Failing State and the Bush Administration: Paradoxes and Perils," paper prepared for the workshop "Failed States, Firenze, Italy, April 2001, 3, www.ippu.purdue.edu/failed_states/2001/papers/Stohl.pdf.

23 See Carnegie Commission on Preventing Deadly Violence, *Preventing Deadly Conflict* (New York: Carnegie Commission of New York, 1997). See also Robert I. Rotberg, "The New Nature of Nation-State Failure," *Washington Quarterly* 25, 3:85–96.

24 Stohl and Stohl, "The Failed and Failing State," 12.

25 Bush, *National Security Strategy*, 17 September 2002.

26 Roland Paris, "Wilson's Ghost: The Faulty Assumptions of Postconflict Peacebuilding," in Chester A. Crocker, Fen O. Hampson, and Pamela Q. Aall, eds., *Turbulent Peace* (Washington, D.C.: United States Institute of Peace, 2001), 765–784.

27 George Packer, "Dreaming of Democracy," *New York Times Magazine*, 2 March 2003, 44Q.

28 Chester A. Crocker, "Engaging Failing States," *Foreign Affairs*, September/October 2003, 32.

29 Major General William Nash, interview by Robert Ricigliano, Milwaukee, 16 October 2003.

30 Robert I. Rotberg, "Failed States in a World of Terror," *Foreign Affairs*, July/August 2002, www.foreignaffairs.org/20020701faessay8525/robert-i-rotberg/failed-states-in-a-world-of-terror.html.

31 National Intelligence Council, *The Global Infectious Disease Threat and Its Implications for the United States*, National Intelligence Estimate 99-17D (Washington, D.C.: National Intelligence Council, 2000).

32 Jordan S. Kassalow, "Why Health Is Important to U.S. Foreign Policy," special report of the Council on Foreign Relations, May 2001, 9, http://www3.cfr.org/pub3946/jordan_s_kassalow/why_health_is_important_to_us_foreign_policy.php.

33 Crocker, "Engaging Failed States," 32.

34 Stohl and Stohl, "The Failed and Failing State," 7.

35 Jeffrey Record, "Collapsed Countries, Casualty Dread, and the New American Way of War," *Parameters* 32, 2 (summer 2002): 5.

36 Crocker, "Engaging Failed States," 43.

37 Campbell and Flournoy, *To Prevail*, 319.

38 Jack Straw, "Failed and Failing States," speech at the European Research Institute, University of Birmingham, Birmingham, England, September 2002.

39 John Bolton, speech at Global Structures Convocation, Washington, D.C., 21 February 1994, cited in Phyllis Bennis, *Before and After: U.S. Foreign Policy and the September 11th Crisis* (Brooklyn: Olive Branch Press, 2003), 218.

40 Campbell and Flournoy, *To Prevail*, 321.

41 Rotberg, "New Nature of Nation-State Failure," 85.

42 Iraq Casualty Coalition, icasualties.org. The Iraq Casualty Coalition Count compiles information from the U.S. Department of Defense and the British Department of Defense, as well as CENTCOM press releases. The casualty figure comes from "U.S. Wounded in Iraq Surpasses 10,000," BBC News, 5 January 2005, http://news.bbc.co.uk.

43 Oklahoma City National Memorial Institute for the Prevention of Terrorism, www.mipt.org.

44 Warren Goldstein, "Justifying a Foreign Policy by Making a Nation Fearful," *Milwaukee Journal Sentinel*, 4 January 2004.

POPULAR CULTURE AND NARRATIVES OF INSECURITY

ANDREW MARTIN

Among the many written acknowledgments of the final episode of the long-running television series *Buffy the Vampire Slayer*, I came across the following remarkable statement: "Buffy deals with uncertainty and the grim side of life better in some ways than many experts in national security."[1] Beyond the fact that the statement appeared in the premier newspaper of the nation's capital, the *Washington Post*, what caught my eye was that its author was Anthony Cordesman, a professional national security expert, media commentator, and chair of the Center for Strategic and International Studies in Washington, D.C. The seemingly nonmainstream implication of Cordesman's argument is that a popular TV show based on the horror film and its subgenre of vampirism has much, if not more, to tell us about national security than have those who are actually responsible for planning and implementing security policies: our elected officials, administrative experts, and policy analysts. In the context of pressing national security threats, this somewhat startling pronouncement—based on a mass cultural fantasy involving a young woman with mystical demon-slaying power—might be written off as a slip of the tongue or the momentary lapse of a busy intellectual. But as it turns out, Cordesman had developed an in-depth analysis of *Buffy the Vampire Slayer* in relation to national security in a lengthy paper that was published online in the days after 9/11.

The immediate fascination is not simply Cordesman's appropriation of a fantasy narrative about a vampire slayer (as Doug Davis explains in his contribution to this collection, the strategic planning conducted today by our national security analysts is always yesterday's fiction). It is rather the way in which such a vampire narrative comes to articulate and then to frame contemporary national insecurities in a post-9/11 world. Cordesman admits that he needed to find a novel way to frame his presentation of a complicated and often arcane discourse about terrorism and biological warfare. For him, *Buffy* is an apt choice with which to set up a serious discussion about "how little we know and how little we can predict" about possible terrorist threats and, equally, how difficult it is "to put biological warfare into perspective." The fact is, Cordesman admits, we have entered "a world we do not yet understand . . . and we are struggling desperately to come to grips with it. In the process, we often seek to deny much of the uncertainty involved. . . . We want a clear course to follow, and a clear course of action." But "the events of September 11 have shown us that even when we think we know a threat, we can get all of the essentials wrong."[2] This is where *Buffy the Vampire Slayer* has much to teach us, both as a reflection of our times and as a cautionary tale.

In the absence of usable analytical tools or workable national strategies, Cordesman approaches national security issues in what he calls "more mundane terms" by thinking about terrorist and biological attacks in terms of a long-running television series. He deems the world of terrorism and biological weapons the "Buffy Paradigm" and asks that we think about many of the problems in the proposed solutions as part of the "Buffy Syndrome." While uncertainty is the dominating motif of the paradigm, Cordesman, in a manner not unlike that of other security analysts, argues that the syndrome has wider implications for U.S. national security:

> The characters in Buffy constantly try to create unrealistic plans and models, and live in a world where they never really face the level of uncertainty they must deal with. They do not live in a world of total denial, but they do seek predictability and certainty to a degree that never corresponds to the problems they face. In short, they behave as if they could create and live with the kind of strategy and doctrine that is typically developed by the US joint chiefs, could develop and implement an NSC decision memorandum, or solve their problems with the equivalent of a Quadrennial Defense Review.[3]

Thus, for Cordesman, popular culture aptly and uncannily illuminates the shortcomings of national policy making. And while he may be unusual among his colleagues in bringing popular cultural figures and narratives to bear on the problem, Cordesman is hardly alone in his more general assessments. Indeed, many commentators have remarked that among the most surprising things about the end of the cold war was that the U.S. security establishment, infatuated as it was with a bipolar model of the balance of power between nation-states, failed to predict it. As Cordesman suggests through the *Buffy* example, U.S. security experts did not have the tools to understand the cultural conditions at work on the ground—which is not to say that neorealist experts lived in total denial, but that in their urge for predictability and certainty, they failed to understand the problems they actually faced. When people power broke loose in Soviet Eastern Bloc countries and then within the Soviet Union itself, neither the security establishment nor its academic backup saw it coming. As one academic commentator put it:

> The end of the cold war, almost overnight, dissolved the structure around which security studies had crystallized in the latter years of the 1980s and promptly precipitated a paradigmatic crisis. The issue— at least for policy makers—was no longer how to manage an arms race and superpower competition, but how to manage the implosion of a superpower and the disintegration of global power structures. Meanwhile, there suddenly reemerged ethnic, nationalist, and other forms of conflict that had been regarded as secondary or marginal phenomena within the universe of security studies.[4]

Nevertheless, the so-called neorealist mindset continued to dominate Western thinking, particularly in the United States, where the assumed triumph of democratic values and the free-market system was celebrated as the "end of history," the final triumph over the "Evil Empire," and the global ascendance of Pax America. Thus, with cold-war plans and models in mind, security officials and scholars failed to predict the next round of struggle and remained for the most part unaware of the levels of resistance and uncertainty and the pervasiveness of a threat that would come back to haunt them on a fateful day in September.

To redress this situation, scholars and commentators have attempted to initiate a broad-based approach to international relations and international studies by combining the insights garnered from an array of disciplines, including anthropology, cultural studies, and postcolonial studies, as well as political science. The aim of this interdisciplinary approach is to turn the paradigmatic assumptions and conventions upside down by insisting that insecurity—and its flip side, security—is a social and cultural construction (rather than "a pregiven" naturalized fact about the world), and that the state, insecurity, and indeed social identities "are produced in a mutually constitutive process."[5]

This formulation and its supporting arguments are of course familiar to scholars of cultural, media, and literary studies. In contrast to a scholarship aimed at policy or prediction, this is a scholarship of illumination and retrospection. For it is within the realm of popular culture that the constructs of national security and global security find some of their most powerful modes of articulation and address. What is of interest in the fictions of popular culture is their circulation and reception—their influence on the ways in which we perceive the world in general and our place within it in particular. This has little to do with claiming a singular influence for popular culture in and on contemporary life (it is certainly not as though it is a single all-powerful entity), but rather with insisting that narratives and representations of popular culture—especially in the United States—are a crucial element in the construction of modern regimes of knowledge and perception, behavior and identity. As such, they are just as deeply entangled in the production of cultural meaning as are those approaches that claim to be separate from mass or popular culture, such as policy making, data collection, and strategic studies. This is why it is important to take popular culture seriously, indeed, as seriously as Cordesman appears to do in his analysis of *Buffy* and the current state of national and global security.

But what this kind of strategic and piecemeal borrowing from popular culture studies might miss is the long-running nature of the story—in other words, how the production of cultural meanings builds upon preexisting narratives, just as a long-running television series does. In the spring of 2003, as the war against Iraq was getting under way, for example, it was surprising to see how often the Vietnam War emerged in journalistic analyses and popular commentaries. Of course, there were also many references to other wars, especially World War II, as one would expect. But whether a commentator was attempting to show how different this war would be or was trying to warn against imperial hubris, regional entanglements, and the like, Vietnam provided a touchstone, signifying a specifically controversial and grim instance of U.S. experience in the modern world. As the war in Iraq has continued, the catchphrases of the Vietnam War continue to be pressed into service: "'search and destroy,' . . . 'winning hearts and minds,' 'the Baghdad triangle,'" and so forth.[6] But what was clear, and became increasingly clear as the Iraq war began, was that this realm of signification was not simply the Vietnam War that took place in the 1960s and early 1970s, but more often than not the war that had been reconstructed and reinscribed within popular culture—through films, for the most part, ranging from the relatively critical *Apocalypse Now* (1979), *Coming Home* (1978), and *The Deer Hunter* (1978) to the revisionist Rambo syndrome in film and *A-Team*, *Tour of Duty*, and *China Beach* on television.

To be sure, mention of World War II has also reemerged in recent years (after Vietnam and after the first Gulf War) in a spate of highly popular histories (Tom Brokaw's best-seller *The Finest Generation*, for instance), as well as in film (*Saving Private Ryan*) and television (*Band of Brothers*). Carl von Clausewitz, famous for claiming that war is politics by other means, also wrote that while war may well generate its own grammar, its rhetorical and representational logic is entirely the product of the domestic culture that produces it. Thus do political discourses find their greatest purchase on the greatest number of people through the narratives and popular culture   particularly, in our own time, as these intermingle with and emerge from film and television. As one news commentator put the case: "There are two conflicts raging—the fight between the antagonists themselves and the pitched battle between journalism and the imperatives of show business. The conflicts are intertwined and the second determines how we view the first."[7]

Popular culture in the United States is where war comes from and where it is made possible—even desirable—and it is where it ends up, as the lived experience of war is fed back to us in displaced forms and narratives. It is one of the key sites where social norms and identities are constructed and valorized; it is where culture in all its complex tangles of residual, dominant, and emergent forms overlaps with and is enfolded back into structures of authority and control. It is through this process that the lived experience of insecurity, of uncertainty about the motives and aims of outsiders (the possible evil ones), are best viewed both as constructs and as constructed.

The journalistic response to the current war in Iraq is instructive in this regard. The first week of the war was full of references to World War II movies; a second "finest generation" was now racing toward Baghdad (Berlin), just like Patton or the Big Red One, John Wayne at the wheel, with thankful locals waving from the sidelines. But then things began to go terribly wrong; a giant sandstorm swept in, the locals were not waving but shooting, and a very different set of references began to appear as the narrative conventions temporarily broke down. Now it was the "quagmire" (an unsubtle code for "Vietnam"), the generals were complaining that they didn't have enough troops and materials (again, an old Vietnam story), and Secretary of Defense Donald Rumsfeld was being compared to Robert McNamara (on the front page of the *New York Times*). Like their "best and brightest" predecessors, Rumsfeld, Vice President Dick Cheney, and Deputy Secretary of Defense Paul Wolfowitz may have enjoyed stellar careers in think tanks, academia, and corporate management, but for the few days that the media conventions of narrative logic broke down, they were portrayed as incompetent war planners who had undercut our fighting men and women. To make matters worse, the U.S. military and the U.S. media did not have total control over the information and images flowing from the war. Unlike the earlier Gulf War, in which a heavy-handed media censorship was maintained, in the war against Iraq the Western media found themselves in competition with the Arab-owned news network Al Jazeera. It was from the latter, more than from any other media source, that pictures of dead and captured U.S. servicemen and -women would flow. In effect, the United States no longer controlled the global reception of its preferred narrative of war.

Toward the end of this time of sandstorms and confusion, the Pentagon planners, the military, and the media got the biggest break of the war: the saving of Private Lynch. Jessica Lynch had been captured during an ambush that, as much as anything, had kicked off the race for references to Vietnam films in the first place. Her convoy of supply trucks had lost its way in the sandstorm and landed in the hands of local Iraqi troops. Pictures of the mangled bodies of U.S. troops quickly turned up on the world's TV and computer screens, and U.S. prisoners were being paraded on Iraqi (and global) television. Under these circumstances, as one reporter put it, the rescuing of Jessica Lynch "provided the nation with a made-for-television catharsis" that "instantly hardened into a Hollywood-style fable of heroism." That the military had videotaped the rescue mission and obligingly provided the news media with selective clips certainly assisted in the process of Lynch's instant stardom. Journalists were now falling over themselves to find the correct movie or TV reference that might best frame their news copy (a play on *Saving Private Ryan* proved very popular). The *Washington Post* even portrayed Lynch as "a teenage Rambo" who continued to fight after being badly wounded, an image that the tabloids and television eagerly adopted.

In short order, Hollywood, the TV networks, and publishing companies were scrambling to offer Lynch exclusive multimedia deals reported to be worth millions. As it turned out, however, most of the story was a fabrication put together by military public relations in an attempt to spin some good news at a time when little existed. Jessica Lynch would eventually have her fifteen minutes of fame, but she used her time to set the record straight. Not only was she unconscious throughout most of the ambush, having been an early victim of the shootout, but an Iraqi doctor was the real hero of the story in that he tended her wounds and was instrumental in summoning help, at great risk to himself, from nearby U.S. forces.[8]

My point here is that journalists are not just being clever when they reach for movie tie-ins or some other reference from popular culture. They are running on automatic pilot in a social environment where the only shared cultural signs and signifiers are the texts of popular culture. Indeed, one might say that popular narratives are embedded in our culture (just as the reporters were embedded in military units in the second Gulf War) to the point where they form a seamless web of naturalized and invisible referents. They are vehicles for working through anxieties and insecurities; they are mechanisms that offer fictive solutions to real social and political contradictions and threats. In this sense, popular narratives are ideological, but not just because they are fabrications or because they dupe and distract. They also work to transform real social and political desires and insecurities into manageable narratives in which these can be temporarily articulated, displaced, or resolved. This is what Fredric Jameson calls the rewriting of the "management of desire in social terms," a process that gratifies desires in the political field that are "intolerable" but also "imperishable . . . only to the degree that they can be laid to rest."[9]

Popular texts and narratives are hardly stable, frozen once and for all within a single possible meaning; and neither are consumers of popular narratives a single decoding entity that endlessly arrives at the same coded message. The texts of popular culture and their consumers enact a complex set of relationships that cannot be reduced to simplistic formulas. A case in point is the films about the U.S. experience in, and of, the Vietnam War (*The Deer Hunter*, *Apocalypse Now*, *Coming Home*, *Cutter and Bone*, *Platoon*, *Full Metal Jacket*, and *Born on the Fourth of July*). When these films were released in the late 1970s and 1980s, they were received by many as critical of the Vietnam War and as offering a variety of ways for understanding its utter madness, its lack of temporal order, its waste of lives and bodies, both U.S. and Vietnamese, and its destructive impact on domestic U.S. culture. But the cultural terrain of the seventies and eighties in which such readings were made possible was subject to a powerful and systemic round of conservative revisionism that accompanied the emergence of Reaganism. Under these new circumstances, the critical knowledge gained from the experience of the Vietnam era gave way to a renewed cycle of cold-war rhetoric. The war in Vietnam, described by author Philip Caputo as "a crime, murder on a mass scale," was reconfigured by President Ronald Reagan as "a noble cause."[10]

To suggest that this process was simply a conservative political intervention against hard-won critical knowledge is to miss the wider cultural changes at work across the 1980s and the way these changes continue to affect our post-9/11 sense of lived experience. Vietnam, civil rights, and an engaged citizenry had exposed some of the most salient truths about what lay behind the cold-war ideology and the institutional systems that were its beneficiaries. Turning this broadly shared critical knowledge aside, and replacing it with a complex of patriotic tropes within a reenergized and interventionist U.S. approach to world affairs, involved an ideological reworking of the U.S. story across the cultural board; it involved the cultural construction of new structures of feeling and new forms of lived ideology, expressed in films from *Rambo* (1982) to *Top Gun* (1989).

By the time of the first Gulf War, as a recent combat biography demonstrates, a completely different reading of the representations of the Vietnam War was possible. In his book *Jarhead*, Anthony Swofford recalls that before going off to the Gulf War, soldiers got themselves fired up for combat by watching these same seventies and eighties Vietnam War films. Swofford writes that "there is talk that many Vietnam films are anti-war, that the message is war is inhumane . . . and terrible. But no matter . . . what Kubrick or Coppola or Stone intended, . . . young soldiers are excited by them, because the magic brutality of the films celebrates the terrible and despicable beauty of their fighting skills. . . . Filmic images of death and carnage are pornography for the military man."[11]

Popular fictions can be read and seen and interpreted in a variety of ways in the course of their reception, and Vietnam's place within this process has never been finally fixed or settled but remains available for use in any number of ways—including critiques of U.S. policies after 9/11. And although the media space for making the connections between earlier critical paradigms, current events, and the spin of popular culture has shrunk considerably, voices of protest did emerge as the George W. Bush administration made what appeared to be a seamless transition from aggrieved victim to global aggressor in a preemptive war against "Evil"—first in Afghanistan and then in Iraq. One independent journalist noted in the *New Statesman* that it was somehow fitting that "the bombing of Afghanistan has been conducted by the same B52 bombers that destroyed much of Indochina 30 years ago."[12]

An accounting of the scale and continuity and consequences of U.S. imperial violence is our elite's most enduring taboo. Contrary to myth, even the homicidal invasion of Vietnam was regarded by its tactical critics as a noble cause into which the United States stumbled and became bogged down. Hollywood has long purged the truth of that atrocity, just as it has shaped, for many of us, the way we perceive contemporary history and the rest of humanity. And now that much of the news itself is Hollywood inspired, amplified by amazing technology and with its internalized mission to minimize Western culpability, it is hardly surprising that many today do not see the trail of blood.

This way of viewing and critiquing the cultural construction of new structures of feeling and new forms of lived ideology is far from dominant and must struggle to find an audience in a crowded media environment and in the face of political and cultural gatekeepers who have grown incredibly powerful compared to their sixties counterparts. Moreover, at a time when U.S. global military strategies are cloaked in a fundamentalist discourse of absolute good versus absolute evil, and in a political atmosphere of open and active hostility toward alternative voices, the places for such critiques have become increasingly rare. That the borders between the news media and popular culture (the institutions of both often contained within a single corporate entity) have become increasingly porous is nonetheless precisely to the point. The taboos that steer both forms of media away from a sustained and serious engagement with U.S. culpability in atrocities and blood trails in the real world most certainly exist. However, there still remains, even if blurry and broadly defined, a division of labor between the conventions of representing news events and narratives of popular culture. Whereas news presentations are restrained from showing in graphic detail the horrific effects of war, violence, and death, the representations of these things are the stock-in-trade of a good deal of popular culture. While the news media dutifully reports on the Bush administration's reliance on a fundamentalist and Manichean justification for its actions in the world, it is in the narratives of popular culture that we find such fantasies acted out and graphically depicted. This returns us to where this essay began, and to popular narratives that indeed manage to illuminate our contemporary notions of security in an age of mounting insecurities.

As I suggested at the outset, Anthony Cordesman of the Center for International and Strategic Studies invokes *Buffy the Vampire Slayer* to argue that we are hampered from creating a truly secure international system by our denial of the dangers that surround us in everyday life. In Cordesman's essay, the bare outlines of the *Buffy* series are appropriated to illuminate this situation and are related to what is for the most part a statistical study of the problems of establishing a measure of homeland security in the face of emergent threats of biological warfare. Indeed, Cordesman is quite explicit about his uses of *Buffy*: He wishes to forward an analysis of the threat of terrorism and biological warfare "to people who seem to be incapable of understanding the subject." *Buffy the Vampire Slayer* in this reading is reduced to a "mundane" example of "pop culture" that might nevertheless help some people understand the "fairly esoteric" and "difficult" analytical language of "modern warfare." In service to this project, then, the entire seven-year series is described accordingly: "A teenage vampire slayer . . . lives in a world of unpredictable threats where each series of crises only becomes predictable when it is over and is followed by a new and unfamiliar one."[13] While this description does capture the original scenario of the show, it misses the complexities of the social world in which Buffy is imagined to live and fight. It also fails to capture the timeliness and the humor of the series and its fraught attempts to be more than the sum of its generic parts.

For Cordesman, it is not that *Buffy* is itself political, or that it offers a plausible strategic model for national defense, but rather that it illustrates, in the form of a cautionary tale, the unpredictable nature of terrorist threats. As I suggested earlier, however, popular culture is sometimes uncanny in the way that it is entangled with and illuminates contemporary social concerns. And it is here that *Buffy the Vampire Slayer* might be approached in ways that take us beyond the dichotomies that structure Cordesman's essay—the opposition between popular culture ("mundane") and national security studies ("esoteric").

When the *Buffy* series appeared in 1997, it was widely celebrated as a particularly good example of "girl-power" or protofeminist narratives, and certainly elements of this theme continued across the entire series.[14] In fact, in the final season's denouement in the spring of 2003, all the potential slayers-in-waiting, young women from all over the world (there can be only one female "chosen one" at any given time) are mystically empowered with the slayer's super strength and fighting skills. But by this time in the show's development, *Buffy* had long outgrown the teenager theme of "school is hell" to investigate darker themes within the imagined world of Sunny Dale, a "one-Starbuck's town" situated over a Hell Mouth (a sort of evil portal between dimensions that is used in the series to account for the continual manifestation of evil forces in one form or another). As the show progressed, the strains of the endless struggle against evil began to take their toll on Buffy and her friends, the overall look of the show became darker, and the pressures within the group intensified. With each passing season, moreover, the evil forces that Buffy must confront became increasingly more complex, powerful, and better organized until the final season, when a powerful force called "the First" begins to make itself felt. What eventually became clear are the global implications of the threat that is focused on Sunny Dale (read, the United States). This particular configuration of the "Big Bad" is international in its ambitions, in that it tries to kill off the potential slayers who might replace Buffy and has also decimated the Watchers Council, which claims global jurisdiction over the slayer's fight against evil. Beyond this attempt to isolate Buffy for a final showdown, the seeds of discontent, ambition, and division have been sown within Buffy's usually tight group of friends and supporters.

By the time these story lines were emerging during the spring of 2003, the United States was gearing up for a war against Iraq with an increasingly zealous rhetoric accompanied by a disastrous attempt at coalition building through the United Nations. At the same time, rumors were rife in the press about serious disagreements between various segments of the government (the Pentagon, the military, the State Department, and so on). The only serious support forthcoming from old allies was offered by Great Britain, and even here it was obvious that such support would arouse strident opposition within Prime Minister Tony Blair's cabinet.

Interestingly, Buffy could also count on an English mentor, Rupert Giles, who across the length of the series offered thoughtful and consistent mentoring that was usually far more coherent and rational than that offered by other (often U.S.) authority figures. It was thanks to Giles that the remaining potential slayers were gathered up and brought to Sunny Dale, where Buffy might guard and train them. When they mixed with Buffy's close-knit circle of friends in a situation of constant pressure, Buffy, too, would find it difficult to negotiate a working battle plan with her international coalition of the willing. Under these circumstances, the language of the show became increasingly militaristic. Buffy found herself constantly called upon to act as a military leader—a demand that flew in the face of the usually relaxed and ad hoc chain of command that marked much of the show's former approach to the weekly manifestation of insecurity. Eventually Buffy and her coalition manage to combine their various strengths and defeat the evil First, but not without casualties and even fatalities among some of the show's long-term characters. But in the end, nothing is left of Sunny Dale, because the entire town has been destroyed and dropped into something resembling a meteor crater. As in the logic of Vietnam, the village was destroyed in order to save it.

Whereas Cordesman reads off the narrative content of *Buffy* and assumes that "we" are no different from the young distracted teenagers who populate the world of Sunny Dale—with their inability to truly understand the scope and sway of the new kinds of evil in a world dominated by the United States and supported by Britain—I would pose the issue in another way. Indeed, *Buffy the Vampire Slayer* is unique in U.S. popular culture in that it at once registers the changed reality of post-cold-war thinking (constant threats in borderless worlds) and proposes a collaborative group effort to examine, research, debate, and dispel these threats. In this regard, of course, I agree with Cordesman that in some ways *Buffy* deals with uncertainties and the grim side of life better than do many experts in national security, which is perhaps not saying so much, given the current state of national response to global security threats. And yet *Buffy the Vampire Slayer* is more than simply a reflection of the Bush security apparatus and less than a throughgoing critique of U.S. unilateralism and military rhetoric. Like popular culture more generally, it provides insights into ways of thinking about security, insecurity, and our globalized world today. But as in all things, the burden of thinking remains our own.

NOTES

1 Rita Kempley, "Fangs for the Memories, Buffy," *Washington Post*, 20 May 2003.

2 Anthony Cordesman, "Biological Warfare and the Buffy Paradigm" (Washington, D.C.: Center for Strategic and International Studies, 29 September 2001), 1, 2.

3 Ibid., 3, 5.

4 Jutta Weldes, Mark Laffey, Hugh Gusterson, and Raymond Duvall, eds., *Cultures of Insecurity: States, Communities, and the Production of Danger* (Minneapolis: University of Minnesota Press, 1999), 3.

5 Ibid., I.

6 Jonathan Schell, "Letter from Ground Zero: Imposing Our Will," *The Nation*, 4/11 August 2003, 10.

7 Frank Rich, "Iraq around the Clock," *New York Times*, 30 March 2003.

8 For summations of the media frenzy over Jessica Lynch, see Alessandra Stanley, "Hoopla over a P.O.W.: A Mirror of U.S. Society," *New York Times*, 18 April 2003, and Daphne Eviatar, "The Press and Private Lynch," *The Nation*, 7 July 2003, 18.

9 Fredric Jameson, "Reification and Utopia in Mass Culture," *Signatures of the Visible* (New York and London: Routledge, 1990), 25

10 Philip Caputo, *Rumors of War* (1977; repr. New York: Ballantine, 1982), 317; Ronald Reagan, quoted in the *Washington Post*, 12 July 1980.

11 Anthony Swofford, *Jarhead* (New York: Scribner, 2003), 4.

12 John Pilger, "An Unconscionable Threat to Humanity," in Phil Scranton, ed., *Beyond September 11: An Anthology of Dissent* (London: Pluto Books, 2002), 21. Originally published in the *New Statesman*, October/November 2001.

13 Cordesman, "Biological Warfare," 3.

14 So much has been written about *Buffy the Vampire Slayer* that it is impossible to cite even a selection of what is available to both the general and the specialized reader. However, three collections of essays offer the interested reader a general view of what is available: Roz Kaveney, ed., *Reading the Vampire Slayer: An Unofficial Critical Companion to Buffy and Angel* (London and New York: Tauris Parke, 2001); Rhonda Wilcox and David Lavery, eds., *Fighting the Forces: What's at Stake in Buffy the Vampire Slayer* (Lanham, Md.: Rowman and Littlefield, 2002); and James B. South, ed., *Buffy the Vampire Slayer and Philosophy* (Chicago: Open Court, 2003).

FEARFUL THOUGHTS

U.S. TELEVISION SINCE 9/11 AND THE WARS IN IRAQ

PATRICIA MELLENCAMP

Within the last few years, the United States has revised and reversed itself, turning from a global economy to a military economy, from internationalism to nationalism, and from peace to war. In this essay, I examine how U.S. popular culture, particularly U.S. television, participated in this revisionism from 1991 to 2003—the interval between the first and second wars in Iraq. I also consider how tales of death and personal sacrifice in war influence other cultural processes and artifacts. Since the current war in Iraq is an ongoing drama, what are some of its aftereffects?

The role played by fear in our current popular culture is palpable, and fear makes us intellectually vulnerable.[1] According to Tyler Volk, who has contributed to a theory of "terror management," immediate awareness of our mortality can lock us into a stringent "worldview" that serves as an antidote to our anxiety about death.[2] Such an intellectual lockdown happened on a national scale after 9/11. More than ten years ago, I elaborated a model of fear and anxiety in U.S. television that I believed was outdated as the cold war ended. It is now once again applicable.[3] In fact, television coverage of the tragedy of 9/11 echoed the magnitude of the U.S. primal catastrophe TV scene—the Kennedy assassination in the 1960s. In both events, the nation as a whole appeared to be in jeopardy.

And yet, the groundwork for the current revival of military heroism was laid in the 1990s. Best-selling books paid tribute to the generation of World War II veterans, our fathers and grandfathers, recreating their war through intimate memories. A short piece in the *New York Times Magazine* argued that this revisionism was indebted to the works of historian Stephen Ambrose, whose popular 1992 book *Band of Brothers* became a 2001–2002 HBO TV series: "Ambrose's significant contribution was to ask us to think about war not as the clash of large . . . forces but . . . as the drama of the fighting man, of brothers helping brothers. In so doing, he helped reshape the war narrative in our time; . . . everything we thought we'd learned about war in the past thirty years has given way to a revisionist theory that seems to have sprung directly from Ambrose's books." "It's about the man next to you" are among the last words spoken in the film *Black Hawk Down*. In a similar process of Vietnam War revisionism, Mel Gibson's film of the book *We Were Soldiers* likewise emphasizes the ideals of brotherhood: "We fought for each other."[4]

An insightful and romantic passage in the book *Black Hawk Down* dramatizes the depth of this emotion. A young soldier in the midst of a terrifying firefight in the central city, surrounded by thousands of angry, armed Somalis, reflects on his experience: "He had been wildly scared . . . he thought he might literally die of fright. His head was filled with sounds of shooting, explosions, and visions of his friends, one by one, going down, blood splashed everywhere, oily and sticky . . . *this is it for me* and then, the fear fell away. His own life no longer mattered. All that did matter were his buddies, his brothers, that they didn't get hurt, that they not get killed. . . . These men around him . . . were more important to him than life itself; . . . he had to keep fighting because the other guys needed him."[5] This is war reporting as personal memory.

Films like *Saving Private Ryan* remember World War II "realistically," as deeply personal and emotional. The film opens with the return of an older veteran to the cemetery in Normandy, a sea of neat white crosses on a green bluff overlooking the ocean. As if paying tribute to the sanctity of this moment and to the privacy of memory, his family humbly follows in a group several feet behind. There is a cut to the older man's lined sad face, remembering, witnessing. The camera dollies in to an extreme close-up of his teary eyes. There is then a cut to young and scared soldiers in landing boats, roiled by the rough sea, nauseous, shelled by German artillery. On the bloody beach, all is chaos, body parts, noise, and carnage, as seen and experienced by the Tom Hanks character. Death is everywhere; it is a random, hellish, brutal slaughter. In stark contrast, the star's death at the end of the film is almost silent and sanctified. Indeed, the film moves from slaughter to sacrifice. Death has taken on ennobled meaning. War has a higher purpose.

Amidst the initial confusion of the landing, Hanks's leadership is steadfast. He is a humble hero, a schoolteacher, who will lead a patrol to rescue another soldier, Private Ryan, whose mother has already lost three sons in this war. The compassionate military command vowed she would not lose another. While the setting is the battle for France, the second world war with Germany is not the issue. While several members of the rescue team will sacrifice their lives, they die not for their country, but for each other.

In this film, war embodies nostalgia for an era when life and death, bravery and self-sacrifice, loyalty and comradeship, were more important than money, greed, and Wall Street competition. Given the context of the 1990s, the novels and films of this time served as admonishment to a culture enthralled with thirty-year-old millionaires riding the stock-market techno-bubble. After all, war was a nobler pursuit than business. Unlike business, war brought out the best in men. War was not self-serving or self-aggrandizing for those who fought and died.

In his best-selling books about the "great generation" of World War II, it was as if Tom Brokaw, the NBC anchor as spokesman, as the son now older, celebrating the courage of the father then younger, was asking: "We fought and died for this?" Brokaw, wearing their mantle, would carry the aura of this period into his coverage of the war in Iraq. The concepts of war as unity, as clarity of belief, as a personal quest and test, were counterpoints to a culture of greed and narcissism, as well as rebukes to a capitalist ideology of selfish individualism. There was a time, we were told, when there was something worth fighting and dying for that was based in personal honor and integrity. There was a time when good and evil were clearly discernible, and notions of freedom, both personal and global, were endangered. With the help of history and popular culture, this belief became the underpinning for a preemptive war against Iraq in 2003.

The scenario of fathers and sons, of the passage of one generation to the next, was the oedipal logic of the larger story. In 2003, George Bush would emulate his father as president and commander-in-chief of the U.S. military, doing what his father did not do in 1991—go all the way to Baghdad and topple Saddam Hussein. Could the century-old theory of Sigmund Freud be so alive in the twenty-first century? The revival of old-fashioned military heroics suggests that psychoanalysis remains entirely relevant.

As Raymond Williams told us years ago, television is not a discrete medium; it is an ongoing drama of flow. TV narratives play out over time.

This war in Iraq, officially begun in March 2003 but planned months in advance, allowing even the TV networks to budget and train for it, is the continuance, perhaps the conclusion, of a long-running serial or obsession; it picks up where the 1991 Gulf War inconclusively left off. The path was not so direct, however. It involves general patterns of thought charted over long periods of television time, with an intricate intertwining of news and entertainment, of reality and fiction.

There are the differences between the 1991 and the 2003 TV wars—the first with a paucity of location reporting, the second with a glut of on-site reporters in uniform. In 1991, journalists were held back from the battlefield in reporter pools. This strategy was cleverly reversed in the second war, as reporters were embedded in military units on the front lines of battle. During the 2003 coverage, the battlefield was blanketed with reporters who, barely able to contain their enthusiasm for their good fortune, agreed to censorship in the name of security. But whether the TV reporters are pooled behind the lines or embedded within combat units, TV war stories are now told from their point of view. Unlike the genre of combat narratives—personal stories told from the soldier's experiential point of view—TV holds the battlefield at arm's length, mediating and even deflecting our involvement. TV reporters, sometimes present but outside the battle, are onlookers, albeit brave and famous spectators. They reveal few if any emotional responses to events they witness or even experience. Because most airtime is focused on images of reporters talking directly to us, we remember the reporters more than the war. One NBC reporter who died coincidentally of an aneurysm was given an on-air funeral peroration by Tom Brokaw, who declared him a national hero.

War in Iraq—I and II

Coverage of the Iraqi oil crisis began in August 1990. Although it was repeatedly denied that oil and money were the cause of the war, TV intercut the military buildup with stock-market reports in a pattern of cause-effect logic, awaiting a war and a recession. In this initial phase, there was no pretense that economics were not the determinant issue or that fear of economic decline was not the real source of national anxiety. CNN's coverage, titled "The Crisis in the Gulf," was particularly direct in this regard, initially interviewing more stock-market experts than government officials. And even with military spokespersons, the economic cost of the action was always at issue. Editorials in newspapers urged the populace not to put off purchasing consumer items; delay would undermine the economy. We were urged to shop regularly as an act of national patriotism and support for the war.

By the time titles were added, the poetic "Operation Desert Storm" was cast not as an economic struggle but as an apocalyptic religious battle between good and evil, Bush versus Saddam (his first name). The war was a robust revival of rugged individualism, with events attributed solely to individual leaders rather than to economic, political, or religious causes. Heroes (Generals Norman Schwarzkopf and Colin Powell, and the U.S. military machine) would rout evil wimps (Saddam and the Iraqi army). (In both wars, the ferocity of the Iraqi army, particularly the infamous "guard," was proclaimed, even vaunted; in both wars it quickly collapsed or surrendered.)

Paradoxically, the strict censorship of coverage in 1991 turned a lusty war into pedagogy and cost accounting. The majority of airtime was devoted to illustrated lectures by retired generals and think-tank talking heads ruminating about strategy, weapons, and the results. This was a war of words (opinions and experts) not bodies (and grunts). It concerned theory more than experience, intellect more than affect, and words more than sights. We watched television to listen to experts and reporters talk about the war.

This was our preparation for the second war, our on-site simulated training. This was true for the war leaders as well as for the general populace. In 2003, we were there, in several Middle Eastern cities, with the anchors or on the battle lines, standing just slightly off to the side, our view mediated by an enthusiastic reporter in camouflage fatigues. In both wars, we watched abstract granular images repeated throughout the day, recontextualized and reinterpreted by different words and opinions. The aerial images of the first war were from the viewpoint of the pilot firing at impersonal targets. The clips lacked specificity and were of such poor quality that they could have been shot anywhere. Because they were bad and barely decipherable, we assumed they must be real—the key attribute of catastrophe coverage's claim on reality.

But bad as they were, these were not amateur images. Instead, they foreshadowed high-tech wars in which the generals have the best seats in the house via live satellite broadcasts of battles, as we learned more than a decade later in the very prescient book and film *Black Hawk Down*. And like the 1993 military action in Somalia, which the book (in 1999) and film (in

2002) recreated, the first war in Iraq did not have a conclusive ending. Iraq just seemed to stop, to run down from twenty-four-hour coverage to an item on the nightly news agenda. The 2003 war, in contrast, had a clear, awaited, and anticipated beginning and a declared ending—initiated and concluded in speeches by George Bush. Paradoxically, the fighting in Iraq continues long after the war has ended. Television's coverage of the beginning of the war, as we waited together for the bombing to start, was clearer than the ending, where the declaration of "mission accomplished" became a contentious political issue. These economic and human aftereffects disfigured the initial congratulatory rush. In a sense, the ending is just beginning.

For both wars, which were planned rather than unforeseen events, TV adopted a catastrophic rather than an educational TV style. The shock of the first war was administered first to a U.S. and then to an international audience on 16 January 1991. Network and CNN journalists on the scene reported about the bombs falling on Baghdad. The 2003 war would also begin in Baghdad, this time with a clear visual image from a stationary surveillance video camera. Paradoxically, however, this was an image with even less visual information and drama. The second war took a long time to begin. We waited patiently for it and even then were unsure if the parking structure we were watching was the "real" beginning. It was a boring image in a deserted noplace. The truly revolutionary technology in this coverage was the old technology—the telephone, a two-way, simultaneous device, unlike the one-way reception of the television screen; and radio, with voices that described maps, charts, graphs, and granular aerial views. It would appear that vision serves sound, which remains the dominant code of television. Sights on television are accompanied by varying facts and opinions, suggesting that words create the context that critically determine meaning. Thus, seeing is not believing.

The real winner in the first Iraq war was CNN, as it stole the networks' prestige. This victory portended the rise of cable TV throughout the 1990s and eventually satellite TV as alternative distribution systems to broadcast TV. CNN has everything to gain from war and catastrophe and constant coverage; the networks have advertising revenue to lose. The former "little channel that could" was catapulted into fame as a twenty-four-hour crisis channel, ever ready when war and nation needed it—although the war of 1991 was fashioned as a reluctant, even petulant, subject, keeping the press at bay while using it as a mechanism of military publicity.

In the 2003 version, the Fox cable news channel beat CNN in the ratings, with its prowar enthusiasm and patriotic outrage often presented by attractive female anchors cheering our boys on. In contrast, in 2003, CNN fired its flashier reporters and coalesced around "serious" journalism. The three networks—initially offering constant coverage but soon shrinking to irregular interruptions, war specials, and half hour regular news formats—lost viewers but held on to the majority of the audience. As in the first war, Tom Brokaw, Peter Jennings, and Dan Rather were at their NBC, ABC, and CBS anchor posts in 2003, looking older but also strangely the same. All three went to the Middle East for the war's opening. Brokaw was there with the troops before the opening salvo, preparing the nation for the war that was coming, granting it a tone of historical continuity.

CNN's international reach in 1990, replicated by Rupert Murdoch's Fox/Star network in 2003, was beginning to look like a version of Marshal Mcluhan's global village. That vision of countercultural video guerrillas in the 1960s and 1970s, dreaming of a satellite network that would bypass national boundaries and differences and directly address the people, had been realized and subverted—in the name of war and nation rather than that of peace and internationalism. Another 1960s memory and protest, opposition to the Vietnam War, was revised yet again, its history lessons vanquished, replaced by the virility of U.S. military might and victory. After years of critique and repentance, war was back in style for much of the U.S. populace.

The most troublesome contradiction, however, was the linkage of military and TV coverage. Embedding reporters within military units rather than pooling them at command central ironically had a censoring effect. The first war's censorship was a top-down command in the name of security; the second war's was a voluntary, almost emergent, strategy to protect the troops, who now included reporters (again, much like World War II). The result was a unitary point of view predicated on a simplistic dichotomy: us versus them, the good guys versus the bad guys. Each network had resident ex-generals as compliant commentators, serving a function comparable to that of scientists during space launches.

There is a third point of view that often goes unremarked—that of the victims of war. Here John Berger's distinction between being a "reporter to the rest of the world" and being "a recorder for those involved in the events" is significant. He makes the distinction between images that are "addressed to those suffering what they depict," and images "to boost the morale of a public, to glorify heroic soldiers or to shock the world press."[6]

The U.S. audience, caught in fear and anxiety, failed to notice the many anomalous incongruities. U.S. tactics were brave and civilized; Saddam's were cowardly. Fifteen thousand bombing sorties against Iraq were sanitized by aerial views and claims for the clinical accuracy of "smart bombs"; fifteen Iraqi missiles fired at Israel were barbaric, their effects viewed from the ground, with casualties. As the 2003 convoy proceeded, Iraqi soldiers were not wearing proper uniforms and hence looked just like average citizens. But perhaps the greatest discrepancy occurred during the initial bombing of Baghdad in 2003. We focused on a deserted parking structure. We saw nothing of war. We could only imagine the horror.

Catastrophe Coverage and Freud's Theory of Anxiety

In his early work on obsession, Freud discusses a mechanism of revision he calls "aftereffects," which disfigure events by turning them into a particular story. One means of distortion is removing an idea from the "situation in which it originated" that made it comprehensible. An interval of time is inserted, like the interruptive flow of TV commercials, leading causal connections astray and "taking the obsession out of its particular setting by being generalized."[7]

We watched the 1991 war from the air, where the effects of the bombs on the ground could not be seen. During the beginning of the 2003 war, we watched a parking structure, seeing flashes of the bombing in the distant background, and hearing the delayed sound of their explosion, much like fireworks—a harmless display of light and sound. The cause-effect logic of dropping bombs on cities and killing people was thus defused, if not denied or repudiated. The claim in both wars that no civilian targets were being hit, and that the bombs hit only their computerized military targets, altered the reality of the images, again derailing cause-effect logic.

In more general terms, the interval of time between the first and second Iraq wars, along with the intervening time between the 2001 World Trade Center and Pentagon tragedies and the 2003 invasion of Iraq after an occupation of Afghanistan, fostered causal links between "Saddam" and terrorism, paradoxically making this wild explanation appear plausible; 9/11 can be seen as an "aftereffect" that played out over the first war, making the second one "logical." In a more literal way, for George W. Bush and the military leadership, Hussein himself was the obsession, taken out of the context of Iraq and into the context of the U.S. war on terrorism.

For Freud, another means by which "obsession is protected against conscious attempts at solution" is the use of indefinite or ambiguous wording, like the military jargon of the generals adopted verbatim by the TV anchors, which works its way into the deliria and furthers misunderstanding. Within hours after each invasion, we began to hear new military terminology—the poetic "Operation Desert Storm" as a euphemism for killing people; "embedded" reporters, cozy and allied with their own fighting units. Reporters and viewers studied and learned new ambiguous wording and phrases of deliria. None was perhaps more ignominious than the BDA, the Bomb Damage Assessment. This close analysis of pilots' footage was constantly promised but forever delayed.

Catastrophe coverage and its reception are remarkably akin to the workings of obsession and compulsion. Simply put, TV causes anxiety (obsessive thought), which necessitates more TV viewing (compulsion), which raises the ante of fear—a loop of viewing triggering anxiety/anxiety triggering viewing, an interchangeability of cause and effect. The key point is that the resultant repression, caused by anxiety, is "effected not by means of amnesia but by a severance of causal connections brought about by a withdrawal of affect" or emotion. By banishing bodies, by eliminating shots of the people on the ground, and in the cool demeanor of third-person reporter-speak, TV withdrew affect, thereby severing causal connections. Yet these repressed memories persist, in another place and time, as endopsychic perceptions. As Freud explained: "Repressed connections appear to persist in some kind of shadowy form . . . transferred, by a process of projection, into the external world, where they bear witness to what has been effaced from consciousness."[8]

The Kennedy assassination set the pattern for catastrophe coverage, creating a new TV genre. What emerged as innovative and unexpected was the constant live coverage, central anchor reporter, appearance of experts and authorities as TV analysts, suspension of regular narrative programming and commercials, serial repetition of the initial event, and updated inclusion of multiple interpretive responses and the anticipation of unpredictable events. This was a veritable disaster array. It has since become the protocol that we have come to expect and that plays into and creates those expectations. One hallmark of that primal television scene was that everyone remembered and recited where they were in real life when they heard and saw the news, and where they were in relation to television. This was a moment when television and our daily lives were separate but merging. While our emotional experience of the event came from television, our psyches and bodies remained distinct from television. "Meaning" occurred to us in specific places, in precise times—as a protection from the shock that we had experienced.

After World War I, Freud began to accord death, fear, and anxiety greater import in his writings. *Inhibitions, Symptoms, and Anxiety* comprises a substantial revision of his earlier analyses of obsession and neuroses, about which Freud wrote more than any other topic.[9] Anxiety, rather than the result of repression, gave way to an understanding that repression is a consequence of anxiety. "Anxiety is a reaction to a situation of danger" predicated on a fear of "being abandoned by the protecting super ego." Anxiety is physical, "something that is felt" with "a very marked character of unpleasure." It is both an "affect" ("every affect . . . is only a reminiscence of an event") and is "freshly created out of . . . the situation."[10] Transposed to our experience of mass media, we respond to TV interruptions of announcements of airline crashes and nuclear accidents with an affect of anxiety, which TV can exacerbate by canceling narrative programming and switching to live catastrophe coverage.

The crucial difference between Freudian theory and televisual logic, however, is that television is simultaneously shock and therapy. It both produces and discharges anxiety; it both administers shock and ameliorates its collective affects. Via repetition of information and constant coverage, TV is at once source and solution, problem and cure. Our anxiety is simultaneously increased and alleviated by watching TV.

Unlike war and other catastrophes, which administer shock, TV simultaneously administers and cushions shocks. It is both the traumatic shock and Freud's notion of the "shield" that "both protects against excess excitation . . . and also transmits excitation from the outside to the inside of the organism." This double function of transmission and protection is temporal and, according to Samuel Weber, is accomplished by narration—"temporizing the traumatic effects of an excess of energy . . . the death drive as another name for a story."[11] Like the joke technique (described by Freud as an envelope or a container), TV envelops the shock, delivering and cushioning us from stimuli, which it regulates at acceptable levels, turning news into story and tragic drama. Rather than an excess of stimuli, which provokes private recollection and memory, such as the Kennedy assassination coverage initially provided, TV now administers then defuses stimuli in containing doses.

Television promises shock and trauma containment, over time, via narration. As Weber explains it, Freud's analysis of abstract time was connected to the psychic real as an aftereffect of events. This aftereffect is separate yet necessarily dependent on the initial event. Aftereffects repeat the event they follow, but they also alter it, and it is precisely this process of repetitive alteration that renders the event psychically "real."[12] TV news stories do not merely repeat an event. They repeat other stories in a sequence that is both successive and simultaneous. Catastrophe coverage over time renders events psychically real through "repetitive alteration" or disfigural representation (the same shot of bombs falling on Baghdad, different voice-overs, the same shot of a Baghdad parking structure, different day and time of day). Through this psychic process of disfiguration, the event morphs. The search for Osama bin Laden, the original goal, is abandoned in the shift to bring down Saddam Hussein.

Abraham Zapruder's one-minute film footage of Kennedy's assassination was endlessly repeated. The thirty-second *Challenger* explosion was run hundreds of times. The World Trade Center crumpled into silent ashes on 11 September 2001. And in 2003 we stared at the deserted parking structure in Baghdad with the occasional car driving past, waiting for war, listening to endless words. Everyday and catastrophic television relies on repetition (an economic "compulsion to repeat") like no other activity or medium. The sheer repetition of coverage serves a hypothetical purpose of "as if"—operating on the pretense that the danger situation still exists.

Freud's descriptions of anxiety help explain the reception of television and digital media more generally. For example, as he often does, Freud tacks on an intriguing addendum that relates "angst" to expectation—"anxiety about something." It has a quality of indefiniteness and a lack of object. As with television itself, a central trait of catastrophe coverage is indefiniteness. Coverage involves a search for the answer, the explanation—in short, the object. What did we see in the BDA footage? Granular, indecipherable ground, without people. What did we see from the side of a tank in Iraq? An embedded reporter in camouflage fatigues. What did we see in the nondescript parking structure? A modern structure that could have been anywhere. Freud differentiates "realist anxiety" about "a known danger" from "neurotic anxiety" about "a danger that has still to be discovered."[13] The current war on terror straddles this divide.

TV vacillates between realistic and neurotic coverage, holding our interest by anticipating something more or something worse. In Iraq, we heard much about Hussein's infamous Republican Guards, their weapons of "mass destruction," and we anticipated the use of chemical weapons or biological weapons. There was no evidence of either, but the line between realistic and imagined neurotic anxiety was blurred, burying the reality completely in fear.

To return to my earlier argument: Freud maintains that "there are two reactions to real danger. One is an affective reaction, an outbreak of anxiety. The other is a protective action." With its strategy of creation/contradiction/cancellation, TV is the outbreak and the protective action, the latter accomplished by repetition, finding answers, and assigning guilt. Like a doctor detailing medical procedures to a patient before and after surgery, information provides a therapeutic service, a ritual akin to prayer or chanting. Cloaked as a desire to know, it soothes our anxiety, protecting us from fear. Thus, information, the raison d'être of coverage, becomes story, therapy, and collective ritual. Later it will become myth. There is no better description of catastrophe coverage than the seemingly convoluted words of Freud: "Anxiety is . . . an expectation of a trauma, and a repetition of it in a mitigated form; . . . expectation belongs to the danger-situation, whereas its indefiniteness and lack of object belong to the traumatic situation of helplessness—the situation which is anticipated in the danger situation."[14] The TV spectator anticipates, fears, and then relishes the danger situation. However helpless, the audience is not passive; it is expectant. Agitated by TV, it is soothed by mundane ritual and contained by contradiction. We become addicted to constant coverage—it becomes part of a collective routine, a daily ritual, a repetition of our ultimate condition of helplessness. As Susan Sontag puts it: "The feeling of being exempt from calamity stimulates interest in looking at painful pictures, and looking at them suggests and strengthens the feeling that one is exempt."[15]

TV News—Since 9/11

Since the horror of 9/11, television, like the nation, has been on catastrophe alert, playing out a series of crises and wars interspersed with reports of suicide bombings in Israel and punctuated by the color-coded warnings of terror alerts, like weather reports or measurements of stress levels. Trying to console us with words about death, TV has taken us from shock and terror to anxiety and fear, accompanying us through anger and grief. We have moved from the 9/11 catastrophe to the search for Osama Bin Laden—which became the war in Afghanistan to displace the Taliban and uproot terrorists, a war involving the formerly covert Delta Forces fighting alongside other military units—to a declared war with Iraq to eliminate Saddam Hussein and his regime as a continuation of the war on terror.

The loss of life on 9/11 has been paralleled by the loss of money on the stock market. The terror of the World Trade Center attacks initially morphed into anthrax, then into Enron, World Com, and other corporate scandals and swindles. After 9/11, economic panic was on the move, illustrating the increasing interconnections between crisis and economics, death and money, and both in terms of loss. As Walter Benjamin taught us so many years ago, moments of crisis and shock are fraught with revolutionary potential; these are moments when history is in the making, when we can see history being made. TV coverage in the United States works by way of a fundamental contradiction, providing us both the shock and its amelioration over time. TV serves a double function: first to soothe us with information and then to keep us watching TV. Over time, the transmission, which has an urgent and a flawed quality, becomes a safe, smooth representation, transformed and tamed by repetition.

Television functions as a desire to know, an epistemephilia, which supercedes the desire to see, a scopophilia, although the latter is invoked as proof, even the conclusive moment of truth (seeing as believing). The vaunted status of the visual and assumed veracity of sight are refigured by repetition, buried in words, and finally discounted. Through denial, disavowal, or repudiation, this logic both proclaims the truth of vision and simultaneously disposes of its veracity. As with a shell game or a sleight of the magician's hand, our eyes are distracted through an ironically relentless focus. The sheer number of sights on TV—of locales, of hundreds of reporters reacting, of twenty-four-hour coverage—ultimately conceals the paucity of meaningful visual information. After months of military action dedicated to uncovering weapons of mass destruction, there is no evidence in Iraq of chemical or biological weapons or of the plants to produce them.

Millions of words, opinions and speculations in an endless repetition of the same, wiped out the original goals of the U.S. war on terrorism—to capture Bin Laden and to find the proverbial smoking gun of biological weapons. We saw very little but we were nonetheless given a great deal to see: reporters in combat fatigues on location or wearing casual clothes and superimposed (or not) over a "foreign" backdrop, in medium frontal shots, all gaining fame in what is either the last gasp of an outmoded heroic image—the intrepid war correspondent—or the messenger announcing (with barely contained glee) the triumphant return of military policy to center stage.

The indelible and horrifying scenario of jet planes crashing into the heart of Wall Street was answered, after a year-long preparatory military takeover of Afghanistan, by the "shock and awe" bombing of Baghdad—a rare moment on U.S. TV without words, without voice-over. For eight long minutes, CNN gave us a vision without commentary. For U.S. audiences, this scene focused on a deserted parking structure in a city that could have been anywhere, with explosions that resembled fireworks on the unlocatable horizon. This time the terror was at a visible and physical distance. We were safe at home in the United States, and the target, the central city, was empty of people, at least on-screen, and on another continent. The mission to search out and destroy Osama Bin Laden and the Taliban morphed into a war to conquer Iraq and destroy Saddam Hussein. The effect and the affect of these twin events depended on point of view (including the resurgence of national identity as "patriotism") and on proximity and personal risk.

The crumbling of the World Trade Center Towers a year earlier ended the decade-long celebration of the high-tech money economy in the United States. This was an international economy, a peace economy. The 9/11 tragedy initiated a monetary nosedive and a national deathwatch labeled a war on terrorism, which reconfigured U.S. politics by resuscitating a national logic of fear, a belief in war and violence, and a military economy. Immediate awareness of death can lock in ideological positions, solidifying worldviews into indisputable truths. This rigidifying happened in the United States almost immediately after 9/11. That sight was so terrifying that it severed seeing from believing.

NOTES

1 See, for example, Strobe Talbott, "Rethinking the Red Menace," *Time*, 1 January 1990, 66–72. In this piece, Talbott remarked that "scenarios for a Soviet invasion of Western Europe have always had a touch of paranoid fantasy about them. . . . Yes, Joseph Stalin 'conquered' Eastern Europe—Exhibit A in the charge of Soviet

expansion—but he did so in the final battles of World War II, not as a prelude to World War III. The Red Army had filled the vacuum left by the collapsing Wehrmacht."

2 Tyler Volk, *What Is Death? A Scientist Looks at the Cycle of Life* (New York: Wiley, 2002), III.

3 See Patricia Mellencamp, *High Anxiety: Catastrophe, Scandal, Age, and Comedy* (Bloomington: Indiana University Press, 1994). This analysis is only a sketch of a much longer elaboration of catastrophe.

4 Anthony Giardina, "The Lives They Lived," *New York Times Magazine*, 29 December 2002; Harold G. Moore, *We Were Soldiers* (New York: Harpers, 1993). Moore's book is less a conventional battle study than a record of the emotional reactions of the GIs to the terror and horror.

5 Mark Bowden, *Black Hawk Down: A Story of Modern War* (New York: Penguin Books, 1999), 120.

6 John Berger, "Uses of Photography," *About Looking* (New York: Pantheon Books, 1980), 58. This essay is "for Susan Sontag."

7 Sigmund Freud, "Sex," *The Complete Psychological Works of Sigmund Freud* (London: Hogarth, 1959), 10:246.

8 Ibid., 231–232.

9 Sigmund Freud, "Inhibitions, Symptoms, and Anxiety," *The Complete Psychological Works of Sigmund Freud* (London: Hogarth, 1959), vol. 10.

10 Ibid., 10:128–133.

11 Samuel Weber, *The Legend of Freud* (Minneapolis: University of Minnesota Press, 1982), 145.

12 Ibid., 147.

13 Sigmund Freud quoted in Susan Sontag, *On Photography* (New York: Dell, 1973), 165.

14 Ibid., 165, 166.

15 Sontag, *On Photography*, 168. This quotation offers a rich nexus of ideas: "A society which makes it normative to aspire never to experience privation, failure, misery, pain, dread, or disease, and in which death itself is regarded not as natural and inevitable but as a cruel, unmerited disaster, creates a tremendous curiosity about these events; . . . partly it is the character of inevitability that all events acquire when they are transmuted into images. In the real world, something *is* happening and no one knows what is *going* to happen. In the image-world, it *has* happened and it *will* forever happen in that way" (167–168).

PLANET PATROL

SATELLITE IMAGING, ACTS OF KNOWLEDGE, AND GLOBAL SECURITY

LISA PARKS

The technological fantasy of planetary control is strangely exemplified in a series of electronics magazine covers from the late 1950s and early 1960s. They feature tiny technocrats standing next to enormous dish receivers and looking out of frame at the vast blue sky, waiting for something to happen (see figures 1 and 2).What is significant is the set of looking relations initiated within these images—that is, the way the human monitor transfers her gaze to a satellite that is out of frame and invisible, investing it with the power to see the world and relay that vision back to the human eye through the dish.[1] They are playfully symptomatic, I think, of an audacious dream to see, sense, and know the world while standing firmly in one place upon it. It was about the same time these magazines hit the shelves that the United States launched its first communications satellites, Echo, Telstar, and Early Bird, as well as its first spy satellite, Corona. Launched as a quintessential cold-war project, Corona was a top-secret spy satellite that snapped coverage of the Soviet Union, China, and areas across the Middle East and Southeast Asia from the late 1950s until 1972.[2] The goal of the Corona project was to assess how rapidly the Soviets were producing long-range bombers and ballistic missiles, and where they were being deployed.[3]

It wasn't until decades later, however, that satellite images of such high resolution became widely available to the public. In 1994, the Clinton administration privatized the remote-sensing industry and U.S. companies such as Spaceimaging and Earthwatch emerged to compete with French and Russian satellite-imaging firms SPOT and Soyuzkarta. A year later, President

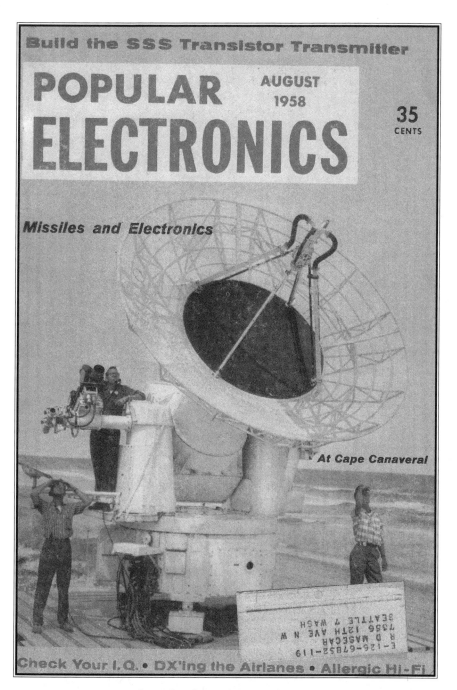

I. Cover of *Popular Electronics* magazine, August 1958

Bill Clinton declassified the Corona project and released more than 860,000 satellite photos gathered between 1960 and 1972. Throughout the 1990s U.S. State Department officials declassified top-secret satellite images on numerous occasions, attempting to visualize global trouble spots that ranged from the war in former Yugoslavia to the refugee crisis in the Congo, from nuclear

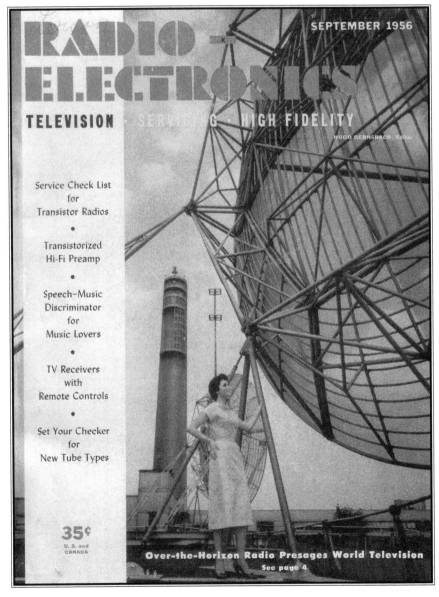

2. Cover of *Radio Electronics* magazine, September 1956

weapons testing in Pakistan to the 9/11 attacks on the World Trade Center and the Pentagon. This occurred most visibly on 5 February 2003, when Secretary of State Colin Powell presented U.S. satellite images to the UN Security Council as "undeniable proof" that Iraq was developing weapons of mass destruction.

Satellite images are typically aligned with official forms of knowledge and have historically been used by the United States to isolate and contain threats to national security and to rationalize U.S. policies and interventions around the world. As the mass distribution of the satellite image increases, however, it can become a productive cultural space that foregrounds often-concealed acts of knowledge and struggles over interpretation. When the satellite image moves beyond official institutions, it appears to most people as an empty visual field, a site of abstraction that must be infused with meaning in order to signify anything other than its own orbital perspective. Satellite images are insecure semiotic fields that must be inscribed within certain agendas. As top-secret intelligence is put on global public display, we become more aware of the knowledge practices that the satellite image participates in and the global securities it is mobilized to defend.[4]

Global Conflicts and Insecure Images

The mass circulation of politically charged satellite images began during the late 1980s as television news producers sought to represent global conflicts from new perspectives.[5] During this time, high-resolution (one-meter) satellite images could be purchased on the global market from the French remote-sensing company Satellite de l'Observation de Terre (SPOT). In 1989, for instance, ABC aired a SPOT image of a Libyan chemical weapons facility that not only visualized this trouble spot from an orbital platform but also worked to dramatize the network's connection to high-level sources and views.[6] The U.S. State Department, however, releases satellite intelligence to the global community only when U.S. officials have a strategic need to produce knowledge about events happening in a particular place. In August 1995, for instance, U.S. secretary of state Madeleine Albright released satellite images of suspected mass graves near Srebrenica, Bosnia, to draw global attention to a massacre that allegedly occurred in a UN-protected safe haven.[7] In 1998, U.S. secretary of defense William Cohen released satellite images of the El-Shifa pharmaceutical plant in Sudan and the Zhawar Kili Al-Badr Camp in Afghanistan to rationalize U.S. bombings of these facilities in retaliation for terrorist attacks on U.S. Embassies in Nairobi, Kenya, and Dar es Salaam, Tanzania.

After the commercialization of remote sensing in 1994, nongovernmental organizations began to press for greater access to U.S. satellite images as a way of exposing global conflicts and advancing particular agendas. In 1996, Refugees International called upon the U.S. government to release satellite images of the Congo so that aid organizations in the region could locate displaced persons and provide better assistance. In 1998, the Federation of American Scientists (FAS) and the Institute for Science and International Security released commercial satellite images of nuclear testing sites in Pakistan to spotlight impending nuclear proliferation in Southeast Asia. In 1999, the FAS developed an initiative called the Public Eye Project, "dedicated to advancing the application by non-governmental organizations and private citizens of these new and emerging [satellite] information systems to the public interest."[8]

Such initiatives were met with a stark wake-up call in October 2001 when, in the aftermath of the 9/11 attacks, the U.S. government exercised its so-called shutter control, banning journalists' and aid workers' access to commercial U.S. satellite images of Afghanistan.[9] When the Clinton administration privatized the remote-sensing industry, it reserved the right to restrict the flow of commercial satellite imagery in the interests of national security. The Bush administration made full use of this provision as part of a broader effort to regulate the flow of information during the U.S. war in Afghanistan. By December 2001, however, the Pentagon calculatingly released a series of before-and-after satellite images of Taliban targets in Afghanistan, flaunting the United States' decisive destruction of enemy military posts.[10]

Whatever the occasion, we can learn as much from the processes by which satellite images become part of public discourse as we can from the images themselves. Because of its remoteness and abstraction, the satellite image functions best as an overview or visual summary, and it draws upon the discursive authority of meteorology, photography, cartography, and state intelligence to produce its reality and truth effects. Since it is digital, the satellite image is only an approximation of an event, not a mechanical reproduction of it or a live immersion in it. While the medium of television trades on its capacity for "liveness," which Jane Feuer and Pat Mellencamp argue involves as much reenactment of the past and forecasting of the future as it does instantaneous access to unfolding events, the satellite image has an altogether different tense.[11] Because it is digital, its ontological status differs from that of the electronic image. The satellite image is encoded with time coordinates that index the moment of its acquisition, but since most satellite-image data are simply archived in huge supercomputers, its tense is one of latency. Satellites are constantly and quietly scanning the earth, but much of what they register is never seen or known. A satellite image is not really produced, then, until it is sorted, rendered, and put into circulation. Satellite-image data become a document of the real and an index of the historical only if there is reason to suspect they have relevance to current affairs. Unless the satellite image is selected and displayed, it remains dormant, gathered as part of an enormous accumulation of image intelligence that can be stored and used retrospectively.

Archives of satellite-image data create the potential for diachronic omniscience—vision through time—because they enable us to generate, in the present, views of the past that have never been known to exist, much less been seen. Our understanding of the temporality of the satellite image should thus be derived more through the process of its selection, display, and circulation than through the instant of its acquisition. This means considering rationales for rendering, viewing, and publicizing the existence of the image.

So long as the public remains un- or misinformed about state and commercial practices of remote sensing, the military-information-entertainment complex can use the satellite image's remoteness and abstraction and the excessive volume of image data gathered (which slows the sorting process) to deny knowledge of events that are in full view. At the same time, however, media and military institutions can use the satellite's constant scanning of the earth to produce what they claim to be uniquely objective and truthful views of events whenever it is strategic to do so. The satellite's gaze is trained on particular places for particular reasons; at the same time, the satellite randomly acquires information about all kinds of places for no apparent reason at all. Therefore, it can be mobilized either as representing the ultimate authority of the state or as a completely abstract and uncertain point of view. It is the ambiguity between these positions that enables the state to use satellites images in what Paul Virilio calls the "strategy of deception."

Virilio suggests that orbital perspectives are increasingly used to reinforce sinister war strategies in which territorial space is replaced by orbital space and in which a system of global telesurveillance is linked to the destructive power of bombers and missiles. Despite the salience of Virilio's arguments, he never looks closely at the image. Instead, he offers critical but ultimately technologically determinist accounts of the satellite and what he calls "terminal-citizens," whose civic engagement is reduced to little more than button pushing at interfaces.[12]

But if state strategies of deception are shifting, then so must practices of witnessing. What might it mean to witness via satellite? The satellite witness draws upon the aesthetics of emptiness and uncertainty embedded within the satellite image in order to highlight its ontological insecurity—to dislocate and destabilize its claims to objectivity, omniscience, and truth. Roland Barthes offers the term "anchoring" to refer to the way that meaning is attached to an image (such as a caption to a news photo) to make it signify in a certain way.[13] Anchoring has the effect of restricting the range of possible meanings by encouraging the viewer to adopt what is prescribed. In a sense, I am arguing for a reversal of this anchoring process: The witness, instead of accepting the state's attempt to anchor the meaning of the satellite image, seizes its emptiness and abstraction as an impetus to infuse it with partiality, situated knowledges, and local tales. The satellite witness engages in a practice of semiotic infusion: The orbital gaze is turned on its head (so to speak) so that claims of top-down military intelligence can be fleshed out. Simply put, it involves a more literal interpretation of the term "remote sensing," exploring how the senses, the sensed, and ways of making sense are related to orbital vision. The satellite witness subjects the military-intelligence apparatus to the same kind of scrutiny and interpretive analysis that this apparatus for decades has applied to the world.

The satellite witness recognizes the ambiguous allure of the orbital view and can use it to expose and attract attention to abuses of power and calculated denials that emanate from a position of seeing and knowing too much.[14] Satellite witnessing involves exposing information-based, simulated, and composite forms of violence that are often trying to hide themselves or pass in seemingly innocent discourses of "monitoring," "peacekeeping," "protection," or "global security." This witness presumes there may be something to see in even the most obscure view and so is in a position similar to that of Sam Weber's television watcher: "To watch carries with it the connotation of a scrutiny that suggests more and less than mere seeing or looking at. To watch is very close to watching out for or looking out for, that is, being sensorially alert for something that *may* happen. . . . It involves watching out for something that is precisely not perceptible or graspable as an image or a representation. To 'watch' is to look for something that is not immediately apparent."[15] The more remote and abstract the satellite image, the more inquisitive the eye, ever aware of the latent temporality of the image's production and the selectivity of its circulation.

Satellite witnessing is a critical practice that refuses to accept the satellite image as an omniscient view, a strategic map, a penultimate perspective, and instead appropriates its abstraction to generate further interrogation, discussion, and inquiry. This practice approaches military image data not as dormant state property but rather as a volatile discursive field that can be used by citizen-viewers to expose, question, and critique military techniques of observation, intervention, action, assistance, or peacekeeping. We need to infuse military satellite images with public debates, countervisions, and situated knowledges precisely because they appear so far removed from spheres of civic and public life—and so far removed from public responsibility and accountability.

Satellite images are fascinating as sites of meaning because they can at once reveal and conceal events that we cannot bear to look at. Their representational codes seem to negate the perspective of the witness altogether. Part of the problem, however, is that we have historically expected the witness to provide comprehensibility and verification. We need to recognize that in the information age, the function of the witness changes: He or she might be exposing misinformation, pointing the finger at an only partly responsible party, exposing the violence and oppression of the gaze/apparatus itself, or simply holding onto an unanchored point of view. In addition to being responsible for what one sees, witnessing involves recognizing horrific acts that are meant not to be seen. Witnessing in the information age involves being able to notice atrocities that might not even be imagined as part of the realm of the visible, things on the "threshold of the visible."[16]

Colin Powell Presents . . .

On 5 February 2003, Secretary of State Colin Powell met with the UN Security Council to present "undeniable proof" of Iraqi weapons treaty violations and to garner international support for a United States-led war against Iraq. Powell's presentation preempted regularly scheduled television programming on the major U.S. networks as he spoke uninterrupted for over an hour. The goal of his presentation was to establish that Saddam Hussein was in material breach of UN Resolution 1441, a unanimous vote by the council to disarm Iraq of weapons of mass destruction. Armed with a flashy audiovisual display entitled "Iraq: Failing to Disarm," Powell insisted that Hussein was developing biological, chemical, and nuclear weapons, expanding Iraq's ballistic missiles capabilities, fostering links to global terrorists, and refusing to cooperate with UN weapons inspectors.[17]

As Powell delivered his address to a roomful of mostly men in suits, television cameras moved in to feature close-ups of officials, some of whom listened discerningly and some of whom displayed skepticism or disbelief. Throughout the presentation, all gazes drifted between Secretary Powell and large projection screens placed on either side of the room where Powell adduced his evidence, which included transcriptions of barely audible telephone exchanges between senior officers of Iraq's Republican Guard and satellite images of alleged weapons facilities. I want to focus in particular on Powell's use of declassified satellite images, which were lifted from the lightboards of intelligence officers and brought into the public sphere, where their meanings could be considered and contested. Powell presented eleven satellite images during the presentation, most of which were intended to bolster the claim that Iraq had evaded the weapons-inspection process.

The first such sequence began when Powell presented a 10 November 2002 satellite image labeled "Chemical Munitions Stored at Taji" (see figures 3 and 4). It was imprinted with eleven yellow circles and four red squares, which, Powell explained, specified the locations of "munitions bunkers" and "active chemical munitions bunkers" respectively. Powell then said: "How do I know that? How can I say that? Let me give you a closer look." He offered a frame displaying comparative satellite views of the same facility on 10 November 2002 and 22 December 2002 labeled "Sanitization of Ammunition Depot at Taji." The first featured one chemical bunker inscribed with yellow arrows indicating the location of a decontamination vehicle and a security post. In the second, yellow arrows pointed out two "sanitized bunkers" and several UN vehicles apparently en route to the site. Powell suggested that when looked at together, the images revealed that the chemical bunker was "cleaned up" and the decontamination vehicle was removed by the time UN inspectors visited the facility on 22 December. Yet it is altogether unclear whether the satellite images represent the same bunker and hence whether they even merit such a comparison. In a commentary after Powell's presentation, London-based satellite-image expert Bhupendra Jasani indicated that it is difficult to accurately identify bases, weapons, and vehicles in these images: "When I look at it I can't be sure what I'm seeing."[18]

Powell continued with three more satellite images representing further Iraqi "housecleaning," each, according to Powell, evidence that Iraq dodged the UN weapons-inspection process when it resumed in November 2002. The first, "Pre-Inspection Al Fatah Missile Removal Al-Musayyib Rocket Test Facility," dated 10 November 2002, relied on yellow arrows and text to indicate cargo trucks moving missiles away from the site. In the second, "Pre-Inspection Materiel Removal Amiriyam Serum and Vaccine Institute," dated 25 November 2002, Powell pointed out a truck caravan that appeared two days before inspectors arrived. And in the final image, "Pre-Inspection Materiel Removal, Ibn al Haytham," dated 25 November 2002, cargo trucks and a truck-mounted crane were allegedly there to move missiles just before an inspection.

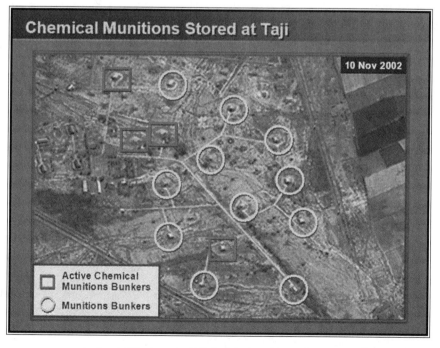

3. A satellite image of Taji dated 10 November 2002, imprinted with yellow circles and red squares to specify locations of alleged chemical munitions facilities. (U.S. State Department)

Powell provided no comparative images of these facilities and left viewers with only his verbal assurance that "days after this activity, the vehicles and the equipment that I've just highlighted disappear and the site returns to patterns of normalcy." Not only were viewers asked to place blind trust in Powell's word, but also they were forced to accept his inconsistent and arbitrary use of satellite images as irrefutable evidence.[19] Why, for instance, did some satellite images have full dates and others only month and year? Why did Powell offer contrasting views of some sites and not others? How could a handful of U.S. satellite images supersede an entire UN weapons-inspection process taking place on the ground? What was at stake, in other words, was the question of visual literacy—that is, we were asked to view and accept satellite images as visual evidence of Iraq's weapons of mass destruction with no conventions or standards among political officials, much less members of the public, for using and interpreting such images in a global political forum. Because of this lack of standards and the public's lack of visual literacy, Powell was able to employ a strategy of obscurity cloaked as clarity.

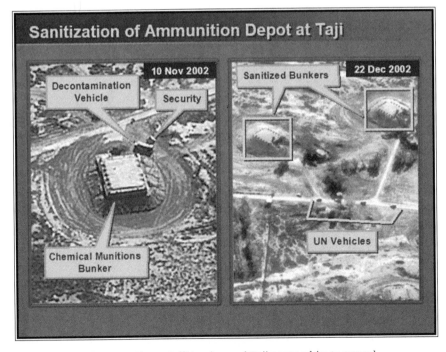

4. Comparative satellite views of Taji zoomed in to reveal alleged changes at a facility between 10 November and 22 December 2002. (U.S. State Department)

The next two satellite images Powell presented were used to allege that chemical weapons were transported from Al-Musayyib in May 2002, and the entire facility was shown as literally covered up with freshly graded earth in a comparative image dated July 2002 (see figures 5 and 6). Since the latter view was presented from a much greater distance and a much different angle, it was virtually impossible, especially for the lay viewer, to determine whether it was actually the same facility. Again we were expected to accept Powell's interpretation of the image: "The topsoil has been removed. The Iraqis literally removed the crust of the earth from large portions of this site in order to conceal chemical weapons evidence that would be there from years of chemical weapons activity."

What was striking about Powell's presentation, at least to a media scholar like me, was his stately use of close analysis. Powell did precisely the kind of thing that I ask my students to do in critical analysis courses—select media content, think about its structure, re-view it, decode it, and formulate a thesis about its meaning and significance that can be defended. What is unique

5. A satellite image used to indicate alleged chemical weapons activity at Al-Musayyib dated May 2002. (U.S. State Department)

about the close analysis of publicly circulated satellite images, however, is that the traces of interpretation are typically inscribed upon them, and these traces in fact signify more than the image data itself. In his presentation, Powell identified the two arrows—not the bunkers themselves—as "sure signs" that bunkers were storing chemical munitions. Discussing another satellite image, he explained: "What makes this picture significant is that we have a human source who has corroborated that movement of chemical weapons occurred at this site at that time. So it's not just the photo and it's not an individual seeing the photo. It's the photo and then the knowledge of an individual being brought together to make the case." Simply put, if these images were not imprinted with red squares and yellow circles and arrows, or anchored by informants on the ground, Powell and his viewers would likely be at a complete loss. As the interpretive process itself becomes an integral part of the satellite image, its ontological status becomes that of a site to be read or a site to be spun.

Because of the semiotic insecurity of the satellite image, Powell invoked the necessity of expert analysis. "Sometimes these images are hard for the

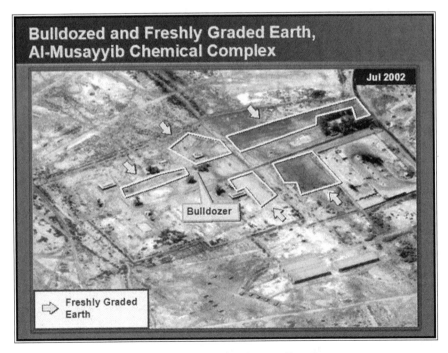

6. A satellite image used to indicate alleged cover-up of chemical weapons activity at Al-Musayyib dated July 2002. (U.S. State Department)

average person to interpret, hard for me," Powell explained. "It takes experts with years and years of experience poring for hours and hours over light-tables" to interpret these images. But his attempts to articulate these images with experts' credibility were ultimately unsuccessful. In the days after his presentation, the press, former intelligence officers, and citizens raised legitimate questions such as, "How do we know those are decontamination vehicles?" "How do we know based on these images what is inside those buildings?" "How do we know cargo trucks were moving materials away to be hidden from weapons inspectors?" The Independent Media Center in Urbana-Champaign even posted a parody of Powell's satellite photos, in which a graduated zoom from the orbital view to a close-up shows the back door of a children's school bus filled with the words "decontamination vehicle" on its backside (see figure 7).

In this case, the circulation of satellite images and the "expert" interpretations imprinted upon them ultimately worked to arouse further concern about U.S. motives and positioned the Bush administration as a potential

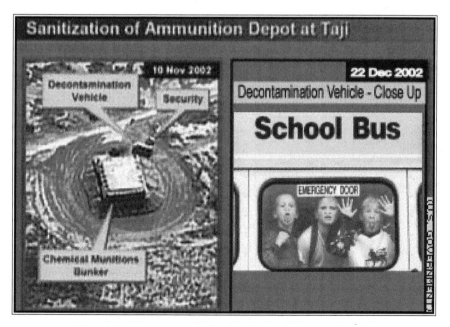

7. A parody of Secretary of State Colin Powell's use of satellite images, posted on the Urbana-Champaign Independent Media Center Web site, 6 February 2003. (Urbana-Champaign Independent Media Center)

threat to global security as great as Iraq, particularly since it seemed willing to go to such extreme lengths to rationalize its desire for military intervention, refused to listen to members of the Security Council, and decided to act audaciously and unilaterally. The credibility of Powell's presentation was further compromised when Britain's Channel 4 reported that much of its content had been based on a British dossier entitled "Iraq—Its Infrastructure of Concealment, Deception, and Intimidation," plagiarized from an essay by graduate student Ibrahim al-Marashi, who had published much of the information in *Middle East Review of International Affairs* months earlier, in September 2002.[20] Despite these disturbing discoveries, Powell remained seemingly beyond reproach. Media critic Norman Solomon suggests that Powell was able to maintain his smooth veneer and confidence only because he functioned in a media bubble that protected him from direct challenge. He rarely had to field any difficult questions during his public presentations, claims Solomon, and engaged in "tacit erasures of inconvenient history—including his own."[21]

In hindsight, what is perhaps most troublesome about Powell's (mis)use of U.S. satellite images is that it boldly undermines the credibility of their future use by the United States in a global forum. This is all the more true given the constant stream of challenges posed to Powell's claims since February 2003. Immediately after his presentation to the UN Security Council, officials from France, Germany, and Russia remained unconvinced and vocally condemned a U.S. preemptive war on Iraq, insisting that UN weapons inspectors be given more time. Despite stalwart resistance from allies, not to mention sheer outrage from world citizens, the United States launched a unilateral attack on Iraq in March 2003 and has led a perilous war of occupation ever since. Troops on the ground, however, have found no tangible evidence of weapons of mass destruction.

In May 2003, with the war fully underway, reports emerged that Powell had met with British foreign secretary Jack Straw at the New York Waldorf Hotel on 4 February 2003, the day before his UN showdown. The two allegedly exchanged comments indicating they had serious doubts about the quality of the intelligence and the claims Powell would make before the UN Security Council.[22] In January 2004 Pulitzer Prize–winning journalist Ron Suskind published a book entitled *The Price of Loyalty*, revealing that Bush's top-level advisors began planning the war against Iraq weeks after the president's inauguration in January 2001.[23] Intelligence analysts came out of the woodwork to comment on Powell's sloppy use of satellite images. Former CIA analyst Ray McGovern insisted that "Powell played fast and loose interpreting the imagery he displayed at the Security Council. You think he would have known better." The online journal *Think & Ask* claims that since no chemical weapons have been found in Iraq, "Powell's presentation amounts to nothing more than a hoax." Finally, in January 2004, former top U.S. weapons inspector David Kay admitted to the Senate Armed Services Committee that "we were almost all wrong—and I certainly include myself here"—in assuming Iraq had weapons of mass destruction; he described the situation as an "unresolvable ambiguity."[24]

When satellite images are contextualized and infused with the wide array of contradictory discourses that surround them, they become sites of contestation and insecurity rather than fields of objective and official truth. Thus, if nothing else, Powell's UN presentation is useful because it forces us to rethink relations between mass media, public education, and global security. To return to the parody of the satellite image and the school bus, what does it mean to have a political administration support the use of "intelligence" in ways that flagrantly violate the virtues of public education? How will the hypothetical kids in the school bus ever learn the importance of concepts such as integrity and truth if these are so frequently abused and denied by top state officials? What is at stake in using arrows, squares, and circles rather than rigorous political debate, negotiation, and diplomacy to assert U.S. strategic agendas in global forums? By now, U.S. state officials have fully internalized the planet-patrol postures with which I began this essay, assuming the role of a global police force that refuses to listen to others, monitors the world from a safe distance, proudly speaks one language, and profits from these activities. Rethinking security involves recognizing the desperate need for political leaders committed to cross-cultural engagement, public education, tolerance, and world peace.

Conclusion

We have several reasons to be skeptical of the use of U.S. satellite images as obvious and irrefutable forms of evidence. First, U.S. satellite intelligence is released in a global forum only under highly strategic and calculated conditions. When satellite images are used to pinpoint a global security threat, they in the process expose the orbital platforms by which the United States secretly monitors the planet. The public release of satellite intelligence is always a risky proposition, then, that must be weighed against national security agendas. Second, rather than provide neutral or objective accounts of global events, satellite images are extremely partial and selective. They may appear to be omniscient views of earthly sites, but satellite images represent only a pass above a target at a given time on a given day. At best, satellite images provide overviews or visual summaries of areas of interest. They do not serve as definitive accounts so much as they invite and require close analysis and interpretation, and quite often they spur ground-based investigation. Third, since satellite images are digital, they do not correspond directly with physical realities. They are simulations or approximations and, like other forms of visual evidence in a digital age, are prone to undetectable doctoring and manipulation. As data sets, satellite images can be rendered to highlight certain elements and conceal others. Finally, the United States has no mandate to use satellite intelligence in the public interest. During the past decade, satellite images have visualized global trouble spots including the war in former Yugoslavia; refugee crises in Central Africa; nuclear weapons testing in Pakistan, India, and North Korea; terrorist attacks on the World Trade Center and the Pentagon; and the war in Afghanistan. Despite their increased circulation, there is little indication that U.S. satellite images are being used to advance public interests. During the war in Bosnia, for instance, the U.S. State Department waited six weeks before releasing satellite images that suggested ethnic-cleansing practices were occurring near the UN-protected safe haven of Srebrenica. During the war in Afghanistan, the U.S. State Department seized exclusive access to satellite images of the region, prohibiting refugee organizations, medical practitioners, human rights workers, and journalists from using them in relief efforts and war reporting. In the case of Iraq, the U.S. State Department spun satellite intelligence into a rationale for a war that many world citizens and heads of state were loath to support.[25] What better place to start rethinking global security than in the terrain of the satellite image—a space that has historically been hardwired to state control but as it circulates more widely has become less and less secure, opening up a field of new intelligibilities, new histories, and new struggles?

NOTES

An earlier version of this paper was presented at the Rethinking Global Security Conference at UW–Milwaukee in April 2003. I thank Patrice Petro, Andy Martin, and Miha Vipotnik for their helpful comments on this manuscript and Mirko Kova-cevic for generously taping the UN Security Council proceedings for me.

1 These covers, in other words, stage the scientist/monitor's psychic investment in the satellite's ability to see and represent the earth from a position that he or she cannot. The images also foreground what Thomas Elsaesser calls the standby mode of television, proudly and patiently waiting for a signal, a vision, and a sound to arrive from elsewhere, to land in the dish, and to provide access to knowledge about something distant. See Thomas Elsaesser, "Digital Cinema: Delivery, Event, Time," in Thomas Elsaesser and Kay Hoffman, eds., *Cinema Futures: Cain, Abel, or Cable? The Screen Arts in the Digital Age* (Amsterdam: Amsterdam University Press, 1998).

2 The 1995 declassification of the Corona project was not a noble gesture of giving forth secrets of intelligence-gathering techniques; it was an attempt to generate income from an enormous archive of satellite images, as users must pay a fee for accessing many of the images.

3 Corona's worldwide coverage was also used to produce global maps and charts for the Defense Department.

4 Seen in this way, the satellite image is a crucial site for reconceptualizing shifts in relations between technology, knowledge, and representation that have emerged in the context of satellite, computer, and television convergence.

5 This can also be understood as part of a broader struggle to compete with the emerging cable news network, CNN.

6 Joseph C. Anselmo, "Remote Sensing to Alter TV News," *Aviation Week and Space Technology*, 5 December 1994, 61.

7 For further discussion, see Lisa Parks, "Satellite Views of Srebrenica: Televisuality and the Politics of Witnessing," *Social Identities* 7, 4 (2001): 585–611. A longer version of this work appears in Parks, *Cultures in Orbit: Satellites and the Televisual* (Durham, N.C.: Duke University Press, 2005).

8 For further discussion of the Congo imaging, see Jo Ellen Fair and Lisa Parks, "Africa on Camera: Televised Video Footage and Aerial Imaging of the Rwandan Refugee Crisis," *Africa Today* 48 (2001): 35–58. See a discussion of the ISIS acquisition of satellite images of Pakistani nuclear experiments at www.isis-online.org/publications/southasia/pakistan%20may%2030%20test%20site/index.html. Also see David Albright, Corey Gay Hinderstein, and Frank Pabian, "New Details Emerge about Pakistan's First Nuclear Test Site," *Earth Observation Magazine*, December 1998/January 1999, www.eomonline.com/Common/Archives/1999decjan/99decjan_gay.html. For the slim remains of the Public Eye Web site, go to www.fas.org/eyeindex.html.

9 Duncan Campbell, "U.S. Buys Up All Satellite War Images," *The Guardian*, 17 October 2001, www.guardian.co.uk/print/0,3858,4278871-103681,00.html.

10 These images are available in the image-intelligence gallery of the Federation of American Scientists Web site, www.fas.org/irp/imint/afghan.htm.

11 Jane Feuer, "The Concept of Live Television: Ontology as Ideology," in E. Ann Kaplan, ed., *Regarding Television: Critical Approaches—An Anthology* (Frederick, Md.: University Publications of America, 1983), 12–22; and Patricia Mellencamp, *High Anxiety: Catastrophe, Scandal, Age, and Comedy* (Bloomington: Indiana University Press, 1992).

12 Paul Virilio, *Strategy of Deception* (London: Verso, 2001).

13 Roland Barthes, "Rhetoric of the Image," *The Responsibility of Forms: Critical Essays on Music, Art, and Representation*, trans. Richard Howard (1964; repr. Berkeley: University of California Press, 1985), 28–29.

14 See, for instance, the work of the Public Eye initiative, which purchases satellite images to expose state secrets and strategic silences, www.fast.org/eye.

15 Samuel Weber, *Mass Mediauras: Form, Technics, Media* (Stanford: Stanford University Press, 1996), 118–119.

16 Ibid.

17 For a full transcript and video recording of Colin Powell's 5 February 2003 presentation to the UN Security Council, www.state.gov/secretary/rm/2003/17300pf.htm.

18 Jasani quoted in Will Knight, "U.S. Intelligence on Iraq 'Compelling' but Limited," *NewScientist.com*, 6 February 2003, www.globalsecurity.org/org/news/2003/030206-unpowell07.htm.

19 It is possible, of course, that Powell had access to further satellite intelligence, which the Bush administration was simply unwilling to share in a global forum as it might expose U.S. intelligence capabilities.

20 William Rivers Pitt, "Blair-Powell UN Report Written by Student," truthout, 7 February 2003, www.truthout.org/docs_02/020803A.p.htm. Also see "Downing St Dossier Plagiarized," Channel 4 News, 6 February 2003, www.channel4.com/news/2003/02/week_1/06_dossier.html; and "UK Accused of Lifting Dossier Text," CNN.com, 7 February 2003, www.cnn.com/2003/WORLD/meast/02/07/sprj.irq.uk.dossier/

21 Norman Solomon, "Colin Powell Is Flawless—Inside a Media Bubble," Champaign-Urbana Independent Media Center, 6 February 2003, www.ucimc.org/newswire/display_any/9342.

22 This conversation is now referred to as the "Waldorf transcript." For further discussion, see Dan Plesch and Richard Norton-Taylor, "Straw, Powell Had Serious Doubts over Their Iraqi Weapons Claims," *The Guardian* (London), 31 May 2003, www.guardian.co.uk/Iraq/Story/0,2763,967548,00.html. The *Guardian* released a statement on 5 June 2003 indicating that Jack Straw claimed such a meeting at the Waldorf never took place, even though a transcript of the meeting was apparently leaked and circulated among NATO officials.

23 Ron Suskind, *The Price of Loyalty: George W. Bush, the White House, and the Education of Paul O'Neill* (New York: Simon and Schuster, 2004).

24 Ray McGovern, "Colin Powell's Blurry Pictures," CounterPunch, 26 February 2003, www.counterpunch.org/mcgovern02262003.html; "Colin Powell 'Iraq Images,' U.S. Intelligence Technology Fail Test of Time," Think & Ask, February 2003 (updated January 2004), www.thinkandask.com/news/colinpowell.html; "David Kay at Senate Hearing: Transcript," 29 January 2004, CNN.com, http://edition.cnn.com/2004/US/01/28/kay.transcript.

25 One of the largest global public protests on record occurred on 15 February 2003, when citizens around the world flooded the streets in a collective outcry against the U.S. war against Iraq.

INTERMEDIA AND
THE WAR ON TERROR

JAMES CASTONGUAY

It is nearly impossible to miss the uncanny similarities between 1950s cold-war paranoia and the cultural anxieties surrounding the "war on terror." The *New York Times* has commented on the "eerily similar" comparisons between the Bush and the McCarthy years,[1] and President George W. Bush went so far as to invoke the ultimate cold war signifier of the mushroom cloud in his 7 October 2002 speech "outlining the Iraqi threat."[2] On the one hand, the capture of Saddam Hussein in Gulf War II, as *Time* magazine called it, provided the denouement for the Gulf War "miniseries" begun by George W. Bush's father.[3] On the other hand, as the president announced the end of the "hot" war in Iraq by prematurely declaring "mission accomplished," he also embarked on an open-ended narrative to prepare the U.S. public for a seemingly endless "war on terrorism."

As I have argued elsewhere, during the 1991 Gulf War, most media scholars analyzed TV news and ignored fictional programming, thus implicitly accepting the generic hierarchies that the television industry both assumes and constructs.[4] In the ongoing Gulf War, although the overwhelming focus has been on news programming and traditional print journalism, some media scholars have begun to analyze nonnews programming while also integrating the Internet into their analyses of the war on terrorism. Nevertheless, a major blind spot in media studies scholarship remains the near neglect of radio, which has been almost completely ignored relative to these other media. This is problematic in light of the widespread use of radio by U.S. and global publics, and in the context of what I call the "convergent intermediality" of our entertainment industries and media culture.[5]

To adequately examine the cultural production of the war on terror, then, it is necessary to examine a wide range of media texts and contexts. Toward that end, this essay explores the ways in which various media formats and genres have propagated the Bush administration's Orwellian nightmare of civil and human rights abuses, militarism, isolationism, and anti-intellectualism, while also actively promoting the war against terrorism at home and abroad for ratings and profit.[6]

The Military-Industrial-Media-Entertainment Network

Although a great deal of media attention was given to criticism by Hollywood celebrities of the wars in Afghanistan and Iraq, the film divisions of the major media conglomerates expressed their eagerness to become part of the war effort from the outset.[7] *Variety* reported in October 2001 that "government intelligence specialists [were] secretly soliciting terrorist scenarios from top Hollywood filmmakers and writers" through "a unique ad hoc working group" at the Institute for Creative Technology at the University of Southern California.[8] Its members were U.S. Army officials and writers and directors of *Die Hard* (John McTiernan, 1988), *MacGyver* (ABC, 1985–1992), and *Delta Force One* (Zito, 1999). In a November meeting with presidential adviser Karl Rove and executives from all the major media conglomerates, the head of the Motion Picture Association of America, Jack Valenti, reminded participants of the global scope of his industry's media imperialism: "We are not limited to domestic measures. The American entertainment industry has a unique capacity to reach audiences worldwide with important messages."[9]

In the wake of 9/11, Valenti announced that Hollywood would not be making films that portrayed Islamic terrorists, in order to prevent a backlash against "the decent, hardworking, law-abiding Muslim community in this country."[10] Hollywood had already done its ideological work in this regard by showing racist, essentialist, and orientalist representations of Arabs and Islam for decades.[11] Indeed, the limited repertoire of images of, and narratives about, Arabs and Islam before and during the war on terror has served to keep much of the U.S. public ignorant about Arab and Islamic culture, thus paving the way for the dehumanizing and demonizing of the "enemy" as part of the inexorable march toward the hot and cold wars on terror. And although the film industry claimed it would absent representations of terrorists, the television production divisions and networks within the media oligopolies have regularly depicted terrorism in both news and entertainment programming.

In an attempt to garner popular support for its existence and budget in the post-Soviet and pre-9/11 era, the CIA actively solicited and nourished intelligence-related TV and film projects by employing a former CIA officer in Latin America as a full-time entertainment liaison officer.[12] Like the underwriting and collaboration by the Congress for Cultural Freedom with artists during the cold war, programs produced with the support of the new collaborators serve as effective propaganda and desirable publicity for the CIA and, more recently, the war on terror.[13]

The canceled CBS series *The Agency* had been developing its scripts in close consultation with the CIA and even shot part of its pilot episode inside CIA headquarters. According to the program's creative supervisor, Wolfgang Peterson (*Das Boot* [1981], *Air Force One* [1997]): "Now that the cold war is over, people are questioning whether we need a CIA and this is a great opportunity to get the word out."[14] As *USA Today* reported on 24 September 2001, however:

> The first episode of a new CBS television series on the CIA cast the intelligence agency as the hero: It thwarted a terrorist bombing of London's Harrods department store by followers of Osama bin Laden. But the episode, scheduled to debut last week, has been scrapped. So has a party that CIA Director George Tenet planned to celebrate the premiere of *The Agency*. Instead, he is hunkered down at headquarters, scrambling to recoup from the worst intelligence failure in US history. In real life, the CIA and other government agencies did not thwart the attacks by bin Laden's terrorist network.[15]

Although the article does point out the pilot's ironic lack of realism, the author takes for granted the complicity between the CIA and CBS. Not surprisingly, throughout its entire run, this CBS-CIA coproduction did not question the validity of the CIA, functioning instead as an uncritical and promotional public relations vehicle for the agency and the Bush administration's war on terrorism. Although the airing of the pilot episode of *The Agency* was postponed because its terrorist plot and reference to bin Laden "too closely resembled reality," focus groups rated the episode much higher after 9/11 because, according to CBS president Leslie Moonves and the *New*

York Times, Americans were in the mood for a "patriotic episode, with bad guys and good guys," in which "the CIA thwarts the evil terrorists."[16]

The ABC series *Threat Matrix*—which refers to the real report the president receives each morning prioritizing threats to the nation—was promoted as "the first prime time series to take on post-9/11 American society, focusing on the heroism and the humanity of people who dedicate their lives to saving the country from ongoing terrorist threats." According to *Broadcasting & Cable*, members of the Department of Defense and of Congress are consultants on the program, which also employs former deputy director of the National Security Agency Bill Crowell. As Cynthia Fuchs has noted: "Any remotely counter-administration thinking that filters into *Threat Matrix* is cut short: patriotism means you toe the line." This positive public relations and propaganda outlet for the Department of Homeland Security, the CIA, and the Bush administration is particularly sinister in the context of the PATRIOT Act.[17]

Similarly, TNT's 2003 "limited series" *The Grid* sets out to capture the nuances of fighting terrorism by representing a range of Muslim characters, as well as showing the emotional toll the war on terror has on the agents who fight it.[18] Similar to the structure of the "coalition of the willing," the production of *The Grid* was a U.S.-led effort (Fox and TNT) with minor additional financial support from the UK (the series also aired on BBC2). Through a collaboration with the British intelligence agency and use of surveillance and other technologies, *The Grid*'s special counterterrorism unit is able to prevent a catastrophic chemical attack in the United States. Like Fox's *24* (2001–), *The Grid* at once exploits cultural anxieties over terrorism, promotes the Bush administration's endless war, and successfully prevents a major act of terrorism in the series finale.[19]

While *The Grid*, *The Agency*, *24*, and *Threat Matrix* exploit reality through fiction, ABC enlisted film and television producer Jerry Bruckheimer (*Crimson Tide* [Scott, 1995], *Armageddon* [Bay, 1998], *Enemy of the State* [Scott, 1998], *CSI* [CBS, 2000–]) along with *Cops* (Fox, 1989–) creator Bertram Van Munster to produce a reality genre series featuring actual soldiers fighting the war in Afghanistan. The short-lived result, *Profiles from the Front Line*, adopted the codes and conventions of the current cycle of reality programs that use follow-up interviews, music soundtracks, fly-on-the-wall recordings of "private" conversations, and "characters" chosen with their narrative potential in mind. As a result of the positive relationship Bruckheimer developed with the Pentagon during the production of *Black Hawk Down* (Ridley Scott, 2001), Dick Cheney and Donald Rumsfeld "signed off on *Profiles* without reservation." "Obviously," Van Munster noted, "we're going to have a pro-military, pro-American stance. We're not going to criticize."[20]

Although the blurring of generic boundaries has been an implicit theme in many post-9/11 shows, the particular conflation of entertainment with news in *Profiles from the Front Line* created tensions between the WB production team that shot the series and the ABC news division, which felt it should have access to any footage considered newsworthy. One could view *Profiles from the Front Line* as a calculated or controlled form of reporter embedding, which in its normal manifestations during the war in Iraq became "most obviously, a next step from *Cops,* when the officer—here the terse, camouflaged troop—pauses in his work to explain what he's doing to an inquiring mind."[21] While scholars have demonstrated the degree to which the U.S. media functioned as cheerleaders for the Bush administration and the U.S. military during and since the World Trade Center and Pentagon attacks, these programs demonstrate the ways in which the entertainment divisions of the Hollywood studios and media conglomerates complemented and surpassed the propagandistic function of TV news. The FCC, the Bush administration, and the U.S. Senate immediately rewarded the media industry for its contributions to the war effort by loosening station-ownership limits by an additional 10 percent and proposing legislation that would greatly increase the criminalization of peer-to-peer network file sharing (or "copyright piracy") through the Protecting Intellectual Rights against Theft and Expropriation Act of 2004, or Pirate Act.[22]

Media Consolidation, Radio, and the Crisis in Democracy

Although the concentration of ownership in the television, print media, and Internet industries has had profound consequences for U.S. political and popular culture, within the context of the entertainment industry, it is the radio sector that has experienced the most radical and undemocratic transformation. Indeed, the increased deregulation contained in the Clinton administration's 1996 Telecommunications Act thoroughly overturned radio broadcasting, with more than half the stations changing ownership as a result of more than one thousand mergers taking place by 2000. That radio is relatively inexpensive for broadcasters and consumers when compared to television and even the Internet would seem to make it "ideally suited for local control and community service," according to Robert McChesney, yet it "has been transformed into an engine for superprofits—with greater returns than any other media sector—for a small handful of firms."[23] In this context, and given that more than 70 percent of Americans used radio as a primary source of information in the weeks following the 9/11 attacks, it is surprising that scholars have largely ignored this medium relative to television, print, and the Internet.[24]

As in other sectors of the entertainment industry during and following the 9/11 attacks, radio executives and programmers had to decide how to respond, including when to return to normal content and commercial programming. After the attacks, music and sports formats were replaced with news reports, and some talk-based stations stopped taking calls to avoid any "inappropriate" comments. National Public Radio's *Morning Edition* host Bob Edwards spoke with affiliate reporters in New York and New Jersey who could see the towers and would later broadcast numerous eyewitness accounts and reactions from across the country in addition to analysis and commentary. Although many commercial stations briefly broke format for live news coverage or to put callers on the air from New York who wanted to communicate with friends and relatives, the *Wall Street Journal* reported on 13 September that "in most places not directly affected by the attacks" stations had already "begun a gradual transition back to music, sports and other fare."[25]

When music stations did return to their regular formats, the most-played song on 12 September 2001 was Lee Greenwood's "God Bless the USA" and other songs that complemented the ethos of the 9/11 aftermath received increased airplay, such as Enrique Iglesias's "Hero," Enya's "Only Time," and Five for Fighting's "Superman (It's Not Easy)."[26] Parody songs with titles like "Die Osama," "Tali Bon Bon,"and "Bombs Will Be Fallin'" soon appeared, and a Memphis station produced a parody program, *The Huntin' Channel: Baggin' Feral Afghans.* Another station held an on-air contest in which the listener who called in with the best way to kill Osama bin Laden won the opportunity to hit an "Osama Pinata" filled with prizes. Several of these stations linked to the many anti-Osama, anti-Taliban, and pro–war on terror Web sites, Flash presentations, and online games dedicated to killing, maiming, and torturing Osama bin Laden and the Taliban as well as other Arabs and Muslims.[27]

Station directors and DJs began to modify their play lists to exclude songs that might appear to be "inappropriate" or in "poor taste" for a variety of reasons, ranging from Radiohead's "Knives Out," Van Halen's "Jump," and Bruce Springsteen's "I'm on Fire" to Cat Stevens's "Peace Train," the Beatles' "Ticket to Ride," and the Cure's "Killing an Arab." Radio-chain giant Clear Channel Communications shared an "unofficial" or "suggested" list of songs for program directors at its more than twelve hundred stations to avoid, filling in the gaps with versions of the "Star-Spangled Banner" and "various montages—intermix[ing] patriotic songs with news radio clips and sound bites of President Bush's speeches"—which were reportedly "a big hit."[28]

While Clear Channel's list was an "informal ban" of "inappropriate" songs, the second-tier radio chain Cumulus Media officially banned the very popular Dixie Chicks' music from its 260 mostly country-format stations in response to lead singer Natalie Maines's statement that she was "ashamed [that] the President of the United States [was] from Texas." Cumulus released statements explaining it banned all Dixie Chicks music "out of respect for the troops, . . . the President of the United States, Country Music and Country Radio, Country Music Fans and the State of Texas." Symptomatic of a proto-fascistic ethos in the United States during the 2003 war in Iraq, a Cumulus-owned country-music station in Shreveport, Louisiana, orchestrated a CD-smashing event at which Dixie Chicks recordings and other band para-phernalia were destroyed by fans and run over by a thirty-three-thousand-pound tractor (similar events were held in other locations).[29]

The most popular nonmusic genre, the call-in political talk show, also had to make adjustments in the wake of the 9/11 attacks. It is widely recog-nized that, since at least the early 1990s, radio talk shows have been domi-nated by the conservative, pro-Republican (and anti-Democratic) political viewpoints of personalities like Rush Limbaugh, Sean Hannity, Bill O'Reilly, Michael Savage, Laura Ingraham, G. Gordon Liddy, Michael Reagan, Glenn Beck, Bob Grant, Alan Keyes, and many other national and regional person-alities.[30] Indeed, although many of these right-wing hosts often propagate the myth of a "liberal bias" in "the media," even they acknowledge that talk radio provides a significant outlet for conservative political views.

Although the talk genre is often viewed as a bastion for angry white men to vent their anger, according to the *New York Times*, in the immediate after-math of 9/11 even these "lowly" and "tasteless" radio programs became more "civil"—including Rush Limbaugh, who "soften[ed] a small bit of late." In its 11 October 2001 editorial entitled "Catering to New Sensitivities," the *Chris-tian Science Monitor* spotted a similar trend: "Americans' shared quest for a constructive response to the Sept. II attacks may be taking some rough edges off popular culture. Consider talk radio, often the purveyor of unfiltered vitriol. A number of hosts have steered discussions away from revenge and bigotry."[31] These observations are part of a broader process of orientalism after 9/11 that presents U.S. citizens participating in "civilized" and democratic discourse in opposition to the "barbaric" and undemocratic behavior and rhetoric of the "Arab (and Muslim) World."[32] In fact, the responses by several prominent right-wing media personalities to the 9/11 attacks were far from sensitive. Conservative pundit Ann Coulter wrote in the 13 September 2001 *National Review Online* that "we should invade [Muslim] countries, kill their leaders and convert them to Christianity." Popular radio-show host Michael Savage would later pick up on this argument, claiming: "Others have written about it, [and] I think these people need to be forcibly converted to Christianity." According to Savage:

> The largest percentage of Americans would like to see a nuclear weapon dropped on a major Arab capital. They don't even care which one. They'd like an indiscriminate use of a nuclear weapon. . . . They want this war over with, and they want it ended like the war against Japan. . . . The American people have had it up to here with this garbage. . . . In fact, Christianity has been one of the great salvations on planet Earth. It's what's necessary in the Middle East. . . . It's the only thing that can probably turn them into human beings. . . . [This is] what Doc Savage recommends as an antidote to [the] kind of poison coming out of the Middle East from these non-humans.[33]

As Anna McCarthy has argued about Coulter's best-selling book *Treason*, even though "it would be a mistake to read Coulter [and Savage] as . . . powerful figure[s] in the Radical Right's core cabal, . . . many who declare themselves more moderate than [they] still benefit from [their] vocal presence in political culture." Indeed, Savage's and Coulter's "tongue-in-cheek agitprop" has consistently "put [their] statement[s] into circulation," and Republicans routinely exploit this kind of "zealotry as the basis for mobilization."[34]

At the same time, these arguments in favor of "forcing Christianity" on the Muslim world resonate with President George W. Bush's description of the war against terrorism as a "crusade," which complement his father's use of medieval icons for Operation Desert Shield and Operation Desert Sword during Gulf War I. As James Carroll has argued, Bush's offhand reference to the war on terrorism as a crusade "expressed [the] exact truth . . . [and] most deeply felt purpose" of a fundamentalist Christian president who regularly elides church and state in his thinking about policy decisions.[35] In addition, Bush's promise to "get Osama dead or alive" at once reinforced his Texas cowboy image and invoked the same conventions of the Hollywood western prevalent during the 1991 "Showdown in the Gulf," CBS's slogan for the *High Noon* scenario set by Bush senior's 15 January 1991 deadline for Saddam Hussein to leave Kuwait.

As the foregoing examples suggest, after the 9/11 attacks, large portions of U.S. culture became increasingly nationalist and militarized precisely because the tropes, conventions, and rhetoric of violent conservatism became more salient and uncritically accepted throughout mainstream U.S. media culture. And even if the tone of talk radio changed slightly and briefly in the immediate days after 9/11, as early as October 2001, one reporter would observe that talk-radio "listeners are venting rage and fear in large numbers" and, according to one radio host, "there [was] not much room for anything but marching in lockstep; . . . If you're not one of us, you're against us—that's the mentality."[36]

One of the most vocal and influential radio proponents of this lockstep promotion of the Bush administration's war agenda has been Rush Limbaugh, who, despite his recent drug scandal, is still the most popular radio talk-show host, with more than twenty million listeners a week on more than 625 stations. Limbaugh's influence among Republican voters and politicians became clear when Vice President Cheney chose Limbaugh's program to respond to Richard Clarke's criticisms of the Bush administration's handling of terrorism before 9/11.[37] Furthermore, in an exclusive interview on Limbaugh's program in August 2004, President Bush told Limbaugh: "You're a good friend and I would hate to let you down," and "it's an honor to talk to you."[38]

While Limbaugh's daily criticisms of Democrats and "liberals" usually go without commentary from the mainstream press, he made headlines for downplaying, justifying, and supporting the abuse of Abu Ghraib prisoners by U.S. soldiers. According to Limbaugh: "This is no different than what happens at the Skull and Bones initiation, and we are going to ruin people's lives over it, and we are going to hamper our military effort, and then we are going to really hammer them because they had a good time. You know, these people are being fired at every day. I am talking about people having a good time . . . ; you ever heard of emotional release? You ever heard of need[ing] to blow some steam off?" Limbaugh has insisted that the prisoners were getting "a taste of [their] own medicine," and likened the photographs and treatment to "anything you'd see Madonna, or Britney Spears do on stage. . . . [or] you can see on stage at Lincoln Center from an NEA grant, maybe on *Sex and the City*—the movie."[39]

After the murder of U.S. hostage Nick Berg, Limbaugh echoed several other conservative radio hosts by insisting on his program and his Web site: "We *Must* Look at Video of 9/11 Horror & Beheadings." According to Limbaugh: "We are made to look at every picture from Abu Ghraib, to see how rotten we are, to see how horrible we are, to see how horrible we can be!. . . . We're starting to forget [9/11] because we're not showing the pictures to ourselves of what happened. [In our] picture-oriented society, . . . if we don't see a picture we don't believe it actually happens." Despite the ease with which photographs can be manipulated in the digital age, for Rush Limbaugh and many other commentators, the veracity of the image or its status as evidence is of less concern than is the overrepresentation and circulation of the "wrong" images. "This [Abu Ghraib] is a pure, media-generated story," he insisted. "I'm not saying it didn't happen or that the pictures aren't there, but this is being given more life than the Waco investigation."[40] For Limbaugh, then, the problem is that "we" (the U.S. public) too readily believe that what we see through mainstream media outlets is newsworthy. Consequently, Limbaugh often uses his considerable (nonvisual) influence on the radio to wrap counterinterpretations around images in an attempt to manage or control their meanings. In addition, Limbaugh has constructed an elaborate Web site (www.rushlimbaigh.com), replete with articles and multimedia content that allow him to continue his spin on issues and events beyond his radio show.

The reports of the beheading of hostages, some of which were explicitly described by the militant groups as revenge for the U.S. treatment of Iraqi prisoners, support the claim made by Limbaugh, Joe Scarborough, Michael Savage, and other conservatives that "Abu Ghraib is nothing compared to what they would do to us," thus presenting the U.S. soldiers' actions as justifiable preemptive torture.[41] Limbaugh's arguments are also part of the larger discursive strategy—facilitated by comments made throughout U.S. media culture—to clearly define the Arab and Muslim enemy as nonhumans who are "not like us" and don't "value life the way we do."

Thus, the Bush administration is allowed to make official statements criticizing U.S. soldiers' behavior, while at the same time endorsing Limbaugh's framing of various issues and interpretations of events through the appearances by the vice-president and the president on his program. It is significant that Limbaugh reaches a large portion of the U.S. military through his broadcasts on American Forces Radio, making him an efficient outlet for getting the administration's message out to the troops, in this case by saying that the commander-in-chief and other military leaders condone the rationalization and endorsement of torture (as well as relentless attacks against Democrats, "feminazis," and "liberals who hate America").

Clear Channel vs. Howard Stern

Rush Limbaugh's program is syndicated on the Premiere Radio Network, Inc., a wholly owned subsidiary of Clear Channel Communications, a media conglomerate that profited more than did any other company from the rapid consolidation of the radio and music industries in the 1990s. Although the San Antonio–based company can be traced back to the early 1970s, Clear Channel's current dominance is a direct result of the Clinton-Gore 1996 Telecommunications Act, which eliminated national radio-station ownership restrictions and significantly relaxed individual market limitations. In 2004, Clear Channel owned 1,250 U.S. radio stations and more than 250 stations internationally, and it is one of the world's largest outdoor advertising companies, with close to eight hundred thousand billboards and transit displays. The company also owns thirty-nine television stations and the Katz Media Group, the largest media-representation firm in the United States, which sells commercial time on behalf of more than four hundred television stations and controls roughly 70 percent of all major live-music events promoted in the United States.[42]

Before the 9/11 attacks, several news articles had already cast Clear Channel as "radio's big bully," blaming its "pay-for-play" or payola practices for why "radio sucks."[43] While these unethical business methods and the overall homogenization of music have serious implications, the *New York Times* and *Guardian* reported in 2003 that Clear Channel sponsored several prowar "Rallies for America" leading up to and during the U.S. war in Iraq. In addition, it was revealed that the company's upper management—including CEO Lowry Mays, president Mark Mays, and vice-chair Tom Hicks—were "close[ly] linked" with George W. Bush as longtime business associates and financial supporters of the Bush family and its political campaigns.[44] Many of the rallies were organized and hosted by conservative talk-radio host Glenn Beck, whose program is also syndicated on more than one hundred stations through Clear Channel.[45]

In addition to these arguments about Clear Channel's political activism, the conglomerate received publicity in 2004 for removing Howard Stern from six major markets. Clear Channel claimed that Stern's removal was part of the company's new "zero tolerance" policy toward indecency, developed in the wake of increased FCC scrutiny after Janet Jackson's 2004 Super Bowl "wardrobe malfunction."[46] According to Stern, however, Clear Channel did not threaten to drop his show for being "vulgar, offensive, and insulting," but because he "came out against Bush. That's when my rights to free speech were taken away. It had nothing to do with indecency."[47]

In September 2001, Stern was encouraging the Bush administration to "make [Afghanistan] a big parking lot," declaring he was "behind the President, but he'd better get violent. We need it in a big way. We have an opportunity to clean up our problems. Don't even think of them as human beings." Indeed, Stern had been a consistent supporter of Republican candidates and policies until, as Eric Boehlert noted, he "emerged almost overnight as the most influential Bush critic in all of American broadcasting, rail[ing] against the president hour after hour, day after day to a weekly audience of eight million listeners. Never before [had] a Republican president come under such blistering attack from a radio talk show host with the influence and national reach Stern has."[48]

As the pressure from the FCC increased, Stern escalated his criticisms, announcing a "radio jihad" against the Bush administration in March 2004, focusing on Bush's religious fundamentalism, his connection with the religious right (whose influence Stern feels is behind the FCC push for "decency"), and Bush's policies on stem-cell research, civil rights, and abortion. The FCC responded with a new method, fining Stern's program and Clear Channel "per utterance," and—using the *Howard Stern Show* as its primary justification—in June 2004 the U.S. Senate voted 99–1 in favor of increasing the fines the FCC may levy against broadcasters for "indecent or lewd content" on the airwaves from $27,500 to $275,000 per incident.[49] In October 2004, Stern announced that he would be leaving broadcast radio in 2006 to begin a five-year, $500 million contract with the subscriber-based Sirius satellite radio network (which, like cable television, is not held to the decency standards of broadcast radio). While the FCC chair, Michael Powell (Colin Powell's son), has led this latest push for "moral decency," he has also aggressively lobbied for deregulation and relaxed ownership restrictions to reward Clear Channel and other conglomerates with increased consolidation and market share.

I am not arguing that Clear Channel's management makes its programming decisions based solely on pro-Republican political criteria. In fact, several Clear Channel stations currently carry the liberal or progressive Air America Radio programs in some cities, suggesting that profit motives will trump political partisanship in the right market.[50] Air America Radio was launched in 2003 in an explicit attempt to combat the right-wing dominance of the talk-radio format, with anti-Limbaugh activist Al Franken as its flagship personality. The Air America–Clear Channel relationships are symptomatic of the problems inherent in an advertising- and profit-driven broadcast system in which the primary obligation is to deliver audiences to advertisers. From Air America's perspective, they are left with little choice but to enter into agreements with radio chains like Clear Channel if they want to be heard and to be profitable.[51] Consequently, the network's very existence becomes dependent on Clear Channel management, which creates an environment of institutionalized censorship that could shift the network's discourse to the Right or away from its purportedly progressive agenda.

Furthermore, in other markets where more risk is perceived and where there is less potential for greater profit, the Air America network is locked out due in part to the oligopolistic or monopolistic structure of station ownership. To break into these other markets, Air America has been targeting ethnic and community radio stations. Many of these stations have had difficulty attracting advertisers and are understandably enticed by the possibility of increasing ratings and revenue through new programming. One could suggest, perhaps, that in the long run these ethnic stations could influence Air America programming in important ways by expanding the agenda of the mainstream U.S. Left to include issues of race, gender, and social class and incorporate disenfranchised voices. The immediate reaction from station employees and listeners, however, has been marked by a sense of abandonment, as Air America has effectively silenced these marginalized voices by usurping the airwaves and stopping the production of ethnic and community radio programming in some regions.[52] This suggests that profit- and advertising-driven progressivism may lead to the institutional or systemic expulsion of already marginalized voices, which is putatively anathema to the progressive agenda.

New Media and Global Insecurities

While the foregoing account documents the ways in which mainstream radio became a site for cultural contestation and war propaganda, a consideration of the mediatization of the war on terror must include alternative and newer media, most notably the increased development of the Internet (Web sites, e-mail, online discussion groups, peer-to-peer file-sharing networks, Weblogs, etc.) and the global proliferation of satellite communication networks. The beginnings of the Internet and the existence of communications satellites date to the 1950s, but the 2003 Gulf War and the ongoing war on terror are the first conflicts in which these technologies have exchanged information in a substantive way, including images and video, to a mass audience both within and outside mainstream media outlets and government channels.

According to *USA Today*, immediately following the 9/11 attacks: "Everyday people . . . increasingly creat[ed] their own personal Web pages to vent anger, frustration and sorrow," calling the trend a kind of "new talk radio, a forum to release our feelings, with digital tools that allow us to add audio, video, photographs and links to others who feel the same way."[53] This "linking to others who feel the same way" unwittingly reveals a major function of the Internet, which despite its theoretical and structural potential for productive dialogue and debate often amounts to insular conversations that preach to the choir and self-police dissenters.[54]

In addition to these forms of self-expression and communal therapy, according to one survey, the percentage of people using the Internet as one of their main sources of information jumped from 64 percent to 80 percent in the two weeks after the 9/11 attacks, overtaking radio (72 percent) but still behind television with 98 percent. Many office workers without access to televisions or radios turned to Internet radio to get news about the attacks because many of the most popular news Web sites were unreachable due to increased server load.[55]

During Operation Iraqi Freedom, the Web became a significant rival to television as a source of information for many U.S. viewers. The cable news channels have increasingly adopted a Web-page aesthetic by cramming text and images into each frame, and the major networks routinely invite viewers to log on to their complementary or supplementary Web sites for more information or multimedia presentations. The inclusion on the CNN Web site of several video feeds (or Webcams) from within Iraq also enabled Gulf War II viewers to choose their own shots, turning TV spectators into interactive armchair imperialists. This is only the latest manifestation in a long history of screen practices that date to at least the apparatus of early cinema and the Spanish-American War in the 1890s that have enabled Americans to participate vicariously in the U.S. imperial project as a mediated and exotic spectacle.[56] In this context, the reception of war can be viewed as a form of interpassivity in which Web users are encouraged to codirect the war(show) on terror, thereby actively embracing and constructing the dominant ideologies of consumerism, nationalism, and hypermilitarism through this new intermediality.

The major television networks have also continued to increase the integration of the Web and the subject of the war on terror into their nonnews programming. For instance, during the initial U.S. attacks on Afghanistan, the conservative family drama *7th Heaven* (WB, 1996–) attempted to "put a real face on the war against terrorism" by including an emotional memorial with the real-life widow and son of a U.S. marine who was killed in a driving accident in Afghanistan. The episode, titled "The Known Soldier," begins with Ruthie, the daughter in the show, producing a video letter to her penpal marine while singing along to the Tom Petty song "I Won't Back Down." The episode concludes with Ruthie's video reprising the song, thus framing the show in the context of the themes of revenge and violence epitomized by the ubiquitous "America Fights Back" news logos used on television coverage during the war in Afghanistan.

More important for my current concerns, the WB network adopted an explicitly pedagogical role for this episode by constructing and promoting a companion Web site on its sister company's TurnerLearning.com. Sponsored by Target (whose logo becomes slightly ironic in the context of this episode) and presented as an "educational guide" for parents, teachers, and administrators, the first link includes a taping-rights agreement that is conditional upon compliance with the curriculum.[57] This is an example of the ways in which a media conglomerate like AOL Time Warner could exploit "convergence" in an explicit attempt to control and contain the *7th Heaven* episode's polysemy in the context of war and is symptomatic of the new intermediality in which the Web has become an integral part of the production and reception of television.

The emergence of the newer media of the Internet and the Web not only has afforded mainstream media such as WB and CNN new modes of representation but also has provided new opportunities for the expression of dissent, new avenues of distribution for audio and video, and alternative representations of war unavailable during previous major U.S. conflicts.[58] To offer one prominent example, the video of the torture and murder of hostages in Iraq, although self-censored by the mainstream media, is consistently uploaded in its entirety to several Web sites and circulated through peer-to-peer file-sharing networks. Video from the cockpit of U.S. helicopters showing the killing of civilians is also readily available online, as are Web sites that challenge the instantaneous electronic historiography of the "fall of Baghdad" by revealing that there were very few celebrants outside the televisual frame during the toppling of Saddam Hussein's statue in central Baghdad. In addition, Arabic and Arab American Web sites offer a wide range of dissenting views, as do online articles and blogs from anti-war libertarians and progressives.[59] Independent videos and community television and radio programs criticizing the war are available over the Web, and the satellite distribution of Al Jazeera and other pan-Arab cable network programming also offered important alternative images to those shown on U.S. networks (most notably images of dead and injured Iraqi civilians).

Shortly after the video of Nick Berg's beheading began to circulate over the Internet, bloggers and Web sites began to question its veracity, claiming, for instance, that the "Nick Berg Video [was] a False Flag Fake" and that Berg was already dead when he was beheaded. The anti-Rumsfeld Web site, Topplerummy.org, offers a close analysis of the video's camerawork, editing, and audio, as well as statements from surgeons and forensic scientists that supported the existence of "over 33 errors with the official story" and "48 problems with the video." Other blogs and Web sites (e.g., www.conspiracyplanet.com, binarycircumstance.typepad.com) offer critiques that question the audio, and the LibertyForum.org discussion board posted a frame-by-frame analysis of the entire video.[60] As is often the case with these kinds of conspiracy sites—like hate group Web sites—they often link to each other, forming an insular Web ring that gives the false impression of more widespread acceptance of their claims.

Internet newsgroups such as alt.culture.iraq, soc.culture.iraq, and alt.religion.islam contain posts from Arab Muslims and others from around the world taunting U.S. participants with statements like "we kicked your ass on

9/11" and reveling in U.S. and coalition deaths of any kind, including military casualties and the killing of civilian hostages. Discussion threads comparing readings of the Bible and the Koran routinely lead to derogatory statements about Jesus or Mohammed, as well as threats of physical violence and murder. To offer just one example, on 12 September 2004, one user posted on alt. religion.islam.one: "George W. Bush will destroy all of the sand-nigger countries one by one until this religion of the devil is eliminated forever! Long live George W. Bush!" This post reflects the mood described and propagated by Michael Savage and Howard Stern in their calls to "nuke" Muslim countries, and although I have already suggested some of the ways in which Savage and Coulter may serve to legitimize Limbaugh and Bush's agenda, the Internet has added an easily accessible outlet for "putting into circulation" an even wider range of extremist and violent rhetoric.

After viewing the videos of hostages being murdered, other Internet users displayed the kind of prowar blood lust that some conservative pundits hoped for. Several users created modified versions of the videos and shared them over peer-to-peer networks, inserting the additional text "FUCK ALL MUSLIMS," and "AMERICANS WORLDWIDE MUST KILL ALL MUSLIMS" at the beginning. On another discussion board for a Web site that hosts pictures of the U.S. military (www.militaryphotos.net), users exchanged ideas for "getting rid of Muslims" in their neighborhood by reporting lies about them to the FBI or INS. That Internet sites tend to be actively sought out by users means that there is a large "preaching to the converted" function with these texts. In addition, given the radical or extreme nature of much of the alternative media available on the Internet and through underground radio, these texts may serve to reinforce presuppositions or alienate those who are confused about their stance on war-related issues.

It would be difficult to exaggerate the degree to which the proliferation of satellite and cable technology in the Middle East, combined with the existence of the Internet, has created new global insecurities and anxieties among U.S. officials about controlling the flow and content of information in the "theater of operations." TNT's TV series *The Grid* illustrates the contradictions and ambivalences that result from the increased role these newer communication technologies and networks play within global media culture. In the series, the Internet, cell phones, and communications satellites not only are tools deployed by the terrorists to recruit, organize, and communicate, but also are shown as essential to the U.S. intelligence community's efforts to protect the world from evil. Terrorists are shown uploading information to their global terrorist network from tents in remote desert locations using laptops, wireless modems, and satellite technology. This emphasis on technology extends to the accompanying Web site for *The Grid*, which includes an online role-playing game, "Terror Tracker," that allows viewers to play their own part in *The Grid* and the war on terror by leading a virtual counterterrorism unit.[61]

The Grid adopted a "ripped from the headlines" approach to its narrative, as articles in the mainstream press documented an actual "electronic jihad" against the United States waged over the Internet, and the Pentagon launched a massive information war during the conflicts in Afghanistan and Iraq to disrupt information flow over the Web and Internet. Ironically, these new global insecurities have their origins in the cold-war desire by the Department of Defense to create a decentralized communications network that could survive a nuclear strike from the Soviet Union.[62] In the new cold war against Islamic terrorism, the Internet's decentralized architecture with its ability to instantly reroute communications traffic to its destination has become the major problem for U.S. intelligence and security efforts.

Capitalizing on anxieties about Internet insecurity at home and abroad, the Bush administration announced in March 2003 that "the war on terrorism [would] include . . . measures to prevent proceeds from pirated movies and music from becoming a vehicle for financing terrorist networks."[63] This tactic of tying illegal activities, such as peer-to-peer file sharing, to terrorism extends the logic of the Bush administration's public service announcements that argue that individual illegal drug use in the United States helps to finance terrorism. Although no concrete proof of any connection between the file sharing of copyrighted material and terrorism was offered at the hearing, MPAA chair and CEO Jack Valenti and Hilary Rose, chair and CEO of the Recording Industry Association of America, testified on Capitol Hill about the "dark paths to which [piracy] profits are put [by] highly organized, violent international criminal groups."[64] The U.S. Senate's proposed Pirate Act is part of broader legislation that resulted from this latest cooperative effort between the military, U.S. government, and the entertainment industries. Like the similarly deliberate anachronism of the PATRIOT Act on which it was modeled, the Pirate Act would grant corporations and the Justice Department increased access to information about citizens.

Digital and satellite technologies along with the Internet have also prob-lematized the Pentagon and Bush administration's efforts to control infor-mation flow and propaganda to troops and civilians in the Middle East. The *New York Times* took notice of the "pervasiveness of popular culture within the military culture," noting that "CD players, MP3s, portable DVD movie systems, satellite dishes and laptop computers with Internet access allow sol-diers to stay current with American music, movies and television" and have "end[ed] [the military's] monopoly over the supply of news and entertain-ment for American troops. . . . When a day's combat patrol or reconstruction mission is over, the troops join the global consumer culture, retreating into the privacy of headphones to recapture a bit of territory in the war zone, free from the collective of military life. . . . 'If a movie has been out in a theater for a week, you can get it here,' said Specialist Michael Trujillo with the 819th Military Police Company."[65] While it is unclear whether the troops are "stay-ing current" by obtaining these illegal copies of MP3s and bootlegged DVDs, the article suggests the degree to which the consumption of entertainment has come to define the "American way of life," eliding identity with media consumption even for the soldier at war. Moreover, the military may be toler-ating Internet use, including illegal downloading, with the hope that it serves to boost morale through mainstream entertainment propaganda rather than to distribute alternative news and dissenting information.

Faith in the power of entertainment to win the "hearts and minds" of Iraqis and Arabs throughout the Middle East is at the center of the latest U.S. propaganda campaign in the region.[66] The proliferation of over 70 Arabic satellite and cable TV networks with accompanying Web sites has forced the United States to upgrade its propaganda effort technologically, rhetorically, and generically. Supported by a $245 million yearly budget, the Bush admin-istration announced the launching of its own Alhurra ("The Free One") satel-lite channel to "cut through the hateful propaganda that fills the airwaves in the Muslim world."[67] Alhurra joins its U.S.-funded Radio Sawa counterpart, which tries to reach younger Arabs through popular music supplemented with talk shows and news.[68] The man in charge of the U.S. media efforts in Iraq is Norman J. Pattiz, chair of Viacom subsidiary Westwood One radio ser-vice, who has reportedly said that shows such as *Friends* "are what's needed to improve the Iraqis' understanding of what we're all about."[69]

There is evidence that Radio Sawa and Alhurra have a large audience throughout the Middle East, but it is difficult to gauge the effectiveness and influence of these new propaganda outlets. Indeed, many Arab and Muslim consumers of U.S.-produced media are aware of the strategy of the use of entertainment as part of a broader campaign of media or cultural imperialism. Still others insist that they are enjoying or using the entertainment value of these channels but ignoring the news programming. Even before the Alhurra network premiered in February 2004, AP correspondent Salah Nasrawi reported that it faced resistance for "attempt[ing] to destroy Islamic values and brainwash the young."[70] While satellite television was illegal under Saddam Hussein's regime, reports of the proliferation of satellite dishes throughout the region during the U.S. occupation suggests that Alhurra could potentially reach and influence a significant part of the Iraqi population.[71]

Just as my accounts of the Internet and the Web suggest a regressive rather than a progressive ideological function, accounts of the Iraqi TV spectator seem to fall along a continuum of resistance and opposition. This theological and ideological resistance to U.S. messages turned into actual violent resistance when Alhurra correspondents and their families became targets of attacks by militant Arab groups in October 2004. These attacks also spread to Arab-funded media when, on 31 October 2004, the Baghdad offices of Al Arabiya, the second largest Arab satellite news network, were also bombed by the militant group 1920 Brigades, who claimed that the station and its staff were "Americanized spies speaking in Arabic tongue."[72]

Conclusion

Lynn Spigel concludes her examination of post-9/11 television by "suggesting some alternative possibilities within the highly consolidated, yet also fragmented, global mediasphere." Spigel briefly mentions BET chat rooms, e-mail from resistance groups, academic Web sites, National Public Radio, and the Al Jazeera news network to justify her qualified optimism about the "hopeful possibilities" for the progressive political potential of "multiple media platforms." These claims seem unconvincing in light of her sustained critique of the regressively orientalist ideological function of U.S. television since 9/11, which is supported by my analysis of other media texts.[73]

Spigel is writing from a television- and media studies tradition that has, at least since the 1980s, tended to highlight the progressive aspects of media culture. By focusing on polysemy, oppositional readings, and the creative potential of interpretive communities, television and media scholars have provided an important antidote to reductive approaches that posited mainstream media as a weapon of hegemonic domination. As Meghan Morris has noted, however, by the late 1980s, much of this cultural studies scholarship amounted to a kind of uncritical populism.[74] More recently, by repeatedly arguing that the Internet provides an escape hatch from mainstream media's ideological influence, cultural studies scholars have unwittingly supported FCC chair Michael Powell's argument that the existence of newer media liberates the broadcasting industry from ownership limits outdated in an era of infinite consumer "choice."

As Spigel suggests: "In the media industries . . . there is both fragmentation and centralization at the same time," and "any attempt to consider the political effects of the multiplication of channels (and fragmentation of audiences) still has to be considered within the overall patterns of consolidation at the level of ownership." Spigel feels that the progressive potential of these multiple channels ultimately outweighs the material constraints, yet I am less optimistic, given the unprecedented structural complicities discussed in this essay. I am certainly sympathetic to a "materialist politics of hope [that would] embrace the new global media environment as an opportunity to listen to 'the third of the world that hates us.'"[75] But I see little material justification for hoping that things will change in any substantive way without legislative and regulatory reform. Under current conditions, although new media may provide spaces for dissenting viewpoints, the complicity between U.S. media conglomerates, the government, and the military create a context of reception with limited possibilities for oppositional or politically progressive readings. In the end, the "war on terror text," like the Bush administration's policy toward Iraq, remains both constrained and managed, offering little room for negotiation.

NOTES

I am grateful to Patrice Petro, Andrew Martin, Anthony Grajeda, Louise Spence, and Dennis Broe for their editorial insights and helpful comments. This project was supported by a Sacred Heart University Research and Creativity Grant.

1 Robert F. Worth, "Truth, Right, and the American Way: A Nation Defines Itself by Its Evil Enemies," *New York Times*, 24 February 2002. See also www.nytimes.com/2002/02/24/weekinreview/24WORT.html.

2 "Bush: Don't Wait for Mushroom Cloud," CNN.com, 8 October 2002, www.cnn.com/2002/ALLPOLITICS/10/07/bush.transcript; and "President Bush Outlines Iraqi Threat," 6 October 2002, www.whitehouse.gov/news/releases/2002/10/20021007-8.html.

3 See the *Time* cover for the 31 March 2003 special issue, www.time.com/time/

covers/110103033I. For a discussion of the 1990–1991 Gulf War as a miniseries, see Douglas Kellner, *The Persian Gulf TV War* (Boulder, Colo.: Westview Press, 1992).

4 An important exception is Susan Jeffords and Lauren Rabinovitz, eds., *Seeing through the Media: The Persian Gulf War* (New Brunswick, N.J.: Rutgers University Press, 1994). See also James Castonguay, "Masquerades of Massacre: Gender, Genre, and the Gulf War TV Star System," *Velvet Light Trap* 39 (1997): 5–22. The discursive field should also be expanded to include less-explicit representations of the "war on terror," such as Disney's *Hidalgo* (2004), in which a nineteenth-century American cowboy and his mustang travel to Saudi Arabia to race against "the World's greatest Arabian horses."

5 The term "convergent intermediality" recognizes the increased concentration of media ownership and synergy (or convergence) across media sectors through vertical and horizontal integration, while also historicizing these developments in relation to the concept of a nineteenth-century intermediality used by scholars of early cinema. For a more detailed treatment of the older and newer intermediality, see James Castonguay, "The Political Economy of the 'Indie Blockbuster': Intermediality, Fandom, and *The Blair Witch Project*," in Sarah Higley and Jeffrey A. Weinstock, eds., *Nothing That Is: Millennial Cinema and the "Blair Witch" Controversies* (Detroit: Wayne State University Press, 2003), 65–85.

6 For an excellent discussion of the regressive policies of the Bush administration, see Douglas Kellner, *From 9/11 to Terror War: Dangers of the Bush Legacy* (Lanham, Md.: Rowan and Littlefield, 2003).

7 Before the U.S. attacks on Afghanistan, Hollywood responded to the terrorist attacks on the World Trade Center with the global broadcast of *America: A Tribute to Heroes* featuring many of the entertainment industry's biggest celebrities. See Lynn Spigel, "Entertainment Wars: Television Culture after 9/11," *American Quarterly* 56.2 (June 2004), pp. 250–255, for a discussion of this TV event. For a detailed analysis of the military-industrial-media-entertainment nexus, see James Der Derian, *Virtuous War: Mapping the Military-Industrial-Media-Entertainment Network* (Boulder, Colo.: Westview Press, 2001).

8 Claude Brodesser, "Feds Seek H'wood's Help," *Daily Variety*, 8 October 2001, 1. For a detailed discussion of the implications of the collaboration between USC's ITC and the military, see Jonathan Burston, "War and the Entertainment Industries: New Research Priorities in an Era of Cyber-Patriotism," in Daya Kishan Thussu and Des Freedman, eds., *War and Media: Reporting Conflict 24/7* (Thousand Oaks, Calif.: Sage, 2003), 163–175.

9 "White House Meets with Hollywood Leaders to Explore Ways to Win War against Terrorism," *PR Newswire*, 11 November 2001, www.findarticles.com/cf_dls/m4PRN/2001_Nov_11/79942648/p1/article.jhtml.

10 Jonathan V. Last, "War? What War?" *Wall Street Journal*, 10 October 2003.

11 See Jack G. Shaheen, *Reel Arabs: How Hollywood Vilifies a People* (New York: Olive Branch Press, 2001), and Akbar S. Ahmed, *Postmodernism and Islam: Predicament and Promise* (London: Routledge, 1992).

12 See Duncan Campbell, "Hollywood Helps CIA Come in from the Cold," *The Guardian*, 6 September 2001.

13 On collaborations with artists during the cold war, see Frances Stonor Saunders, *The Cultural Cold War: The CIA and the World of Arts and Letters* (New York: New Press, 1999).

14 Campbell, "Hollywood Helps CIA," 15.

15 Barbara Slavin and Susan Page, "CIA Recovering after Failure to Prevent Attacks," *USA Today*, 24 September 2001.

16 Caryn James, "Television, Like the Country, Loses Its Footing," *New York Times*, 4 November 2001. As the only military drama on TV before 9/11, *JAG: Judge Advocate General* (CBS, 1995–) also saw a boost in ratings after the attacks on the World Trade Center, jumping from twenty-eighth to twelfth. *JAG*'s characters have fought the Taliban in Afghanistan, held terrorism tribunals, and participated in the rebuilding process in Iraq. One of the show's main characters lost a leg saving an Iraqi child from a minefield. CBS also premiered the *JAG* spin-off *Navy NCIS* in fall 2003.

17 See the TV Tome Web site on *Threat Matrix* at www.tvtome.com/tvtome/servlet/ShowMainServlet/showid-16750/; Paige Albiniak, "Post-9/11 Becomes a Television Plot: Threat Matrix Feeds on New Interest in National Security, *Broadcasting & Cable*, 13 October 2003, 22; Cynthia Fuchs, "Smoke 'Em Out," Popmatters.com, 29 September 2003, www.popmatters.com/tv/reviews/t/threat-matrix.shtml.

18 It appears that the industry has replaced the term "mini" with the less diminutive "limited."

19 For a discussion of the way *24* "took on a different cast following the declaration of the war on terror" and began to "support [Bush's] 'endless' war," see Dennis Broe, "Fox and Its Friends: Global Commodification and the New Cold War," *Cinema Journal* 43, 4 (2004): 97–102.

20 See Josef Adalian and Michael Schneider, "Alphabet Targets Battlefront Reality," *Daily Variety*, 20 February 2002, 1.

21 Cynthia Fuchs, "The 'Real World' War," Alternet.org, 2 April 2003, www.alternet.org/story.html?StoryID=15539.

22 For more information on the Pirate Act, see Declan McCullagh, "'Pirate Act' Raises Civil Rights Concerns," CNET News.com, 26 May 2004, http://news.com.com/Pirate+Act+raises+civil+rights+concerns/2100-1027_3-5220480.html; and Xeni Jardin, "Congress Moves to Criminalize P2P," *Wired News*, 26 March 2004, www.wired.com/news/digiwood/0,1412,62830,00.html.

23 Robert W. McChesney, *Rich Media, Poor Democracy* (New York: New Press, 1999), 75–76.

24 "Harris Interactive Survey Shows Internet's Growth as Primary Source of News and Information in Weeks Following September 11 Attacks," HarrisInteractive.com, 5 October 2001, www.harrisinteractive.com/news/allnewsbydate.asp?NewsID=371.

25 Anna Wilde Matthews, "Radio Stations Slowly Return to Normal Formats," *Wall Street Journal*, 13 September 2001; on breaking format, see Chris Jenkins, "Sports Talk Radio Takes News Slant," *USA Today*, 12 September 2001.

26 Anna Wilde Mathews, "Radio Stations Turn Back Clock for Songs to Capture Nation's Mood after Attacks," *Wall Street Journal*, 14 September 2001.

27 Jon W. Sparks, "How Low Can You Go? Radio Rules That Turf," *Memphis Commercial Appeal*, 28 September 2001, E1.

28 "Disk Jockeys Changing Playlists out of Sensitivity to Terrorist Attacks," Associated Press State and Local Wire, 20 September 2001.

29 See Paul Krugman, "Channels of Influence," *New York Times*, 25 March 2003.

30 Until his recent anti-Bush turn, Howard Stern would have been included in this list of pro-Republican radio personalities.

31 Timothy Egan, "Talk Radio, a Medium Noted for Vitriol, Shows Some Restraint," *New York Times*, 25 September 2001; "Catering to New Sensitivities," *Christian Science Monitor*, 11 October 2001.

32 Similar to the articles about talk radio in the mainstream press, Bruce A. Williams identifies increased "civility" as one of the major characteristics of post-9/11 Internet chat-room discussions, including radical hate-group sites like the neo-Nazi Stormfront.org. Williams concludes with an important qualification: "This spirit of tolerance, even when it did emerge, was quite short-lived." Bruce A. Williams, "The New Media Environment, Internet Chatrooms, and Public Discourse after 9/11," in Thussu and Freedman, eds., *War and the Media*, 187. As I demonstrate in this essay, there is much evidence to suggest that intolerance and incivility increased within the United States immediately following the events of 9/11.

33 "Savage: Arabs Are 'Non-humans' and 'Racist, Fascist Bigots,'" *Media Matter for America*, 14 May 2004, http://mediamatters.org/items/200405140003.

34 Anna McCarthy, "The Limits of the Cold War Analogy," *Cinema Journal* 43, 4 (summer 2004): 124.

35 James Carroll, *Crusade: Chronicles of an Unjust War* (New York: Metropolitan Books, 2004), 3. As Chalmers Johnson has noted, Bush's statement that "moral truth is the same in every culture, in every time, in every place" is "demonstrably untrue but . . . , in the mouth of the president of the United States, amount[s] to the announcement of a crusade." See Chalmers Johnson, *The Sorrows of Empire: Militarism, Secrecy, and the End of the Republic* (New York: Metropolitan, 2004), 286.

36 Joel Selvin, "Giving Voice to Opinions on Attacks: Talk Radio Waves Heat Up as Public Vents Its Feelings," *San Francisco Chronicle*, 5 October 2001.

37 Joe Klein, "Sending Out the Smite Squad," *Time*, 5 April 2004, 25.

38 See www.rushlimbaugh.com/home/daily/site_083104/content/eib_interview. guest.html (text), and http://mfile.akamai.com/5020/wma/rushlimb.download. akamai.com/5020/clips/04/08/083104_bush.asx (audio).

39 Transcriptions and audio excerpts available on the Media Matter for America Web site, mediamatters.org.

40 Mark Follman, "Limbaugh: Abu Ghraib Was Just a Big Frat Party!" Salon.com, 6 May 2004, www.salon.com/politics/war_room/2004/05/06/limbaugh. See also "Rush Limbaugh Continues to Justify Iraqi Prison Torture, *America's Intelligence Wire*, 11 May 2004.

41 Of course, the military trains and prepares soldiers to kill the enemy, and the process of dehumanizing the enemy in preparation for battle facilitates torture. In addition, official government documents and administrative actions implicitly—and at times explicitly—condoned the mistreatment of prisoners as a matter of policy. See Oliver Burkeman, "Bush Team 'Knew of Abuse' at Guantanamo," *The Guardian*, 13 September 2004; Dave Moniz and Donna Leinwand, "Iraq Abuse Report Holds Top Officials Responsible," *USA Today*, 25 August 2004; and Seymour M. Hersh, *Chain of Command: The Road from 9/11 to Abu Ghraib* (New York: HarperCollins, 2004).

42 See Damien Cave, "Inside Clear Channel: How the Company's Domination Has Made the Airwaves Blander and Tickets Pricier," *Rolling Stone*, 13 August 2004, www.rollingstone.com/news/story/_/id/6432174?pageid=rs.Home&pageregion= single1&&rnd=1096721454244&has-player=true. See also the *Columbia Journalism Review*'s "Who Owns What" Web site: www.cjr.org/tools/owners/clearchannel. asp.

43 See www.dir.salon.com/ent/feature/2001/04/30/clear_channel/index.html. Clear Channel has also purchased SFX, the largest concert promotion business in the United States.

44 See Paul Krugman, "Channels Of Influence," *New York Times*, 25 March 2003, 17. See also Oliver Burkeman, "War in the Gulf: Bush Backer Sponsoring Pro-War Rallies," *The Guardian*, 26 March 2003. A map of the connections between Bush, Hicks, and Clear Channel can be found on the Take Back the Media Web site, www.takebackthemedia.com/radiogaga.html.

45 Frank Ahrens, "'Rallies for America' Draw Scrutiny: Critics Question Clear Channel's Ties," *Washington Post*, 26 March 2003. See also Amy Goodman (with David Goodman), *The Exception to the Rulers: Exposing Oily Politicians, War Profiteers, and the Media That Love Them* (New York: Hyperion, 2004); and David Walsh, "Right-wing Campaign against U.S. Country Music Group," www.wsws. org/articles/2003/mar2003/chic-m22.shtml.

46 According to press releases posted on the Clear Channel Web site (www. clearchannel.com) in September 2004: "In our view, industry-developed guidelines should be as effective as Government-imposed regulations without running afoul of the First Amendment protections that we all respect. . . . Clear Channel also has volunteered to fully participate with other representatives of the broadcast, cable and satellite industries to develop an industry-wide response to indecency and violence in the media." Janet Jackson's breast was revealed on a live national broadcast, outraging FCC chair Michael Powell, who was reportedly watching with his wife and children.

47 *The Howard Stern Show*, 19 March 2004. Clear Channel was not Stern's primary syndicator and consequently did not have nearly as much invested in Stern's program as did its main distributor, Infinity Broadcasting. Infinity continued to support Stern even after he announced that he would be leaving broadcast radio for satellite, most likely to keep their options open with Stern in the future.

48 Stern quoted in David Hinckley, "Rants in Their Pants: Talk Radio Took the Public's Pulse after Sept. 11—But at What Price?" *New York Daily News*, 30 September 2001, "Showtime" sec., 15; Eric Boehlert, "Howard Stern's Schwing Voters," Salon. com, 12 March 2004. www.salon.com/news/feature/2004/03/12/stern/.

49 See "FCC Fines Clear Channel $495,000," *Tech Law Journal Daily E-Mail Alert*, No. 874; and Glynn Wilson, "Senate Votes 99–1 to Increase FCC's Indecency Fines," Hollywoodreporter.com, 23 June 2004, www.hollywoodreporter.com/thr/article_ display.jsp?vnu_content_id=1000542803.

50 According to UPI reports, the popularity of Michael Moore's *Fahrenheit 911* was a strong determinant of which markets Clear Channel considered for carrying Air America programming. See "Clear Channel Picks Up 'Air America'," United Press International, 23 July 2004.

51 Air America got off to a disastrous financial start that included the resignation of upper management. See Julia Angwin and Sarah McBride, "Radio Daze: Inside Air America's Troubles," *Wall Street Journal*, 21 June 2004.

52 See Karen Juanita Carrillo, "Kicked off the Dial," *Colorlines Magazine* 7, 3 (fall 2004): 34–36.

53 Jefferson Graham, "As America Vents, Free Web Pages Thrive," *USA Today*, 29 October 2001.

54 In addition, the Internet is being economically restructured in similar ways to television and radio by many of the existing media industry conglomerates. See McChesney's chapter, "Will the Internet Set Us Free?," in *Rich Media, Poor Democracy*, 119–188.

55 "Harris Interactive Survey Shows Internet's Growth as Primary Source of News and Information in Weeks Following September 11 Attacks," HarrisInteractive. com, 5 October 2001, www.harrisinteractive.com/news/allnewsbydate.asp?News ID=371. Some Internet radio broadcasters experienced increases as high as 8,900 percent in their total listening or streaming time on the day of the attacks. See "MeasureCast: Office Workers Turn to Internet Radio for News of Terrorist Attacks," *Business Wire*, 18 September 2001, www.businesswire.com.

56 See my discussion of the Spanish-American War and film in *American Quarterly*'s Project for Hypertext Scholarship in American Studies, chnm.gmu.edu/aq. See also James Castonguay, "The Spanish-American War in U.S. Media Culture," in J. David Slocum, ed., *Hollywood and War: The Film Reader* (New York: Routledge, forthcoming); Charles Musser, *The Emergence of Cinema: The American Screen to 1907* (New York: Scribner, 1990); and Amy Kaplan, *The Anarchy of Empire in the Making of U.S. Culture* (Cambridge: Harvard University Press, 2002).

57 See www.turnerlearning.com/thewb/7thheaven/knownsoldier/index.html.

58 For a discussion of the use of the Internet and Web during Operation Desert Storm and the Bosnian War, see James Castonguay, "Representing Bosnia: Human Rights Claims and Global Media Culture," in Mark P Bradley and Patrice Petro, eds., *Truth Claims: Representation and Human Rights* (New Brunswick, N.J.: Rutgers University Press, 2002), 157–185.

59 See, for example, www.arabnews.com, http://albawabaforums.com, http://english.aljazeera.net, www.cafearabica.com, www.adc.org, www.antiwar.com, http://thememoryhole.org, www.iraqbodycount.net, and www.alternet.org.

60 Here is a representative example analysis of one shot from the video:

> Shot video time 02:18:33 to 02:18:43 synced audio; Nick sitting in chair, giving his details, different angle
> This is *not* a second angle on the first shot. Nick has clearly moved in between these two shots, as illustrated by the change in his voice tone while reciting his details, and the change in the pattern of folds and clothing position under his harms [sic] and on his chest. This clearly shows a careful edit has been made, and we cannot know how long apart these two shots were taken. It also shows that the editor as [sic] at least some basic editing skills.
> We also hear a door squeak at 2:18:41
> We see the reflection of a horizontal light in the top left of screen.
> questions:
> Why did they shoot the scene twice?
> Was Nick's "performance" not up to scratch?

Why did they go to such lengths to make it look like it was shot at the same time?

Did they get him to replicate his hand position is that just coincidence?

See also www.libertyforum.org/showflat.php?Cat=&Board=news_international &Number=1471708&view=collapsed&sb=5&o=21%E2%88%82=1.

61 See www.tnt.tv/title/0,,540146,00.html. Described by its creators as a "multiplatform experiment," *The Grid* prompted one trade journal to claim that its overall aesthetic and its elaborate multimedia and "after-marketing" plan "presents a template for made-for-DVR and VOD [video on demand] programming . . . [and] a model for multiple media opportunities across the digital landscape." See Gary Arlen, "TNT's Multi-Platform Experiment: Limited Thriller Series 'The Grid' Is Built to Accommodate DVRs and DVDs," *Multichannel News*, 23 August 2004, 6.

62 See Gene I. Rochlin, *Trapped in the Net: The Unanticipated Consequences of Computerization* (Princeton: Princeton University Press, 1997). The origins of the Internet cannot be traced to one originary impulse or motivation. The point here is that the ethos during the cold war lent itself to the development of the Internet, which was from its inception funded in large part by the Department of Defense through DARPA (Defense Advanced Research Projects Agency).

63 Pamela McClintock, "Piracy Perils Pervasive," *Daily Variety*, 13 March 2003, 50.

64 Although Valenti resigned days after the passage of the Pirate Act, his successor has made copyright piracy a flagship issue for his agenda. See "Valenti Calls on Congress to Battle Theft of Intellectual Property, Cites Role of Organized Crime in Piracy Abroad," 13 March 2003, www.mpaa.org/jack/2003/2003_03_13A.htm.

65 Thom Shanker, "G.I.'s in Iraq Tote Their Own Pop Culture," *New York Times*, 13 April 2004.

66 To defray the costs of the new media outlets, the Broadcasting Board of Governors, which also operates Voice of America radio, has drastically cut the VOA news staff and existing radio broadcasts, prompting more than 450 VOA employees (more than half) to sign a petition protesting these decisions.

67 Teresa Castle, "TV Programs to Join U.S. Radio in Offering American Spin," *San Francisco Chronicle*, 5 May 2002. The United States has also launched the Pentagon-funded Iraqi Media Network (IMN)—with Al Iraqiya as the flagship channel—built in part out of the remaining infrastructure of Iraq's state-run television network. According to the Center for Media and Democracy, the "IMN [has] faced credibility issues [for being] too closely associated with the [Coalition Provisional Authority]" and has been unable to compete with the popular Al Jazeera and Al Arabiya satellite channels. See the entry for "Iraq Media Network" at the Center for Media and Democracy's SourceWatch Web site: www.sourcewatch.org/index.php?title=Iraqi_Media_Network.

68 According to VOA officials: "Radio Sawa and Alhurra are attempting the twin tasks of reporting the news honestly and reminding their Arab audiences of all the good America does." See "U.S. Raising New Voices to Counter Arab Media: Old VOA Hands Say Alhurra TV, Radio Sawa Are Less News Than Propaganda," *Baltimore Sun*, 1 August 2004.

69 Pattiz quoted in Vinay Menon, "Iraq Braces for Cultural Bombardment," *Toronto Star*, 26 April 2003.

70 Salah Nasrawi, "U.S.-Government Satellite TV Station Draws Arab Fire Even before Its Debut," Associated Press, 12 February 2004.

71 Valentinas Mite, "Iraq: Once-Outlawed Satellite Dishes Sprouting Like Mushrooms on Baghdad's Rooftops," Radio Free Europe/Radio Liberty, 28 May 2003, www.rferl.org/features/2003/05/28052003163456.asp.

72 "Huge Blast outside Al Arabiya Station in Baghdad," www.aljazeera.com/cgi-bin/news_service/middle_east_full_story.asp?service_ID=5435. The documentary *Control Room* (Noujaim, 2004) offers evidence that the U.S. military deliberately bombed an Al Jazeera news facility, killing veteran correspondent Tarik Ayoub, and claims that similar attacks were made on other Arab news outlets and journalists. Linda Foley, president of the Newspaper Guild, has accused the U.S. military of deliberately targeting American and Arab journalists: "It's not just U.S. journalists . . . They target and kill journalists from other countries, particularly Arab countries, at news services like Al Jazeera, for example. They actually target them and blow up their studios, with impunity. This is all part of the culture that it is OK to blame the individual journalists, and it just takes the heat off of these media conglomerates that are part of the problem." See John Leo, "Stories Not Told," *U.S. News & World Report* 13 June 2005, 76.

73 Spigel, "Entertainment Wars," 260. To be sure, Spigel acknowledges that what alternative media outlets "will amount to in terms of democracy and citizenship remains a complex historical question" (261).

74 See Meaghan Morris, "Banality in Cultural Studies, " *Discourse* 10, 2 (1988): 3–29.

75 Spigel, "Entertainment Wars," 260, 263.

Remapping the Visual War on Terrorism

"U.S. Internationalism" and Transnational Citizenship

WENDY KOZOL AND REBECCA DECOLA

The "Human" in the War on Terrorism

In the spring of 2004, photographs of torture by U.S. soldiers and civilian contractors, taken at the Abu Ghraib prison in Iraq, dominated news coverage in the United States and elsewhere. As other commentators have noted, photographing these atrocities was not simply about documenting an event but was itself a form of torture.[1] Many people assume that rather than furthering such acts, publishing these "shocking" pictures was instrumental in exposing human rights violations by the U.S. military. The lack of impact on subsequent U.S. policies, however, foregrounds the limitations of the power such claims invest in photography. The appropriate response, however, should not be to turn away in revulsion from the images. Rather, pictures of abuse foreground the need for what Judith Butler terms the "double path," that is, working with and being skeptical of the available means of representing "the local conceptions of what is human," including acts of warfare and torture.

> The local conceptions of what is human or, indeed, of what the basic conditions and needs of human life are, must be subjected to reinterpretation. . . . We have to follow a double path in politics; we must use this language to assert an entitlement to conditions of life in ways that affirm the constitutive role of sexuality and gender in political life, and we must also subject our very categories to critical scrutiny.

We must find out the limits of their inclusivity and translatability, the presuppositions they include, the ways in which they must be expanded, destroyed, or reworked both to encompass and open up what it is to be human and gendered.[2]

Butler is concerned with the politics of visibility in determining access to social, cultural, legal, economic, and political rights and privileges. As she argues, the language of identities and rights that constitute recognition on the basis of humanness also structures exclusions, invisibilities, and demonizations. The Abu Ghraib photographs expose U.S. militarized violence, which may be a necessary precursor to rights advocacy. At the same time, the voyeurism central to the power of these images is predicated on the erasure of Iraqi prisoners' subjectivities. Thus, who is visibly "human" in these pictures is at stake in the politics of representing abuse.

Visual news media have been crucial in the production of war rhetoric for Americans typically distant culturally and geographically from Afghanistan and Iraq. One way to work within the double path suggested by Butler is to recognize the value of news photography for representing marginalized and oppressed people and yet to resist reading any image as an unmediated document. We analyze here how visual representations available to U.S. viewing publics constitute Afghan and Iraqi subjectivities. We reviewed photographs produced or published by mainstream and progressive news media from 7 October 2001 when the United States starting bombing Afghanistan to 30 June 2004 when the United States officially "turned over power" to the Iraqi interim government.[3] While Afghanistan and Iraq have distinct historical trajectories, the U.S. government and the U.S. news media tend to collapse the two under the rubric of the "war on terrorism," making it relevant to talk about an archive that oscillates between these two war zones and cultural imaginaries. In rejecting this visual and rhetorical flattening, we investigate instead the politics of representing Iraqis and Afghans as citizen-subjects in the designated territories of "war zones" and "at home" in this moment of what U.S. president George Bush has called "American internationalism."[4]

Media scholars today debate whether the proliferation of news sources, including Internet and satellite, has led to diversity in the global media field.[5] More sites of news production, especially those that cross national boundaries, effectively mean less state control. Yet, the "transnationalization of media organizations" has also intensified pressure for commercially appealing products.[6] Limited access to news sources and the consolidation of media outlets into global communications networks has further diminished divisions between types of media institutions. Distinctions between mainstream news organizations like the *New York Times* and progressive sites like *Z-Net*, however, continue to be useful in the current polarized political climate, in which both politicians and the news media mobilize political differences to appeal to segmented audiences. Whether simply marketing niches or sites that produce varied constituencies, distinctive editorial perspectives on the war on terrorism remain identifiable.

In contrast to the print media, the visual archive consists of fewer editorial distinctions, because the same types of images appear across the spectrum of news organizations. Throughout the twentieth century, visual culture became increasingly important in the representation of military conflicts. The mechanical nature of the camera reinforces claims of authenticity and thus accords photojournalism the cultural authority to document war. Over time, certain representational forms have come to dominate the visual coverage of military conflicts, including such conventions as the heroic figure of the wounded male soldier and the mother-and-child dyad.[7] The persistence of identifiable representational forms across different time periods and wars indicates that broader cultural scripts inform photographers' and editors' fields of view. The continuity that we observed across this archive supports the findings of earlier studies of war reportage, such as Michael Griffin and Jongsoo Lee's analysis of the Gulf War, in which they argue "that photographers, photo agencies, and newsmagazine editors operated from the outset within parameters and expectations that conform to long-standing conventions of war illustration."[8]

The burgeoning visual archive of the war on terrorism includes pictures of beheadings, masked insurgents, and U.S. troops engaged in combat. Others will most certainly examine the spectacular images of violence and heroism, such as the beheadings and their influence on Americans' perceptions and anxieties about the Arab world. In this essay, we look instead at a subgenre of photographs of ordinary Afghan and Iraqi women. Along with narratives about national security, rhetorical justifications for the war on terrorism have pivoted around claims of rescue from religious or political oppression and the promise of Western-style democracy. In pictures of Afghan women purchasing consumer goods in the marketplace, for instance, nameless subjects stand in for, or become synecdoches for, the presumably

now liberated nation. Whatever the intentions of the photographers, reporters, or editors, be it to expose the violence of militarism and occupation or to
justify the war itself, the ideological work of visual representation marks the
figures as Afghan and Iraqi citizen-subjects operating within local, national,
and transnational political structures.

Photographs of noncombatant Afghan and Iraqi women constitute citizenship as a marker of subjectivity at moments of extreme violence and displacement. What, we ask, can citizenship entail when the United States has
destroyed the state structures of Afghanistan and Iraq? What does it mean
to label the subjects of pictures in this archive "Iraqis" or "Afghans" when
they exist in this stateless geography, or in what many now refer to as "failed
states"?[9] As synecdoches of "failed states," these women embody highly contested concepts of identity and community, enemy and ally, and even more
abstract notions, such as transnational ideals of "liberal democracy" and
"new sovereignty."

The visual archive of the war on terrorism contains a broad range of predictable enough themes, given the varied geographical, political, and social
contexts of this war. We concentrate on two prominent themes in the depiction of Afghan and Iraqi women, because they offer specific insights into
the representation of citizenship. The first consists of Afghans and Iraqis
who appear as primitive or barbaric peoples to whom liberation promises
to bring modernity and equality.[10] Gender and sexuality significantly structure this rescue narrative, just as in earlier moments of orientalist fervor.[11]
For instance, when Laura Bush spoke for the first time on the radio, on 17
November 2001, she declared support for U.S. military action in Afghanistan with the promise that it would liberate women oppressed by the Taliban. At the time, many criticized the administration's sudden interest in
Afghan women as a cynical use of women's human rights.[12] In the wake
of post-9/11 militarism, U.S. mainstream news media continue to promote
and reinforce this racialized and gendered story. Afghan and Iraqi women,
especially veiled women, are prominent symbols of gendered imprisonment
and lack of equality or agency. This rescue narrative, we will argue, is closely
intertwined with the Bush administration's stated objective of "American
internationalism," producing an ideal of the transnational citizen freed
from barbarism and able to participate in the global marketplace. Cameras
have been crucial in the representation of both Afghanistan's primitive
patriarchal culture and the benefits of liberation and modernization. In the

days after Kabul fell, for instance, pictures proliferated of women wearing nail polish and getting their hair styled as evidence of the success of their rescue.

Photographers frequently turn to women for pictures of citizens responding to war, because domestic spaces appear within U.S. cultural frameworks as less political (and thus less contested) than public spaces, which are presumed to be occupied by men. Additionally, liberal political ideologies have historically positioned women as performing a critical role in the reproduction of an ideal citizenry. Circulating around the individual person and property, women's maternal and marital capacities serve an integral educational function of training children toward "civilized" behavior. As in other wars, women and children who are "civilized" or "civilizable" can be constructed as innocent victims and thus continue to provide symbolic justification for current military conflicts. In the visual archive of this war, men more typically appear as leaders, soldiers, or outsiders/terrorists, as in photographs of (seemingly) large groups of male protestors with raised fists shouting anti-U.S. slogans. The Bush administration, largely uncontested by the media, has represented oppositional responses as outside the state and hence outside citizenship. In contrast, depictions of women in mourning, women in the marketplace, or women seeking the release of jailed family members perform citizenship through their representative roles as civilians or noncombatants.

Nothing has challenged this construction of the U.S. delivery of democracy to the woman/citizen/nation more than has Abu Ghraib. As we show, the violence visible in the prison photos depends upon denying markers of citizenship, a denial that facilitates the movement of prisoners outside the category of human. Even though these photographs were taken by soldiers and not by professional photojournalists, they circulated within some of the same cultural spaces as photographs of Iraqi and Afghan women. Considering the Abu Ghraib photographs alongside pictures that mark citizenship provides an opportunity to examine how the visual archive operates dialogically to constitute the boundaries of self and other, enemy and friend, and most specifically, liberatory or coercive ideals of citizenship.

A second identifiable theme that can be found in representations of gendered citizenship are photographs whose polysemic elements destabilize any linear or coherent trajectory from primitivism to modernity. While many news photographs of Iraqi and Afghan women produce an ideal of citizenship that conforms to U.S. foreign policies, others configure notions of local and national subjectivities that differ from these narratives. Not surprisingly, many photographs do not conform to U.S. militarized rhetoric, because historical conditions complicate representational strategies that attempt to produce a neat linearity. Gender politics and feminist movements, for instance, have a long and diverse history in the Middle East that is too often elided in the representation of Arab men as "universally oppressive to women."[13] Likewise, in Afghanistan, a more complexly layered gender society exists than either the pro-Bush nationalist narratives of rescue or the progressive antimilitaristic narratives often promote.[14] The multiple meanings of citizenship embedded in images of Iraqi and Afghan women demonstrate that the media provides more than a single representation of subjectivity in relationship to U.S. imperial power.

Surely, Afghan and Iraqi women deserve the rights and privileges of citizenship. Yet, as Butler reminds us, we need to explore how U.S. media representations of subjectivity, identity, and citizenship align with, privilege, or challenge U.S. internationalist claims of inclusion based on narrowly constrained concepts of democracy and rights. In taking up Lila Abu-Lughod's call to do the "hard work involved in recognizing and respecting difference," this essay considers both visual rescue narratives and challenges to that story in order to understand when and how women's bodies are mobilized within the (collapsing) geographical, religious, political, and historical fields of inclusion and exclusion.[15] As spectatorship is a critical dimension of this process, we aim to provide a perspective that does not just "consume the trauma" at Abu Ghraib or elsewhere, but rather explores the contingent possibilities for looking as a form of political literacy.[16]

Violence and Citizenships

The smiling faces of U.S. soldiers that proudly stare at the camera over the naked bodies of Iraqi prisoners in Abu Ghraib prison are trophy pictures that display U.S. domination over a subordinated Arab population.[17] In the Abu Ghraib pictures, U.S. soldiers, who function in Iraq as representatives of the United States, repeatedly gesture to the camera with a thumbs up that signals triumph over the enemy. Such smiles in the context of torture and death hail a community of viewers who presumably share the objectives of these soldiers. At a time when Iraqis were struggling against the occupation and attempting to reconstitute citizenship rights, these images also publicly punish nonwhite, and non-U.S., citizens by visualizing acts of sexual and physical violence and humiliation.

For a country at war or under occupation, formal citizenship is an unstable and often untenable position. At times of violent social conflict, "victim" and "victimizer," like "rescuer" and "rescued," connect to citizenship as terms that define who represents, speaks for, or acts on behalf of or against the state or the community. In turn, these concepts, and indeed citizenship itself, are produced through contested meanings around race, gender, sexuality, and nation. We rely here on the language of citizenship, rather than of humanity, because of our concern that the term "humanity" invokes a universalism that elides specific historical conditions.[18] While citizenship can be understood variously in terms of legal status, rights, political activity, and identity, we are interested in how visual images produce concepts of citizenship as identity.[19] Citizenship is a historicizing concept that foregrounds power and inequality and thus provides a framework through which to understand how photographs mark or label their subjects. These markers mobilize concepts of belonging and exclusion that form the basis of identifying subjects as members of one or more communities.

The U.S. news media most typically framed Abu Ghraib as a scandal or an exceptional event outside ordinary practices. One common explanation argued that the soldiers are "rogue" individuals whose deviant behavior positions them outside the normative boundaries of "civilized" citizenship in the war on terrorism, in effect, outside the boundaries of the nation. In this reading, the photographs show the spectator that conditions are so bad in Iraq that decent folks are turned into monsters, making it possible to conclude that the solution to such abuses is further empowerment of the state and military: more supervision, better training, better prisons, more staffing. A U.S. commission in the fall of 2004 charged with investigating the prison situation came to just this conclusion.[20] In this reading, the military, along with the imagined community of the nation, and the organizing logic of imperialism, are left immune to critical accountability. Framing Abu Ghraib as a scandal or an exceptional narrative precludes discussion of the connections between this abuse and incarceration practices in U.S. prisons or the ways in which colonial powers have historically included sexual violence as a key practice among the larger repertoire of weapons of domination.[21]

Many commentators, however, did focus on the appalling violations of human rights. An outpouring of condemnation about both the prison scandal and the photographs persisted for several months. This outcry, which had little apparent impact on the Bush administration or the 2004 presidential election, has subsequently diminished. Although the reasons for this lack of attention are mostly beyond the scope of this paper, we would like to identify one argument that did more to reinforce than to undermine the logic of this war. Namely, both progressive and mainstream critics claimed that the sexual abuse visualized in these photographs would be more horrific to Muslims than to others because of Islamic intolerance of homosexuality, and it could result in torture victims being shunned by their communities.[22] For instance, Seymour Hersh, in the article that first reported on Abu Ghraib, wrote that "homosexual acts are against Islamic law and it is humiliating for men to be naked in front of other men."[23] Frances Hasso notes that such representations reproduce "Orientalist fantasy of a degraded, repressed society. . . that in turn allows [the writer] to see him/herself in oppositional terms whereby 'out' queers, undressed bodies, and public sexual expression and displays of affection symbolize the pinnacle of modernity and advancement."[24] Disturbingly, this phantasm of Muslims as primitive homophobes continues to circulate, even among leftist critics who were more likely to mobilize than to condemn this homophobic and racist narrative.[25] By focusing on the individual pathology of the torturers and the imagined homophobic Muslim-community response, in effect these critics assent to a concept of the citizen-subject that they were attempting to unravel. In criticisms of supposedly antimodern Islamic homophobia, "the Muslim community," like the torturers, stands outside the ideals of liberal humanism and hence as an obstacle to a possible future ideal democratic statehood.

Much of the critical reception of the Abu Ghraib photographs has attempted to look beyond the pictures to the historical experiences of Iraqi prisoners and of the devastations wrought by the U.S. occupation. While this is crucial historical and political work, such critiques often leave unquestioned a central tenet of human rights discourse: that mobilizing shame by publicizing atrocities will produce oppositional acts. We share Thomas Keenan's skepticism of this faith in publicity when he asks: "What would it mean to come to terms with the fact that there are things which happen in front of cameras that are not simply true or false, not simply representations and references, but rather opportunities, events, performances, things that are done and done for the camera, which come into being in a space beyond truth and falsity that is created in view of mediation and transmission?"[26]

In calling attention to moments when acts of torture are performed for the camera (as in Abu Ghraib), Keenan refutes the commonsense faith that the mimetic qualities of photographs can in themselves promote social change, even as he recognizes the performative nature of the camera and its political significance. Similarly, we examine the Abu Ghraib photographs, not as scandalous evidence but to understand how the images produce politically meaningful categories of identity. Citizenship, we argue, is effaced in these pictures by denying "local conceptions of what is human."

To simply condemn the visual content in the Abu Ghraib photographs ignores how the camera sets up the viewer's gaze to look with the photographer at the prisoners' naked and abused bodies. Photographs such as the widely circulated picture of a U.S. woman soldier, Lynndie England, holding a prisoner by a leash pronounce that the U.S. military has literally tamed Iraqis by conquering that spectral figure of the dangerous Arab terrorist. This operation of power also implicates the viewer through an interpellative process that produces citizens and noncitizens. In many of the pictures, the only visible faces are those of the soldiers smiling at the camera, beckoning the viewer to look with them at what is represented as abject. News organizations blurred prisoners' faces to comply with the Geneva Convention, but the net result is that Iraqi prisoners appear in these pictures without faces, identities, or other markers of subjectivity. Compositions that encourage viewers to identify with the subjects—the smiling faces of the soldiers—operate within the tradition of Western portraiture. As Butler explains: "There is already not only an epistemological frame within which the face appears but an operation of power; . . . under what conditions do some individuals acquire a face, a legible and visible face, and others do not?"[27] This visual economy of subjectivity produces the soldiers as political agents, while the prisoners remain unrecognizable outside of the frame of victimization. In contrast, smiles and thumbs up provide a representation of agency and citizenship based on identification with a clearly defined community, whatever the conditions of military command may be that currently structure U.S. soldiers' experiences. In addition, facial expressions and hand gestures hail the viewer, making it difficult to locate oneself outside the voyeurism that is a fundamental aspect of the abuse of the prisoners. The composition and gestures leave little space to look other than at and with the smiling soldiers.

In discussing interpellation, moreover, we must be cautious about assuming a unified gaze. What does it mean for Americans from historically oppressed communities, such as African Americans or Arab Americans, to look at the picture of England holding an Iraqi prisoner by a leash? Surely spectators' multiple and differential social positions shape the historical resonances of this image. This understanding, however, should not lead to an essentialist assumption that such spectators are naturally in possession of a resistant gaze. Americans from marginalized communities have been coercively recruited by the U.S. military to participate in the war on terrorism with the promise of socioeconomic advancement and the privileges of citizenship. Given this current historical context, the costs and benefits involved in identifying with visual representations of the war on terror must not be underestimated.[28]

The voyeurism of the Abu Ghraib photographs visualizes an extralegal supranational authority over the bodies of Iraqi men. Lauren Berlant argues that ideals of intimacy established in the private sphere increasingly form the basis for citizenship claims in the United States.[29] If gender, racial, and sexual concepts of the heteronormative family structure the ways in which citizens and noncitizens are imagined in relationship to each other in the nation, it should not be difficult to imagine that these same conceptualizations hold true when the frame is extended to global contexts. The Abu Ghraib photographs claim U.S. citizenship for the soldiers (and the presumed viewers) through a violent, sexually abusive intimacy that is relationally bound to the visual erasure of Iraqi citizenship. These photographs strip Iraqi prisoners of their local rights and identities as citizens of a nation through the forced erasure of their faces by the hoods and the men's immobility, either through the piles of bodies that makes movement impossible or through the chains that lock prisoners to the bars of their cells. The abasement of these prisoners' masculinity marks U.S. citizenship as that of domination and power. Similar to the "uncanny" space of Guantánamo, the Abu Ghraib photographs remain a haunting challenge to occupation claims to civilize Iraq, precisely because there is no visible sign of Iraqi political agency.[30]

Widening the scope of the visual, however, locates these representations of abuse within other contexts of identity and citizenship in occupied Iraq. Associated Press photographers took a series of pictures of Iraqi protesters outside the Abu Ghraib prison in the months after the publication of the abuse images.[31] Many of these pictures feature women either calling for the release of their family members or struggling with their grief and anger. For instance, one picture shows a line of women in black chadors walking away from the camera toward the perimeter fence outside the prison (see figure 1). The third woman in the row, closest to the viewer, has turned back and stares directly at the camera. The stare works as a representative gesture of political agency for the rest of the group, which looks away. This composition visualizes a political subjectivity that groups of women performed, transforming this public space into one of torture and protest, violence and resistance, isolation and community. Thus, the photograph depicts the agency of the women at Abu Ghraib, not as a pure act of resistance, but as spatially, legally, and culturally bounded by the occupation. Moreover, the barbed wire in the foreground locates the women within a separate cultural geography distant from the viewer. In so doing, these photographs complexly reshape and rehistoricize the space of Abu Ghraib in contrast to the abuse photographs that deterritorialize Iraq. As horrific as the Abu Ghraib photographs are, and as much as they may implicate us as spectators, it is crucial that we do not look away but instead explore the possibilities of publicizing the abuse

1. Iraqi women line up behind razor wire, waiting to find out whether their family members would be among the prisoners released from Abu Ghraib prisons in Baghdad, Iraq, Monday, 14 June 2004. (Courtesy of David Guttenfelder/Associated Press)

and victimization of Iraqi prisoners. Moreover, photographs like those of the women outside the prison provide the critical tools with which to resist reductive renderings of the human and those excluded from that category.

Rescue, "American Internationalism," and Transnational Citizenship

Rescue and liberation have been central tenets of the Bush doctrine since 9/11. The Bush administration most clearly articulated its civilizing mission of "American internationalism" in the *National Security Strategy* (*NSS*), released in September 2002. The document unapologetically claims the U.S. "aim is to make the world not just safer but better. . . . And this path is not America's alone. It is open to all."[32] The *NSS* spells out the justifications for military actions anywhere in the globe by envisioning the supranational threat posed by terrorists, a term that since 9/11 has become associated the specter of pan-Islamic fanaticism. In contrast, the document promises U.S. protection and aid to nations who remain compliant allies, implicitly denying the possible presence of terrorists that may be 'homegrown,' such as white-supremacist groups.[33]

Though the *NSS* explicitly claims to be a doctrine of national security and identifies the borders of a national citizenship, it necessarily also produces a transnational citizen-subject who needs U.S. assistance not only to combat terror in its local geography but to be civilized into the "American international" community. The *NSS* recognizes that there are "finite political, economic, and military resources to meet [the United States'] global priorities" and states that "the United States should be realistic about its ability to help those who are unwilling or unable to help themselves. Where and when people are ready to do their part, we will be willing to move decisively."[34]

The rescue scenario articulated in this document is predicated on the promise that Afghans and Iraqis will abandon religious fanaticism and become part of the transnational community that the *NSS* calls "American internationalism."[35] Linda Bosniak challenges Western liberal political theory that presumes an inherent link between citizenship and the nation-state. Rather, she argues, the concept of "global or transnational or postnational citizenship [can be used] to characterize the collective identifications and commitments that people maintain with others across national boundaries." In other words, citizenship is a form of inclusion in a network of affective ties of identification. That does not mean, however, that representations of citizenship enact a progressive ideal. As Bosniak states, citizenship has an "enormous legitimizing function" that is "neither desirable nor dangerous per se."[36] If citizenship is about affective identification or belonging, then rescue promises to incorporate Afghans or Iraqis into the modern global community.

Along with the beheadings by terrorist groups, or the faceless prisoners of Abu Ghraib, the media continually represents the visible face of those to be rescued or the "now-liberated." The destruction of Iraq as a nation-state through invasion and occupation has left the process of reconstituting citizenship treacherously unstable at the moment. Once U.S. troops had some control over parts of Iraq in spring 2003, one story that gained prominence reported the unearthing of a mass grave in Mahaweel, sixty miles south of Baghdad, left by the brutal reign of Saddam Hussein. News coverage of the mass graves in Iraq explicitly links the visualization of atrocities with exposure of the tyranny of Hussein's rule. Problematically, however, such coverage offers a script of Iraqi national mourning as part of a U.S. liberation narrative that precludes U.S. audiences from gaining a historical perspective on these traumas. One photograph taken by an AP photographer shows the shovel marks of a ditch digger in the foreground, while several women in chadors stand in the background.[37] Significantly, these women lack any individuated subjectivity, for their faces are not visible. The women at Mahaweel perform a type of citizenship as the symbolic representation of the nation in mourning and in search of evidence of the violation of human rights by the Hussein regime. The shovel marks signify the act of uncovering evidence and, with it, the promise of knowledge. And yet, the violence of digging up the earth speaks to the problematics of recovering evidence, and the inaccessibility of history and memory about these human rights violations.[38]

Complicating this image further, the AP photographer took this picture in the moments after the United States had declared victory. By encouraging reporters to publicize the unearthing of mass graves, the U.S. military recognized the value of ontologizing the remains of the dead to herald a new liberation. Hence, images of Iraqis mourning their dead from the period of the Ba'athist rule cannot be seen as transparent reflections of suffering. Instead, the photographs ask viewers to gaze at two types of victims: the dead (signified by the empty grave) and the women mourners. Such a gaze promotes an intimate political fellowship based on a gendered and racialized narrative of Arab women as victims of oppression. In this way, the Mahaweel pictures participate differently in the politics of war rhetoric than do the images of women protestors at Abu Ghraib, which visualize citizenship practices in opposition to the occupation. Here, the public spectacle of mourning functions as an act of citizenship that reinforces the imperial logic of current U.S. military strategies.

The rescue of civilian populations from repressive political regimes has been a central justification by the Bush administration for military intervention. Rescue, however, has also been mobilized in the context of socioeconomic arguments linked to the promise of global consumer citizenship. This type of representation is most evident in news coverage of Afghanistan, where justifications for U.S. intervention have been more widely accepted. It is less that news personnel are intentionally adopting Bush doctrine (although some news organizations are demonstrably supportive of current foreign policies) than that an orientalist logic of modernity and primitivism structures both the media and foreign policy. From the AP and the *New York Times* to *Ms.* and *Mother Jones*, news organizations in the fall of 2001 and since have published pictures of Afghan women with faces uncovered that reinforce a narrative of once-immobilized and now-liberated bodies (women couldn't go out of their houses, couldn't move, couldn't work, couldn't clothe themselves, couldn't move their bodies through space, and now they can). In one AP picture, in the middle of a group of veiled women walking on a city street, one woman has uncovered her face and smiles at the camera. Offering at once a before-and-after scene of liberation, the photograph seems to suggest that even the smile did not exist before the U.S. invasion. Such scenarios equate Afghan women's new ability to move through public space with political agency and citizenship. In this way, the photograph visualizes a political fellowship based on ideals of the private sphere that, Berlant argues, is crucial to contemporary concepts of liberal citizenship. If the burqa operates within the logic of orientalism as a symbol of fundamentalism, throwing off the veil becomes the sign of liberation, democratization, and women's equality. With women figured as the most victimized members of Afghan society, changing conditions for them are "increasingly taken as an index of the democratization and development of a society."[39]

The novelty highlighted here—women's newfound mobility—invokes what Ella Shohat calls "dischronicity"—the orientalist segregation of temporalities into an ahistorical or anthropological past and a historical, modern, and progressive present.[40] Dischronicity, which Shohat argues is integral to the logic of modernity, becomes visible in the rescue scenario through the representation of the split figures of the smiling woman and her still-burqa-clad companions. Such representations work metonymically to signify female oppression within indigenous patriarchy, which the anthropological gaze can immediately identify and locate as the past. Looking proceeds from this preexisting anthropological orientation by juxtaposing past and present in the image of both veiled and unveiled women. Though this photograph of the smiling woman represents the movement of Afghan women through public space (an ability critical to the concept of liberal citizenship), the image visually closes down opportunities for recognizing the particular subjectivities and complex citizenships of women in present-day Afghan.

Rescue scenarios, in other words, connect modernity to the global marketplace through rhetorics of liberal citizenship premised on tropes of mobility. The *NSS* promises modernity, civilization, and security to those who support the United States through a commitment to global free trade that includes progrowth legal and regulatory policies, tax incentives for capital investment, and other processes to ensure the growth of market economies favorable to Western investment. "Our long-term objective should be a world in which all countries have investment-grade credit ratings that allow them access to international capital markets and to invest in their future," states the *NSS*. This twinning of global militarism and economics reveals that what is at stake in the war on terrorism goes beyond the image of the masked Muslim fanatic. The document makes clear that nations with economic systems unreceptive to free trade do not accord their people "freedom": "This is real freedom, the freedom for a person—or a nation—to enter the market as an autonomous agent. To promote free trade the United States has developed a comprehensive strategy . . . including 'seize the global initiative.'"[41] The Bush doctrine outlines an agenda not just to combat "Muslim terrorists" but also to restructure errant nations to be more cooperative with U.S. capital investments.[42]

Crucially, in the months after the fall of the Taliban, many photographs visualized Afghan women as newly constituted citizens through their participatory acts in a global commercial culture, such as the purchase of consumer products or attendance at beauty parlors. Captions celebrated the fact that women could now go unaccompanied to the market. One AP photograph from 24 February 2004 shows two Afghan women standing in front of a market stall in Kabul looking at nail polish. In contrast to a woman standing behind them wearing the face covering to her burqa, the two women in the center foreground have uncovered their faces and draped the cloth over their heads and shoulders (see figure 2). In case the viewer does not get the point, the caption explains that conditions have improved for women since the overthrow of the Taliban regime, although it does qualify this claim by stating that "strict Islamic culture still inhibits women from a greater role outside of their homes." Such descriptions encourage the viewer to peer at these women's faces for signs of exploitation or evidence of relief from suffering. Women are configured here as now-liberated agents in the marketplace, in contrast to the specter of indigenous masculinity found repeatedly in U.S. hegemonic discourses on terrorism.

As eye-catching advertisements for newly expressed public sexualities, locating Muslim women in the marketplace as the ideal transnational citizen-subjects reinforces an imperial narrative of liberation through neoliberal economic and military policies. Notably, this gendering of transnational citizenship underscores, as Kandice Chuh reminds us, "the history of coercion embedded in the very notion of the transnation."[43] Despite the wide range of veiling practices and their different political and social histories, photographs that depict the veil as monolithically oppressive circulate within a

2. Afghan women compare nail polish at an outdoor stall selling cosmetics in Kabul, Afghanistan, Tuesday, 24 February 2004. (Courtesy of Ed Wray/Associated Press)

broader field of cultural production, oriented by the anthropological gaze that invests this mode of dress with a culturally static premodern value. This, though, is not the only representation of gendered citizenships and subjectivities in present-day Afghanistan and Iraq.

Disruptions and Dischronicities

The news media have a tendency to conflate Afghanistan and Iraq as one geopolitical space. One of the many dangers in this conflation is that such representations often produce a nondistinct veiled female body that promises to show the place, the nation, and its people through a realist (and anthropological) gaze. Such representations constrain spectators' abilities to recognize citizenships that are noncompliant with the agendas of the *NSS* and uncritical liberal humanism. As much as narratives of rescue attempt to position Iraqi and Afghan women within a modernizing logic, other photographs contain polysemic signifiers that trouble such reductive concepts of citizenship. In the last section, we used the framework of dischronicity to explore how images such as the one of the mourners at Mahaweel or the Afghan woman in the burqa who smiles at the camera restage U.S. military actions as liberation. And yet, what are they being liberated from? Since the smiling woman continues to wear a burqa, to read this as only an orientalist depiction of a woman embracing secular modernity erases the complexities of the representation of this woman's subjectivity and agency. Here, to explore the politics of these depictions of citizenship, we reconsider how terms like "woman," and "citizen" are figured in the visual archive. It has been much harder in Iraq than in Afghanistan for the media and the Bush administration to make the case for liberation, especially since the widening of resistance and insurgency after the proclaimed victory in Iraq in May 2003. Pictures that challenge or disrupt the orientalist logic of rescue include those that do not conform to the stereotype of veiled women as imprisoned by religious practices. The veil as the symbol of gender oppression is a problematic narrative in Iraq for several reasons, including a longer history of feminist activism and the legal rights that women had under the Hussein regime. Moreover, secularism and religion have a very different historical trajectory in Iraq than in Afghanistan.[44] Finally, the extensive and violent resistance to U.S. invasion and occupation by Iraqi men and women has made the visual rescue scenario more difficult to secure.

A picture of thirty Iraqi Shiite women from the al-Medhi Army wearing pink- and green-colored chadors with green face veils protesting the U.S. occupation appeared on the front page of the *New York Times* in April 2004 (see figure 3). During a period of increasing opposition to the U.S. troops, images of women who have taken to the streets to decry the occupation clearly challenges at least one of the Bush administration's justifications for invasion. The scene of veiled Muslim women using their bodies in public protest also disrupts any simplistic narrative of veiling as a sign of oppression. Furthermore, these Shiite women's demands for the end of occupation and for Iraqi sovereignty are not, at least visually, based on individualism, one of the core tenets of Western concepts of citizenship. Rather, the visual rhetoric of anonymous women protesters in public space claims a citizenship that privileges community and religion over individualism.

Yet protesting in the streets does not necessarily mean an absence of exploitation or oppression. In avoiding reductive assumptions about either agency or exploitation, progressive and feminist critics face the challenge of producing social critique without reproducing orientalist narratives about Muslim patriarchy. Attempts to avoid this narrative, unfortunately, have

3. Female members of the al-Mehdi Army march in military formation during a military parade through the streets of the Sadr City neighborhood in East Baghdad, Iraq, 3 April 2004. (Courtesy of Scott Nelson/Getty Images)

often resulted in a defense of religious or cultural differences that ignores debates and contestations, especially feminist ones, within religious communities.[45] For critics of U.S. policies in the Middle East, it is crucial to resist either romanticizing or revictimizing women's positions within varied Islamic practices, both of which simplify understandings of race, religion, class, gender, and sexual identities.

In the photograph of the Shiite women protestors, one woman in the last visible row wears eyeglasses over her veil. Common sense tells us that people select various modes of dress, yet the U.S. news media rarely circulate photographs of Muslim women wearing eyeglasses in this manner. It does not fit either the representation of Islamic women embracing religious authority and rejecting modernity or the representation of women awaiting rescue and liberation. Rather than a uniform Muslim otherness, this small gesture of a woman veiled but not "hidden" reminds the viewer of the multiplicities of social and political practices that constitute identity. To state the obvious, one can both engage in religious practices and global culture, wear the veil and wear eyeglasses, and be a member of a particular community and a citizen of a nation-state.

The photograph of the women of the al-Medhi Army depicts not a static Islamic tradition but rather women who occupy multiple social positions, roles, and responsibilities, and who move through local, national, and transnational geographical, political, and cultural spaces of citizenship at once. As Lila Abu-Lughod writes in her discussion of Western feminists' relationships with non-Western women: "We may want justice for women, but can we accept that there might be different ideas about justice and that different women might want or choose different futures from what we envision as best? We must consider that they might be called to personhood, so to speak, in a different language."[46] The necessity of engaging with different languages of justice and rights is apparent in this picture of women who belong to an oppositional group that has participated in violence as a means of social change. Such images force us to confront the complex intersections between gender and aspects of identity formations that are themselves always tied to social structures of power.

A "different language" of citizenship is also apparent in several AP photographs taken on 1 March 2003 that feature a procession of Iraqi Shiite women in a public square in Baghdad walking toward the Al-Khullani Mosque at the beginning of the ten-day festival of Ashoura, a commemorative celebration of a saint, Imam Hussein. The pictures show women guarding the procession with AK-47 rifles, while the caption explains: "Security has been tightened around Iraq as Iraqi Shiites freely observed Ashoura which was banned during the regime of toppled dictator Saddam Hussein." In one picture, two women in the foreground stand in front of the crowd, holding their rifles across their bodies in confident postures of command (see figure 4). Their bodies and their rifles block the viewer from full access, as one must look past them to see the procession. These women neither smile in welcome nor angrily reject the camera. Instead, they stand in this public space and gaze out with vigilant, even grim, expressions. Disrupting Western assumptions about Muslim gender conventions, the guards claim citizenship rights in a space that the viewer is not invited to enter.

4. Iraqi women, armed with AK-47s guard the procession toward the Al-Khullani Mosque on the eve of the 10-day Shiite festival of Ashoura, the mourning of the death of one of their most important saints, Imam Hussein in Baghdad, Iraq, Monday, 1 March 2004. (Courtesy of Khalid Mohammed/Associated Press)

The ambivalence in these pictures resists simplistic readings and raises questions that cannot be answered without historical context. Most importantly, why the need for security if the Shiites are now free to observe this holy event? Is security required to guard against other Iraqis? Or are these women guarding their religious beliefs against the occupation forces? At the least, the presence of women with guns signals the violence that has accompanied U.S. military policies and indicates a broad range of social and religious civic practices that U.S. media rarely if ever explain. Most significantly, the image disrupts a racist vision of Islamic patriarchy, as these women occupy a public space of gendered citizenship based on belonging to a religious community. With this in mind, we can reconsider pictures such as the smiling Afghan woman who has removed the face covering of her burqa and the women purchasing nail polish. While these photographs conform more readily to the rescue scenario, they too depict women's political subjectivities within, not outside, religion.

The Ashoura photographs explicitly visualize a gendered Muslim citizenship that enables us to rethink the politics of inclusion and exclusion in media representations of the current war in Iraq. Paying attention to these complexities facilitates a transnational feminist practice that begins with the recognition of third-world women's embodied political subjectivities, including the complex interactions between victimization and agency. Lest we end up imagining women's agency as devoid of multiple and often exploitative constraints, however, we need to engage further with the ambiguities in the Ashoura photographs. As much as the women's rifles may protect participants, the picture also calls attention to the question of who in the procession is in attendance willingly. The photograph suggests protection from an outside threat but can also be read as an act of control over the crowd. The intimacy central to a liberal construction of citizenship is evident, as we pointed out earlier, in scenes of Afghan women shopping, whereby the private becomes the marker for participation in the public sphere. In the Ashoura photographs, women's protective, and perhaps coercive, position as guards armed with rifles visualizes a public sphere with tightly circumscribed boundaries. Analyzing the depiction of women's agency within specific social contexts and not simply assuming that it is a function of resistance enables us to grapple with the visual strategies by which U.S. news media represent the dynamics of globalization, militarization, and citizenship.

Conclusion

In uncanny anticipation of the Abu Ghraib photographs, the World Press Photo of the Year for 2003 features an Iraqi prisoner with a hood over his face sitting on the ground behind barbed wire with his four-year-old son in his lap.[47] In the photo, taken in Najaf, Iraq, on 31 March 2003, the photographer, Jean-Marc Bouju, depicts the father gently comforting his young son with his hand on the boy's forehead (see figure 5). As a response to the war and captivity, the intimacy of this gesture visualizes the man as a father, as an Iraqi, as a prisoner, and as a citizen of a nation at war. Even though we cannot see the man's face, we can approach the complexities of this historical moment through the suffering in his son's expression. Moreover, this moment of tender care challenges racist constructs of Arab men as brutal, patriarchal terrorists.

World Press Photo is an annual exhibition that features award-winning photojournalism in a variety of categories. The 2004 show traveled to approximately eighty cities; visitors walked into a variety of exhibition spaces, but all confronted an over-life-size reproduction of Bouju's photograph as the

5. An Iraqi prisoner comforts his son near Najaf, Iraq, 31 March 2003. (Courtesy of Jean-Marc Bouju/Associated Press)

first image of the show. As this picture circulates in a global cultural market, it performs different work in different venues. Globalization, transnational cultural, political, and economic mobilities, and current hegemonic news practices all necessitate a contingent reading of the visual archive on the war on terrorism. Proceeding from this recognition of looking as a contextualized act, it is possible to understand that the palimpsestic meanings of this image will become visible and traceable at different moments and to different spectators. Imagining the migration of this picture in these varied spaces troubles critiques that deploy simplistic binarisms of East/West, first/third world, colonizer/colonized.

Bouju's photograph foregrounds the ambivalent relationship between political subjectivity and spectatorship in the circulation of visual information in contemporary global media. One could read the intimacy of the father and son as a representation of progressive masculinity. Yet the framing of the sentimental family as the synecdoche for the captive nation limits the possibilities for a radical or alternative vision. If viewed through the frame of individual sentiment, the photograph can more easily serve as a moment of universal suffering. The picture emblematically calls for human rights: a call that need pay little attention to the material circumstances of this particular man and his son.

If viewed within the context of publication and in dialogue with other images circulating in global communications networks, however, this depiction of the captive father and son connects to local, national, and transnational geographical, political, and cultural spaces. Neither suffering nor political subjectivity, including citizenship, exists in isolation or outside historical contexts. Interestingly, the photographer refuses the conventional representation of the bound prisoner as abject and humiliated, while using the barbed wire in the foreground to distance the viewer from the subjects. The viewer can recognize the prisoner's political subjectivity as an Iraqi national under arrest, yet this distancing troubles any easy move of empathy since it positions the viewer in the same location as the soldiers with whom the photographer is embedded. The terms of citizenship mobilized here thus do not invoke an ideal status (for instance, freedom or liberty) but are fraught with the tensions of belonging to a community, in this case a community at war.

In exploring representations of gendered citizenship in U.S. news coverage, this essay argues that the rhetorical aspects of the war on terrorism include varied, and sometimes competing, visual depictions of citizenship. The portrait of the prisoner and his son is an example of how this archive contains various representational webs of citizenship such as national, transnational, global consumer, religious, and oppositional identities.

Like the eyeglasses in the photograph of the Shiite woman protester, the boy's sneakers that sit unattended in the foreground of Bouju's photograph serve as a reminder of the intersections of the quotidian and brutal aspects of life during military conflicts. When turning to news coverage of the war on terrorism, which too often suppresses how people live within the interstices of multiple citizenships and belongings, these small elements remind us to consider the relationship between visibility and political knowledge. In the visual archive of the war on terror, the representational politics of the everyday constitute citizenship in varied and not always predictable ways, alongside the policy formations that confer privileges of access and belonging.

NOTES

Working collaboratively has been an enriching experience for both of us. In addition, we are grateful to Meredith Raimondo, Rachel Buff, Joe Austin, Haley Pollack and Steven Wojtal for their support and critical feedback. We also appreciate the opportunity to present this work at the 2004 American Studies Association meeting, Oberlin College, the History Department at the University of Wisconsin, Milwaukee, and the Media Studies Program at the University of Sussex. Most of all, many, many thanks to Andrew Martin and Patrice Petro.

1 See for example, Luc Sante, "Tourists and Torturers," *New York Times*, 11 May 2004; and Susan Sontag, "Regarding the Torture of Others," *New York Times Magazine*, 23 May 2004, 24–29.

2 Judith Butler, *Undoing Gender* (New York: Routledge, 2004), 37.

3 For this study, we reviewed Associated Press photographs of Afghanistan and Iraq from the AccuNet/AP Multimedia Archive, because it is one of the two largest producers of visual news in the world. See. e.g., Ted Madger, "Watching What We Say: Global Communication in a Time of Fear," in Daya Kishan Thussu and Des Freedman, eds., *War and the Media: Reporting Conflict 24/7* (London: Sage, 2003), 28–44. In addition, we surveyed a range of progressive online and print publications about the war on terrorism using the same time frame, including *Electronic Iraq*, *Ms.*, *Mother Jones*, *Nation*, *Salon.com*, and *WarTimes.com*.

4 The 2002 National Security Strategy states in the introduction that "the United States security strategy will be based on a distinctly American internationalism that reflects the union of our values and our national interests. The aim of this strategy is to help make the world not just safer but better. Our goals on the path to progress are clear: political and economic freedom, peaceful relations with other states and respect for human dignity" (*The National Security Strategy of the United States of America*, September 2002, 1, www.whitehouse.gov/nsc/nss.html).

5 See for example, Thussu and Freedman, eds., *War and the Media*; and Lynn Spigel, "Entertainment Wars: Television Culture after 9/11," *American Quarterly* 56, 2 (June 2004): 235–270.

6 Robin Brown, "Spinning the War: Political Communications, Information Operations, and Public Diplomacy in the War on Terrorism," in Thussu and Freedman, eds., *War and the Media*, 87–100.

7 See, e.g., Caroline Brothers, *War and Photography: A Cultural History* (London: Routledge, 1997); Michael Griffin, "The Great War Photographs: Constructing Myths of History and Photojournalism," in Bonnie Brennen and Hanno Hardt, eds., *Picturing the Past: Media, History, and Photography* (Urbana: University of Illinois Press, 1999), 121–157; and Wendy Kozol, "Domesticating NATO's War in Kosovo: (In) Visible Bodies and the Dilemma of Photojournalism," *Meridians: Feminism, Transnationalism, Race* 4, 2 (2004): 1–38.

8 Michael Griffin and Jongsoo Lee, "Picturing the Gulf War: Constructing an Image of War in *Time, Newsweek*, and *U.S. News & World Report*," *Journalism and Mass Communication Quarterly* 72, 4 (winter 1995): 821.

9 See, e.g., John Beverly, *Testimonio: On the Politics of Truth* (Minneapolis: University of Minnesota Press, 2004), 27.

10 Melanie McAlister persuasively argues that U.S. cultural representations since the 1950s often depict the Middle East in ways that continue to produce racist discourses but work outside the logic of orientalism; see *Epic Encounters: Culture, Media, and U.S. Interests in the Middle East, 1945–2000* (Berkeley: University of California Press, 2001). One of the notable elements of the visual archive of the war on terrorism, however, has been the revitalization of an orientalist scenario. Alison Donnell, for instance, argues that an earlier orientalist gaze in which the veiled woman is an object of exoticism and eroticism has been replaced since 9/11 by a more xenophobic and specifically Islamaphobic "gaze through which the veil, or headscarf is seen as a highly visible sign of despised difference" ("Visibility, Violence, and Voice? Attitudes to Veiling Post-11 September," in David A. Bailey and Gilane Tawadros, eds., *Veil: Veiling, Representation and Contemporary Art* [Cambridge: MIT Press, 2003], 122–123).

11 See, e.g., Lila Abu-Lughod, "Do Muslim Women Really Need Saving? Anthropological Reflections on Cultural Relativism and Its Others," *American Anthropologist* 104, 3 (2002): 783–790; and Annabelle Sreberny, "Unsuitable Coverage: The Media, the Veil, and Regimes of Representation," in Tasha G. Oren and Patrice Petro, eds., *Global Currents: Media and Technology Now* (New Brunswick, N.J.: Rutgers University Press, 2004), 171–185.

12 See, e.g., Sharon Smith, "Using Women's Rights to Sell Washington's War," *International Socialist Review* 21 (January–February 2002); Abu-Lughod, "Do Muslim Women Really Need Saving?"; and Amy Farrell and Patrice McDermott, "Claiming Afghan Women: The Challenge of Human Rights Discourse for Transnational Feminism," in Wendy Hesford and Wendy Kozol, eds., *Just Advocacy? Women's Human Rights, Transnational Feminisms, and the Politics of Representation* (New Brunswick, N.J.: Rutgers University Press, 2005), 33–55.

13 Therese Saliba, "Military Presences and Absences: Arab Women and the Persian Gulf War," in Susan Jeffords and Lauren Rabinovitz, eds., *Seeing through the Media: The Persian Gulf War* (New Brunswick, N.J.: Rutgers University Press, 1994), 263–284. Among the extensive field of Middle East and North African feminist

studies, see, e.g., Lila Abu-Lughod, ed., *Remaking Women: Feminism and Modernity in the Middle East* (Princeton, N.J.: Princeton University Press, 1998); and Saud Joseph and Susan Slyomvoics, eds., *Women and Power in the Middle East* (Philadelphia: University of Pennsylvania Press, 2001).

14 Shahnaz Khan, "Between Here and There: Feminist Solidarity and Afghan Women," *Genders 33* (2001), www.genders.org.

15 Abu-Lughod, "Do Muslim Women Really Need Saving?" 787.

16 Patricia Yaeger, "Consuming Trauma; or the Pleasures of Merely Circulating," in Nancy K. Miller and Jason Tougaw, eds., *Extremities: Trauma, Testimony, and Community* (Urbana: University of Illinois Press, 2002), 25–54.

17 Seymour Hersh first reported the story in "Torture at Abu Ghraib: American Soldiers Brutalized Iraqis: How Far Does the Responsibility Go?" *New Yorker*, 10 May 2004. The *Washington Post* had some of the most extensive reporting on the photographs; see, e.g., Christian Davenport, "New Prison Images Emerge," www.Washingtonpost.com, 6 May 2004.

18 See Butler, *Undoing Gender*, 37

19 See Lauren Berlant, *The Queen of America Goes to Washington City: Essays on Sex and Citizenship* (Durham, N.C.: Duke University Press, 1997); Linda Bosniak, "Citizenship Denationalized," *Indiana Journal of Global Legal Studies* 7 (spring 2000): 447; and Leti Volpp, "The Citizen and the Terrorist," in Mary L. Dudziak, ed., *September 11 in History: A Watershed Moment?* (Durham, N.C.: Duke University Press, 2003), 147–162.

20 See "AR 15-6 Investigation of the Abu Ghraib Prison and the 205th Military Intelligence Brigade," 24 August 2004. For the Executive Summary of this investigation, see www.defenselink.mil/news/Aug2004/d20040825fay.pdf.

21 Jasbir K. Puar, "Abu Ghraib: Arguing against Exceptionalism," *Feminist Studies* 30, 2 (summer 2004): 522–534.

22 For critiques of this commentary, see Puar, "Abu Ghraib;" and Frances Hasso, "Reflections on Sexuality, Gender, Race, Orientalisms, and Empire: The Tortures of Iraqis in Abu Ghraib and Elsewhere," paper presented at "Transnational Feminist Sociologies: Current Challenges, Future Directions" conference, University of California, Berkeley, 13 August 2004.

23 Hersh, "Torture at Abu Ghraib." Subsequent reporting has continued to reproduce this stereotype of Muslim homophobia.

24 Hasso, "Reflections on Sexuality."

25 See, e.g., Patrick Moore, "Weapons of Mass Homophobia," *The Advocate*, 8 June 2004, www.advocate.com; and Barbara Ehrenreich, "What Abu Ghraib Taught Me," *AlterNet*, posted 20 May 2004, www.alternet.org.

26 Thomas Keenan, "Mobilizing Shame," *South Atlantic Quarterly* 103: 2/3 (spring/summer 2004): 435.

27 Judith Butler, "Giving an Account of Oneself," *Diacritics* 31, 4 (February 2004): 23.

28 See Catherine Lutz, *Homefront: A Military City and the American 20th Century* (Boston: Beacon Press, 2001), who discusses the promise of citizenship through military service offered to soldiers of color.

29 Berlant, *The Queen Goes to America*, esp. 1–24.

30 On Guantánamo, see Amy Kaplan, "Homeland Insecurities: Transformations of Language and Space," in Dudziak, ed., *September 11 in History*, 55–69.

31 See AccuNet/AP Multimedia Archive online database.

32 *National Security Strategy*, 1.

33 Volpp, "The Citizen and the Terrorist." See also Kaplan's analysis of the Bush administration's use of terms like "terror," "terrorism," and "homeland security" in "Homeland Insecurities."

34 *National Security Strategy*, 9.

35 Diana Taylor's discussion of "scenario" provides a useful theoretical frame to understand how rescue narratives can reproduce enduring orientalist tropes while continuously responding to historical currents; see *The Archive and the Repertoire: Performing Cultural Memory in the Americas* (Durham, N.C.: Duke University Press, 2003), 28.

36 Bosniak, "Citizenship Denationalized," 483, 489, 493. Bosniak also warns of the difficulties with claims of transnational citizenship that are linked to international human rights regimes. As she notes, such claims risk "overstating the degree to which the international human rights regime actually protects the individual" (469).

37 Alexander Zemlianichenko, "Iraqi women walk passing plastic bags containing remains of bodies pulled from a mass grave in Mahaweel, 60 miles south of Baghdad, central Iraq, Thursday, May 15, 2003," Associated Press, AccuNet/AP Multimedia Archive online database.

38 For a discussion of the problematics of documenting trauma in visual culture, see, e.g., Andrea Liss, *Trespassing through Shadows: Memory, Photography, and the Holocaust* (Minneapolis: University of Minnesota Press, 1998).

39 Sreberny, "Unsuitable Coverage," 175.

40 Ella Shohat, "Rupture and Return: Zionist Discourse and the Study of Arab Jews," *Social Text* 21, 2 (summer 2003): 49–74.

41 *National Security Strategy*, 17–18.

42 This agenda has become evident most recently in Iraq, where the Coalition Provisional Army established laws favorable to foreign investment. See, e.g., Mary Lou Malig, "War: Trade by Other Means: How the U.S. Is Getting a Free Trade Agreement Minus the Negotiations," *Znet*, 20 July 2004, www.zmag.org.

43 Kandice Chuh, "Transnationalism and Its Pasts," *Public Culture* 9, 1 (1996): 94.

44 See, e.g., Saliba, "Military Presences and Absences"; Abu-Lughod, "Do Muslim Women Really Need Saving?"; and Sreberny, "Unsuitable Coverage."

45 Madhavi Sunder, "Piercing the Veil," in Hesford and Kozol, eds., *Just Advocacy*, 266–290. See also Abu-Lughod, "Do Muslim Women Really Need Saving?"

46 Abu-Lughod, "Do Muslim Women Really Need Saving?" 787–788.

47 *World Press Photo 04* (New York: Thames and Hudson, 2004), 4–5.

PICTURING TORTURE

GULF WARS PAST AND PRESENT

TONY GRAJEDA

A series of public events unfolded in April 2004 that pointed to the significance of image culture in what had become a media war over the war in Iraq.
The first involved news coverage of the siege of Fallujah, where fierce fighting
had claimed the lives of at least a dozen U.S. marines and, by many accounts,
more than six hundred Iraqi civilians, including women and children. As
reported by Knight Ridder Newspapers on 11 April military spokesperson
Brigadier General Mark Kimmitt addressed the growing crisis during a regular news briefing in Iraq. An Iraqi journalist asked the senior U.S. military
officer about televised images broadcast on Arabic-language newscasts,
in particular that of grisly footage showing dead Iraqi civilians. Kimmitt
responded: "My solution is change the channel."[1]

Later in the month, photographs of flag-draped coffins of U.S. soldiers,
loaded onto a cargo plane from Iraq to be transported to Dover Air Force Base
in Delaware, were published by the *Seattle Times* and posted on the Memory
Hole Web site. The cargo workers who had taken the photos were swiftly
fired by their employer, Department of Defense contractor Maytag Aircraft
Corporation, reportedly for violating the Pentagon's strict ban on images of
dead soldiers.[2] By the end of April, two more media events would add fuel to
the fire in the battle over images in this "war on terror." First, the ABC News
show *Nightline* aired a special program, "The Fallen," in which anchor Ted
Koppel read a solemn roll call of the more than seven hundred U.S. service
people killed in Iraq to date. The Sinclair Broadcast Group, which owns sixty-
two U.S. television stations in thirty-nine markets, ordered its ABC affiliates
to preempt the broadcast, issuing a statement that the program "appears to

be motivated by a political agenda designed to undermine the efforts of the United States in Iraq."[3] Then, at the end of the month, photographs emerged of Iraqi prisoners held at Abu Ghraib Detention Facility. These photos revealed abuse, if not torture, at the hands of U.S. military personnel.

Both the production and suppression of images—their subsequent circulation and reception that have been so crucial to the representation and perception of the Iraq War—are not new developments. Indeed, a struggle over images was also very much at stake in the Gulf War in 1991. In the wake of that war, as James Castonguay has argued, "studies of Gulf war TV have focused on news programming in an attempt to expose lies, document the complicity of the networks with the global postindustrial-military-media complex (and the Bush administration), and reveal the formal conventions and representational strategies of Gulf war news." Yet, as Castonguay also notes, such scholarly work "has been done at the expense of any sustained examination of fictional programming."[4] What intervened in the years between the wars in the battle over what could and couldn't be shown publicly included a handful of intriguing fictional accounts of the first Gulf War that staged this very dispute over the image. What concerns me in this essay, then, is not only the actual wars erupting within and across the terrain of global media but also the fictional forms of those wars and, moreover, the possibility that a work of critical fiction can at least momentarily interrupt the circuit of mass-mediated representations.

Consider, for example, David O. Russell's 1999 film *Three Kings*, one of the few U.S. films to date about the first Gulf War and one that offers a rather unflattering depiction of U.S. motives. Of course, what we might now call the first Gulf War triggered a good deal of popular and academic commentary dominated by notions of postmodern spectacle—war as video game, simulacra, and the limits (if not the impossibility) of representation. Perhaps working against this notion of a purely virtual war, *Three Kings* foregrounds the ways in which what took place in 1991 was a "media war," with the real war obscured or rendered invisible by commercial media and high theory alike. *Three Kings* thus contributes to the historical memory of first Gulf War in a fairly critical way and, given the extent to which the current Gulf War echoes the first, I want to suggest how the film's afterimage anticipates or at least resonates with Gulf War II. Indeed, by visualizing the death and destruction that the military managed to conceal, as well as providing a back story of historical context to U.S. involvement in Iraq, the film not only questions U.S.

ambitions behind such interventions but also insists that the war itself was not beyond the realm of representation.

More specifically, *Three Kings* challenges the blinding spectacle of a technowar seemingly without bodies by explicitly focusing on bodies in pain. This attempt to return casualties of war to the field of vision has a visceral resonance in light of the "shock and awe" campaign of the second Gulf War, in which a concerted erasure of bodies has once again haunted our screens. Until, that is, the pictures of torture emerged from Abu Ghraib prison. In comparison to the interrogation scenes in *Three Kings*, in which a U.S. soldier is tortured not for information but for (re)education, the photographs of U.S. soldiers torturing Iraqi prisoners signify something else altogether. Against the idea of "torture warrants" that rationalizes the gathering of intelligence as that which is extracted from a body (fictionalized, for instance, in the now-cancelled ABC series on Homeland Security, *Threat Matrix*, as well as in the suddenly all-too-relevant film *The Battle of Algiers*), the Abu Ghraib imagery reveals a regime of signification closer to sadistic racism and sexualized violence.

The photographs themselves also demand that we revisit the debate on the ontology of the image. As digital photos circulating throughout various media channels, these images must be read within the larger context of digital technology's destabilization of the relation between the referent and its representation, and the apparent indeterminacy of the image in postmodern media culture. In spite of attempts by the military and some media organizations to recontextualize and deconstruct the images (highly reminiscent of the struggle over meaning with the Rodney King video, this time augmented by a certain strain of conspiratorial chatter on the Web), I suggest that such pictures of torture have provided irrefutable "bodies of evidence," signifying unambiguously a politics and logic of forcing a body under duress to surrender meaning—not as information or intelligence but as proof of the brutal display of power and domination. As such, these images could be said to bear witness to the repressive apparatus of the global war on terror, in effect raising questions around an ethics of seeing.

"This is a Media War": The Gulf War on Film

On 1 May 2003, President George W. Bush landed aboard the U.S.S *Abraham Lincoln* to immodestly declare before the cameras: "Mission accomplished." Not long afterward, a story surfaced that U.S. soldiers had been caught attempting to sneak out of Iraq with "war booty." According to *Time* magazine, soldiers of the Third Infantry Division guarding Saddam International Airport had "helped themselves to items in the duty-free shop, including alcohol, cassettes, perfume, cigarettes and expensive watches." A U.S. military official is quoted as saying: "Soldiers do this stuff all the time, everywhere. It's warfare. . . . These are just bored soldiers."[5] This story was mostly lost amidst all the reports of widespread looting following the fall of Baghdad, especially the looting of the National Museum of Iraq. In this regard, it's worth noting that an engineer for Fox News, Benjamin James Johnson, who had been embedded with U.S. troops, was caught smuggling monetary bonds and some twelve paintings from Iraq.[6]

This incident of military looting recalled one of the narrative threads in the film *Three Kings*, in which U.S. soldiers pursue gold bullion "boosted" from Kuwait by Iraqi forces. What this and other such examples suggest is that the film has acquired something of a second life, or afterimage, in the wake of the more recent Gulf War. This notion of the film's afterimage should not be mistaken for Jean Baudrillard's ruminations on the simulacrum. For Baudrillard, the representation, as with his example of *The China Syndrome*, preceded the real; thus the disaster at Three Mile Island was only a simulation of what had already taken place on film.[7] I want to argue not for a mere reversal in the sequence, but for a critical recognition of the mutual imbrication and circulation of texts, in which, for example, a work such as *Three Kings*—narrating the role of mainstream media during the Gulf War and thus foregrounding its own status as a mediated text—occasions a moment of reflection on the processes and procedures of mediation at large. It thus allows attention to be drawn toward the otherwise underacknowledged media amnesia accruing around the latest conflict, and thereby potentially returns us to the ground of history itself.

Short of wondering whether we have always been at war with Iraq, the events leading up to March 2003 could be confused, if one didn't know better, with those leading up to January 1991. After all, the principal players returned—Dick Cheney, Donald Rumsfeld, Colin Powell, Paul Wolfowitz—while a President Bush is once more commander-in-chief. And lest we forget, the shifting series of rationales for the first Gulf War are also back: from humanitarian intervention against Iraqi aggression and brutality (recall the Free Kuwait lobby and the manufactured baby-incubator story); followed by an argument that the impending war was to protect oil reserves (or U.S. "interests" in the region); and finally, the demonization of Saddam himself, with Bush the First calling him "Hitler revisited" and hyperbolizing Saddam's efforts to acquire weapons of mass destruction, including nuclear weapons.[8]

My point is that a theory propounding how the reality of war has disappeared behind a screen of empty signs seems seductive, and at the very least, it is abetted by a mostly decontextualized and ahistorical universe of mass-media news. The true scandal, then, has been the corporate media's refusal or reluctance to draw sufficient attention to the parallels between the two wars, in particular the rationales marshaled by the administrations for why the country needed to go to war in the first (and second) place.

As countless commentators have noted, the 1991 Gulf War was presented as a grand spectacle—a dramatic made-for-TV movie broadcast live, with round-the-clock coverage by CNN, among other outlets, framed by stunning graphics and portentous music, and featuring, of course, eye-popping special effects. In short, it seemed ready-made for a big-screen treatment. Yet the Gulf War has for the most part eluded a Hollywood makeover. It's not as if the past decade or more has been bereft of war movies, since the genre is clearly flourishing, not only with such nostalgic epics on World War II as *Saving Private Ryan* and *Pearl Harbor* but also with its eternal return to Vietnam, an evidently never-ending battleground between, on the one hand, redeeming the war (*Forrest Gump* or *We Were Soldiers*) and, on the other, recalling it as trauma and nightmare (e.g., *Tigerland*). These more familiar narrative tropes, however, have gained little footing in telling the tale of the Gulf War, encountering a difficulty in being translated into what Colin MacCabe calls "classical realist cinema," which privileges the personal over the political. As George Gerbner argues: "The war in the Persian Gulf was an unprecedented moving picture spectacular," and yet the kind of technowar on display in 1991 did not lend itself to the genre's reliance on personalized experiences (those individual acts of heroism demanded by narrative cinema).[9]

One exception is Edward Zwick's *Courage Under Fire* (1996). In this rather conventional war movie, the issue of friendly fire plays a pivotal role. As such, the film contributes to the tradition of narcissism that underwrites so many Vietnam films, since here the real tragedy of the Gulf War is U.S. soldiers killing each other. The plot of *Courage Under Fire* involves an investigation into the merits of a posthumous candidate for the Congressional Medal of Honor, a nominee who would be the first woman to be awarded the nation's highest recognition for bravery. The drama issues from competing and conflicting testimony from various witnesses to the event in question. While highlighting the function of memory and interpretation in the search for what really happened, in the end, as might be expected, the truth will out. In *Courage Under Fire*, the military can be trusted to police itself—to restore honor, order, truth itself—in the process extending the Gulf War triumph of restoring the military's own image.[10]

Against such moral certainty, as well as the political rhetoric of the day— "a line in the sand"—*Three Kings* serves to blur the line, offering a far more ambiguous treatment of the war. It does so on several fronts: by sundering American uniformity behind U.S. involvement in the Gulf region, the film depicts tension and division within the ranks; by deprivileging the grunt's-eye view that typically provides access to otherwise inaccessible knowledge of the conflict, the film renders those on the ground in a perpetual state of confusion and ignorance; against the narcissistic tradition of U.S. war movies (to which we might now add *Courage Under Fire*), the film offers at least two counterperspectives from competing Iraqi interests. *Three Kings* answers the constructed spectacle of a technowar without bodies by grimly depicting bodies in pain, representing the carnage that the U.S. military had censored so skillfully. Finally, within and against the spectacle itself, the film foregrounds the extent to which, as one character puts it, "this is a media war."

A number of these issues are set in motion with the opening credits. *Three Kings* opens with a title—"March 1991. The war just ended." This is followed by a bleached-out shot of a few U.S. soldiers patrolling what's identified as the Kuwaiti desert. Sergeant Troy Barlow (Mark Wahlberg) spots what appears to be an Iraqi soldier in the distance. Barlow asks his comrades, "Are we shooting people, or what?" No one seems to know. Noticing that the man is waving a white flag ambiguously attached to a gun, Barlow opens fire and runs up to find the man convulsing on the ground, gasping for air, and spitting blood. Barlow turns away with his head in his hands, as another soldier eagerly has his snapshot taken with the body. Along with a gruesome death, then, the film already suggests a far messier portrait of the Gulf War than the military's sanitized package featuring precision aerial bombing and smart bombs that turned out to be not so smart after all.[11]

As a counterargument to the war as a clear-cut battle of good versus evil, where *we* are indivisible, *Three Kings* stitches divisiveness within the ranks, implying as much from the outset through its soundtrack. Shots of

U.S. soldiers celebrating the announced ceasefire (and the official end of
the war) are accompanied by a diegetic montage of three pop songs: Lee
Greenwood's "God Bless the U.S.A.," the 1984 country hit that became the
unofficial anthem of the Gulf War; Public Enemy's "I Can't Do Nuttin' for
Ya Man," a track from, significantly, 1990's *Fear of a Black Planet*; and Rare
Earth's "(I Just Want to) Celebrate," that crestfallen farewell to the coun-
terculture with its memorable line, "Put my faith in the people, but the
people let me down." The incongruous mix here, in which the songs overlap
but remain distinct, signifies through sound a sense less of unity than of
unease, not harmony but dissension—the audible dimensions of the ambiguity of this war.

Such ambivalence gives way to chaos as the film dives into the turmoil
of a complicated regional conflict fatally oversimplified for domestic U.S.
consumption. Here one might point to the ways in which *Three Kings* also
cuts against the grain of film history, especially the view of history offered by
those Vietnam films that reduce geopolitical mappings to the ground-level
grasping of the common soldier. In what might be called a "grunt epistemology," such films as *Platoon* privilege personal experience over historical
understanding.[12] The grunts in *Three Kings*, however, are largely ignorant of
the politics that brought them to the Gulf—both a Southern lumpen-cracker
and a Northern postindustrial prole are equally oblivious to wider events.

At the same time, the purpose behind the war is repeatedly called into
question, as when a pair of officers argues about what they have accomplished. "I don't even know what we did here," says Special Forces major
Archie Gates (George Clooney). "The war is over and I don't know what the
fuck it was about," to which his fellow officer responds, "Do you want to
occupy Iraq and do Vietnam all over again?" Similar questions are raised
by one of the reporters in the film, who begins interviewing an officer with
another loaded refrain: "They say you exorcised the ghost of Vietnam with a
clear moral imperative"—a distinct reference to remarks by General Norman
Schwarzkopf and George H. W. Bush that reverberate into the current debate
on Iraq becoming a "quagmire."

The role of the media is crucial here. *Three Kings* offers a form of skepticism not inconsistent with an old-fashioned project of demystification. For
example, it draws attention to the media-pool system and the military's
success at channeling the flow of information. As the TV reporter Adriana
Cruz (Nora Dunn) complains: "I was managed by the military," extending her

analysis to include the "sexual politics of this business"—that is, commercial media—that favors style over substance. While not exactly self-reflexive, the film does feature several moments of frames within frames, in particular of television sets that inhabit the mise-en-scène, seeming to appear everywhere, even in the desert. One scene juxtaposes a TV set broadcasting news with TV news in the process of production. Iraqi soldiers are shown watching "NBS" on TV (the stand-in CNN network) as it airs the reporter's piece taped earlier in the film of U.S. soldiers celebrating. This is juxtaposed with Adriana's attempts to start a new report, interrupted at first by her own cameraman, who points out that she already used the phrase "gritty city," before Iraqi soldiers step in to stop the taping, at which point one says to the other: "She's much shorter in person." Another embedded TV appears in a scene of Iraqi soldiers relaxing in a bunker, watching the Rodney King video footage. The sight of a body being beaten is no accident. One of the more radical gestures offered by *Three Kings* is simply a return to the body, the visibility of which has been very much at stake—then and now.

Casualties of war in *Three Kings* are indeed returned to the field of vision—unblinking shots of death and dying, of bodies in distress, of corpses scorched beyond recognition. At one point there is a discussion of what wasn't shown on CNN, such as Iraqi soldiers being buried alive. This is followed by an in-country anatomy lesson on what happens when a bullet pierces flesh, illustrated by a graphic shot zooming through a body (much like a bullet itself). In *Three Kings* the internal view of a body and the sight of damaged organs has the visceral effect of revealing what technowar aims to conceal, reminding us that the purpose of war is, in Elaine Scarry's words, "to alter (to burn, to blast, to shell, to cut) human tissue."[13]

As Douglas Kellner explains in regard to the first Gulf War: "The military and media kept daily tally of the score of Iraqi tanks and equipment eliminated, though the sanitized war coverage contained no 'body count'; figures and images of wounded or dead soldiers were strictly forbidden." And as Douglas Kahn points out in a piece called "Body Lags," the "surgical war" in the Gulf was successful to the extent that "bodies, tens upon thousands of them, were removed from representation." A dozen years later, in the "shock and awe" campaign of the second Gulf War, a similar erasure of bodies haunts our screens. The "spectacularly televised air-strikes," as Cynthia Fuchs notes, conveniently failed to "produce bodies for TV," thus satisfying official policy in which "the U.S. military, in charge of this version of embedded TV, refuses to 'keep track of civilian casualties'."[14] As General Tommy Franks famously stated, "We don't do body counts."

While repeatedly drawing attention to the image of bodies that at the time were "removed from representation," *Three Kings* also enacts an aspect of war that almost without fail remains hidden from view—the sight of torture. In one of its more pronounced afterimages, as a text that anticipated the crisis around Abu Ghraib, the film stages a quite brutal interrogation scene that illuminates a range of issues under examination here.

The scene opens with a close-up on the face of Troy Barlow, who has been captured by Saddam Hussein's Republican Guards and is being held in a bunker. As an Iraqi soldier wraps around Barlow's ears and chin bare wire that is connected to an electrical device, an interrogator, Captain Said (Said Taghmaoui), begins his questioning by asking Barlow, "What is the problem with Michael Jackson?" Barlow is perplexed. Said, appropriating American slang and speaking in slightly broken English, insists: "Michael Jackson is Pop King of sick fucking country." Barlow protests, "That's bullshit," to which Said replies: "It is so obvious: The black man make the skin white and the hair straight. You know why? Your sick fucking country make the black man hate himself, just like you hate the Arab and the children you bomb over here." When asked if his army cares about the children in Iraq, whether or not they are coming back to help, Barlow says: "No, they're not coming back." Said then signals to the soldier working the electrical equipment, and the shot cuts to a close-up of his hand turning a knob on the console; at once the camera races down the wire as if chasing the voltage rushing to Barlow's body. A close-up of Barlow gnashing his teeth and struggling against the electrical charge is cut with a close-up of the Iraqi soldier at the console, who can barely bring himself to look upon the scene of torture. Averting his eyes, covering them with his hand, this witness is anything but pleased. He is clearly afraid to look directly upon the horror; what comes over his face is an unmistakable look of shame that will haunt many such scenes that follow.

Stopping the electrical shock, Said tells Barlow that his own infant son was killed in the bombing. Barlow responds that since he has an infant girl, they share the experience of being fathers. Said then asks: "Can you think how it feels inside your heart if I bombed your daughter?" "Worse than death," cries Barlow. "That's right," says Said. "Worse than death." The interrogation then turns more explicitly political, as each soldier relates the economic reasons motivating their decisions to join the army—"to make a good living for my family" and "for the extra cash." Said then informs Barlow that he received his "training" from Americans during Iraq's war with Iran. "What did they train you in?" asks Barlow. "Weapons, sabotage, interrogation." A final discussion entails the reasons behind the Gulf War, with Barlow insisting that the United States was fighting to "save" Kuwait and to "stabilize the region." Said disabuses him of this fiction by pouring crude oil into his mouth. "This is your fucking stability, my main man."

Here and elsewhere, the film ties U.S. racism to U.S. imperialism, which in turn is tied to the globalization of Western commodity culture, while reminding us of U.S. complicity historically in Saddam Hussein's power over Iraq. What is also offered is a moment of, dare one say, humanist connection between the two figures, articulated precisely through the subjectivity of class—that in fact what mobilizes soldiering has more to do with economic desperation than with the ideological imperatives of God and country.[15]

An altogether different scene of torture appeared in the short-lived ABC TV show on homeland security, *Threat Matrix*. In an episode that aired in October 2003 (precisely when the Abu Ghraib crimes were first being documented), an "enemy combatant" held by the unnamed "counterterrorism" team at Guantánamo Bay dies during interrogation (rather benignly, since his interrogators merely deny him medicine). The prisoner, identified as an Algerian national, surrenders vital information before dying, and this leads to the interception of a terrorist act, thus serving to justify the torture at a time when the idea of "torture warrants" had been floated as a reasonable route to security.[16] In comparison, the scene in *Three Kings* regards the use of torture not to extract information but rather to (re)educate. In yet a third scene of torture, from a nearly forty-year-old film that has suddenly returned with something of a vengeance, the practice itself is sundered, like that of the body subjected to it, as a "method" that might work in the short term but, regardless of ethical concerns, will inevitably fail, irreparably if unevenly distributing its damage to tortured and torturer alike.

"A Cruel Necessity": Watching Torture and The Battle of Algiers

In late summer 2003, the Pentagon held a screening of *The Battle of Algiers*, Gillo Pontecorvo's 1966 film portraying the Algerian struggle for independence from French colonial rule, a war that stretched from 1954 to 1962. As reported in the *New York Times*, the screening was promoted with a flier that offered the following enticement: "How to win a battle against terrorism and lose the war of ideas. Children shoot soldiers at point-blank range. Women plant bombs in cafes. Soon the entire Arab population builds to a mad fervor. Sound familiar? The French have a plan. It succeeds tactically, but fails strategically. To understand why, come to a rare showing of this film."[17]

According to the *Times*, the screening was attended by about forty officers and civilian experts associated with the Directorate for Special Operations and Low-Intensity Conflict. It prompted a discussion of the "implicit issues" of the film, in particular, "the problematic but alluring efficacy of brutal and repressive means in fighting clandestine terrorists in places like Algeria and Iraq," along with "the advantages and costs of resorting to torture and intimidation in seeking vital intelligence about enemy plans."[18]

Revisiting Pontecorvo's film when the Iraq War has mutated from "mission accomplished" to unending "quagmire" is indeed instructive, but in ways perhaps the Pentagon would just as soon not advertise. *The Battle of Algiers* stages the historical events of 1954–1957, focusing on the 1957 siege of the Casbah, the city's old Muslim quarter, when the French called in their military to crush an insurgency organized by the National Liberation Front (FLN). Led by Colonel Mathieu (Jean Martin), the character based on General Jacques Massu (the actual military commander of the French forces in Algeria), the colonial response to the "terrorism" of the colonized is not only militarization but also rationalization, a process that ultimately leads to the practice of torture as a rational form of the empire's defense.

Before delineating their enemy's tactics and organizational structure, during an initial military briefing with his officers, Mathieu holds a movie screening of his own, here of surveillance film taken by the local police. Military headquarters becomes a makeshift theatre, as shades are drawn and a movie projector operated for the assembled audience. Mathieu's mostly off-screen voice works to narrativize the silent footage of people in the streets or being searched at police checkpoints, interspersed with seemingly random images of daily life during wartime:

> Anonymous and unrecognizable, it [the enemy] mingles with the crowd. It is everywhere: in the cafes, in the alleys of its ghetto, in the streets of the French city, in stores, in work areas. Films were taken by the police with hidden cameras. The police thought these films could be useful. And they are. They demonstrate the futility of certain methods and their disadvantages. I deliberately chose these films

taken just before several recent terrorist incidents. Therefore, the culprits are among these Arab men and women. Which ones are they? How can we recognize them? Checking identification is ridiculous. If anyone's papers are in order, it's the terrorists'.

The footage accompanying these questions posed by Mathieu is of a scene from earlier in *The Battle of Algiers*, when one of the Algerian women, Hassiba (Fasia El Kader), having dyed her hair blonde and Westernized her look with makeup and dress, passes as a European to elude detection, even flirting with a French soldier as she is en route to planting a bomb in a café.[19]

This film within a film takes on additional significance in its current appropriation by the U.S. military, given that Pontecorvo includes several shots of the officers themselves watching the surveillance footage. But the mirror of identification aligning the French elite forces with the Pentagon's is only "useful," as Mathieu stated, for its uselessness in showing what it could never discover: the very identity of the "enemy."

Following the screening, Mathieu indicates that to "destroy" the enemy, the military needs to gather information on the structure of the FLN: "The method: interrogation. But interrogation is a method only when it guarantees a reply. To succumb to humane considerations only leads to hopeless chaos." A shot of Mathieu gesturing to a graph on a wall that depicts increasing incidents of violence is followed by a close-up shot of a young officer's face looking noticeably anxious. Here too we might wonder if any of the assembled for the Pentagon screening of *The Battle of Algiers* would have recognized a similar sense of dread over the need to exchange "humane considerations" for "interrogation."

The Battle of Algiers did not shrink from showing what General Massu, years after leading the French suppression of the Algerian insurgency, called "a cruel necessity."[20] One scene of an interrogation room shows a prisoner badly beaten, shirtless, and cowering on a chair as he surrenders information into a tape recorder. Suspects are subsequently rounded up. And following the apprehension of Larbi Ben M'Hidi, one of the leaders of the FLN, Mathieu holds a press conference to address the supposed suicide of M'Hidi in his prison cell. A reporter asks about the "methods" used by the military that have proven so successful in quelling the insurrection. After Mathieu's evasive answer, another reporter insists that "it's better to speak—frankly—and use the word 'torture.'" In a response that, reverberating into the present, could have been delivered by the U.S. secretary of defense, Mathieu states: "The word 'torture' doesn't appear in our orders. Questioning is the only valid method in a police operation against a clandestine group."[21] Mathieu proceeds to lecture the reporters on the efficacy of such "methods" and the lack of "respect for legality" shown by the enemy. After defending the soldiers asked to defend the empire, some of whom joined the Resistance and some of whom "survived Dachau and Buchenwald," Mathieu implicates the fourth estate: "Is France to remain in Algeria? If your answer is still yes, you must accept all the consequences."

The consequences depicted in *The Battle of Algiers* include a series of gruesome shots of torture: an interrogator applies a hand-held torch to the bare chest of a man who writhes in agony, as another bloodied prisoner dangles from a suspended wood frame; still another prisoner, shown having electrodes clipped to his ears, convulses with the shocks delivered. But one of the most arresting shots in this sequence is not of torture itself, which is harrowing enough, but of a passive participant bearing witness who exhibits a dramatically different demeanor than the face of fear on the witness to torture in *Three Kings*. As one soldier violently holds a prisoner's head under water, the shot cuts to a close-up of another soldier (who appears to be, as we often forget, remarkably young in age) looking upon the scene of horror. The shot lingers for a moment, allowing the film's spectator to take in this young face as the soldier looks on in silence, sitting passively, barely moving to take a drag from his cigarette, even as, finally, a subtle look of amusement creeps over his face. Calling attention to this mute witness, who could be standing in for the spectator of the film itself, Pontecorvo is already alluding to what we would come to learn about the scene of torture.[22]

Framing Torture: The Spectacle of Brutality in an Era of Unreality

In "The Logic of Torture," one of a series of articles published in the *New York Review of Books* since the Abu Ghraib scandal erupted, Mark Danner writes that "a simple truth" lies behind the entire event: "that since the attacks of September 11, 2001, officials of the United States, at various locations around the world, from Bagram in Afghanistan to Guantánamo in Cuba to Abu Ghraib in Iraq, have been torturing prisoners." Indeed, as Danner posits: "What is difficult is separating what we now know from what we have long known but have mostly refused to admit."[23] Certainly, revelations of abuse and torture of detainees at the hands of U.S. military personnel had already come to light, in particular, in a *Washington Post* report in December 2002 of interrogation methods used on suspected al Qaeda members held at the Bagram air base in Afghanistan. As one CIA officer put it: "After 9/11 the gloves come off."[24] The declared war on terror had apparently now made such measures necessary, functioning as a righteous justification for national security. Yet this report, and several related accounts in the mainstream news media on similar incidents at Guantánamo and other U.S. military facilities, had barely registered in public debate. It wasn't until the photographs from Abu Ghraib appeared that torture became an unavoidable social text. As Donald Rumsfeld admitted: "It is the photographs that give one the vivid realization of what actually took place. Words don't do it."[25] In other words, it was the *sight* of torture that provided the profound, horrific impact that previous reports, dependent on a medium given to words on a page, could not approximate.

The political firestorm that ensued (momentarily threatening to engulf the Bush administration's entire foreign policy) was met by an array of attempts to contain and control the meaning of the photographs, from the military's closing ranks by floating a bad-apple strategy to outright efforts at denial and disavowal through discourse, as in Rumsfeld's refusal to use the word "torture." But more widespread, if less organized, efforts at containment were mounted across a range of media platforms, geared toward what might be called recontextualization. Perhaps most notoriously, Rush Limbaugh, on his widely aired radio program, characterized the photos as merely revealing frat-boy shenanigans, amounting to little more than an exuberant form of hazing. Although Limbaugh's interpretation appeared to gain little traction beyond his dedicated following, the recontextualization proved to have some mileage. For as former Secretary of Defense James Schlesinger stated in one of the army's reports on Abu Ghraib, the imagery could be summed up as "Animal House on the night shift."[26] While such efforts to hijack, or at least neutralize, the probable meanings of the images have taken on the air of predictability—given the political bearings of these sources—what overrides these specific ideological impulses is the sheer human will to torture the photos themselves into signifying anything but that to which the images bear witness.

Another, perhaps less predictable, attempt at reading against the grain involved Army Reserve Pfc. Lynndie England, one of the seven soldiers from the 372nd Military Police Company who faced a court-martial for "mistreatment" of prisoners at Abu Ghraib. The twenty-one-year-old England had appeared in several of the more widely circulated photographs, including one image of her holding a dog leash around the neck of a naked prisoner lying on the ground and another of her pointing at the genitals of a naked, hooded prisoner, giving a thumbs-up sign and smiling while a cigarette casually dangles from her lips (see figure 1).

During a press conference in England's hometown of Fountain, West Virginia, and aired on CNN the week that the story erupted, family members and friends defended England's honor and duty to country, stressing that the photos didn't depict the person they knew and loved. The most intriguing statements, however, were made by family attorney Roy G. Hardy, who, in a vernacular treatment of image analysis, exclaimed that we can't tell what might be happening outside the frame of the photograph or, for that matter, what took place before or after the snapshot was taken.[27] Trying to cast doubt not on what the images themselves convey but rather on decontextualizing the image, England's defender actually pointed to the larger problematic of

1. Army Reserve Pfc. Lynndie England, sans cigarette, all smiles, *60 Minutes II*, CBS, 28 April 2004

grasping the meaning of even a lone image in isolation, once nested within a continuum of time and place.

Asking what resides just beyond the frame or ruminating on the temporal and spatial dimensions that allow emplotment of the image conjures another contested social text—that of the Rodney King beating in 1991 captured on George Holliday's amateur videotape. In his analysis of how the referentiality of the footage had been undermined by "close reading" from defense attorneys who "essentially turned Holliday's long take into a montage by 'deconstructing' and decomposing it into isolated parts," Frank Tomasulo takes a certain strain in contemporary theory to task for effectively evacuating the historical "facticity" of events that constitute the real. "Attorneys defending the L.A. police officers at this first trial," writes Tomasulo, "were able to provide sophisticated 'spin control' of the beating by repeatedly showing the infamous home video recording (in slow motion) and by telling the jury that Rodney King was behaving irrationally and was resolutely disobeying the officers' commands to stop moving—a classic instance of the 'reading against the grain', 'structuring absence' methodology valorized by many film and video scholars." For Tomasulo, this "recent tendency to dissolve events into a nihilistic specter of postmodernist nonmeaning" is symptomatic of a troubling trend in academic thinking toward radical historical relativism, whereby the privileging of "textuality" and the "endless play of signifiers" serve to obscure if not deny "the very existence of historical 'facts' and realities outside the realm of visual mediation and other mediating discourse."[28]

Yet this challenge to questions chiefly of epistemology is also aggravated by the increasingly dominant digital technologies of representation and their impact on the status of the referent. "We (the audience) no longer believe in images," claims Wheeler Winston Dixon, "since computer-generated images make any effect possible. . . . The veracity of the moving image has been hopelessly compromised; the demarcation line between the real and the engineered (both aurally and visually) has been obliterated. All is construction and fabulation. All is predetermined; nothing natural remains."[29] But not all images, we might say, are created equal. It's one thing to say that the high-tech special effects of a fiction film serve to remove it from the plane of the real, and another when it comes to, say, the documentation of real bodies in the work of photojournalism, especially of those that a certain regime of power decrees don't count.

This more specific concern is addressed by Fred Ritchin, who discusses the challenge posed by computer technology to "photography's reputation for verisimilitude and objectivity," a challenge to its very capacity for a reliable "representation of 'reality.'" Computerized manipulation of the image, far more efficient than "conventional retouching techniques," Ritchin asserts, "allows modifications that appear virtually seamless." Moreover, computer-generated imagery and digital-compositing techniques usher in a "modification of time" by executing, for instance, a shift in the angle from which the picture was taken, "a kind of retroactive repositioning of the photographer." This ability to "reach backward in time," to "rephotograph," unsettles not only the ontological connection between the image and its referent but also the temporal connection between the image and its historical framing.[30]

As digital technologies accelerate this destabilization of the relation between reality and its representation, "what matters in this fluctuating multimedia landscape," as Lynne Kirby advises, "is not so much the medium itself as the institutions of mass media." Since the Rodney King video "reminds us all too painfully [that] no picture really speaks for itself," the increasingly uncertain status of the image now more than ever "require[s] contextualization."[31] In a similar vein, Vivian Sobchack discusses the 1994 film *Forrest Gump* and its use of a digital "apparition," a technical process that cleverly inserted the central character into recognizable documentary footage. Although this film would seem to acutely illustrate the postmodern "crisis of historicity" thesis, deliberately confusing "the fictional with the historically 'real' in an absolutely seamless representation," Sobchack argues that the film's humor and visual pleasure depend on audience awareness of this very disjunction. While "this loss of a 'fix' on History and of the stable temporal and spatial framing of events as 'historical'" is cause for concern, Sobchack contends, it also provides us with an opportunity: "This loss of a firm grasp of its object forces into the foreground of our current existence the constitutive quality of consciousness as it engages the objective world." Moving then from object to subject, Sobchack reminds us that "we are subjectively implicated in and responsible for the histories we tell ourselves or others tell us."[32]

Insofar as computerization and digital technologies have intensified this indeterminacy of the image in postmodern culture, what is being called for here is a shift in attention either to the politics of media institutions (Kirby) or to the historical nature of subjectivity (Sobchack). Yet neither axis of consideration enables unproblematic access to the truth-value of the Abu Ghraib photos. For viewed in light of the larger context from which the images have emerged, this photographic testimony arrives at a time deeply riven by a culture of suspicion, a vague but pervasive sense of distrust accruing around powerful and far-reaching institutions of government and media alike. For example, the discernible pattern of secrecy that shrouds both domestic and foreign policy issuing from the Bush White House has coalesced around the ruthless campaign of disinformation and deception over the Iraq war, from unfounded claims about weapons of mass destruction to outright lies linking Saddam Hussein's Iraq to the 9/11 attacks.

As for the standing of media institutions, we must now recognize the role of the Internet: Where Vietnam was held to be the first televised war, and where the first Gulf War was aired live through satellite communications and round-the-clock news coverage, the Iraq war has been splayed out across the World Wide Web, coursing throughout what one critic has termed "webs of conspiracy." From the struggle over how to estimate the number of Iraqi civilian deaths due to the war, to conflicting claims over the kidnapping of U.S. Marine corporal Wassef Ali Hassoun, to rampant doubts over the beheading of Nicholas Berg, the Internet has functioned as a never-ending circuit of rumor, a perpetual-motion machine contributing the world over to a politics of paranoia.[33] Yet in spite of this confluence of forces—from intellectual discourses of dissimulation to technologies of fabrication to institutional apparatuses of propaganda and conspiracy—in spite of all this, what has refused to disappear behind the fog of war is a mere handful of photographic images that bear the weight of history in their capacity to speak to the spectacle of brutality.

Picturing Torture: Abu Ghraib and the Politics of Shame

In his recent article "Torture in the Algerian War," Tzvetan Todorov examines a French television program aired in 2002 by Patrick Rotman called "L'ennemi intime" (The intimate enemy), in which Rotman interviews former soldiers in the French Army, some of whom practiced the use of torture during Algeria's war for independence. Todorov asks, as does Rotman: "How is it that torture, while rejected officially and condemned generally by one and all, could have happened on such a wide scale?" Refraining from turning the torturer into an extreme other, Todorov considers the ways in which the "refinements of torture" are rather a product of rationalization, not entirely inconsistent with the logic of a "civilization" based on the exercise of power in which the ends justify the means. In a chilling passage, Todorov discusses one of Rotman's interviewees, who, recalling that his military lodging in Algeria was "papered with pornographic photos," narrated a particularly unbearable scene of horror involving a twelve-year-old son forced to torture his own father with electricity. "What I felt was a kind of fascination," admits the witness. "One could also feel something akin to jubilation at watching things that extreme. Today I connect that feeling to the porno pictures I used to see in the mezzanine, and I tell myself, yes, there is an obvious relationship between the two, in the instrumentalization of the body: one makes a body do one's bidding."[34]

The "pornographic" element of this recollection has become part of the discourse around Abu Ghraib. In her analysis of these images, Susan Sontag argues that "most of the torture photographs have a sexual theme, as in those showing the coercing of prisoners to perform, or simulate, sexual acts among themselves." Further, "the pictures seem part of a larger confluence of torture and pornography," leading Sontag to "wonder how much of the sexual tortures inflicted on the inmates of Abu Ghraib was inspired by the vast repertory of pornographic imagery available on the Internet." Although I argue against this reading of the Abu Ghraib photos as rooted in and thus contained by the imagery of pornography, I turn to Sontag's insightful account of the appearance of the perpetrators in the photos themselves, the *presence* of the perpetrators shown "posing, gloating, over their helpless captives." What is truly appalling, then, is all the grinning—"the expression of satisfaction at the acts of torture"—that illustrates what for Sontag is a "culture of shamelessness."[35]

To begin, we need to distinguish between what can be considered two distinct sets of images that initially escaped from the prison: Arab victims with their faces more or less concealed and U.S. perpetrators with their faces exposed, often exhibiting, as Sontag notes, gleeful expressions. The first set of images have taken on iconographic status: While alluding to a specific historical memory (and in contrast to Sontag's reading of the other set of images, which recall the pictorial legacy of U.S. lynching), at least one of the Abu Ghraib images has become something of a universal statement, its very iconicity allowing it to be adapted across cultures and language (see figures 2–4). Erasing the boundaries of cultural translation, the implicit meaning of this Abu Ghraib image—conjuring the ghost of U.S. racism—and its iconic recognizability have fueled a cross-cultural discourse, gathering force across currents of global media as a pointed critique of the racist dimension of U.S. empire.

The second set of photos is marked by the presence of U.S. faces, functioning in part within the repertoire of self-portraits, which provide a kind of shock of recognition: The sight of happy U.S. faces that appear to announce

——————— 2. The iconicity of Abu Ghraib, *New Yorker*, 10 May 2004, 42 ———————

3. The global memory of U.S. racism, captioned "Torture: Bush et Rumsfeld face a une affaire d'Etat," *Le Monde,* 11 May 2004

glee in the company of death allows paradoxically for an uneasy process of identification, an unkind suturing that, indeed, torturers are us (see figure 5). As such, we are implicated in the spectacle of torture, drawn into the photos as bearing witness, not unlike those witnesses to other scenes of torture, caught between the ethical responses of shame or indifference.

Such shamelessness in the face of brutality is compounded by the utter visibility of recording the event. This too is not necessarily an aberration. As Elaine Scarry has written: "It is not accidental that in the torturers' idiom the room in which the brutality occurs was called the 'production room' in the Philippines, the 'cinema room' in South Vietnam, and the 'blue lit stage' in Chile: built on these repeated acts of display and having as its purpose the production of a fantastic illusion of power, torture is a grotesque piece of compensatory drama." Similarly, as Todorov discloses in the French practice of torture: "One of Rotman's interviewees drew attention to another feature of the process in which he was then involved. To defend himself against the feelings that could assail him, the torturer or the witness would very gradually come to see the surrounding world as a fiction or a spectacle: 'I was a spectator. I felt like I wasn't there. . . . It gave me the impression I was watching a film. . . . Things seemed pretty unreal. . . . We thought it was a game.' 'We turned reality into something we could accept.'" Perhaps it is not accidental either that a Red Cross report on the condition of prisoners at

Abu Ghraib found evidence of cultural markers not far removed from these earlier accounts: "Detainee-14 was detained in a totally darkened cell measuring about 2 meters long and less than a meter across, devoid of any window, latrine or water tap, or bedding. On the door the [Red Cross] delegates noticed the inscription 'the Gollum,' and a picture of the said character from the film trilogy 'Lord of the Rings.'"[36]

4. The political mobilization of Abu Ghraib imagery.
(Courtesy of Richard Serra, www.BloodForOil.org)

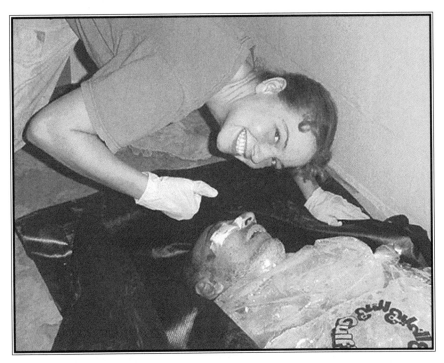

5. Not ashamed: Spc. Sabrina Harman, with the body
of Manadel al-Jamadi, *ABC News*, 19 May 2004

Such referencing of a fictional world of representation appears to reveal that the torturer inures himself or herself to the reality of torture through a process of dissociation, in which, to quote Todorov, "real acts become no more than fiction, seen from the outside, as if by a spectator."[37] Yet this process of objectifying oneself as an actor in the "drama" and as a spectacle of torture—of turning self into other—does not easily translate in the case of Abu Ghraib. Even if the compulsion to render the act of torture as a visible display of power remains constant, the actors of Abu Ghraib seem to signal selves unburdened by a need for dissociation. The utter shamelessness of the perpetrators being caught in the act, then, their signs of pleasure for the entire world to see, must now be viewed as the mirror image of the shame perpetrated on the victims, in which the work of shaming the victims is precisely the mechanism of torture.

In his critique of the U.S. Army's "few bad apples" defense, Mark Danner unearths the systemic nature of U.S. torture, tracing specific forms of interrogation back to the CIA, which, since the late 1950s, has been developing techniques that produce "a kind of psychological shock" that "is very likely to create feelings of fear and helplessness." According to the CIA's manual *KUBARK Counterintelligence Interrogation* (1963), if forced to comply under such duress, "the subject will experience a feeling of guilt. If the 'questioner' can intensify these guilt feelings, it will increase the subject's anxiety and his urge to cooperate as a means of escape." Such techniques, as Danner argues, "seem clearly designed to exploit the particular sensitivities of Arab culture to public embarrassment, particularly in sexual matters." The reading and containment of the Abu Ghraib photos as depictions of aberrant behavior or as merely pornographic simulation is therefore something of a cover, since torment through shame has been precisely the point all along. Moreover, as Danner notes, "the *public* nature of the humiliation is absolutely critical." Endemic to what he calls "staged operas of fabricated shame," the agency or weapon of torture was in fact the presence of the digital camera—its flash and sound no doubt exacerbating the detainee's "guilt feelings"—which functioned to potentially publicize the humiliation beyond control, serving as a kind of "shame multiplier."[38]

What this suggests, finally, is a form of cultural terrorism, a highly sophisticated project of power—calculating, formalized, systematic—that attends to the specific subjectivity of its victims and therefore, not unlike the French tactics that came before it, is thoroughly "rational." Yet by casting the scandal of Abu Ghraib as an isolated incident rather than a systemic policy, the military, perhaps ironically, set the stage for a much larger drama.[39] By projecting the problem onto wayward individuals as a way of rescuing the system itself, the military and its apologists have personalized Abu Ghraib and helped create the conditions for its reception—that those recognizable villains are our people, that we are they, that torturers are us. What remains uncertain, of course, is the afterimage of this shock of recognition, especially for spectators who would disavow the gaze staring back at them.

NOTES

I want to thank Julia Lesage for sharing an early version of her electronic resource project on Abu Ghraib, since posted on the *Jump Cut* Web site. For feedback and advice along the way, I want to thank Jay Haffner, Daniel Freire, Daniel Beck, Kevin Meehan, Laila Farah, Victoria Mosher, and Cynthia Fuchs, as well as our editors, Andrew Martin and Patrice Petro. Finally, I would like to dedicate this work to the memory of Charles Haynie.

1 Matthew Schofield, "Combat Limited in Fallujah, but Fighting Erupts Elsewhere in Iraq," *San Jose Mercury News*, 11 April 2004. See also Dan Murphy, "Siege

of Fallujah Polarizing Iraqis," *Christian Science Monitor*, 15 April 2004, www.csmonitor.com/2004/0415/p01s02-woiq.html; and Virginia Tilley, "The Carnage According to Gen. Kimmitt: Just Change the Channel," *CounterPunch*, 14 April 2004, www.counterpunch.org/tilley04152004.html. Among the numerous eerie echoes from the past, Kimmitt's irritated recommendation to "change the channel" recalls Norman Schwarzkopf's irritation, from his own account in *It Doesn't Take a Hero*, over the Pentagon's inability during the first Gulf War to suppress media coverage of the "highway of death," the devastated convoy of Iraqis fleeing Kuwait City that appeared to be little more than a massacre: "Though many Iraqis in the convoy had died, most had jumped out of their vehicles and run away. I felt irritated—Washington was ready to overreact, as usual, to the slightest ripple in public opinion. I thought, but didn't say that the best thing the White House could do would be to turn off the damned TV in the situation room." Quoted in Margot Norris, "Only the Guns Have Eyes: Military Censorship and the Body Count," in Susan Jeffords and Lauren Rabinovitz, *Seeing through the Media: The Persian Gulf War* (New Brunswick, N.J.: Rutgers University Press, 1994), 295–296.

2 Bill Carter, "Pentagon Ban on Pictures of Dead Troops Is Broken," *New York Times*, 23 April 2004. For the Memory Hole Web site coverage: www.thememoryhole.org/war/iraqis_tortured/index.htm. See also Mike Whitney, "Where Have They Been for the Last Year? Flag-Draped Coffins and the *Seattle Times*," *CounterPunch*, 28 April 2004, www.counterpunch.org/whitney04282004.html.

3 Elizabeth Jensen, "'Nightline' Fuels Iraq Images Feud," *Los Angeles Times*, 29 April 2004, http://fairuse.1accesshost.com/news1/latimes133.html. See also Al Tompkins, "Koppel Defends 'The Fallen,'" *Poynteronline*, 29 April 2004, www.poynter.org.

4 James Castonguay, "Masquerades of Massacre: Gender, Genre, and the Gulf War TV Star System," *Velvet Light Trap* 39 (spring 1997): 6. See also Castonguay, "Conglomeration, New Media, and the Cultural Production of the 'War on Terror,'" *Cinema Journal* 43, 4 (summer 2004): 102–108. I want to thank Jim for sharing this paper with me prior to its publication.

5 Quoted in Simon Robinson, "Grounding Planes the Wrong Way," *Time*, 14 July 2003, 34. See also "U.S. Charged with War Crimes," posted on the Information Clearing House Web site, www.informationclearinghouse.info/article3465.htm.

6 BBC News, "Newsman on Iraq Looting Charge," 23 April 2003, http://news.bbc.co.uk/go/pr/fr/-/2/hi/entertainment/2966345.stm.

7 Jean Baudrillard, "The China Syndrome," *Simulacra and Simulation*, trans. Sheila Faria Glaser (Ann Arbor: University of Michigan Press, 1994). For a persuasive critique of Baudrillard's commentaries on the Gulf War, collected as *The Gulf War Did Not Take Place*, trans. Paul Patton (Bloomington and Indianapolis: Indiana University Press, 1995), see James Castonguay, "Hollywood Goes to Washington: Scandal, Politics, and Contemporary Media Culture," in Adrienne L. McLean and David A. Cook, eds., *Headline Hollywood: A Century of Film Scandal* (New Brunswick, N.J., and London: Rutgers University Press, 2001), 273–297.

8 For thorough accounts of the first Gulf War, see Bradley S. Greenberg and Walter Gantz, eds., *Desert Storm and the Mass Media* (Cresskill, N.J.: Hampton Press, 1993); and W. Lance Bennett and David L. Paletz, eds., *Taken By Storm: The Media,*

Public Opinion, and U.S. Foreign Policy in the Gulf War (Chicago and London: University of Chicago Press, 1994).

9 Colin MacCabe, "Realism and the Cinema: Notes on Some Brechtian Theses," *Screen* 15, 2 (summer 1974): 7–27, and "Theory and Film: Principles of Realism and Pleasure," *Screen* 17, 3 (autumn 1976): 7–27; George Gerbner, "Instant History—Image History: Lessons of the Persian Gulf War," *Velvet Light Trap* 31 (spring 1993): 4. For a still-relevant treatment of the modern evolution toward technowar, see Paul Virilio, *War and Cinema: The Logistics of Perception*, trans. Patrick Camiller (London and New York: Verso, 1989). For perceptive analysis of the war genre's limits as a "classic realist text," especially with regard to Vietnam films, see Andrew Martin, *Receptions of War: Vietnam in American Culture* (Norman and London: University of Oklahoma Press, 1993). The genre's dependence, as Martin demonstrates, on "a narrative form that hinges on private, personal dramas, while suppressing wider social or political dimensions" (129), is precisely the route taken by the U.S. military in its handling of the Abu Ghraib crisis, a route of personalization that, as I argue later, paradoxically engendered greater access to (and potential identification with) the otherwise abhorrent acts in evidence.

10 For an acute analysis of the gender politics of the film, see Yvonne Tasker, "Soldiers' Stories: Women and Military Masculinities in *Courage Under Fire*," *Quarterly Review of Film and Video* 19, 3 (July–September 2002), 209–222.

11 On the deadly inaccuracy of laser-guided precision bombing and the military marketing of a clean war, see Gerbner, "Instant History"; and Philip M. Taylor, *War and the Media: Propaganda and Persuasion in the Gulf War* (Manchester and New York: Manchester University Press, 1992).

12 See Tony Grajeda, "The (Un)Reality of War: Reconsidering Stone's *Platoon*," *disClosure* 1 (fall 1991): 41–57. See also Thomas Prasch, "*Platoon* and the Mythology of Realism," in William J. Searle, ed., *Search and Clear: Critical Responses to Selected Literature and Films of the Vietnam War* (Bowling Green: State University Popular Press, 1988). For a similar argument on the "secret knowledge" acquired through the experience of war, see James Campbell, "Combat Gnosticism: The Ideology of First World War Poetry Criticism," *New Literary History* 30 (1999): 203–215.

13 Elaine Scarry, *The Body in Pain: The Making and Unmaking of the World* (New York: Oxford University Press, 1985), 64.

14 Douglas Kellner, *Media Culture: Cultural Studies, Identity, and Politics between the Modern and the Postmodern* (London and New York: Routledge, 1995), 211 (see also Kellner, *From 9/11 to Terror War: The Dangers of the Bush Legacy* [Lanham, Md.: Rowman and Littlefield, 2003]); Douglas Kahn, "Body Lags," in Nancy J. Peters, ed., *City Lights Review: War after War* (San Francisco: City Lights Books, 1992), 45 (for a comprehensive account of a "war apparently without bodies," see John Taylor, "The Body Vanishes in the Gulf War," *Body Horror: Photojournalism, Catastrophe, and War* [Washington Square, N.Y.: New York University Press, 1998]); Cynthia Fuchs, "The 'Real World' War," *PopMatters*, 24 March 2003, www.popmatters.com/features/030324-iraq-fuchs.shtml. For an early but indispensable account of the Iraq war's mediatization, see David Miller, ed., *Tell Me Lies: Propaganda and Media Distortion in the Attack on Iraq* (London and Ann Arbor: Pluto Press, 2004).

15 Although *Three Kings* ends by capitulating to genre conventions—consistent with post–Vietnam War movies in the wish fulfillment of redeeming the

soldiers even if the war itself is beyond redemption—its farcical but ultimately sympathetic gesture toward the class configuration of modern soldiering is even more relevant to the current Iraq war, underwritten as it is by what Arundhati Roy calls a "poverty draft"; see *Public Power in the Age of Empire* (New York: Seven Stories Press, 2004), 57. For a critique of the film's liberal ideology, see John Carlos Rowe, "Culture, U.S. Imperialism, and Globalization," *American Literary History* 16, 4 (winter 2004): 575–595.

16 I am referring to Alan Dershowitz's promotion, since 1989, of "torture warrants" and the debate this has incited since 9/11. See Dershowitz, "Torture of Terrorists: Is It Necessary to Do—and to Lie About?" *Shouting Fire: Civil Liberties in a Turbulent Age* (Boston: Little, Brown, 2002); and William F. Schulz, "The Torturer's Apprentice," *The Nation*, 13 May 2002, 25–27. See also Sanford Levinson, ed., *Torture: A Collection* (Oxford and New York: Oxford University Press, 2004), especially Elaine Scarry's chapter, "Five Errors in the Reasoning of Alan Dershowitz."

17 Michael T. Kaufman, "What Does the Pentagon See in 'Battle of Algiers'?" *New York Times*, 7 September 2003. See also Stephen Hunter, "The Pentagon's Lessons from Reel Life: 'Battle of Algiers' Resonates in Baghdad," *Washington Post*, 4 September 2003; and J. Hoberman, "Revolution Now (and Then)!" *American Prospect* 15, 1 (January 2004): 63–65. The parallels between the film of Algeria's past and the real of Iraq's present are explored in "*The Battle of Algiers*: A Case Study," a 2004 taped conversation among counterterrorism experts (including former national coordinator for security and counterterrorism Richard A. Clarke) accompanying the DVD release of *The Battle of Algiers* (Criterion Collection, 2004).

18 Kaufman, "What Does the Pentagon See."

19 For an incisive reading of this scene, see Ella Shohat and Robert Stam, *Unthinking Eurocentrism: Multiculturalism and the Media* (London and New York: Routledge, 1994), 253–255.

20 Michael T. Kaufman, "Jacques Massu, 94, General Who Led Battle of Algiers," *New York Times*, 31 October 2002. In his 2001 published memoirs, General Paul Aussaresses, a Special Services officer who served under Massu in Algeria from 1955 to 1957, insists torture was not only common but also condoned by the French government of Guy Mollet. For his unapologetic account of the use of torture and summary executions, including admission of personally strangling to death FLN leader Larbi Ben M'Hidi, see General Paul Aussaresses, *The Battle of the Casbah: Terrorism and Counter-Terrorism in Algeria, 1955–1957*, trans. Robert L. Miller (New York: Enigma Books, 2002). See also Adam Shatz, "The Torture of Algiers," *New York Review of Books*, 21 November 2002, 53–57.

21 During a press conference held shortly after the Abu Ghraib scandal broke, Secretary of Defense Donald Rumsfeld stated: "My impression is that what has been charged thus far is abuse, which I believe technically is different from torture. And therefore I'm not going to address the 'torture' word." Quoted in Susan Sontag, "Regarding the Torture of Others," *New York Times*, 23 May 2004.

22 Film scholars have tended to overlook this shot of the young soldier in this sequence, focusing instead on the shots of "the sympathetic woman observer," as Robert Stam notes, "who cries as she witnesses torture and empathizes with the victim." Stam, "Fanon, Algeria, and the Cinema: The Politics of Identification,"

in Ella Shohat and Robert Stam, eds., *Multiculturalism, Postcoloniality, and Transnational Media* (New Brunswick, N.J., and London: Rutgers University Press, 2003), 40.

23 Mark Danner, "The Logic of Torture," *New York Review of Books*, 24 June 2004, 70. Danner's articles for the *Review*, along with other relevant documents, have subsequently been published in Danner, *Torture and Truth: America, Abu Ghraib, and the War on Terror* (New York: New York Review Books, 2004). See also Julia Lesage's comprehensive electronic resource project, "Abu Ghraib and Images on Abuse and Torture," *Jump Cut: A Review of Contemporary Media*, www.ejumpcut.org/currentissue/links.html.

24 Dana Priest and Barton Gellman, "U.S. Decries Abuse but Defends Interrogations: 'Stress and Duress' Tactics Used on Terrorism Suspects Held in Secret Overseas Facilities," *Washington Post*, 26 December 2002. See also Joseph Lelyveld, "In Guantánamo," *New York Review of Books*, 7 November 2002, 62–68; and Eyal Press, "In Torture We Trust?" *The Nation*, 31 March 2003, 11–16.

25 Rumsfeld quoted in Kristian Williams, "When Journalists Call for Self-Censorship," *Extra!* 17, 4 (July/August, 2004): 21.

26 James Schlesinger quoted in Mark Danner, "Abu Ghraib: The Hidden Story," *New York Review of Books*, 7 October 2004, 44. See also Frank Rich, "The War's Lost Weekend," *New York Times*, 9 May 2004, "Arts and Leisure" sec. 2, 1, 12; and Dick Meyer, "Rush: MPs Just 'Blowing Off Steam,'" CBSNews.com, 6 May 2004. In May 2004 hearings before the Senate Armed Services Committee, Senator James Inhofe, Republican from Oklahoma, stated: "I'm probably not the only one up at this table that is more outraged by the outrage than . . . by the treatment. The idea that these prisoners—you know, they're not there for traffic violations. If they're in cell block 1A or 1B, these prisoners—they're murderers, they're terrorists, they're insurgents. Many of them probably have American blood on their hands. And here we're so concerned about the treatment of those individuals." Quoted in Christopher Brauchli, "'The Object of Torture Is Torture': From Wallens Ridge to Abu Ghraib," *CounterPunch*, 21 May 2004.

27 "No one has the full story of what was going on in those pictures," Roy G. Hardy said during the news conference, adding: "They don't show what was behind her, beside her or what was going on behind the scenes." CNN Evening News, 7 May 2004.

28 Frank Tomasulo, "'I'll See It When I Believe It': Rodney King and the Prison-House of Video," in Vivian Sobchack, ed., *The Persistence of History: Cinema, Television, and the Modern Event* (New York: Routledge, 1996), 75–76, 84, 72. See also Hamid Naficy, "King Rodney: The Rodney King Video and Textual Analysis," in Jon Lewis, ed., *The End of Cinema as We Know It: American Film in the Nineties* (New York: New York University Press, 2001).

29 Wheeler Winston Dixon, "Twenty-five Reasons Why It's All Over," in Jon Lewis, ed., *The End of Cinema as We Know It: American Film in the Nineties*, 358–59.

30 Fred Ritchin, "Photojournalism in the Age of Computers," in Carol Squiers, ed., *The Critical Image: Essays on Contemporary Photography* (Seattle: Bay Press, 1990), 28–31. For a more optimistic take on the use of these new techniques for historical representation, see Barbara Allen, "Digitizing Women's History: New Approaches to Evidence and Interpretation in Museum Exhibits," *Radical History Review* 68 (spring 1997): 103–120. For a thorough account of "the digital-imaging

revolution," see William J. Mitchell, *The Reconfigured Eye: Visual Truth in the Post-Photographic Era* (Cambridge: MIT Press, 1992). See also Kevin Robins, "Will Images Move Us Still?" *Into the Image: Culture and Politics in the Field of Vision* (London and New York: Routledge, 1996).

31 Lynne Kirby, "Death and the Photographic Body," in Patrice Petro, ed., *Fugitive Images: From Photography to Video* (Bloomington and Indianapolis: Indiana University Press, 1995), 74, 76. John Berger's work in general has made this case for an "alternative use of photographs" that emphasizes its context: "The aim must be to construct a context for a photograph, to construct it with words, to construct it with other photographs, to construct it by its place in an ongoing text of photographs and images. . . . Such a context replaces the photograph in time—not its own original time for that is impossible—but in narrated time. Narrated time becomes historic time when it is assumed by social memory and social action." Berger, "Uses of Photography," *About Looking* (New York: Pantheon Books, 1980), 60–61.

32 Vivian Sobchack, "Introduction: History Happens," in Sobchack, ed., *The Persistence of History*, 3, 6. See also Stephen Prince, "True Lies: Perceptual Realism, Digital Images, and Film Theory," *Film Quarterly* 49, 3 (spring 1996): 27–37; and Arild Fetveit, "Reality TV in the Digital Era: A Paradox in Visual Culture?" *Media, Culture, and Society* 21, 6 (1999): 787–804. On the "apparitions" of digitalization, see Vilem Flusser, "Digital Apparition," in Timothy Druckrey, ed., *Electronic Culture: Technology and Visual Representation* (New York: Aperture Foundation, 1996).

33 See Kareem Fahim, "Lost in America: From Nicholas Berg to Abu Ghraib, the Search for Something to Trust," and Gary Indiana, "No Such Thing as Paranoia: On the Culture of Conspiracism," *Village Voice*, 26 May 2004. For a concise treatment of how "conspiracy haunts our thinking about the Web," see Jodi Dean, "Webs of Conspiracy," in Andrew Herman and Thomas Swiss, eds., *The World Wide Web and Contemporary Cultural Theory* (New York and London: Routledge, 2000).

34 Quoted in Tzvetan Todorov, "Torture in the Algerian War," trans. John Anzalone, *Salmagundi* 135/136 (summer/fall 2002), 20. For a harrowing account of the victims of torture in Algeria at the time, see Frantz Fanon, "Colonial War and Mental Disorders," *The Wretched of the Earth*, trans. Constance Farrington (1961; New York: Grove Press, 1968).

35 Sontag, "Regarding the Torture of Others," 27. For a similar reading of the Abu Ghraib photographs, see Susan J. Brison, "Torture, or 'Good Old American Pornography'?" *Chronicle of Higher Education*, 4 June 2004, B10.

36 Scarry, *The Body in Pain*, 28; Todorov, "Torture in the Algerian War" 18; for the Red Cross report, Mark Danner, "Abu Ghraib," 49.

37 Todorov, "Torture in the Algerian War," 20.

38 Danner, "The Logic of Torture," 71–72. For further evidence of the exploitation of sexual humiliation aimed specifically at Arabs and Muslims, see Seymour M. Hersh, "The Gray Zone," *New Yorker*, 24 May 2004, 38–44; and Mark Matthews, "Abuse Tailored to Arabs, Experts Say," *Baltimore Sun*, 23 May 2004, posted at www.cageprisoners.com. See also Don Van Natta Jr., "Questioning Terror Suspects in a Dark and Surreal World," *New York Times*, 9 March 2003. For related work on the CIA's history of torture and its evolution from the practice

of physically brutalizing a body to more "scientific" forms of psychological torment, see Lisa Haugaard, "Textbook Repression: U.S. Training Manuals Declassified" (originally published in *Covert Action Quarterly*, 1 September 1997); and Thomas Blanton and Peter Kornbluh, "Prisoner Abuse: Patterns from the Past," 12 May 2004, posted on the Web site for School of the Americas Watch, www.soaw.org.

39 As Danner adds: "How isolated could the so-called 'Animal House on the night-shift' abuses of the military police have been from military intelligence when, as we learn in the Fay report, one of the most notorious images, that of 'several naked detainees stacked in a "pyramid",' served as a 'screen saver' on one of the computers in the military intelligence office?" Danner, "Abu Ghraib," 49.

NOTES ON CONTRIBUTORS

MIKE ALLEN is a professor and chair of the department of communication at the University of Wisconsin–Milwaukee. His research and teaching interests examine the various means of social influence processes. He has published numerous articles in such journals as *Communication Monographs*, *Communication Theory*, *Law and Human Behavior*, *Journal of Homosexuality*, and *Psychological Bulletin*.

MARCUS BULLOCK is a professor of English at the University of Wisconsin–Milwaukee. He is coeditor of *Walter Benjamin: Selected Writings, Volume I, 1913–1926* (1997) and author of *The Violent Eye: Ernst Jünger's Visions and Revisions on the European Right (1992)* and *Romanticism and Marxism: The Philosophical Development of Literary Theory and Literary History in Friedrich Schlegel and Walter Benjamin* (1987). His teaching areas include eighteenth- to twentieth-century European literature and the Frankfurt School.

JAMES CASTONGUAY is an associate professor and chair of media studies and digital culture at Sacred Heart University in Fairfield, Connecticut. He is the former information technology officer for the Society for Cinema and Media Studies and has published on war and the media in *American Quarterly*, *Bad Subjects*, *Cinema Journal*, *Discourse*, and the *Velvet Light Trap*. He is currently completing a manuscript on war and global media culture from the Spanish-American War to the war on terror.

DOUG DAVIS is an assistant professor of English at Gordon College in Georgia. He received his PhD in literary and cultural studies from Carnegie Mellon University in 2003. He is currently completing his book manuscript, "Strategic Fictions: Tales of Mass Destruction in the Cold War and the War on Terror."

REBECCA DECOLA is a graduate of Oberlin College who plans to pursue her academic interests in feminist critical studies, epistemology, and theories of globalization and human rights in graduate school one day.

TONY GRAJEDA is an assistant professor of cultural studies in the department of English at the University of Central Florida. He has published on Vietnam War films, popular music, and cultural studies of technology. He is currently completing a manuscript, "Machines of the Audible: A Cultural History of Sound, Technology, and a Listening Subject," as well as a coedited collection on film sound.

WENDY KOZOL is an associate professor of gender and women's studies at Oberlin College. She is the author of *Life's America: Family and Nation in Postwar Photojournalism* (1994) and the coeditor (with Wendy Hesford) of *Haunting Violations: Feminist Criticism and the Crisis of the "Real"* (2001) and *Just Advocacy? Women's Human Rights, Transnational Feminisms, and the Politics of Representation* (Rutgers University Press, 2005).

MARY N. LAYOUN is a professor and chair of the department of comparative literature at the University of Wisconsin–Madison. She is the author, most recently, of *Wedded to the Land? Gender Boundaries and Nationalism in Crisis* (2001) and is working on two projects: a study of race, gender, sexuality, and citizenship in early postwar Japan and the United States, "Occupying the National Family"; and a study of visual and verbal narrative in comic books, "Graphic Words and Telling Images: Stories of History in Comic Books."

ANDREW MARTIN is an associate professor of English and film studies at the University of Wisconsin–Milwaukee, where he also serves as chair of the English department. He is the author of *Receptions of War: Vietnam in American Culture* (1995). He has written and taught extensively on issues of culture and representation and the implications of both for understanding our world today.

PATRICIA MELLENCAMP, formerly Distinguished Professor of Art History at the University of Wisconsin–Milwaukee, is the author of *A Fine Romance: Five Ages of Film Feminism* (1996), *High Anxiety: Catastrophe, Scandal, Age, and*

Comedy (1992), and *Indiscretions: Avant-Garde Film and Video* (1990). She is the editor of *Logics of Television: Essays in Cultural Criticism* (1990).

LISA PARKS is an associate professor of film and media studies at University of California–Santa Barbara. She is the author of *Cultures in Orbit: Satellites and the Televisual* (2005) and coeditor of *Planet TV: A Global Television Reader* (2002). She is writing a book, "Mixed Signals: Media Technologies and Cultural Geographies."

PATRICE PETRO is a professor of English and film studies at the University of Wisconsin–Milwaukee, where she is also director of the Center for International Education. She is the author, editor, and coeditor of numerous books, most recently, *Aftershocks of the New: Feminism and Film History* (Rutgers University Press, 2002) and, with Tasha Oren, *Global Currents: Media and Technology Now* (Rutgers University Press, 2004).

ROBERT RICIGLIANO is an adjunct professor of communication and director of the Institute of World Affairs at the University of Wisconsin–Milwaukee, where he directs the Peace Studies Program. He was a founding board member of the Alliance for International Conflict Prevention and Resolution, former executive director of the Conflict Management Group, and associate director of the Harvard Negotiation Project and is the cochair of the Theory and Practice Committee for the Alliance for International Conflict Prevention and Resolution. He has written extensively on negotiation and peace processes.

INDEX

David F. O'Connell, PhD
Eileen P. Beyer, PsyD
Editors

Managing the Dually Diagnosed Patient
Current Issues and Clinical Approaches

Second Edition

Pre-publication
REVIEWS,
COMMENTARIES,
EVALUATIONS . . .

"Treating patients who suffer from dual diagnosis is the greatest challenge facing addiction treatment today. This book offers both theoretical and practical insights into the therapeutic process with this difficult population."

Sheila Blume, MD, CAC
*Medical Director, Alcoholism
and Chemical Dependency
and Compulsive Gambling Programs,
South Oaks Hospital,
Amityville, NY*

"Managing the Dually Diagnosed Patient provides teachers, supervisors, practitioners, and students with a comprehensive and highly informative update on the major issues associated with diagnostic and treatment considerations when working with the dually diagnosed population. Through this edited work, Drs. O'Connell and Beyer have provided a synthesized and very timely update of chemically dependent clients who have comorbid psychiatric vulnerabilities. Included among the many highlights are insights about dual diagnosis in relation to gender, adolescence, treatment adherence, major psychiatric disorders, and guidelines for effective program management in time-sensitive clinical settings. Clinicians who are practicing, supervising, researching, or teaching in the area of substance abuse counseling will reap quick benefit from the quality of information contained within this text."

Jed Yalof, PsyD, ABPP
*Professor and Chair,
Department of Graduate Psychology,
Immaculata College, PA*

Managing the Dually Diagnosed Patient
Current Issues and Clinical Approaches

Second Edition

THE HAWORTH PRESS
New, Recent, and Forthcoming
Titles of Related Interest

Managing the Dually Diagnosed Patient
Current Issues and Clinical Approaches
Second Edition

David F. O'Connell, PhD
Eileen P. Beyer, PsyD
Editors

The Haworth Press®
New York • London • Oxford

The Haworth Press, Inc., 10 Alice Street, Binghamton, NY 13904-1580.

Cover design by Marylouise E. Doyle.

Library of Congress Cataloging-in-Publication Data

Managing the dually diagnosed patient : current issues and clinical approaches / David F. O'Connell, Eileen Beyer, editors.—2nd ed.
    p. cm.
    Includes bibliographical references and index.
    ISBN 0-7890-0876-9 (alk. paper) — ISBN 0-7890-0877-7 (alk. paper)
    1. Narcotic addicts—Mental health. 2. Mentally ill—Substance use. I. O'Connell, David F. II. Beyer, Eileen.
    [DNLM: 1. Diagnosis, Dual (Psychiatry). 2. Substance-Related Disorders—complications. 3. Mental Disorders—therapy. 4. Substance-Related Disorders—therapy. WM 270 M2664 2002]
RC564 .M256 2002
616.86—dc21
                                                                                    2001043367

CONTENTS

ABOUT THE EDITORS

David F. O'Connell, PhD, is a consulting psychotherapist at the Caron Foundation, an internationally recognized addictions treatment facility. He is a licensed psychologist in private practice specializing in executive/corporate counseling and development and is listed in the National Register of Health Service Providers in Psychology. He received his PhD from Temple University in 1986. Dr. O'Connell is an attending psychologist at St. Joseph's Hospital in Reading, Pennsylvania. He is the editor/author of four books on chemical dependency treatment, including *Dual Disorders: Essentials for Assessment in Treatment, Self Recovery: Treating Addictions Using Transcendental Meditation and Maharishi Ayurveda,* and *Awakening the Spirit.*

Dr. O'Connell has contributed to numerous professional journals, including *Alcoholism Treatment Quarterly, Journal of Chemical Dependency Treatment,* and *The Journal of College Student Personnel.* He is the co-author of an audiotape series entitled *True Spirituality* and serves on the editorial board of the *Journal of Adolescent Chemical Dependency.* He is also a board member of the Institute for Science, Technology, and Public Policy. Dr. O'Connell is listed in *Who's Who in Science and Engineering* and *Who's Who in the World.* He resides in Womelsdorf, Pennsylvania.

Eileen P. Beyer, PsyD, CAC Diplomate, has sixteen years of experience in the field of substance abuse treatment as a clinician, administrator, presenter, author, and researcher. She graduated with her doctorate in clinical psychology from Immaculata College in 1998. Dr. Beyer specializes in addiction and women's issues in her private practice and organizational consulting work. As the former Director of Women's Services at the Caron Foundation, she led the development and growth of female-sensitive addiction treatment services through program initiatives and staff training/supervision. Prior to the Caron Foundation, she was clinical coordinator of the University of Pennsylvania's Addiction Treatment Research Center where she facilitated the integration of addiction treatment research into their outpatient addiction treatment program. With K. Carnabucci, she co-authored the chapter "Group Treatments with Substance Abusing Women" for the *Handbook of Addiction Treatment of Women: Theory and Practice* (2002). She has also contributed to the *Journal of Substance Abuse Treatment* and the *Journal of Addictions Nursing.* She can be contacted at <gebeyer@msn.com>.

CONTRIBUTORS

John A. Conahan, ACSW, CAC, Health Care Consultant, Ephrata, Pennsylvania.

Dennis C. Daley, PhD, Associate Professor of Psychiatry; Chief, Drug and Alcohol Services, Western Psychiatric Institute and Clinic, University of Pittsburgh Medical Center, Pittsburgh, Pennsylvania.

Peter J. Garito, PhD, private practice of psychology, Reading, Pennsylvania.

George S. Layne, MD, private practice of psychiatry, Philadelphia, Pennsylvania.

A. Majid Malik, MD, Chief Resident, Department of Psychiatry, Texas Tech University Health Services Center, Lubbock, Texas.

Razia T. Malik, PharmD, Clinical Pharmacist, Covenant Medical Center, Lubbock, Texas.

John Ramirez, PhD, Psychologist, Behavioral Health Services, Holy Spirit Hospital, Camp Hill, Pennsylvania.

Barbara W. Reeve, MD, private practice of psychiatry, Ellsworth, Maine.

Micah R. Sadigh, PhD, F.I.C.P.M., Assistant Professor of Psychology, Cedar Crest College, and Behavioral Medicine Psychologist, Good Shepherd Hospital, Allentown, Pennsylvania.

Ihsan M. Salloum, MD, Associate Professor of Psychiatry; Medical Director, Drug and Alcohol Services, Western Psychiatric Institute and Clinic, University of Pittsburgh, Pittsburgh, Pennsylvania.

Russell Smith, MA, Clinical Psychologist, Chief Psychologist (retired), State Correctional Institution Graterford, Pennsylvania State Department of Corrections, Graterford, Pennsylvania.

Richard L. Weddige, MD, Professor, Department of Psychiatry, Texas Tech University Health Services Center, Lubbock, Texas.

Foreword

One cannot read this book without being impressed by the diversity of substance abuse patients. This book covers a broad array of psychiatric problems that often coexist with substance use disorders. Although the chapters are heavily oriented toward psychological approaches, this orientation is not incompatible with the collaborative use of medication in the management of these complex cases.

It would be helpful to integrate psychotherapeutic approaches with information about specific medication that might be required by the psychopathology. That is clearly not the purpose of this book. What is impressive is that it reviews a wide variety of treatment approaches and by its nature illustrates the need for matching of patient to treatment. This matching need not occur according to a theoretical construct but rather according to the patient's needs as determined by a diagnostic interview and complete biopsychosocial evaluation. Clearly the rigid adherence to a dogmatic treatment program would not be helpful to this broad range of diverse patient problems.

These chapters are a testimony to the fact that the treatment of addictive disorders has entered a new era. It must be more results oriented and consumer oriented. Modern treatment is evidence-based so that the results of randomized clinical trials determine the efficacy of treatments whether they be for heart disease or for alcoholism. This places an added burden on the clinician. It is no longer ethically acceptable to continue to provide the same treatment to our patients that we learned when we were students or trainees. Rather, we must keep up with the literature and learn which of the new approaches are effective and which are not. We also must be willing to test our most cherished traditional treatments in controlled trials and see whether they meet the standard of efficacy now required of all treatments. The diversity demonstrated in this book also makes clear that a treatment that worked for one type of patient may not work for another. Indeed, the same intervention that was helpful to one patient in recovery can even be detrimental to another. The concept of patient-treatment matching based on the individual needs of the patient is one that should be uppermost in the minds of all clinicians as we do the initial evaluation on any new patient.

This is a challenge that faces today's clinician in the field of substance abuse. This book, edited by David O'Connell and Eileen Beyer, will help to provide the information to meet that challenge. The dually diagnosed patient is the most complicated of all patients with addictive disorders and unfortunately, it is also the most common.

Charles P. O'Brien, MD, PhD
Kenneth Appel Professor;
Vice Chair of Psychiatry
University of Pennsylvania;
Chief of Psychiatry
Philadelphia VA Medical Center

Preface to the Second Edition

Since its publication in 1990, *Managing the Dually Diagnosed Patient: Current Issues and Clinical Approaches* has been adopted widely as a graduate text in addictions studies and to a lesser extent in undergraduate courses. It has found its usefulness as a reference text for research into managing psychiatric comorbidity in addicted populations. The second edition of this book continues the emphasis on research-based, diagnostic and therapeutic practices, programs, and approaches to managing chemically dependent patients who show co-existing psychiatric disorders.

The new edition reflects numerous developments in the field of comorbidity over the past decade. Important research has led to the recognition of the chemically dependent patient population as an extremely heterogeneous group, with psychiatric comorbidity as one of the many variables necessary to consider in understanding and treating this group of patients. Depending on the study, between 25 and 80 percent of chemically dependent patients manifest at least one additional psychiatric disorder in addition to chemical dependency, with mood and anxiety schizophrenic disorders predominating. Many patients show multiple psychiatric disorders, and clinical experience has shown that patients presenting for addictions treatment are often maintained on multiple psychiatric medications targeted to treat various psychiatric symptoms.

The arrival of managed care has had definite effects on diagnostic and treatment practices with dually diagnosed patients. Clinical care has of necessity been streamlined, and rapid, accurate diagnosis of both chemical dependency disorders and psychiatric disorders is the order of the day. Inpatient care is now reserved for patients with the most acute and severe chemical withdrawal states or psychiatric conditions, and addictions programs have had to accommodate these patients through designing and reconfiguring clinical programming as well as enhancing professional continuing education programs for addictions therapists.

The literature on dual diagnosis treatment is replete with the descriptions of new, innovative programs that strive to provide appropriate, adequate treatments for both chemical dependency and psychiatric disorders. The best of these have adopted an integrated approach to the problem, blending appropriate psychotherapies, pharmacotherapies, and twelve-step group involvement in an individualized, comprehensive, and continuous system of care.

Addressing the unique needs of special populations such as female and adolescent patients has also been in ascendancy over the past decade. Research studies show a high rate of psychiatric comorbidity in both of these populations. The second edition of the text includes a special focus on both of these patient subpopulations and in general has attempted to recognize the complexities of these patients and present research-based approaches to clinical management.

The discovery of the frequency of psychiatric disorders in chemical-dependent patient populations has led to a demand for greater, broader training of addiction professionals and the realization that addictions treatment is more complicated and in general now requires a more complex skill set. The editors of this book now consider psychiatric training as an absolutely essential skill for addictions clinicians; this text is one resource available to assist in this process. Clearly, the professional preparation of addictions therapists needs to move from a more insular, specialized focus to a more generalist model that is akin to professional degree and continuing education programs for mental health professionals.

The research included in this second edition of the text indicates great strides in understanding and treating dually diagnosed patients. Future research should focus on a number of areas including studies to gain a much greater understanding of substance-induced psychiatric syndromes. These disorders have barely been addressed by researchers thus far. Likewise, the advent of integrated or complementary and alternative medicine (CAM) has had a major impact on other medical subspecialties but has barely scratched the surface in addictions medicine. Areas such as spirituality and spiritual technologies, meditation, and Chinese and Ayurvedic medicine have much to offer patients suffering multiple chronic disorders, and they should be fully investigated. On a more conventional note, we see the development of disease management procedures and modified clinical pathways to deal with dual diagnosis as important areas for research and program development, especially in inpatient environments with their dwindling lengths of stay and high rates of psychiatric severity and acuity. There is still the need to develop and test innovative strategies and community living arrangements that provide for the continued treatment connection and compliance of the most chronic dually diagnosed patients.

We hope the reader will find this second edition of *Managing the Dually Diagnosed Patient* as useful and practical as its predecessor, and that it will continue to serve as a reliable, sought-out graduate and reference text.

David F. O'Connell
Eileen P. Beyer

SECTION I:
THEORETICAL AND
PROGRAMMATIC ISSUES

Chapter 1

Managing Psychiatric Comorbidity in Inpatient Addictions Treatment

David F. O'Connell

The purpose of this chapter is to assist clinical managers, program administrators, and therapists in inpatient addictions treatment programs with the practical management of the problems associated with ever-increasing levels of psychiatric impairment, severity, and acuity in chemically dependent patient populations. It is based on my own experiences at Caron Foundation, a large (235-bed) inpatient primary addictions treatment program in southeastern Pennsylvania, as well as suggestions and treatment guidelines that I have found useful drawn from extant clinical research on psychiatric comorbidity (e.g., Osher, 1996; Polcin, 1992; Zweben, 1993; Brady, et al., 1996). Caron Foundation is an internationally known and respected addictions treatment facility. Caron Foundation is a free-standing, nonprofit addictions treatment program that offers a full continuum of adult and adolescent addictions programs including detoxification, short-term stabilization, primary care, intensive chronic relapse treatment, extended care for adolescents and adults, inpatient codependency and family-of-origin issues treatment, family counseling and education, as well as specialized inpatient programs to treat such problems as nicotine dependence, compulsive eating, and pathological grief and loss. Caron also maintains a large outpatient program. As its clinical director, I have struggled to address the problems presented in this chapter and I offer the reader practical strategies to manage psychiatric comorbidity in the inpatient environment. This chapter offers guidance, suggestions, and advice as well as procedures to manage psychiatric comorbidity in three areas of inpatient treatment, including recommended policies and procedures for intake and screening of new admissions, tips on diagnosis and assessment, and treatment protocols for several co-occurring psychiatric disorders. Also included are suggestions for initiatives to improve treatment efficacy and quality of delivery of inpatient addictions care.

A number of developments over the past decade have dramatically changed how inpatient addictions treatment is conceived, designed, and delivered. These changes include appreciably shorter lengths of stay in inpatient care, a higher level of psychiatric impairment in chemically dependent patients presenting for inpatient treatment, clinical staff downsizing, and an increase in the volume and complexity of clinical documentation necessary to maintain the treatment status of patients in inpatient treatment. In addition, psychodiagnostic and treatment practices in psychiatry and clinical psychology have changed in part as a response to the changes and demands associated with managed care. First, there appears to be a change in diagnostic practices with a trend toward *inclusiveness* in psychiatric diagnosis in contrast to a more traditional focus on *exclusiveness* and a more parsimonious explanation of a patient's symptom picture (O'Connell, 1999). This practice has resulted in greater numbers of patients presenting for inpatient addiction treatment with multiple psychiatric diagnoses. For example, patients entering inpatient treatment with three or four Axis I diagnoses is not uncommon. Second, prescription practices appear to have shifted toward targeting and treating psychiatric symptoms rather than treating psychiatric syndromes and conditions. This trend has been made possible in part by recent pharmacological advances that have seen the development of a wider variety of psychiatric medications with increasing specificity of action. According to my studies (O'Connell, 1999), patients are regularly treated with multiple medications both within and across medication types such as antidepressants and mood stabilizers. These studies indicate that it is not uncommon for a patient in inpatient chemical dependency treatment to be receiving two to three antidepressants, one to two antipsychotics, and at least one mood stabilizing agent or anti-anxiety agent. The trend toward multiple psychiatric diagnoses and multiple medications has made the practice of psychiatric evaluation, monitoring, and clinical management more complex and complicated. In my experience, pharmacological treatment of psychiatric diseases has, again partly in response to managed care demands, moved to a first order of treatment for many psychiatric disorders rather than a second order of treatment behind psychotherapy and other nonpharmacological approaches to the treatment of psychiatric disorders. Most psychiatric medications are prescribed by primary care physicians and pharmacotherapeutic approaches are often the only treatment a patient is receiving for a psychiatric condition.

Advances and changes in pharmacological treatments have also occurred specifically in the field of addictions medicine, leading to increased use of psychiatric medications to treat addictive syndromes directly (Graham, Schultz, and Wilford, 1998). According to my own internal studies on quality improvement (O'Connell, 1999), the number of patients in inpatient chemical dependency treatment maintained on a chemical agent to manage an addictive disease, such as agents to reduce alcohol cravings and consumption, control stimulant addiction, or prevent relapse to opioids or nicotine use, has risen appreciably over the past five years.

These developments reflect a trend toward the remedicalization of addiction as a psychiatric and medical illness that places medical treatment at the forefront of approaches to addictions therapy. This is a dramatic departure from traditional approaches to addictions treatment, which relied primarily on verbal psychotherapeutic and educational interventions to resolve and manage addictive disorders. Addictive disorders, as well as many other psychiatric disorders, are increasingly being conceptualized as brain diseases that require medical care (Leshner, 1998).

The greater numbers of patients entering inpatient addictions care with psychiatric disorders, as well as the generally higher levels of psychiatric impairment with such patients, has resulted in a shift in focus for addictions therapists from individual patient and patient community recovery concerns to the more serious and immediate concerns of identifying, managing, and treating high-risk, acute, potentially lethal patient behavior, such as suicidal and parasuicidal behaviors, explosive and aggressive behaviors, and other disruptive behaviors often seen in inpatient psychiatric treatment environments. Many inpatients addictions clinicians now find themselves in the business of psychiatric stabilization and many of the patient management problems traditionally addressed in inpatient psychiatric programs now are regularly attended to in primary addictions treatment.

These dramatic changes and trends have placed greater demands on addictions professionals both in terms of professional training and education and in daily clinical responsibilities. Addictions therapists now need a sensitivity to and sophistication about complex clinical cases involving severe, often multiple addictive disorders and multiple psychiatric conditions. Having a background in frontline psychiatric treatment, preferably inpatient treatment, is absolutely essential for an addictions counselor in today's inpatient treatment climate (O'Connell, 1998). Indeed the need for intensive psychiatric training is now being recognized by health organizations at the state and national levels (MISA Consortium, 1999). Skill sets that have traditionally fallen outside of the professional preparation of addictions counselors are now essential. For example, training in passive physical restraint and other conflict management skills to manage patients in acute psychiatric distress should be considered a prerequisite for effective functioning in an inpatient addictions treatment environment. All addictions therapists should be capable of identifying psychiatric symptoms and syndromes and need solid skills in brief and emergency psychotherapy as well as crisis management skills (O'Connell, 1998).

CLINICAL MANAGEMENT POLICY AND PROCEDURE GUIDELINES

Intake and Admission

Entry into the inpatient treatment system by patients who are inappropriate for intensive chemical dependency services emerges as a major concern for those responsible for patient management. Several variables can be identified that complicate admissions decisions. For example, patients requesting an admission to an inpatient chemical dependency program may greatly underreport psychiatric impairment and the acuity and severity of their symptoms and problems. Patients' family members and even professional referral sources can also collude in this effort. Transfers from inpatient psychiatric hospitals can be particularly problematic. Continuing care personnel in these programs are often anxious and eager to place a patient whose treatment days have been expended and for whom a transfer to a less restrictive level of care is necessary. Often patients are not clinically ready for such a transfer. It is very difficult for addictions intake personnel to get an accurate, valid assessment of the nature of a patient's psychiatric problems and current level of functioning under these conditions.

It is recommended that an up-to-date psychiatric or psychological evaluation on a patient transferred from a hospital precede the patient to addictions treatment so that a reasonable decision regarding admission can be offered. However, even having current psychiatric data in hand presents problems. The quality and completeness of patient records can fluctuate greatly among institutions. This complicates the decision-making process for admission and can reduce the validity of subsequent psychiatric evaluations upon admission to a chemical dependency program.

I have found that patients with an extensive history of acting-out behaviors such as suicidality, self-mutilation, or violence—especially a recent history (e.g., while a patient on a psychiatric ward)—who have a history of multiple trials on various psychiatric medications with poor compliance and/or poor clinical response, and who are emotionally reactive in stressful situations (such as the entry into a new treatment system) are the most problematic and lead to a high level of psychiatric management problems in the inpatient addictions environment. Consequently, intake decisions should be based on an awareness of this profile and every effort should be made to keep such patients from premature entry into the inpatient's addictions environment.

Exhibit 1.1 depicts a set of guidelines and principles devised for intake and admission personnel at Caron Foundation to assist with guidance and direction in the admissions process. Intake counselors (who are not clinicians) are oriented to these guidelines as are all clinical department heads. Intake decisions are based on these principles and are made on a case-by-case basis in conjunction with the clinical director.

Exhibit 1.2 shows an intake questionnaire on psychiatric comorbidity developed by the clinical director for intake personnel. This questionnaire operationalizes the guidelines and principles from the previous exhibit. If a potential admission shows a history of psychiatric problems, the intake counselor uses this questionnaire and asks the appropriate questions from one or more of the sections on various psychiatric disorders. If two or more responses are affirmative in any of these areas, the intake counselor then consults the clinical director for further guidance in deciding on admission. The questions in this format were derived from my own clinical experience with patients who did poorly in the chemical dependency inpatient treatment environment and showed problems such as poor treatment compliance,

EXHIBIT 1.1.

Guidelines for Screening Dual Diagnosis Admissions

The following are three main areas of concern and possible problems:

1. *Acute Suicidality:* Patients coming to our facility transferred from a psychiatric hospital or dual diagnosis unit who have attempted suicide while on the unit one or more times are considered the highest risk. Also, the more violent and severe the suicide attempt, the greater the concern, especially if there is a lengthy history of such attempts and there is a history of self-mutilating behavior. Attempts that occur when the individual is alone in a nontoxic state with a highly lethal method are the greatest concern. *Do not admit a patient who has had one or more serious suicide attempts while in an inpatient setting.*

2. *Violence and Aggression:* Patients who are applying for admission to Caron Foundation who have had serious multiple episodes of violent acting out in an inpatient setting are of the greatest concern. Patients who have had to be put in physical restraints (for example, leathers) and who voice homicidal and sadistic thoughts and impulses and have a history of acting out on them are of great concern. Patients who have a history of poor response to aggression controlling medications, such as Depakote, and are not currently medicated are of great concern. *Do not admit a patient who has had one or more recent violent episodes in an inpatient setting and is not currently stabilized on an antiaggression medication.*

3. *Medication:* Patients who have a history of multiple trials on various antipsychotic medications or mood-stabilizing medications, such as lithium, are of the greatest concern. Be especially wary of a patient who is on two or more antipsychotic medications and who continues to show breakthrough psychotic symptoms. In general, the longer the history of psychosis and the poorer the response to the medications prescribed, the greater the likelihood of psychotic behavior in inpatient care. Be particularly wary of patients on Mellaril. *Do not admit a patient who is actively psychotic while maintained on one (1) or more antipsychotic medications.*

Other Areas of Concern

1. *Eating Disorders:* Of greatest concern are anorexic patients who are medically unstable. Second, be wary of bulimic patients who have active serious medical problems associated with bulimia. Also, patients who are showing regular daily binges and purges and a past poor response to eating disorder treatment or no treatment at all are of great concern. *Do not admit a patient who is medically unstable and/or one who suffers from severe daily binge and purging behavior.*

2. *Adolescents:* In general, the guidelines for adolescents are the same as for adults. In addition, be alert for patients who suffer from severe attention deficit hyperactivity disorder (ADHD) with significant comorbidity, such as

(continued)

(continued)

conduct disorder and learning disorder/impulse control disorders. In general, if patients cannot function adequately without medications to control hyperactivity, they are not appropriate for treatment here. *Do not admit an adolescent patient with severe ADHD who cannot function without medication.*

3. *Cognitive Disorders:* This includes patients with severe organic problems such as dementia and patients with moderate to profound mental retardation. Such patients do not have the requisite cognitive ability to learn in treatment. *Do not admit patients with severe organicity and/or moderate to profound mental retardation.*

4. *General Guidelines and Principles:* In general, the level of functioning of the patient is much more important than the patient's admitting diagnosis. For example, the diagnosis borderline personality disorder raises serious concerns; however, there are high functioning borderlines who have stopped self-mutilating and can control suicidal impulses and have at least a moderate response to mood-stabilizing and antidepressant medications. Consequently they are appropriate for admission. Another example is major depression; most patients with this diagnosis can and do benefit from primary inpatient addictions treatment, depending on the level of functioning and severity of depressive symptoms. Severely depressed patients require inpatient psychiatric care. Mildly to moderately depressed patients with an adequate response to medication are appropriate here.

In regard to suicidality, most of our patients have probably thought of or even attempted suicide in the past. Again, the concern is their *current* level of functioning and that is best assessed by their *recent behavior* in a hospital or other inpatient setting. The rule of thumb is that past behavior predicts future behavior. The same is true for violence. Patients who simply cannot control their impulse or urge to strike out at others or at inanimate objects are a danger to themselves and others here. More often than not, however, patients with a history of violence can control themselves with the social pressure that comes with living in an inpatient environment.

In regard to medications, it is important to ask questions about patients' *compliance* and *duration*. In general, the longer the patient has been on medications without interruptions, serious side effects, and with at least a mild to moderate response with good compliance, the greater the chance that they will be easily managed here.

Patients who carry a serious personality disorder, such as paranoid, borderline, or antisocial personality disorder often have problems adjusting to the treatment community and are eventually therapeutically discharged. However, all such patients deserve a chance to attempt treatment here. It is very difficult to predict the clinical course in inpatient care for a patient with a personality disorder. In reality, most function adequately.

EXHIBIT 1.2.
Assessment Questions for Dual Diagnosis Admissions

Suicidality

1. Was this a recent attempt (within the past month)? Yes No
2. Was this a serious, potentially lethal attempt (serious overdose, Yes No
   hanging, deep gash in the wrists, carbon monoxide or other
   poisoning)?
3. Has this been a recurring, long-standing, serious problem? Yes No
4. Did this patient attempt suicide or serious self-mutilation while Yes No
   in a hospital setting?
5. Has this patient attempted suicide in a nonintoxicated state? Yes No

If you are getting a lot of "Yeses" to the above questions, this is a
serious situation. Call me and we will discuss.

Violence and Aggression

1. Has this patient ever shot or stabbed anyone? Yes No
2. Has this patient been jailed or arrested for violence? Yes No
3. Is this patient violent even when off drugs? Yes No
4. Does this patient have a history of psychiatric treatment and Yes No
   medication for violence?
5. Has this patient recently (within the past month) threatened to Yes No
   strike or kill anyone?
6. Do others in this patient's life describe the patient as seriously Yes No
   dangerous?
7. Has this patient refused to take medication for aggression con- Yes No
   trol or had a very poor response to it?
8. Has this patient ever had to be put in physical restraints in a Yes No
   hospital setting?
9. Does this patient report that he or she cannot control his or her Yes No
   aggressive impulses?

If you are getting a lot of "Yeses" to the above questions, call me
and we will discuss.

Psychosis

1. Is this patient currently experiencing psychotic signs such as Yes No
   hallucinations, delusions, or ideas of reference or influence?
2. Has this patient ever become violent in a psychotic state? Yes No
3. Does this patient have a poor history of tolerating and comply- Yes No
   ing with antipsychotic medication?
4. Has this patient been on antipsychotic medication only for a Yes No
   brief time (less than two weeks)?
5. Does this patient report psychotic symptoms even when on Yes No
   antipsychotic medication?
6. Is this patient on more than one antipsychotic medication? Yes No
7. Has this patient been hospitalized frequently for psychotic Yes No
   breaks?
8. Has this patient ever tried to kill himself or herself in a psychotic Yes No
   episode?
9. Does the patient feel antipsychotic medications do not reduce Yes No
   or eliminate psychotic symptoms?

Psychotic patients should be cleared by a psychiatrist before they come
here. If you are getting a lot of "Yeses" to the above questions, call me.

(continued)

(continued)

Mood Disorders (Bipolar Disorder, Atypical Bipolar Disorder, Hypomania)

1. Does this patient have problems with medication compliance?   Yes   No
2. Does this patient have a lot of bad side effects with medication?   Yes   No
3. Has this patient been on medications for less than a week?   Yes   No
4. Does this patient experience mood swings even though he or   Yes   No
   she is on medications?
5. Does this patient get violent when he or she has mood swings?   Yes   No
6. Has this patient been violent, arrested, or psychotic during a   Yes   No
   manic episode?

If you are getting a lot of "Yeses" to the above questions, call me. Patients should be on mood-stabilizing medication at least a week before coming to Caron. We should have a psychiatrist clear them before admittance.

Eating Disorders

1. Does this patient have any medical problems associated with   Yes   No
   the eating disorder, such as dangerously low weight, electrolyte imbalances, severe gastrointestinal distress?
2. Has this patient been bingeing/purging three to four times per   Yes   No
   week or more over the past month?
3. Has this patient had a poor response or inadequate response   Yes   No
   to past eating disorder treatment?
4. Does this patient have no history of previous eating disorder   Yes   No
   treatment?
5. Does this patient or someone close to the patient feel the eating   Yes   No
   problems are out of control?
6. Does this patient have a poor response to medications to con-   Yes   No
   trol bingeing and purging behavior?

If you are getting a lot of "Yeses" to the above questions, the patient is probably not appropriate. Give me a call. In general, patients who regularly binge and purge are not appropriate for admission.

For Adolescents

1. Does this patient have a history of serious fire setting (e.g.,   Yes   No
   burning a building, furniture, room, etc.)?
2. Has this patient ever been accused of/charged with rape?   Yes   No
3. Does this patient have a history of serious animal cruelty (e.g.,   Yes   No
   torturing or killing family pets, birds, frogs)?
4. Does this patient have a serious history of gang membership   Yes   No
   and violence?
5. Does this patient have a history of heavy inhalant abuse (glue,   Yes   No
   solvent cleaners, etc.)?
6. Has this patient ever been accused of/charged with making a   Yes   No
   bomb threat or death threat?
7. Does this patient have a history of stalking?   Yes   No

If you get a "Yes" to *any* of these questions, call the clinical director or a designated psychologist immediately to discuss. Do not routinely admit any patient with a history of fire setting, violence, or bomb threats.

aggressiveness, self-mutilating and suicidal behaviors, decompensation to florid psychosis or other regressed emotional states (such as dissociative), or any problem that necessitated a return to inpatient psychiatric care. Intake workers can utilize this questionnaire either to screen out inappropriate admissions or to identify high-risk patients for intensive case management and risk management procedures and strategies upon admission.

Because of the unreliability of important patient information necessary to make an admissions decision, it is recommended that any patient with serious psychiatric disease, especially patients transferring from a psychiatric facility, have a *recent* psychiatric as well as medical evaluation. The report should precede the patient to inpatient addictions care.

The types of patients referred to or seeking admission to an inpatient addictions program will be determined in part by the particular program's philosophy of care about treating patients who present psychiatric comorbidity. This is particularly important for nonhospital-based inpatient addictions programs that are not licensed to provide psychiatric treatment. It is recommended that such programs have a clear, comprehensive written policy on dual diagnosis admissions.

Exhibit 1.3 is an example of Caron Foundation's policy on psychiatric comorbidity. All program personnel are made aware of this policy, particularly marketing personnel. It is important to give a clear message about dual diagnosis admissions to potential patients and referral sources. This can help clear up, minimize, or preempt confusion about which patient profiles are appropriate for our particular inpatient program.

To further refine and promote the effectiveness of the intake and admissions screening process for dual diagnosis patients, Caron Foundation developed a special admissions study team for our adolescent inpatient continuum. Quality improvement studies conducted by the clinical director revealed that the majority of psychiatric management problems realized in the inpatient environment occurred in the adolescent program, and significantly greater numbers of psychiatrically impaired adolescent patients were escaping detection by the intake screening process. After consultation with the clinical leadership at the Betty Ford Center who have utilized a similar process for years, a clinical team consisting of the medical director, the clinical director, a nurse, the clinical coordinator of the adolescent contin-

---

EXHIBIT 1.3.
Caron Policy on Dual Diagnosis Cases—Residential Treatment

David F. O'Connell, PhD
Clinical Director

Caron Foundation strives to address all the unique needs of chemically dependent patients. It recognizes that alcohol- and drug-dependent patients present with a variety of problems including legal, medical, occupational, and psychological difficulties. Caron Foundation recognizes that many addicted patients present for treatment with coextensive psychiatric disorders. Many such patients can be treated in our residential setting. Patients who present with co-occurring psychiatric disorders that are subacute and do not seriously interfere with the capacity of the patient to function in a nonpsychiatric, residential setting are appropriate for assessment and treatment. Patients with acute psychiatric problems that are severe in nature are most appropriately treated in a psychiatric setting. In many cases patients who are stabilized psychiatrically following inpatient mental health treatment, who are compliant with their medications and psychiatric treatments, and who are not a danger to themselves or others can come to Caron Foundation for addictions treatment. For patients who are not appropriate for Caron's setting, Caron makes every effort to place the patient in an appropriate psychiatric treatment setting such as a dual diagnosis program or a mental health ward in a general hospital setting.

Although it is difficult to make a general statement about the entire spectrum of psychiatric disorders and the nature and level of patients' functioning, patients who are not floridly psychotic, seriously suicidal or self-destructive, do not present with serious violence issues, do present problems of moderate severity, who are compliant with psychiatric medications, and show evidence of psychiatric stabilization are appropriate candidates for treatment at our inpatient facility.

---

uum, and an addictions therapist was assembled to meet regularly to address, on a case-by-case basis, appropriateness of special admissions to the inpatient environment. Figure 1.1 presents a scale developed by the clinical director, which is utilized to guide the admissions decision-making process.

The preadmission patient profile is essentially a rating by each member of the admissions study team on seven variables found to be of particular importance in assessing appropriateness for an admission to inpatient addictions treatment for patients with psychiatric comorbidity. The first variable is *impulsivity/dyscontrol*. Patients with a history of and high potential for acting out on impulses are rated on this subscale. Patients who rate high on this scale are currently violent and/or cannot inhibit self-destructive behavior, such as self-mutilative, parasuicidal and suicidal impulses, or other high-risk behaviors (e.g., fire setting, bridge jumping).

PATIENT: _____

	Impulsivity (Acting Out)/ Dyscontrol	Acuity	Recency	Severity	Non-compliance	Chronicity (History)	Non-responsiveness to Treatment
HIGH 7 6 5							
MEDIUM 4 3 2							
LOW 1							

FIGURE 1.1. Preadmission Patient Profile

14

Acuity is a subjective rating of the immediacy and seriousness of a patient's symptoms and behaviors. For example, suicidal behavior can be acute or subacute, as can, for example, psychotic symptoms. The intent is to admit patients who present in the subacute range of difficulties. Patients with acute problems may be more appropriate for inpatient psychiatric care.

Recency is an important variable to consider in predicting the patient's response to inpatient addictions treatment. Generally, immediate past behavior predicts future behavior. For example, a patient who cuts himself on a psychiatric ward one week prior to coming to addictions treatment shows a high risk for such behaviors in the inpatient addictions environment. For the purposes of this scale, recency includes problems that have occurred within thirty days of consideration for admission to addictions treatment.

Severity is a subjective rating of psychiatric and behavioral impairment across diagnostic categories. Most psychiatric diagnoses present varying levels of severity, such as mild, moderate, or severe. Severity also encompasses psychiatric impairment. Chemically dependent patients with significant psychiatric impairment may be so dysfunctional that they will not be able to take advantage of the inpatient addictions treatment experience.

Noncompliance refers to the patient's interest in and motivation for addictions treatment as well as compliance with previous treatment recommendations, such as psychotropic medications and behavioral self-control management methods. Generally, we have found that patients who show low motivation for or resistance to treatment are not likely to comply with treatment recommendations in the inpatient environment. They may pose significant clinical management problems that may render them inappropriate for inpatient addictions treatment.

Chronicity is a measure of the duration and frequency of a particular problem, symptom, or diagnostic syndrome. Chronic problems, by definition, are persisting and are of great clinical concern. Patients presenting with chronic suicide attempts, self-mutilation, or purging behaviors are very unlikely to show abrupt changes in these behaviors in inpatient addictions treatment. Often these symptoms are aggravated by the intensity of the inpatient treatment environment.

Nonresponsiveness to treatment refers to any history of poor response to treatments, particularly psychiatric medications. Patients who show little or no improvement in psychotherapy and counseling or show problems that are treatment refractory also fall in this category. Patients who score high in this variable often are described as unimproved patients in previous treatments and may have a history of leaving treatment against medical advice.

At Caron we have found the scale to be quite useful in structuring admissions decision discussions, and our quality improvement studies indicate that it has significantly refined the process, resulting in an appreciable drop in the admission of inappropriate patients to our adult and adolescent programs.

ASSESSMENT

Diagnostic Issues

Rapid, accurate, and comprehensive psychiatric and psychological assessment of a dual diagnosis patient is highly desirable for appropriate psychiatric and addictions care. However, as seasoned diagnosticians in the addictions field know, diagnostic clarity and conclusiveness is difficult to achieve with a substance-abusing patient, especially early in treatment during detoxification and stabilization. Furthermore, the former rule of thumb (O'Connell, 1998) to wait two weeks after detoxification until assessing a patient is no longer practical or tenable. In many inpatient programs, patients may have a length of stay from only three to seven days and would be long gone before they were properly evaluated and diagnosed. In addition, demands from managed care organizations for immediate diagnosis and treatment planning render the "wait and see" approach to diagnosis a luxury. In today's inpatient clinical practice, patients present with many coexisting psychiatric disorders and often multiple severe addictive disorders as well as serious medical problems. Although a questionable practice, psychiatric diagnosis often must be established during acute withdrawal from alcohol and other drugs of abuse. Complicating the picture is the fact that very little research on substance-induced psychiatric disorders and few clinical principles and guidelines on diagnosis for the practicing diagnostician exist (Goldsmith and Ries, 1998). It is my experience (O'Connell, 1998) that dual diagnosis patients often show complex, fluctuating symptom pictures. Symptoms may abate and then abruptly reappear. Also, a greater frequency of atypical clinical syndromes appear with this patient population (O'Connell, 1999). This combination of pressure for early (often premature) psychiatric diagnosis; complex, multi-symptom, clinical presentations; the frequency of atypical syndromes; and the lack of clinical and research literature on the assessment of substance-induced disorders greatly complicates the psychiatric assessment process in the context of addictions treatment. In the following section, common presenting diagnostic problems for the mental health professional are addressed along with clinical advice on resolving them.

General Diagnostic Guidelines

Substance-Induced and Primary Psychiatric Disorders

The clinician should keep in mind that the presence of a chemical dependency disorder usually exacerbates the symptoms of a psychiatric disorder. Much less often a substance dependence disorder can mimic the symptom picture of a primary psychiatric disorder. However, although much has been written about the difficulty of accurately diagnosing a psychiatric condition in a newly recovering chemically dependent patient, the likelihood of a substance-induced disorder *fully* replicating or manifesting as clinically indistinguishable from an autonomous major mental disorder is extremely remote in my experience. Most commonly the presence of a substance dependence disorder exacerbates and exaggerates the acuity and severity of an existing psychiatric condition. Substance-induced psychiatric conditions actually clear rather quickly. As Penick et al. (1990) note, research has shown that psychiatric symptoms initially seen in alcoholics and addicts are absent or nearly absent in the majority of patients after two weeks of abstinence. Moreover, as I point out in a later discussion on diagnostic considerations, substance-induced psychiatric symptoms are usually clinically identifiable and distinguishable from autonomous psychiatric disorders to the experienced diagnostician. Patients with substance-induced syndromes can look initially quite psychiatrically disturbed but rapidly compensate within three to five days following abstinence.

The issue of conceptualizing psychiatric and addictive disorders as primary versus secondary merits some discussion here. According to

Blume (1997), the primary disorder is that which occurs first in the patient's life and the secondary disorder occurs at a later time. Either a psychiatric disorder or a substance abuse disorder can be primary or secondary. However, this distinction does not imply causality, and addictions as well as psychiatric diseases can arise from common etiologies or independent, separate causes. Regardless of whether a specific disorder is designated as primary or secondary, *both disorders require appropriate treatments,* since failure to treat either can lead to relapse of one or both disorders. Many professionals find the primary versus secondary distinction of little clinical utility and exhort diagnosticians to consider *both* disorders primary disorders that require specific and appropriate interventions (MISA Consortium, 1999).

In assessing a patient, a prudent diagnostic practice is to assume that presenting symptoms are due to a medical or physiological cause until such causes are ruled out. Since it may be impossible to rule out entirely the physiological contributions of substances of abuse with dual diagnosis patients, the nature of the abuse substance's impact on the clinical presentation of patients should be taken into consideration. The diagnostician should be very familiar with the predictable, common clinical manifestations of the major psychoactive substances of abuse. In addition, physiological syndromes can be ruled out or diminished in importance by discussion with the patient of his or her reaction to and interpretation of the patient's symptoms. Often the patient has had significant experience with intoxification and withdrawal from his or her drug(s) of abuse and is intensely familiar with the nature and course of psychiatric symptoms and experiences. For example, the patients may tell you they "always feel" or "act this way" when they are coming off drugs and never show particular symptoms when not intoxicated. The clinician should also vigorously explore periods of abstinence and sobriety. Relevant questions are, for example, "Under what conditions are your symptoms less intense? More intense? Exacerbated?" The clinician should become intimately familiar with the patient experiences with acute or postacute withdrawal symptomatology. Predictable symptoms that occur only in the context of excessive drug or alcohol use, intoxication, or withdrawal are likely to be substance induced, transient, and of less clinical importance in arriving at an accurate psychiatric diagnosis.

With experience the diagnostician can begin to regularly and reliably distinguish between psychiatric symptoms such as depression, anxiety, psychic disorganization, and character issues that are directly precipitated by the presence of an addictive disease, from those syndromes and disorders, primary or secondary, that are coextensive with, but diagnostically unrelated to, an addictive disease.

Research (for example, Schuckit et al., 1997) has shown that gender is an important consideration in arriving at a differential diagnosis especially with regard to the primary and secondary distinction. General research has shown that for males the substance abuse disorder more often than not predates the mental disorder. The reverse is true for female patients. There also appear to be differences with regard to diagnostic groups. For example, affective disorders are more frequently diagnosed *subsequent* to the manifestation of an addictive disorder with females, and depression is most often found to be the primary or initially occurring diagnosis in males. In females, findings are different for anxiety disorders. However, in both men and women the anxiety disorders are overwhelmingly the primary diagnosis in cases of dual diagnosis (Kessler et al., 1996). Severe personality disorders such as antisocial personality disorder and borderline personality disorder also appear to be much more frequently diagnosed as the primary disorder both in male and female patients, respectively.

In my experience and in the absence of more specific research-based clinical guidelines for diagnosticians, I have found definite trends in the nature of the patient's presenting symptoms and the patient's emotional and behavioral presentation at the time of assessment that can assist the clinician with a more valid, accurate diagnosis of an autonomous versus a substance-induced psychiatric syndrome. The following guidelines are a summary of my own findings and guidelines for diagnosis, grouped according to major diagnostic categories.

Anxiety disorders. I have found that patients with a substance-induced anxiety disorder complain about *physical* symptoms much more than cognitive ones, are angrier and more impatient than individuals with primary anxiety disorders, and more often than not do not show an anxious or "neurotic" temperament such as self-consciousness, rejection sensitivity, emotional sensitivity, and intropunitiveness. Unlike patients with a primary anxiety disorder, these patients have not accommodated to their anxiety symptoms. Anxiety is often intense and acute, but the patient also has periods of near complete remission if only for a brief period. Often what is seen during periods of anxiety with these patients is an Axis II disorder that becomes aggravated by the addiction, such as histrionic, avoidant, or dependent personality. In contrast to patients with primary anxiety disorders I have found that patients with substance-related anxiety are often extremely irritable, angry, demanding, or emotionally reactive.

Affective disorders. I have found that unlike patients with primary depression, patients with a substance-induced depression report a greater number of situational stressors, complain about their depression more, exaggerate symptoms more, show much anger and irritability, and show a greater number of cognitive complaints as opposed to neurovegetative signs of depression. These patients often present as more "actively hopeless" than patients with an autonomous major depressive disorder who, in my experience, present as more resigned and passive. Another clue for identifying substance-induced affective disorders is that these patients often have a history of extensive use of antidepressants with no clear response to any of them, poor medication compliance, and often many complaints of side effects. Often these patients describe antidepressants as "worthless."

When an autonomous depression co-occurs in this population, it is often in my experience an atypical syndrome. I have also seen a high frequency of "characterological" depression. These patients report depressive symptoms for most of their lives that are usually subacute. They show a history of poor response to both medications and psychotherapy. Psychiatric medications usually reduce only the intensity of their dysphoria and emotional overreactivity rather than eliminate it. These patients often have excessive expectations from psychiatric medications or hostile antitherapeutic transference attitudes toward the therapists, which can camouflage or undermine the effects of psychiatric medications that are usually headed in a positive direction. Such patients can show a kind of masochistic triumph and in the psychotherapeutic relationship work at undermining the treatment experience. Often these patients are chronically depressed by their own report but only intermittently depressed by independent, objective clinical observation.

Bipolar disorder is common with this patient population and there should be a high index of suspicion for this disorder. I have found a great deal of rapid cycling and ultrarapid cycling in chemically dependent patients.

Psychotic disorders. I have found that schizophrenia is usually rare with this patient population and, in general, this disorder is not usually difficult to diagnose. When it is present, these patients often use drugs of abuse to offset the negative symptoms of schizophrenia, such as apathy, lethargy, feelings of deadness, depersonalization, etc. I very rarely see overt, florid psychosis. I commonly see periods of psychic fragmentation characterized by loss of reality testing, disorganized behavior, and brief psychotic symptoms, chiefly visual hallucinations followed by paranoid symptoms. Most of these patients show rapid compensation following detoxification. Most of these patients eventually show significant Axis II pathology. I have found psychotic syndromes in the context of drug abuse, intoxication, and withdrawal much more common with adolescent patients. These syndromes are most often characterized by hyperexcitability and explosive behavior as well as manic symptoms.

I have never seen psychoactive drug use, even psychotomimetic drugs, produce a syndrome that was indistinguishable from schizophrenia. It is well recognized that abuse of methamphetamine, for example, can produce psychotic states resembling schizophrenia, but I have found these syndromes to be dominated by visual hallucinations and rarely present as fully mimicking schizophrenia. Likewise in hallucinogen abusers, psychotic symptoms and complaints are usually easily distinguishable from schizophrenia to the experienced diagnostician.

Personality disorders. Early thinking about diagnosis in the chemical dependency field equated addictive diseases with character disorders. Although research (e.g., Nace, 1990) has shown that personality disorders are common in substance abuse populations and the index of suspicion for a personality disorder should be high, I have found that substance abuse exaggerates personality flaws and negative traits. Nace (1987) has described the syndrome of personality disorder secondary to substance abuse. This syndrome is characterized by impulsivity, decreased frustration, tolerance, grandiosity, self-centeredness, and affect intolerance. I have found this constellation of symptoms to be frequent with this population and the intensity and severity of the symptoms greatly abate with abstinence and treatment. Although research has shown that approximately one-half of alcoholics and two-thirds of addicts have a personality disorder, my own diagnostic experience and QI (quality improvement) studies on several psychological and psychiatric reports do not show a high prevalence of Axis II diagnoses with this patient population. Research does show that addicts and alcoholics who have a personality disorder show an earlier onset of addiction, comparatively greater severity of addiction, a pattern of polydrug dependence, higher levels of suicidal and self-destructive behavior, as well as poorer treatment outcomes (Nace, 1990).

Following these guidelines and considerations as well as reviewing existing, albeit scant, research on diagnosis with chemically dependent patients, the clinician may significantly refine and upgrade his or her skills at accurate, valid, reliable, and clinically useful diagnostic approaches. In general, the index of suspicion of a psychiatric disorder should be high with this patient population, both adult and adolescent. The likelihood that the psychiatric symptomatology the clinician is observing in a patient is a direct manifestation or exacerbation of a primary psychiatric disorder rather than the symptom of a substance-induced psychiatric disorder is high. A chemical dependency disorder can only rarely account for the presence of an identifiable psychiatric disorder. In my experience, the psychiatric impairment brought on by substance abuse is rather global and diffuse in its impact and results more in general impairment in patient functioning, such as compromised decision making, self-care, reality testing, judgment, frustration tolerance, the capacity for autonomy of mood, mood stability, and adequate ego defense and regulation. Only further research into the nature, course, and natural history of substance- induced syndromes and disorders will bring greater clarity and accuracy to diagnostic practices with this complex patient population.

CLINICAL MANAGEMENT AND TREATMENT OF COEXISTING PSYCHIATRIC DISORDERS IN INPATIENT ADDICTIONS TREATMENT

In my experience, the primary concern with treating comorbid psychiatric impairment in primary inpatient addictions treatment settings is the decision about how much time, attention, and focus should be allotted to the management and treatment of the psychiatric condition(s). This is particularly important since the average length of stay in inpatient care is dwindling precipitously. Many patients now have less than fourteen days of inpatient care and a growing population of patients are seen in short-term stabilization with treatment stays ranging from three to seven days (O'Connell, 1999). This is barely enough time to meet even minimal treatment goals for the addictive disorder, which, of course, is the top priority in the inpatient addictions treatment environment. In my experience, addictions therapists generally conceptualize psychiatric disorders as secondary concerns and are chiefly interested in how they affect the clinical course of the addictive disorder.

Another important consideration is the level of experience with psychiatric impairment of the addictions staff and their skills with the treatment of psychiatric disorders. In my experience, even highly experienced master's level addictions clinicians are rarely skilled enough to assess and treat psychiatric disorders. Competency in psychiatric diagnosis and treatment is not commonly a part of the skill set of addictions therapists.

Of necessity, the treatment approaches for psychiatric comorbidity must be modified appropriately to the goals and objectives of primary addictions treatment. While acknowledging the importance of identifying and viewing both the psychiatric disorder and the addictions disorder as primary disorders requiring appropriate treatments, the reality of day-to-day clinical management is that in addictions settings most of the time, attention, and energy of the therapist and the patient will be devoted to ameliorating the addictive disorder. The dilemma for the clinical manager, program director, and therapist is developing strategies that can accomplish the dual task of adequately addressing both disorders.

The appendix to this chapter is a compendium of treatment plan problems and methods of intervention for selected major psychiatric disorders that commonly occur in chemically dependent populations. The reader will note that these strategies have a strong behavioral and cognitive behavioral focus to them. The nature and type of these suggested problems and interventions are based on research on cognitive-behavioral therapy for substance abuse disorders. Beck et al. (1993) have developed research-based cognitive strategies in a comprehensive system to address both addictive disorders and associated psychiatric dysfunction. Cognitive behavioral research in treating addictions has also been carried out by Finney et al. (1998) and Ouimette, Finney, and Moos (1997). This research indicates that a cognitive-behavioral approach to treating problems is an effective treatment for both addictive and psychiatric disorders as well as a complementary treatment for a primarily twelve-step approach common in many addiction treatment programs. I have found (O'Connell and Patterson, 1996) cognitive therapy to be the treatment of choice for addictive disorders, especially when dealing with short-term stabilization and in time-limited, outpatient services for addicted patients. I consider skill in cognitive-behavioral therapy to be absolutely essential for addictions clinicians working in inpatient treatment.

The treatment plan strategies listed here are active, practical, observable, and measurable as well as labor intensive for the patient. With these strategies, the bulk of time and energy for the treatment of psychiatric comorbidity is placed on the patient in the form of treatment plan activities that keep the patient focused, active, and intensely involved in the treatment process. Utilizing this scheme, the therapist's primary duty is to monitor the patient's progress with treatment tasks and goals as the patient addresses his or her experiences with the treatment plan activities in individual, group, or family therapy sessions. I have found that treatment plan activities that are guided by the principles and practices of active training (Silberman, 1990) are the most clinically useful and practical approaches to patient care in inpatient addictions treatment. The patient typically finds these activities to be helpful and pleasurable, and the therapist enjoys devising creative ways to address recurring, common psychiatric problems encountered in day-to-day clinical practice. This active training approach is also recommended in light of research by Timko and Moos (1998), which suggests that programs encouraging active patient involvement in treatment and community activities, a practical approach to treating problems, and the opportunity for individual patient personal expression were related to better patient outcomes, including higher levels of patient functioning, higher levels of patient involvement in the activities in the treatment facility and community, and greater patient use of health treatment services and social recreation activities. Timko and Moos note that these aspects of the treatment milieu were especially beneficial for patients with higher levels of psychiatric impairment. The active training approach to patient treatment and education keeps the patient focused on a variety of learning activities both didactic and experiential. At Caron we have found that treatment activities carried out in this way lead to increased levels of learning and utilization of learned material, both in the immediate inpatient environment and in continuing care. Research has shown (e.g., Kaskutas, Marsh, and Kohn, 1998) that experiential approaches to knowledge acquisition and life-skills development for psychiatric and chemically dependent patients may be a useful addition to inpatient care and this has been found to be the case at Caron Foundation.

The strategies and approaches described in this chapter are also consonant with research results on treatment matching (e.g., McLellan et al., 1997), which indicate that matching patients to treatments based on presenting clinical problems and patient needs can increase the effectiveness of chemical dependency treatment. Research on behavioral approaches to treating dual diagnosis (e.g., Ridgely and Jerrell, 1996) indicates that strategies to modify patient problem behavior can be quite effective with this population, and Ridgely found behavioral approaches superior to intensive case management and twelve-step approaches to dual diagnosis treatment.

In designing and delivering psychosocial treatments for patients with psychiatric comorbidity in primary addictions treatment, several considerations arise. Following are examples of these considerations, along with recommendations drawn from experience at Caron Foundation.

There is no substitute for good clinical and case management. This patient population, like any population, is best served when therapists practice good integrated clinical care (Minkoff, 1989). The ingredients of such care include a comprehensive patient assessment, individualized treatment planning, ample time for individual contact with the patient, being emotionally and physically available to the patient during times of crisis, listening to and addressing patients' concerns, and providing for patient safety and stability (Curley, 1999). Patients with a dual diagnosis should have daily contact with the therapist even if for only a few minutes. Regular individual counseling sessions, even brief ones, can be associated with dramatic decreases in patient acting-out behaviors such as suicidal, parasuicidal, and violent behavior.

Match treatments according to patient's readiness for change, the type of program, and the patient's level of functioning. It is recommended that all dually diagnosed patients receive psychoeducation regarding the problems of both psychiatric disorders and addictive diseases as well as their interaction. Addictions counselors should provide liberal supportive psychotherapy to patients early in the treatment stay and to patients undergoing emotional crisis. Brief cognitive and cognitive-behavioral therapies are appropriate for patients involved in brief lengths of stay, such as short-term detoxification and stabilization. Patients who have a history of significant trauma and possess adequate levels of ego strength can be involved in evocative and expressive therapy such as psychodrama. At Caron Foundation we have found this to be a particularly useful approach for patients in our relapse treatment unit, many of whom have had several previous psychiatric and addictions treatment experiences. Adolescent and young adult patients presenting with problems such as conduct disorder and attention deficit hyperactivity disorder require programs that provide a lot of activity, such as extra recreational time or outdoors experiences. Patients involved in extended care or halfway house arrangements require ongoing psychiatric management and programs that develop life skills and coping skills to meet the daily challenges of early recovery. Research and clinical programming mentioned previously by Brady et al. (1996) has shown that well-planned, appropriate therapeutic interventions tailored to individual patients' needs based on their unique characteristics have a greater potential for increasing patient functioning than approaches that are not planned or well designed.

Recommendations for Improving Clinical Programming

It would appear that treatment of psychiatric comorbidity with chemically dependent patients will increase in its effectiveness as inpatient addictions programs begin to utilize existing research on dual diagnosis in the design, development, and operation of the delivery of clinical care. Patients with a dual diagnosis will also benefit from the dramatic developments in psychopharmacology with newer, more effective agents having significantly decreased side effect profiles. Such patients will also benefit from the development of new behavioral psychotherapeutic approaches, such as eye movement, desensitization, and retraining (EMDR) and thought field therapy. For enhanced quality of clinical care, in my opinion, addictions therapists should also be skilled psychotherapists and should have a strong background in inpatient psychiatric care.

Directors of addictions programs are encouraged to develop a process to ensure that clinicians in the field investigate, understand, and utilize research on treatment effectiveness. At Caron Foundation the decision was made to form a professional advisory council consisting of leaders in addictions research. These individuals would offer guidance, advice, consultation, and direction in identifying and applying empirical addictions research and translating it into enhanced clinical programs and practices. Several illuminaries in the field were sought for the council. Examples include Charles O'Brien, MD, PhD, chief of psychiatry at the University of Pennsylvania, a prolific researcher in the field of addictions and dual diagnosis; Sheila Blume, MD, a researcher, writer, and expert in the field of the treatment of female patients; and David Melee, MD, developer of the American Society of Addiction Medicine placement criteria. The professional advisory council meets two to three times per year with clinical and administrative leaders of Caron Foundation and offers training and education on the latest research on addictions treatment and its implications for clinical program improvement.

Complementary and Alternative Medical Approaches

In 1994, a book titled *Self-Recovery: Treating Addictions Using Transcendental Meditation and Maharishi Ayurveda* was published (O'Connell and Alexander, 1994) as a special four-volume edition of *Alcoholism Treatment Quarterly.* It included a summary, interpretation, and meta-analysis of outcome studies on the application of transcendental meditation (TM) to the treatment of addictions. Meta-analysis results revealed that the practice of transcendental meditation was 1.6 to 9 times more effective in treating addictions than conventional approaches to addictions treatment. The book also presented several previously unpublished studies on the effectiveness of TM and also medical and clinical case studies on the applications of Maharishi Ayurveda to addictions and mental health problems. This bold, innovative approach to the treatment of addictions and psychiatric problems has been largely ignored by the addictions field. I have found this lack of interest in these treatment approaches to be part of a larger trend in the addictions field of ignoring the strategies and approaches of complementary and alternative medicine (CAM) despite the fact that there is a growing body of research on a number of such approaches including acupuncture, herbal remedies, yoga, homeopathy, aromatherapy, prayer, and other contemplative practices (Graham, Schultz, and Wilford,

1998). Given the high relapse rates for patients with psychiatric comorbidity and the severe, often chronic, problems they face, continuing to ignore complementary and alternative medical approaches to treating addiction and psychiatric problems would appear to be unwise and unfair to patients. This patient population, in fact, needs all the help that can be given to them. In the case of transcendental meditation, early research (e.g., Bloomfield, 1975) showed that the practice of this effortless, natural meditation technique led to significant, often dramatic improvements with severely impaired psychiatric patients, including marked symptom reduction, improvements in level of functioning, as well as a markedly decreased need for psychiatric medications. A meta-analysis by Eppley, Abrams, and Shear (1989) revealed that the practice of transcendental meditation is twice as effective as other meditation and relaxation techniques in the treatment of trait anxiety. Based on these data and data drawn from over 600 other studies on the transcendental meditation technique, TM would easily emerge as a treatment of choice for many psychiatric and addictive disorders. However, this has not yet transpired.

In my opinion, future research and program development for patients presenting with a dual diagnosis should include a consideration of the effects of a broader array of therapies including innovative psychotherapies and therapies from complementary and alternative medicine (CAM). This certainly would entail some risk and discomfort. Both are a necessary part of innovation, growth, and development.

APPENDIX: CLINICAL PROTOCOLS FOR THE TREATMENT OF SELECTED PSYCHIATRIC DISORDERS

This appendix contains concise, concentrated useful information on selected major mental disorders, several representative problem areas, as well as suggested treatment plan activities designed to address them. This appendix can serve as a quick clinical reference and treatment strategy guide for addictions therapists who desire to gain greater understanding of and comfort with treating commonly occurring psychiatric disorders in chemically dependent patient populations.

Clinical Protocol for the Management of Mood Disorders (Major Depression, Dysthymic Disorder, Depressive Disorder, Not Otherwise Specified)

Clinical Management

This class of disorders is frequently found in chemically dependent populations. Substance-induced depression tends to clear relatively rapidly (within three to five days) and differential diagnosis is sometimes difficult. Symptoms of depression include: low appetite, deep sadness, grief, low energy, poor concentration, isolation, suicidal thoughts and urges, and strong feelings of hopelessness, worthlessness, or inappropriate guilt. The course of depression tends to fluctuate and rate of relapse to a depressive episode is high.

The depressed patient should be kept busy in treatment. He or she should keep a daily log of feelings and moods. At least once weekly, the therapist should meet for an individual session with the depressed patient. The mood picture should be periodically (every three to five days) evaluated with a Beck Depression Inventory. Psychological evaluation would be considered routine with these disorders, and psychiatric consultation and medication an option in severe cases. If suicidal thoughts or urges are present, they should be evaluated using the recommended suicide protocol. Our protocol for treating mood disorders involves a combination of supportive therapy, education about depression, cognitive therapy, and scheduled physical activity.

Problem Area	Treatment Plan Activity
Patient lacks understanding of depressive illness.	Patient will read handout titled "Understanding Depression" (Greenberger and Padensky, 1995), write down key concepts, and discuss in individual therapy session.
Patient shows dysfunctional thoughts and beliefs that accompany depressed mood.	Patient will read handouts on cognitive distortions (Burns, 1989) and will describe five situations in which one or more distortions are utilized and discuss them in individual therapy.
Patient lacks effective coping strategies for depressing thoughts and beliefs.	Patient will identify five depressive thoughts and develop five rational counters to these thoughts, using the triple column technique and discuss results and experiences in therapy group.
Patient lacks awareness of underlying dysfunctional assumptions and beliefs associated with depression.	Patient will complete dysfunctional attitude scale (Burns, 1989) and discuss results with therapist in individual therapy session.

Patient lacks cognitive and behavioral skills to offset irrational thinking associated with depression.	Patient will read handout titled "10 Ways to Untwist Your Thinking" (Burns, 1989) and will develop an action plan to implement these suggestions.
Patient lacks consistent daily structure and routine.	Patient will develop a daily plan of activities including exercise, a work schedule, learning activities, and meal planning and practice them in treatment and discuss in therapy group.
Patient has history of significant loss and grief.	Patient will complete feelings letter to appropriate persons/situations involved in loss and discuss in therapy group.
Patient lacks knowledge of and plan for dealing with relapse to depression.	Patient will review history of depressive episodes listing those feelings, thoughts, situations, and stresses that accompany the episodes and develop an action plan including self-help, professional support, and daily activities for relapse prevention.
Patient needs information on medication effects, side effects, and dosing.	Patient will meet with nursing/medical staff and review guidelines for medication compliance.

Clinical Protocol for the Management of Anxiety Disorders

Clinical Management

The anxiety disorders include generalized anxiety disorder, agoraphobia, panic disorder, social anxiety disorder, obsessive compulsive disorder, posttraumatic stress disorder, and simple phobia. All of these disorders have in common both cognitive and physiological symptoms of pathological fear (anxiety). They are the most common psychiatric illnesses. They occur relatively frequently in chemically dependent populations. The existence of one of these disorders rarely precludes participation in inpatient or outpatient addictions treatment. Most patients will be pharmacologically managed with antidepressants. These patients tend to be compliant and are fairly easily managed. Our treatment protocol involves a combination of supportive counseling, educational information on the psychology and physiology of anxiety, cognitive restructuring, relaxation/meditation techniques, worry and time management, working through avoidance behaviors, and pharmacological management. These disorders usually predate the onset of chemical addiction and are relatively easy to differentiate from substance-induced anxiety. These patients' lives are dominated by fear. In general, both clinical management interventions and treatment plan strategies are designed to reduce fear and build coping skills. Transcendental meditation has been shown by research to be the most effective meditation for anxiety; however, its prescription involves a specialized program that is not feasible in inpatient care. Other meditation techniques such as quieting reflex training, mindfulness meditation, and progressive muscle relaxation have been found useful in the treatment of chronic anxiety problems.

Problem Area	Treatment Plan Strategy
Patient lacks understanding of the medical and psychological aspects of anxiety disorders.	Patient will read handout titled "The Causes of Anxiety Disorders" (Bourne, 1990) and discuss in individual therapy session. Patient will read handout "Understanding Anxiety" (Burns, 1989) and discuss in individual session.
Patient lacks effective program for reducing symptoms of tension, rapid breathing, rapid heart rate, and other indicators of anxiety.	Patient will practice mindfulness meditation (Kabat-Zinn, 1994) for twenty minutes twice daily, keep a log of experiences, and discuss in individual therapy session.
Patient lacks understanding of cognitive components of the anxiety response.	Patient will read handout titled "Irrational Self Talk" and keep a log of situations in which the patient uses such examples (Bourne, 1990).
Patient lacks cognitive coping skills for anxiety-arousing situations.	Patient will use triple column technique (Bourne, 1990) and develop three rational coping statements to offset anxiety and discuss results in individual session.
Patient reports chronic worry and concern.	Patient will construct a list of common worries, rank them for level of anxiety, and develop a plan of action to deal with them including cognitive coping statements and relaxation procedures.
Patient shows chronic controlling behaviors.	Patient will meet with therapist and discuss the language of letting go and surrender, and will discuss the fears associated with this in individual therapy session and group session.
Patient reports being overwhelmed by daily work and family obligations.	Patient will develop a time management procedure listing daily activities and obligations and prioritize them for completion.
Patient reports flashbacks of past trauma.	Patient will develop action plan to offset flashbacks including developing rational coping statements, practicing relaxation, and writing a feelings letter to person/situations/memories evoking anxiety response. Discuss results in therapy group.
Patient lacks adequate understanding of role of medications in treatment of anxiety.	Patient will meet with appropriate nursing/medical staff and discuss the effects, side effects, and appropriate use of antianxiety medication to ensure medication compliance.

| Patient reports significant anxiety and avoidance behaviors in social situations. | Patient will develop a list of fears and concerns that arise in group therapy and other community activities and will develop a list of coping strategies for each fear. Discuss in individual and in group therapy sessions. |

Clinical Protocol for the Management of Personality Disorders

Clinical Management

These disorders are common in chemically dependent populations. The general goal of our clinical management strategies is to keep the patient focused on primary addictions treatment with minimal disruptive behavior in the treatment community. Keep in mind we cannot change these patients' personalities. We can, however, make some inroads in behavior and attitudinal change, and we can increase their ability to get along with other people. This is of immense importance if they are to take advantage of twelve-step and other therapies in continuing care. Personality disorders are arranged in clusters. Cluster A includes paranoid, schizoid, and schizotypal personality. Cluster B disorders are probably the most difficult to treat and include antisocial, borderline, histrionic, and narcissistic personality disorder. Cluster C disorders are probably the least difficult to treat and include avoidant, dependent, and obsessive-compulsive personality disorder. Keep in mind that any patient can exhibit any of these traits and behaviors in any combination. Caron's clinical protocol for these disorders involves strong focus on twelve-step character defect work, and a labor-intensive treatment plan for the patient involving much self-evaluation and getting feedback from other patients in the treatment community. The treatment strategies listed here involve a strong component of reality testing to augment the patient's perception of self and relationships with others, and to decrease disruptive impulsive behavior as well as irrational thinking and emotional expression.

Problem Area	**Treatment Plan Strategy**
Paranoid Personality Disorder	
Patient shows lack of trust in interpersonal relationships.	Patient will list fears involved with trust and present them in therapy group.
Patient shows excessive anger in response to benign events.	Patient will practice identifying hurt in anger-provoking situations and share experiences in group.
Patient shows irrational suspicious pattern of thinking with no evidence to document concerns.	Patient will keep a log of negative self-talk and irrational thinking social encounters and provide justification for them. Discuss in individual therapy.

Patient anticipates being abused or attacked unjustly in intimate relations.

Patient will interview three other patients and discuss their feelings about conflict resolution and handling criticism.

Schizoid Personality Disorder

Patient lacks adequate social support system and shows low desire to develop one.

Patient will interview one new patient per day and discuss interests/similarities and discuss in therapy group.

Patient spends inordinate amount of time in solitary pursuits.

Patient will assume leadership/responsibility function in community and discuss experiences in group.

Patient lacks adequate feeling vocabulary and skills to express needs and desires.

Patient will review a feelings list and describe one personal situation for each feeling and share in group therapy.

Patient lacks awareness of impact of his or her behavior on others.

Patient will ask for personal feedback daily in group therapy and keep a log of responses.

Schizotypal Personality Disorder

Patient is defocused onto internal thoughts/perceptions.

Patient will practice switching to here and now focus when defocusing behavior is identified and share experiences in group.

Patient lacks awareness of eccentric behaviors.

Patient will keep daily written log of his or her thoughts/reactions to therapy and share in individual session.

Patient reports high level of social anxiety/ineptness.

Patient will interview three patients and discuss their fears/concerns in group activities and identify common concerns and similarities.

Antisocial Personality Disorder

Patient lacks appropriate concern for others' rights and feelings.

Patient will describe situations where he or she was discounted/neglected and share in therapy group.

Patient shows chronic pattern of lying, misrepresentation, and manipulative behaviors.

Patient will assess the effects of manipulative behaviors and generate alternative methods of need attainment.

Patient lacks consistent, responsible behavior in work and family commitments.

Patient will practice responsible behaviors for one day and discuss reactions in therapy group.

Patient lacks adequate planning and time management skills.

Patient will interview three patients and discuss their methods of daily time/routine management and discuss in individual session.

Borderline Personality Disorder

Patient lacks ability to control self-destructive impulses/behaviors.

Patient will commit to a suicide and self-mutilation prevention plan and will review guidelines for hospital admission.

Patient lacks capacity to modulate/control expression of moods and feelings.	Patient will practice time out and relaxation procedures as needed. Discuss results in individual therapy.
Patient shows pervasive pattern of rage and violent behavior to self and others.	Patient will recognize and write down anger-provoking situations/thoughts and practice cognitive coping skills.
Patient lacks stable, interpersonal relations with others.	Patient will analyze current intimate relations and list his or her contributions to problems and discuss in individual session.

Histrionic Personality Disorder

Patient engages in disruptive attention-seeking/ seductive behavior.	Patient will model and role-play rational, assertive problem-solving behaviors in group therapy.
Patient lacks ability to modulate extremes in feelings and moods.	Patient will learn and practice mindfulness meditation/relaxation (Kabat-Zinn, 1994; Stroebel, 1983) techniques and discuss in individual therapy.
Patient shows poor conflict containment skills.	Patient will model a staff member or patient who has developed rational, adaptive conflict resolution skills and discuss in group.
Patient lacks deep, significant intimate relations with others.	Patient will interview five patients and record their thoughts about what constitutes intimacy and discuss in group.

Narcissistic Personality Disorder

Patient lacks stable realistic self-image.	Patient will practice nonjudging, nonevaluating behaviors with self and others for one day and discuss experiences in group.
Patient shows deep fears of self-disclosure and exposure in relations with others.	Patient will imagine his or her worst fear happening and discuss how he or she would cope with it and discuss in group.
Patient shows deficits in capacity for sensitivity/empathy with others.	Patient will repeat and defend the statement "I am the center of the universe" and discuss in group.

Avoidant Personality Disorder

Patient shows excessive anxiety in social situations.	Patient will identify and define catastrophizing behaviors and keep a log of fears in social interaction.
Patient reports deep fears of criticism and rejection in interpersonal relations.	Patient will identify emotional reasoning behavior and defend this statement: "If I feel it, it must be true."
Patient lacks strong social support network.	Patient will discuss the benefits/liabilities of loneliness and discuss in group therapy.

Dependent Personality Disorder

Patient lacks self-care/reliance skills.	Patient will list twenty reasons why he or she is helpless and cannot get needs met and discuss in group.
Patient avoids taking responsibility for meeting his or her needs.	Patient will list liabilities of looking to others for need fulfillment and discuss fears of being independent.
Patient lacks effective conflict management skills.	Patient will role-play three conflict situations and ask group members for assistance in developing alternative methods of coping.

Obsessive-Compulsive Personality Disorder

Patient is excessively perfectionistic.	Patient will discuss the emotional price of perfectionism and practice being imperfect for one day and discuss in therapy group.
Patient shows compulsive work behaviors and attitudes.	Patient will identify what fears/conflicts he or she is avoiding through workaholism and discuss in therapy group.
Patient lacks capacity to identify and express positive affects.	Patient will list perceived dangers of showing positive feelings. Patient will discuss the most positive experience in his or her childhood and discuss in therapy group.

Clinical Protocol for the Management of Eating Disorders

Clinical Management

Eating disorders such as anorexia nervosa and bulimia are common in chemically dependent populations and often have serious psychological and medical effects. Patients may come into chemical dependency treatment actively bingeing, purging, and engaging in other efforts to control weight or may experience a relapse to such behaviors as a result of the experience and stress of inpatient treatment. In either case, the dysfunctional eating and weight-controlling habits need to be vigorously addressed. Patients should be medically cleared for treatment to address potential problems such as fluid imbalances, cardiac abnormalities, kidney dysfunction, and gastrointestinal disturbances, which can result from laxative, diuretic, and other medication abuse, as well as bingeing and purging behavior. Referrals to the dietitian should be considered routine. This professional can correct the often distorted and peculiar beliefs that anorexics and bulimics have about nutrition, dieting, fasting, exercising, and other efforts at weight control. In this context they can also learn about the effects of these behaviors on the patient's emotional life. All patients should be administered the Diagnostic Survey of Eating Disorders (DSED) (Garner and Garfinkel, 1985). This provides a wealth of information on patient symptoms and can be used for focusing treatment plans. It is also a good educational experience for the patient and can heighten the patient's awareness of dysfunctional eating patterns and dysfunctional beliefs about eating and weight control. Our treatment protocol involves a combination of medical management, nutritional education and guidance, cognitive therapy, and behavior therapy, all designed to restore normal eating patterns, body weight, realistic body perception, and good physical and psychological health. Appropriate patients can be referred to twelve-step groups such as Overeaters Anonymous. Patients with eating disorders should be routinely referred to outpatient, or in some cases inpatient, treatment of their eating disorder as a part of their continuing care plan.

Problem Area	Treatment Plan Strategy
Patient shows ongoing urges to binge, purge, and fast.	Patient will learn and utilize distracting, delaying, and cognitive self-coping behaviors to manage urges. Keep a log of experiences and discuss with therapist in individual session.
Patient lacks adequate coping strategies to manage dysphoric moods.	Patient will interview five other patients/staff and learn four strategies to cope with negative emotions that can precede binge/purge.
Patient lacks knowledge of the relationship of irrational beliefs and thoughts to onset of bingeing/purging behavior.	Patient will review list and examples of cognitive distortions and discuss with therapist in individual session.
Patient shows dysfunctional beliefs and thoughts about weight control and emotional health.	Patient will review handout "Ten Ways to Untwist Your Thinking" (Burns, 1989), practice at least three techniques, write down experiences, and discuss with therapist in individual and group session.
Patient shows overevaluation of control and perfectionism.	Patient will list the benefits and liabilities of these behaviors and attitudes, evaluate personal outcomes with these behaviors, and discuss with therapist in individual sessions.

| Patient demonstrates strong feelings of fear of failure and inadequacy. | Patient will meet with therapist and discuss the meaning of these concerns and the role of personal beliefs and thoughts and how to sustain them. Discuss in individual session. |

Clinical Protocol for the Management of Psychotic Disorders (Schizophrenia, Schizophreniform Disorder, Schizoaffective Disorder, Brief Psychotic Disorder, Delusional Disorder, and Psychotic Disorder Not Otherwise Specified)

Clinical Management

Patients presenting for treatment at Caron with a psychotic disorder are a small but growing subpopulation of patients. Psychotic symptoms include delusions; hallucinations; disorganized speech, thinking, and behavior; ideas of reference and influence; inappropriate affect; as well as negative symptoms of psychosis, which include: flat affect, feelings of emptiness, amotivation, avolition, apathy, poor attention, asociality, and anhedonia. The most common psychotic disorders encountered at Caron include: schizoaffective disorder, psychotic disorder not otherwise specified, and schizophrenia. Substance abuse and dependence is common among patients with a diagnosis of schizophrenia. Chemicals are often used to offset the negative symptoms of schizophrenia, which may not respond well to antipsychotic medications. Drugs such as cannabis and alcohol, the most favored drugs among schizophrenic patients, can induce a sense of liveliness and excitation in a patient who may otherwise feel flat, empty, and unhappy. There is a definite wide range in symptom and syndrome severity, acuity, and level of functioning with psychotic patients. Most psychotic patients respond at least partially to antipsychotic medication. However, a significant portion of psychotic patients are not well managed on psychiatric medications. Medication compliance is often poor with this diagnostic group. Chemically dependent psychotic patients can experience a relapse to active psychotic illness when they resume drug and alcohol use, which generally lowers the efficacy of psychiatric medications and exacerbates and provokes psychotic symptomatology. Psychotic patients are generally underemployed and have a poor, underdeveloped social life. Psychotic patients are especially stress sensitive, particularly to interpersonal stress, and may quickly regress to overt psychotic disease during stressful periods in their lives.

Transient, substance-induced psychotic symptoms are not uncommon among intoxicated chemically dependent patients. With substance-induced disorders, however, these symptoms clear fairly rapidly with abstinence. In general, psychotic patients who use drugs show a poorer prognosis, increased number and length of hospital stays, as well as increased institutionalization and diminished socioeconomic status compared with psychotic patients who are not chemically abusive or dependent. Nearly half of patients who are schizophrenic show a chemical dependency disorder. Psychotic conditions can be induced by medical conditions. Examples are tumors, disturbances in endocrine functioning, electrolyte imbalances, liver or renal failure, autoimmune disorders, as well as cognitive disorders such as delirium and dementia. Drugs can also cause psychotic episodes including stimulants, sedatives, designer drugs such as ecstasy, high doses of marijuana, hallucinogens, and phencyclidine. Corticosteroids, certain cardiovascular medications, antihypertensives, anticonvulsants, and certain anesthetics can also induce psychosis occasionally. Psychotic disorders, in particular schizophrenia, are generally considered to be genetically based neurophysiological illnesses and are thought to involve a disturbance in the dopaminergic system of the brain. Magnetic resonance imaging (MRI) studies reveal neuroanatomical correlates of schizophrenia such as widened sulci, cortical atrophy, and ventricular enlargement, as well as deficiencies in the frontal and temporolimbic areas of the brain. Schizophrenia, in particular, and often other psychotic disorders are chronic and show a fluctuating course of the illness including periods of quiescence, relapse to florid psychosis, and a remission of psychotic symptoms. Nearly all psychotic patients will benefit from antipsychotic medications and other medications (e.g., antidepressants, antianxiety drugs). These patients do best with a combination of individual and group therapy. The prognosis for these patients is almost always guarded. Psychotic patients are appropriate for this level of care only if they are adequately managed on antipsychotic and other medications. Patients who are schizophrenic should be in *social remission,* which is the state in which psychotic symptoms are absent and the patient can act appropriately in groups. Caron's protocol for managing psychotic disorders includes appropriate antipsychotic and other medications, psychiatric management, group therapy supplemented with individual counseling sessions, and relapse prevention and education to impact on relapse to either active chemical dependency or overt psychotic illness.

Problem Area	Treatment Plan Strategy
Patient shows overt psychotic symptoms despite current regimen of antipsychotic medications.	Patient will receive a psychiatric evaluation and medication assessment from staff psychiatrist.
Patient shows evidence of social withdrawal and discomfort in informal social situations.	Patient will discuss social fears with therapist in individual supportive counseling session.

Patient shows signs of cognitive disorganization when addressing treatment assignments and other tasks.	Patient will meet with therapist for individual counseling session and develop a concrete, practical approach to organizing and executing treatment plan assignments.
Patient shows poor medication compliance which leads to relapse to active psychotic illness.	Patient will read informational handouts on antipsychotic medications (American Psychiatric Press, 1994), write down any questions or comments about them, and discuss concerns with psychiatrist/psychologist in individual consultation session.
Patient shows fear of intimacy and closeness and interpersonal relationships.	Patient will interview five other patients in treatment community, solicit their concerns about intimacy and ways they have dealt with the problem. Discuss in group therapy session.
Patient has history of decreased capacity to manage stress and manage lifestyle.	Patient will meet with therapist and develop a comprehensive plan to address relapse to psychosis/addiction, simplify lifestyle, and manage daily stressors.
Patient shows evidence and history of self-medicating negative symptoms of psychosis with drug and alcohol use.	Patient will complete "Understanding Schizophrenia and Addiction" (Daley and Montrose, 1993) and discuss results with therapist in individual counseling session.

Clinical Protocol for the Management of Impulse Control Disorders (Intermittent Explosive Disorder, Impulse Disorder Not Otherwise Specified)

Clinical Management

This is a diagnostically diverse group of disorders characterized chiefly by a failure to resist an impulse (for example: stealing, setting fires, gambling, hair pulling, and committing acts of violence). Two of the impulse control disorders, intermittent explosive disorder and impulse disorder not otherwise specified (NOS), are of primary concern in our inpatient environment and these alone are the focus of clinical management and treatment planning in this protocol. Individuals who engage in violent acting out present obvious dangers to both patients and staff; therefore, controlling, inhibiting, and preventing violent acting out is the chief focus of treatment plan interventions. Eighty percent of patients with these disorders are male. These patients come to treatment with a history of problems that can include both focal and diffuse neurological abnormalities, a history of seizures, legal problems, attention deficit hyperactivity disorder, head trauma, learning disabilities, a diagnosis of antisocial personality disorder, and a family history of violence. Patients with acute problems with violence are not appropriate for admission to Caron and every opportunity is made to screen them out at intake. However, patients with a history of violence and rage reactions who are successfully managed on appropriate psychotropic medication may be appropriate for placement here. A variety of medications are used to treat impulse control disorders including lithium, Depakote, beta-blockers such as Inderal, neuroleptics, and selective serotonin reuptake inhibitors (SSRIs), as well as psychostimulant medications. It is imperative that patients comply with their medications. Patients with a history of violent behavior who present concerns to the staff should be referred for a psychiatric evaluation and medication review. A psychological consultation is also advisable to gain specific advice on how to manage the patient. General clinical management principles include avoiding evocative, effectively stimulating experiential work, such as family sculpting, psychodrama, and anger-release work. These procedures may overstimulate the patient and inadvertently precipitate a rageful or violent reaction. In general, our clinical protocol focuses on imparting behavioral and emotional control. Patients with these disorders often lack the capacity to modulate anger and other troubling affects. In addition, they impulsively act before they think, which often has serious consequences. Typically these patients react to hurt, guilt, shame, and other dysphoric affects with anger and violence. They often have unidentified or unacknowledged vulnerabilities, frailties, and inadequacies, which can leave them at risk for violent acting out. Treatment planning at Caron aims at ensuring medication compliance, fostering the development of affective awareness as well as awareness of somatic and cognitive cues for violent behavior, addressing underlying hurt and character flaws, and assisting the patient to anticipate and predict potential violent situations so as to preempt or prevent them. Our clinical protocol for the management of impulse control disorders has a strong cognitive-behavioral focus designed to assist the patient to proactively identify and effectively deal with violence and rage before it erupts. Treatment plans also aim at reducing impulsivity and assisting the patients to understand and assume responsibility for the consequences of their behaviors. Continuing care plans should routinely include referral of patients with impulse control disorders to a competent psychotherapist. Long-term cognitive-behavioral and insight-oriented therapy is almost always necessary for the successful treatment of these disorders, as is ongoing pharmacotherapeutic management. In addition to the clinical management and treatment planning guidelines listed here, therapists are referred to the guidelines on preventing and managing patient violence for assistance in this area.

Problem Area	Treatment Plan Strategy
Patient shows history of rage/violent behavior and lacks understanding of how violent behaviors are triggered.	Patient will complete written violence history listing triggers for violence, feelings/thoughts/behaviors during violent episodes, and the consequences of each episode. Discuss in individual therapy session.
Patient lacks understanding of affective somatic and cognitive clues for rage/violent behavior.	Patient will complete "When I Get Angry" chart (Brasswell and Bloomquist, 1991) for five days. Discuss information in individual therapy session.
Patient lacks ability to anticipate and prevent situations that lead to violent behavior.	Patient will interview three other patients and solicit their advice on handling anger/conflict. Patient will complete "Anger Combat Chart" (Brasswell and Bloomquist, 1991) for five days. Discuss in group therapy.
Patient shows poor capacity to modulate and control anger, irritability, agitation, and other affects.	Patient will develop five cognitive coping statements (see Exhibit 1.4) and practice them daily for five days. Discuss results in group therapy.
Patient has not acknowledged or identified hurt that underlies and leads to violent/rage behavior.	Patient will verbalize the statement "When I get angry it means that I am hurt. Please understand and help me on a daily basis" in group therapy and community meetings. Patient will discuss what assistance he or she has received with this intervention in therapy group.
Patient shows pattern of impulsive (acting before thinking) behavior in response to stress.	Patient will read handout on anger aggression control (see Exhibit 1.5), brainstorm with therapy group methods to control and reduce anger and aggression, and discuss results in therapy group.
Patient lacks full awareness of the consequences of violent behavior.	Patient will complete "Cost Benefit Analysis" form (Burns, 1989) listing both the short- and long-term positive and negative consequences of engaging in violent behavior. Discuss in group therapy session.
Patient lacks appreciation of the importance of medication compliance.	Patient will meet with appropriate medical/nursing personal and discuss the patient's medications including affects, side effects, tolerance of medications, and medication compliance guidelines.

EXHIBIT 1.4.
Cognitive Coping Statements for Alleviating Rage/Violence

- I'm starting to feel angry; it's time for me to back off.
- It's time to take a "time out."
- Don't jump to conclusions.

(continued)

(continued)
- I don't have to be at the mercy of my impulses; I have options.
- Just because somebody is yelling at me doesn't mean I have to respond.
- Is there something else I can do in this situation?
- Ignoring them takes away their power and this might be the best way to get back at them.
- If I get angry and violent I will have to face the consequences.
- This too shall pass.
- Just because I feel angry doesn't mean there is something to be angry about.
- They probably didn't mean to hurt my feelings.
- They really don't know what I feel inside.
- It's time to take a walk and practice my relaxation skills.
- What am I feeling right now?
- It's time to talk to my therapist or group members.
- I don't have to do anything right now; I can always get angry later.
- I can handle this; I just have to cool down.
- Nothing good has ever come of my being violent.
- It's time for me to begin thinking about my problems rather than hitting someone.
- It just isn't worth getting mad about.
- Why should I blow everything I've worked for?

Source: O'Connell, D.F. (1999). Wernersville, PA: Caron Foundation.

EXHIBIT 1.5.
Anger/Aggression Control Approaches

1. *Problem definition*—What is the problem? The patient is prompted to identify what led up to the problem, what are the provoking stimuli, situational variables, and internal anger cues.

2. *Generation of alternative solutions*—What can I do? During this phase the individual brainstorms all possible responses to the problem.

3. *Consequence evaluation*—What will happen if . . . ? The patient is prompted to identify the most probable consequences occurring subsequent to each of the responses generated in phase two. Both positive and negative consequences and both long- and short-term results are delineated.

4. *Choosing a problem solution*—What will I do? The patient ranks all solutions according to their desirability or undesirability or severity of the consequences described above. The ideal choice is the solution that optimizes positive consequences, minimizes negative consequences, and solves the problem.

5. *Feedback*—How did it work? Was it effective? If not, a second choice solution is then implemented.

Source: Adapted from Brasswell and Bloomquist (1991). *Cognitive behavioral therapy for ADHD children.* New York: Guilford.

REFERENCES

American Psychiatric Press (1994). *Practical psychiatric practice.* Washington, DC: American Psychiatric Press.

Beck, A.T., Wright, F.D., Newman, C.F., and Liese, B.S. (1993). *Cognitive therapy of substance abuse.* New York: Guilford.

Bloomfield, H.H. (1975). Some observations on the uses of the transcendental meditation program in psychiatry. Institute of Psychophysiological medicine. San Diego, CA.

Blume, S.B. (1997). *Dual diagnosis in women,* Twentieth Anniversary SAA Conference on Alcohol and Drug Abuse, Reykjavik, Iceland. October 1997.

Bourne, E.J. (1990). *The anxiety and phobia workbook.* Oakland, CA: New Harbinger.

Brady, S., Hiam, C.M., Saemann, R., Humbert, L. (1996). Dual diagnosis: A treatment model for substance abuse and mental illness. *Community Mental Health Journal,* 32(6), 573-578.

Brasswell, L. and Bloomquist, M.L. (1991). *Cognitive behavioral therapy with ADHD children,* p. 296. New York: Guilford.

Burns, D. (1989). *The feeling good handbook,* pp. 97-119. New York: William and Morrow.

Curley, R. (1999). Taking the "dual" out of dual diagnosis. *Behavioral Healthcare Tomorrow.* December, 14-47.

Daley, D. and Montrose, K. (1993). Understanding schizophrenia and addiction. Center City, MN: Hazelden.

Eppley, K.R., Abrams, D., and Shear, J. (1989). Differential effects of relaxation on trait anxiety: A meta analysis. *Journal of Clinical Psychology,* 45(6), 957-974.

Finney, J.W., Noyes, C.A., Coutts, A.I., and Moos, R.H. (1998). Evaluating substance abuse treatment process models: Changes on proximal outcome variables during 12 step and cognitive behavioral treatment. *Journal of Studies on Alcohol,* 59(4), 371-380.

Garner, D.M. and Garfinkel, P.E. (Eds.) (1985). *Handbook of psychotherapy for anorexia nervosa and bulimia.* New York: Guilford.

Goldsmith, R.J. and Ries, R.K. (1998). Substance induced mental disorders. In A.W. Graham, T.K. Schultz, and B.B. Wilford (Eds.), *Principles of addiction medicine,* Second edition, pp. 969-982. Chevy Chase, MD: American Society of Addiction Medicine.

Graham, A.W., Schultz, T.K., and Wilford, B.B. (Eds.) (1998). *Principles of addiction medicine, Second edition.* Chevy Chase, MD: American Society of Addiction Medicine.

Greenberger, D. and Padensky, C.A. (1995). *Mind over mood: A cognitive therapy treatment manual for clients,* pp. 3-14. New York: Guilford.

Kabat-Zinn, J. (1994). *Wherever you go, there you are: Mindfulness meditation in everyday life.* New York: Hyperion.

Kaskutas, L.A., Marsh, D., and Kohn, A. (1998). Didactic and experiential education in substance abuse programs. *Journal of Substance Abuse Treatment,* 15(1), 43-53.

Kessler, R.C., Nelson, C.B., McGonagle, K.A., Edlund, M.J., Frank, R.G., and Leaf, P.J. (1996). The epidemiology of co-occurring addiction and mental disorders: Implication for prevention and service utilization. *American Journal of Orthopsychiatry,* 66(1), 17-30.

Leshner, A.L. (1998). What we know: Drug addiction is a brain disease. In A.W. Graham, T.K. Schultz, and B.B. Wilford (Eds.), *Principles of addiction medicine,* Second edition. Chevy Chase, MD: American Society of Addiction Medicine.

McLellan, A.T., Grissom, G.R., Zanis, D., Randall, M., Brill, P., and O'Brien, C.P. (1997). Problem-service matching in addiction treatment. A prospective study in 4 programs. *Archives of General Psychiatry,* 54(8), 730-735.

Minkoff, K. (1989). An integrated treatment model for dual diagnosis of psychosis and addiction. *Hospital and Community Psychiatry,* 40(10), 1031-1036.

MISA Consortium (1999). *Recommendations for a system of care for persons with co-occurring mental illness and substance use disorders (MISA).* Harrisburg, PA: Commonwealth of Pennsylvania, Departments of Public Health and Public Welfare.

Nace, E.P. (1987). *The treatment of alcoholism.* New York: Brunner/Mazel.

Nace, E.P. (1990). Substance abuse and personality disorder. In D. O'Connell (Ed.), *Managing the dually diagnosed patient: Current issues and clinical approaches* (pp. 183-198). Binghamton, NY: The Haworth Press.

O'Connell, D.F. (1998). *Dual disorders: Essentials for assessment and treatment.* Binghamton, NY: The Haworth Press.

O'Connell, D.F. (1999). *Report on psychiatric and psychological utilization to the Caron Foundation Quality Improvement Committee.* Wernersville, PA: Caron Foundation.

O'Connell, D.F. and Alexander, C.N. (1994). *Self-recovery: Treating addiction using transcendental meditation and Maharishi Ayurveda.* Binghamton, NY: Harrington Park Press.

O'Connell, D.F. and Patterson, H.O. (1996). Recovery maintenance and relapse prevention with chemically dependent adolescents. In M. Reineke, F. Dattilio, and A. Freeman (Eds.), *Cognitive therapy with children and adolescents: A casebook for clinical practice* (pp. 79-102). New York: Guilford.

Osher, N.C. (1996). A vision for the future: Toward a service system responsive to those with co-occurring addictive and mental disorders. *American Journal of Orthopsychiatry,* 661, 71-76.

Ouimette, P.C., Finney, J.W., and Moos, R.H. (1997). Twelve step and cognitive behavioral treatment for substance abuse: A comparison of treatment effectiveness. *Journal of Consulting and Clinical Psychology,* 65(2), 230-240.

Penick, E.C., Nickel, E.J., Cantrell, P.F., Powell, B.J., Read, M.R., and Thomas, M.M. (1990). The emerging concept of dual diagnosis: An overview and implication. In D. O'Connell (Ed.), *Managing the dually diagnosed patient: Current issues and clinical programs* (pp. 1-54). Binghamton, NY: The Haworth Press.

Polcin, D.L. (1992). Issues in the treatment of dual diagnosis clients who have chronic mental illness. *Professional Psychology: Research and Practice,* 23(1), 30-37.

Ridgely, S.M. and Jerrell, J.M. (1996). Analysis of three interventions for substance abuse treatment of severely mentally ill people. *Community Mental Health Journal,* 32(6), 561-572.

Schuckit, M.A., Tipp, J.E., Bergman, M., Reich, W., Hesselbrock, N., and Smith, T.L. (1997). Comparison of induced and independent major depressive disorders in 2,945 alcoholics. *American Journal of Psychiatry,* 154(7), 948-956.

Silberman (1990). *Active training: A handbook of techniques, designs, care examples and tips.* San Diego: Lexington Books.

Stroebel, C. (1983). *Quieting reflex training for adults.* Audiotape. New York: Guilford.

Timko, C. and Moos, R.H. (1998). Outcomes of the treatment climate in psychiatric and substance abuse programs. *Journal of Clinical Psychology,* 54(8), 1137-1150.

Zweben, J.E. (1993). Dual diagnosis: Key issues for the 1990s. *Psychology of Addictive Behaviors,* 7(3), 168-172.

Chapter 2

Improving Treatment Adherence Among Patients with Comorbid Psychiatric and Substance Use Disorders

Dennis C. Daley
Ihsan M. Salloum

INTRODUCTION AND OVERVIEW

This chapter discusses the issue of treatment adherence or compliance among patients with the dual disorders of a psychiatric illness and substance use. It begins by defining adherence and delineating the ways in which adherence problems show. Factors contributing to adherence problems as well as effects of poor adherence on patients, families, caregivers, and payors are then discussed. Then, clinical and systems strategies aimed at enhancing adherence among patients with dual disorders are discussed. This chapter is based on a review of clinical and empirical literature; my experiences in dual diagnosis inpatient, partial hospital, and outpatient programs; and studies conducted in programs related to the areas of adherence and motivation.

THE PROBLEM OF POOR TREATMENT ADHERENCE

Adherence refers to the extent to which the patient follows the agreed upon behavioral health plan developed with a professional caregiver. Adherence involves patient behaviors related to attending ses-

The preparation of this manuscript was supported in part by grants from the National Institute on Drug Abuse (DA-09421) and National Institute on Alcohol Abuse and Alcoholism (AA 11929-01A2).

sions, taking prescribed medications, or following other aspects of the treatment plan. Adherence is important for patients to gain optimal benefits from psychological, psychosocial, and pharmacological interventions. Adherence to attending sessions, taking medications as prescribed, and following the treatment plan generally are associated with improvement of specific symptoms of the disorders, as well as physical, psychological, occupational, and interpersonal functioning of the individual (Daley and Zuckoff, 1999). It is also associated with improvement in the quality of life of the affected individual and, in many cases, the family.

Problems with adherence have been documented across a range of medical (Meichenbaum and Turk, 1987; Krasnegor et al., 1993), psychological (Walitzer, Dermen, and Connors, 1999), psychiatric (Hatfield, 1990; Chen, 1991), substance use (Hser et al., 1997; Onken, Blaine, and Boren, 1997; Carroll, 1998), and dual diagnosis disorders (Stark, 1992; Bartels, Drake, and Wallach, 1995; Daley and Zuckoff, 1998). Adherence problems include:

1. *Delay or failure to follow through with an initial scheduled assessment.* Numerous studies show low rates of treatment entry with up to 50 percent or more of patients failing to show for the initial assessment required to enter treatment (Matas, Staley, and Griffin, 1992; Chen, 1991; Orme and Bowell, 1991; Hser et al., 1997; Festinger et al., 1995; Simpson et al., 1995).

2. *Failure to make the transition from one level of care to another (e.g., from inpatient to outpatient).* Aftercare following psychiatric hospitalization or residential addiction treatment is important regardless of the problems or disorders of the patient. Although participation in aftercare is associated with lower incidence of use and improved psychiatric outcomes, improved functioning, and lower rehospitalization rates, many patients fail to adhere to their initial aftercare session and thus do not receive treatment following inpatient care or a visit to a psychiatric emergency room (Tomasson and Vaglum, 1998; Solomon and Gordon, 1988; Miner et al., 1997; Daley and Zuckoff, 1998). Dual diagnosis patients are less likely than patients with psychiatric disorders only to make the transition successfully to outpatient care following hospital discharge (Daley and Zuckoff, 1999; Swanson, Pantalon, and Cohen, 1999). In one of our recent studies of 229 consecutively discharged psychiatric inpatients, we found that the major clinical predictor of failure to attend aftercare, defined as

making the initial outpatient appointment within thirty days of hospital discharge, was having any type of substance use disorder. While 86 percent of psychiatric patients without comborbid substance use disorders attended their initial aftercare appointment, only 51 percent of dual diagnosis patients complied with their initial appointment (Daley, 1999).

3. *Missing scheduled treatment sessions and early attrition.* Studies show low rates of outpatient or aftercare attendance and high rates of early dropout from treatment (Stark, Campbell, and Brinkerhoff, 1990; Simpson, Brown, and Joe, 1997), particularly for patients with dual disorders (Mueser, Bellack, and Blanchard, 1992; Daley and Zuckoff, 1999). Our study of discharged psychiatric patients mentioned above included 102 patients with psychiatric disorders only (P–) and 127 patients with psychiatric disorders and comborbid substance use disorders (P+). Our analysis of ninety-day outpatient treatment completion rates between the P+ and P– groups showed significant differences. While 65 percent of the 86 P– patients who entered treatment by attending the initial aftercare session completed a ninety-day course of outpatient care, only 25 percent of the 65 P+ patients who attended at least one aftercare session completed ninety days. The difference in ninety-day treatment completion rates was quite significant, with the dual diagnosis patients clearly being at much higher risk for early dropout from aftercare following psychiatric hospital discharge. When we compared ninety-day attendance rates for individual and medication sessions between the two groups, we found significant differences between the two groups as well. P– patients attended a greater number and percentage of treatment sessions than P+.

4. *Failure to adhere to medication regimens, stopping medications prematurely, or mixing medications with alcohol or other drugs.* Many dual diagnosis patients are prescribed medications for their psychiatric or substance use disorders. Poor adherence to medication plans leads to reduced effectiveness of the medication to treat the target symptoms and contributes to relapse and subsequent rehospitalization (Carpenter et al., 1985; Casper, Romo, and Fasnacht, 1991; Swartz et al., 1998; Keck et al., 1998).

5. *Failure to attend self-help programs or other community support programs as agreed upon between patient and caregiver.* Patients may not attend these programs at all, attend erratically, or drop

out before sufficient exposure. Involvement in support groups has long been considered an important component of recovery for substance use disorders (Nace, 1987). We believe mental health support groups (e.g., Recovery Incorporated and groups for specific disorders) and dual diagnosis support groups (e.g., Double Trouble, Dual Recovery Anonymous) can play a significant role in a patient's recovery. Patients who are not oriented and prepared for support groups may be more prone to fail to attend or to drop out early.

6. *Failure to abstain from alcohol or other drugs.* Studies show high rates of relapse among treated substance abusers (Daley and Marlatt, 1997a). Many patients lapse or relapse one or more times, particularly those with more chronic and severe forms of substance dependency. Relapse may occur regardless of the level of motivation of patients regarding acceptance of abstinence, although those who accept abstinence and follow their recovery plan are less likely to return to substance use.

7. *Failure to make lifestyle changes (e.g., diet modification, exercise, meditation, etc.) as agreed upon between patient and caregiver.* Recovering from dual disorders involves making lifestyle changes based on the problems and issues of a given patient (Daley and Thase, 2000; Daley, 2000). Although patients may adhere to treatment sessions, they may fail to adhere to the plan to make specific lifestyle changes needed to facilitate long-term recovery.

8. *Failure to involve the family or significant others.* Dual disorders affect the family system and individual members in many ways (Daley and Moss, 2002; Daley and Salloum, 1997). Although much literature addresses the importance of family involvement in psychiatric treatment (Anderson, Reiss, and Hogarty, 1986; Lefley and Waslow, 1994; Daley, Bowler, and Cahalane, 1992) and addiction treatment (Stanton, 1996; Stanton and Shadish, 1997), there is a paucity of dual diagnosis literature addressing the importance of the family in recovery. Patients may refuse to involve family members or sabotage their efforts to be part of the treatment or recovery process. Professionals may also contribute to a lack of family involvement by failing to explore the effects of dual disorders on the patient's family, engage the family in assessment or treatment sessions, or facilitate family participation in self-help programs.

9. *Failure to self-disclose problems in treatment sessions.* A patient may adhere to treatment in terms of attending sessions but not

make optimal use of therapy by limiting self-disclosure. Self-disclosure refers to the patient's sharing of important information, such as problems, internal struggles or conflicts, thoughts, feelings, and experiences. Self-disclosure is a prerequisite to insight and change.

10. *Failure to complete individualized therapeutic assignments.* Therapists often assign recovery-oriented tasks aimed at educating patients, changing their attitudes, managing symptoms of their disorders, or making personal or lifestyle changes. These include, for example, completion of daily monitoring logs (feelings, thoughts, cravings for substances), bibliotherapy assignments, or behavioral assignments such as attending self-help meetings, developing a plan to structure time, asking for a sponsor, practicing assertive behavior, or expressing feelings openly and honestly to another person. It is not unusual for patients to fail to complete assignments as a result of low motivation or because these assignments seem too complex or overwhelming.

Adherence is particularly problematic for patients receiving more expensive psychiatric or dual diagnosis inpatient hospital care, medical detoxification, or residential addiction care, as many of these patients either fail to enter aftercare or drop out of treatment prior to completion (Verinis and Taylor, 1994; Lash, 1998; Solomon, 1987; Tomasson and Vaglum, 1998). Many of the gains made during the inpatient treatment are negated and these poorly compliant patients often experience clinical deterioration and psychosocial problems, and subsequently seek rehospitalization for exacerbation of their psychiatric symptoms or relapse to substance abuse (Haywood et al., 1995). Poor treatment adherence among discharged inpatients from psychiatric and addiction treatment settings represents a significant health problem for patients and families, and a challenge for professional caregivers and treatment providers.

Aftercare adherence is increasingly important in the current treatment environment, as managed care organizations limit the number of inpatient hospitalizations as well as the number of days of inpatient care approved for funding. Outpatient care represents the primary source of aftercare referrals for discharged psychiatric and dual diagnosis patients and is an important component of the continuum of care needed for ongoing treatment of these patients, many of whom have recurrent or chronic disorders requiring long-term treatment.

DETERMINANTS OF TREATMENT ADHERENCE

Adherence problems can be viewed on a continuum from total adherence to total nonadherence. Although many patients are partially compliant and benefit from treatment participation, these benefits could be maximized by improved adherence. A combination of several factors rather than one alone contributes to poor or partial adherence in any given case. Factors impacting on adherence include patient, relationship, social support, and treatment-related and system variables (Nace, Davis, and Gaspari, 1991; McKay et al., 1998; Miner et al., 1997; Daley and Zuckoff, 1999).

Patient Variables

Patient variables affecting adherence include motivation to change and participate in treatment or self-help activities, beliefs about illness and treatment, stigma associated with having one or more disorders, expectations of treatment, personality characteristics, problem-solving skills, and life events or problems. A dual diagnosis patient with a depressive disorder and cocaine dependency who minimizes the drug problem is at high risk for failure to follow through with outpatient care following inpatient treatment. Adherence behaviors are also affected by specific symptoms of a psychiatric or substance use disorder, such as poor judgment, cognitive impairment, affective instability, obsessions with drugs or alcohol, or severe social anxiety. An individual with schizophrenia who also has an alcohol and marijuana abuse problem may fail to attend self-help meetings or outpatient group sessions as a result of paranoia or delusions. A patient with a social phobia may fail to attend group therapy or self-help groups due to a high degree of social anxiety.

Relationship and Social Support Variables

Relationship and social support variables impacting on adherence include current social and family support networks, problems in family or interpersonal relationships, life events, as well as living situations. An individual with serious family conflicts whose recovery efforts are not supported at home and who is subject to persistent criticism from family members is more vulnerable to relapse as well as decreased adherence with treatment. Homeless patients often fail to keep treatment appointments or get medications refilled.

Patients who lack meaningful social supports or whose social networks are comprised of active substance abusers are prone to social pressures to use substances, which in turn impacts relapse and poor adherence. Family members or others can also discourage adherence to therapy or medications. For example, the authors have treated patients who were told by family members that medications they were taking for psychiatric illness were unnecessary, medications taken for addiction were a "crutch," or that therapy or self-help programs were not needed. In one instance, a spouse actually discarded a patient's antidepressants.

Treatment and Systems Variables

The literature has focused on adherence primarily from the perspective of the patient, focusing on patient variables contributing to adherence problems and ways in which the patient can improve adherence. However, therapist or caregiver variables are important factors mediating patient adherence. In recent years, increased attention has been directed to delivering empirically based treatments according to guidelines or manuals that describe the clinical interventions of a particular treatment model such as cognitive-behavioral therapy, twelve-step counseling, motivational enhancement therapy, and group drug counseling, to name a few (National Institute on Alcohol Abuse and Alcoholism [NIAAA], 1997; National Institute on Drug Abuse [NIDA], 1991; Daley, Mercer, and Carpenter, 1998; Daley and Marlatt, 1997b; Kendall and Chambless, 1998). Yet compliance with delivering the treatment can be a problem for the therapist as well (Carroll, 1998; NIDA 2000, 2002).

Treatment and systems variables related to caregivers and treatment agencies impacting on adherence include the following (Simpson et al., 1997; Gariti et al., 1995; Smoller et al., 1998):

- Problems in the therapeutic alliance between patient and caregiver
- Competence of treatment providers
- Access to treatment
- Expense of treatment

- Characteristics of the treatment system
- Duration, intensity, and appropriateness of the treatment regimen
- Continuity of care
- Availability of ancillary services to address other problems such as vocational, housing, or economic problems
- Medication side effects, unrealistic expectations of the purpose and efficacy of medicine, lack of adequate response, complicated medication regimens, and adverse interactions with alcohol or other drugs

For example, a patient who experiences a significant decrease in libido following initiation of an antidepressant medication may become noncompliant by stopping the medication completely despite actual or potential positive effects on mood symptoms. A patient who is put on a waiting list for outpatient treatment services may fail to show for the intake evaluation as a result of an unreasonable delay in getting the initial appointment.

EFFECTS OF POOR ADHERENCE

Poor adherence affects patients with dual disorders, their families, professional caregivers, and payors. As a result of poor adherence to therapy and/or psychiatric medications, patients are more likely to drop out of treatment early and, hence, not experience the potential full benefits. They are also at higher risk for relapse to their psychiatric and/or substance use disorder as well as subsequent hospitalizations in a psychiatric or addiction treatment facility. These patients are more vulnerable to experiencing any of the numerous problems associated with dual disorders, such as suicidality; homocidality; legal, and familial, interpersonal, occupational, spiritual, and financial difficulties (Salloum et al., 1996; Mueser, Bellack, and Blanchard, 1992; Clark, 1994; Cuffel and Chase, 1994; NIAAA, 1997). In addition, some of these patients who engage in high-risk behaviors such as intravenous drug use, sharing needles or paraphernalia, prostitution, unprotected sex, sex with strangers, or promiscuous sex with multiple partners are at increased risk for HIV transmission or acquisition (Freeman, Rodriguez, and French, 1994; Fitterling et al., 1993; Hoffman et al., 1998).

Families of dual-disordered patients may become upset, angry, frustrated, and worried about their loved one who shows poor treatment adherence. Anxieties about decompensation, substance use or psychiatric relapse, suicidal behaviors, and rehospitalization are common. Family members may also experience concerns related to potential problems such as loss of job and income if the dual-disordered member is the major source of economic support for the family.

Providers and caregivers often have to deal with the clinical crises that occur when patients are poorly compliant. They may feel frustrated as well. In addition, since most providers rely on fees for services as their major source of revenue, missed treatment sessions lead to lost revenue. In some instances, this can create a major burden for the provider as it becomes difficult for clinicians to meet productivity requirements if a high percentage of patients fail to show for scheduled appointments.

Finally, payors are affected because patients with poor adherence who drop out of treatment often return and request higher levels of care that are more expensive, such as medical detoxification, inpatient rehabilitation, or acute-care psychiatric hospitalization. This leads to using a disproportionate amount of limited treatment dollars for more expensive levels of care.

STRATEGIES THAT IMPROVE ADHERENCE

The empirical and clinical literature document a variety of clinical and systems strategies that impact positively on patient adherence with both psychological and pharmacologic treatment. Three recent major reviews report a host of strategies (Onken, Blaine, and Boren, 1997; Carroll, 1998; Daley and Zuckoff, 1999).

Clinical Strategies

1. *Attend to the therapeutic alliance.* Expressing empathy, providing support, being optimistic about change, being nonjudgmental, and facilitating patient self-disclosure of thoughts, feelings, and problems help build a therapeutic alliance between patient and therapist. Engaging the patient in a discussion of how the therapy is progressing, promptly exploring problems such as lateness or missing ses-

sions, and working collaboratively on the patient's problems also help the therapist strengthen the alliance and intervene early when problems exist in the therapeutic relationship.

2. *Anticipate and prepare for nonadherence among high-risk patients.* High-risk patients are those with a history of poor adherence or those with low levels of motivation. The therapist can review intrapersonal, interpersonal, and systems barriers to adherence based on past treatment episodes and develop strategies to address these issues before they occur rather than wait until they occur. For example, a patient highly ambivalent about abstinence who is reluctant to attend treatment sessions can be asked to examine advantages and disadvantages of abstinence and treatment attendance. The patient can be encouraged to stick with treatment for an agreed-upon period of time or number of sessions despite ambivalent feelings. A patient with a history of poor adherence can be asked to identify barriers to treatment participation and can be engaged in a discussion of problem-solving strategies aimed at overcoming these barriers.

3. *Focus on the early phase of recovery, especially the first thirty to ninety days.* Dropout rates are the highest in the first thirty to ninety days of treatment (Carroll, 1998; Onken, Blaine, and Boren, 1997) so it makes sense for the clinician to view this as a critical period in terms of engaging the patient. In a study of discharged inpatients, we found that psychiatric patients with and without comorbid substance use disorders who attend four outpatient sessions have significantly higher rates of completing a ninety-day course of outpatient care compared to patients who attend less than four sessions. Other reports in the literature confirm the effect of keeping patients in treatment for at least three or four sessions (Stanton and Shadish, 1997). Findings from studies of drug-abusing patients indicate that at least ninety days in outpatient care is needed for patients to benefit from treatment (Onken, Blaine, and Baren, 1997; Simpson, Brown, and Joe, 1997).

4. *Provide transitional counseling prior to discharge from a residential or hospital facility.* When patients move from one level of care to another (e.g., from an inpatient psychiatric hospital to a partial hospital or outpatient program), the therapist can discuss differences between the various levels of care, identify the benefits of participating in this next level of care, identify potential roadblocks that could contribute to a failure to follow up with ongoing care, and develop

strategies to overcome these roadblocks. In our work with dual diagnosis inpatients, we have found that a single session with an outpatient clinician prior to discharge from the hospital leads to a significant increase in the percentage of patients who keep their initial aftercare appointment (Daley and Zuckoff, 1998). This brief transitional counseling session has a positive impact whether conducted in an individual or small group session, at the inpatient facility, or at the outpatient program where the patient is referred for aftercare services. As part of our ongoing quality improvement activities, we tracked compliance rates for 240 inpatients discharged to our dual diagnosis outpatient clinic. Of these 240 patients, fifty-seven received a single individual or small group (two to four patients) transitional session with an outpatient clinician prior to hospital discharge. The other 183 patients received the usual referral to aftercare at our clinic and did not have contact with an outpatient clinician prior to hospital discharge. Only 40.4 percent ($n = 74$) of the 183 patients receiving the usual discharge interventions showed for their initial outpatient appointment compared to 64.9 percent ($n = 37$) of the fifty-seven patients receiving the predischarge intervention. The effects of this intervention were greatest when conducted in an individual session at the outpatient site prior to hospital discharge.

5. *Address adherence problems as soon as they arise in the treatment process.* Immediate attention to adherence problems conveys the message that this is an important issue that will be discussed rather than avoided, that the therapist is aware of potential problems in the relationship with the therapist which show in adherence behaviors, and that the therapist wants to work with the patient to resolve adherence problems. Lateness for sessions, missing sessions, and failure to complete therapeutic assignments or follow through with agreed-upon plans for change are common indicators of an adherence problem. Early identification and exploration of problems may lead to improved trust in the therapist and ability of the patient to take responsibility for addressing adherence issues early. This, in turn, may help to decrease treatment dropout rates, particularly during the first several weeks of treatment when dropout rates are the highest.

6. *Involve the family.* Inviting the family to sessions provides a context for members to share important information about the patient, the family system, and ways in which family members communicate and relate. These sessions also provide the opportunity for the

family to receive support from professionals. Families can gain information about illness and recovery, ways to cope with the dual-disordered member (e.g., setting limits, reducing enabling behaviors), as well as their own issues (e.g., anger, hurt, distrust) and how support programs such as Al-Anon, Nar-Anon, or the National Alliance for the Mentally Ill can help them. By providing support, offering help during times of crisis, setting limits, and conveying the expectation that the patient is responsible for making positive changes, the family may directly or indirectly influence the patient to adhere to the treatment plan. Family members who are a part of the patient's treatment team may be able to avert a small crisis from becoming a major disaster by intervening early in the process of substance use lapse or psychiatric relapse.

7. *Change the intensity of treatment.* Patients who are not benefiting from a particular level of treatment can be offered more intense treatment or a different level of care. For example, if weekly outpatient treatment is insufficient in helping a depressed alcoholic establish a stable mood or period of sobriety, an intensive outpatient or partial hospital program can be considered. Patients often opt for less involved treatment due to low motivation or a belief that more extensive treatment is not needed. The therapist can negotiate a plan with the patient in which the patient's choice is respected and followed with the understanding that if certain benchmarks are not met, the patient will agree to enter a different level of care. This allows the patient to have a choice in determining treatment needs and learning from real world consequences of the disorders. However, in cases in which the therapist strongly believes that the patient's choices are not appropriate given the current level of symptomatology or difficulty with the recovery process, the therapist should be forthright in giving recommendations and the rationale behind them to the patient. The patient ultimately has the final decision, but knowing why the therapist believes a certain course of treatment is needed can help the patient consider more than one option. The same holds true for self-help participation. If a patient is struggling with recovery and attending few or no support group meetings, the clinician may recommend increasing the level of involvement. As the patient experiences improvement due to a change in level of involvement in treatment or self-help programs, adherence may increase. On the other hand, there may be times in which decreasing treatment frequency or intensity

may benefit the patient. For example, a patient who is not consistent in attending a partial hospital or intensive outpatient program may be advised to move to a lower level of outpatient care with less frequent sessions.

8. *Provide options regarding the treatment program or self-help programs.* There are many different ways to recover and change. When making recommendations for treatment programs, medications, or self-help programs, the clinician can provide the patient with various options, helping to examine the advantages and disadvantages of each. Patients who feel they have a say in their plan are more likely to follow it than those who are mandated to a program. However, when a therapist feels strongly that a particular treatment option is in the best interest of the patient, he or she should convey this. For example, one patient, a very depressed alcoholic health care professional, continued to feel persistent depression despite initiating and maintaining sobriety. Initially, this patient refused recommendations for antidepressant medications and chose the option of psychotherapy. Although this therapy helped the patient with alcohol abstinence, the depression improved only moderately. The therapist then strongly recommended the option of medication evaluation and treatment. The patient reluctantly agreed and started taking an antidepressant, leading to a significant improvement in mood symptoms, continuation of sobriety, and improvement in the patient's ability to function at work and home. Although initial treatment options presented may be refused, the therapist can revisit them, particularly if the current plan is not effective after a reasonable period of time.

9. *Use motivational interventions.* Adherence often improves as the patient's level of readiness or motivation to change increase. As a result, patients are more likely to enter treatment, remain in treatment, or follow the change plan. Approaches such as motivational interviewing (Miller and Rollnick, 1991), motivational enhancement therapy (Miller et al., 1995), motivational therapy (Daley et al., 1998), and compliance therapy (Miner et al., 1997) have been successfully used to improve motivation and patient compliance. These approaches have been used with substance use disorders, psychiatric disorders, and dual disorders. As mentioned before, a single motivational session provided prior to hospital discharge has a significant positive effect on aftercare treatment entry rates (Daley and Zuckoff, 1998; see Daley and Zuckoff, 1999, for a detailed description of this approach).

In a small pilot study of outpatients with cocaine dependence and depression, patients receiving an experimental motivational therapy (MT) approach did significantly better than patients receiving a comparison control treatment-as-usual (TAU) condition in terms of compliance with treatment sessions and completion of one and three months of outpatient care. In addition, in the year following entry into outpatient care, MT patients were six times less likely than TAU patients to return to a psychiatric hospital (Daley et al., 1998). Preliminary results from a randomized clinical trial comparing outpatient adherence between MT with TAU patients indicates that MT patients attend almost twice as many sessions as TAU patients during the first three months of outpatient care. Numerous studies have also demonstrated that motivational interventions enhance treatment entry, retention, and completion rates among diverse groups of patients with alcohol use disorders (Bien, Miller, and Tonigan, 1993; Miller, Benefield, and Tonigan, 1993), opiate dependency (Saunders, Wilkinson, and Phillips, 1995), obesity and diabetes (Smith et al., 1997), and psychotic disorders (Miner et al., 1997).

10. *Use psychotherapy preparation techniques.* These include role induction, therapy pretraining, and experiential pretraining (see Walitzer, Dermen, and Connors, 1999, for a description of these). These techniques familiarize the patient with rationale and process of treatment, prepare the patient for a positive expectancy of treatment, and align the patient's and therapist's expectations of treatment. Walitzer and colleagues conducted an extensive review of twenty-nine studies and believe that these techniques impact positively on both treatment adherence and outcome.

11. *Provide incentives or reinforcements for compliant behaviors.* Recent studies show that providing cocaine patients with reinforcements in the form of financial incentives for clean urinalysis reports lead to improved adherence to abstinence from cocaine (Higgins et al., 1994; Higgins and Silverman, 1999; Carroll, 1998). While these studies were supported by grant funding, making it possible to pay for incentives, therapists could provide free recovery literature, bus tickets, lunch vouchers, or other small items as reinforcement for patients adhering to medications, to session attendance, or to sobriety. An incentive program could be used with higher-risk patients who evidence a poor history of compliance with treatment. Reinforcers are commonly used in twelve-step programs in the form of

tokens or chips or key chains for reaching a designated period of abstinence, and in the form of public acknowledgements. In our structured intensive outpatient program, we provide patients with a certificate of treatment completion. During the ceremony, the patient also receives feedback and supportive statements from other program participants. Patients report that they value receiving this certificate of treatment completion, particularly since many of them have prior histories of early termination from treatment. Many patients have stated that this was one of the few programs they ever completed. Although we have not studied the effect of the certificate or group feedback on adherence, we believe that they serve as an incentive for some dual diagnosis patients and, hence, improve adherence to treatment sessions.

SYSTEMS STRATEGIES TO IMPROVE ADHERENCE

Since poor treatment adherence is a significant problem among dual diagnosis patients, treatment programs could routinely address this as part of their quality improvement activities. Monitoring patient adherence rates in the program and among individual therapists will provide information about how a particular program and the staff are doing in relation to patient adherence. For example, if a review of a clinic's adherence rates finds that clinicians average a 65 to 70 percent show rate for scheduled individual appointments, but two clinicians average only 45 percent adherence, it makes sense for the clinical supervisor to explore the potential reasons for such low compliance rates for these clinicians. Strategies can then be identified and implemented to improve adherence rates of the patients of these clinicians.

Staff training on motivational and compliance enhancement strategies are often helpful in addressing adherence problems in a treatment program. Such training not only provides clinical skills but also challenges therapists to examine their beliefs about adherence problems as well as how they clinically address these issues with their patients.

A number of other treatment system strategies have been used in various clinical programs to improve adherence to the initial treatment session, aftercare following psychiatric hospitalization, ongoing treatment appointments, and medication regimens.

1. *Use case managers* (Ashery, 1992). Dual-disordered patients often have numerous psychosocial problems related to employment, living arrangements, finances, and involvement in other systems (legal, child welfare, etc.). Since therapists may not have the time or expertise to address these other problems, a referral to a case manager (CM) can be initiated if this service is available and the patient meets eligibility criteria. Case managers traditionally are used to help patients with severe and persistent psychiatric disorders address other significant problems that contribute to relapse or cause distress or impairment for the patient. The CM can help the patient in numerous ways: advocating on behalf of the patient, facilitating use of community resources (medical, social, spiritual, economic, housing, legal, recreational, educational, or vocational), serving as a liaison between patient and treatment team, accompanying the patient to support group meetings, and helping the patient learn problem-solving skills or life skills, such as using public transportation, shopping for food, or budgeting. In addition, the CM can visit patients in their homes and intervene early when they fail to make their treatment appointments. These CM interventions can have a positive impact on adherence to therapy, medications, and self-help program attendance.

2. *Provide prompt and easy access to treatment.* Although many treatment programs are experiencing a reduction of resources while caseloads expand, a delay in an initial appointment often leads to the prospective patient failing to attend the appointment and enter treatment. The longer the wait for the appointment, the greater the likelihood of the patient missing the appointment. Initial sessions held within a day or so of the call for help have much better outcomes than sessions scheduled later, particularly if the initial appointment is scheduled a week or longer after the call. The same is true for aftercare appointments. Patients seen promptly after hospital discharge are more likely to comply with the session compared to those who have to wait weeks or longer. Easy access to treatment implies that patients have minimal barriers to scheduling sessions. Offering evening hours and flexible appointment times, especially for patients who work or have child care responsibilities, may make the difference in whether a given patient attends or misses treatment sessions.

3. *Use reminders of the appointment.* Telephoned or written reminders a day before the initial appointment often lead to an improvement in the show rate for evaluations. This conveys the message

that the clinic is very interested in meeting with the individual to help with the presenting problems. For high-risk patients with more severe and chronic disorders or those with prior histories of poor compliance, phone calls can also be used the day before the scheduled individual or group session as a prompt. Once a patient establishes a consistent pattern of adherence, reminders can be discontinued.

4. *Use outreach for poorly compliant patients.* Calling patients who miss sessions and inviting them to return to treatment, sending friendly letters conveying concern to poorly compliant patients who do not have telephones, or having case managers make home visits are outreach strategies that can improve adherence. Outreach efforts convey the message that the patient's welfare is important and that the therapist wants the patient to return for treatment.

5. *Use contracts for adherence.* A written adherence plan can be used for the patient who is repeatedly noncompliant with treatment. This plan can state the problem, steps the patient will take to address the problem, and consequences if the plan is not followed. For example, a contract may state that if the patient misses a certain number of individual treatment sessions, the scheduling of future sessions will be contingent upon attending a specified number of group sessions. In open treatment clinics for dual-diagnosis clients, the authors have had moderate success with some poorly compliant patients by not offering additional individual sessions until they attend a certain number of group sessions (usually two to four group sessions).

6. *Assess reasons for poor compliance or early termination from treatment.* Since many dual-disordered patients have had multiple experiences in treatment, programs can use quality improvement surveys to ask patients reasons for poor compliance or early attrition during previous episodes of treatment. Usually, patients report a variety of personal reasons (e.g., they did not want to stop using substances, time problems, problems improved, etc.) and systems variables (e.g., long delays in getting appointments, dislike of therapist, not finding treatment helpful, etc.) as factors contributing to prior compliance problems.

7. *Provide integrated treatment.* There are three paradigms for understanding and treating dual-disordered patients described in the literature: *parallel, sequential,* and *integrated* (Minkoff, 1989; Ries, 1995).

The *parallel model* involves the patient receiving treatment for the psychiatric disorder in a mental health system, and treatment for the substance use disorder in a drug and alcohol system. Involvement in two agencies reduces the chances of adherence since the patient must keep appointments and develop a relationship with two different caregivers and may be exposed to conflicting philosophies of treatment. It is not unusual, for example, for mental health professionals to view treatment much differently than substance abuse treatment professionals.

The *sequential treatment model* involves treating the most acute disorder first, then addressing the other disorder. However, it is often difficult to distinguish between primary and secondary disorders, and the various relationships among disorders and the effects of substance use on masking, precipitating, or exacerbating psychiatric symptoms. For example, a dual-diagnosis patient with depression receiving treatment from a substance abuse agency may find that the depression is not addressed at all or is seen as secondary to the substance use disorder. If the depression is untreated and unremitting, the patient will continue suffering and could be at increased risk for suicide. The authors have had numerous complaints from patients over the years that substance abuse treatment professionals did not acknowledge, address, or facilitate treatment of their mental health disorders, and mental health professionals did not acknowledge, address, or facilitate treatment of their substance use disorders.

Although any of these three treatment paradigms may be useful in a given case, the *integrated treatment model* is generally viewed as the most appropriate approach to taking care of patients with dual disorders. This approach involves addressing both psychiatric and substance use symptoms, issues, and related problems by the same treatment team in the same location. Although this is a relatively new area and little research has been conducted, the available evidence suggests patients receiving integrated treatment have higher rates of adherence and better clinical outcomes compared to patients receiving parallel or sequential treatment, especially those with more persistent and chronic forms of mental disorders (Hoffman, 1993; Drake et al., 1996, 1998).

CONCLUSIONS AND RECOMMENDATIONS

Poor adherence is a common problem among patients with dual disorders. Adherence problems occur in multiple ways related to professional service and self-help group program utilization, including failure to enter treatment after scheduling an evaluation, failure to continue with aftercare (professional and/or self-help) following hospital discharge, missing scheduled treatment program or self-help activities, early attrition from treatment or self-help programs, and failure to take medications as prescribed.

Adherence problems also occur related to the process of recovery, such as failure to abstain from substances, make personal or lifestyle changes agreed upon with the therapist, or complete recovery-oriented therapeutic tasks. Adherence is affected by a variety of interacting patient, family, and treatment systems variables. Poor adherence has adverse effects on the patient (e.g., increased rates of substance abuse relapse or psychiatric symptom exacerbation, rehospitalization, and involvement in high-risk activities such as intravenous drug use, sharing needles or paraphernalia, or engaging in unprotected or promiscuous sex), family (e.g., anger, worry, anxiety, fear), and providers of service (e.g., frustration, low morale, reduced productivity, and reduced generation of clinical revenues to cover costs of staff). In addition, payors spend money to fund treatment in higher levels of care such as inpatient facilities when patients decompensate due to poor treatment adherence. By implementing clinical and systems strategies to enhance motivation and readiness to change, providers can make a positive impact on adherence, which will lead to improved clinical outcomes for dual-diagnosis patients. Clinicians, supervisors, administrators, and researchers all need to address this serious problem from multiple perspectives if this problem is to be reduced.

SUGGESTED PATIENT EDUCATIONAL VIDEOS

The following videos are part of the *Living Sober Series III: Improving Motivation and Compliance.* Each video focuses on one or more specific areas of interest to clinicians who deal with adherence and motivational problems in their clinical work. Each video is brief (less than fifteen minutes) and can be used in individual or group sessions to stimulate the patient(s) to explore specific types of motivational and/or adherence issues. Videos include an introduction by a narrator, brief dramatic vignettes illustrating common problems associated with adherence and motivation, testimonials by men and women dealing with the problems discussed, and comments by Dennis Daley and Allan Zuckoff.

The first video focuses on motivational and adherence issues pertinent to entering aftercare following discharge from inpatient care, and related to attending outpatient treatment (Daley, 1999c). The second video explores struggles of low motivation to seek treatment that are common among many individuals, and issues related to the need for a higher level of care for patients not benefiting from their current treatment plan (Daley, 1999d). The third video focuses on problems in the patient's relationship to the individual therapist or treatment group that impact on adherence (Daley, 1999e). The fourth video explores issues pertinent to taking medications to treat a psychiatric disorder or facilitate recovery from addiction (Daley, 1999b). This video also explores common issues in self-help program attendance. The final video in this series addresses adherence and motivational issues from a broader, lifestyle perspective. Exercise, smoking, and diet are addressed (Daley, 1999a).

Daley, D.C. (1999a). *Compliance with lifestyle changes*. Wilmette, IL: Gerald T. Rogers Productions, (800) 227-9100.

Daley, D.C. (1999b). *Compliance with medications or self-help programs*. Wilmette, IL: Gerald T. Rogers Productions, (800) 227-9100.

Daley, D.C. (1999c). *Compliance with aftercare/outpatient counseling*. Wilmette, IL: Gerald T. Rogers Productions, (800) 227-9100.

Daley, D.C. (1999d). *Low motivation to change or seek treatment*. Wilmette, IL: Gerald T. Rogers Productions, (800) 227-9100.

Daley, D.C. (1999e). *Relationship to therapy and treatment group*. Wilmette, IL: Gerald T. Rogers Productions, (800) 227-9100.

REFERENCES

Anderson, C., Reiss, D., and Hogarty, G. (1986). *Schizophrenia and the family*. New York: The Guilford Press.

Ashery, R.S. (Ed.) (1992). *Progress and issues in case management*. Rockville, MD: National Institute on Drug Abuse.

Bartels, S.J., Drake, R.E., and Wallach, M.A. (1995). Long-term course of substance use disorders among patients with severe mental illness. *Psychiatric Services, 46*(3), 248-251.

Bien, T.H., Miller, W.R., and Tonigan, J.S. (1993). Brief interventions for alcohol problems: A review. *Addiction, 88*(3), 315-336.

Carpenter, M.D., Mulligan, J.C., Bader, I.A., and Meinzer, A.E. (1985). Multiple admissions to an urban psychiatric center: A comparative study. *Hospital and Community Psychiatry, 36*(12), 1305-1308.

Carroll, K.M. (1998). *A cognitive-behavioral approach: Treatment of cocaine addiction.* Rockville, MD: National Institute on Drug Abuse.

Casper, E.S., Romo, J.M., and Fasnacht, R.C. (1991). Readmission patterns of frequent users of inpatient psychiatric services. *Hospital and Community Psychiatry, 42*(11), 1166-1169.

Chen, A. (1991). Noncompliance in community psychiatry: A review of clinical interventions. *Hospital and Community Psychiatry, 42*(3), 282-287.

Clark, R.E. (1994). Family costs associated with severe mental illness and substance abuse. *Hospital and Community Psychiatry, 45*(8), 808-813.

Cuffel, B.J. and Chase, P. (1994). Remission and relapse of substance use disorders in schizophrenia: Results from a one-year prospective study. *The Journal of Nervous and Mental Disease, 182*(6), 342-348.

Daley, D.C. (1999). A comparison of aftercare compliance and rehospitalization rates between psychiatric patients with and without comorbid substance use disorders. Unpublished manuscript.

Daley, D.C. (2000). *Dual diagnosis workbook: Recovery strategies for addiction and mental health problems.* Independence, MO: Herald House/Independence Press.

Daley, D.C., Bowler, K., and Cahalane, H. (1992). Approaches to patient and family education with affective disorders. *Patient Education and Counseling, 19*(2), 163-174.

Daley, D.C. and Marlatt, G.A. (1997a). Relapse prevention. In J.H. Lowinson, P. Ruiz, R.B. Millman, and J.G. Langrod (Eds.), *Substance abuse: A comprehensive textbook,* Third edition (pp. 458-466). Baltimore, MD: Williams and Wilkins.

Daley, D.C. and Marlatt, G.A. (1997b). *Therapist's guide to managing your alcohol and drug problem.* San Antonio, TX: Psychological Corporation.

Daley, D.C., Mercer, D., and Carpenter, G. (1998). *Group drug counseling manual.* Holmes Beach, FL: Learning Publications, Inc.

Daley, D.C. and Moss, H.M. (2002). *Dual disorders: Counseling clients with chemical dependency and mental illness,* Third edition. Center City, MN: Hazelden.

Daley, D.C. and Salloum, I.M. (1997). The family factor. *Professional Counselor, 11*(4), 51-54.

Daley, D.C., Salloum, I.M., Zuckoff, A., and Kirisci, L. (1998). Increasing treatment compliance among outpatients with depression and cocaine dependence: Results of a pilot study. *American Journal of Psychiatry, 155*(11), 1611-1613.

Daley, D.C. and Thase, M.E. (2000). *Dual disorders recovery counseling: Integrated treatment for substance use and mental health disorders,* Second edition. Independence, MO: Independence Press.

Daley, D.C. and Zuckoff, A. (1998). Improving compliance with the initial outpatient session among discharged inpatient dual diagnosis clients. *Social Work,* *43*(3), 385-480.

Daley, D.C. and Zuckoff, A. (1999). *Improving treatment compliance: Counseling and system strategies for substance use and dual disorders.* Center City, MN: Hazelden.

Drake, R.E., Mercer-McFadden, C., Mueser, K.T., McHugho, G., and Bond, B. (1998). A review of integrated mental health and substance abuse for patients with dual disorders. *Schizophrenia Bulletin, 24*(5), 589-608.

Drake, R.E., Mueser, K.T., Clark, R.E., and Wallach, M.A. (1996). The course, treatment, and outcome of substance disorder in persons with severe mental illness. *American Journal of Orthopsychiatry, 66*(1), 42-51.

Festinger, D.S., Lamb, R.J., Lountz, M.R., Kirby, K.C., and Marlowe, D. (1995). Pretreatment dropout as a function of treatment delay and client variables. *Addictive Behaviors, 20*(1), 111-115.

Fitterling, J.M., Matens, P.B., Scotti, J.R., and Allen, J.S. Jr. (1993). AIDS risk behaviors and knowledge among heterosexual alcoholics and non-injecting drug users. *Addiction, 88*(7), 1257-1265.

Freeman, R.C., Rodriguez, G.M., and French, J.F. (1994). A comparison of male and female intravenous drug users' risk behaviors for HIV infection. *American Journal of Drug and Alcohol Abuse, 20*(2), 129-157.

Gariti, P., Alterman, A.I., Holub-Beyer, E., Volpicelli, J.R., Prentice, N., and O'Brien, C.P. (1995). Effects of an appointment reminder call on patient show rates. *Journal of Substance Abuse Treatment, 13*(3), 207-212.

Hatfield, A.B. (1990). *Family education in mental illness.* New York: The Guilford Press.

Haywood, T.W., Kravitz, H.M., Grossman, L.S., Cavanaugh, J.L., Davis, J.M., and Lewis, D.A. (1995). Predicting the "revolving door" phenomenon among patients with schizophrenic, schizoaffective, and affective disorders. *American Journal of Psychiatry, 152*(6), 856-861.

Higgins, S.T., Budney, J.A., Bicket, W.K., Foerg, F.E., Donham, R., and Badger, G.J. (1994). Incentives improve outcome in outpatient behavioral treatment of cocaine. *Archives of General Psychiatry, 51*(7), 568-576.

Higgins, S.T. and Silverman, K. (1999). *Motivating behavior change among illicit-drug abusers.* Washington, DC: American Psychological Association.

Hoffman, G.W. Jr. (1993). Three-month follow-up of 28 dual diagnosis inpatients. *American Journal of Drug and Alcohol Abuse, 19*(1), 79-88.

Hoffman, J.A., Klein, H., Clark, D.C., and Boyd, F.T. (1998). The effect of entering drug treatment on involvement in HIV-related risk behaviors. *American Journal of Drug and Alcohol Abuse, 24*(2), 259-284.

Hser, Y., Maglione, M., Polinsky, M.L., and Anglin, M.D. (1997). Predicting drug treatment entry among treatment-seeking individuals. *Journal of Substance Abuse Treatment, 15*(3), 213-220.

Keck, P.E., McElroy, S.L., Strakowski, S.M., West, S.A., Sax, K.W., Hawkins, J.M., Bourne, M.L., and Haggard, P. (1998). Twelve-month outcome of patients with bipolar disorder following hospitalization for a manic or mixed episode. *American Journal of Psychiatry, 55*(5), 646-652.

Kendall, P.C. and Chambless, D.L. (Eds.) (1998). Empirically supported psychological therapies. *Journal of Consulting and Clinical Psychology, 66*(1), 1-209.

Krasnegor, N.A., Epstein, L., Johnson, S.B., and Yaffe, S.J. (Eds) (1993). *Developmental aspects of health compliance behavior.* Hillsdale, NY: Lawrence Erblaum Associates.

Lash, S.J. (1998). Increasing participation in substance abuse aftercare treatment. *American Journal of Drug and Alcohol Abuse, 24*(1), 31-36.

Lefley, H.P. and Waslow, M. (Eds.) (1994). *Helping families cope with mental illness.* Chur, Switzerland: Harwood Academic Publishers.

Matas, M., Staley, D., and Griffin, W. (1992). A profile of the noncompliant patient: A thirty-month review of outpatient psychiatry referrals. *General Hospital Psychiatry, 14*(2), 124-130.

McKay, J.R., McLellan, A.T., Alterman, A.I., Cacciola, J.S., Rutherford, M.J., and O'Brien, C.P. (1998). Predictors of participation in aftercare sessions and self-help groups following completion of intensive outpatient treatment for substance abuse. *Journal of Studies on Alcohol, 59*(1), 152-162.

Meichenbaum, D. and Turk, K. (1987). *Facilitating treatment adherence: A practitioner's guidebook.* New York: Plenum Press.

Miller, W.R., Benefield, G., and Tonigan, J.S. (1993). Enhancing motivation for change in problem drinking: A controlled comparison of two therapist styles. *Journal of Consulting and Clinical Psychology, 61*(3), 455-461.

Miller, W.R. and Rollnick, S. (1991). *Motivational interviewing: Preparing people to change addictive behavior.* New York: The Guilford Press.

Miller, W.R., Zweben, A., DiClemente, C.C., and Rychtarik, R.G. (1995). *Motivational enhancement therapy manual: A clinical research guide for therapists treating individuals with alcohol abuse and dependence.* Rockville, MD: National Institute on Alcohol Abuse and Alcoholism.

Miner, C.R., Rosenthal, R.N., Hellerstein, D. J., and Muenz, L.R. (1997). Prediction of compliance with outpatient referral in patients with schizophrenia and psychoactive substance use disorders. *Archives of General Psychiatry, 54*(8), 706-712.

Minkoff, K. (1989). An integrated treatment model for dual diagnosis of psychosis and addiction. *Hospital and Community Psychiatry, 40*(10), 1031-1036.

Mueser, K.T., Bellack, A.S., and Blanchard, J.J. (1992). Comorbidity of schizophrenia and substance abuse: Implications for treatment. *Journal of Consulting and Clinical Psychology, 60*(6), 845-856.

Nace, E.P. (1987). Alcoholics anonymous. In J.H. Lowinson, P. Ruiz, R.B. Millman, and J.G. Langrod (Eds.), *Substance abuse: A comprehensive textbook,* Third edition (pp. 383-389). Baltimore, MD: Williams and Wilkins.

Nace, E.P., Davis, C.W., and Gaspari, J.P. (1991). Axis II comorbidity in substance abusers. *American Journal of Psychiatry, 148*(1), 118-120.

National Institute on Alcohol Abuse and Alcoholism (NIAAA) (1997). *Ninth special report to the U.S. Congress on alcohol and health.* Rockville, MD: U.S. Department of Health and Human Services.

National Institute on Drug Abuse (NIDA) (1991). *Drug abuse and drug abuse research.* Rockville, MD: U.S. Department of Health and Human Services.

National Institute on Drug Abuse (NIDA) (2000). *Approaches to drug abuse counseling.* Rockville, MD: U.S. Department of Health and Human Services.

National Institute on Drug Abuse (NIDA) (2002). *Group drug counseling for cocaine dependence: The cocaine collaborative model.* Therapy manuals for drug addiction. Manual 4. Rockville, MD: U.S. Department of Health and Human Services.

Onken, L.S., Blaine, J., and Boren, J. (Eds.) (1997). *Beyond the therapeutic alliance: Keeping the drug-dependent individual in treatment.* Rockville, MD: National Institute on Drug Abuse.

Orme, D.R. and Bowell, D. (1991). Brief report: The preintake dropout at a community mental health center. *Community Mental Health Journal, 27*(5), 375-379.

Ries, R. (1995). *Assessment and treatment of patients with coexisting mental illness and alcohol and other drug abuse.* Rockville, MD: U.S. Department of Health and Human Services.

Salloum, I.M., Daley, D.C., Cornelius, J.R., Kirisci, L., and Thase, M.E. (1996). Disproportionate lethality in psychiatric patients with concurrent alcohol and cocaine abuse. *American Journal of Psychiatry, 153*(7), 953-955.

Saunders, B., Wilkinson, C., and Phillips, M. (1995). The impact of a brief motivational intervention with opiate users attending a methadone program. *Addiction, 90*(4), 415-424.

Simpson, D.D., Brown, B.S., and Joe, G.W. (1997). Treatment retention and follow-up outcomes in the drug abuse treatment outcome study (DATOS). *Psychology of Addictive Behaviors, 11*(4), 294-307.

Simpson, D.D., Joe, G.W., Rowan, G., and Greener, J. (1995). Client engagement and change during drug abuse treatment. *Journal of Substance Abuse, 7*(1), 117-134.

Simpson, D.D., Joe, G.W., Rowan-Szal, G.A., and Greener, J.M. (1997). Drug abuse treatment process components that improve retention. *Journal of Substance Abuse Treatment, 14*(6), 565-572.

Smith, D.E., Heckemeyer, C.M., Kratt, P.P., and Mason, D.A. (1997). Motivational interviewing to improve adherence to a behavioral weight-control program for older obese women with NIDDM. *Diabetes Care, 20*(1), 52-54.

Smoller, J.W., McLean, R.Y.S., Otto, M.W., and Pollack, M.H. (1998). How do clinicians respond to patients who miss appointments? *Journal of Clinical Psychiatry, 59*(6), 330-338.

Solomon, P. (1987). Receipt of aftercare services by problem types: Psychiatric psychiatric/substance abuse and substance abuse. *Psychiatric Quarterly, 58*(3), 180-188.

Solomon, P. and Gordon, B. (1988). Outpatient compliance with psychiatric emergency room patients by presenting problems. *Psychiatric Quarterly, 59*(4), 271-283.

Stanton, M.D. (1996). The role of family and significant others in the engagement and retention of drug dependent individuals. In L.S. Onken, J.D. Blaine, and J.J. Boren (Eds.), *Beyond the therapeutic alliance: Keeping the drug dependent individual in treatment* (pp. 157-180). Rockville, MD: National Institute on Drug Abuse.

Stanton, M.D. and Shadish, W.R. (1997). Outcome, attrition, and family-couples for drug abuse: A meta-analysis and review of the controlled, comparative studies. *Psychological Bulletin, 122*(2), 170-191.

Stark, M.J. (1992). Dropping out of substance abuse treatment: A clinically oriented review. *Clinical Psychology Review, 12*(1), 93-116.

Stark, M.J., Campbell, B.K., and Brinkerhoff, C.V. (1990). "Hello, may we help you?" A study of attrition prevention at the time of the first phone contact with substance-abusing clients. *American Journal of Drug and Alcohol Abuse, 16*(1), 67-76.

Swanson, A.J., Pantalon, M.V., and Cohen, K.R. (1999). Motivational interviewing and treatment adherence among psychiatric and dually-diagnosed patients. *Journal of Nervous and Mental Disease, 187*(9), 630-635.

Swartz, M.S., Swanson, J.W., Hiday, V.A., Borum, R., Wagner, H.R., and Burns, B.J. (1998). Violence and severe mental illness: The effects of substance abuse and nonadherence to medication. *American Journal of Psychiatry, 155*(2), 226-231.

Tomasson, K. and Vaglum, P. (1998). Psychiatric comorbidity and aftercare among alcoholics: A prospective study of a nationwide representative sample. *Addiction, 93*(3), 423-431.

Verinis, J.S. and Taylor, J. (1994). Increasing alcoholic patients' aftercare attendance. *The International Journal of the Addictions, 29*(11), 1487-1494.

Walitzer, K.S., Dermen, J.H., and Connors, G.J. (1999). Strategies for preparing clients for treatment: A review. *Behavior Modification, 23*(1), 129-151.

Chapter 3

Psychopathology and Substance Abuse: A Psychoanalytic Perspective

Russell Smith

Soon her eye fell on a little glass box that was lying under the table: she opened it, and found in it a very small cake, on which the words "EAT ME" were beautifully marked in currants. "Well, I'll eat it," said Alice, "and if it makes me grow larger, I can reach the key; and if it makes me grow smaller, I can creep under the door: so either way I'll get into the garden, and I don't care which happens!"

From *Alice's Adventures in Wonderland*
by Lewis Carroll

LIBIDO AND PERSONALITY DEVELOPMENT

Psychoanalysis offers a highly deterministic vision of behavior. For analysts, the child is father of the man. The personality core is thought to evolve from infantile and childhood experiences during crucial, inevitable, developmental phases. Sigmund Freud postulated that libido, the primal sexual drive, becomes centered on oral, anal, and genital areas of the body in successive early stages of life. He believed that this sequence was biologically destined and universal.

To illustrate: at a meeting of the Vienna Psychoanalytic Society, Freud was in the audience while an analyst/anthropologist was presenting field studies of the rearing practices of a jungle tribe. He said

The author is indebted to David Smith for his technical assistance in the preparation of this chapter.

that his observations corroborated the oral and genital erogenous phases, but he found no evidence of the anal. Freud, known for his scatological and mischievous wit, interrupted, exclaiming, "What's the matter with these people? Don't they have assholes?"

The infant's relationship with the mother is considered to be of singular importance, while somewhat later the relationship with the parent of the opposite sex is viewed as paramount. The perceptions, drives, attitudes, and emotions of an adult are derived from—though not completely governed by—the events of childhood. The degree of self-determination or free will of an individual is dependent on maturity and ego strength. The ego (the central organizing or executive agency in the personality) flourishes if, in the early years, a healthy balance between nurturance and frustration is established. On the other hand, the ego can be enfeebled by childhood trauma. If trauma and fixation occur after the ego has formed a vital foundation (after the age of three or four), neurotic symptoms may ensue. In neurosis the ego becomes entangled in a conflict between the id (the instinctual, hedonistic force) and the superego (conscience). The symptoms are a manifestation of the ego's compromise. For example, a phobia may be a symbolic way of avoiding a wish; a compulsion may be a method of undoing or controlling a drive such as hostility.

If, however, infants or very young children are subjected to environments that seem to threaten their very existence either by deprivation, rejection, abandonment, physical harm, or perceived annihilation, the development of the ego may be so weakened that its ability to deal with the internal or external world is severely handicapped. Such conditions may dispose individuals toward psychosis or the erection of drastic defensive measures against the disintegration of the ego. In some cases, depending on the stage of fixation and the nature of the defenses employed, a person may manifest symptoms of a character disorder, such as a narcissistic or borderline personality. The latter is characterized by unstable, chaotic interpersonal relationships, identity problems, and an intense need for external distraction or stimulation ("stimulus hunger"), among other symptoms. Persons whose behavior is primarily unlawful, immoral, or exploitive are thought to have deficient superegos and are diagnosed with the roughly synonymous terms psychopath, sociopath, antisocial personality, or impulse disorder. Analysts, like most clinicians, generally view drug abuse as an expression of a personality disorder (though most see more utility in a psychodynamic description than a diagnostic classification). That the personality disturbance often encompasses some antisocial features is not surprising, since most substance abuse is illegal and all substance abuse is socially condemned—though there are many cultural inconsistencies and double standards in this regard. Whether drug users as a group have a multiplicity of antisocial traits is not clear.

Early analytic descriptions of drug dependence were framed in terms of libidinal theory and erogenous zones. Freud, who used cocaine himself for a while early in his career, believed at one time that addiction was a form or derivative of masturbation. That notion, which never gained acceptance, and which Freud in later writings made little reference to, seems quaint in the light of contemporary analytic thought. However, whether drug abuse and masturbation are related, there are points of comparison, the most obvious being that both are sources of intense, self-indulgent pleasure; in addition, some users of drugs that induce a "rush" describe this experience as orgasmic. E. Hopper (1995), for one, finds a sexual basis for drug use. Based on the psychoanalytic treatment of "at least twelve men and women," he has found that the state of intoxication allows the user to indulge in otherwise repressed homosexual fantasies. He concludes, "Drugs are used to facilitate masturbation fantasies and masturbation" (p. 1139).

EARLY VERSUS LATER PSYCHOANALYTIC THOUGHT

Until relatively recently few analysts, or clinicians in general for that matter, seemed interested in drug dependence and certainly not because there have not been prior epidemics in the Western world. The lack of attention may have been because it was identified as more of a social problem than a reflection of intrapsychic processes and thus was not treated by analytic therapists. Furthermore, perhaps because of the time, money, and effort involved in psychoanalysis, there has been an elitist sensibility in patient selection. Analysts, like most therapists, prefer patients who are troubled by their symptoms. Behavior that is purely self-gratifying and unattended by conflict (ego syntonic) is considered refractory to treatment.

However, a few eminent psychoanalysts have offered some theoretical comments. For example, Abraham (1960) and Rado (1933) believed that hedonism is central to drug use. As Rado (p. 3) put it: "The patient doesn't suffer from his illness, he enjoys it." They viewed addiction as a regressive phenomenon, a reversion to infantile forms of gratification. Glover (1932) used libidinal theory in his formulation but departed from his contemporaries with his belief that drug use could be a "defense" against aggressive, destructive urges. This view of addiction as having an internal regulative and adaptive function anticipated later ego-psychological thought. In contemporary analytic writings on the subject, several authors emerge as most influential. These writers, such as Edward Khantzian, Leon Wurmser, and Henry Krystal, are indebted to classical or neoorthodox theorists such as Anna Freud, Margaret Mahler, Heinz Hartmann, Otto Kernberg, Melanie Klein, and Heinz Kohut. They see addiction as a prismlike phenomenon that can split the psyche into its component parts.

Khantzian, Wurmser, and Krystal all believe that substance abusers suffer from defects in personality development, structure, and organization which render them vulnerable to powerful, painful, and destructive emotions (affects). Substance abusers are inadequately defended against affects such as rage, fear of abandonment, helplessness, and shame. Because of primitive ego development, sometimes their experience of these emotions is not well differentiated and therefore not comprehended or even acknowledged, a condition known as hyposymbolization or alexithymia.

These three analysts also generally agree that the personality impairment found in drug abusers is due to the lack of opportunity in the formative years to identify with (introject) a nurturing, benevolent parent. This may lead to a narcissistic insult—an injury to the person's fundamental sense of worth, competence, and identity. Krystal (1977, p. 92) states that, as a result, "drug-dependents may not *want* control of appropriate self functions" (original emphasis). He goes on to say that drug users "wall off" the maternal image (presumably because of rejection or neglect) and are then unable to adopt for themselves the caring functions of the mother. These functions find external embodiment in the form of drugs, which provide comfort, support, emotional analgesia, and a symbolic fusion with a fantasized benevolent mother personified by the drug. This is a reaffirmation of what Krystal and Raskin (1970) had previously stated to the effect that drugs represent love, and that drug use is an attempt to repair early important relations fractured by ambivalence. According to this hypothesis, the ego of the drug user has been fragmented by a destructive love-hate relationship with the mother. Drugs may serve to resolve, at least temporarily, these conflicting feelings and reduce anxiety, tension, and rage. Krystal and Raskin add that while the main palliative effect of drugs is tension reduction, an increase in *pleasurable* tension (thrills) can also result.

Frosch and Milkman (1977) express a similar idea about drugs as psychological nourishment, stating "self esteem is dependent on supplies of food and warmth; the drug represents these supplies" (p. 152).

Otto Kernberg (1975) has been an influential proponent of object relations theory, which deals with this process of an internalized and permanent psychic representation of a nurturant parent(s). The word *object* here refers to the image of the mother formed by the infant. This image is internalized and becomes part of the infant's psyche. Kernberg asserts that if a mother is perceived as threatening, the psychic image of her will be divided into two representations, the good mother, which is the one needed for survival, and the feared, hated, bad mother. He says that this division, called "ego splitting," will not attain internal, symbolic status in the ego because this risks destruction of the good by the more powerful bad. These perceptions remain externalized, incarnated, and reincarnated repeatedly in the form of persons with whom the so-called borderline personality becomes closely involved. The borderline comes to perceive others as sometimes all good and sometimes all bad when they cannot live up to the perfection required of the former. Relationships become tumultuous, conflict ridden, and usually short-lived. This person, who already suffers from psychic desolation and intense feelings of loneliness, creates nothing but misery and havoc in all relationships. As Woody (1977) reports, Kernberg believes that euphoria-producing drugs are used to relieve the emptiness of such a life. The drugs also provide an illusion of being loved and a sense of being whole and real. The abuser's narcissism is thus artificially bolstered. Drug use is further reinforced by a feeling of magical control over the environment during the intoxicated state.

Heinz Kohut (1977) is another analyst who supports the notion that drug use is a symbolic attempt at merging with a love object, the illusive warmth of the good mother longed for during infancy. Kohut states that the user is soothed by the drug but that since no developmental progress or growth in the "self" results, the solution is transitory at best. Goldman and Gelso (1997), using Kohut's ideas, tried to quantify changes in the healthy and morbid narcissism of adolescent addicts in treatment. Psychological inventories were employed to assess three aspects of negative narcissism: *pseudoautonomy*, characterized by withdrawal and rebellion; *defensive grandiosity*, expressed by superiority, dominance, and needs for perfection; and *defensive idealized parent* (referring to relationships with figures of authority) as manifested by low frustration tolerance and rage.

Two dimensions of positive narcissism were measured: *healthy grandiosity*, as reflected by confidence and self-assertion, and *healthy idealized parent*, in which there is empathy, humor, acceptance of one's limitations, and admiration for the realistic virtues of others.

They found that narcissistic functioning did improve somewhat with treatment, especially in pseudoautonomy (counterdependent acting out was reduced) and healthy grandiosity (self-confidence increased).

Much of Edward J. Khantzian's work, like Krystal's, is centered on the failure to internalize the function of self-care (Khantzian's equivalent of good mothering). As a result, the addict seems oblivious to risk and danger. He indicates that the addicts' lack of concern for their welfare especially applies to the drug use itself "where despite obvious deterioration and imminent danger as a result of their drug use, there is little evidence of fear, anxiety, or realistic assessment about their substance involvement" (1977, p. 108). He is not referring here to the addicts who are primarily self-destructive or who may seek out danger in order to prevail over their fears (the counterphobic addict). Rather, he is discussing the addict who lacks what Freud (1926) called "signal" or "real" anxiety. Khantzian says that this insouciance or recklessness poses one of the most serious problems in trying to treat addiction.

THE BORDERLINE PERSONALITY

Based on behavioral and psychodynamic considerations, the analysts reviewed in this article would all probably diagnose drug abusers as borderline personalities who rely on drugs as a reaction to childhood trauma and as a means of establishing or shoring up psychological defenses. Krystal (1977) believes that addicts use narcotizing substances in an effort to subdue their aggression (resulting from frustration of the need for love) and their grief over the perceived loss of a loving parent. He states that if users abstain—while in therapy, for example—they will invariably go through a depressive phase as their emotions surface. Greenspan (1977) would concur, stating: "The substance abuse . . . is a defense against separation anxiety and its accompanying depression" (p. 78). Greenspan also notes that drugs may serve an adaptive purpose by promoting a psychic equilibrium not attained in childhood because of psychological wounds.

Hartmann (1969) also views underlying depression and a need to counteract painful feelings arising from deprivation of affection as causal elements in drug abuse. Like Kohut, he sees dependence on drugs as offering relief in the short term, but ultimately highly maladaptive and contributory to arrested character development.

However, in his study of adolescent drug abusers, Hartmann could not identify any unique developmental events or clinical syndromes that predisposed adolescents to drug abuse rather than some other behavioral or psychological abnormality. Furthermore, he believes that object relations problems, low frustration tolerance, and other psychic turbulence are found in all adolescents and therefore are not predictive of drug abuse. Anna Freud (1965) commented on this same phenomenon: "adolescence produces its own symptomatology which, in the more severe cases, is of a quasi-dissocial, quasi-psychotic, borderline order . . . [which] disappears when adolescence has run its course" (p. 164).

Wurmser (1974, 1977), on the other hand, after years of studying compulsive drug users from an analytic perspective, concluded that severe psychopathology characterized by regressive tendencies and defective regulation of powerful emotions is an antecedent of substance dependence. He postulates that the most disturbing emotions that overwhelm potential drug abusers are rage, shame, alienation, and disappointment—all the result of "narcissistic frustration" (unfulfilled needs). Overcome with psychic pain, tortured and sickened by their emotions, they are reduced to a state of terror and despair before turning to drugs. Wurmser believes, as do other writers (Frosch, 1970; Milkman and Frosch, 1973; Frosch and Milknan, 1977; Greaves, 1980; Wikler, 1973a,b; Spotts and Shontz, 1980) that various drugs are used for their differential abilities to alleviate certain emotional states as well as for their ability to satisfy needs arising from developmental fixation. According to Wurmser (1977), depressants help deny rage and shame; hallucinogens counteract emptiness, anomie, and boredom; stimulants relieve depression and promote feelings of mastery, control, and power; alcohol helps overcome shyness, facilitates the release of anger, and blunts loneliness.

Wurmser (1974) indicates that without drugs the needs, primitive drives, and psychopathology of the user will be revealed. The narcotics addict will become violent; the stimulant user depressed; the psychedelic user apathetic and existentially sad. He states (1977) that the addict often does not experience emotions in a well-defined way but rather in the form of diffuse tension. As noted earlier, many clinicians are similarly aware of addicts' inability to articulate their feelings.

To review his position, Wurmser views drug use as a form of self-medication—an exogenous, chemical defense that establishes or amplifies defenses of denial, dissociation (ego splitting), acting out of internal conflict, and the related defense of externalization, which involves the projection of symbolic, infantile emotions and needs. Narcotics and alcohol serve the purposes of denial; hallucinogens induce dissociation; stimulants release aggression.

In terms of ego structure and psychodynamics, he focuses much attention on the defenses of splitting and externalization, which he believes are fundamental to the psychic operations and behavior of the drug user. His notion of splitting is consistent with Kernberg's described previously; as noted there, splitting results in a dichotimized view of others as all good (perfect) or all bad (punitive, rejecting, destructive). Splitting has a pervasive effect on perceptions and attitudes. Continuums such as mind-body, past-present, moral-immoral, and hate-love become rigidly compartmentalized. A frequently observed symptom of splitting is the verbalization of contradictory thoughts in a narrow space of time. For example, an intense interest in reaching a certain goal might be expressed (e.g., get a certain job, obtain a diploma, start a family, quit drugs) while a few statements later the person will indicate no interest whatsoever in that goal. In the borderline personality Wurmser and Kernberg write about this as not a manifestation of ambivalence or indecisiveness but rather a reflection of ego fragmentation. A listener—whether a psychotherapist or an acquaintance—trying to follow such unpredictable and contradictory thoughts is likely to be more than a little puzzled and irritated.

Wurmser (1977) states that splitting leads to experiences of depersonalization and derealization: "Drug abuse thus seems like an artificial depersonalization coupled with . . . externalization, which is so characteristic for 'sociopaths'" (p. 55).

By externalization Wurmser means the acting out of an unconscious conflict or problem. Things or other persons come to represent some aspect of—or solution to—the internal, dynamic source of the distress. In this way drugs are experienced as magical and omnipotent cures for an ongoing psychological difficulty. Similarly, authoritarian institutions or persons (parents, police, teachers, therapists) may become substitutes for the individual's conscience. Through externalization a material enemy is established and can be struggled against or submitted to, as the case may be. In addiction—and here Wurmser extends the concept to compulsive behavior such as television watching, gambling, and overeating—the addictive substance or compulsive ritual represents an illusory means of control over externalized forces. He summarizes the nature of this mechanism he considers so basic to the drug user, stating "an external conflict situation and action ward off the internal conflict and the archaic overwhelming affects stemming from it" (1977, p. 58).

The same concepts, ego splitting and externalization, are fundamental to Otto Kernberg's (1975) formulation, though he uses the term *projective identification* instead of externalization.

In any event, Wurmser concludes by categorically stating that all of the drug-dependent patients whom he has examined fit the diagnosis of borderline personality.

All of the theorists discussed in this article believe that drug dependence is a result of psychological imbalance, conflict, frustration, and failure of coping mechanisms. Though it creates its own secondary social and psychological problems, drug use is an attempt at intrapsychic remediation, a form of self-medication. The user's drug of choice is a reflection of specific psychodynamic and affective needs. As Khantzian (1980) states, "preference . . . is the result of the drug of choice and its distinctive psychopharmacologic effects interacting with the unique personality organization and reactive patterns of an individual" (p. 31).

A FEW NONANALYTIC IDEAS

It is worth noting that these metapsychological ideas are not incompatible with other formulations. Pandina, Johnson, and Labourie (1992) use a neurochemical model to explain drug choice as a function of affect regulation. They propose that differential use is governed by needs for increased neurological stimulation, overstimulation resulting from excessive activation, or chronic deprivation of positive reinforcement (pleasure). Greaves (1980), writing from an existential viewpoint, states, "The taking of drugs in an attempt to rectify an abnormal state of personality is a form of auto-medication, and forms the cornerstone of all drug dependency" (p. 26). He also says that, outside of drug use, the drug dependent do not know how to find enjoyment in life. He decries methods of treatment based on self-denial or "asceticism" as he calls it. In his opinion, many treatment programs are misguided in their insistence that the addicts give up their only source of enjoyment "while offering little in return except vague, distant promises of a better life and improved self-esteem" (p. 27). Similarly, Freud in *Civilization and Its Discontents* (1930) seems more existential than analytic when he states that drugs are used because: "Life, as we find it, is too hard for us; it brings us too many pains, disappointments and impossible tasks. In order to bear it we cannot dispense with palliative measures" (p. 22). Finally, Krystal and Raskin (1970), who mainly rely on psychodynamic concepts to explain drug selection, note that some persons—otherwise normal—may fall prey to drug dependence because they are starved for pleasure, perhaps because they overwork, to cite one possibility. Sometimes—just sometimes—the reason might be this simple.

COMMENTS

Freud's Influence on the Theory

In 1895, Freud wrote a paper titled "Project for a Scientific Psychology" (1953) in which he proposed the objective investigation of mental and emotional processes in an effort to elevate psychology to the realm of the natural sciences. In that paper, Freud, being a neurologist, emphasized the neuronal basis of psychic functions. In time he saw less need for neurological explanations of behavior. Instead, he developed a model of the mind as composed of various structures (id, ego, superego) that interact in very complex ways. The nature of these structures and their interaction form the personality, which, to a great extent, is determined by a sequence of developmental experiences occurring in the first few years of life.

Freud collected his data using an idiographic approach—that is, he studied the individual. In his clinical practice, he attempted to reconstruct the life experiences of his patients, from which he drew conclusions about the pathogenesis of psychological disorders, mainly neuroses. He relied on inductive reasoning whereby broad principles are derived from the particular. He thought of himself as a scientist, though he spurned the scientific method of experimentation believing it was neither relevant to nor necessary for his work.

Freud's approach to the study of psychology established precedents which are evident in modern psychoanalysis. Behavior, motivation, emotion, and psychopathology are conceptualized in metapsychological terms, also known as psychodynamics. Freud's language, drawn from literature and mythology, is still used in describing warring psychological and social forces. The main drives are the Darwinian notion of survival and procreation—embodied in the libido, and the aggressive instinct.

Freud and other early psychoanalytic writers have clearly influenced the theorists reviewed herein. They view drug use as the behavioral manifestation of personality aberrations arising from frustration, deprivation, and emotional pain. Drug use is also thought to be purposeful and, in the short-term, adaptive: the user generally feels better when intoxicated.

The observations of analysts on drug use and behavior in general are humanistic and well integrated within a comprehensive theory of psychology. Their writings are erudite and imaginative, eloquent and forceful. Their method of collecting and interpreting data, however, is a problem in its almost exclusive reliance on retrospective information, lack of controls, and disdain for testable propositions. In addition, the terminology is often esoteric and unstandardized. Thus, even Wurmser—who lapses into some very cryptic metapsychology—writing about the formulations of certain other analysts complains that their "theoretical expositions are very abstract and difficult to understand" (1977, p. 54).

Experimental Findings

Direct laboratory experimentation with humans taking addictive drugs, while it has been done (Fischman and Schuster, 1982; Griffiths, Bradford, and Brady, 1979; Henningfield et al., 1987; Mello and

Mendelson, 1980; Wikler, 1952), poses obvious problems of ethics and liability. Those who do conduct such studies are either behaviorists or pharmacologists and rarely are naive subjects (those having no history of drug dependence) used, so analysts cannot be faulted for not experimenting directly with borderlines and nonborderlines. However, the utter disregard for a comparison group and for statistics—for all of its pitfalls and misuses—seems arrogant. In this vein, Wurmser's assertion—that every drug addict he had ever examined was a borderline personality—smacks of self-selection or some other form of bias. Numerous psychological studies, in which no personality abnormalities were found among habitual drug users, refute his contention (Gilbert and Lombardi, 1967; Hill, Haertzen, and Glaser, 1960; Ling et al., 1973; McDonald, 1965; Messinger and Zitrin, 1965; Mirin, Meyer, and McNamee, 1976; Olson, 1964; Sheppard et al., 1972; Stefanis et al., 1976; Sutker, Allain, and Cohen, 1974), while others offer some support or at least find some form of severe psychopathology in addicts (Gay et al., 1972; Gerard and Kornetsky, 1955; Halikas, Goodwin, and Guze, 1972; Kaufman, 1974; Monroe, Ross, and Bergins, 1971; Robbins, 1974; Senay, Dorus, and Meyer, 1976; Sheppard et al., 1973).

Animal studies, though of debatable relevance to human behavior and motivation, do provide examples of controlled experimentation. Some of these studies (Deneau, Yanagita, and Seevers, 1969; Johanson, Balster, and Bonese, 1976; Johanson and Schuster, 1981; Pickens, Meisch, and Thompson, 1978; Schuster and Thompson, 1969) clearly indicate that exposure to certain drugs such as amphetamine, barbiturates, morphine, diazepam (Valium)—*not* psychopathology—is all that is required to produce continued self-administration (the animal equivalent of dependence).

Furthermore, some researchers (Bozarth and Wise, 1985; Deneau, Yanagita, and Seevers, 1969; Dworkin et al., 1987; Johanson, Balster, and Bonese, 1976) have found that given unlimited access to cocaine, animals will continue taking this drug until it proves fatal, while Winger and Woods (1973) reported the same result with unlimited access to ethanol (alcohol). There is a striking congruity between drugs animals seem to be attracted to and those human use. At face value, then, this would seem to argue for a biologically reinforcing mechanism involved in drug use. If so, doubt is cast on the importance of concepts such as "ego splitting" or "narcissistic impairment." On the other hand, animals are notorious gluttons. They are not taught (or genetically programmed) to curb their appetites. What if people were given unlimited access to cocaine? As noted, this is not feasible to study under controlled conditions. However, a natural lab is available: the demimonde of drug trafficking, where there is cocaine galore.

Working in a prison setting, the author has had the opportunity to interview well over 1,000 convicts who have been involved in cocaine sales—from the runners ("mules"), to street-corner sellers, to suppliers. Based on their statements, and keeping in mind possible problems of veracity, three categories emerge: those who become dependent, which seem to constitute the majority of sellers; those who use with varying degrees of frequency short of habituation; and those who abstain. The abstainers tend to be found on a higher rung of the distribution ladder. They see themselves as businessmen, though they have nothing but contempt for the end users of their product. In addition, they often explain their abstinence with a shuddering fear of the drug, noting precisely the devastating effects of drug dependence. The author concludes, therefore, that there are differences between animals and humans in the potential for addiction. In humans mere exposure—even to the most powerful euphoria-producing drugs—is not sufficient to produce addiction or habituation.

Occasional Use of Addictive Drugs

In seeking to identify predisposing factors in human drug dependence, two analytically oriented investigators, Zinberg and Shaffer (1985), concluded that sociological processes have a strong influence on drug use. They state that to the extent that drugs become more available and normative "there is less likelihood that users who have disturbed personalities will predominate" among the universe of users (p. 70). Zinberg (1984), in a very interesting study comparing heroin addicts with occasional opiate users, found that addicts were more prone to distort reality and that a much greater number of addicts used opiates to relieve depression and satisfy a need for risk taking. More occasional users indulged in opiates for social purposes, recreation, and enjoyment of the "high." He found no significant differences in history of trauma, predrug use maladjustment, or social class. He does believe that personality variables (the "set") are important factors in determining who uses opiates and how often, but he indicates that the social circumstances of use (the "setting") are at least of equal importance. Thus he found that chronic users were much more likely to use opiates in the company of other chronic users, whereas most occasional users (67 percent), while indulging, kept to the company of other nonaddicted users. Zinberg further found that occasional users were much more likely to have ritualistic rules governing when and where they used than the addicted subjects. He concludes, "Setting variables were found to be a major, if not the primary element in determining degree of control" (1984, p. 81).

A Few Problems of the Psychoanalytic Theory

In most of the work done by analysts, however, there is rarely an attempt to isolate variables by comparing one group of subjects with another. To the contrary, their inferences are almost always based on subjects in treatment. In terms of science, this is chasing one's tail. That psychoanalysis is lacking in methodological rigor is a frequently registered criticism that applies in varying degrees to other theories of personality. After all, psychoanalysis, like the study of history, is based on the reconstruction of events and, as one eminent historian once said, few things happen at the right time, the rest never happens at all; it is the duty of the historian to correct these defects of subject.

Wurmser (1977) does note many of the problems for the psychoanalytic exploration of drug abuse, including distortion of personal history by the patient, resistance to long-term treatment, the influence of cultural and familial processes, and the rareness of a well-defined transference (reenactment of the past) in therapy. In view of all of these serious obstacles it is no small wonder that Wurmser learned as much as he did about the psyches of drug abusers.

A particularly difficult problem for analytic theory—and any other theory that relies on ideas of drug use as self-medication—is the fundamental notion that drug selection is a function of specific developmental and ego anomalies. It is hard to reconcile this with the epidemiology of drug use. Specific habit-forming drugs (alcohol and marijuana aside) seem to have gained ascendance at different times in recent decades: heroin and hallucinogens in the 1960s and early 1970s; hypnotics (especially Quaalude and Doriden) and methamphetamine through the 1970s and early 1980s; and cocaine as the widespread drug of choice in the 1980s and 1990s. Some individuals do, in fact, seem to be loyal to a specific drug or pharmacological class of drugs (e.g., euphorics, central nervous system depressants, stimulants, hallucinogens), but polydrug abuse, both concurrent and sequential, seems so common that the idea of a match between drug and pathological state, and therefore the whole principle of self-medication, may be moot.

IMPLICATIONS OF THE THEORY
FOR THE NONANALYTIC CLINICIAN

If psychoanalysis is vulnerable to criticism on grounds of scientific laxity, it merits respect for bringing discipline to the therapeutic setting. This discipline is based on any number of considerations, the most important of which is the understanding of the phenomena of transference and countertransference. The former refers to the emotions and reenactments from the remote past that the patient experiences in relation to the analyst as a parental figure. The latter is the constellation of attitudes and feelings aroused in the analyst because of past events or the personal needs of the analyst. Since countertransference is influenced to some extent by the traits and strivings of the patient, it provides the analyst another door to the patient's psyche. The therapy is efficacious to the extent that the transference allows problems from the past to be worked through while the analyst maintains tight control over countertransference reactions.

Transference and countertransference will arise in any therapeutic relationship regardless of the therapist's technique, training, or personality. They will occur in the most egalitarian treatment settings where everybody is on a first name basis, sessions are informal, and the therapist reveals almost as much personal information as the client does. However, under these circumstances, where the authority, expertise, and objectivity of the therapist are rejected, transference phenomena become extremely contaminated, distorted, and impossible to use constructively.

On the other hand, therapists who understand manifestations of transference and the need for firm boundaries between themselves and their clients will be better able to establish rapport and empathy and facilitate the growth and curative processes. Analytic tools can thus provide a framework for eliciting and comprehending the emotional life, fantasies, and formative experiences of the habitual drug user as they play out on the therapeutic stage.

In this context is it not preferable, more helpful, *and* safer for the therapist to take the role of Greek chorus, bringing clarity, commentary, and—dare one say—sanity to the situation, rather than to play a major character? Under these conditions all of the addict's tangled emotions and drives—rage, shame, loneliness, inadequacy, emptiness, boredom, search for excitement, need to exploit, need for constant euphoria, desperation, and self-destruction—can emerge and be treated without frightening or consuming the patient or the therapist. This is one of the monumental contributions of psychoanalysis. An understanding of it can be useful to any therapist regardless of theoretical orientation.

Finally, in an age of biological reductionism ("it's all in your genes") and cognitive reductionism ("it's all in your mind"), analysis is there as a reminder of the complexity of human behavior and of the human heart and soul.

GLOSSARY

acting out: The behavioral expression or discharge of a drive, psychological conflict, or tension usually engendered by trauma. It often denotes the conversion of the psychic (memory, thoughts, needs) into the motoric either as a defense against recognition of the drive or because of affective flooding.

affect: An emotion derived from an instinct. Also, a manifest mood that may or may not correspond with the actual feeling reported.

borderline personality: A disorder originally thought of as a form of schizophrenia but which has become widely described as a primitive personality disturbance characterized by grossly unstable social and psychological functioning, severe identity problems, self-destructive behavior, and rapidly shifting or contradictory perceptions and attitudes.

countertransference: *See* transference.

defense: A mechanism in service to the ego to protect against unpleasant emotions or dangerous impulses. Denial, repression, reaction formation, projection, and sublimation are some examples.

depersonalization: A feeling, often accompanied by anxiety and confusion, that one's self has changed. The feeling may be a vague bodily sensation or pertain to personal/social identity.

derealization: The feeling that one's immediate environment has changed and is thus rendered unfamiliar or unreal.

dissociation: A process, such as amnesia, by which psychological material is detached from the ego. Also, the fragmentation of the ego into disharmonious elements. Term is sometimes used interchangeably with "ego splitting" (quod vive).

ego: In psychoanalysis, that agency of the personality that functions as a mediator between biological urges (the id) and the conscience (superego), or between hedonistic drives and the demands of society and limits of the real world. One of the primary tasks of the ego is reality testing. Adaptation, affect regulation, cognition, and identity are other important ego processes.

ego psychology: A modern movement within psychoanalysis that ascribes more importance to ego functioning than to libido in the determination of behavior. The manner in which the ego maintains psychic equilibrium through the use of defenses is considered of special interest in understanding normal as well as pathological conditions.

ego splitting: The division of the ego into unintegrated parts or subsystems. Splitting often results in dichotomized perceptions of everything in terms of good and bad. Erratic fluctuations in the experience of love-hate, trust-mistrust, and dependence-autonomy occur. Splitting is viewed by some as a defense, and by others as a nonadaptive defect in personality integration.

externalization: Usually, the displacement of a psychological conflict onto things or persons in the outer world that symbolically come to represent aspects of the conflict. The defense of projection is often involved and is sometimes used synonymously with externalization.

id: The part of the personality encompassing the biological drives or instincts. It operates according to the pleasure principle, which dictates immediate gratification of needs either in the real world or in fantasy.

introjection: Sometimes known as internalization, the process by which things external to the ego become part of the ego through a kind of psychic ingestion. Identification and introjection are often used interchangeably with incorporation though some writers draw fine distinctions among these terms.

libido: Broadly speaking, the basic life force or energy. The libido becomes attached to specific erogenous zones during critical developmental stages.

narcissism: The focusing (cathexis) of libidinal energy on the self. In normal early development this is a healthy process that later in life is manifested by a sense of worth, competence, and desirability as a love object. Narcissism that is damaged or insulted may lead to a defective sense of self, while excessive narcissism might engender feelings of omnipotence, superiority, and entitlement. Paradoxically, either condition can produce the same demanding, egocentric behavior. For the person with deficient narcissism the behavior is compensatory. In the person with excessive narcissism the behavior represents infantile fixation and self-love.

object relations: The "object" usually is a reference to the nurturant mother especially as she is eventually perceived by the infant/child to have existence separate from its needs. An object relationship generally refers to the mature and reciprocal relationship a psychologically healthy person is capable of and enters into because of love, fondness, or other emotional investment. "Object relations theory" deals with the psychic representation of others within one's ego. Through the processes of libidinal attachment (cathexis) and internalization, those we are close to in childhood become part of our selves.

psychodynamics: The personality forces that arise from the interaction of the psychic structures (id, ego, superego). The study of these forces is called metapsychology.

separation anxiety: Dread of or distress from being separated from the mother. As a morbid condition the separation is construed by the infant/child as abandonment or death.

superego: Conscience. Societal standards and values. Often, though not exclusively punitive, the superego is considered to be the source of guilt feelings.

transference: Feelings, perceptions, and reactions from childhood that emerge in treatment as a product of a patient's relationship with a therapist. Countertransference is the displacement of the therapist's needs and emotions from the past and from the therapist's personal life to the treatment setting. Transference and countertransference are inevitable and essential parts of the therapeutic process.

REFERENCES

Abraham, K. (1960). *The psychological relation between sexuality and alcoholism. Selected papers of Karl Abraham.* New York: Basic Books.

Bozarth, M.A. and Wise, R.A. (1985). Toxicity associated with long-term intravenous heroin and cocaine self-administration in the rat. *Journal of the American Medical Association,* 253, 81-83.

Deneau, G., Yanagita, T., and Seevers, M.H. (1969). Self-administration of psychoactive substances by the monkey. *Psychopharmacologia,* 16, 30-48.

Dworkin, S.I., Goeders, N.E., Grabowski, J., and Smith, J.E. (1987). In Harris, L.S. (Ed.), *Problems of drug dependence 1986* (pp. 221-225). National Institute on Drug Abuse Research Monograph 76. DHHS no. ADM 87-1508. Washington, DC: U.S. Government Printing Office.

Fischman, W.M. and Schuster, G.R. (1982). Cocaine self-administration in humans. *Federation Proceedings,* 41, 241-246.

Freud, A. (1965). *Normality and pathology in childhood.* New York: International Universities Press, Inc.

Freud, S. (1895). *The standard edition of the complete psychological works,* Volume I. Strachey, J. (Ed.). London: Hogarth Press, 1953.

Freud, S. (1926). Inhibitions, symptoms, and anxiety. *The standard edition of the complete psychological works,* Volume XX. Strachey, J. (Ed.). London: Hogarth Press, 1953.

Freud, S. (1930). *Civilization and its discontents.* Strachey, J. (Ed.). New York: W. W. Norton and Company, 1961.

Frosch, W.A. (1970). Psychoanalytic evaluation of addiction and habituation. *Journal of the American Psychoanalytic Association,* 18, 209-218.

Frosch, W.A. and Milkman, H. (1977). Ego functions in drug users. In Blaine, J.D. and Julius, D.A. (Eds.), *Psychodynamics of drug dependence* (pp. 142-156). National Institute on Drug Abuse Research Monograph 12. DHEW no. ADM 77-470. Washington, DC: U.S. Government Printing Office.

Gay, G.R., Wellisch, D.K., Wesson, D.R., and Smith, D.E. (1972). *The psychotic junkie.* New York: Insight Publishing Company.

Gerard, D.I. and Kornetsky, C. (1955). Adolescent opiate addiction: A study of control and addict subjects. *Psychiatric Quarterly,* 29, 457-486.

Gilbert, J.G. and Lombardi, D.N. (1967). Personality characteristics of young male narcotic addicts. *Journal of Consulting Psychology,* 31(5), 536-538.

Glover, E. (1932). On the aetiology of drug addiction. *International Journal of Psychoanalysis,* 13, 298-328.

Goldman, G.F. and Gelso, C.J. (1997). Kohut's theory of narcissism and adolescent drug abuse treatment. *Psychoanalytic Psychology,* 14, 81-94.

Greaves, G.B. (1980). An existential theory of drug dependence. In Lettieri, D.J., Sayers, M., and Pearson, H.W. (Eds.), *Theories on drug abuse* (pp. 24-28). National Institute on Drug Abuse Research Monograph 30. DHHS no. ADM 84-967. Washington, DC: U.S. Government Printing Office.

Greenspan, S.I. (1977). Substance abuse: An understanding from psychoanalytic developmental and learning perspectives. In Blaine, J.D. and Julius, D.A. (Eds.), *Psychodynamics of drug dependence* (pp. 73-87). National Institute on Drug Abuse Research Monograph 12. DHEW no. ADM 77-470. Washington, DC: U.S. Government Printing Office.

Griffiths, R.R., Bradford, L.D., and Brady, J.V. (1979). Predicting the abuse liability of drugs with animal drug self-administration procedures: Psychomotor stimulants and hallucinogens. In Thompson, T. and Dews, P.B. (Eds.), *Advances in behavioral pharmacology,* Volume 2 (pp. 163-208). New York: Academic Press, Inc.

Halikas, J.A., Goodwin, D.W., and Guze, S.B. (1972). Marijuana use and psychiatric illness. In Miller, L. (Ed.), *Marijuana: Effects on human behavior* (pp. 265-302). New York: Academic Press, Inc.

Hartmann, D. (1969). A study of drug-taking adolescents. *Psychoanalytic Study of the Child,* 24, 384-398.

Henningfield, J.E., Nemeth-Coslett, R., Katz, J.L., and Goldbert, S.R. (1987). Intravenous cocaine self-administration by human volunteers: Second-order schedules or reinforcement. In Harris, L.S. (Ed.), *Problem of drug dependence 1986* (pp. 266-273). National Institute on Drug Abuse Research Monograph 76. DHHS no. ADM 87-1508. Washington, DC: U.S. Government Printing Office.

Hill, H.E., Haertzen, C.A., and Glaser, R. (1960). Personality characteristics of narcotic addicts as indicated by the MMPI. *Journal of General Psychology,* 62, 127-139.

Hopper, E. (1995). A psychoanalytic theory of drug addiction. *International Journal of Psychoanalysis,* 76, 1121-1142.

Johanson, C.E., Balster, R.L., and Bonese, K. (1976). Self-administration of psychomotor stimulant drugs: The effects of unlimited access. *Pharmacology Biochemistry and Behavior,* 4, 45-51.

Johanson, C.E. and Schuster, C.R. (1981). Animal models of drug self-administration. In Mello, N.K. (Ed.), *Advances in substance abuse: Behavioral and biological research,* Volume 2 (pp. 219-297). Greenwich, CT: IAI Press.

Kaufman, E. (1974). The psychodynamics of opiate dependence: A new look. *American Journal of Drug and Alcohol Abuse,* 1(3), 349-370.

Kernberg, O.F. (1975). *Borderline conditions and pathological narcissism.* New York: Jason Aronson.

Khantzian, E.J. (1977). The ego, the self, and opiate addiction: Theoretical and treatment considerations. In Blaine, J.D. and Julius, D.A. (Eds.), *Psychodynamics of drug dependence* (pp. 101-117). National Institute on Drug Abuse Research Monograph 12. DHEW no. ADM 77-470. Washington, DC: U.S. Government Printing Office.

Khantzian, E.J. (1980). An ego/self theory of substance dependence: A contemporary psychoanalytic perspective. In Lettieri, D.J., Sayers, M., and Pearson, H.W. (Eds.), *Theories on drug abuse* (pp. 29-33). National Institute on Drug Abuse Research Monograph 30. DHHS no. ADM 84-967. Washington, DC: U.S. Government Printing Office.

Kohut, H. (1977). Preface. In Blaine, J.D. and Julius, D.A. (Eds.), *Psychodynamics of drug dependence* (pp. vii-ix). National Institute on Drug Abuse Research Monograph 12. DHEW no. ADM 77-470. Washington, DC: U.S. Government Printing Office.

Krystal, H. (1977). Self- and object-representation in alcohol and other drug dependence: Implications for therapy. In Blaine, J.D. and Julius, D.A. (Eds.), *Psychodynamics of drug dependence* (pp. 88-100). National Institute on Drug Abuse Research Monograph 12. DHEW no. ADM 77-470. Washington, DC: U.S. Government Printing Office.

Krystal, H. and Raskin, H.A. (1970). *Drug dependence: Aspects of ego function.* Detroit, MI: Wayne State University Press.

Ling, W., Holmes, E.D., Post, G.R., and Litaker, M.B. (1973). A systematic psychiatric study of the heroin addicts. In National Association for the Prevention of Addiction to Narcotics, *Proceedings of the Fifth National Conference on Methadone Treatment.* Volume 1 (pp. 429-432). New York: The Association.

McDonald, L. (1965). Psychopathology of narcotic addiction: A new point of view. In Harms, E. (Ed.), *Drug addiction in youth* (pp. 56-66). New York: Pergamon Press.

Mello, N.K. and Mendelson, J.H. (1980). Buprenorphine suppresses heroin use by heroin addicts. *Science,* 207, 657-659.

Messinger, E. and Zitrin, A. (1965). A statistical study of criminal drug addicts. *Crime and Delinquency,* 11(3), 283-292.

Milkman, H. and Frosch, W.A. (1973). On the preferential abuse of heroin and amphetamine. *Journal of Nervous and Mental Disease,* 156(4), 242-248.

Mirin, S.M., Meyer, R.E., and McNamee, H.B. (1976). Psychopathology, craving, and mood during heroin acquisition: An experimental study. *International Journal of the Addictions,* 11(3), 525-544.

Monroe, J.J., Ross, W.F., and Bergins, J.I. (1971). The decline of the addict as "psychopath": Implications for community care. *International Journal of the Addictions,* 6(4), 601-608.

Olson, R.W. (1964). MMPI sex differences in narcotics addicts. *Journal of General Psychology,* 71, 257-266.

Pandina, R.J., Johnson, V., and Labourie, E.W. (1992). Affectivity: A central mechanism in the development of drug dependence. In Glantz, M. and Pickens, R. (Eds.), *Vulnerability to drug abuse.* Washington, DC: American Psychological Association.

Pickens, R., Meisch, R.A., and Thompson, T. (1978). Drug self-administration: An analysis of the reinforcing effects of drugs. In Iversen, L.I., Iversen, S.D., and Snyder, S.H. (Eds.), *Handbook of psychopharmacology,* Volume 12 (pp. 1-37). New York: Plenum Press.

Rado, S. (1933). The psychoanalysis of pharmacothymia. *Psychoanalytic Quarterly,* 2, 1-23.

Robbins, P.R. (1974). Depression and drug addiction. *Psychiatric Quarterly,* 48(3), 374-386.

Schuster, C.R. and Thompson, T. (1969). Self-administration of and behavioral dependence on drugs. *Annual Review of Pharmacology,* 9, 483-502.

Senay, E.C., Dorus, W.W., and Meyer, E.P. (1976). Psychopathology in drug abusers. Preliminary report. Department of Psychiatry, University of Chicago, Chicago, Illinois.

Sheppard, C., Fracchia, J., Ricca, E., and Merlis, S. (1972). Indications of psychopathology in male narcotic abusers, their effects and relation to treatment effectiveness. *Journal of Psychology,* 8(12), 351-360.

Sheppard, C., Ricca, E., Fracchia, J., and Merlis, S. (1973). Indications of psychopathology in applicants to a county methadone maintenance program. *Psychological Reports,* 33, 535-540.

Spotts, J.V. and Shontz, F.C. (1980). A life-theme theory of chronic drug abuse. In Lettieri, D.J., Sayers, M., and Pearson, H.W. (Eds.), *Theories on drug abuse* (pp. 59-70). National Institute on Drug Abuse Research Monograph 30. DHHS no. ADM 84-967. Washington, DC: U.S. Government Printing Office.

Stefanis, C., Liakas, A., Boulougouris, J., Fink, M., and Freeman, A. (1976). Chronic hashish use and mental disorder. *American Journal of Psychiatry,* 133(2), 225-227.

Sutker, P.B., Allain, A.N., and Cohen, G.H. (1974). MMPI indices of personality change following short-term and long-term hospitalization of heroin addicts. *Psychological Reports,* 34, 495-500.

Wikler, A. (1952). A psychodynamic study of a patient during self-regulated readdiction to morphine. *Psychiatric Quarterly,* 26, 270-293.

Wikler, A. (1973a). Dynamics of drug dependence: Implications of a conditioning theory for research and treatment. *Archives of General Psychiatry,* 28, 611-616.

Wikler, A. (1973b). Sources of reinforcement for drug using behavior. A theoretical formulation. In Pharmacology and the Future of Man. *Proceedings of the Fifth International Congress on Pharmacology, San Francisco, 1972,* Volume 1 (pp. 18-30). Basel, Switzerland: Karger.

Winger, G.D. and Woods, J.H. (1973). The reinforcing property of ethanol in the rhesus monkey: Initiation, maintenance, and termination of intravenous ethanol-reinforced responding. *Annals of the New York Academy of Sciences,* 215, 162-175.

Woody, G.E. (1977). Psychiatric aspects of opiate dependence: Diagnostic and therapeutic research issues. In Blaine, J.D. and Julius, D.A. (Eds.), *Psychodynamics of drug dependence* (pp. 156-178). National Institute on Drug Abuse Research Monograph 12. DHEW no. ADM 77-470. Washington, DC: U.S. Government Printing Office.

Wurmser, L. (1974). Psychoanalytic considerations of the etiology of compulsive drug use. *Journal of the American Psychoanalytic Association,* 32, 820-843.

Wurmser, L. (1977). Mr. Pecksniff's Horse? (Psychodynamics in compulsive drug use.) In Blaine, J.D. and Julius, D.A. (Eds.), *Psychodynamics of drug dependence* (pp. 36-72). National Institute on Drug Abuse Research Monograph 12. DHEW no. ADM 77-470. Washington, DC: U.S. Government Printing Office.

Zinberg, N.E. (1984). *Drug, set, and setting: The basis for controlled intoxicant use.* New Haven, CT: Yale University Press.

Zinberg, N.E. and Shaffer, H.J. (1985). The social psychology of intoxicant use: The interaction of personality and social setting. In Milkman, H.B. and Shaffer, H.J. (Eds.), *The addictions: Multidisciplinary perspectives and treatments.* Lexington, MA: D.C. Heath and Company.

SECTION II:
TREATMENT CONSIDERATIONS
WITH SPECIAL POPULATIONS

Chapter 4

Females with Dual Diagnoses: Implications for Specialized Clinical Approaches

Eileen Beyer
John A. Conahan

INTRODUCTION

It is a well-established clinical and research observation that women present to addiction treatment with a greater number of psychiatric problems than do men. They present as more complex than do men, with more coexisting cognitive, emotional, medical, and relationship problems that need to be assessed and addressed in order to attain and maintain sobriety. Therefore, case conceptualizations are more complicated and points of intervention are broader. Women are more likely to present with mental health complaints to physicians or mental health practitioners and not admit to using substances to cope or that their substance use is out of control.

Understanding dual diagnosis issues with women entails learning the essential differences between men and women regarding addiction and recovery as well as the gender differences in the manifestation of coexisting psychiatric diagnoses. This chapter will overview these essential differences as well as provide key factors in the assessment and treatment of the major dual diagnosis issues affecting women: depression, dissociative disorders, and eating disorders. A philosophy of care for dual-diagnosis women will be articulated through incorporation of feminist models of addiction treatment and mental illness. The importance of developing specialized dual diagnosis treatment for women will be justified using the latest research on barriers to treatment entry and need for comprehensive, gender-specific programs that address the increased level of burden that these women carry.

GENDER DIFFERENCES IN ADDICTION

Next to nicotine, alcohol is the most widely used substance for both men and women. Biological differences in how women metabolize alcohol make it more likely that they will develop physical consequences more rapidly, even with lower intake. Women have higher blood alcohol levels (BAC) than men do for a given amount consumed (Jones and Jones, 1976). Although this had been primarily attributed to alcohol being more dilute in the bodies of men who have more water and less fat cells, this effect is now primarily attributable to women having less of the stomach enzyme alcohol dehydrogenase, which begins the metabolism of alcohol (Frezza et al., 1990). Much less alcohol is digested and therefore more of it goes directly to body tissues. Therefore, it is not surprising that women are likely to react more intensely to a given dose of alcohol and that the effects are less predictable (Blume, 1997). Due to women's proportion of fat and less water than men, which increases with age, benzodiazepines and barbiturates have longer half-lives (Barry, 1986) and marijuana takes longer to clear. This is significant for anticipating withdrawal responses and assessing urine drug-testing results.

The physical effects of alcohol and drugs have a more severe course and more rapid onset in women, probably due to the increased chronic concentrations in their systems (Blume, 1997). For instance, alcoholic women develop liver cirrhosis through lower levels of alcohol intake and over shorter periods of time than do men (Gavaler, 1982). Alcoholic women may begin a pattern of abusive drinking later in life due to the stigma associated with heavy drinking among women, but they typically begin treatment at the same time as males with the same severity of illness, although the women often already have begun experiencing greater physical consequences (Blume, 1997). For women, there are fewer years between landmark symptoms and progression to a later stage of illness. This has been termed the "telescoping effect" of the progression of the disease in women (Corrigan, 1980; Piazza, Vrbka, and Yeager, 1989). It is particularly pronounced for women who are depressed before the onset of their alcoholism (Smith and Cloninger, 1981). Lewis et al.'s (1996) analysis of the Epidemiological Catchment Area (ECA) nationwide community data collected in 1982 supported prior findings that the rapid accrual of alcoholic symptoms in females is independent of both psychiatric comorbidity and the amount of alcohol consumption. Their research also supported the idea of a culturally mediated protection for women, which delays the onset of problematic drinking.

Alcohol and drugs interfere with women's fertility and can exacerbate gynecological disorders (Blume, 1997). The presence of premenstrual dysphoria has been associated with increased quantity and frequency of alcohol and marijuana use, and women with diagnosable premenstrual syndrome have higher rates of alcohol abuse and dependence (Tobin, Schmidt, and Rubinow, 1994). Unsafe sex associated with trading sex for drugs or relationships with addicted partners is related to increases in sexually transmitted diseases. Sexual dysfunction, such as lack of sexual desire, inability to orgasm, and painful intercourse, can cause a woman to use alcohol or drugs to cope, or these issues may be consequences of addiction. Although women may feel less sexually inhibited under the influence and even report greater desire, their physical responsiveness is actually diminished (Malatesta et al., 1982). This subjective sense of needing alcohol or drugs in order to perform sexually may lead many newly recovering women to avoid sexual relations, despite research that indicates the quality of sexual relations in recovery is likely to improve (Blume, 1997). Contrary to popular opinion, alcoholic women are not necessarily more promiscuous under the influence. Only 8 percent of surveyed women who drank reported being less particular about their sexual partner. In contrast, 60 percent of these women drinkers were likely to experience sexual aggression by someone else who had been drinking (Wilsnack, Wilsnack, and Klassen, 1986). In the research summarized by Blume (1997), 16 percent of alcoholic women are raped during their drinking history, and alcoholic women are more likely to experience violence from their spouses. Thus, the inaccurate stereotype of women made more promiscuous by alcohol results in continued promotion of their sexual victimization.

Double standards for women who abuse alcohol have been evident for a long period of time. Power differentials between men and women and subsequent vulnerability to victimization attack a woman's self-image as a female and seem to invite substance abuse. Despite research dispelling the stereotype of increased promiscuity, alcoholic and addicted women typically internalize the shame that they have "fallen from grace" and are "whores" who have self-inflicted their own pain (Blume, 1997). They suffer from the underlying cultural standard that mothers should be pure vessels of reproduction that remain unpolluted for the good of their fetuses. The shame of not living up to this expectation has prevented many addicted women from seeking treatment.

The impoverished environment often associated with illegal drug use, as well as the stigma (and possible loss of custody) associated with substance use while pregnant, decreases use of prenatal care and creates the conditions necessary for poor fetal and infant outcomes. Although "crack babies" brought heightened public awareness to the consequences of addiction to offspring, and heroin-addicted moms are vilified for producing addicted infants who need to be withdrawn, it is the legal drug, alcohol, that has been shown to be teratogenic, a direct cause of birth defects. Fetal alcohol syndrome is the leading cause of mental retardation, and less severe alcohol effects such as physical abnormalities and neurological impairment are all too common (Institute of Medicine, 1995). Like crack, nicotine is proven to cause low birth weight in babies and increase the chances for miscarriage, premature delivery, and birth complications. Smoking during pregnancy is also associated with the development of attention deficit hyperactivity disorder, conduct disorder, and substance abuse in offspring (Weissman et al., 1999).

Across all socioeconomic groups, addiction has severe effects on maternal-infant bonding that can have lifelong ramifications. The shame, guilt, loss, and fear of separation from their infants that addicted mothers feel can create significant barriers to treatment entry and less than optimal connection and compliance. Unresolved maternal grieving of abortion or of the effects of addiction on infants and/or loss of custody is a significant treatment issue that can contribute to depression and behavioral management problems in addicted women (Raskin, 1992). Women often do not readily acknowledge their shame, guilt, and loss because of societal stigma against their actions. Denial of their pain may cause them to act as if they do not care. Assessment of depression or personality dynamics should include evaluation of maternal role and grief issues.

According to a large national study of gender differences in drinking practices, Wilsnack, Wilsnack, and Klassen (1986) found that women who lack or who have lost significant relationships are at most risk for alcoholism. Young women ages twenty-one to thirty-four who were "roleless" (i.e., never married, no children, less than full-time employment) were at most risk for alcohol problems. Women in their middle years from thirty-five to forty-nine who experienced a "lost role" through separation or divorce, children living apart from them, or who were unemployed were the highest proportion of heavy drinkers. Older women (fifty to sixty-four) who felt they were trapped in their role (i.e., married and not working) or who were empty nesters drank the most. An interesting correlation is that women who lived with their partners were more likely to be heavy drinkers than those who were married. Women's drinking patterns also highly correlate with those of their significant others more so than for men. Most addicted women begin their use with the influence of a significant male in their lives (Hser, Anglin, and McGlothlin, 1987), typically their "darling, dealer, or doctor" (cited in Ettorre, 1992; Johnson and Auerbach, 1984). It was also determined that women progress more quickly from initiation to addiction than do men (Anglin, Hser, and McGlothin, 1987). In contrast, males are much more likely to begin addicted use in the context of male peer relationships. Addicted women presenting to treatment are more likely than addicted men to have an addicted partner, whose use patterns these women parallel (Jacob and Brenner, 1986; Griffin et al., 1989). Women are also more likely to be divorced or separated, and described their existing relationships as less happy and supportive (Schilit and Gomberg, 1987). It is important to recognize that women who enter treatment experience more opposition from friends and families and report greater conflict with them than men do (Beckman and Amaro, 1986). When support for treatment was identified, it was typically from their children and parents.

It is suggested that female substance abusers are more likely to come from dysfunctional families of origin. There are higher rates of mental illness, alcoholism, and depression in early family life of alcoholic women than in alcoholic men (Straussner, 1985). Glenn and Parson (1989) found that the rate of maternal alcoholism for men was reported as 11 percent; for women it was 25 percent. The rate of paternal alcoholism for men was reported as 36 percent; for women it was 50 percent. Daughters of alcoholics are likely to have had more frequent experiences of sexual abuse over a longer period of time.

Surprisingly in alcoholic families, the father was not usually the aggressor. Rather, the chaotic and secretive nature of the family system created a lack of protection for the female child, who was abused by other males (Miller and Downs, 1986). Women in addiction treatment are known to have high rates of past sexual, physical, and psychological abuse and demonstrate high rates of post-traumatic stress disorders, depression, and other mental health disorders (Gil-Rivas et al., 1997).

Overall, alcohol and cocaine dependent women date the onset of problematic use to a stressful life event, typically one involving a relationship trauma or loss (Griffin et al., 1989). As precipitating factors to their addiction, women typically identify significant life events such as miscarriage, loss of contact with children, mastectomy, hysterectomy, infidelity, separation, and divorce. It is detrimental to their connection to treatment when women are chastised for blaming their addiction on these events. Rather, it is important to empathize with the impact of this precipitant in the process of explaining how it promoted the disease process. Primary motivators for women to enter treatment are physical and emotional concerns as well as family issues, while men are most influenced by job and legal problems (Blume, 1997). Thus, women are motivated by more internal and relational factors and men by more external interventions.

CONTEXT OF COMORBIDITY: RELATIONAL PERSPECTIVE

Relational Model of Development

In the late 1970s, the psychological and social development of females began to be studied by progressive thinkers such as Jean Baker Miller (1976), Carol Gilligan (1982), and their colleagues at the Stone Center at Wellesley College (www.wellesley.edu/WCW). Their qualitative research suggested that female development occurs in the context of relationships, with mutually empathic and giving relationships being both a source and a goal of development. This contrasts traditional developmental theories that ignored or pathologized much of women's experience by studying males and generalizing their experience to females. These theories failed to describe the uniqueness of feminine values and means of expression.

According to the female-specific theories, women's focus on relationships is seen as natural and necessary rather than pathologized as dependence or lack of a sense of self. According to Carol Gilligan, the primary task of moral development for girls and women is to achieve a balance between self-nurture and care of others, not separation and autonomy. This balance fosters a heightened awareness and appreciation of self. Societal pressures to distance from family relationships and meet unrealistic standards of beauty contribute to adolescent girls' vulnerability to devalue themselves and lose their "voice." In a later work, Mary Pipher (1994) noted that junior high-age girls face enormous struggles not to succumb to media and peer pressure to conform to feminine roles that objectify their bodies and limit their power. Female teens also face the increasingly difficult task of protecting themselves from an escalating incidence of violence in their peer and family relationships. A feminist view of development gives significant weight to contextual influences from the media and peers. The significant changes in expectations and negative influences that girls face when they transition into puberty increase their vulnerability to drug and alcohol use and mental illness.

Relationship with Substance

Stephanie Covington (1999), who is a pioneer in integrating the relational development theory into addiction treatment, has conceptualized the process of addiction and recovery as a spiral. As the disease of addiction progresses, it constricts the woman's life until she is totally focused on the drug. The dependence on the substance becomes the primary relationship in the woman's life to the exclusion of self-care and participation in other relationships and activities. Recovery is a process of transformation that allows her to expand her sphere of focus to encompass healthy relationships and other positive activities that promote her self-esteem.

According to the self-medication hypothesis of Edward Khantzian (1985; 1997), people initially choose certain substances because of their self-medicating effects. The specific drugs provide some physiological change or way of coping that the person inherently lacked. This theory supports the practical application of trying to understand and treat the target symptoms and subjective distress that people report to self-medicate. Understanding the impact of relationship history has significant implications on the understanding of women's addictive behavior. Many women use substances to numb painful feelings, thoughts, and memories or to cope with problems or relationships over which they feel little control. According to Covington (1999), women may use substances to alter themselves to fit into their available relationships (i.e., to engage in sex, manage addiction in a partner, cope with violence). Imbalances of power or responsibilities can significantly decrease a woman's self-esteem. Substances may provide energy, a sense of power, and relief from confusion, compensating for what the relationship is not providing. Relationship dissatisfaction, conflict, and loss can precipitate heavier use and contribute to the maintenance of active addiction or relapse.

When women in treatment are asked what their substance of choice did for them, they typically are able to state what attracted them to the substance and how it helps them to cope. It is easy for women to conceptualize their relationship with a substance. Eileen Beyer asks female patients to write "Dear John" letters to their substance of choice to stimulate grieving the loss of the relationship with the substance. Women easily respond to the task of writing what attracted them to the substance, how it helped them, how it hurt them, and why they need to say good-bye. Because of this strong relationship association, women with coexisting mental disorders need to have the ability to acknowledge the positive things that the substance did for them in order to more fully grieve the need to let go. Focusing solely on the consequences of their use may not get at their alliance with the substance.

Expansion of the Disease Model of Addiction to Include the Relational Context

When viewing addiction as a primary disease, a common tenet of treatment is to steer the recovering persons away from blaming people or circumstances for their addiction, and to minimize self-blame by viewing addiction as primarily a product of hereditary predisposition or physiological vulnerability. The recovering persons are guided toward emotional acceptance of their powerlessness over the disease and assisted to accept responsibility for their own recovery. Although there are many practical benefits to this philosophy, many recovering women are left with little support to deal with precipitating issues and to grieve their consequences. As described earlier, most addicted women date the onset of their heaviest use to some stressful event. To ignore or discourage them from talking about the meaning of this event because it would foster self-pity instead of self-responsibility ignores the contextual factors that are so important to women. Although there is more interest and understanding in the mental health field to acknowledge precipitating events and understand the meaning of their impact, the rise of psychopharmacological interventions fosters the primacy of a medical model, which focuses on the management of symptoms and does not address contextual variables. Women can best move from a stance of feeling victimized by their circumstances and justifying their use of substances to cope when their experiences are given voice and empathetically received.

Relational Model: Implications for Addiction Treatment

Relational theory is supported by the philosophy and delivery of twelve-step-based addiction treatment for girls and women but also calls for change (Covington, 1999). Twelve-step meetings and the therapeutic community model of treatment have always prioritized making connections, and have even elevated the value of relationships by emphasizing their spiritual nature, thus in many ways fostering a feminist approach. However, in an attempt to simplify the process, guidance may be imposed in ways that ignore women's unique problems and issues in early recovery and their need for less hierarchical, more collaborative relationships with sponsors or treatment providers. Also, women's relationship focus may not always be sensitively addressed through traditional addiction approaches. Women may still be told that they have to work a "selfish program." For instance, many women are still given the guidance to do ninety meetings in ninety days or attend a certain number of meetings a week without regard for the impact of competing forces within them not to sacrifice their relationships in order to fulfill recovery and work or school commitments.

Relationship Focus versus Codependency

Recovering women who struggle in their attempts to balance care of self with others are often viewed as being relationship dependent, codependent, or externally focused (having an external locus of control) when in reality their struggle with priorities is well within the realm of normal for women. When the relational model of development is applied to recovery, it contends that rebuilding and strengthening relationships is essential to relapse prevention and is not a competing force to self-understanding and self-advocacy. Therefore, women's focus on relationships can be used to enhance motivation for recovery. Women can be counseled on how they sacrifice too much of themselves in order to mold themselves to fit into relationships with persons who are unwilling or unable to change without pathologizing their relationship desires and commitment. For a more complete history and critique of the codependency concept see Collins, 1993; O'Gorman, 1993; Uhle, 1994; and Favorini, 1995.

GENDER DIFFERENCES AND SIMILARITIES IN PSYCHIATRIC COMORBIDITY

Large-scale, national studies using community samples show some consistent gender differences in overall co-occurrence of psychiatric disorders (Regier et al., 1988; Kessler et al., 1994). Anxiety and affective disorders are most likely to co-occur in women while substance disorders, conduct disorders, and antisocial personality disorder are the most likely to co-occur in men (Kessler et al., 1997). Data from the National Comorbidity Survey (NCS), collected in 1994 (Kessler et al., 1997), have been analyzed to derive specific gender differences and similarities in psychiatric comorbidity among the problem-drinking community subgroup.

The majority of people in the NCS community sample with an alcohol disorder had at least one psychiatric disorder as well. Furthermore, the co-occurrence was stronger among women than in men (Kessler et al., 1997). The lifetime prevalence of alcohol abuse was 12.5 percent for men and 6.4 percent for women. Lifetime alcohol dependence rates were 20.1 percent and 8.2 percent, respectively. Over the course of a lifetime, drug dependence co-occurred with alcohol dependence in 29.5 percent of men and 34.7 percent of women. Furthermore, larger portions of women than men with alcohol abuse or dependence report prior anxiety disorders, affective disorders, and drug use disorders. The presence of prior psychiatric disorders was predictive of alcohol dependence, especially among women. Lifetime co-occurrence was positively associated with the persistence of alcohol dependence in both men and women.

Several studies have shown significant differences in psychopathology between men and women who seek help for chemical dependency (Brady et al., 1993; Magura et al., 1998). In Brady et al.'s (1993) descriptive study of 100 inpatient substance abusers, women were significantly more likely to have another current Axis I disorder in addition to substance abuse. This is consistent with the Epidemiological Catchment Area (ECA) study of the general population, which found that Axis I diagnoses were twice as prevalent in women (Regier et al., 1988). Women had almost twice the number of current anxiety disorders as men, particularly panic disorder (18 percent versus 10 percent) and post-traumatic stress disorder (PTSD) (46 percent versus 24 percent). These rates are substantially higher than the ECA data of the general population of women. For both men and women, social phobia and PTSD predated the onset of substance dependence in the majority of cases, which would support a self-medication hypothesis. No significant differences were found in the rates of affective disorders between male and female substance abusers, which is in contrast to ECA data in which major depression is twice as common in women as in men (Weissman and Klerman, 1977). In addition, the majority of addicted men experienced the onset of depression after the onset of substance abuse, indicating a more substance-induced condition in men. There were more pronounced gender differences within primary alcoholics. Female alcoholics had substantially more anxiety and affective disorders than males, the ratios of which are consistent with ECA data. Panic disorder was significantly more likely to predate alcoholism in women, supporting the use of alcohol to self-medicate. In contrast, within the primary cocaine dependent group, no significant differences in psychopathology were found between genders. Cocaine was found to precipitate depressive episodes that outlasted intoxication and withdrawal, thereby minimizing any gender differences. There were no differences in Axis II diagnoses between genders.

Magura et al. (1998) studied a sample of 212 methadone patients who were dually addicted to opiates and cocaine. Similar to the population data from the National Comorbidity Survey (Kessler et al., 1994), women addicts were more likely than men to present with concurrent mood and anxiety disorders. Methadone-dependent women with an antisocial personality disorder were likely to continue their opiate abuse and were less likely to have a concurrent alcohol use disorder.

Patients presenting to detoxification and dual diagnosis inpatient treatment were studied by Westreich et al. (1997). A review of 156 randomly selected charts revealed mostly demographic similarities between genders, except that women were more likely than men to report being victims of crime, especially interpersonal violence, though they were more likely to have a home. Men were more often admitted with a diagnosis of schizophrenia than women, who were more likely to have an affective disorder. There were also a greater percentage of women in the psychiatric diagnosis category of "other," which included psychosis, substance-induced hallucinosis, and borderline personality disorders. Furthermore, the higher number of women in detoxification with previous psychiatric treatment seems to suggest that women were directed to psychiatric services rather than addiction services. Women also reported being fearful of treatment due to the belief that they could lose their children or there would be inadequate care for their children.

The findings of Westreich et al. (1997) replicate the results of an earlier study of dually diagnosed outpatients (Comtois and Ries, 1995), which also found that men were more often diagnosed with schizophrenia and women with affective disorders. An interesting finding of this study was that women were less likely to attend group treatments, even when directed to do so.

Studies of alcoholic (Cornelius et al., 1995) and addicted patients (Grilo et al., 1997) presenting to psychiatric hospitals revealed many similar findings to previously mentioned studies of patients presenting to addiction treatment, especially when primary substance is taken into account. In their study of 604 alcoholics presenting for evaluation at a psychiatric diagnostic evaluation center, Cornelius et al. (1995) found that major depression was more commonly diagnosed with females and antisocial personality disorder with males. This is consistent with both Brady et al.'s (1993) data on primary alcoholics and the ECA community data (Regier et al., 1988). Standardized psychiatric symptom assessment revealed that these alcoholic females had significantly higher rates of depressed mood, general anxiety, unstable and intense interpersonal relationships, and overly dramatic behavior. An interesting finding is that reversed neurovegetative "atypical depressive" symptoms of weight gain, hypersomnia, and increased appetite were more severe in females than in males and approached significance. Overall, women had more psychiatric severity on fifteen symptoms while men were more severe only on homicidal ideation, other antisocial behavior, and suspiciousness. Female alcoholics were also more likely to have experienced recent marital difficulties and to have come from a broken home.

Grilo et al. (1997) studied young adults with polysubstance use who were psychiatric inpatients; no gender differences in rates of depression or anxiety were found. This is consistent with the Brady et al. (1993) study subsample of cocaine dependents, but not with ECA general population data (Regier et al., 1988). Men, however, had higher proportions of major depression and anxiety disorders than expected, given the general population sex-ratio data. It is yet to be determined whether this leveling effect between the genders with higher rates of depression and anxiety in male drug addicts indicates a substance-induced phenomenon, a self-medication effect, or that men who are clinically depressed or anxious are more likely to be induced to seek treatment. This study did show higher rates of dysthymia and eating disorders in women with substance use disorders. Males had higher rates of cluster A personality disorders (paranoid, schizotypal, and schizoid), suggesting that they used substances to cope with their general social ineffectiveness, characterized by odd behaviors. Antisocial personality disorder was not significantly more prevalent in this sample of males with substance use disorders, supporting the observation that female addicts are more likely to engage in antisocial behaviors than female alcoholics.

Level of Severity: Liabilities of Viewing Dually Diagnosed Women As Sicker

The relational model suggests a different perspective on women's psychological problems and how they should be addressed. Since first documented by Aristotle in Western culture, society has viewed women as weaker psychologically and thus prone to psychiatric disorders. In fact, a foundational study by Broverman et al. (1970) concluded that traits attributed to mentally healthy individuals were predominantly masculine (i.e., independence, self-determination, assertiveness, competitiveness). Females who adhered to stereotypically feminine traits were considered deviant and mentally unhealthy. It has also been suggested that the *Diagnostic and Statistical Manual of Mental Disorders'* classification reinforces negative perceptions of women's mental health and sexist bias in diagnosis. There may also be gender bias in the prevalence of diagnostic categories, which is inherent in the diagnostic classifications (i.e., borderlines as female, antisocials as male) (Nuckolls, 1997; Paris, 1997).

It has been argued that our diagnostic classification system scrutinizes and pathologizes many feminine traits, which are products of socialization or coping with power imbalances in relationships (dependent and histrionic personality disorders) and ignores exaggerated male forms of dependency on females or of severely restricted social functioning (Stiver, 1991; Nuckolls, 1997). This system also minimizes the impact of trauma on identity and behavior in relationships (borderline personality disorder) in favor of more inherent or early developmental attributions (Saunders and Arnold, 1991). The diagnostic description of PTSD may most accurately describe the experience of war or natural disaster survivors rather than the complex form of PTSD that is postulated to exist in trauma survivors, which may encompass borderline personality disorder (Herman, 1992).

It is clinically observable and supported by previously described research that women presenting to addiction treatment have more psychiatric symptomatology and diagnosable psychiatric problems than men do. This has led to common assumptions that they are sicker, which can imply weaker. As stated earlier, because of physiological differences in metabolizing substances, chemically dependent women are more likely to enter their first treatment with more severe physical and brain-related mental complications. The majority of chemically dependent women have experienced significant abuse, loss, or disruption in relationships which created significant changes in their view of themselves and their world. Methods of coping are developed that may help a woman to survive but now interfere with her healing and growth. These features increase women's vulnerability to the development of symptoms characterizable as mental illness.

Thus, chemically dependent females' higher proportion of psychiatric concerns may be most compassionately viewed as a product of relationship victimization and disconnection or perhaps physical vulnerability rather than inherent psychological vulnerability or character pathology. It is also important to factor in the common generalization that women tend to internalize their pain (i.e., depression, anxiety) and men tend to show external manifestations (irritability, explosive behavior). Men often receive more compassionate responses and validation that their pain must have been severe in order to be internalized (depression) or acted out (antisocial).

Focusing on the severity and complexity of their illnesses may foster or reinforce a self-fulfilling negative prophecy that they have due to prior treatment failures or lack of empowerment or validation in the social systems in which they operate. In addition, focusing on the generalization that dually diagnosed women are sicker, rather than have more complicated problems, reinforces the heightened stigma that chemically dependent women face as failing to remain the moral standard bearers of society. As described earlier, chemically dependent women face a triple stigma: that their addiction is self-afflicted, that they have "fallen from grace," and that they are promiscuous (Blume, 1997). The consequences of their addiction and mental illness are often seen as worse, less acceptable, and less forgivable than men's because a higher moral standard is expected from them. Therefore, dually diagnosed women may be more likely to be viewed as morally or psychologically weak instead of as suffering from two illnesses.

Although there is greater acceptance of the need to treat both illnesses simultaneously, there still exists the bias to directly or indirectly pathologize women's experience by attributing their difficulties to inherent weakness, lack of motivation, or codependency, thus ignoring the impact of contextual variables such as dysfunctional support systems and cultural attitudes toward women. Difficulties in recovery have traditionally been attributed to lack of motivation, effort, or ability to work the "right" recovery program, which has been viewed as successfully focusing one's efforts on one's own recovery and opening oneself up in trust to the help of others and a spiritual force that has greater power. It is obvious how these expectations may not be appropriate for women with histories of victimization.

Because they typically do not conform to traditional expectations of addiction recovery, dually diagnosed women are frequently perceived as being more problematic and difficult to treat. Repeated treatment episodes reinforce negative staff perceptions that these women's problems are primarily internal or even self-inflicted. Rather than focus on the inadequacies of treatment programs to meet their special needs, dually diagnosed women are typically blamed for their own failures. It is incumbent on those who treat dually diagnosed women to become more acutely aware of personal and systemic sexist biases that can maintain the status quo in programs and limit assessment accuracy, therapeutic connection, and treatment effectiveness.

MAJOR PSYCHIATRIC COMORBIDITIES IN ADDICTED WOMEN: DEPRESSION, DISSOCIATIVE DISORDERS, AND EATING DISORDERS

Depression

The estimates of affective disorders of alcoholics in treatment have been reported in the National Comorbidity Study (NCS) as 32 percent of a community sample having a co-occurrence of alcoholism and a major depressive episode (Kessler et al., 1997). Due to a limited amount of data, no consensus has been reached on the best way to identify comorbid depressive disorders in alcoholics. This is due to the possibility of confusing the symptoms of major depression with alcohol withdrawal-related mood symptoms. The delivery of chemical dependency services to men and women who also demonstrate symptoms of depression fails to determine if the depression is primary or secondary. Furthermore, if the depression is identified, treatment recommendations often include abstinence during the first ninety days then an assessment for depression. The reverse is also common. This implies that the chemical dependency is dismissed as a symptom of depression.

Brady et al. (1993), in their study on gender differences in substance use disorders, found that men were more likely to have affective disorders than women. Upon further examination the male population symptoms of depression were identified after the onset of chemical dependence. Women experience symptoms prior to the onset of chemical dependency.

Even though chemical dependency treatment populations have men outnumbering women, there is a significant incidence of depressive disorder in the female gender in both alcoholic and nonalcoholic treatment samples (Pettinati et al., 1997). Furthermore, the National Comorbidity Study documented that depressed alcoholic samples include more females than males (Kessler et al., 1997). The occurrence of lifetime comorbid depression was twice as likely in female alcoholics than in male alcoholics (Pettinati et al., 1997). The Epidemiological Catchment Area survey identified that the occurrence of comorbid depression was four times more prevalent in female than in male alcoholics (Lewis et al., 1996). The results of the study reported by Pettinati et al. (1997) supported the overall findings and prior literature of a relationship between comorbid depression with alcoholism and a more severe clinical picture at treatment entry than uncomplicated cases of alcoholism. Furthermore, depressed female alcoholics can be considered more severely depressed than male alcoholics, as was demonstrated by the greater intensity and number of depressive symptoms reported by females than males.

Goldman and Bander (1990) suggest that a good prognosis is possible when the differences in males and females are recognized in chemical dependency treatment and the severity of depression in females is identified and monitored throughout the early phases of treatment. In addition, Goldman and Bander studied dysthymic-disordered alcoholics who reported high and persistent levels of depressive symptomatology well into treatment and into sobriety. They found that in spite of the ongoing mood disturbance, female alcoholics had achieved and maintained abstinence. This is consistent with the findings of Rounsaville et al. (1987), that alcoholic women with major depression had better treatment outcomes on drinking-related measures than women without a comorbid diagnosis.

Depression and other affective disorders in women have significant implications for assessment and treatment, treatment retention, and improving outcomes. Depression in women seeking chemical dependency treatment has been consistently reported in the literature (Goldman and Bander, 1990; Meehan et al., 1996; Pettinati et al., 1997; Schutte, Hearst, and Moos, 1997).

Schutte, Hearst, and Moos (1997) found a notable relationship among women with depressive symptoms and alcohol consumption. Over a three-year period Schutte and colleagues found that more depression predicted heavier alcohol consumption among women. Pettinati et al. (1997) found that depressed males had a more severe clinical profile with respect to their alcoholism. However, depressed females were more severely depressed. Meehan et al. (1996) compared recovering men and women to nonaddicted men and women and found that addicted persons had higher scores for depression, shame, and maladaptive guilt. Furthermore, Goldman and Bander (1990) ascertained that abstinent dysthymic alcoholic women scored as depressed as nonabstinent alcoholics at intake, three months, and six months of treatment. This suggests that alcoholics with a history of dysthymia could remain depressed and need continued monitoring.

These findings clearly imply that the treatment of women with chemical dependency with comorbid depression is not necessarily more difficult to treat as much as it is different. These differences exist in the assessments, treatment strategies, gender-specific or gender-separate services. Differences are further illustrated by Davis and DiNitto (1996), who support what has been referred to as the "double whammy" phenomenon, which suggests that family and social difficulties are greater in alcoholic women than men. Female alcoholics have more familial alcoholism than male alcoholics do and significantly more women experience psychiatric hospitalizations.

Davis and DiNitto (1996) also reported high rates of depression among females, and 69 percent of those identified never received medication for their disorder. Evaluation for depression medication in the first month of sobriety is still very controversial given the perception that most symptoms disappear. However, these studies suggest that symptoms of persons with comorbid diagnosable major depression and dysthymia are not as likely to remit and that medication may be a necessary adjunct to make the initial transition to an abstinent lifestyle and connection to treatment easier.

Implications from this body of research for the treatment of women with chemical dependency and other depressive disorders are that matching the most effective services to the areas assessed is critical if the clinician is to have impact upon treatment retention, treatment planning, individualized assessments, and improved outcomes. Furthermore, relapse prevention strategies should include continued assessment of level of depression, use of medications, and coaching to build support systems for women to fill the void of spouses and family members who have withdrawn their support, and cognitive-behavioral strategies to deal with stresses of life that have been avoided or numbed by their use of chemicals.

Dissociative Disorders

A primary dissociative disorder is likely to go unrecognized by clinicians who treat addiction (Kolander and Frances, 1993; McDowell, Levin, and Nunes, 1999). The presenting symptoms may mask behavior of active addiction. "Failure to address DID or substance abuse will likely have negative impact on the patient" (McDowell, Levin, and Nunes, 1999, p. 72).

It is commonly accepted that dissociation occurs on a continuum from the comparatively normal experience of going on autopilot while driving to the more severe manifestation of dissociative identity disorder (DID) in which at least two separate personality states periodically take full control of the person. DID is thought to derive directly from severe, repeated, and often life-threatening incest, or physical or emotional abuse beginning at an early age. Symptoms are present before the age of twelve and often before the age of five (McDowell, Levin, and Nunes, 1999). Thoughts, feelings, memories, and perceptions are split off.

This primary author has experienced that persons with the most severe dissociation tend to deny any childhood trauma history or present with only vague suspicions. This may occur because the host personality that is presenting to treatment either has no knowledge of the traumatic events, the person's memory is so fragmented, or because the host is being threatened with serious harm if the secrets are divulged. For an excellent glossary of terms related to dissociative identity disorder that addiction professionals may be unfamiliar with, see McDowell, Levin, and Nunes (1999).

It is common for persons with DID to have drug abuse that is severe and begins at an early age (Ellason et al., 1996). While DID is thought to be present in 1 percent of the general population, the prevalence of DID in addicted patients may be as high as 15 percent (Ross, 1997).

Dissociation is more common than is currently acknowledged and patients are typically misdiagnosed as borderline, PTSD, or bipolar. I have been most likely to see people in early abstinence who meet criteria for dissociative disorder not otherwise specified (NOS), because without overexposing the patient, I do not gather enough evidence to conclude that two or more alters periodically take full control. While the physiological effects of intoxication occur no matter which alter is in control, it is common for an alter personality to be the "addicted one" or for more than one alter personality to have a preference for or addicted use of different substances. Polysubstance dependence is common in persons with DID (McDowell, Levin, and Nunes, 1999).

Persons presenting with coexisting dissociative disorders and substance use disorders are notable for their history of multiple prior treatments (often both psychiatric and substance use), multiple diagnoses, and use of multiple medications (McDowell, Levin, and Nunes, 1999). Almost half of all patients with DID have been previously diagnosed and treated for schizophrenia (Ellason and Ross, 1997).

Confusion lies among the experience of blackouts, the anterograde amnesia caused by alcohol and other sedative drugs, and the episodes of time loss associated with dissociation (Kolander and Frances, 1993). Blackouts from substances typically occur after the person has ingested enough of the substance to experience a "buzz." They typically last from a few hours to the length of a binge. The start of blackouts often hails the transition from experimental use to more regular, problematic use. Although people with a genetic predisposition to alcoholism may experience blackouts early in their addiction, blacking out (not passing out) during a person's first alcohol use is rare and may be dissociation. Another marker for dissociation occurs when a patient reports lack of recall of events after entering a bar or after the first drink, especially if this occurs on almost every occasion of use. Persons with a dissociative disorder present as poor historians, with fragmentary recall of life events and large gaps in history before substance abuse.

Time loss related to dissociation may begin at the start of an episode of substance use and may indicate that an alter personality took control. Dissociation should be suspected when clinicians begin to conceptualize the patients as "pathological liars" because they deny significant consequences of their substance abuse even when corroborated by external sources (DUIs, arrests, rapes). They also appear to demonstrate a level of denial that is even more pervasive than is typically seen with substance abuse (Kolander and Frances, 1993).

Persons with addiction commonly experience the narrowing of their social network to persons who also use or enable their use. Probing into relationship networks with DID patients often uncovers that they have social circles in which they operate as if they were two different people, with the addiction not seeming to permeate certain spheres of relationships or functioning. The chronic mistaken identity experience of being called by different names or being told they did things that they do not remember doing can all too easily be mistakenly attributed to manifestations of active addiction (McDowell, Levin, and Nunes, 1999). Although fluctuations in skills, habits, and knowledge are common to both disorders, persons with DID may show spheres of normal or above-average functioning that remain untouched by addiction. Work behavior is often the last to be affected by addiction, but an astute counselor can often poke holes in a patient's denial that there has not been any diminishing of functioning (McDowell, Levin, and Nunes, 1999).

Patients with dissociation tend to tune out during emotionally charged group sessions or have difficulty staying focused in individual sessions. They may appear easily distracted, especially if they are aware of inner dialogue between their personality states. This distracted state may lead the clinician to explore a diagnosis of ADHD instead of a trauma-related disorder.

The hallucinations and delusional states of dissociation can be typically distinguished from the acute psychotic states associated with substance intoxication and withdrawal. The hallucinations of primary addicted persons often manifest as olfactory, tactile, or visual hallucinations. The auditory hallucinations of addicted or thought-disturbed individuals typically are perceived to come from external sources rather than the internal dialogue that dissociative disorder patients report occurring inside their heads. Differentiation of dissociation from thought disturbance can be made by noting the paucity of negative symptoms of schizophrenia, such as pervasive lethargy, emotional flatness, and lack of motivation (Ross, 1997).

It is the first author's suspicion that many dissociative patients are mislabeled as bipolar or cyclothymic because of their moodiness, unpredictability, and extreme behavior. Typically, they are first diagnosed as rapid cycling bipolar II with psychotic features. Ineffective, adverse, or inconsistent responses to mood stabilizing medication with known significant history of trauma are indicators that dissociation needs further exploration. While there are reported cases of bipolar illness in patients with DID and borderline personality disorder (Alarcon, 1990; Wills and Goodwin, 1996), concurrent dissociation is likely to be missed when bipolar illness is considered the primary diagnosis. However, use of the Dissociative Experiences Scale (Bernstein and Putnam, 1986) did appropriately distinguish, by level of severity of dissociation, patients with DID, other dissociative disorders, and bipolar disorder (Nihenhuis et al., 1997). Failure to adequately diagnose dissociation can significantly impact psychiatric and addiction treatment outcomes. While pharmacotherapy is the treatment of choice for bipolar illness, psychotherapy is still the principal treatment for dissociation (Alarcon, 1990).

Evidence is accumulating that childhood trauma affects neurobiological development and can increase the risk of developing mood and anxiety disorders (Heim and Nemeroff, 2001). Much media attention has been paid to the more current use of the early-onset bipolar label with children and adolescents. Lynn (2000, p. 41) described the occurrence in these children of a "limbic wave" in which normal consciousness is taken over by "rage, obsession, and wildness" that "begins slowly, builds to a crescendo, and releases pressure in an explosive affect and rapid drop off of energy after the explosion, sometimes resulting in sleep." These rage attacks typically occur for no apparent reason but once activated, take a predictable course. Hallucinations, gory thinking, irrationality, and paranoia are often present during the "explosive phase" of the escalation (p. 60). Lynn stated that children and adolescents "report rage almost as an entity that takes them over or that is clearly localized as a presence" (p. 54) and that afterward, they do not remember what happened during the rage attack.

It has been this author's clinical experience that bipolar disorder may have been the most probable diagnosis in a few adults she mistakenly concluded were dissociating, given their reports of time lapses during rages. These anecdotal reports suggest the need for heightened diligence in obtaining evidence of alters before being convinced that one is dealing with DID. Also, dissociation that occurs during rage or obsession episodes may be best attributable to the brain activity associated with bipolar disorder, and thus most amenable to other medication and behavioral management strategies. However, if dissociation is the primary phenomenon, it will be evident during varied moods, circumstances, and substance use patterns.

Identification of true dissociation is important because it is necessary to alter therapeutic interventions to develop and maintain communication between the split-off aspects of the patient's self and the therapist so that the most cooperation possible takes place in the service of stabilization in sobriety. Also, it is healing and motivating for patients to be acquitted of intentionally lying about aspects of their substance use or behavior over which they had little awareness. Identification of true dissociation is important because it is necessary to alter therapeutic interventions to develop and maintain communication between the split-off aspects of the patient's self and the therapist so that there is the most cooperation as is possible in the service of stabilization in sobriety. Also, it is healing and motivating for patients to be acquitted of intentionally lying about aspects of their substance use or behavior over which they had little awareness.

It is important for addiction treatment providers to ascertain whether different parts of a person are "the users" and whether the host personality that typically presents for treatment has the ability to communicate with these alters. If little or no communication exists or if these parts have too much power, verbal agreements for abstinence and safety are unlikely to be kept if made with the host, who typically is amenable to treatment and open to change. Suicidal ideation and self-mutilation are extremely common in these dually disordered patients, and it is important to ascertain which alter is behind the suicidal thoughts and behaviors (McDowell, Levin, and Nunes, 1999). Typically a persecutory alter, often identified with the patient's perpetrator, seeks to punish or destroy the patient if secrets are revealed or if self-abusive behavior is stopped.

Screening and diagnostic tools have been proven to be very effective in detecting clinically significant levels of dissociation in substance-abusing patients (Dunn, Ryan, and Paolo, 1994; Kolander and Frances, 1993; McDowell, Levin, and Nunes, 1999). The first author has found the Dissociative Experiences Scale (DES) (Bernstein and Putnam, 1986), available in the public domain, to be exceptionally useful in screening for the presence of clinically significant dissociation in substance-abusing women. It is a twenty-eight-item self-report instrument that asks respondents to indicate the percentage of time, from 0 to 100, that an experience of dissociative or PTSD symptoms occurs for them. Substance-abusing patients can be asked to answer with regard to times when they are not under the influence of substances or make note that they experience it under the influence. A cut-off score of 30, which is the average of percentile responses for all questions, is considered highly suggestive of a dissociative disorder or PTSD with significant dissociative features in substance-abusing patients (Kolander and Frances, 1993). The higher the score, the more severe level of dissociation. Adolescents tend to score higher than adults. It has been the author's experience that women with dissociative disorders score exceptionally high and can give unequivocal descriptions of the experiences they positively endorsed. Scores under 30 are considered normal, because the DES also asks about nonpathological, common forms of dissociation. Therefore, a very low score may indicate intentional minimization of responses due to distrust or paranoia. Interestingly, patients with dissociative disorders tend not to underreport or exaggerate their symptoms, conceivably because they perceive their experiences as normal.

A benefit of the DES is that addiction counselors can be taught to explain to patients the rationale for administration and then administer, score, and ask patients for clarifying examples of positive responses. Screens with scores above 30, along with counselor generated clarifications of responses, should then be passed to the psychologist or psychiatrist to do further evaluation to make the differential diagnosis and make recommendations for management of symptoms and long-term treatment integrated with addiction recovery. Preferably, patent feedback will occur with the addiction counselor present, given the complicated nature of the course of recovery.

According to McDowell, Levin, and Nunes (1999), treatment for dissociative disorders should assist the patient toward the goal of more integrated functioning, at a pace that is determined as much as possible by the patient. The processing of traumatic events can occur by uncovering memories, emotional catharsis, and creating a narrative account of the patient's experiences that is made up of the perspective of the different aspects of self. Desensitization can also be used to lessen the response to affectively charged memories. The importance of corrective emotional experiences in therapy and in current relationships cannot be overestimated. Progress can be measured by symptom stabilization, control of dysfunctional behaviors, and relationship improvement.

Dissociation is the most complicated disorder to treat concurrently with substance abuse. With intensive psychotherapy being the treatment of choice for dissociation, it is very easy to lose focus on addiction being a primary illness that will not automatically resolve if greater integration of personality states occurs. Specialists in the treatment of dissociation are still heavily influenced by belief in the need to thoroughly process trauma by becoming consciously aware of and grieving abuse experiences and less influenced by cognitive-behavioral stabilization strategies that can be so useful in recovery, especially in early sobriety.

Eating Disorders

Within settings that primarily treat substance use disorders (SUD) or eating disorders, there still exists much ambivalence and avoidance of addressing these disorders concurrently. This results from a lack of understanding of the similarities and differences between these two disorders and their treatment methods. Practitioners who specialize in either of these two disorders may avoid addressing the coexisting issues because concurrent management seems too difficult, or approaches to management seem too divergent. Very few dual-diagnosis programs address both or provide specialized treatment tracks. General mental health practitioners often suffer from the denial, minimization, or avoidance of diagnosing and learning how to treat these two disorders because of lasting stereotypes that stigmatize patients with either of these two disorders as being too difficult or treatment refractory. This section highlights current research on the prevalence and progression of this comorbidity and discusses theoretical controversies as well as provides assessment and treatment guidelines based on model programs.

Prevalence of Eating Disorder/Substance Abuse Comorbidity

Comorbidity findings suggest that the association between eating disorders with bulimic features and substance abuse is much stronger than that with restricting anorexia. In a review of fifty-one studies of primarily eating disorder patients, Holderness, Brooks-Gunn, and Warren (1994) found that bulimics had rates of alcohol abuse and dependence ranging from 14 to 49 percent and drug abuse and dependence rates from 8 to 36 percent (Lilenfeld and Kaye, 1996). Restricting anorexics had a prevalence of alcohol abuse or dependence of 0 to 6 percent, which is less than the general population rate of 12 percent (Kessler et al., 1997). This can be explained by the anorexics' unwillingness to take in extra calories from alcohol. Because of anorexics' tendency to abuse amphetamines as a means of weight control, their rates of drug abuse and dependence range from 5 to 19 percent (Lilenfeld and Kaye, 1996). Severity of binge eating has been associated with tranquilizer use, while severity of purging was most closely associated with alcohol, cocaine, and nicotine use (Wiederman and Pryor, 1996). Caffeine, laxative, and cigarette use was highest among bulimics and anorexics who are also bulimic (Lilenfeld and Kaye, 1996).

In Lilenfeld and Kaye's (1996) summary of research on primarily women alcoholics, 15 to 32 percent had a history of an eating disorder at some point in their lives. Of those with current eating disorder diagnoses, 12 to 20 percent had bulimia nervosa or the bulimic subtype of anorexia, whereas only 2 to 10 percent of alcoholic women had the restricting-only subtype of anorexia nervosa. In the majority of comorbid cases, the eating disorder preceded the onset of the substance use disorder. Young women are likely to present to substance abuse treatment with a concurrent eating disorder, with rates ranging as high as 72 percent in a large sample of Japanese alcoholic women under the age of thirty (Higuchi et al., 1993).

Research in a twelve-step-based thirty-day for-profit residential addiction rehab center found that 14 percent of 100 adult females were diagnosed with bulimia with 50 percent of them being cocaine addicts and 36 percent alcoholics (Walfish et al., 1992). Gordon et al. (2001) found a 14.8 percent positive rate of screening for eating disorders using the Eating Attitudes Test (EAT-26) (Garner et al., 1982) on 115 adolescent and adult patients in both inpatient and outpatient settings at the Caron Foundation. The Walfish and Gordon studies produced screening prevalence rates consistent with the approximately 15 percent of adolescent and young adult women in the general population who score at or above the twenty point cut-off score on the EAT-26 determined by Garner and colleagues, which is used to indicate the need for diagnostic evaluation. Similar to the Walfish study, Gordon and colleagues found that primary cocaine patients had significantly higher rates of eating disorder symptoms than did alcohol, opiate, or marijuana patients.

Young women are socialized to control their weight and appetite through media images which portray the "heroin chic" look as the standard of beauty as well as through the continued objectification of women's bodies in advertising. Heroin use is on the rise in young females (Gordon, 2001). It has been considered a "masculine" drug and is often chosen by girls who are thrill seeking and rebellious, rejecting standards of feminine purity (Ettorre, 1992). Over the years, heroin has become more potent and dangerous and it can be inhaled and smoked as well as used intravenously. Heroin addicts who have an eating disorder may become conditioned to vomit spontaneously, mimicking the symptoms of heroin withdrawal and masking bulimic behavior.

Although anorexics typically do not abuse alcohol because it is high in calories, some restrictors do drink regularly before meals to disinhibit their control so that they can eat. Others may use alcohol to increase control through its effect on decreasing their appetite and food consumption. Use of a substance to decrease appetite or induce vomiting indicates the eating disorder is primary; the substance is being used in the service of the eating disorder. Heroin is an appetite suppressant and induces vomiting. Stimulants such as nicotine, amphetamines, and cocaine are known appetite suppressants and may be used to suppress binge behavior or to induce fasting after binge eating. When the eating disorder is secondary, the binge/purge cycles become a substitute way to numb or space out, similar to the experience of an alcohol binge. Often the substance disorder may be secondary to a trauma-related disorder and there is an obvious self-medication effect.

Relationship Between Sexual Abuse, Substance Dependence, and Eating Disorders

While a causal relationship between sexual abuse and eating disorders has not been empirically justified, research has demonstrated that rates of sexual abuse vary by subtype of eating disorder and whether or not there is comorbid substance abuse (Deep et al., 1999). The research of Deep and colleagues (1999) supported prior findings that bulimic women with a history of substance abuse, without a history of restricting, had the highest rates of sexual abuse (65 percent), with rape being the most common form of sexual abuse in this group (50 percent). In comparison, only 37 percent of non–substance-abusing bulimic women had a history of sexual abuse, which was most likely to be reported as incest (19 percent). Anorexics without any history of bulimic symptoms had a sexual abuse rate of 23 percent and were most likely to have experienced fondling by a nonfamily member (12 percent). This rate of sexual abuse in anorexics is comparable to the 10 to 30 percent rates of sexual abuse found in the general population of women (Connors and Morse, 1993, cited in Deep et al., 1999), though only 7 percent of the control group in the Deep study reported sexual abuse.

Deep and colleagues (1999) cited prior research that bulimic, substance dependent women had poor impulse control and affective liability, which seemed to be characterological in nature. They suspected that poor impulse control predated the onset of substance dependence and that drug and alcohol use, along with the failure to foresee the potential consequences of risky behavior, put this subgroup at an even higher risk for traumatic sexual experiences than the typical teenage girl who uses substances. This view was congruent with the hypothesis of Lacey and Evans (1986) that "multiple self-damaging behaviour reflects a general personality trait marked by loss of control" (Evans and Lacey, 1992, p. 643). Other behaviors thought to be related to this "multi-impulsive personality" were self-mutilation, suicide attempts through overdose, violence toward others, stealing, and promiscuity (Evans and Lacey, 1992), all of which resemble the key features of borderline personality disorder. Koepp et al. (1993) found that the significantly higher rate of alcohol abuse in patients with eating disorders, particularly bulimics, was accounted for by the subgroup of patients who also had borderline personality disorder. Because alcohol abuse correlated with borderline personality disorder rather than with eating disorders, this study supports the idea of a primary multi-impulsive personality that is similar conceptually to borderline personality disorder.

Deep and colleagues (1999) determined that substance dependence and sexual abuse typically occurred at age sixteen, one year prior to the onset of bulimia. This is useful data to support the need for comprehensive assessment and early intervention within substance abuse treatment settings to prevent the possible onset of bulimia in high-risk young women, especially those who demonstrate multi-impulsive behaviors. Evans and Lacey (1992) maintained that it is essential to uncover the full range of impulse control problem behaviors in order that they may be addressed comprehensively and simultaneously. While obtaining sobriety is the initial priority, it is recommended that "the treatment regime must address the general issues of impulse control and displacement of dysphoric affect" (p. 646) in order to prevent "revolving door" relapses that occur as a result of behavioral substitution. Lacey (1993) described an eclectic inpatient treatment program that was designed to treat multi-impulsive bulimic patients. This program was deemed effective in outcome studies and may be useful as a model to develop progamming to treat this problematic subgroup of dual diagnosis patients.

Similarities and Differences Between Substance Dependence and Eating Disorders

Many similarities exist between chemical addictions and binge/purge disorders. Both are chronic conditions with high rates of relapse. With each there are intense cravings to consume the food or substance, especially to regulate one's emotional state or relieve negative affect. There is a growing sense of loss of control over intake with repeated attempts to stop the behavior. Preoccupation with the behavior increases, along with attempts to hide it as feelings of shame predominate. The compulsive behavior continues despite adverse consequences such as physical deterioration, cognitive dysfunction, and social isolation. Denial and minimization are predominant defenses against seeking help to change (Jonas, 1992).

Although there are many similarities between binge-type eating disorders and chemical addiction, the use of the term "food addiction" is very controversial. Addiction specialists often use it in an effort to warn patients about the dangers of substituting compulsive behaviors for their drug of choice. This oversimplification ignores the research indicating that eating disorders are psychological conditions; they are dysfunctional behaviors related to irrational fears of weight gain and distorted body image (APA, 1994). Chemical addiction has been demonstrated to be a primary disease which results from the addictive properties of the substance while acknowledging that social learning processes contribute to the severity of physical dependence. It is most correct to refer to the similarities between these two disorders as addictive behaviors, though this subtle distinction is often lost in staff and patients who have the need to simplify their approach to recovery.

An addiction model of eating disorders typically fails to discriminate differences between types of eating disorders and obese binge eaters. It is often unfairly assumed that obese persons are addicted to food. In an addiction model, differences between persons involved in binge/purge behavior and restriction are ignored or minimized. Understanding differences in ego congruency are useful in articulating differences between addiction and eating disorders. This understanding has assessment and treatment implications. Susan Gordon, Director of Research and Training at the Caron Foundation, described chemical addiction as being mostly ego dystonic, with the person liking the initial feeling of the drug and perhaps the self-medication effects but not liking the stigma of being out of control as they increasingly use just to feel normal (personal communication, December 1999). Anorexics experience their behavior as ego syntonic. They like what they are doing and experience the ultimate sense of control. Bulimia is only partially ego syntonic in that bulimics typically do not like the physical consequences of the binge/purge cycle but like the weight loss and believe that this is the only way to achieve or maintain it. The emotional release, numbing, and feelings of mastery associated with purging, overexercise, or laxative abuse are reinforcing.

Another liability of the addiction model of eating disorders is that it assumes that the typical craving for a high carbohydrate diet in early recovery signals the vulnerability to developing an addiction to carbohydrates. For a discussion on dietary influences on alcohol intake and early recovery eating habits see Forsander (1998). No evidence supports the idea that the desire to binge eat is a direct biochemical result of consuming a toxic nutrient. There are not enough mood-altering qualities in any food to cause physical addiction to it. There is no evidence that an uncontrollable biochemical reaction from any food causes loss of control over consuming it. However, coming from an addiction model of eating disorders, total abstinence from psychoactive substances is frequently sought alongside abstinence from carbohydrates. Though not directly attributable to the foundational philosophy of Overeaters Anonymous (OA), the "no white flour or sugar" rule has become strongly associated with OA. Though carbohydrate restriction may work for some people with binge eating, this approach is totally contrary to the mainstream treatment of eating disorders, which focuses on the development of moderation in eating a wide variety of foods. Also, OA focuses on individuals' relationships to food while eating disorder treatment focuses on the emotions that eating disorder behaviors mask.

Course of Illness and Recovery

Herzog, Nussbaum, and Marmor (1996) summarized the research on the course of the illness and recovery of eating disorders. Recovery rates for anorexia nervosa are around 50 percent when measured by recovery of weight to above 85 percent of ideal, and resumption of eating behavior and regular menstrual cycles. Even when these criteria are achieved, the majority of anorexics remain impaired in physical, psychological, and social functioning. Anorexia is considered a chronic disorder, with a typical weight loss relapse rate of 41 percent in the first year after treatment. With a mortality rate of 6 to 7 percent, anorexia nervosa death rates are among the highest of all psychiatric disorders. Suicide accounts for 24 percent of deaths. Predictors of positive outcome are early age of onset, brief interval before hospitalization, and a low number of hospitalizations. Poor prognostic indicators include very low body weight, purging, and disturbed family relationships. The process of recovery has been described as coming to a turning point at which the individual becomes bored and tired of the disease and is ready to relinquish the symptoms. This process of change is similar to that described with substance abuse (Prochaska, DiClemente, and Norcross, 1992). Helpful factors include having meaningful relationships with a therapist, partner, or friend; positive job or school experiences; distance from family; and group therapy. Cognitive-behavioral strategies and sometimes the use of antipsychotic medication can assist anorexics to gain more flexibility and objectivity in their thinking regarding their weight and body image.

Bulimics tend to improve over time whether or not in treatment, with recovery rates ranging from 13 to 71 percent (Herzog, Nussbaum, and Marmor, 1996). The lowest recovery rate of 13 percent was noted in a sample of thirty bulimics who were considerably impaired (40 percent depression, 30 percent suicidal ideation, 37 percent drug abuse, 20 percent alcohol abuse, 33 percent shoplifting). One reason that the range of recovery rates is so variable is because the definitions of recovery have become less stringent due to growing recognition that the disorder is characterized by multiple episodes of relapse and remission. Rather than total abstinence, a more acceptable definition of recovery is a patient who binges and purges only once per month. Relapse definitions include return to bulimic symptoms weekly over a two-month period or eight times during a four-week period. Given these definitions, relapse rates range from 28 percent to 41 percent. Some evidence demonstrates a bimodal pattern of relapse, with periods of vulnerability at nine to eighteen weeks and thirty-six to forty-six weeks following intake. Herzog, Nussbaum, and Marmor (1996) suggest that a recurrence be considered a return to diagnostic criteria of binge/purge behavior of two times a week for three months.

Much is still to be learned about the recovery process of bulimia. "Hitting bottom" and fearing medical, social, and work-related consequences appear to be primary motivators for change. Those patients who hate the physical consequences of vomiting also fare better. Supportive relationships are critical. Poor prognostic indicators include frequency of vomiting at baseline, extreme weight fluctuations, comorbidity, impulsivity, low self-esteem, history of sexual abuse, and suicidal behavior.

Clinical experience indicates that actively anorexic and bulimic women with concurrent substance use disorders, including nicotine dependence, have a harder time maintaining abstinence from both behaviors due to concerns about gaining weight and vulnerability to using these methods to cope with the changes experienced during early recovery. Women with a history of restricting or purging before escalation of substance abuse are also vulnerable to renewing eating disorder behavior. Weight gain is common in chemical dependency recovery as people resume more normal and healthy eating patterns. In women who have body image concerns and fear of gaining weight, this normal weight gain can be a significant relapse trigger to renewed substance use. Restricting or bulimic behavior may escalate in response to perceived weight gain. A woman may attempt to avoid return to purging by restricting intake or through excessive exercise. Therefore, these women must receive nutritional guidance that addresses the normal weight gain in recovery from substances, and therapeutic coaching on how to learn to tolerate it for their greater good.

If women are prone to use substances to numb their feelings, they may begin to reengage in eating disorder behavior as a substitute way to escape. In the one- to four-month residential addiction treatment offered at the Caron Foundation, vulnerability to return to eating disorder behavior seems to occur around the third week of treatment, when weight gain is noticed and the patients are actively dealing with core issues. Transfer to less intensive levels of care is also a vulnerable time, perhaps due to disruption of therapeutic relationships and adjustment to a new recovering community. Bulimic patients are vulnerable to relapse during the extended care phase of residential treatment, which lasts from five to seventeen weeks. This is consistent with the vulnerability to relapse between nine and eighteen weeks discussed in Herzog, Nussbaum, and Marmor (1996). Women seem to be particularly vulnerable to eating disorder relapse when they are actively working in therapy on issues of trauma, grief and loss, or dysfunctional relationships. Therefore, the timing of undertaking the more intensive work of remembering and mourning is very critical. As described previously, early treatment should focus on the development of safety and coping skills for women. With this foundation, women are less likely to resort to eating disorder behavior in order to cope with the increase and lability of feelings and realizations that typically occur in the first six months of abstinence from chemicals.

Monitoring and Relapse Prevention

In a substance abuse treatment setting, it is important to regularly monitor for recurrence or increase in eating disorder behavior, especially during the vulnerable times mentioned previously. In eating disorder treatment settings, it is important to regularly assess the level of craving for substances and their use as well as substituting one method of coping for another. Whichever treatment setting patients with these two disorders are involved, it is important to regularly ask them about their vulnerability. It may be helpful to ask them to rate on a scale of 1 to 10 how difficult it is for them to resist the behavior. That way, they will develop a language with which to communicate their level of distress and know when to try certain coping strategies or to ask for help. This type of monitoring is particularly useful with multi-impulsive patients who have self-destructive impulses.

Traditional relapse prevention strategies that focus on greater awareness of how thoughts, feelings, and behavior can trigger a process of relapse to substances are very useful when they are applied concurrently with relapse to eating disorder behavior. Specific relapse signs to look for are loss of weight, preoccupation with weight gain, increased focus on food (especially on resuming a strict vegetarian diet), excessive exercise, and missing therapy sessions. Reports of restricting or purge behavior often come through secondary sources, though openness can be encouraged early in the therapeutic relationship by honestly discussing risks to relapse to eating disorder behavior and conveying an attitude of acceptance and hope.

The patients must understand the "abstinence violation effect," in which the person has a slip back into substance use and becomes so guilt ridden and hopeless over loss of control that he or she gives up trying to prevent the relapse from progressing (Marlatt and Gordon, 1985). A colloquial way of describing this is, "The hell with it. I blew it. I might as well keep going." With comorbid eating disorders and substance abuse, this effect is generalizable to both, in that relapse to eating disorder behavior could be used to justify relapse to substance abuse or vice versa. Given the refractory nature of purge behavior, it is best to coach patients not to "throw in the towel" should this happen. In this case, it may be beneficial to make abstinence from substance use a primary goal as the patients do not want to restart the physical addictive process to the substance. It is important to convey the belief that even though they vomited again, they can learn to stop and to focus on the development of alternative coping skills.

It is often much more difficult to recognize a return to eating disorder behavior than it is to recognize a return to substance use. Eating disorder patients may have what appear to be legitimate excuses: "I have a cold and I'm not hungry. My cramps are worse now that I'm sober, and I have no appetite. I'm still throwing up from heroin withdrawal. Exercise helps me cope with my craving." Eating disorder patients are prone to convey the message that "My body did it to me" rather than believe that they have some responsibility and ability to intervene in the relapse process.

It is typically unrealistic to expect that a patient can achieve total abstinence from substance use and purging behavior at the same time, especially in a substance abuse treatment center that is not set up for tight monitoring of eating disorder behavior. Therefore, patients need reality-based counseling in which warning signs are openly and regularly discussed with acknowledgment of the chronicity of their comorbid conditions and with an eye to how relapse is most likely to occur.

If eating disorder behavior reemerges, it must be treated seriously and proactively to prevent progression without a response of panic or catastrophizing, which can induce further shame and compulsion. Addiction treatment centers need to acknowledge that although eating disorder behavior is a relapse trigger to substance use, patients have not failed in their addiction recovery if they relapse to eating disorder behaviors. An attitude of guarded tolerance is most helpful to encourage patients' continued honesty and motivation to change. Ultimatums about abstinence from purging behavior typically serve only to increase secretiveness and progression. Behavioral contracts may be appropriate to modify restricting behavior, especially if there is medical risk, but are best applied within a multidisciplinary approach to care.

Treatment Options

Few dual disorder units specialize in substance dependence and eating disorder treatment. Eating disorder treatment settings typically assess for substance abuse but do not typically provide much assistance with medical detoxification. Some may have a substance abuse track, but due to the various differences in treatment philosophy, many eating disorder treatment centers still do not provide or encourage twelve-step meetings for addiction or offer specialized groups for substance abusers. The typical course of treatment is for patients first to be sent to a substance abuse residential treatment center to withdraw from their substance use and obtain a foundation of sobriety, and then be transferred to eating disorder treatment. This transition may not occur if the patient's eating disorder is not acknowledged and managed appropriately in the substance abuse treatment setting. Addiction treatment centers without protocols for dealing with eating disorders are likely to be overwhelmed with the management of eating disorder behavior and may discharge these patients prematurely due to noncompliance. Active eating disorder behavior interferes with patient progress and the stability of the therapeutic community. "Copycat" behavior occurs in substance abuse treatment settings, where dominant females in the patient community affect the eating habits and purge behavior of other residents. If this dominant patient is a restrictor, the facilities' food bills could drastically reduce (Sharon O'Boyle, Caron Foundation dietitian, personal communication, 1999).

Krahn (1991) asserts that the question of which type of treatment should come first "is based less on what is appropriate for the patient and more on what care providers feel comfortable treating" (p. 249). Much misunderstanding still exists about treatment philosophies between these two specialties, which fosters beliefs of incompetence or unwillingness to treat the "other" disorder. Even though addiction and eating disorder treatment centers typically have defined admission criteria for these comorbidities, the final decision often appears to be made based on speculation about how difficult the patient will be to treat. Patients with more severe personality disorders or multi-impulsive traits are less likely to be accepted even if they meet criteria for stabilization of either behavior. This differential treatment probably reflects the fear of not being able to successfully treat very complicated patients who have problems with compliance and forming therapeutic attachments. It would be helpful for all of those involved in admission and intake processes if these issues were addressed more directly, rather than referring to more arbitrary exclusion criteria such as length of sobriety or frequency of purging.

Multidisciplinary Assessment and Management

For licensing and legal reasons, as well as philosophical misunderstanding, most addiction or eating disorder treatment centers will not say that they "treat" the other disorder. This means that unless the facility has a "dual disorder" license, treatment centers need to focus on developing management strategies. With growing numbers of young females presenting to addiction treatment with active eating disorders, a standardized identification and management approach is essential.

Assessment should include specific questions targeted to cardinal symptoms of each disorder during the initial medical and biopsychosocial intake evaluations. History as well as current symptoms need to be assessed due to relapse vulnerabilities mentioned previously. To accurately assess for bulimia, it is important to ask about use and severity of dependence on diuretics, emetics (agents that induce vomiting), laxatives, and phenylpropanolamine (diet pills). For a thorough discussion of the effects, toxicity, detection, tolerance, and withdrawal characteristics of many over-the-counter preparations that are associated with weight control in eating disorders, see Bulik (1992). Even in substance abuse treatment settings where detailed histories of substances are the norm, the breadth of over-the-counter medications used for weight control are often overlooked. Synthroid, a thyroid medication, can also be abused if individuals take more than prescribed in an attempt to lose weight. If patients are found to be dependent on any of these substances, expect this to affect the withdrawal process from their primary substance of dependence, as well as add to the discomfort of their detoxification experience.

Patients need help especially dealing with water weight gain, physical discomfort, and emotional responses regarding body image. Helping patients deal with craving and reactivity to environmental triggers is a compatible treatment approach. Bulik maintains that abuse of these substances needs to be treated with supervised discontinuation, electrolyte replacement, if necessary, and psychoeducation regarding the medical risks and how return to use of these substances can trigger eating disorder or chemical dependency relapse. Differing viewpoints exist on how to handle medical supervision of cessation of laxative dependence. At the Caron Foundation, patients dependent on laxatives do not abruptly discontinue their use, as the distress could significantly affect the patients' connection to treatment. Instead, they are typically tapered with less harsh substitutes, such as prune juice.

Eating disorder symptoms checklists such as the EAT-26 (Garner et al., 1982) may provide a useful screening tool for restricting and purging behavior for females but should not be thought of as a substitute for a thorough diagnostic evaluation by a trained professional. As part of the Caron Foundation eating disorder assessment and management protocol, it is recommended that all adolescent and adult females be routinely screened using the EAT-26 during their first three days of treatment. Other points of assessment intervention include medical assessments (nursing and physician assistant physical) and the biopsychosocial intake evaluation done by a therapist. Some patients may deny eating disorder behavior initially but then admit to staff that they are bingeing, purging, or restricting, or this behavior comes to the attention of the staff or patient community. The primary therapist who coordinates the care of the patient compiles this information and includes it in the seventy-two-hour evaluation that is presented to the treatment team.

The primary therapist makes referrals for assessment by the dietitian and psychologist during this first seventy-two hours. The dietitian sees the patient within the next seventy-two hours and conducts a nutritional and eating disorder symptom assessment and provides psychoeducation and basics of management. The dietitian contacts the therapist, psychologist, and/or medical director with relevant information and confers with them after their evaluations, if necessary. The dietitian confers with medical staff about physical consequences and may activate a medical protocol to include an eating contract if the person is under 85 percent of ideal body weight or shows signs of significant malnutrition.

The psychologist sees the patient within one week of referral unless there are possible medical consequences that necessitate more immediate attention. The psychologist provides diagnostic clarification and evaluates for medication appropriateness, which would then necessitate referral to the medical director or psychiatrist. The psychologist also assesses the presence of cognitive impairment and depression related to metabolic consequences. This is likely to occur if the person is below 85 percent body weight or has an electrolyte imbalance. The psychologist also obtains information that may be useful in medical contracting. This information is routinely conveyed back to the primary therapist, and findings that warrant immediate intervention are verbally reported to the medical director.

Given a positive eating disorder diagnosis or history of such, which would indicate vulnerability to relapse in sobriety, the primary therapist continues with the eating disorder management protocol. This involves gathering the details from the dietitian, psychologist, psychiatrist, and medical team to clarify the nature of the patient's eating disorder and develop a treatment plan that addresses management of the eating disorder and related relapse prevention issues. The therapist initiates recheck of the patient with the relevant initial evaluators at fourteen and twenty-one days from admission due to the possibility of reemergence or intensification of symptoms. The therapist also requests a specialized continuing care plan and ensures that the eating disorder is mentioned in the discharge summary.

Implementation of this protocol occurs after all levels of clinical staff receive training in the identification and management of eating disorders. This management philosophy includes individualized assessment and intervention to reduce the shaming and "copycat" behavior that can occur when behavior is confronted in a group or community setting. Conversely, in settings that treat eating disorders, confrontation of behaviors occurs almost exclusively in the group or community setting. Decreasing bulimic symptoms should be addressed as a goal in the treatment plan, but behavioral contracting is not used unless the purge behavior is excessive (greater than three times a day). Contrary to many eating disorder treatment centers, use of the "buddy system" is not recommended to decrease purging or restricting behavior due to potential problems with manipulative or colluding behaviors. Instead, it is recommended that purging patients be asked to remain with the community and not go to the bathroom for one hour after meals, and that bathroom breaks be monitored with staff standing outside while the patient talks or sings (to show that the voice is being used and therefore no vomiting is taking place).

The dietitian conducts regular psychoeducation sessions with patients that address how to prevent or manage treatment weight gain. Discussion also includes how to manage thinking and feeling states that produce poor body image and could lead to relapse. The impact of societal standards on producing unrealistic body image expectations is also discussed.

Increased physical activity supervised by trained recreation counselors is important to lessen excessive treatment weight gain, especially with adolescents. Recreation counselors are trained to recognize exercise compulsion and to report this behavior to the primary therapist who will confer with the multidisciplinary team about exercise restrictions.

NEED FOR SPECIALIZED WOMEN'S TREATMENT

The traditional view is that chemically dependent persons are more similar than different, that an addict is an addict. However, research over the past twenty years summarized previously suggests that gender differences are physiological, psychological, social, and familial. In addition to specialized approaches to treat dual diagnoses, certain aspects of women's roles should be addressed in the content and context of treatment in order to attain the best outcomes. Lemay (1980) contended that women's roles in their families and society play a critical part in the development and maintenance of alcoholism, especially the psychological aspects. According to feedback given during Lemay's interviews with addiction counselors, it is important for a woman to grow to understand her conflicts with her own gender role and to learn to take responsibility to define her own role. It is also important for a woman to ascertain if she has sexuality conflicts and to determine what she wants from sexual relationships. The belief that a woman needs a perfect relationship to be happy should be examined as well as her need for approval from others to validate her self-concept. Becoming aware of her basic personal rights and transcending feelings of overall powerlessness can be aided by learning how to express anger and appropriate assertiveness. Developing the life skills to live effectively should be considered an integral part of treatment. Counselor identified that their own prejudices against women can interfere with their ability to assist women to broaden their choices as well as scapegoat women for behavior (i.e., flirtatiousness) that would be more tolerated in men. Counselors' own biases regarding sexuality also impact their effectiveness. Ignorance of women's health issues and the differences in addiction between men and women were seen as significant impediments to effective treatment.

The Lemay article was published over twenty years ago, so why is it that so few programs provide specialized services for women and why is it that so few women have access to treatment? This is partly due to philosophical issues, barriers to care, complexity of women's issues, and program design.

One of the critical influences on effectiveness is that males dominate most treatment programs in terms of number of patients and program leadership, and the treatment delivery system is also male based (Weisner and Schmidt, 1992). Best estimates based on the National Drug and Alcohol Treatment Unit Survey (NDATUS) and National Prevalence Data (cited in Engs, 1990) indicate that one out of three alcohol-abusing persons in the United States is a woman, and that only one out of twenty of these women is in treatment in a given year. Of the other drug users, two of five are women, but only one of fifty of these women is in treatment in a given year. In spite of the consistent call for specialized treatment programs for women, only 27 percent of treatment units offer such specialized programs, and the proportion of treatment units with specialized women's programs is not increasing (Engs, 1990).

A study conducted by Wallen (1992) to examine male and female treatment needs in an inpatient drug and alcohol setting with 75 percent men confirmed that women were more likely to report symptoms of emotional distress and a willingness to seek help for emotional problems. Also, Wallen (1992) suggested that women would benefit from specialized treatment that addresses childhood trauma, particularly childhood physical abuse and feelings related to anger and victimization. Wallen (1992) also reported that women were significantly less employed than men but less likely to be arrested. Women were found to enter treatment later in the course of their chemical dependency than men and were more likely to seek treatment in mental health settings as opposed to alcohol-specific treatment (Weisner and Schmidt, 1992).

Barriers to Treatment Entry

Copeland (1997) suggests that the barriers women experience are social stigma, labeling, lack of awareness of treatment options, concerns about child care, and confrontation models of treatment. What is working for women? Bushway and Heilman (1995), in their literature review up to and through 1985, profiled women in treatment and treatment implications. They described patterns of drug and alcohol abuse, physical health needs and education, mental health issues coexisting with their dependence, decrease in self-esteem as addictive behaviors increase, significant drug and alcohol use of family members compared to nonaddicted women, poor impulse control, genetic vulnerability, and racial differences. The implications for comprehensive and specialized treatment may seem overwhelming and cost prohibitive for treatment providers. However, one program cannot be all things to all clients. Therefore, Bushway and Heilman (1995) identified the variables that impact outcome and their implications for treatment in their review of the literature. The variables identified as improving outcomes are gender-specific programs, higher levels of education or job security, and the ability to connect and trust other women. To improve quality and effectiveness, they recommended provision of gender-separate services along with a gender-specific approach.

Program Components/Service Delivery

The comprehensive program that Bushway and Heilman (1995) recommended included the following: the provision of health care, including physicals; sexuality education and advocacy on the part of the providers to help women access health care services; utilization of psychological services including diagnostic evaluations and medication; relapse prevention focused on coping skills to handle stressors; education regarding self-esteem issues addressing self-perception; and healthy female behavior and interactions modeled in order to encourage a sense of value and hope. Women were encouraged to identify their family of origin issues, including their own definition of family since family issues and stressors tend to trigger relapse. Child care needs must be actively addressed and provisions made since this is a significant stressor in retaining women in treatment. Environmental factors must also be addressed as this relates to appropriate female role models, support groups, and identification of life stressors that could lead to relapse. Sensitivity to and understanding of racial issues and the diversity that exists within the cultures that present themselves in treatment is also an important contextual ingredient.

Very little data are available to compare female-only versus coed treatment. However, there are many theoretical rationales for treating women within a women-centered model versus the traditional coed model that dominates the treatment field. The outcomes of treatment of chemically dependent women are sparse, but despite what is known about the documented differences in the female addictive population, many treatment programs remain relatively disinterested in the need for specialized services. The findings from a study conducted by Nelson-Zlupko et al. (1996) identified the following significant conclusions: female clients reported experiencing negative stereotyping and sexual harassment in mixed-gender treatment. Women requested greater respect from their individual counselors regardless of setting. Women viewed themselves as having a unique set of needs pertaining to parenting, child care, and sexuality that largely went unmet. Furthermore, coed groups did not provide opportunity to discuss issues such as child rearing, sexuality, and relationships. Last, treatment programs that attempted to implement women services over a traditional male-oriented philosophy were not sufficiently responsive to the needs of the female.

Philosophy of Care

Given the review of needs and barriers that women are experiencing, the existing model of addiction treatment certainly has its shortcomings. The implications of the disease model and the concept of powerlessness given these gender issues is also problematic. The framework and ideology of alcoholism as a disease is quite valuable. However, the significance of the factors that influence women's use of mood-altering chemicals is lacking. Therefore, with the focus on illness, the disease model is incomplete for women. Psychosocial, environmental, and medical issues are overlooked and minimized (Burman, 1994). The treatment field is inadvertently promoting weakened self-concept and overlooking conscious efforts to establish personal empowerment and to take responsibility. Treatment recommendations based on literature and needs of women suggest that recognition must occur in viewing the ideological factors in recovery needs for women, which are significantly different from those of men. Second, treatment must be consistent with its philosophical view of chemical dependency. Third, given the analysis of traditional drug and alcohol services and the needs of women, gender-specific and gender-separate programs are clearly recommended. Fourth, the services should be matched to the needs of women. At a minimum services should include the following: nicotine cessation, victimization issues, health education, education on how to access health care, sexuality issues relating to roles, identity and dysfunction, and parenting skills. Fifth, investment in staff training should ensure competency in assessing and treating the needs of women. Sixth, a high degree of emphasis should be placed upon empowerment in the philosophical design of services.

Kirkpatrick (cited in Kaskutas, 1994) strongly urges the development of programs and self-help groups separately designed for women. Her rationale is that females need more than AA because the chemically dependent woman has an inner sense of failure as a wife, mother, daughter, and woman. The research conducted by Brown, Melchior, and Huba (1999) encourages a comprehensive treatment model that engages women with dual disorders early in the treatment process. Second, their emphasis is on treatment preparedness and longer length of treatment to help women learn how to connect and participate in treatment. The prognosis for addicted women can be positive if engaged in a comprehensive, well-structured program.

Level of Burden and Treatment Retention Outcomes

Brown, Huba, and Melchior (1995, p. 339) expanded on the observation of Lidz and Platt (1995) that "multiply diagnosed individuals may not be able to withstand the burden of integrating the different clinical approaches utilized to treat their substance abuse and psychiatric conditions." Brown, Huba, and Melchior (1995) defined level of burden as the cumulative number and severity of psychological, cognitive, health, and social problems thought to affect treatment outcome that could be experienced by substance-using women and the program staff that treat them. Five hundred seventy-seven women who participated in a comprehensive and specialized long-term residential treatment program for addicted women and their children were assessed to determine their level of burden, which was correlated with treatment retention and exit interview data (Brown, Melchior, and Huba, 1999). This was an expansion of data from an earlier study (Brown, Huba, and Melchior, 1995) which found that highly burdened women, those with multiple co-occurring disorders, were most likely to drop out early in the course of addiction treatment. It was "hypothesized that these women may be more easily overwhelmed by the transition required in entering a structured therapeutic community" (Brown, Melchior, and Huba, 1999, p. 38). In Brown and colleagues' 1999 study, they reported that only women with the most severe mental illness, such as schizophrenia and bipolar disorders, were likely to drop out earlier than other women in the program. In contrast, this study did not replicate previous research that showed high early dropout rates for women with borderline personality disorder or PTSD (Root, 1989).

Brown, Melchior, and Huba (1999) suggested that women with borderline personality disorder or PTSD stayed longer and did better in their program because it was designed to be very women sensitive. It had highly trained, multicultural female staff who emphasized the maintenance of a safe and nonthreatening environment that accommodated women with children. The therapeutic philosophy emphasized "safety first" for women who suffered from trauma and addiction. This research also suggested that dropout rates for all women declined when women were prepared for the initial transition, to decrease feeling overwhelmed when participating in a treatment community and complying with rules. Brown, Melchior, and Huba (1999) recommended that potential residents visit the program facility prior to intake to speak with other residents and program personnel, and that preadmission and intake appointments be accompanied by outreach workers or treatment advocates. Other connection-enhancing strategies included treatment readiness groups and stabilization on medications prior to admission.

It has been well documented that longer retention in addiction treatment is associated with positive outcomes. In the Brown, Melchior, and Huba (1999) study, women who stayed in treatment over 180 days were perceived by staff as doing better and were almost six times more likely to be clean and sober and five times more likely to have plans to get a job or go to school. Women with severe mental illness who did not stay for 180 days were perceived to have disorganized thoughts and no specific plans to manage their lives after they left the program. However, women with severe mental illness who stayed in treatment had outcomes similar to other addicted women. Treatment outcomes of employment, sobriety, and housing were similar to women who had less severe disorders. This research supports the view that women with severe disorders can be engaged in treatment and that they can learn how to participate in specialized programs if their individual needs are met in the context of a women-sensitive therapeutic community that bolsters their typically impoverished social support systems.

SUMMARY OF IMPLICATIONS FOR SPECIALIZED TREATMENT APPROACHES

In order for the effective implementation of services to meet the specific needs of dually diagnosed women, treatment programs must be designed around the needs of these women. This includes a commitment and a vision by the leadership of treatment organizations, their decision to allocate the necessary resources to meet the needs of this population, and their commitment to apply research to practice. The philosophy of care, treatment components, and service delivery should be based on addressing the differences in recovery needs for dually diagnosed women and men, which are fully supported by research findings. At a minimum, gender-specific and preferably gender-separate programs are recommended. Treatment services can be most effective and attract more women to treatment if specially designed services are matched to the needs of women. To accomplish this, a shift is needed to a paradigm that provides for a comprehensive and holistic view of women's needs. This view, based on the relational model of development, provides a mechanism for understanding the dynamics of dual disorders, as well as developing assessment techniques, treatment strategies, and program designs that adequately address gender differences of addiction and mental illness.

This chapter provides strong evidence to support the allocation of greater resources and leadership commitment to enhance treatment systems for dually diagnosed females through the provision of individualized treatment within a philosophical and program context that validates women's unique needs in recovery and relational focus. This is in contrast to a traditional chemical dependency treatment field clinical focus on commonality between the genders regarding addiction and recovery issues as well as a minimization of the importance of concurrently dealing with mental health concerns. Based on research, there are strong indications that enhancement of services will increase access to treatment as well as improve retention and outcomes. Although it may be overwhelming for programs to determine how to address all of the issues identified, failure to recognize these differences through the development of specific strategies to reach out to this population only perpetuates the barriers to successful outcomes that dually diagnosed women have been experiencing. This, in effect, would be continuing to blame the victim of addiction or mental health treatment systems that are often more interested in maintaining their philosophical territory than developing treatments that are most effective.

REFERENCES

Alarcon, R.D. (1990). Pseudomultiplicity: A clinical manifestation of rapid cycling affective disorder in borderline personality? *Annals of Clinical Psychiatry, 2*(2), 127-133.

American Psychiatric Association (APA) (1994). *Diagnostic and statistical manual of mental disorders* (DSM-IV) (Fourth edition). Washington, DC: Author.

Barry, P.P. (1986). Gender as a factor in treating the elderly. *NIDA Research Monograph, 65:* 65-69.

Beckman, L. and Amaro, H. (1986). Personal and social difficulties faced by women and men entering alcoholism treatment. *Journal of Studies on Alcohol, 47*(2): 135-145.

Bernstein, E.M. and Putnam, F.W. (1986). Development, reliability, and validity of a dissociation scale. *Journal of Nervous and Mental Disease, 174*(12): 727-735.

Blume, S.B. (1997). Women: Clinical aspects. In J.H. Lowinson, P. Ruiz, R.B. Millman, and J.G. Langrod (Eds.), *Substance abuse: A comprehensive textbook,* Third edition, (pp. 645-654). Baltimore: Williams & Wilkins.

Brady, K.T., Grice, D.E., Dustan, L., and Randall, C. (1993). Gender differences in substance use disorders. *American Journal of Psychiatry, 150*(11): 1707-1711.

Broverman, I.K., Broverman, D.M., Clarkson, F.E., Rosenkrantz, P.S., and Vogel, S.R. (1970). Sex-role stereotypes and clinical judgments of mental health. *Journal of Consulting and Clinical Psychology, 34*(1): 1-7.

Brown, V.B., Huba, G.J., and Melchior, L.A. (1995). Level of burden: Women with more than one co-occurring disorder. *Journal of Psychoactive Drugs, 27*(4): 339-346.

Brown, V.B., Melchior, L.A., and Huba, G.J. (1999). Level of burden among women diagnosed with severe mental illness and substance abuse. *Journal of Psychoactive Drugs, 31*(1): 31-40.

Bulik, C. (1992). Abuse of drugs associated with eating disorders. *Journal of Substance Abuse, 4*(1), 69-90.

Burman, S. (1994). The disease concept of alcoholism: Its impact on women's treatment. *Journal of Substance Abuse Treatment, 11*(2), 121-126.

Bushway, D. and Heilman, L. (1995). Women in treatment for addiction: What's new in the literature? *Alcoholism Treatment Quarterly, 13*(4), 83-96.

Collins, B. (1993). Reconstruing codependency using self-in-relation theory: A feminist perspective. *Social Work, 38*(3): 470-476.

Comtois, K.A. and Ries, R.K. (1995). Sex differences in dually diagnosed severely mentally ill clients in dual-diagnosis outpatient treatment. *American Journal on Addictions, 4*(3): 245-253.

Connors, M.E. and Morse, W. (1993). Sexual abuse and the eating disorders: A review. *International Journal of Eating Disorders, 13*(1): 1-11.

Copeland, J. (1997). A qualitative study of barriers to formal treatment among women who self-managed change in addictive behaviors. *Journal of Substance Abuse Treatment, 14*(2): 183-190.

Cornelius, J.R., Jarrett, P.J., Fabrega, H., Haas, G.L., Jones-Barlock, A., Mezzich, J.E., and Ulrich, R.F. (1995). Gender effects on the clinical presentation of alcoholics at a psychiatric hospital. *Comprehensive Psychiatry, 36*(6): 435-440.

Corrigan, E.M. (1980). *Alcoholic women in treatment.* New York: Oxford University Press.

Covington, S. (1999). *Helping women recover: A program for treating addiction.* New York: Guilford Press.

Davis, D.R. and DiNitto, D.M. (1996). Gender differences in social and psychological problems of substance abusers: A comparison to nonsubstance abusers. *Journal of Psychoactive Drugs, 28*(2): 135-145.

Deep, A.L., Lilenfeld, L.R., Plotnicov, K.H., Pollice, C., and Kaye, W. (1999). Sexual abuse in eating disorder subtypes and control women: The role of comorbid substance dependence in bulimia nervosa. *International Journal of Eating Disorders, 25*(1): 1-10.

Dunn, G.E., Ryan, J.J., and Paolo, A.M. (1994). The need to screen for dissociative symptoms and disorders in patients being treated for substance abuse. *Psychotherapy in Private Practice, 13*(1): 55-67.

Ellason, J. and Ross, C. (1997). Positive and negative symptoms in dissociative identity disorder and schizophrenia: A comparative analysis. *Journal of Nervous and Mental Disease, 183*(4): 236-241.

Ellason, J.W., Ross, C.A., Sainton, K., and Mayran, L.W. (1996). Axis I and II comorbidity and childhood trauma history in chemical dependency. *Bulletin on the Menninger Clinic, 60*(1): 39-51.

Engs, R.C. (Ed.). (1990). *Women: Alcohol and other drugs.* Debeque, IA: Kendell/ Hunt Publishing.

Ettorre, E. (1992). *Women and substance abuse.* New Brunswick, NJ: Rutgers University Press.

Evans, C. and Lacey, J. (1992). Multiple self-damaging behavior among alcoholic women: A prevalence study. *British Journal of Psychiatry, 161*(Nov): 643-647.

Favorini, A. (1995). Concept of codependency: Blaming the victim or pathway to recovery? *Social Work, 40*(6): 827-830.

Forsander, O.A. (1998). Dietary influences on alcohol intake: A review. *Journal of Studies on Alcohol, 59:* 26-31.

Frezza, M., DiPadova, C., Pozzato, G., Terpin, M., Baroona, E., and Lieber, C.S. (1990). High blood alcohol levels in women: The role of decreased gastric alcohol dehydrogenase activity and first-pass metabolism. *New England Journal of Medicine, 322*(January 11): 95-99.

Garner, D.M., Olmsted, M.P., Bohr, Y., and Garfinkel, P.E. (1982). The Eating Attitudes Test: Psychometric features and clinical correlates. *Psychological Medicine, 12*(4): 871-878.

Gavaler, J.S. (1982). Sex-related differences in ethanol-induced liver disease: Artificial or real? *Alcoholism Clinical and Experimental Research:* 182-196.

Gilligan, C. (1982). *In a different voice: Psychological theory and women's development.* Cambridge, MA: Harvard University Press.

Gil-Rivas, V., Fiorentine, R., Anglin, D., and Taylor, E. (1997). Sexual and physical abuse: Do they compromise drug treatment outcomes? *Journal of Substance Abuse Treatment, 14*(4): 351-358.

Glenn, S. and Parson, O. (1989). Alcohol abuse and familial alcoholism: Psychosocial correlates in men and women. *Journal of Studies on Alcohol, 50*(2): 116-127.

Goldman, D. and Bander, K. (1990). Six-month course in depression in female alcoholics. *Journal of Substance Abuse, 2*(3): 375-380.

Gordon, S. (2001). *Heroin: Challenge for the 21st Century.* Wernersville, PA: The Caron Foundation.

Gordon, S., Hagan, T., Beyer, E., and Snyderman, R. (2001). Eating disorders prevalence for female chemical dependence patients. *Journal of Addictions Nursing, 13*(3/4): 211-216.

Griffin, M.L., Weiss, R.I., Mirin, S.M., and Lang, U. (1989). A comparison of male and female cocaine abusers. *Archives of General Psychiatry, 46*(2): 122-126.

Grilo, C.M., Martino, S., Walker, M.L., Becker, D.F., Edell, W.S., and McGlashan, T.H. (1997). Psychiatric comorbidity differences in male and female adult psychiatric inpatients with substance use disorders. *Comprehensive Psychiatry, 38*(3): 155-159.

Heim, C. and Nemeroff, C.B. (2001). The role of childhood trauma in the neurobiology of mood and anxiety disorders: Preclinical and clinical studies. *Biological Psychiatry, 49*(12): 1023-1039.

Herman, J. (1992). *Trauma and recovery.* New York: Basic Books.

Herzog, D.B., Nussbaum, K.M., and Marmor, A.K. (1996). Comorbidity and outcome in eating disorders. *Psychiatric Clinics of North America, 19*(4): 843-858.

Higuchi, S., Suzuki, K., Yamada, K., Parrish, K., and Kono, H. (1993). Alcoholics with eating disorders: Prevalence and clinical course—A study from Japan. *British Journal of Psychiatry, 162*(March): 403-406.

Holderness, C.C., Brooks-Gunn, J., and Warren, M.P. (1994). Co-morbidity of eating disorders and substance abuse: Review of the literature. *International Journal of Eating Disorders, 16*(1): 1-34.

Hser, Y., Anglin, M., and McGlothlin, W. (1987). Sex differences in addict careers: I. Initiation of use. *American Journal of Drug Abuse, 13*(1-2): 33-57.

Institute of Medicine (1995). *Fetal alcohol syndrome: Research base for diagnostic criteria, epidemiology, prevention, and treatment.* Washington, DC: National Academy Press.

Jacob, T. and Brenner, D.A. (1986). Assortive mating among men and women alcoholics. *Journal of Studies on Alcohol, 47*(3): 219-222.

Johnson, M. and Auerbach, A.H. (1984). Women and psychotherapy research. In L.E. Walker (Ed.), *Women and Mental Health Policy* (pp. 59-78). Beverly Hills, CA: Sage Publications.

Jonas, J. (1992). An examination of eating disorders and addictions: Is there an association? *Newsletter of the American Anorexia-Bulimia Association Inc.,* September 1, 3-4.

Jones, B.M. and Jones, M.K. (1976). Women and alcohol: Intoxification, metabolism, and the menstrual cycle. In M. Greenblatt and M.A. Schuckit (Eds.), *Alcohol problems in women and children* (pp. 103-136). New York: Grune & Statton.

Kaskutas, A.L. (1994). What do women get out of self-help? Their reasons for attending Women for Sobriety and Alcoholics Anonymous. *Journal of Substance Abuse Treatment, 11*(3): 185-194.

Kessler, R.C., Crum, R.M., Warner, L.A., Nelson, C.B., Schulberg, J., and Anthony, J.C. (1997). Lifetime co-occurance of DSM-III-R alcohol abuse and dependence with other psychiatric disorders in the National Comorbidity Survey. *Archives of General Psychiatry, 54*(4): 313-321.

Kessler, R.C., McGonagle, K.A., Zhao, S., Nelson, C.B., Hughes, M., Eshleman, S., Wittchen, H.U., and Kendler, K.S. (1994). Lifetime and 12-month prevalence of DSM-III-R psychiatric disorders in the United States. Results of the National Comorbidity Study. *Archives of General Psychiatry, 51*(1): 8-19.

Khantzian, E.J. (1985). The self-medication hypothesis of addictive disorders: Focus on heroin and cocaine dependence. *American Journal of Psychiatry,* *142*(11): 1259-1264.

Khantzian, E.J. (1997). The self-medication hypothesis of substance use disorders: A reconsideration and recent applications. *Harvard Review of Psychiatry, 4*(5): 231-244.

Koepp, W., Schildbach, S., Schmager, C., and Rohner, R. (1993). Borderline diagnosis and substance abuse in female patients with eating disorders. *International Journal of Eating Disorders, 14*(1): 107-110.

Kolander, G. and Frances, R.J. (1993). Recognizing dissociative disorders in patients with chemical dependency. *Hospital and Community Psychiatry, 44*(11): 1041-1043.

Krahn, D.D. (1991). The relationship of eating disorders and substance abuse. *Journal of Substance Abuse, 3*(2): 239-253.

Lacey, J.H. (1993). Multi impulsive bulimia: Description of an inpatient eclectic treatment programme and a pilot follow-up study of its efficacy. *European Eating Disorders Review, 1*(1): 22-31.

Lacey, J.H. and Evans, C.D. (1986). The impulsivist: A multi-impulsive personality disorder. *British Journal of Addiction, 81*(5): 641-649.

Lemay, D. (1980). The need for an awareness of specialized issues in counseling alcoholic women. *Personnel and Guidance Journal, 59*(2): 103-115.

Lewis, C.E., Bucholz, K.K., Spitznagel, E., and Shayka, J.J. (1996). Effects of gender and comorbidity on problem drinking in a community sample. *Alcoholism: Clinical and Experimental Research, 20*(3): 466-476.

Lilenfeld, L.R. and Kaye, W.H. (1996). The link between alcoholism and eating disorders. *Alcohol Health & Research World, 20*(March 1): 94-100.

Lynn, G.T. (2000). *Survival strategies for parenting children with bipolar disorders.* Philadelphia: Jessica Kingsley Publishers.

Magura, S., Kang, S.-Y., Rosenblum, A., Handelsman, L., and Foote, J. (1998). Gender differences in psychiatric comorbidity among cocaine-using opiate addicts. *Journal of Addictive Diseases, 17*(3): 49-61.

Malatesta, V.J., Pollack, R.H., Crotty, T.D., and Peacock, L.J. (1982). Acute alcohol intoxication and female orgasmic response. *Journal of Sex Research, 18*(1): 1-16.

Marlatt, G.A. and Gordon, J.R. (1985). *Relapse prevention: Maintenance strategies in the treatment of addictive behavior.* New York: Guilford Press.

McDowell, D.M., Levin, F.R., and Nunes, E.V. (1999). Dissociative identity disorder and substance abuse: The forgotten relationship. *Journal of Psychoactive Drugs, 31*(1): 71-83.

Meehan, W., O'Connor, L., Berry, J., Weiss, J., Morrison, A., and Acampora, M. (1996). Guilt, shame and depression in clients recovering from addiction. *Journal of Psychoactive Drugs, 28*(2): 125-134.

Miller, B.A. and Downs, W.R. (1986). *Conflict and violence among alcoholic women as compared to a random household sample.* Paper presented at the thirty-eighth meeting of the American Society of Criminology, Atlanta, GA.

Miller, J.B. (1976). *Toward a new psychology of women.* Boston: Beacon Press.

Nelson-Zlupko, L., Dore, M.M., Kauffman, E., and Kaltenbach, K. (1996). Women in recovery: Their perceptions of treatment effectiveness. *Journal of Substance Abuse Treatment, Jan-Feb 13*(1): 51-59.

Nihenhuis, E.R.S., Spinhoven, P., van der Hart, O., de Graaf, A., and Knoppert, E.A.M. (1997). Dissociative pathology discriminates between bipolar mood disorder and dissociative disorder. *British Journal of Psychiatry, 170.*

Nuckolls, C. (1997). Allocating value to gender in official American psychiatry. Part II: Psychiatric training and practice. *Anthropology and Medicine, 4*(3): 245-271.

O'Gorman, P. (1993). Codependency explored: A social movement in search of definition and treatment. *Psychiatric Quarterly, 64*(2): 199-211.

Paris, J. (1997). Antisocial and borderline personality disorders: Two separate diagnoses or two aspects of the same pathology? *Comprehensive Psychiatry, 38*(4): 237-242.

Pettinati, H., Pierce, J., Wolf, A., Rukstalis, M., and O'Brien, C. (1997). Gender differences in comorbidity in depressed alcohol-dependent outpatients. *Alcoholism: Clinical and Experimental Research, 21*(9): 1742-1746.

Piazza, N.J., Vrbka, J.L., and Yeager, R.D. (1989). Telescoping of alcoholism in women alcoholics. *International Journal of Addictions, 24*(1): 19-28.

Pipher, M. (1994). *Reviving Ophelia: Saving the selves of adolescent girls.* New York: Ballantine Books.

Prochaska, J.O., DiClemente, C.C., and Norcross, J.C. (1992). In search of how people change: Applications to addictive behaviors. *American Psychologist, 47*(9): 1102-1114.

Raskin, V.D. (1992). Maternal bereavement in the perinatal substance abuser. *Journal of Substance Abuse Treatment, 9*(2): 149-152.

Regier, D.A., Boyd, J.H., Burke, J.D., Rae, D.S., Myers, J.K., Kramer, M., Robins, L.N., George, L.K., Karno, M., and Locke, B.Z. (1988). One month prevalence of mental disorders in the United States. *Archives of General Psychiatry, 45*(11): 977-986.

Root, M.P. (1989). Treatment failures: The role of sexual victimization in women's addictive behavior. *American Journal of Orthopsychiatry, 59*(4): 542-549.

Ross, C. (1997). *Dissociative identity disorder: Diagnosis, clinical features, and treatment of multiple personality* (Second edition). New York: John Wiley and Sons.

Rounsaville, B., Dolinsky, Z., Babor, T.F., and Meyer, R.E. (1987). Psychopathology as a predictor of treatment outcome in alcoholics. *Archives of General Psychiatry, 44*(June): 505-513.

Saunders, E.A. and Arnold, F. (1991). Borderline personality disorder and childhood abuse: Revisions in clinical thinking and treatment approach. *The Stone Center of Wellesley College Work in Progress Series, 51.*

Schilit, R. and Gomberg, E. (1987). Social support structures of women in treatment for alcoholism. *Health and Social Work, 12*(3): 187-195.

Schutte, K., Hearst, J., and Moos, R. (1997). Gender differences in the relationship between depressive symptoms and drinking behavior among problem drinkers: A three-wave study. *Journal of Consulting and Clinical Psychology, 65*(3): 392-404.

Smith, E.M. and Cloninger, C.R. (1981). Alcoholic females: Mortality at twelve-year follow-up. *Focus on Women, 2,* 1-13.

Stiver, I.P. (1991). The meaning of care: Reframing treatment models. In J.V. Jordan, A.G. Kaplan, J.B. Miller, I.P. Stiver, and J.L. Surrey (Eds.), *Women's Growth in Connection* (pp. 250-267). New York: Guilford Press.

Straussner, S. (1985). Alcoholism in women: Current knowledge and implications for treatment. *Alcoholism Treatment Quarterly, 5*(2): 139-155.

Tobin, M.B., Schmidt, M.D., and Rubinow, D.R. (1994). Reported alcohol use in women with premenstrual syndrome. *American Journal of Psychiatry, 151*(10): 1503-1504.

Uhle, S.M. (1994). Codependence: Contextual variables in the language of social pathology. *Issues in Mental Health Nursing, 15*(3): 307-317.

Walfish, S., Stenmark, D., Sarco, D., Shealy, J.S., and Krone, A. (1992). Incidence of bulimia in substance misusing women in residential treatment. *International Journal of the Addictions, 27*(4): 425-433.

Wallen, J. (1992). A comparison of male and female clients in substance abuse treatment. *Journal of Substance Abuse Treatment, 9*(3): 243-248.

Weissman, M.M. and Klerman, G.L. (1977). Sex differences and the epidemiology of depression. *Archives of General Psychiatry, 34*(1): 98-111.

Weissman, M., Warner, V., Wickramaratne, P., and Kandel, D. (1999). Maternal smoking during pregnancy and psychopathology in offspring followed to adulthood. *Journal of the American Academy of Child and Adolescent Psychiatry, 38*(7): 892-899.

Weisner, C. and Schmidt, L. (1992). Gender disparities in treatment for alcohol problems. *Journal of the American Medical Association, 268:* 1872-1877.

Westreich, L., Guedj, P., Galanter, M., and Baird, D. (1997). Differences between men and women in dual-diagnosis treatment. *American Journal on Addictions, 6*(4): 311-317.

Wiederman, M.W. and Pryor, T. (1996). Substance use among women with eating disorders. *International Journal of Eating Disorders, 20*(2): 163-168.

Wills, S.M. and Goodwin, J.M. (1996). Recognizing bipolar illness in patients with dissociative identity disorder. *Dissociation: Progress in the Dissociative Disorders, 9*(2): 104-109.

Wilsnack, S.C., Wilsnack, R.W., and Klassen, A.D. (1986). Epidemiological research on women's drinking, 1978-1984. *Women and alcohol: Health-related issues. National Institute on Alcohol Abuse and Alcoholism. Research monograph no. 16* (Vol. Publication no. (ADM)86-1139, pp. 1-68). Washington, DC: Department of Health and Human Services.

Chapter 5

Assessing and Treating Psychiatric Comorbidity in Chemically Dependent Adolescents

Peter J. Garito

Adolescence, stress, and drugs form a witch's brew of trouble for teens in the United States. Passage from childhood to adulthood is a turbulent time of profound change, adventure, and rebellion. It involves an exploration of teenagers' inner selves and of the new world opening up around them. One of the dangers of that world is the availability of drugs. Talking to any middle or high school student in America today will elicit a ready awareness of availability and incidence of substance use. If the students do not know who uses illegal drugs or where to get them, they know somebody who does. A recent major statewide survey of public school students in Minnesota (Harrison, Fulkerson, and Beebe, 1998) found that of the students who reported any substance use in the past twelve months, 8.2 percent of ninth graders and 10.5 percent of twelfth graders met the diagnosis of substance dependence. Completing the troubling mix is stress. When asked why they use drugs, the most frequent reasons given were related to stress reduction (Singer and White, 1991). Since high levels of stress are often associated with emotional distress, it is not surprising that most teens who enter treatment for substance issues also have one or more psychological or comorbid disorders.

The purpose of this chapter is to focus a greater awareness on the serious problem of comorbidity with adolescent substance disorders. The first part of the chapter provides an overview of the field including a literature review and general guidelines for the assessment and treatment of comorbid disorders. The second part presents four conditions that typically co-occur with substance abuse in adolescents:

conduct disorder, attention deficit hyperactivity disorder, mood disorders, and anxiety disorders. Assessment, treatment, and interactive factors related to each problem are reviewed.

LITERATURE REVIEW

In their extensive review of the literature on the topic of comorbidity of substance abuse and other psychiatric disorders in adolescence, Bukstein, Brent, and Kaminer (1989) strengthened the link between these two forms of psychopathology and emphasized their mutual importance in the etiology, treatment, and prognosis of these disorders. They had to draw on the literature from adult studies because of the limited studies on adolescents at the time and so recommended more research. Suggested areas of study included prevalence of comorbidity in adolescents, types of co-occurring psychiatric disorders, the study of the development of the disorders, and other genetic or familial factors.

Results of studies using community and clinical samples of adolescents have shed light on the prevalence of comorbidity and have suggested the frequency of the psychiatric diagnoses co-occurring with substance abuse. In a large survey of the general population, Kessler et al. (1996) found significantly high probabilities of comorbidity between alcohol and drug abuse and anxiety, mood, and conduct disorders among adolescents and adults. Rohde, Lewinsohn, and Seeley (1996) found that more than 80 percent of a community sample of adolescents who abused alcohol had an additional form of psychopathology. Increased alcohol use was associated with increased co-occurrence of mood disorders, behavior disorders, and other drug use.

Among patient samples, DeMilio (1989) reported the following comorbid conditions among adolescents in treatment for substance abuse: conduct disorder (42 percent), major depression (35 percent), and attention deficit hyperactivity disorder (14 percent). Greenbaum et al. (1991) sampled a large number of adolescents in treatment for mental health problems and found significant rates of co-occurrence between alcohol and marijuana use and conduct disorder, depression, and attention deficit hyperactivity disorder. Among 156 adolescent inpatients, Bukstein, Glancy, and Kaminer (1992) found that 70.5 percent of the sample had comorbid substance abuse and conduct disorder, and 51.3 percent had comorbid substance abuse with mood disorders. Stowell and Estroff (1992) found comorbid substance abusing adolescents also had mood disorders (61 percent), conduct disorders (54 percent), and anxiety disorders (43 percent). In a sample of adolescent inpatients, Grilo et al. (1995) reported that the most frequent comorbid diagnosis with substance abuse was conduct disorder, followed by mood disorders and attention deficit hyperactivity disorder, with anxiety disorders occurring least often.

The prevalence questions Bukstein, Brent, and Kaminer (1989) posed appear to be answered: There is a significant amount of co-occurrence of substance abuse disorders and psychiatric disorders among adolescents, and the two most frequent comorbid diagnoses are conduct disorder and mood disorders followed by either attention deficit hyperactivity disorder or anxiety disorder. The answer to the primacy question also seems to be showing a pattern—in their samples of community subjects, both Kessler et al. (1996) and Rohde, Lewinsohn, and Seeley (1996) comment that the substance abuse disorder followed the onset of the comorbid psychiatric disorder. Primarily investigating the association between attention deficit hyperactivity disorder and age of onset of substance abuse disorders in an adult population, Wilens, Biederman, Mick, et al. (1997) reported that psychiatric disorders commonly emerged before the onset of the substance abuse disorders. Young et al. (1995) described the relationship of various forms of co-occurring psychopathology, including conduct disorder and substance abuse in adolescent males and reported that the conduct disorder symptoms began over three years before regular use of drugs.

One method of exploring familial or genetic factors has been to look at gender patterns. The results of these studies have been less straightforward. In their clinical sample, Bukstein, Glancy, and Kaminer (1992) reported significantly more adolescent females with comorbid mood disorders and substance abuse, and significantly more males with comorbid conduct disorder and substance abuse. Looking at a large community sample of all ages, Kessler et al. (1997) reported that anxiety and mood disorders and alcohol abuse were the most frequent co-occurring disorders among females, and conduct disorder and alcohol abuse were the most frequent co-occurring disorders among males. The results of a study by Whitmore et al. (1997) were equivocal. They examined the prevalence and severity of various psychiatric disorders and substance abuse by gender. Data analysis revealed no gender differences in severity of substance use, mood disorders, or attention deficit hyperactivity disorder, but males had more severe conduct disorder. In females, major depressive disorder was the only diagnosis significantly associated with severity of substance abuse.

Other studies found no gender effects. Lewinsohn, Rohde, and Seeley (1995) reported no significant gender differences among adolescents with comorbid substance abuse and either depression, anxiety, or disruptive behavior disorder. Grilo et al. (1998) examined adolescent psychiatric inpatients with alcohol use disorder. They reported that the proportion of females and males with mood disorders and conduct disorder did not differ significantly.

More research on gender factors as well as other factors in adolescent comorbidity is needed. However, sufficient data exist to indicate that this is a high-risk population, susceptible to serious emotional and behavioral problems.

ASSESSMENT

The assessment of comorbidity of adolescent substance abuse with another form of psychopathology remains a two—and sometimes multiple—step process. Diagnoses are made based on the initial symptomatology presented, after which the clinician considers comorbid disorders based on what is presented in the subsequent interviews. In effect, there is no unified method to assess for comorbidity of disorders so that the process is piecemeal or sequential.

Developmental Issues

Adding to the complexity of the diagnostic process is the influence of the naturally occurring turmoil of adolescence itself. Children are evolving into the adults they will become (Malmquist, 1985). Ego identity is formed and lifelong patterns of behavior may be set. Self-esteem is refined and solidified based on choices that are made and the success of experiences matched to expectations. Achievement in vocational, academic, community, social, and athletic endeavors shape self-image. How appetites, needs, and impulses are handled often determines degree of success in endeavors and self-esteem. Development of problem-solving skills enhances feelings of well-being in contrast to chronic experiences of frustration and anger. Coping strategies impinge on teens' emotional states. Character structure is formed through beliefs and values. A higher sense of morality may begin to influence decisions and behavior. Characteristic social relations and response to peer influences, probably the most powerful factors during adolescence, take form. It is a very stressful time, as imposed and perceived societal demands require attention and resolution.

First signs of potential psychopathology typically are expressed in some breakdown of an adolescent's dealing with academic and psychosocial functioning. By the time the dysfunction is noticed by parents, adolescents have likely tried unsuccessfully to solve the problem themselves, often by using drugs. They feel overwhelmed by pressures to succeed or conform (Segal and Stewart, 1996) or may be self-medicating to relieve unresolved traumas or losses. Using street chemicals to reduce stress provides an unfortunate irony for teens, since it typically produces a greatly enhanced but opposite effect of the one intended. Negative consequences of use begin to exacerbate and exceed previous stressors. As addiction progresses, substance use becomes less useful as self-medication, and a vicious cycle of dependency is created. Windows of opportunity for intervention and treatment occur when adolescents or their families begin to acknowledge the severity and the escalation of dysfunctional behavior.

General Parameters

Detailed procedures have been published for the diagnostic assessment of various disorders of adolescence by the American Academy of Child and Adolescent Psychiatry (AACAP, 1997). These include substance abuse, anxiety disorder, conduct disorder, bipolar disorder, and attention deficit hyperactivity disorder. Each procedure provides recommendations for differential diagnosis and diagnosis of possible co-existing disorders, as well as instruments, questionnaires, and checklists. However, the process is still very dependent on careful information analysis and on clinical expertise.

No matter what the initial reason or complaint, the evaluation must be thorough and comprehensive. It is essential that the evaluation probe various domains of functioning in the adolescent's life, including substance use behaviors, psychological and behavior problems, school or vocational achievement, family relations, social relations and peer interactions, civil or legal offenses, and leisure and recreational activities—the more information, the better. Do not overlook the school and previous service providers and especially the adolescents themselves (O'Donnell et al., 1998). They may minimize their drug use or leave out information, so having several levels or opportunities of data gathering over time could provide a clearer picture. Structured interview techniques or other instruments may be used to aid in the assessment process (Weinberg et al., 1998).

The diagnosing of substance abuse involves a combination of DSM-IV (American Psychiatric Association, 1994) criteria as well as functional indicators regarding the teen's drug use. The latter includes a pattern of use, onset, types of chemicals used, and negative consequences. It should also include context of use, self-medication effects, paradoxical reactions to substances, and amount of control over use including the outcomes of any attempts to stop. Once a substance abuse disorder has been established, the focus should move to evaluating possible psychological problems.

Clinical experience suggests a vigilant but cautious approach in diagnosing a co-occurring condition. Adolescents coming for treatment have typically been through much distress and could have many reactive symptoms such as sleep disturbance, dysphoria, tension, underlying anger, appetite and energy dysfunction, perceptual distortions, etc. These could occur even after the acute effects of the drugs and subsequent withdrawal symptoms have abated. Often these symptoms will clear with time and abstinence. Symptoms of authentic comorbid conditions tend to persist after the secondary chemical effects have ended (Clark and Neighbors, 1996).

Signs of the comorbid condition often appear early in life, before the first chemical use. This information can be used to confirm the comorbid disorder. Check for behavior problems or underachievement in school, excessive fighting, or acting out in the early grades. Adolescents coming for treatment often already have additional diagnoses and have been given medication for these disorders. Symptoms of mood disorders and anxiety disorders are commonly reported and may have been previously treated. Note the onset of these symptoms or the start of any treatment or medication. Routine evaluation should include asking about a history of prior trauma, especially sexual and physical abuse or significant losses such as the death or estrangement from loved ones. These losses initially may be minimized or denied but become clearer as greater trust and connection are attained in the therapeutic relationship or community.

Clinical Consistency

As with any competent clinical assessment, the information should have an internal consistency and fit conclusions and diagnoses. There should be a logical connection among the data that then leads to the final interpretation. Assessing adolescents poses unique challenges in that regard since their lives and behaviors can be chaotic and troubled, and their veracity of reporting questionable. Adolescents who abuse drugs tend to have a typical pattern of dysfunction that encompasses most aspects or domains of their lives. If the information deviates significantly from that pattern, the chances are high that something is missing or in error. For example, if an adolescent claims to be getting poor grades in school, not getting along very well with his or her family, and is on probation with the criminal justice system but claims to be using drugs only occasionally, more information is needed. A female adolescent with heavy drug use, such as using heroin or other narcotics, who has a history of running away from home, poor school attendance and underachievement, minor delinquent behavior, several boyfriends who maltreated her, and sleep and appetite disturbance, yet who does not report any past trauma or current affective disturbance needs to be monitored closely and reinterviewed after a time in treatment. In some cases, it may be impossible to verify diagnostic impressions based on available data, and treatment must proceed. The clinician's experience is a significant factor in assessment of comorbidity in adolescents.

TREATMENT

One of the early difficulties in the treatment of clients with comorbid disorders was the dichotomy in training and treatment philosophy between the traditions of chemical dependency and mental health (Penick et al., 1990; Belfer, 1993). Most practitioners now agree that a combined or comprehensive approach is needed and is the most helpful in treating comorbid disorders (Gregorius and Smith, 1991; Parrish, 1994; Weinberg et al., 1998; Wodarski and Feit, 1997).

As with assessment, there is as yet no universally accepted, unified set of standards for comorbidity treatment but rather combinations of interventions based on the initial assessment of problems. The American Academy of Child and Adolescent Psychiatry (1997) recommends the following for adolescents with substance use disorders: Addiction treatment should be multimodal—that is, combined with other modalities that fit the needs of the adolescent. Treatment components should be of adequate intensity and duration; comprehensive, focusing on all domains of dysfunction; include the family; foster a drug-free lifestyle; encourage self-help groups (AA or NA); sensitive to cultural and socioeconomic factors; coordinate with local systems of care; and include aftercare or follow-up treatment.

Two such programs on inpatient settings described in the literature (Kaminer and Frances, 1991; Singer and White, 1991) include an array of treatment modalities: individual, group, and family therapy; community support services and twelve-step programs; relapse prevention, social skills, and problem-solving training; and medication when indicated. Treatment occurred in a specially designed therapeutic environment with specific rules and expectations that were matched to the adolescents' developmental level and approach to life. Program goals were to foster abstinence from chemical abuse, to alleviate the symptoms of the psychological disorder, and to provide the adolescent with a range of improved skills to cope with life problems and internal distress.

Outcome Studies

Reviewing the research on efficacy of specific interventions for substance-abusing adolescents, Weinberg et al. (1998) noted that family-oriented therapies have been investigated the most and have shown some utility in reducing drug use. Strong family bonding has been shown to be associated with a decrease in alcohol use (Bahr, Marcos, and Maughan, 1995). Kennedy and Minami (1993) reported that 47 percent of substance-abusing adolescents were abstinent one year after treatment in an inpatient program which included a wilderness phase. Participation in aftercare support programs was very important: teens not attending AA meetings were 4.5 times more likely to relapse. Azrin et al. (1994) found that behavioral treatment was much more effective than supportive counseling among substance-abusing adolescents receiving outpatient treatment. Nine percent of the supportive group versus 73 percent of the behavioral group was abstinent during the final month of the six-month program. The behavioral approach targeted family and peer relations, and drug use was measured by drug screens and personal reports. Kaminer et al. (1998) reported that cognitive-behavioral group treatment was more effective than interactional group treatment. Dually diagnosed teens participated in an outpatient program; after three months, the cognitive therapy group showed a significant reduction in substance abuse.

Summary

Treatment of substance-abusing adolescents with comorbid psychiatric disorders needs to be a team effort led by the direct treatment providers and should include family, school personnel, community agencies, and peers. The treatment approach should match the adolescent's level of development and motivation for change. Therapeutic status and readiness for change needs to be monitored regularly to allow for modifications in the treatment plan. Cognitive-behavioral models of intervention seem to be effective since their core involves a didactic, skills-building, and practical approach that attempts to anticipate problems and gives the adolescent the tools to deal with potential problems in the community. Clinical experience suggests keeping gender differences in mind in treatment. Providing separate treatment may produce less acting out by removing one more distraction or chance to be impulsive. Interactional groups should not be discounted as they help to foster learning, sharing, identification with others, and opportunities to refine relationship skills. Groups also prime the teen to utilize aftercare support groups that have been shown to aid in relapse prevention. Activities that boost self-esteem can be valuable. General educational programs that enhance academic achievement, provide vocational information, and counsel, as well as therapeutic recreational activities, add to the overall effectiveness of the treatment process.

CONDUCT DISORDER

The key diagnostic factors for conduct disorder are behaviors that show a repetitive, persistent pattern of misconduct in which the fundamental rights of others are violated. Basic societal and age standards of behavior are not followed and actions of very high risk or poor judgment occur. Common types of such behaviors include rebellion toward authority (running away, school defiance, disobedience toward parents); covert acts (stealing, smoking, substance abuse, vandalism) and overt acts (fighting, more serious crimes, violence). Risk factors range from the constitutional to the environmental, leading to the view that it is a heterogeneous disorder. A suggested model is that of a genetic liability triggered by environmental risk and mediated by factors such as poor coping skills (AACAP, 1997).

It is the most common comorbid disorder with substance abuse, but it is also very highly correlated with other externalizing disorders such as attention deficit hyperactivity disorder (Arredondo and Butler, 1994). Among adolescents diagnosed with attention deficit hyperactivity disorder, conduct and bipolar disorders were the key predictors of substance abuse (Biederman et al., 1997). In another study, adolescents diagnosed with substance abuse disorder were much more likely to be also diagnosed with conduct disorder rather than oppositional defiant disorder or anxiety disorder (Grilo et al., 1995). Interestingly, however, even among the non–substance-abuse group, conduct and disruptive behavior disorders were the most prevalent problems, highlighting the common limit-testing attitude of adolescence.

Another issue related to the assessment of comorbidity of conduct disorder with substance abuse disorder is that both are externalizing conditions. The essential features for identifying the problems depend on outward signs and, to some degree, the symptoms overlap. The main indicator for conduct disorder is a disregard for appropriate social norms. Substance use among adolescents is almost always illicit. Adolescence is a time of high risks and foolish acts, so that the combination of adolescence and substance abuse can easily lead to behaviors that could be considered indicative of conduct disorder (Bukstein, Brent, and Kaminer, 1989). These behaviors often begin at the same time as the drug-abusing behaviors and may be related to, if not caused by, drug-seeking behavior (Brown et al., 1996). Conduct disorder behaviors may dissipate with sobriety. However, even without early signs, a negative pattern of behavior can occur and a basic disregard for individual and societal rights can be adopted as a consistent lifestyle, even if it is only in service to the addiction.

Treatment Issues

The fundamental goal in treating an adolescent with comorbid conduct and substance abuse disorders is to reestablish a sense of respect for the rights of others. This entails developing an awareness of another person's feelings, expressions, and behaviors as special and important. It also involves an inhibition of impulses that, when expressed, would ignore those feelings or expressions, or in the case of larger society, its rules and standards. Another view is to reduce the risk function in the adolescent and increase resilience function. Strengthen the factors that increase the likelihood of positive behavior. Specific targets would be to improve social relations, improve problem-solving skills, provide knowledge of proper actions, teach impulse control, and handle feelings appropriately.

Few treatment outcome studies have been reported. One study assessed adolescents who were dually diagnosed and treated in an inpatient setting for four to six weeks. Over 75 percent completed treatment, but of the noncompleters, most had a comorbid conduct disorder diagnosis (Kaminer, 1992). Another residential treatment program found that earlier onset and more severe conduct disorder symptoms and greater drug dependence predicted poor treatment outcomes on follow-up. There were improvements in conduct disorder behaviors but not in substance use (Crowley et al., 1998).

The intervention focus must be multidimensional, long enough in duration, and suited to the individual. It must target each of the problem areas identified, thus necessitating a proper and thorough assessment. Intervention should then occur as part of a continuum of care by a coordinated team that would modify strategies and goals as needed. Whether inpatient or outpatient, the treatment for comorbid substance abuse and conduct disorder must embrace family, school, and peer group environments. In general, the externalizing nature of the primary manifestations of this problem across the spectrum of the adolescent's functioning warrant the use of interpersonal and psychoeducational approaches in addition to intrapsychic and psychopharmacological methods (AACAP, 1997). Treatment approaches should complement and augment each other because they are interrelated as part of the overall clinical picture and treatment plan.

Specific Methods

Family Treatment

Family treatment includes family therapy and parenting training as well as encouraging treatment for any parent's psychopathology. Negative relational patterns need to be changed, communication improved, and feelings safely shared so that parents can once again be considered a positive resource rather than another source of tension. Parents need to learn to explain their expectations and be consistent and fair in their limit setting—while remaining flexible.

Individual and Group Treatment

In addition to providing information, improving communication skills, and receiving feedback about themselves, individual and group treatment modalities can alter the adolescent's attitude and feelings toward others and the community. Anger can be reduced, hurt expressed, and psychic controls strengthened. Cognitive-behavioral, supportive, and confrontive approaches can be employed. Other techniques include the use of a daily journal, letters, music and art therapy, recreational therapy, relaxation, and meditation.

Skills Training

Special emphasis is needed to change behavioral tendencies for this population. Prosocial problem-solving techniques and socially appropriate interactions must be learned. Assertiveness training, anger management, relapse prevention, psychodrama, role-playing, thought stopping, and other anticipatory or rehearsal type methods can be used to develop the adolescents' capacity to think before they act.

School Programs

Most teens with these problems have been doing very poorly in school and restoring their academic competence will help not only in their future endeavors but boost their self-esteem as well. This training could also entail life and independent living skills.

Community and Social Services

The juvenile justice system can be a powerful ally in providing an external level of restraint for the adolescent, which may be crucial in the early stages of the treatment process. The expectation would be that the locus of control of behavior would revert to inner, personal controls and motivation. It is important to access other service providers and work cooperatively. Mentoring, placement, and protective services can all be used.

Therapeutic Community

This is primarily for residential settings but the same mind-set can be used when the adolescent is in the community. Inpatient treatment typically involves a highly structured, reward-based system to help restore a sense of order and routine in what usually has been a chaotic, needs-driven lifestyle.

Interactive Factors

The combination of substance abuse and conduct disorder in an adolescent can be very detrimental to the individual and can present special challenges in treatment. Although some of these issues can occur in outpatient settings, they have a greater influence in inpatient treatment. Conduct-disordered adolescents can be very disruptive in treatment. They can promote an atmosphere of rebellion or persistently complain about and question the rules or therapy conditions. Acting-out behaviors can occur in either a covert or overt fashion and possibly incite others to do so. Incidences can be minor, such as stealing small objects or invading space or privacy, to more serious acts of theft and fighting. Conduct-disordered teens can be manipulative and can instigate problems or confrontations without being directly involved. They also can be insensitive to others' needs or feelings, which can hamper another's progress in therapy. Anticipating and then watching for these behaviors can smooth the therapy process for the entire community as well as confirm early diagnosis.

This group of adolescents must learn the interactional effects of drugs on their psychological problems. Chemicals generally have a disinhibitory effect on behavior, allowing impulses freer reign. What may have been detained without drugs becomes an almost automatic behavior with drugs. There is also a blunting of feelings, permitting easier disregard for one's own doubts and the feelings of others. Chemicals also dull cognitive functioning, reducing any chance of rationality or common sense being utilized in a situation.

ATTENTION DEFICIT HYPERACTIVITY DISORDER

The essential feature of ADHD is impulsiveness either in behavior or in the ability to focus mentally on a task or stimulus. The behavioral aspect is often manifested by an inability to sit still or remain seated. Adolescents with ADHD tend to be fidgety or active even when in a resting position. The inability to focus mentally is expressed in many ways but primarily through inattention and high distractibility. ADHD teens cannot concentrate because they cannot maintain a consistent sensory vigilance to acquire information in coherent, understandable units. Under these conditions, learning is extremely difficult so learning disabilities are common. They also show very poor skills in organization and may be hard to discipline or manage. Such children and adolescents are very trying to engage in the classroom, at home, or in other settings. Since at least some of the symptoms must be present before the age of seven in order to make the diagnosis, adolescents often will already have been labeled when coming for treatment for a substance abuse disorder and are likely to have been on medication in the past.

ADHD and Substance Abuse

The majority of evidence posits a relationship between ADHD and substance abuse but the exact nature is not clear (Wilens, Biederman, and Spencer, 1996). Studies that have evaluated adults with substance abuse disorders for signs of ADHD in childhood have generally found that the ones with ADHD symptoms have a higher prevalence of substance abuse as adults (Milin et al., 1997; Biederman et al., 1998). This was the case with and without comorbidity of other disorders, though conduct disorder and bipolar disorder were better predictors of substance abuse than ADHD alone (Wilens, Biederman, Abrantes, et al., 1997). Mannuzza et al. (1998) studied ADHD children into adulthood and found that they had a higher rate of non-alcohol substance abuse than non-ADHD children. Interestingly, there was a low rate of ADHD diagnosis among all the subjects upon reaching adulthood (4 percent of the sample), though a larger percentage had ADHD symptoms.

When adolescents have been studied, some similarities result, but also much inconsistency. Adolescents with ADHD— 50 percent of the sample—tended to have earlier onset and more severe substance abuse than non-ADHD subjects (Horner and Scheibe, 1997), more comorbidity with other disorders (Thompson et al., 1996), and no difference in prevalence rates between boys and girls (Rounds-Bryant et al., 1998). A study of siblings of adolescents with ADHD found at a four-year follow-up that ADHD and male gender accounted for higher rates and earlier onset of substance abuse—risk was higher if mediated by conduct disorder (Milberger et al., 1997). However, while studying substance abusing and non–substance-abusing adolescents for comorbidity with other disorders, Wilens, Biederman, Abrantes, et al. (1997) found a significantly greater percentage of behavioral disorders, mood disorders, and panic disorder among the substance-abusing group compared to the non–substance-abusing group. The two groups did not differ significantly on ADHD even though occurrence was high in both groups: 61 percent of the sample of the substance-abusing group and 57 percent of the sample of the non–substance-abusing group. In a large study of children and adolescents seen at baseline and after four years, there was no difference between ADHD subjects and controls in rates of substance abuse. Both groups had abuse rates of 15 percent (Biederman et al., 1997). In contrast, a recent study by Biederman et al. (1999) reported that only 25 percent of the fifty-six boys diagnosed with ADHD and treated with psychostimulants for about four years had at least one substance abuse disorder compared to 75 percent of the nineteen boys diagnosed with ADHD but not treated. A control group of non-ADHD boys produced 18 percent with a substance abuse disorder. Biederman et al. concluded that treating ADHD can result in a significant reduction in risk (84 percent) for developing substance abuse disorders.

Assessment

The diagnosis of ADHD is based on clinical judgment from a careful review of information provided by parents, the individual, and other sources such as the school. Signs of inattention include missing details, making careless mistakes, losing things, general inattention, frequent daydreaming, easy distractibility, and forgetfulness. Behavioral impulsiveness is expressed through general hyperactivity, excessive climbing or running, constant talking, difficulty taking turns, and frequent interrupting, or intruding. Information from family members is very important since they would be in a position to provide data about the early life and behavior of the adolescent, both developmental and early school material. Impressions from the school and the adolescent can give anecdotal information about achievement, work habits, classroom and personal demeanor, and social relations (AACAP, 1997).

Encountering an adolescent suspected of abusing substances and possibly having ADHD requires careful inquiry about comorbidity. This is another externalizing disorder with some overlap in symptomatology with substance abuse. With no prior information, it is best clinically to look for substance abuse and then assess the ADHD. If the adolescent comes into treatment with an ADHD diagnosis, inquire when the diagnosis was made and by whom. Adolescents with substance abuse typically do very poorly in school both in achievement and comportment. They also show many acting-out behaviors, all of which could be considered evidence of ADHD. It is important to look for ADHD signs that started in childhood and have occurred independently of the onset or occurrence of the substance abuse.

It is important to assess whether the use of substances provides any self-medicating effects for the symptoms of ADHD or consequences of the disorder. Often stimulants such as amphetamines, cocaine, nicotine, and caffeine provide paradoxical effects of calming hyperactivity and focusing attention (Khantzian, 1997). Alcohol and opiates may be used to provide relief from dysphoric feelings associated with underachievement and being labeled as lazy, stupid, or rebellious. Substances may be used to ease social anxiety and mask social inadequacies.

Treatment Issues

A most common and effective treatment for ADHD has been psychopharmacology, mostly use of psychostimulant medication (AACAP, 1997). This poses a dilemma for adolescents with comorbid substance abuse and ADHD. They may have been taking medication for a long time and developed reliance on it to function effectively. Many teens, however, have abused their medication or have been involved in other misuse of the medicine, e.g., selling it. Therefore, treatment of this comorbid condition should involve discussion and a decision regarding initiation or continuation of medication. Medical or psychiatric consultation is indicated as well as coordination with attending providers. As an alternative to psychostimulants, the use of nonabusable medications such as pemoline or bupropion may be considered and have been effective in reducing ADHD symptoms (Riggs, 1998). Treatment for comorbidity should address the apprehension in giving up the self-medicating properties of abusable substances and should promote the development of compensatory coping strategies for difficulties not alleviated by medication treatments.

As with all of these problems, a team approach works best by including family, school, and psychological and medical clinicians. The key factors in treating this disorder are to help the adolescent gain greater control of impulses and to help increase the ability to focus more consistently. It is usually best to identify specific target behaviors in cooperation with the adolescent who becomes an integral part of the treatment process. The more the adolescent knows about ADHD, the better. The more that interventions can be shown to produce success for the adolescent, the greater the cooperation. Specific targets of intervention include improving organizational skills, learning to control impulses and delay gratification, learning to extend and heighten attention, and developing more careful self-monitoring of thought and behavior.

ADHD has a very long course, and continual monitoring of behaviors and adjustment of goals is necessary. The limited evidence of treatment outcome on subjects with comorbid substance abuse and ADHD suggests that the ADHD tends to prolong treatment in adults (Wilens, Biederman, and Mick, 1998) and in adolescents (Adams and Wallace, 1994). If the adolescent is medicated, stable medication compliance, a strict administration regimen, and ample instruction for the adolescent concerning potential misuse are needed. If medication is not used in treatment, the core symptoms related to impulsivity, inattention, and hyperactivity must be modified in other ways. A highly structured environment or one that is composed of very clearly defined routines and expectations for behavior may be necessary. This entails intervention with family members to train them about the disorder so that they become part of the clinical team helping the adolescent stay on track. Collaboration with teachers and other school staff is also essential so that everyone maintains a common approach to reinforcing acceptable behavior. A coordinator may need to be designated to monitor progress. Other interventions may be needed. Family therapy or individual therapy should occur if coaching on management of behaviors or dealing with the consequences of behaviors is needed. Skills training in social interaction, referral to support groups, and ancillary training such as recreational activity may be helpful.

Interactive Factors

Adolescents with combined ADHD and substance abuse may have a more benign view of taking drugs than other adolescents and may resist considering treatment without medication. If they can be convinced to go without medication for a time, either to aid in differential diagnosis or as part of the treatment regimen, their impulsive symptoms may return, making overall treatment difficult. Such adolescents can be very disruptive in treatment, much like the conduct-disordered teens. These teens are susceptible to heightened stimulation. They act out, interrupt, intrude, or otherwise interfere with their own group therapy. This can be disruptive in a therapeutic community. They also may have difficulty absorbing new techniques or therapeutic information. They may require more specific guidelines and need more time to acquire skills. It is important for them to learn that certain chemicals can make their behavior worse and that more, not less, personal control is needed.

MOOD DISORDERS

These disorders are characterized by a disturbance in mood, the effects of which reverberate throughout the body. Emotional signs include feelings of sadness, guilt, hopelessness, and worthlessness. Social indicators could be isolation and avoidance as well as irritability and moodiness. Cognitive manifestations take the form of lowered concentration, poor decision making, low self-esteem, and suicidal thoughts or thoughts of death. Personal signs of an affective disorder may be fatigue, weight loss, poor appetite, psychomotor agitation, sleep disturbance, and general anhedonia. Types of mood disorder range from major depressive disorders to dysthymia to adjustment disorders with depression (APA, 1994).

Mood Disorders and Substance Abuse

Mood disorders co-occur frequently among substance-abusing adolescents. Percentages range from 50 to 60 percent among adolescents entering treatment (Stowell and Estroff, 1992). Depressed substance-abusing adolescents also have additional comorbid disorders such as conduct disorder and anxiety disorders (Arredondo and Butler, 1994; King et al., 1996; Riggs et al., 1995). Although it is not clear that these adolescents harm themselves to a greater degree than other groups, teens who have committed suicide typically have experienced a recent stressor for which treatment is not sought (Rich, Sherman, and Fowler, 1990). The greatest risk for suicide is an intoxicated white male who does not seek professional help (Kaminer, 1992).

Mood disorders have a significant cognitive component. The negative thought patterns and maladaptive attitudes tend to perpetuate the sad mood and dismal outlook. Inpatient adolescents with multiple comorbid conditions were found to have the most cognitive distortions among various diagnostic groups tested, with the depression group scoring as high as the comorbid group. Catastrophizing and personalizing were prominent distortions (Kempton et al., 1994). Calache et al. (1994) compared depressed and nondepressed substance-abusing adolescents along with a control group using scores on the Dysfunctional Attitude Scale. The depressed group produced higher scores than the nondepressed group, suggesting a strong connection between faulty thinking, depression, and substance abuse.

Assessment

Since this is an internalizing disorder, more emphasis is placed on information provided by the adolescent directly during the initial aspect of assessment. Careful delineation of symptoms, their onset, intensity, and duration is important. Assessment for risk of suicidality is essential and the completion of a behavioral contract regarding telling someone before action is taken should be used if active suicidal ideation is endorsed. Family history, school history, past treatment information, and medication history are also necessary. Information from the family, school, and other treaters can fill in details and yield an accurate diagnostic picture. Rating scales can be used to indicate current intensity of symptoms and then as a monitoring tool as treatment proceeds to measure the effectiveness of the treatment regimen (AACAP, 1997).

It is important to determine what type of depressive disorder is present. Whether a depressive disorder is present or whether symptoms are secondary to substance abuse is difficult to determine. In reviewing the list of symptoms for mood disorders, it is very likely that an adolescent entering treatment for substance abuse will exhibit or report many of these symptoms. If only because of the basic physical effects chemicals can have on the body, there will probably be disturbances of routine functions—sleep, appetite, energy, and thinking. Feelings of guilt, regret, and shame about foolish behaviors also are common. Their lives by this point have been so disrupted and caused so much trouble that feelings of hopelessness and self-harm are usual. This has led to the notion of primary and secondary depression in people with comorbid substance abuse (Schuckit, 1985). The distinction is based on onset of depression: onset prior to substance abuse is primary; onset after the start of substance abuse is secondary. In time and with abstinence, secondary depressive symptoms clear up and only primary symptoms continue and can be treated appropriately. However, unlike in adults, this may not occur in adolescents. Bukstein, Glancy, and Kaminer (1992) found that adolescents with secondary depressive symptoms did not remit their symptoms over time; nonremitters outnumbered remitters nearly two to one.

Assessment of adolescent psychopathology can be challenging and uncertain. While comprehensive histories and accurate clinical data are essential, teens with comorbid depression and substance abuse need to be followed consistently in treatment. Depressive signs should be taken seriously from the start and treated diligently.

Treatment Issues

Since most adolescents report using drugs and alcohol to feel better, the main treatment goal of adolescents with comorbid substance abuse and depression is to help them find other ways to maintain their sense of well-being and normal mood. Often the first step is to help them recognize their depression and learn more about the problem. They need to learn that there are many treatment modalities and the outlook is positive for improvement. The focus of treatment is on the individual primarily, with family, peers, and other life connections as adjuncts in the process. Treatment needs to raise the adolescents' mood but, more important, modify the cognitive distortions that generate their unhappiness. Emphasizing strengths, teaching new skills, accepting limitations, and setting plans for future achievement are methods that can be used to boost self-esteem, which is typically low. Often significant losses in these adolescents' lives have never been resolved and warrant attention.

Depression can impede treatment in this patient population. Dobkin et al. (1998) studied treatment completers and noncompleters among comorbid substance-abusing depressed adolescents. Noncompleters were significantly different from completers in measures of alienation and social maladaption; on follow-up, teens who did not improve on remission of substance abuse had greater depressive symptoms. As with other comorbid conditions, treatment should target all relevant disorders. An effective modality for this comorbid condition is cognitive-behavioral therapy. Kaminer et al. (1998) demonstrated its effectiveness for substance abuse in outpatient therapy groups, and cognitive therapy has long been known to help in depression (Stein and Davis, 1982).

The cognitive-behavioral model can be used in individual or group therapy, in outpatient or inpatient settings, and in conjunction with family therapy. Negative thinking patterns can not only lead to sad emotions, but can justify imprudent behavior. Other techniques include problem-solving training, assertiveness training, and methods to encourage sharing of feelings. These methods can serve to improve success in life functioning and also to improve ability to anticipate and prevent depression. Another method is to assist the adolescent in designing a course of action that will lead back to a sense of normalcy or productive endeavors. School failure, legal problems, and familial conflict may all need to be dealt with; this can be overwhelming for the adolescent. A plan of action could aid in building self-worth, and stressing positive attributes could achieve similar ends. Significant losses contribute to the adolescent's depression, and grief work may be in order. The clinician should check for absent parental figures and deaths in the family or among friends. Abusing drugs can be life threatening. It is not uncommon for substance-abusing teens to have had a relative or friend die directly or indirectly as a result of chemical abuse, such as in motor vehicle accidents, by suicide, or from long-term negative health effects. These adolescents may not have had an opportunity to grieve the loss and may need time in counseling to do so.

In some families, depressive symptoms provide the first alert to parents that something may be wrong with their adolescent. Initial treatment often is with the family doctor who diagnoses depression and may prescribe an antidepressant. Clinical experience finds many adolescents coming for treatment for substance abuse already taking such medication. Appropriate consultation is needed to decide to continue medication. Precipitating factors, symptom intensity and duration, treatment history, and response to medication will figure in the decision. Reliance on any chemicals—even prescription ones— to alter mood must be weighed carefully in the decision to medicate.

Interactive Factors

It is important for the adolescent with comorbid depression and substance abuse to appreciate the complex interplay of the various forces involved in this condition. A cyclical pattern of causality perpetuates the depression and substance abuse. Drugs are taken to dull unhappiness, avoid painful thoughts and life problems, as well as alter negative self-image. Continuing this pattern generates more negative thoughts, low self-esteem, and more depression. Often, reminding the adolescent that being in treatment is their affirmation of wanting a better lifestyle can enhance recovery. Results can be slow with this comorbidity; much needs to change in their lives to counter negative perspectives. Despondency can easily reoccur. They can be fragile, so sufficient support should be built into the treatment plan.

ANXIETY DISORDERS

The commonality of experience in this group of disorders is an uncontrolled feeling of fear, usually irrational, and often, but not always, associated with specific events or circumstances. Manifestations vary from sudden onset of terror (panic attack) to fear of separation from attachment figures (separation anxiety disorder) to specific objects or social situations (specific and social phobias). Obsessive-compulsive disorder is marked by recurrent and persistent anxious thoughts and repetitive behaviors meant to reduce the anxiety. Generalized anxiety disorder involves multiple symptoms such as restlessness, poor concentration, and irritability. Post-traumatic stress disorder (PTSD) is a reaction following a trauma, identified by symptoms of reexperiencing the trauma, by avoidance or numbing behaviors, and signs of increased arousal (sleep problems, hypervigilance) (APA, 1994).

Anxiety Disorders and Substance Abuse

The co-occurrence of anxiety disorders with substance abuse disorders in clinical populations varied from 7 percent (DeMilio, 1989) to 15 percent (Greenbaum et al., 1991) to over 40 percent (Stowell and Estroff, 1992). More recent research suggests an even higher prevalence: 67 percent of adolescents with substance abuse presenting for treatment at an inpatient rehab center were comorbid with anxiety disorders (Deas-Nesmith, Brady, and Campbell, 1998). In the same study, the rate of comorbidity for teens was 33 percent whether they presented at an inpatient or outpatient psychiatric facility. Wilens, Biederman, Abrantes, and Spencer (1997) found a significantly higher rate of panic disorders among substance-abusing teens versus a non–substance-abusing group. In a study investigating prevalence of comorbid substance abuse and PTSD, Deykin and Buka (1997) reported rates of 29.6 percent lifetime and 19.2 percent current. Comorbid substance abuse and anxiety disorders can also co-occur with depression (Riggs et al., 1995) and ADHD (Thompson et al., 1996).

Assessment

The assessment for comorbid anxiety disorder among substance-abusing adolescents generally follows that for other comorbid conditions, namely taking a solid history with information from the adolescent, family, school, and other providers and sources. A mental status evaluation is needed to determine the current level of anxiety and history of previous symptoms. Developmental information is important.

Signs indicating shyness, social discomfort, problems in friendship, childhood fears, fearful temperament, and inability to separate all should be noted. Check for family or individual stresses, frequent moving, or significant losses. Also consider recurrent or chronic minor ailments as signs of past or current anxiety. Rating scales can be used to assess current anxiety level and measure responsiveness to treatment (AACAP, 1997). Differential diagnosis can be made based on symptoms, though a period of time may be needed for adjustment in inpatient settings. Separation anxiety may be homesickness; social phobia may be uncertainty at sharing in group therapy.

For this comorbid condition, it is essential to search for physical and sexual abuse in the teen's history, especially among girls. In a study comparing a group of sexually abused adolescents girls with an unabused group, significantly higher measures on substance abuse were found with the sexually abused group compared to the controls (Hussey and Singer, 1993). Abuse is often initially denied due to not recalling the event, minimizing its importance or effect, or deliberately keeping it secret. Reasons for the latter include fear of reprisal by the abuser, wanting to protect the abuser, or a sense of self-recrimination. Strong feelings of shame, guilt, embarrassment, or foolishness may also play a role in preventing the adolescent from reporting the abuse.

Even with a history of trauma, diagnosis of PTSD depends on careful analysis of symptoms. Substance-abusing teens often have disturbances of arousal and concentration, numbed or restricted feelings, lack of hope for the future, and a sense of detachment. However, if they have avoided talking about the trauma even with sufficient opportunity and there are clear signs of reexperiencing the situation, PTSD may be occurring. Although the research evidence is sparse, clinical experience suggests that adolescent girls who consistently use heroin or other narcotics are most likely to be covering up a trauma or dealing with PTSD.

Treatment Issues

As with depression, this internalizing disorder focuses on the individuals. It is also critical to differentiate the symptoms of anxiety secondary to the substance abuse. By the time they reach treatment, their lives may be filled with trouble and multiple sources of worry and fear related to their addiction. The initial phase of treatment for an adolescent with a comorbid anxiety disorder is to identify the sources of stress and then develop methods to deal with each one, a process akin to the so-called Serenity Prayer—deciding what needs to be changed and then changing it. The core issue in anxiety disorders is fear, and all treatment endeavors should be aimed at reducing apprehensions.

No outcome studies have been identified. Anxiety disorders in adolescents respond well to a variety of treatments but cognitive-behavioral approaches appear the most effective (AACAP, 1997). As with mood disorders, the technique is to identify the faulty thinking that generates the fear and modify the cognitive distortion. Concomitant procedures include using strategies to solve stress-causing problems and developing different perspectives from which to view the stressors. Other methods serve to lessen the anxiety directly, such as relaxation, meditation, and thought stopping. Other forms of therapy have been used, such as psychodynamic and family therapy (AACAP, 1997).

An important ingredient in the treatment of anxiety disorders is for individuals to feel more in control of their lives and not to feel alone. Specific therapeutic techniques should be provided as a way to empower individuals. Since anxiety is often anticipatory, just having the knowledge of effective methods to cope is often sufficient to reduce tension. Encouraging and providing support groups and networks is also very helpful. Specialized groups may be needed for PTSD or specific phobias. As with other comorbid disorders, the decision to use psychoactive medications in treatment is a complex one. The severity of symptoms and the efficacy of certain medications must be weighed against the potential harm to the individual who has used drugs to solve problems and feel better. Certain classes of medications (such as benzodiazepines) present greater possible risks for abuse to the adolescent with comorbid anxiety disorder, thus warranting consultation with an addictions specialist in medicine.

Interactive Factors

Therapeutic messages should include conveying the understanding that life stressors do not arise only from substance abuse, and that treatment methods learned will be needed to cope with future stressors. Frustration and tension may have resulted from unrealistic expectations on the part of the adolescents themselves or from the family regarding unmet achievements, so the treatment process should contain goals that fit the adolescents' resources. Past issues may affect treatment. Memories or indications of prior abuse or traumatic events may surface and detract from focusing on current stressors, increasing vulnerability to relapse. Dealing therapeutically with several disorders could in itself cause stress. There also may be a reluctance or fear to reach out—to support groups, networks, or other resources—inherent to the anxiety disorder.

CONCLUSIONS

The field of comorbidity of substance abuse with other psychological disorders among adolescents has been emerging over the past decade. Adolescent substance abusers coming for treatment today are viewed as being clinically different from previous ideas about adolescent abusers. There is a greater awareness of the psychological forces interacting with their conditions and generally a more sophisticated approach to providing treatment. The complexity of the problem has fostered greater cooperation among various providers, since a multimodal approach has been shown to work best. The ultimate result has been to provide this clinical population with more effective and humane care.

APPENDIX:
SELECTED TREATMENT PROTOCOLS
FOR COMORBID DISORDERS

Conduct Disorder

Problem Area	Treatment Plan Strategy
Patient shows significant hostility bias and overinterpretation of events and experiences as aggressive or provocative in nature.	Patient will record three situations in which he or she felt threatened or angered and share experiences in therapy group. Patient will ask three other patients to describe their own reactions to and interpretations of the events/situations. Discuss in therapy group.

Patient shows a history of and current impulses to engage in violent/intimidating behavior.	Patient will complete cost/benefit analysis and list the positives and negatives, as well as short-term and long-term results of engaging in violent and intimidating behavior. Discuss results in therapy group.
	Patient will review personal history of violence and write down which situations provoked the violence, what thoughts and feelings the patient experienced prior to and after the violence. Patient will brainstorm five ways future violent situations can be preempted/managed.
	Patient will learn and practice the five-step aggression control procedure and discuss experiences in therapy group.
	Patient will develop five cognitive coping statements to modulate/inhibit angry/aggressive behaviors. Discuss in therapy group.
Patient has a history of vandalism, truancy, running away, and associated maladaptive behaviors.	Patient will meet with therapist for individual insight-oriented psychotherapy session and explore feelings, conflicts, beliefs, and thoughts that precipitated acting-out behaviors.
Patient shows extremely limited conflict containment skills.	Patient will interview three patients and learn three ways of defusing anger/hostility other than through aggressive or intimidating behaviors. Discuss results in therapy group.
Patient shows history of impulsively responding in conflict situations.	Patient will read "Causal Thinking," discuss concepts with therapist in individual session, and list three ways this information can assist patient with decreasing impulsive behavior.
Patient has history of abuse, neglect, and maltreatment.	Patient will meet with therapist in individual psychotherapy session and discuss issues related to anger, hurt, loss, and grief, and will complete feelings letter and discuss in group therapy session.

These protocols were developed by David F. O'Connell, PhD, Clinical Director, Caron Foundation. Reprinted with permission. Additional protocols for affective and anxiety disorders are located in the Appendix to Chapter 1.

Attention Deficit Hyperactivity Disorder

Problem Area	Treatment Plan Strategy
Patient needs appreciation/understanding of importance of stable medication administration regimen.	Patient will read "Help Is Only a School Nurse Away," summarize main points, and discuss in individual session and adhere to a regular and appropriate medication administration schedule.
Patient lacks knowledge of abuse potential of stimulant medication and its effects on primary relapse.	Patient will identify negative consequences of abusing stimulant medication and practice five-step self-instruction plan to address medication abuse/relapse. Discuss in therapy group.
Patient lacks effective strategies to manage interpersonal conflict, anger arousal, and poor effort behaviors.	Patient will interview three other patients and discuss their methods of coping with anger, self-motivation, and problem solving. Discuss in group therapy.
Patient shows poor organizational skills in home, treatment, and school environments.	Patient will read "Getting Organized" and "Tips for School Success" handouts. Summarize and discuss in invidual therapy session.
Patient lacks awareness of and has not addressed comorbid problems.	Patient will discuss emotional/social problems associated with ADHD in individual therapy session.
Patient lacks skills to manage ADHD symptoms and related problems.	Patient will learn and use five-step self-instruction plan for three problems and discuss results in therapy group.
Patient lacks effective verbal coping skills for managing ADHD-related emotional/behavioral problems.	Patient will identify and challenge self-defeating, ineffective self-talk in three problem situations and develop alternative coping strategies. Discuss in individual therapy session.

REFERENCES

Adams, L. and Wallace, J. (1994). Residential treatment for the ADHD adolescent substance abuser. *Journal of Child and Adolescent Substance Abuse, 4*(1), 35-44.

American Academy of Child and Adolescent Psychiatry (AACAP) (1997). Practice parameters for the assessment and treatment of children and adolescents with substance use disorder. *Journal of the American Academy of Child and Adolescent Psychiatry, 36*(10 Supplement), 140s-156s.

American Psychiatric Association (APA) (1994). *Diagnostic and statistical manual of mental disorders, Fourth edition (DSM-IV)*. Washington, DC: American Psychiatric Association.

Arredondo, D. and Butler, S. (1994). Affective comorbidity in psychiatrically hospitalized adolescents with conduct disorder or oppositional defiant disorder: Should conduct disorder be treated with mood stabilizers? *Journal of Child and Adolescent Psychopharmacology, 4*(3), 151-158.

Azrin, N., Donohue, B., Besalel, V., Kogan, E., and Acierno, R. (1994). Youth drug abuse treatment: A controlled outcome study. *Journal of Child and Adolescent Substance Abuse, 3*(3), 1-16.

Bahr, S., Marcos, A., and Maughan, S. (1995). Family educational and peer influences on the alcohol use of female and male adolescents. *Journal of Studies on Alcohol, 56*(4), 457-469.

Belfer, M.L. (1993). Substance abuse with psychiatric illness in children and adolescents: Definitions and terminology. *American Journal of Orthopsychiatry, 63*(1), 70-79.

Biederman, J., Wilens, T.E., Mick, E., and Faraone, S. (1997). Is ADHD a risk for psychoactive substance abuse disorders? Findings from a 4-year prospective follow-up study. *Journal of the American Academy of Child and Adolescent Psychiatry, 36*(1), 21-29.

Biederman, J., Wilens, T., Mick, E., Faraone, S., and Spencer, T. (1998). Does attention-deficit hyperactivity disorder impact the developmental course of drug and alcohol abuse and dependence? *Biological Psychiatry, 44*(4), 269-273.

Biederman, J., Wilens, T., Mick, E., Spencer, T., and Faraone, S. (1999). Pharmacotherapy of attention-deficit/hyperactivity disorder reduces risk for substance use disorder. *Pediatrics, 104*(2), e20.

Brown, S., Gleghorn, A., Schuckit, M., Myers, M., and Mott, M. (1996). Conduct disorder among adolescent alcohol and drug abusers. *Journal of Studies on Alcohol, 57*(3), 314-324.

Bukstein, O.G., Brent, D.A., and Kaminer, Y. (1989). Comorbidity of substance abuse and other psychiatric disorders in adolescents. *American Journal of Psychiatry, 146*(9), 1131-1141.

Bukstein, O.G., Glancy, L.J., and Kaminer, Y. (1992). Patterns of affective comorbidity in a clinical population of dually diagnosed adolescent substance abusers. *Journal of the American Academy of Child and Adolescent Psychiatry, 31*(6), 1041-1045.

Calache, J., Martinez, R., Verhulst, S., Bourgeois, M., et al. (1994). Dysfunctional attitudes in depressed and non-depressed substance abusers: An exploratory study. *European Psychiatry, 9*(2), 77-82.

Clark, D. and Neighbors, B. (1996). Adolescent substance abuse and internalizing disorders. *Child and Adolescent Psychiatric Clinics of North America, 5*(1), 45-57.

Crowley, T., Mikulich, S., MacDonald, M., Young, S., and Zerbe, G. (1998). Substance dependent, conduct-disordered adolescent males: Severity of diagnosis predicts 2-year outcome. *Drug and Alcohol Dependence, 49*(3), 225-237.

Deas-Nesmith, D., Brady, K., and Campbell, S. (1998). Comorbid substance use and anxiety disorders in adolescents. *Journal of Psychopathology and Behavioral Assessment, 20*(2), 139-148.

DeMilio, L. (1989). Psychiatric syndromes in adolescent substance abusers. *American Journal of Psychiatry, 146*(9), 1212-1214.

Deykin, E. and Buka, S. (1997). Prevalence and risk factors for posttraumatic stress disorder among chemically dependent adolescents. *American Journal of Psychiatry, 154*(6), 752-757.

Dobkin, P., Chabot, L., Maliantovitch, K., and Craig, W. (1998). Predictors of outcome in drug treatment of adolescent inpatients. *Psychological Reports, 83*(1), 175-186.

Greenbaum, P., Prange, M., Friedman, R., and Silver, S. (1991). Substance abuse prevalence and comorbidity with other psychiatric disorders among adolescents with severe emotional disturbances. *Journal of the American Academy of Child and Adolescent Psychiatry, 30*(4), 575-583.

Gregorius, H.H. and Smith, T.S. (1991). The adolescent mentally ill chemical abuser: Special consideration in dual diagnosis. *Journal of Adolescent Chemical Dependency, 1*(4), 79-113.

Grilo, C., Becker, D., Fehon, D., Walker, M., Edell, W., and McGlasham, T. (1998). Psychiatric morbidity differences in male and female adolescent inpatients with alcohol use disorders. *Journal of Youth and Adolescence, 27*(1), 29-41.

Grilo, C., Becker, D., Walker, M., Levy, K., Edell, N., and McGlasham, T. (1995). Psychiatric comorbidity in adolescent inpatients with substance use disorders. *Journal of the American Academy of Child and Adolescent Psychiatry, 34*(8), 1085-1091.

Harrison, P., Fulkerson, J., and Beebe, T. (1998). DSM-IV substance use disorder criteria for adolescents: A critical examination based on a statewide school survey. *American Journal of Psychiatry, 155*(4), 486-492.

Horner, B. and Scheibe, K. (1997). Prevalence and implications of attention deficit hyperactivity disorder among adolescents in treatment for substance abuse. *Journal of the American Academy of Child and Adolescent Psychiatry, 36*(1), 30-36.

Hussey, D. and Singer, M. (1993). Psychological distress, problem behaviors, and family functioning of sexually abused adolescent inpatients. *Journal of the American Academy of Child and Adolescent Psychiatry, 32*(5), 954-961.

Kaminer, Y. (1992). Psychoactive substance abuse and dependence as a risk factor in adolescent-attempted and completed suicide: A review. *American Journal on Addictions, 1*(1), 21-29.

Kaminer, Y., Burleson, J., Blitz, C., Sussman, J., and Rounsaville, B. (1998). Psychotherapies for adolescent substance abusers: A pilot study. *Journal of Nervous and Mental Diseases, 186*(11), 684-690.

Kaminer, Y. and Frances, R. (1991). Inpatient treatment of adolescents with psychiatric and substance abuse disorders. *Hospital and Community Psychiatry, 42*(9), 894-896.

Kempton, T., Van Hasselt, V., Bukstein, O.G., and Null, J. (1994). Cognitive distortions and psychiatric diagnosis in dually diagnosed adolescents. *Journal of the American Academy of Child and Adolescent Psychiatry, 33*(2), 217-222.

Kennedy, B. and Minami, M. (1993). The Beech Hill Hospital/Outward Bound adolescent chemical dependency treatment program. *Journal of Substance Abuse Treatment, 10*(4), 395-406.

Kessler, R., Crum, R., Warner, L., Nelson, C., Schulenberg, J., and Anthony, J. (1997). Lifetime co-occurrence of DSM-III-R alcohol abuse and dependence with other psychiatric disorders in the National Comorbidity Survey. *Archives of General Psychiatry, 54*(4), 313-321.

Kessler, R., Nelson, C., McGonagle, K., Edlund, M., Frank, R., and Leaf, P. (1996). The epidemiology of co-occurring addictive and mental disorders: Implications for prevention and service utilization. *American Journal of Orthopsychiatry, 66*(1), 17-31.

Khantzian, E.J. (1985). The self-medication hypothesis of substance use disorders: A reconsideration and recent applications. *Harvard Review of Psychiatry, 4*(5), 231-244.

King, C., Ghaziuddin, N., McGovern, L., Brand, E., Hill, E., and Naylor, M. (1996). Predictors of comorbid alcohol and substance abuse in depressed adolescents. *Journal of the American Academy of Child and Adolescent Psychiatry, 35*(6), 743-751.

Lewinsohn, P., Rohde, P., and Seeley, J. (1995). Adolescent psychopathology: III. The clinical consequences of comorbidity. *Journal of the American Academy of Child and Adolescent Psychiatry, 34*(4), 510-519.

Malmquist, C. (1985). *Handbook of adolescence.* New York: Jason Aronson.

Mannuzza, S., Klein, R., Bessler, A., Malloy, P., and LaPadula, M. (1998). Adult psychiatric status of hyperactive boys grown up. *American Journal of Psychiatry, 155*(4), 493-498.

Milberger, S., Biederman, J., Faraone, S., Wilens, T., and Chu, M. (1997). Associations between ADHD and psychoactive substance use disorders: Findings from a longitudinal study of high-risk siblings of ADHD children. *American Journal on Addictions, 6*(4), 318-329.

Milin, R., Loh, E., Chow, J., and Wilson, A. (1997). Assessment of symptoms of attention deficit hyperactivity disorder in adults with substance use disorders. *Psychiatric Services, 48*(11), 1378-1380, 1395.

O'Donnell, D., Biederman, J., Jones, J., Wilens, T., Milberger, S., Mick, E., and Faraone, S. (1998). Informativeness of child and parent reports on substance use disorders in a sample of ADHD probands, control probands, and their siblings. *Journal of the American Academy of Child and Adolescent Psychiatry, 37*(8), 752-758.

Parrish, S. (1994). Adolescent substance abuse: The challenge for clinicians. *Alcohol, 11*(6), 453-455.

Penick, E.C., Nickel, E., Cantrell, P., Powell, B., Read, M., and Thomas, M. (1990). The emerging concept of dual diagnosis: An overview and implications. In D. O'Connell (Ed.), *Managing the dually diagnosed patient* (pp. 1-54). Binghamton, NY: The Haworth Press.

Rich, C., Sherman, M., and Fowler, R. (1990). San Diego suicide study: The adolescents. *Adolescence, 25*(100), 855-865.

Riggs, P.D. (1998). Clinical approach to treatment of ADHD in adolescents with substance use disorders and conduct disorder. *Journal of the American Academy of Child and Adolescent Psychiatry, 37*(3), 331-332.

Riggs, P., Baker, S., Mikulich, S., Young, S., and Crowley, T. (1995). Depression in substance-dependent delinquents. *Journal of the American Academy of Child and Adolescent Psychiatry, 34*(6), 764-771.

Rohde, P., Lewinsohn, P., and Seeley, J. (1996). Psychiatric comorbidity with problematic alcohol use in high school students. *Journal of the American Academy of Child and Adolescent Psychiatry, 35*(1), 101-109.

Rounds-Bryant, J., Kristiansen, P., Fairbank, J., and Hubbard, R. (1998). Substance use, mental disorders, abuse and crime: Gender comparisons among a national sample of adolescent drug treatment clients. *Journal of Child and Adolescent Substance Abuse, 7*(4), 19-34.

Schuckit, M. (1985). The clinical implications of primary diagnostic groups among alcoholics. *Archives of General Psychiatry, 42*(11), 1043-1049.

Segal, B. and Stewart, J. (1996). Substance use and abuse in adolescence: An overview. *Child Psychiatry and Human Development, 26*(4), 193-210.

Singer, M. and White, W. (1991). Addressing substance abuse problems among psychiatrically hospitalized adolescents. *Journal of Adolescent Chemical Dependency, 2*(1), 13-27.

Stein, M. and Davis, J. (1982). *Therapies for adolescents.* San Francisco, CA: Jossey-Bass, Inc.

Stowell, R.J. and Estroff, T.W. (1992). Psychiatric disorders in substance-abusing adolescent inpatients: A pilot study. *Journal of the American Academy of Child and Adolescent Psychiatry, 31*(6), 1036-1040.

Thompson, L., Riggs, P., Mikulich, S., and Crowley, T. (1996). Contribution of ADHD symptoms to substance problems and delinquency in conduct-disordered adolescents. *Journal of Abnormal Child Psychology, 24*(3), 325-347.

Weinberg, N., Rahdert, E., Collier, J., and Glantz, M. (1998). Adolescent substance abuse: A review of the past ten years. *Journal of the American Academy of Child and Adolescent Psychiatry, 37*(3), 252-261.

Whitmore, E., Mikulich, S., Thompson, L., Riggs, P., Aarons, G., and Crowley, T. (1997). Influences on adolescent substance dependence: Conduct disorder, depression, attention deficit hyperactivity disorder, and gender. *Drug and Alcohol Dependence, 47*(2), 87-97.

Wilens, T., Biederman, J., Abrantes, A., and Spencer, T. (1997). Clinical characteristics of psychiatrically referred adolescent outpatients with substance use disorder. *Journal of the American Academy of Child and Adolescent Psychiatry, 36*(7), 941-947.

Wilens, T., Biederman, J., and Mick, E. (1998). Does ADHD affect the course of substance abuse? Findings from a sample of adults with and without ADHD. *American Journal on Addictions, 7*(2), 156-163.

Wilens, T., Biederman, J., Mick, E., Faraone, S., and Spencer, T. (1997). Attention deficit hyperactivity disorder (ADHD) is associated with early onset substance abuse. *Journal of Nervous and Mental Disease, 185*(8), 475-482.

Wilens, T., Biederman, J., and Spencer, T. (1996). Attention deficit hyperactivity disorder and the psychoactive substance use disorders. *Child and Adolescent Clinics of North America, 5*(1), 73-91.

Wodarski, J. and Feit, M. (1997). Adolescent preventive health: A social and life group skills paradigm. *Family Therapy, 24*(3), 191-208.

Young, S., Mikulich, S., Goodwin, M., Hardy, J., Martin, C., Zoccolillo, M., and Crowley, T. (1995). Treated delinquent boys' substance use: Onset, pattern, relationship to conduct and mood disorders. *Drug and Alcohol Dependence, 37*(2), 149-162.

SECTION III:
ASSESSMENT AND TREATMENT
OF MAJOR MENTAL DISORDERS

Chapter 6

A Guide to the Assessment of Psychiatric Symptoms in the Addictions Treatment Setting

Barbara W. Reeve

INTRODUCTION: CURRENT SYMPTOMS AND BEHAVIORS AS A GUIDE TO ADDICTIONS TREATMENT PLANNING

Many clients in chemical dependency treatment programs are being found to have serious mental illnesses in addition to problems with drugs and/or alcohol (Balcerzak and Hoffmann, 1985). While existing treatment approaches for addictions in the absence of mental illness can claim relative success, the presence of psychiatric symptoms has been associated with poor treatment response and, no doubt, has limited the overall success rate of otherwise effective treatment programs (McLellan et al., 1983; Rounsaville et al., 1987). An understanding of psychiatric symptoms can help the addictions counselor

1. to form realistic treatment plans,
2. to make appropriate referrals to specialized treatment programs,
3. to identify the need for psychiatric consultation,
4. to know when to request psychological testing, and
5. to help the patient get the most from the available treatments.

A popular belief holds that it is necessary to determine which illness is considered to be the *primary* condition in order to appropriately treat the individual with both mental illness and substance abuse (Ewing, 1980; Powell et al., 1987). In the author's experience, the focus on this "chicken and egg" dilemma has more often *prevented* the individual from receiving appropriate treatment. Individuals are often shuttled back and forth between addictions programs and mental health programs without receiving adequate treatment for either problem. Certain conditions do need to be addressed before others may be accurately diagnosed or effectively treated. For example, most patients entering alcohol treatment centers meet the criteria for major depression and 80 percent of these resolve within two weeks without any specific treatment other than abstinence (Dakis et al., 1986). A diagnosis of major depression cannot be made within the first few weeks of treatment for alcoholism. Many of the depressive symptoms seen in drinking alcoholics are caused by the direct effects of alcohol; however, little is gained by speculating at the time of admission which came first. Whether the depression or the alcoholism occurred first, the initial treatment is the same: abstinence.

The essential purpose of *diagnosis* is to form the basis for *treatment* planning; the diagnosis provides a tool for determining the appropriate treatment(s). The diagnosis should be made with available data but should be considered tentative (working diagnosis) and be revised when additional data (history, clinical observations, treatment response) are available (Lieberman and Baker, 1985).

What follows is a "decision tree" to be used by addictions or mental health professionals in a variety of settings, including emergency rooms, outpatient treatment, and residential treatment programs. A "current symptom" focus will assist the evaluation of patients seeking, or currently in, treatment for chemical dependency and will provide a means of identifying special treatment needs and defining treatment priorities. Special attention will be given to situations in which psychiatric symptoms prevent the patient from making use of available treatments.

A DECISION TREE FOR ASSESSING PSYCHIATRIC SYMPTOMS IN THE CHEMICALLY DEPENDENT INDIVIDUAL

Assessing the Potential for Violence

The most alarming situations for any clinician are those in which the patients indicate, by words or actions, that they may be physically dangerous to themselves or others. These types of situations arise in almost any context: in emergency treatment centers where the patient may be seen following suicide attempts, during individual counseling where the client may confide thoughts of homicide or suicide, or in residential treatment centers where persons may express threats of violence. It is important for the clinician to keep in mind that any and all such expressions must be treated with the utmost seriousness. Suicidal, homicidal, or otherwise violent ideation is not a joking matter. Laws exist in each state that permit the practitioner to isolate individuals who are believed to be at risk of hurting themselves or others (Slovenko, 1985; Tancredi, Lieb, and Slaby, 1975). Usually, this involves certification to involuntary hospitalization by more than one professional (e.g., psychologist or physician) licensed to perform such a function. Addictions counselors should familiarize themselves with the local laws and with the mechanisms (such as the law enforcement agencies or emergency services) by which an individual believed to be dangerous may be detained or isolated.

Evaluation of Violent Expressions
in an Acutely Intoxicated Individual

In this, as in many of the situations to follow, an accurate mental status examination cannot be performed while the patient is intoxicated; however, a great deal of assessment *can* be done while the patient is intoxicated. If an actual act of violence has taken place (this includes any form of suicide attempt, such as overdose, or any assaultive behavior toward others), a secure holding environment is needed until the acute intoxication has passed and a more accurate mental status examination may be performed. If, however, such violent ideation is being verbalized but has not yet been acted upon, other indicators can be used to determine the potential risk (Patterson et al., 1983). In general, if any doubt exists on the part of the practitioner, a careful, complete, and rapid evaluation should be conducted by a professional capable of hospitalizing and/or medicating the patient. The following is a guide for gathering information to be used in such an evaluation:

Symptoms indicating poor reality testing or poor impulse control. Symptoms such as *command hallucinations* (these are often described as "voices telling me to kill myself") or *delusions* (e.g., a belief that a neighbor is a Nazi and must be annihilated) indicate that an acute psychotic process, such as PCP psychosis or schizophrenic illness, may be occurring, and most certainly are indicators that the individual is out of touch with reality. Regardless of the presumed cause of such symptoms, the temptation to dismiss them on the basis of recent drug or alcohol ingestion must be resisted. The expression of violent intent in the context of altered reality calls for a complete and rapid evaluation in a secure area. Most suicides occur while the individual is under the influence of drugs or alcohol (Fowler, Rich, and Young, 1986).

History of violence. A prior history of violence increases the risk of violent ideation being acted upon (Kreitman, 1986). Again, the temptation must be resisted to dismiss current suicidal or other violent ideation on the basis of prior similar events. "He always says things like this" is not sufficient reason to take such expressions lightly.

History of mental illness. A history of mental illness or treatment consistent with major depression or psychotic illness should be noted in an unbiased manner. An individual's actions must not be dismissed on the basis that "He's just crazy." On the other hand, keep in mind that a psychiatric diagnosis is not to be feared. Mental illnesses can result in unusual or upsetting behaviors but they *are* illnesses, which can be treated. In addition, consider all prior diagnoses as tentative until a new clinical evaluation with complete history and mental status examination confirms or establishes the diagnosis. An example of potential unhappy consequences comes from a case in a general hospital:

A psychiatric consultation was requested by the nursing staff on a surgical ward. The request was to "evaluate and medicate this sixty-seven-year-old schizophrenic woman who is incontinent following surgery to stabilize an arm with multiple fractures." The "diagnosis" was given in the consult request: schizophrenia. This diagnosis was considered tentative and a careful chart review and examination were completed. No history or symptoms of schizophrenia were found. What *was* found was an elderly woman with fluctuating levels of awareness, with an irritable temper, and without orientation for place or time. This lady was experiencing a postsurgical delirium as a result of sedatives received during and following surgery. (A more complete discussion of delirium will follow in the section called Assessing the Risk of Medical Danger.) The "diagnosis" of schizophrenia was given by the nursing student who was frustrated with the constant demands being made by this confusing patient and her symptoms. If the consultant had accepted the "diagnosis" of schizophrenia without conducting a complete evaluation, the sedatives may have been continued and the "schizophrenia" may have remained a problem.

This case illustrates the problems of using diagnostic labels to describe behavior. An accurate description of observable symptoms and behaviors and any known response of these symptoms to prior treatments (medications) is usually more helpful than a diagnostic label.

Secondary gain. Consider whether the patients have something to gain by expressing violent ideas. For example, do they need a place to spend the night and know that hospital admission often follows suicidal expressions? The issue of secondary gain is another that can lead the practitioner into taking violent expressions less seriously. Intoxication impairs judgment sufficiently to lead some manipulative patients to act on violent thoughts to "get back at" people who turn them away. Again, a cautious attitude is recommended.

Available support system. Are family or friends available to provide physical protection until a sober state is achieved and a more complete evaluation can be made? It is important to respect any fears that family members may express about their own safety. Limited resources for the referral of the potentially violent patient often result in "the system" pushing the patient onto the family for protection when the family may not be equipped to provide the necessary structure. Before releasing an individual into the care of family or friends, inquire about details of the environment. For example, are there any weapons? Will someone be available around the clock to transport the patient to emergency services if the situation should worsen?

Evaluation of Violence After a Detoxification or Sobering Up

It is possible that the violent ideation will subside and the patient will express regret or amnesia for these thoughts or gestures. In these cases, use firm confrontation, emphasizing (1) the need to prevent recurrence of this type of situation and (2) the patient's responsibility for his or her actions while under the influence. "I didn't mean it; I was just drunk" *is not* a sufficient response. One must wonder how many of the 8,000 suicides committed in this country each year by persons under the influence of psychoactive substances were "unintended" (Miles, 1977).

Evaluation of Violence in Nonintoxicated Individuals

The same principles apply to nonintoxicated people as in the evaluation of intoxicated individuals; however, a more accurate mental status examination can be conducted and the evaluation can take place with the full participation of the patient.

Symptoms indicating poor reality testing. As in the case of intoxicated individuals, the presence of symptoms that would indicate a loss of touch with reality or an inability to control one's actions must be considered. Hallucinations and delusions as mentioned previously are this type of indicator. Other symptoms of serious concern include the belief or experience of having thoughts inserted into one's mind (thought insertion). This can range from a delusional belief that "Martians have implanted a radio receiver in my head" to a sense or feeling that thoughts of suicide or death are intruding when unwanted and cannot be pushed aside. It is important to inquire openly about these symptoms; the avoidance of such material can add to the patient's perception that these thoughts themselves are powerful or controlling. A direct, matter-of-fact approach can elicit the needed information and, in some cases, can be reassuring to the patient.

Seriousness of intent. It is important to distinguish between general violent ideation and clear intent. Most individuals who find themselves in a treatment setting talking about such ideas *do* want help. Assume that they will talk about any plans or means which they may have to act on violent impulses; so ask about these. It is also important to have a frank discussion of the risks involved in attempting to block out such ideas by resuming drug or alcohol use. Remember, most suicide attempts take place while the individual is intoxicated.

History of violence. Obtaining a history of any prior violence is important. In the nonintoxicated individual, additional information may be obtained including the patient's feelings and reactions to prior episodes, any similarities to the current situational factors, any unpleasant consequences that may have resulted, or insights that were gained. These can be used to assess the individual's current ability to control his or her impulses.

T.W. is a twenty-six-year-old man with a ten-year history of alcohol and sedative abuse. He has had five hospital admissions for suicide attempts in the past. All of these hospitalizations were brief, and he has never taken medication for depression. T.W. has been attending a weekly outpatient alcohol treatment group for the past year in addition to attending Alcoholics Anonymous (AA) several times per week. He is proud of the nine months of sobriety he has achieved.

T.W. just learned that he is being laid off from his job because of "general cutbacks." His employer was careful to explain that his work record for the past six months was good, but he had the least seniority and he had to be let go. T.W. reported to his group that he feels worthless and that "it is useless to work so hard to do good." He said life is "too hard" and he "may as well be dead." The group leader, recalling T.W.'s history of suicide attempts, responded promptly:

LEADER: T., I see you are really discouraged by all this, but do you think you really want to die?

T.W.: I don't know. It all seems so hopeless.

LEADER: Have you thought about what you would do if you decided you really did want to give up?

T.W.: Oh, I don't have to think about it; I've done it plenty of times. First, I would buy a bottle.

LEADER: A bottle?

T.W.: Yeah, when I felt like this before, I would get drunk, then somehow I would find a way to overdose.

LEADER: Then what?

T.W.: Well, I guess the next thing I'd know, I would be in some emergency room having my stomach emptied.

The group joined in and gave T.W. their views of his situation. Some members agreed he had a right to feel down; some shared that they had had similar experiences. None thought it was a good idea for T.W. to take his life over this.

During the session, T.W. realized that he did not want to die; he also realized that he *did* want to take a drink. With the support of the group, T.W. decided to attend two AA meetings daily and to make an appointment with the clinic doctor to request Antabuse. He also made an agreement with the group that if he felt like he could not resist the urge to drink, he would call someone in AA or the twenty-four-hour emergency hotline. T.W. had identified a key factor (alcohol) in his feelings-thoughts-actions cycle. He had learned that, for him, discouraged feelings can lead to suicidal thoughts and that he can prevent these thoughts from being translated into action by removing the alcohol "link."

This case provides an example of how an expanded history of prior violence can (1) help the clinician to assess risk and (2) lead the patient into more self-awareness.

History of mental illness. In addition to eliciting a history of prior violent events, it is important to obtain a good history of prior treatment for major illnesses, which may indicate the need for medication. Suicide has been associated with a number of major mental illnesses including major depression, bipolar disorder (manic-depression), and schizophrenia. If a client mentions medications that are unfamiliar, record the names of these as accurately as possible but, more important, record a description of the symptoms the medications were intended to help. The patient's assessment of how helpful these medications were, as well as any adverse effects experienced, is valuable information. This can be passed on to another professional who is knowledgeable about medications and illnesses and can be useful in arriving at a decision about the current need for medication.

Situational factors. Life situation is important to consider when assessing the potential for violence. The individual may need help in identifying recent events that may have contributed to current thoughts and feelings. For example, it may have "slipped" his "mind" that an old friend walked past him on the street without speaking, or he may consider it unimportant that his mother locked him out of the house last night because he came home late. If the patient is agreeable to a dialogue, spend some time attempting to identify precipitating events and to help the patient to identify solutions to the situation other than violence. As in the case of the intoxicated individual, a supportive family can provide needed structure and protection until the crisis passes. Other community supports include friends, AA, Narcotics Anonymous (NA), or other self-help groups. However, bear in mind that mere attendance at groups may not provide sufficient support. Some individuals attend many meetings but obtain a minimal amount of support because of little interpersonal interaction.

Treatment context. Treatment context is another life situation that deserves separate attention. Every residential rehabilitation, detox, or group home program has rules of conduct, which can be used as a guide to determine appropriate action in any individual case. For example, some programs consider verbal threats of violence toward another individual so disruptive that the consequences are the same as actual physical violence: discharge. The underlying message is, "If you cannot control your verbal expressions, then we cannot trust you to control your actions." Of course, this is clearly explained in the orientation to the program and written in the rules.

Review with the patients the details of their "contract" and make certain they clearly understand the potential consequences of their actions. Helping the individuals to see the potential consequences of their actions may be especially useful in the context of individual or group counseling. In the case of T.W., he was able to recall the unpleasant consequences of prior suicide attempts ("woke up in the emergency room") and to resolve to avoid repeating these (or less reversible) consequences. An effort can be made to determine what the patients are "really saying," and to help them gain a broader perspective on the situation, but if the patients are unable to understand these connections and, as a consequence, to control their actions, the need for external controls continues.

Assessing the Risk of Medical Danger

In the patient with major mental illness and alcohol or drug abuse, the signs and symptoms of intoxication, overdose, or withdrawal can be difficult to evaluate. *Delirium* is an alteration of mental functioning resulting from injury or metabolic insult to the central nervous system. Delirium can result from drug overdose, drug or alcohol withdrawal, head trauma, or infections such as HIV encephalitis. Delirium tremens (alcohol withdrawal) is a serious medical illness and, untreated, may result in death (Behnke, 1976). It is important to distinguish between life-threatening syndromes (such as delirium tremens or drug overdose) and simple intoxication. The practitioner must know when to make rapid referral to medical emergency services and to gather any important information that may be useful in medical assessment.

Signs and Symptoms of Delirium

Elevated pulse rate, blood pressure, temperature (vital signs), or profuse sweating. Although intoxication with some stimulants may cause some rapid pulse and elevated blood pressure, the above symptoms in conjunction with a history of recent abstinence generally indicate the autonomic nervous system hyperactivity found in alcohol or sedative withdrawal (Leroy, 1979). These are often seen in conjunction with confusion and hallucinations in the full delirium tremens syndrome. However, the absence of confusion or hallucinations should not delay immediate medical attention. Remember, total abstinence is not required for withdrawal; individuals may reduce their alcohol intake significantly but continue to drink and experience withdrawal. Elevated vital signs may be the only way to distinguish a withdrawal delirium from intoxication or functional psychosis.

Disorientation. Confusion or disorientation regarding time, place, or person is an indicator of serious metabolic, traumatic, or other injury to the central nervous system such as acute intoxication, withdrawal, or head trauma. Functional mental illness without physical origins (e.g., schizophrenia) seldom results in the inability to orient oneself; however, symptoms such as hallucinations or delusions may interfere with the examiner's ability to obtain an accurate assessment of orientation. Another potentially misleading feature of delirium is that it involves a *fluctuating course*. In delirium it is possible to be oriented and coherent at one time and disoriented a short time later. The less experienced practitioner often misconstrues this mixed picture to indicate a volitional component on the part of the patient and therefore does not treat this symptom with the seriousness it deserves. Disorientation or changing mental status, regardless of metabolic signs, always needs medical assessment.

Alterations in perception. Perceptual distortions, illusions, and hallucinations are associated with acute intoxication with hallucinogens (PCP, LSD, marijuana), cocaine, amphetamine, and occasionally alcohol; they are also found in withdrawal delirium. Drug or alcohol intoxication or withdrawal can occur in individuals with serious mental illnesses; these illnesses can also have hallucinations as symptoms. In general, visual or tactile (involving the sense of touch) hallucinations are rarely found in functional mental illness; rather, these types of hallucinations are considered indicators of an organic involvement such as delirium or intoxication. The visual hallucinations of delirium tremens often are rather simple in nature and rarely elicit an emotional response. On the other hand, hallucinations accompanied by elaborate delusional ideation are more often found in functional illnesses. (See the section on Hallucinations.)

Tremors and physical agitation. These classic signs of early delirium tremens can be evident in a number of other illnesses. In general, early withdrawal from any addictive substance may result in tremor, agitation, and/or sleeplessness. These symptoms may accompany intoxication with stimulants or functional psychiatric illnesses such as bipolar disorder, attention deficit disorder, or anxiety disorders. Again, careful assessment of other symptoms is needed to determine the need for medical intervention.

History of Recent Events

In assessing the potential for medical danger due to overdose, withdrawal, or head trauma, a complete history of recent events is of key importance. In many cases a great deal of detail may not be available; however, any information regarding recent activities may be helpful to the clinician in making an evaluation. Family, friends, or acquaintances may be able to provide useful information about drug, alcohol, or medication ingestion, including time of last drink. Keep in mind that some over-the-counter preparations taken in excess or in combination with alcohol can result in metabolic disturbance (Gardner and Hall, 1982). Record any information that may indicate recent head trauma (e.g., "found at roadside unconscious"). Past history of delirium tremens is important to know, but it does not confirm the diagnosis; a complete medical evaluation is needed. In a similar manner, a history of serious mental illness may be helpful to know but, as mentioned, does not explain confusion or metabolic signs if they are present.

Assessing Symptoms That May Interfere with the Patients' Ability to Participate in Treatment for Addictions

Situations often arise in the treatment of drug or alcohol abuse in which the patient does not seem to be benefiting from the treatment being offered. Lack of progress is often considered an indicator that "the client is not ready for change" or "has not reached bottom." Lack of sufficient motivation to enter into and follow through with treatment is certainly the most common reason for lack of progress in treatment among substance abusers without other mental illness. However, serious mental illness introduces a number of additional factors that may impact on the individuals' suitability for a given type of treatment and their ability to make use of available treatments. In addition, the effects of long-term substance abuse (especially alcohol) result in impaired cognition including difficulty in learning and organizing new facts in ways that can be applied to life situations.

Isolation, Withdrawal, or Difficulty Relating to Others

These symptoms, in the extreme, can keep an individual homebound. Withdrawal from interpersonal interactions can have at its basis many factors including paranoia, anxiety, depression, or personality traits. Conditions that can be involved include paranoid disorder, schizophrenia, bipolar disorder, social phobia, agoraphobia, major depression, post-traumatic stress disorder, and personality disorder. If an individual has engaged in some form of treatment and is observed to become withdrawn during its course, this is unlikely to be due to a personality disorder or paranoid disorder. The symptoms of these conditions are stable and relatively unchanging (Hoffmann,

1971; Hoy, 1969). In the case of an observed change in behavior, it is important to inquire about reasons rather than to assume "avoidance" or "denial."

In the case of depression, the patients may only be able to describe low energy, disinterest, or hopelessness; they may even refer to themselves as "lazy" for lack of a better explanation. Inquire about the specific symptoms of depression including change in sleep or appetite, tearfulness, irritability, hopelessness, worthlessness, ruminations on themes of death, or suicidal ideation. Some of these symptoms are common during withdrawal from chemicals and the early recovery process; however, if they persist past two or three weeks or if they develop during the course of active treatment for addictions, they should be more fully evaluated. Eighty percent of patients who enter alcoholism treatment with symptoms of depression improve within two weeks. Conversely, 20 percent have depressive symptoms that do not spontaneously resolve and, therefore, may have major depressions in need of treatment with medication.

Isolation or withdrawal may also occur during an active psychotic illness. Usually, other symptoms will be present, which will indicate the need for psychiatric evaluation; however, this is not always the case. For cases in which delusions and/or hallucinations lead to social withdrawal, direct inquiry may yield an explanation. For example, if a paranoid schizophrenic has begun isolating himself because he fears his family is trying to poison him, he may reveal this to his counselor, depending on whether the counselor has been included in the delusional thinking. He may remark, "If I tell you what is going on, you will tell my parents." It is important to be direct with the patients about the way their behavior (e.g., withdrawal) is interfering with their treatment and to try to have them explore this with you. Individuals with impaired reality testing may be surprisingly frank when asked about their symptoms and may provide the counselor with sufficient information to allow for appropriate referral.

Social isolation associated with anxiety specific to going into public places is a characteristic of social phobia, when scrutiny by others is feared, or agoraphobia, when impeded escape is feared. Posttraumatic stress disorder is another condition that may lead to social isolation. Individuals may avoid situations that remind them of the traumatic event. Emotional blunting, increased startle response, flashbacks, and/or bad dreams are characteristic of this condition. Usually individuals with these conditions are genuinely distressed by their symptoms and are willing to be referred for specialized help. On the other hand, some anxiety about participating in the treatment process is almost universal. Every individual feels some anxiety about talking in groups until these skills are repeatedly practiced.

In the case of individuals who have not yet engaged in the active treatment process, evaluation of the symptom of isolation or withdrawal is not so straightforward. An example would be a man who was detoxified after a motor vehicle accident and transferred to a residential treatment facility for the first time. Again the approach needs to be direct: ask for an explanation. If a direct inquiry does not provide an adequate explanation, a thought disorder may be present but remaining undetected. Psychological testing may be useful in uncovering serious pathology about which the patient is unable or unwilling to talk. If psychological testing is unavailable or if no thought disorder is found, assume the patient is not aware of the problem his behavior causes to others and to his recovery process. He should be given an opportunity to correct his behavior. Explain the nature of the therapeutic/recovery process as one that necessitates interaction with others. If he is unable to correct his behavior with education, support, and limits, look at this behavior in the context of the whole individual: Does he show the ability to interact appropriately? Are his interactions provocative? Does he have a history of poor relationships? If his patterns of interactions have been unsatisfactory in the past, a personality disorder is likely. The methods of presenting clear, consistent limits with carefully defined consequences are well known to addictions counselors. These methods provide the individual with character pathology, the structure necessary to tolerate the formation of positive relationships in the therapeutic environment (Zarcone, 1978).

Extremes of Mood, Mood Swings, Labile Mood

Depression, irritability, and sleeplessness are common among drinking alcoholics and barbiturate users and are often a part of the "crash" following cocaine use (Gawin and Kleber, 1986). The patient who first presents for treatment while actively using drugs or alcohol and depressed should be advised to undergo detox first. Accurate assessment of mood symptoms cannot be made while the individual is still using substances. (Violent or suicidal ideation should be handled in the manner outlined in the previous sections.)

When depression and related symptoms occur during the early addiction recovery process, the patient is usually guided through this phase by reassurance about the time-limited nature of these symptoms and by the support of others in recovery who have had similar symptoms and found them to decrease in frequency and intensity as the length of abstinence increases. Most severe symptoms of mood disturbance pass after about two weeks of abstinence, but many milder symptoms may persist for several weeks or months. For patients with major depression, sleeplessness, sadness, low energy, lack of interest in activities, or poor attention span may continue for several weeks to the extent that they interfere with daily activities, such as the ability to go to meetings or to work, or the ability to read or concentrate on an interesting television program. In these cases, a referral should be considered for a psychiatric evaluation to assess the usefulness of medication in controlling these symptoms. Other factors that would suggest the likelihood of major depression are a history of severe depression prior to drug or alcohol use, a history of significantly improved symptoms with prior treatment with antidepressants, or the presence of depression or manic-depressive illness in a close relative.

Increased physical activity, impulsiveness, euphoria, and rapid thoughts are all symptoms of cocaine or amphetamine abuse. However, mood swings or the emergence of an extremely irritable or euphoric mood with prolonged abstinence may be due to mental illness requiring medication. The symptoms of attention-deficit disorder (ADD, a childhood disorder that can persist into adulthood) and of bipolar disorder may resemble stimulant intoxication (Cocores et al., 1987). As with depression, if these symptoms persist or worsen after several weeks of abstinence and interfere with normal functioning, a psychiatric evaluation should be conducted to determine the usefulness of medication. A history of similar symptoms prior to any drug or alcohol use or a positive family history will be helpful in the evaluation.

Finally, a brief mention will be made regarding *labile affect*. Mood swings are common in early recovery; however, labile affect is a particular kind of mood swing in which, quite rapidly and often for no apparent reason, the mood may switch from elation to tearfulness or from euthymia (normal mood) to irritability. Several moods may be observed during a single conversation and often the patients are not aware of their own inconsistency. This labile mood is most often associated with an organic disturbance such as intoxication; when it persists beyond detoxification, other organic etiologies should be considered. In these cases, the labile mood is often accompanied by deficits in cognition and may be the result of permanent neurologic damage. A full discussion of these conditions is found in the following sections.

Hallucinations

Disordered perception has been discussed in the previous sections about violence and delirium. This discussion will help to put this symptom into a broader perspective. As noted previously, disordered perception may occur with auditory, visual, or tactile senses. The conditions in which hallucinations are found are numerous; they include intoxication, withdrawal delirium, delirium of other etiologies, schizophrenia, bipolar illness, and major depression. Visual and tactile hallucinations are most often indicators of an organic process (e.g., the snakes on the wall or the bugs on the skin as often reported in delirium tremens). Auditory hallucinations are more often associated with functional (i.e., psychiatric without clear organic origin) illness. One exception to this is the frequently reported experience of persons in withdrawal or early recovery to believe they have heard their named called. In fact, this is such a common and relatively unalarming symptom that even the reader may recall such experiences, especially when tired or distracted.

The best way to find out about hallucinations is to ask. If individuals are having difficulty concentrating on educational material presented as part of their treatment, or if they are having difficulty joining in with the activities, or if they seem easily distracted from conversation by nothing in particular, or if they have difficulty expressing their thoughts in a coherent, goal-directed manner, ask if thoughts or other experiences are making it difficult to concentrate. The interviewer may suggest that some people who have trouble concentrating are hearing voices inside or outside their head or are seeing distracting things around them. In these cases, as in the case of unexplained isolation or social withdrawal, psychological testing may be useful in identifying disturbance in thought or perception, which is difficult for the patient to report directly. Any report of hallucinations should be referred for more complete evaluation. Again, it is helpful to find out if there is a history of similar experiences. If there has been prior treatment, ask what medications were used and if they helped. In addition, inquire about other family members who may have similar symptoms and any known diagnosed illnesses and/or treatments.

Delusions

To the student of psychopathology, delusions are the most bizarre and fascinating symptoms of altered mental status. As with many of the symptoms previously discussed here, delusions may stem from a number of conditions. Delusions may occur in any condition that has altered reality testing: schizophrenia, bipolar illness, major depression, paranoid disorder, toxic psychosis (cocaine, PCP, LSD), delirium, or dementia. In general, delusions are beliefs held by an individual that are inconsistent with external reality. Delusions may be quite organized and elaborate, such as "The neighbors are beaming X rays into the house and any attempt to block these rays results in feedback to the neighbors and they increase the intensity of the rays." Delusions may be disconnected beliefs about being "bad" or that the police are watching, or that "My brain is melting."

Some delusions, referred to as secondary delusions, are developed to "explain" perceptual distortions (hallucinations) resulting from a delirium. An example would be the belief that "The little man behind the door is spying on me," developed in response to a visual hallucination induced by medication overdose. In secondary delusions, the patient is usually willing to listen to reason. Such is not the case with most other types of delusions. Do not waste your time trying to talk patients out of a delusional belief (Wallen and Weiner, 1988); at the same time, do not allow them to think you share their belief. When delusional material emerges during the course of treatment, encourage discussion only as far as necessary to determine the degree of organization of the belief system. In addition, try to determine how long the delusion has been active and any other accompanying symptoms or experiences (e.g., "I know there is a radio receiver in my head because I hear the voices").

Ideas of reference are another type of delusion. In this case, usual environmental cues are misinterpreted in a personal way. For example, a man sees a group of people talking and assumes that they are talking about him. In general, ideas of reference are less firmly held and interfere less with normal functioning. They may or may not be associated with psychiatric conditions. As with the previously discussed symptoms, if this is noted to cause distress or to interfere with routine life, a more complete evaluation is indicated.

Poor Memory, Limited Attention Span, Poor Concentration

Some symptoms that may interfere with attention or concentration have been mentioned, including the hallucinations of a psychotic process or the distractibility of attention-deficit disorder (ADD). More often, these types of problems are indicators of cognitive impairment resulting from neurologic damage (dementia). The most common cause of neurologic impairment found in addiction is alcoholic dementia. Keep in mind that many other things can lead to dementia including Alzheimer's disease, stroke, small strokes (multi-infarct), vitamin deficiency, HIV infection, or head trauma.

A full assessment of cognitive functioning is needed to determine the usefulness of various forms of treatment (Becker et al., 1986). For example, a treatment that relies heavily on an educational approach in which the patient is expected to learn new material quickly would be unsuccessful for someone with impaired memory, or an approach that relies on teaching problem-solving skills would have limited benefit for an individual with impaired abstract thinking ability. Neuropsychologic testing can determine which of the various cognitive functions are impaired, including immediate, recent, and long-term memory; ability to abstract; judgment; visual-spatial coordination; and expressive and receptive language. If specific deficits are identified in an otherwise motivated patient, treatment approaches can be developed to compensate for that deficit (Ryan and Butters, 1986; Tarter and Edwards, 1987). Consideration may be given regarding mental retardation in individuals who do not seem to have the intellectual capacity to process information effectively. Again, psychological testing is helpful in assessment and treatment planning.

OTHER FACTORS TO CONSIDER IN ASSESSING THE MENTALLY ILL SUBSTANCE ABUSER

The previous section provides a framework by which to evaluate psychiatric symptoms as they appear in the context of substance abuse evaluation and treatment. A number of other factors may influence that assessment process including the background or attitudes of the evaluator, the context of the assessment, the treatment options available, and the availability of other assessment instruments.

Background or Attitudes of the Evaluator

Each of us brings to our clinical work personal attitudes, knowledge, and feelings. These generally have a positive influence on the clinical outcome; however, sometimes personal attitudes, known as *countertransference,* may cloud the clinical picture or impede the progress of treatment. Effective professional training provides the practitioner with the valuable skill of identifying personal feelings as they develop in response to a patient. Some guidelines are offered here addressing the special countertransference issues that arise when working with mentally ill substance abusers.

When in Doubt, Obtain a Consultation

If clinical symptoms or issues do not seem to add up, if the therapeutic process seems stalemated, or if the clinician has strong negative or positive feelings toward the client, much can be gained by obtaining a second opinion. The best of clinicians have some "blind spots" or occasionally try to fit a type of treatment to a patient who is not ready to receive it or capable of benefiting from it. The results can be frustrating for the therapist or counselor. Another view of the situation can illuminate issues or factors that may have been overlooked, or provide confirmation for the appropriateness of the current treatment. In almost any situation, a second opinion will provide information that will lead to more effective and less frustrating interactions with the client.

The Patient Is Responsible for Compliance with Treatment

Occasionally, a mentally ill substance abuser will attempt to elicit a permissive attitude from the counselor by highlighting his or her unhappy condition of mental illness. "He's sick; he can't help himself," would be a statement representative of this attitude. An analogy may be drawn between the conditions of mental illness and that of chemical dependency. Each of these conditions can be considered a treatable disease; each involves features that temporarily render confrontation techniques ineffective (e.g., intoxication in alcoholism and psychotic symptoms in schizophrenia); each may involve denial; and in each the ultimate responsibility for obtaining and complying with treatment lies with the individual. In mental illness, as with chemical dependency, after a careful assessment has been done, effective treatment established (often done during psychiatric hospitalization), and basic education about the illness and about the recommended treatment provided, the patient can be considered to have the elements necessary to control his or her symptoms. Approaches similar to those employed in alcohol and drug counseling can be effective with mentally ill substance abusers in helping them to move past their denial to a more responsible attitude toward their mental illness.

One sixty-two-year-old woman had been diagnosed as having major depression, which responded well to antidepressant medication. She also had a history of alcoholism for many years. During residential rehabilitation for a drinking relapse following eighteen months of sobriety, she reported that she drank because she was depressed. Her counselor inquired about the sequence of events leading to relapse and found she had stopped taking her antidepressant medications two months prior to the return of symptoms of depression. She had then stopped attending AA, had become increasingly withdrawn and hopeless, and had begun to drink in an effort to "kill myself with booze." On further examination of the events surrounding discontinuation of medication, the patient admitted that she had begun to feel neglected by her family and thought that she could gain more of their attention if she was no longer "doing so well." Appropriate confrontation led the patient to see that she has as much responsibility to control her symptoms of depression by proper use of medication as she has to control her alcoholism through abstinence.

Situational Factors

The influence of situational factors (such as availability of various types of treatment programs, financial constraints, and resource limitations within treatment programs) on clinical findings and recommendations has not been well studied. However, these influences are inevitable. How often have we thought, "What he really needs is . . . a long-term residential program . . . or an opiate detox on a psychiatric unit . . . or a supportive family"? We learn to "make do" with limited resources and services without question. However, it is the dually diagnosed individuals who seldom have sufficient social and emotional reserves to apply this "make do" attitude. These are the individuals who lack the social skills needed to make themselves feel comfortable in an AA meeting, who find themselves scapegoated in residential settings ("I may be a drunk, but at least I'm not crazy like him"), and in some cases, lack the intellectual capacity to make use of the usual educational and confrontational techniques used extensively in the treatment of addictions. Those of us who accept the challenge of developing treatment approaches with the dually diagnosed need to resist the "make do" attitude that has failed these complicated cases. Some questions to keep in mind when assessing dual diagnosis clients and their treatment needs may help to resist the "make do" attitude and its limiting influence on our thinking:

What would happen with no intervention? "Some treatment is better than no treatment" is not always the case. When determining if the individual is in need of a therapeutic intervention or when assessing the effectiveness of a current treatment, this question may help to clarify the issues.

Is enough known to make a decision/diagnosis? We never seem to have enough information in the form of psychiatric or substance use history, clinical mental status examination, psychological testing, and knowledge of social and family factors to be certain that our assessment and treatment approach are accurate. The assessment process needs to be ongoing, treatment response reviewed periodically, and treatment approach revised as needed.

What are the treatment goals? To assess the effectiveness of treatment, we need to have a clear idea of what outcome is expected. Is abstinence a sufficient goal? Is employment? Is probation compliance? When working with clients in a residential program, we are aware of the need to assist them in the development of the skills necessary to maintain sobriety prior to discharge from a protected environment. When working with dually diagnosed patients, we may want to consider what skills or emotional factors are lacking (e.g., difficulty relating to others or poor verbal skills) and make the acquisition of these factors an initial goal of treatment.

Can existing treatments be modified to meet the special treatment needs of the patient without disruption to the treatment program or the counselor? In our zealous efforts to include mentally ill substance abusers in treatment programs, we need to be cautious about disrupting the integrity of these programs or overextending resources. Some elements may be relatively simple to add to existing programs, such as adding a psychologist consultant to assess distracting intrapsychic symptoms, social skills, or cognitive functioning and to participate in treatment planning; adding a psychiatrist consultant to assess patients for the usefulness of psychotropic medications and to monitor these; or adding an educational group to teach the hazards of alcohol, drug, and medication combinations. Other modifications, such as maintaining supervision of acting out psychotic patients or suicidal patients, would require significant changes in staffing patterns or specialized training for staff.

In the end we will serve our clients and society by assessing as objectively as possible the symptoms and behaviors indicating the special treatment needs of clients and in assessing the realistic ability of the existing treatment programs to meet these needs. As we learn to see patients and their needs without the "blinders" of limited resources, we will be better equipped to garner resources to meet these needs.

CONCLUSION

This chapter provides the clinician in addictions referral and addictions treatment settings with some practical guidelines for the assessment of psychiatric and behavioral symptoms as they may influence treatment planning and treatment response. A "current symptom" focus is advocated with the belief that, in most cases, a hierarchy of treatment needs can be determined from the presenting clinical picture. Also emphasized is the need for periodic reassessment of symptoms and of treatment response to determine emerging problems or resolving issues.

REFERENCES

Balcerzak, W.S. and Hoffmann, N.G. (1985). Dual treatment rationale for psychologically disordered and chemically dependent clients. *Alcoholism Treatment Quarterly, 2,* 61-67.

Becker, J.T., Butters, N., Rivoira, P., and Miliotis, P. (1986). Asking the right questions: Problem solving in male alcoholics and male alcoholics with Korsakoff's syndrome. *Alcoholism: Clinical and Experimental Research, 10,* 641-646.

Behnke, R.H. (1976). Recognition and management of alcohol withdrawal syndrome. *Hospital Practice,* NOV, 79-84.

Cocores, J.A., Patel, M.D., Gold, M.S., and Pottash, A.C. (1987). Cocaine abuse, attention deficit disorder, and bipolar disorder. *Journal of Nervous and Mental Diseases, 175,* 431-432.

Dakis, C.A., Gold, M.S., Pottash, A.L.C., and Sweeney, D.R. (1986). Evaluating depression in alcoholics. *Psychiatry Research, 17,* 105-109.

Ewing, J.A. (1980). Editorial: Alcoholism—Another biopsychosocial disease. *Psychosomatics, 21,* 371-372.

Fowler, R.C., Rich, C.L., and Young, D. (1986). San Diego suicide study: II. Substance abuse in young cases. *Archives of General Psychiatry, 43,* 962-965.

Gardner, E.R. and Hall, R.C.W. (1982). Psychiatric symptoms produced by over-the-counter drugs. *Psychosomatics, 23,* 186-190.

Gawin, F.H. and Kleber, H.D. (1986). Abstinence symptomatology and psychiatric diagnosis in cocaine abusers. Clinical observations. *Archives of General Psychiatry, 43,* 107-113.

Hoffmann, H. (1971). Personality changes of hospitalized alcoholics after treatment. *Physiological Reports, 29,* 948-950.

Hoy, R.M. (1969). The personality of inpatient alcoholics in relation to group psychotherapy, as measured by the 16-P.F. *Quarterly Journal of Studies in Alcoholism, 30,* 401-407.

Kreitman, N. (1986). The critical assessment and management of the suicidal patient. In A. Roy (Ed.), *Suicide* (pp. 181-195). Baltimore, MD: Williams and Wilkins.

Leroy, J.B. (1979). Recognition and treatment of the alcohol withdrawal syndrome. *Primary Care, 6,* 529-539.

Lieberman, P.B. and Baker, F.M. (1985). The reliability of psychiatric diagnosis in the emergency room. *Hospital and Community Psychiatry, 36,* 291-293.

McLellan, A.T., Luborsky, L., Woody, G.E., O'Brien, C.P., and Druley, K.A. (1983). Predicting response to alcohol and drug abuse treatments: Role of psychiatric severity. *Archives of General Psychiatry, 40,* 620-625.

Miles, C.P. (1977). Conditions predisposing to suicide: A review. *Journal of Nervous and Mental Disease, 164,* 231-246.

Patterson, W.M., Dohn, H.H., Bird, J., and Patterson, G.A. (1983). Evaluation of suicidal patients: The SAD PERSONS scale. *Psychosomatics, 24,* 343-349.

Powell, B.J., Read, M.R., Penick, E.C., Miller, N.S., and Bingham, S.F. (1987). Primary and secondary depression in alcoholic men: An important distinction? *Journal of Clinical Psychiatry, 48,* 98-101.

Rounsaville, B.J., Dolinsky, Z.S., Babor, T.F., and Meyer, R.E. (1987). Psychopathology as a predictor of treatment outcome in alcoholics. *Archives of General Psychiatry, 44,* 505-513.

Ryan, C. and Butters, N. (1986). The neuropsychology of alcoholism. In D. Wedding, A.M. Horton, and J. Webster (Eds.), *The Neuropsychology Handbook:Behavioral and Clinical Perspectives* (pp. 376-409). New York: Springer.

Slovenko, R. (1985). Law and psychiatry. In H.I. Kaplan and B. J. Sadock (Eds.), *Modern Synopsis of Comprehensive Textbook of Psychiatry/IV* (pp. 1960-1990). Baltimore: Williams and Wilkins.

Tancredi, L.R., Lieb, J., and Slaby, A.E. (Eds.) (1975). *Legal Issues in Psychiatric Care.* Hagerstown, MD: Harper And Row, Medical Dept.

Tarter, P.E. and Edwards, M.L. (1987). Brief and comprehensive neurological assessment of alcohol and substance abuse. In L.C. Hartlage, M.J. Asken, and J.L. Hornsby (Eds.), *Essentials of Neuropsychological Assessment* (pp. 138-162). New York: Springer.

Wallen, M. and Weiner, H. (1988). Guidelines for individual counseling with dually diagnosed patients. Presented at "The Mentally Ill Substance Abusing Person: Yours, Mine, or Ours?" The Medical College of Pennsylvania, May 19 and 20, Philadelphia, PA.

Zarcone, V.P. Jr. (1978). Residential treatment for drug dependence. In R.J. Craig and S.L. Baker (Eds.), *Drug Dependent Patients: Treatment and Research* (pp. 67-89). Springfield, IL: Charles C Thomas.

Chapter 7

Affective Disorders and Affective Symptoms in Alcoholism

A. Majid Malik
Richard L. Weddige
Razia T. Malik

ALCOHOLISM: MORE OFTEN THE CAUSE OR THE RESULT OF DEPRESSION?

The past fifteen years have seen increasing clinical interest in the effective management of patients who are comorbid for alcoholism and other major psychiatric disorders. In the case of individuals with schizophrenia or with antisocial personality disorders who are also comorbid for alcoholism, it has often been more efficacious to focus on the nonalcohol-related diagnosis first. For example, many young adults with antisocial personality disorder engage in drunkenness by decision; once mature enough to control their impulsive behavior, they are able to resume social drinking. Similarly, once their psychosis and their living arrangements are controlled, many people with schizophrenia cease uncontrolled drinking.

This situation is quite different for depressive disorders. Among clinicians there is a widespread belief that alcohol abuse and depressive disorder occur together, principally because depressed patients self-medicate with alcohol to relieve their depression. This belief is supported by the assertion of many alcoholics who explain their abuse on the basis of preexisting depression, and such assertions make good intuitive sense to their clinicians. The empirical clinical evidence, however, militates against the likelihood that self-medica-

The authors thank Covenant Medical Center in Lubbock, Texas, for providing them with research material for this chapter.

213

tion can fully explain the association between alcohol abuse and clinical depression.

Prospective studies are gradually teaching clinicians the astonishing fact that most of the psychopathology seen in alcoholics is the *result,* not the cause, of alcohol abuse. Originally, three premorbid personality types were repeatedly postulated to play an etiological role in alcoholism: the emotionally insecure, anxious, and dependent personality; the depressed personality; and the sociopathic and/or the minimally brain-damaged personality. Not until several prospective studies were available could the hypothesis be seriously entertained that the "alcoholic personality" might be secondary to the disorder. Prospective studies by Jones (1968) and by Kammeier, Hoffmann, and Loper (1973) concurred that premorbid traits of dependence do not increase the risk of alcoholism.

Similarly, Morrison (1975) and Cloninger, Reich, and Wetzel (1979) have all presented evidence from family pedigree studies that alcoholism and affective disorders are transmitted independently. Weissman et al. (1984) and Merikangas and Gelernter (1990), have further clarified the fact that from a genetic standpoint, alcoholism and major depressive disorders are separate disorders. In a series of general population studies, they reported that alcoholism was no more common among the 2,003 first-degree relatives of 335 individuals with major depressive disorder than it was among individuals who were not affected with depression.

INCIDENCE OF MAJOR DEPRESSION IN ALCOHOLICS

Schuckit, Irwin, and Smith (1994) examined the relationship between alcoholism and depression by evaluating the incidence of new episodes of major depressive disorders among alcohol-dependent men during the year following treatment. One year following discharge from an alcohol treatment program, structured face-to-face interviews were conducted with 239 primary alcoholic men, as well as additional informants. Approximately 4 percent of the men developed depressive episodes while drinking heavily, but only 2.1 percent demonstrated major depression independent of heavy drinking.

PREVALENCE OF MAJOR DEPRESSION
IN ALCOHOLICS

No agreement is found in research or clinical findings about the prevalence of primary depression among alcohol-dependent persons. Studies report the prevalence of depression as ranging from 3 to 90 percent.

Depressive symptoms are common in alcoholism, with estimates of sadness among alcoholics ranging from 28 to 98 percent (Keeler, Taylor, and Miller, 1979; Weissman and Meyers, 1980). This wide span reflects a variety of factors including diagnostic heterogeneity of the patients (Hesselbrock, Meyer, and Keener, 1985; Schuckit, 1985); differences in instruments used to measure depressive symptoms; as well as the impact of recent drinking (Hesselbrock, Meyer, and Workman, 1983).

Two major epidemiological surveys have studied the prevalence of psychiatric disorders in community samples. The first was the National Institute of Mental Health Epidemiological Catchment Area (ECA) Study (Regier et al., 1990) conducted in the early 1980s. The second study was the National Comorbidity Study (NCS) conducted in 1991 (Kessler et al., 1994).

Data from the ECA study estimated the lifetime prevalence for alcohol abuse and dependence to be 13.5 percent. Among those with any affective disorder, 32 percent had a comorbid addictive disorder. Of the individuals with major depression, 16.5 percent had a comorbid alcohol abuse use diagnosis and 18 percent had a comorbid other drug use disorder. Of those individuals with any bipolar diagnosis, 46 percent had a comorbid alcohol diagnosis.

Data from the NCS estimated a lifetime prevalence of 14.1 percent for alcohol dependence and 19.3 percent for any affective disorder. The odd ratio was calculated to determine the relative risk of co-occurence of any mental disorder and addictive disorders (Kessler et al., 1997). The odd ratio of finding any lifetime substance use disorder in a person with mood disorder was 2:3 and the twelve-month odd ratio was 3:0. Among those with a diagnosis of major depression, the odd ratio of comorbid substance abuse disorder was approximately 2.7 for lifetime co-occurrence. The odd ratio of lifetime comorbid alcohol dependence in a person with bipolar disorder was 9.7.

ECONOMICS

Alcoholism is a common disorder posing a heavy burden on patients, their families, and society. The economic cost to society from alcohol abuse and alcoholism in the United States was an estimated $148 billion in 1992 (Harwood, Fountain, and Livermore, 1998). Epidemiological studies indicate that alcoholism will affect approximately 10 percent of Americans at some time in their lives, with men affected more than women. This is a high prevalence rate compared with many other diseases and highlights the public health significance of alcohol dependence. In addition to the estimated 100,000 U.S. citizens who die each year due to alcohol-related causes (including traffic collisions and cirrhosis of liver), alcoholism costs the nation an estimated $166 billion annually in direct and indirect health and social costs (Harwood, Fountain, and Livermore, 1998).

It is estimated that 45.1 percent of costs are borne by alcohol abusers and/or members of their household, 38.6 percent are borne by the government, 10.2 percent by private insurance, and 6.0 percent by victims of alcohol-related trauma (Harwood, Fountain, and Livermore, 1998).

TYPES OF DEPRESSION

Primary versus Secondary

The sadness associated with alcohol dependency is often described in terms of clinical depression and the relationship between alcoholism and depression has been the focus of study and debate within the profession for years.

It is important to distinguish between the three types of depression before discussing the significance of depression within any alcoholic population since type of depression is a critical factor in determining appropriate diagnosis and interventions in a treatment setting. Using the psychiatrically defined physical, behavioral, emotional, and cognitive symptoms, depression can be categorized as primary, secondary, or withdrawal.

Depression is termed primary when it exists independent of other psychiatric conditions. If depression coexists with alcoholism, it can be considered primary only when it existed prior to alcohol dependence and can be diagnosed three to four weeks postdetoxification, using the standard DSM-IV criteria.

Although secondary depression has the same symptoms of primary depressive disorder, it is defined as occurring after the onset of alcoholism. Depression usually arises in the course of chronic alcohol misuse as an understandable reaction to the social, psychological, and physical problems of the drinker. Studies of intoxication show that alcohol exerts a direct chemical depression effect, even if the individual has not been otherwise predisposed to depression. These neurochemical changes remain obscure, although the dopaminergic system could have been involved. The reduction of 5-hydroxytryptamine has been postulated to direct a depression effect (Pietrasjek et al., 1991). Usually such depressive symptoms improve within two to four weeks after cessation of drinking and do not require additional treatment.

The depressive syndrome, which accompanies detoxification, is known as withdrawal depression. This type of depression is clearly the product of primary alcoholism, and its symptoms and distress clear with detoxification.

DIAGNOSIS OF AFFECTIVE DISORDER IN ALCOHOLISM

The consumption of alcohol and occurrence of alcohol-related problems are extremely common in Western societies. For example, 90 percent of people in the United States drink alcoholic beverages (Schuckit, 1985), and perhaps one-third to one-half experience some temporary alcohol-related life problem. While drinking, most people have experienced some intense level of depression as might be observed during grief. The high prevalence of drinking and sadness means that a very large proportion of individuals in Western cultures has had experience with alcohol, and some of them have experienced depression secondary to alcohol use on a regular basis. Schuckit (1994) stresses the importance of distinguishing these experiences from the severe and persistent alcohol-related life problems that form the core of alcohol dependence and the intense experience of months of debilitating, vegetative symptoms consistent with major depressive disorders.

A study of a consecutive series of 577 male alcoholics (Schuckit, 1985) entering a treatment program revealed that the rate of coexisting depressive symptoms varied with the definitions used. Over 80 percent of these patients reported that they had been "very sad" at some point in their lives. However, one-third of these individuals reported being depressed for two or more weeks at a time to the point of interference with life functioning, a condition that at first glance resembles a major depressive episode. However, when a careful history was gathered, only approximately 5 percent reported experiencing a major depression, and this rate is similar to that found in the general population.

In view of this, Schuckit and Irwin (1989) proposed a simple time line approach to make the distinction between depressive episodes that occur only in context of heavy alcohol or drug use and those depressive episodes that appear to be independent of alcohol consumption. The first step in this method is to place on the time line the age at which the major life problems related to alcohol began to cluster. This indicates the approximate age at which alcohol dependence was severe enough to be an ongoing phenomenon. Second, any periods of time when the individual was abstinent or near abstinent for three or more consecutive months are also placed on the time line. This establishes periods during which abstinence had been long enough for an independent depression, if present, to be observed. If a review of the information does not clearly reveal that major depressive episodes occurred either before the onset of alcohol dependence, or that such episodes occurred for a period of at least two weeks while the individual had been dry for an extended period of time, then it is presumed that the individual has alcohol dependence but suffers only from an alcohol-related depression. An independent major depressive disorder is diagnosed at this point only if the depression was truly independent of the heavy drinking. Thus, even if our patients tell us they drink "because" they are depressed, there are few convincing data indicating that a substantial proportion of individuals with major depressive disorders are likely to develop alcohol dependence.

THE RELATIONSHIP BETWEEN ALCOHOLISM AND AFFECTIVE DISORDERS

The relationship between alcohol and depression has long been of clinical and scientific interest. Although many studies have sought to clarify the nature of this relationship, it still is a complicated issue that remains poorly understood, and more research is needed. The two basic ideas of a possible connection are, on one hand, symptomatic alcoholism with a preexisting depression and, on the other hand, alcoholism leading to a symptomatic depression. Literature reveals a great variability of results with regard to this problem.

Conventional wisdom holds that patients suffering from depression frequently self-medicate with alcohol. Because alcohol itself is a depressant, it is easy to presume that a vicious cycle could then develop in which depressed alcoholics continue to drink to obtain relief, only to worsen both their depression and alcoholism. Conventional wisdom also often presumes that chronic heavy drinking represents a "depressive equivalent" and that mood disorders may represent a broad spectrum of phenomenology, with a common genotypical etiology expressed in a variety of phenotypical clinical presentations, including alcoholism. As we will see, conventional wisdom is wrong on both accounts.

Raimo and Schuckit (1998) explored the complex relationship between alcohol dependence and mood disorders. They conclude that although many alcoholics present with substance-induced depression, once appropriate methodological controls are used, there does not appear to be a significant relationship between independent unipolar depression and alcohol dependence.

Schuckit et al. (1997) performed a study comparing induced and independent major depressive disorders in 2,945 alcoholics. Major depressive episodes with an onset before the development of alcohol dependence or during a subsequent long length of abstinence (i.e., independent depression) were observed in 15.2 percent of the alcoholics, while 26.4 percent reported at least one substance-induced depressive episode. According to logistic regression analysis, the subjects with independent (as compared to substance-induced) major depressive episodes were more likely to be married, Caucasian, and female. These subjects also reported less drug use and had less treatment for alcoholism. They were more likely to have attempted suicide and to have a close relative with a major mood disorder.

Holdcraft, Iacono, and McGue (1998) found a weak association between alcohol dependence and depression but a strong relationship with antisocial personality disorder. Merikangas, Weissman et al.

(1985) showed that depressed alcoholics and pure depressives had similar risk for depression in their children.

FAMILIAL TRANSMISSION OF ALCOHOLISM AND AFFECTIVE DISORDERS

The concept of depression spectrum disease, in which probands present with depression and a strong family history of alcoholism, supports the notion that perhaps a familial and possible genetic relationship exists between alcoholism and depression. A number of studies have rejected this notion, demonstrating that the etiology of the two disorders is heterogeneous and that they are not the manifestations of the same illness. Weissman et al. (1984) found no evidence for familial aggregation between alcoholism and depression.

Scherrer and colleagues (1996) studied the influence of familial and nonfamilial factors on the association between major depression and substance abuse/dependence. This study examined the lifetime association of major depression with alcohol, cannabis, amphetamine, and cocaine (DSM-III-R criteria) before and after controlling for familial factors in a nonclinical sample in 1,874 middle aged, monozygotic male twin pairs. A lifetime diagnosis of major depression was significantly associated with lifetime diagnosis of alcohol and illicit substance use prior to accounting for familial factors. After employing a co-twin analytic technique to control for familial factors, a lifetime major depression remained significantly associated only with a lifetime diagnosis of cannabis, amphetamine, and sedative abuse. These results suggest that the association between major depression and alcohol is influenced by familial factors. In contrast, the association between major depression and illicit substances is largely explained by nonfamilial factors.

Merikangas, Leckman, et al. (1985) studied the familial transmission of depression and alcoholism in a case-controlled study of first-degree relatives of normal and depressed probands. The findings indicated that the relatives of probands with primary unipolar affective disorders had significantly greater rates of alcoholism (14.45 percent) than relatives of normal probands (9 percent). However, relatives of severely depressed (hospitalized) probands did not have significantly higher rates of either alcoholism or depression than relatives of mildly depressed (nonhospitalized) probands. The results of this study confirm those of previous studies, which demonstrated that depression and alcoholism are not alternate manifestations of the same underlying disorder. The findings indicate that depressives without alcoholism did not transmit alcoholism, and probands with depression and alcoholism transmitted both.

Dawson and Grant (1998) analyzed self-report data from a sample of 42,862 U.S. adults (25,043 women) by means of multiple logistic regression models that predicted the odds of various combinations of DSM-IV alcohol dependence and major depression. Their findings supported more familial alcoholism among persons with comorbid depression and alcohol dependence than among those with alcohol dependence alone. Adoption studies have tended to confirm an independent transmission for depression and alcoholism. Goodwin et al. (1973) showed that adoptees of alcoholic biological parents who were raised by nonalcoholic parents had no increase in depression, but did have increased alcoholism. It concludes that depression and alcoholism are independent disorders, and alcoholism is not a masked form of depression.

Some studies do, however, establish the relationship between alcohol dependence and major depression. Winokur and Coryell (1991) tested the hypothesis that a familial relationship exists between alcoholism and primary depression. Their results indicated higher rates of alcoholism in the families of depressed women but not in the families of depressed men.

GENETIC RELATIONSHIP BETWEEN ALCOHOLISM AND AFFECTIVE DISORDERS

Twin Studies

Kendler et al. (1993) conducted a twin study of the causes of comorbidity between alcoholism and major depression in women. Personal interviews were conducted with 2,163 female twins from a population-based twin registry. Twin analysis found no evidence of familial environmental factors for either major depression or alcoholism. However, significant genetic correlations between major depression and alcoholism were found.

Prescott and Kendler (1999) conducted a population-based study of 3,516 male twins from the United States and concluded that genetic factors played a major role in the development of alcoholism among males, with similar influence for alcohol abuse and alcohol dependence. In this population-based sample, environmental factors shared by family members appeared to have little influence in the development of alcoholism in males.

CEREBROSPINAL FLUID

Roy et al. (1991) studied depression among alcoholics in relationship to clinical and cerebrospinal fluid variables. One hundred eleven of the 339 alcoholics had a history of major depression. Significantly more of the female than male alcoholics had a history of depression. Depressed alcoholics were younger, had an earlier onset of heavy drinking, and had a greater daily intake of alcohol. Also, depressed alcoholics had significantly lower cerebrospinal fluid concentration of homovanillic acid and gaba-amino butyric acid than never-depressed alcoholics.

DEXAMETHASONE SUPPRESSION TEST

Additional biological evidence that alcoholism is not a symptom of primary depressive disorder was provided by a study by Schlesser, Winokur, and Sherman (1980). Using the dexamethasone suppression test (DST) to differentiate biologically based (for example, primary) depression from that induced by the environmental (for example, secondary) causes, they examined a group of patients who met the *Diagnostic and Statistical Manual of Mental Disorders* (DSM-III) (APA, 1987) criteria for primary depression and who had first-degree relatives with antisocial personality disorder or alcoholism but no relatives with depressive illness. They compared the DST response of these patients to a group of patients with primary unipolar depression who also had depressive relatives, and a group of patients with secondary depression. The vast majority (93 percent) of depressed patients with alcoholic relatives and all patients with secondary unipolar depression showed suppression of serum cortisol after the DST. In contrast, only 20 percent of patients with familial or bipolar depression had a normal DST response.

SUICIDE IN DEPRESSED ALCOHOLICS

Two mechanisms are found in suicide attempters and in suicide among alcohol misusers. The first results from the disinhibitory effects of alcohol on behavior and is precipitated abruptly during intoxication. The second involves a more prolonged buildup of depression and self-incriminatory ideas. Earlier understanding of depressed mood promotes further understanding of patients and can prevent a lethal outcome.

Suominen et al. (1997) examined the differences in hopelessness, impulsiveness, and suicide intent between suicide attempters with either major depression or alcohol dependence, and those without these disorders. A sample of 114 patients from consecutive cases of attempted suicide referred to a general hospital in Helsinki were interviewed and diagnosed according to DSM-III-R criteria. Suicide intent was measured by the Suicide Intent Scale (SIS) and hopelessness was assessed by the Beck Hopelessness Scale (BHS). Impulsiveness of the suicide attempt was measured by two items of the SIS. Suicide attempters with major depression without comorbid alcohol dependence had higher suicide intent and lower impulsiveness than attempters with nondepressive alcohol dependence. Suicide attempts may differ between subjects with major depression, alcoholism, or both disorders in terms of impulsiveness and suicide intent.

Roy et al. (1990) reported that of 298 alcoholic subjects, 57 subjects (19.1 percent) had histories of attempted suicide. Thirty-eight had one attempt; ten had two attempts; and nine had made three or more attempts. Compared with nonattempters, suicide attempters were significantly more likely to be the following: female, in a lower socioeconomic status, younger, a heavy drinker, and have an early age onset of alcohol-related problems. They were also more likely to consume a greater amount of alcohol when drinking, and have an additional lifetime psychiatric diagnosis of major depression, antisocial personality disorders, substance abuse, or a generalized anxiety disorder. Also, significantly more suicide attempters had first- or second-degree relatives who abused alcohol. In a study by Whitters, Cadoret, and Widmer (1985), alcoholics with and without histories of suicide attempts were examined, and Whitters and colleagues found that a significantly greater proportion of attempters had abused drugs and experienced episodes of major depression.

Salloum, Mezzich, and Cornelius (1995) reported that combined alcohol use disorder-major depression had a strikingly higher rate of suicidal indicators as compared to alcohol use disorder or major depression alone. Biro, Bursic, and Kapamadzija (1991) reported that depressive disorders appear significantly more often in alcoholics who manifest suicidal behavior than in those who do not.

Alcoholism and depression in combination increases the risk of suicide more than if each entity is considered alone.

REMISSION OF ALCOHOLISM
AND AFFECTIVE SYMPTOMS

Rumpf et al. (1998) reported preliminary results of their ongoing study to examine triggering factors and maintenance factors in remission from alcoholism without professional help. The analysis of the subsample in their study shows that adverse consequences from drinking in the domains of health, work, family, and drunk driving are relevant triggering factors in remitting from alcohol dependence without formal help, and social support can be regarded as a significant maintenance factor. Furthermore, social support is related to higher alcohol abstinence self-efficacy, lower temptation to drink, and specific cognitive methods of coping.

PERSISTENCE OF AFFECTIVE DISORDERS
IN ALCOHOLISM

Brown et al. (1995) compared the severity of and the change in depressive symptoms among men with alcohol dependence, affective disorder, or both disorders during four weeks of inpatient treatment. After their primary and secondary psychiatric disorders were defined with the use of criteria based on the chronology of symptoms, fifty-four unmedicated men entering treatment for alcohol dependence or affective disorders were assessed for four consecutive weeks with the

Hamilton Depression Rating Scale. This study demonstrated that men with primary alcoholism, regardless of secondary affective disorder, displayed marked reductions in their depressive symptoms compared to men with primary affective disorder throughout the four-week inpatient treatment program. The patient with primary alcoholism evidenced a 49 to 63 percent reduction in Hamilton depression scale scores by the fourth week of treatment. In contrast, there was a 14 to 16 percent reduction in these scores among the unmedicated patients with primary affective disorder.

Brown et al. (1995) and Schuckit et al. (1988) assessed the incidence, rate, and pattern of change of depressive symptoms among primary alcoholics with no prior major psychiatric diagnosis. One hundred ninety-one alcoholics were administered the Hamilton Depression Rating Scale within forty-eight hours of admission and again during each of the four weeks of treatment. Results indicate that 42 percent of alcoholics have clinically significant levels of depression (Hamilton score > 20) at intake and only 6 percent remain clinically depressed at week four. Results suggest that antidepressant medication should not be considered prior to four weeks of abstinence. If the depression started before the onset of alcoholism (primary depression), then antidepressant medications can be considered in two to four weeks or less, depending upon the seriousness of the depression.

DRINKING OUTCOME IN AFFECTIVE DISORDER

Davidson and Blackburn (1998) studied comorbid depression and drinking outcome in patients with alcohol dependence. Depressed and nondepressed (preadmission and postdetoxification) alcohol-dependent patients were followed up on two occasions over a period of five months following detoxification from alcohol. Detailed measures of alcohol consumption, alcohol-related problems, and abstinence status were taken throughout the follow-up period. No significant differences were found between those with the diagnosis of depression and those with alcohol dependence alone, regardless of whether diagnosis of depression was made postdetoxification or preadmission, on any drinking outcome measure including abstinence status, alcohol consumption, pattern of drinking, or alcohol-related problems. Neither a diagnosis of depression in the postdetoxification period nor in the preadmission episode was related to drinking outcome at follow-up, which suggests that comorbid depression does not necessarily confer a worse outcome in those with alcohol dependence.

Schuckit (1985) found no differences in drinking outcomes between depressed and nondepressed alcoholics.

Hodgkins et al. (1999) followed eighty-four alcohol-dependent patients seeking treatment for three years in a naturalistic, prospective design. Their study showed no evidence that drinking precedes or initiates depressive episodes or that depressive episodes precipitate heavy drinking.

PHARMACOLOGICAL TREATMENT OF ALCOHOL DEPENDENCE

The treatment of alcoholism consists of psychosocial intervention, pharmacological intervention, or both. Garbutt et al. (1999) examined the efficacy of five categories of drugs used to treat alcohol dependence: disulfiram, the opioid antagonists, naltrexone and nalmefene, acamprosate, and various serotonergic agents including SSRIs and lithium. The results of 375 studies on the pharmacological treatment of alcoholism focused on the following.

Naltrexone

Of the seventy-seven research articles identified, three controlled studies evaluated the efficacy of naltrexone with alcohol-dependent patients. Although the overall sample size of the three naltrexone 50 mg/day studies is modest ($n = 271$ randomized patients), the trials are recent and of good quality, with consistent results on relapse rates and drinking frequencies. Among all patients in the first two trials, relapse rates at the end of the trials were higher for the placebo groups (54 percent and approximately 80 percent) than for the naltrexone groups (23 percent and approximately 40 percent). In a third trial, end-of-study relapse rates for all subjects were 53 percent and 35 percent for placebo and naltrexone patients, respectively; however, for compliant patients, the figures were 52 percent and 14 percent.

Volpicelli et al. (1992) studied the effects of administrating the opiod antagonist naltrexone to treat alcohol dependence. Their preliminary study included thirty alcohol-dependent men who were out-patients at a Veterans Administration hospital. The fourteen patients who in this experiment group received naltrexone and intensive psychosocial treatment were less likely to experience an alcoholic relapse and drank on fewer days than the sixteen patients who received placebo.

In the second study, O'Malley et al. (1992) studied 104 alcohol-dependent men and women who were randomly assigned to one of four treatment groups. Patients received either naltrexone or placebo in combination with either coping skills therapy or supportive therapy. Compared with placebo-treated patients, naltrexone-treated patients consumed one-third of the number of drinks during treatment and drank on half as many days. Naltrexone-treated patients were more likely to remain abstinent and less likely to resume heavy drinking than were placebo-treated patients.

Nalmefene

The nalmefene trial randomized twenty-one subjects to placebo and two nalmefene dosage groups (10 mg/d and 40 mg/d); eight subjects completed the study. The results indicated a significantly lower relapse rate in the high dosage nalmefene group.

Acamprosate

Data were abstracted from nine studies of the thirty-seven acamprosate studies identified in the literature. A total of 2,170 patients were enrolled; all studies used a double-blind method and one used a crossover design. The most consistent finding in the acamprosate trials has been its effect on drinking frequency; nondrinking days were typically increased by 30 to 50 percent (e.g., from 162 to 225 nondrinking days). Several studies also found that acamprosate nearly doubled abstinence rates, although a majority of patients eventually returned to drinking while taking acamprosate. Whitworth et al. (1996) conducted a one-year, multicenter study of acamprosate in Austria. They concluded 18 percent of acamprosate-treated subjects sustained abstinence versus 7 percent of placebo-treated patients.

Selective Serotonin Reuptake Inhibitors (SSRIs)

The SSRI fluoxetine has been studied in five double-blind placebo controlled trials (n = 227 subjects). Outcomes are mixed regarding the efficacy of fluoxetine for alcohol-dependent patients. Trials among patients who also had depression or anxiety totaled 179 subjects (n = 51 for fluoxetine trials; n = 128 for two buspirone trials). Depressed alcohol-dependent patients taking fluoxetine showed improved amount and frequency of drinking compared with those receiving placebo; buspirone studies showed one positive change in drinking outcomes (time of first drink).

Odansetron

One trial of odansetron (n = 57), using a double-blind, placebo-controlled design with random assignment to high dosage (4 mg/d) or low dosage (0.5 mg/d) found that low dosage odansetron reduced drinking only among light drinkers.

Lithium

Six trials (n = 83) have appeared on the effects of lithium in alcohol-dependent subjects with and without depression or bipolar disorders. All trials report comorbid depression in subjects; only two studies controlled for depression in their data analyses. The strongest and largest trial found no positive effect for lithium in either depressed or nondepressed alcohol-dependent subjects. One study (not controlling for comorbidity) found improved drinking outcomes in subjects with high lithium levels.

The advances in the pharmacology of alcohol dependence are valuable developments, but the treatment of alcoholism should continue to incorporate a biopsychosocial and spiritual perspective in an effort to change a life from the pattern of addiction to a pattern of sobriety and improved physical, mental, and social well-being.

TREATMENT STRATEGIES
FOR AFFECTIVE DISORDER IN ALCOHOLISM

Tricyclic Antidepressants

Merikangas and Gelertner (1990) analyzed a number of studies that have examined the efficacy of tricyclic antidepressants and lithium in the treatment of alcoholism complicated by major depression. Five double-blind, placebo-controlled studies of tricyclic antidepressants in the treatment of alcoholics examined the efficacy of these agents in reducing depressive symptoms, but did not address the question of whether they reduced alcoholic relapse rates. The results of these studies are as follows: Imipramine is superior to placebo (Butterworth, 1971). Doxepin is superior to diazepam (Butterworth and Watts, 1971). Amitriptyline is superior to mesoridazine and chlordiaxepoxide (Overall, 1973, cited in Merikangas and Gelertner, 1990).

Because depressive symptoms of alcoholics usually abate quickly with abstinence, use of antidepressants before two to four weeks after detoxification should be considered cautiously. Caution should also be exercised on the outpatient basis where impaired judgment associated with intoxication could result in lethal overdose of medication.

Several studies of tricyclic antidepressants in alcoholic populations have indicated that antidepressant treatment may be helpful in the treatment of individuals with comorbid substance use and depression. McGarth and colleagues (1996) conducted a twelve-week, placebo-controlled trial of imipramine treatment in actively drinking alcoholic outpatients with depression. They found that imipramine treatment was associated with improvement in depression, and patients whose mood improved showed a more marked decrease in alcohol consumption.

Selective Serotonin Reuptake Inhibitors

Research investigating the use of selective serotonin reuptake inhibitors (SSRIs) in the treatment of alcoholism has shown recent promise. The serotonin system has been implicated in control of alcohol intake (Amit, Smith, and Gill, 1991). A number of SSRIs have been shown to have a modest effect in decreasing alcohol consumption in problem drinkers and alcoholics (Gorelick and Paredes, 1992). Cornelius et al. (1997) completed the first double-blind trial of the SSRI fluoxetine with patients who were comorbid for alcohol dependence and major depression. Fifty-one patients received between 20 and 40 mg of fluoxetine or placebo daily, as well as standard weekly treatment of supportive psychotherapy. Following twelve weeks of treatment, fluoxetine-treated subjects enjoyed more pronounced improvement in depression than the placebo group. Furthermore, the number of drinking days was significantly reduced by 48 percent.

Lithium

Evidence of lithium as an effective treatment for alcoholic inpatients with depression is equivocal. In the following four studies lithium was compared with placebo in the treatment of drinking behavior among alcoholic patients. The results of these studies are lithium superior to placebo (Kline et al., 1974); lithium superior to placebo in alcoholics with depression only (Reynolds, Merry, and Coppen, 1977); lithium superior to placebo (De la Fuente et al., 1989); and no difference between lithium and placebo (Dorus et al., 1989).

CONCLUSION:
SUMMARY AND TREATMENT PROTOCOLS

Although it is tempting to assume that individuals become clinically depressed and then self-soothe and self-medicate with alcohol, it is now generally accepted that alcohol use precedes the development of depressive symptoms for most individuals. Both major depression and predisposition to develop alcohol dependence seem to be inherited as separate diseases (with some overlap) and run separate longitudinal courses.

Either affective syndromes or affective disorders appear to be most universal among individuals with alcoholism. Some patients suffer from primary affective symptoms (affective symptoms occurring before the onset of alcohol abuse) such as major depression and bipolar disorder. Other patients develop secondary affective symptoms (the depressive symptoms developing after the onset of alcohol abuse).

Examples of secondary affective symptoms would be those occurring in individuals who are comorbid for alcoholism and personality disorders, and in those patients who experience grief, mourning, and symptoms of loss after they have given up their "friend," alcohol.

Outpatient Treatment Protocols

Patients with affective symptoms and alcoholism who present for outpatient evaluation are initially evaluated for the appropriateness of inpatient versus outpatient treatment. Individuals with serious suicidality (suicidal plan, past suicide attempts, and marked alcohol use or personality-induced inhibition) are admitted to a mental health unit for stabilization. Patients with serious comorbid medical conditions (delirium, pancreatitis, or hepatitis) are admitted to an intensive care unit or medical floor for detoxification. Poststabilization patients are transferred to a mental health unit or an inpatient alcohol treatment unit for continued differential diagnosis.

Following discharge, the nonsuicidal, medically stable patient can be managed as an outpatient. A waiting period of three to four weeks is suggested before treating the affective symptoms, which may meet diagnostic criteria for dysthymic disorder or adjustment disorder with depressive features. These symptoms are secondary to the chemical depressant effect of alcohol and/or to the social system, interpersonal, vocational dissolution secondary to the behavioral effects of the alcohol.

Persistent depressive symptoms may be approached in the supportive milieu of the AA community and with a sponsor. Patients who remain depressed may benefit from a specific type of individual psychotherapy such as grief counseling, cognitive-behavior therapy, or dynamic therapy with a self-psychology approach.

An initial efficacious approach is to encourage transference development to a multidisciplinary staff or to an AA community rather than to an individual therapist. Pharmacotherapy may also be indicated for patients with affective symptoms after a three- to four-week waiting period if they meet the diagnostic criteria for major depression or bipolar disorder.

Some outpatients will also be comorbid for alcoholism plus personality disorder (borderline, antisocial, histrionic) and will manifest symptoms of affective illness as a part of their underlying personality structure. These affective symptoms are also termed secondary depression and may be treated with antidepressant medication or individual psychotherapy.

Inpatient Treatment Protocols

Patients with coexisting affective disorder and alcoholism who meet previously discussed criteria for hospital admission are admitted to the appropriate inpatient unit for the establishment of differential diagnosis and treatment.

Following the resolution of a withdrawal syndrome, delirium tremens, other concomitant medical illnesses, or psychosis, the patient is further evaluated for the specificity of affective symptoms. Major depressive syndromes are treated with appropriate therapies (antidepressants, mood stabilizers, or electroconvulsive therapy) following alcohol withdrawal and detoxification. Two to three weeks following withdrawal should be an adequate time interval to ascertain the persistence of a major depressive syndrome.

Treatment of the major depressive syndrome as an inpatient may occur simultaneously with the beginning phases of alcohol rehabilitation within the hospital setting. A consultation from the alcohol rehabilitation specialist is obtained with subsequent treatment planning, which may include transfer to a contiguous alcohol treatment unit or group participation in the program of an alcohol rehabilitation unit located within the hospital. The patient can continue psychotropic medication while participating in a multidisciplinary alcohol treatment process.

Be sure that the patients are discharged to an outpatient Alcoholics Anonymous (AA) group that supports the use of psychotropic medication in this population. Members in some AA settings discourage the use of these therapeutic medications because they believe that the patient is still abusing a substance.

The prognosis is good for the affective component in alcoholism. When affective symptoms persist, they can be effectively managed from a grief/loss aspect of alcoholism or as a separate, distinct illness with its own distinct clinical longitudinal natural course history. In this respect, both alcohol dependence and the affective syndrome must be treated as separate illnesses. The prognosis for each can be excellent.

BIBLIOGRAPHY

American Psychiatric Association (APA) (1987). *Diagnostic and Statistical Manual of Mental Disorders,* Third Edition. Washington, DC: American Psychiatric Association.

Amit Z, Smith BR, and Gill K (1991). Serotonin uptake inhibitors: Effects on motivated consummatory behaviors. *Journal of Clinical Psychiatry 52*(Supplement), 55-60. Review. PMID: 1752861 [PubMed - indexed for MEDLINE]

Berner P, Lesch O, and Walter H (1986). Alcohol and depression. *Psychopathology, 19,* Suppl. 2, 177-183.

Biro M, Bursic S, and Kapamadzija B (1991). *The role of depressive disorder in the suicidal behavior of alcoholics.* Yugoslovia: Hogrefe and Huber Publishers.

Bowen R, Cipywnyk D, Arcy C, and Keegan D (1984). Types of depression in alcoholic patients. *Canadian Medical Association Journal, 130,* 869-874.

Brown S, Inaba R, Gillin C, Schuckit M, Stewart M, and Irwin M (1995). Alcoholism and affective disorder: Clinical course of depressive symptoms. *American Journal of Psychiatry, 152*(1), 45-52.

Brown S and Schuckit M (1988). Changes in depression among abstinent alcoholics. *Quarterly Journal of Studies on Alcohol, 49*(5), 412-417.

Butterworth A (1971). Depression associated with alcohol withdrawal: Imipramine therapy compared with placebo. *Quarterly Journal of Studies on Alcohol, 32*(2), 343-348.

Butterworth AT and Watts RD (1971). Treatment of hospitalized alcoholics with doxepin and diazepam. *Quarterly Journal of Studies on Alcohol, 32*(1), 78-81.

Cloninger CR, Reich T, and Wetzel (1979). Alcoholism and affective disorders: Familial associations and genetic models. In Goodwin DW, Erikson CK (Eds.), *Alcoholism and affective disorders: Clinical, genetic, and biochemical studies.* New York: SP Medical and Scientific Books.

Cornelius JR, Salloum IM, Ehler JG, Jarrett PJ, Cornelius MD, Perel JM, Thase ME, and Black A (1997). Fluoxetine in depressed alcoholics. *Archives of General Psychiatry, 54*(8), 700-705.

Davidson K and Blackburn I (1998). Comorbid depression and drinking outcome in those with alcohol dependence. *Alcohol and Alcoholism, 33*(5), 482-487.

Davidson K and Ritson E (1993). The relationship between alcohol dependence and depression. *Alcohol and Alcoholism, 28*(2), 147-155.

Dawson D and Grant B (1998). Family history of alcoholism and gender: Their combined effects on DSM-IV alcohol dependence and major depression. *Quarterly Journal of Studies on Alcohol, 59*(1), 97-106.

De la Fuente J, More R, Niven RG, and Ilstrup DM (1989). A controlled study of lithium carbonate in the treatment of alcoholism. *Mayo Clinic Proceedings, 64,* 177-180.

Dorus W, Ostrow D, Anton R, Cushman P, Collins JF, Schaefer M, Charles HL, Desai P, Hayashida M, Malkerneker U, et al. (1989). Lithium treatment of depressed and nondepressed alcoholics. *Journal of the American Medical Association, 262*(12), 1680-1681.

Fawcett J, Clark D, Gibbons R, Aagesen CA, Pisani VD, Tilkin JM, Sellers D, and Stutzman D (1984). Evaluation of lithium therapy for alcoholism. *Journal of Clinical Psychiatry, 45*(12), 494-499.

Frederick P (1992). The depressed alcoholic. *General Hospital Psychiatry, 14*, 258-264.

Garbutt J, West S, Carey T, Lohr K, and Crews F (1999). Pharmacological treatment of alcohol dependence. *Journal of the American Medical Association, 281*(14), 1318-1325.

Goodwin DW, Schulsinger F, Hermansen L, Guze SB, and Winokur G (1973). Alcohol problems in adoptees raised apart from alcoholic biological parents. *Archives of General Psychiatry, 28*(2), 238-243.

Gorelick DA and Paredes A (1992). Effect of fluoxetine on alcohol consumption in male alcoholics. *Alcoholism: Clinical and Experimental Research, 16*(2), 261-265.

Greenfield S, Weiss R, Muenz L, Vagge LM, Kelly JF, Bello LR, and Michael J (1998). The effect of depression on return to drinking: A prospective study. *Archives of General Psychiatry, 55*(3), 259-265.

Harrington R, Fudge H, Rutter M, Pickles A, and Hill J (1990). Adult outcomes of childhood and adolescent depression. *Archives of General Psychiatry, 47*(5), 465-473.

Harwood H, Fountain D, and Livermore G (1998). *The consequences of alcoholism: Recent developments in alcoholism.* New York: Plenum Press.

Hesselbrock MN, Meyer RE, and Keener JJ (1985). Psychopathology in hospitalized alcoholics. *Archives of General Psychiatry, 42*, 1050-1055.

Hesselbrock M, Meyer T, and Workman L (1983). Methodological consideration in the treatment of depression in alcoholics. *Journal of Clinical Psychology,* 401-405.

Hirschfeld R, Kosier T, Keller M, Levori P, and Endicott J (1998). The influence of alcoholism on the course of depression. *Journal of Affective Disorders, 16*, 151-158.

Hodgkins D, Gluebaly N, Armstrong S, and Defour M (1999). Implications of depression on outcome from alcohol dependence: A three-year prospective follow-up. *Alcoholism: Clinical and Experimental Research, 23*(1), 151-157.

Holdcraft I, Iacono W, and McGue M (1998). Antisocial personality disorder and depression in relation to alcoholism. *Quarterly Journal of Studies on Alcohol, 59*, 222-226.

Jones MC (1968). Personality correlates and antecedents of drinking patterns in adult males. *Journal of Counsultant Clinical Psychology, 32*(1), 2-12.

Kammeier M, Hoffman H, and Loper R (1973). Personality characteristics of alcoholics as college freshmen and at time of treatment. *Quarterly Journal of Studies on Alcohol, 34*, 390-399.

Keeler M, Taylor C, and Miller W (1979). Are all recently detoxified alcoholics depressed? *American Journal of Psychiatry, 136*(4B), 586-588.

Kendler K, Heath A, Neale M, Kessler R, and Eaves L (1993). Alcoholism and major depression in women: A twin study of the causes of comorbidity. *Archives of General Psychiatry, 50*(9), 690-698.

Kessler RC, Crum RM, Warner LA, Nelson CB, Schulenberg JS, and Anthony JC (1997). Lifetime co-occurrence of DSM-III-R alcohol abuse and dependence with other psychiatric disorders in the National Comorbidity Survey. *Archives of General Psychiatry, 54*(4), 313-321.

Kessler RC, McGonagle KA, Zhao S, Nelson CB, Hughes M, Eshleman S, Wittchen HU, and Kendler KS (1994). Lifetime and 12-month prevalence of DSM-III-R psychiatric disorders in the United States. Results from the National Comorbidity Survey. *Archives of General Psychiatry, 51*(1), 8-19.

Kline NS, Wren JC, Cooper TB, Varga E, and Canal O (1974). Evaluation of lithium therapy in chronic and periodic alcoholism. *American Journal of Medical Sciences, 268*(1), 15-22.

Lesch O and Walter H (1996). Subtypes of alcoholism and their role in therapy. *Alcohol and Alcoholism, 31*(1), 63-67.

Litten R and Allen J (1999). Medications for alcohol, illicit drug, and tobacco dependence. An update of research findings. *Journal of Substance Abuse Treatment, 16*(2), 105-112.

Lynskey M (1998). The comorbidity of alcohol dependence and affective disorders. *Drug and Alcohol Dependence, 52,* 201-209.

Maden J (1993). Alcohol and depression. *British Journal of Hospital Medicine, 50*(5), 262-263.

Maier W, Litchterman D, and Minges J (1994). The relationship between alcoholism and unipolar depression: A controlled family study. *Journal of Psychiatric Research, 28*(3), 303-317.

Mann K, Chabac S, Potgieter P, and Saas H (1995). Acamprosate improves treatment outcome in alcoholics: A polled analysis of 11 randomized placebo-controlled trials in 3,338 patients. Poster presented at the annual conference of the American College of Neuropsychopharmacology, Puerto Rico.

McGarth PJ, Nunes EV, Stewart JW, Goldman D, Agosti V, Ocepek-Welikson K, and Quitkin FM (1996). Imipramine treatment of alcoholics with primary depression. *Archives of General Psychiatry, 53,* 232-240.

McGovern T and Weddige R (1991). Depression and grief. *The Counselor,* January/February, 29-30.

Merikangas K and Gelernter C (1990). Comorbidity for alcoholism and depression. *Psychiatric Clinics of North America, 13*(4), 613-632.

Merikangas K, Leckman J, Prusoff B, Pauls DL, and Weissman MM (1985). Familial transmission of alcoholism and depression. *Archives of General Psychiatry, 42,* 367-372.

Merikangas KR, Weissman MM, Prusoff BA, and Leckman JF (1985). Depressives with secondary alcoholism: Psychiatric disorders in offsprings. *Quarterly Journal of Studies on Alcohol, 46*(3), 199-204.

Morrison Jr. (1975). The family histories of manic depressive patients with and without alcoholism. *Journal of Nervous Mental Disorders, 160*(3), 227-229.

Nakamura M, Overall E, and Hollister E (1983). Factors affecting outcomes of depressive symptoms in alcoholism. *Alcoholism: Clinical and Experimental Research, 7(2)*, 188-193.

O'Malley S. (1996). Opiod antagonists in the treatment of alcohol dependence: Clinical efficacy and prevention of relapse. *Alcohol and Alcoholism, 31*(S1), 177-811.

O'Malley S, Jaffe AJ, Chang G, Schottenfeld R, Meyer RE, and Rounsaville B (1992). Naltrexone and coping skill therapy for alcohol dependence. A controlled study. *Archives of General Psychiatry, 49*(11), 881-887.

Pietrasjek MH, Urano T, Sumioshi K, et al. (1991). Alcohol-induced depression: Involvement of serotonin. *Alcohol Alcohol, 26,* 155-159.

Prescott C and Kendler K (1999). Genetic and environmental contributions to alcohol abuse and dependence in a population-based sample of male twins. *American Journal of Psychiatry, 156*(1), 34-40.

Raimo EB and Schuckit MA (1998). Alcohol dependence and mood disorders. *Addiction Behavior, 23*(6), 933-946.

Regier DA, Farmer ME, Rae DS, Locke BZ, Keith SJ, Judd LL, and Goodwin FK (1990). Comorbidity of mental disorders with alcohol and other drug abuse. Results from the Epidemiologic Catchment Area (ECA) Study. *Journal of the American Medical Association, 264*(19), 2511-2518.

Reynolds CM, Merry J, and Coppen A (1977). Prophylactic treatment of alcoholism by lithium carbonate: An initial report. *Alcohol: Clinical and Experimental Research 1*(2), 109-115.

Roy A, DeJong J, Lamparski D, George T, and Linnoila M (1991). Depression among alcoholics. Relationship to clinical and cerebrospinal fluid variables. *Archives of General Psychiatry, 48*(5), 428-432.

Roy A, Lamparski D, DeJong J, Moore V, and Linnoila M (1990). Characteristics of alcoholics who attempt suicide. *American Journal of Psychiatry, 147*(6), 761-765.

Rumpf HJ, Hapke U, Dawedeit A, Meyer C, and John U (1998). Project 5: Triggering and maintenance factors of remitting from alcohol dependence without formal help. *European Addict Research, 4*(4), 209-210.

Salloum I, Mezzich J, and Cornelius J (1995). Clinical profile of comorbid major depression and alcohol use disorders in an initial psychiatric evaluation. *Comprehensive Psychiatry, 36*(4), 260-266.

Scherrer JF, Linn N, Eisen SA, Goldber J, True WR, Lyons MJ, and Tsuang MT (1996). The association of antisocial personality with marijuana abuse/dependence. A monozygotic co-twin study. *Journal of Nervous Mental Disorders 184*(10), 611-615.

Schlesser M, Winokur G, and Sherman B, (1980). HPA activity in depressive illness: Its relationship to classification. *Archives of General Psychiatry, 37*(7), 737-743.

Schuckit MA (1985). Epidemiology of alcoholism. In Schuckit M (Ed.), *Alcohol patterns and problems* (pp. 1-42). New Brunswick, NJ: Rutgers University Press.

Schuckit MA (1994). Alcohol and depression: A clinical perspective. *Acta Psychiatrica Scandinavica, 377*, 28-32.

Schuckit MA and Irwin M (1989). An analysis of the clinical relevance of type 1 and type 2 alcoholics. *British Journal of Addiction, 84*(8), 869-876.

Schuckit MA, Irwin MR, Howard T, and Smith T (1988). A structured diagnostic interview for identification of primary alcoholism: A preliminary evaluation. *Quarterly Journal of Studies on Alcohol, 49*(1), 93-99.

Schuckit MA, Irwin M, and Smith T (1994). One-year incidence rate of major depression and other psychiatric disorders in 239 alcoholic men. *Addiction, 89*(4), 441-445.

Schuckit M, Tipp J, Bergman M, Reich W, Hesselbrock V, and Smith T (1997). Comparison of induced and independent major depressive disorders in 2,945 alcoholics. *American Journal of Psychiatry, 154*(7), 948-957.

Spring G and Rothgery J (1984). The link between alcoholism and affective disorders. *Hospital and Community Psychiatry, 35*(8), 820-823.

Suominen K, Isometsa E, Henriksson M, Ostama A, and Lonnqvist J (1997). Hopelessness, impulsiveness and intent among suicide attempters with major depression, alcohol dependence, or both. *Acta Psychiatrica Scandinavica, 96*(2), 142-149.

Swift R (1999). Drug therapy for alcohol dependence. *The New England Journal of Medicine, 340*(19), 1482-1488.

Vaillant G (1993). Is alcoholism more often the cause or the result of depression? *Harvard Review of Psychiatry, 1*, 94-99.

Volpicelli J, Alterman A, Hayashida, and O'Brien (1992). Naltrexone in the treatment of alcohol dependence. *Archives of General Psychiatry, 49*(1), 876-880.

Weissman MM, Gershon ES, Kidd KK, Prusoff BA, and Leckman JF (1984). Psychiatric disorders in the relatives of probands with depressive disorders. *Archives of General Psychiatry, 41*(1), 13-21.

Weissman M and Meyers K (1980). Clinical depression in alcoholism. *American Journal of Psychiatry, 137*(3), 372-373.

Whitters AC, Cadoret RJ, and Widmer RB (1985). Factors associated with suicide attempts in alcohol abusers. *Journal of Affective Disorders, 9*(1), 19-23.

Whitworth A, Fischer F, Lesch OM, Nimmerrichter A, Oberbauer H, Platz T, Potgeiter A, Walter H, and Fleischhacker, WW (1996). Comparison of acamprosate and placebo in long- term treatment of alcohol dependance. *Lancet, 347*(9013), 1438-1442.

Winokur G and Coryell W (1991). Familial alcoholism in primary unipolar major depressive disorder. *American Journal of Psychiatry, 148*(2), 184-187.

Chapter 8

Chemical Addictions
and Anxiety Disorders:
When Adaptive Mechanisms Go Awry

John Ramirez

INTRODUCTION

The study and treatment of comorbid addictive and psychiatric disorders has received growing interest in the past decade. This trend has been facilitated by findings from epidemiological studies (e.g., Regier et al., 1990) as well as clinical studies (e.g., Ross, Glazer, and Germanson, 1988), showing an elevated (higher than expected) co-occurrence of substance use disorders with other psychiatric illness. The functional nature of this relationship continues to occupy considerable research and speculation, particularly regarding the diagnosis and treatment of comorbid disorders.

This chapter will examine the relationship between the various anxiety disorders and chemical addiction. The guiding principle for our discussion will be the ANOVA statistical procedure, which distinguishes between main effects and interaction effects. Thus, the main effects of addiction will be examined first. A model will be presented that seeks to explain how addiction to psychoactive substances unfolds and manifests itself as a disease of the mind and body. The main effects of anxiety will be explored through a review of the common understanding of the etiology and diagnosis of the major anxiety disorders. I will then demonstrate how understanding of these two classes of disorders is enhanced when the manner in which they interact with each other is examined. Indeed, it has been argued elsewhere that the effective treatment of dually diagnosed patients must address the complex interaction between the patients' addictive and psychiatric disorders, and that this will require a synthesis of the knowledge base pertaining to both disorders (Pincus and Ramirez, 1997).

THE DISEASE OF ADDICTION

Perhaps the most significant positive trend in the treatment of addictive disorders has been the wide acceptance of the disease concept of chemical addiction. This concept has led us to abandon the view that addicts are moral degenerates possessing lack of will and poor moral fiber. Instead, they are seen as suffering from a chronic, progressive, and potentially fatal disease, which was contracted through excessive consumption of addictive psychoactive substances. Physical and psychological dependence on the substance will develop when one's excessive consumption becomes chronic and will get progressively worse with continued use. This progression will be reflected in increasingly negative biopsychosocial consequences. The only way to stop this degenerative biopsychosocial process is to discontinue the consumption of the substance altogether. However, abstinence will progress to recovery from addiction when the addicts accept that they have a serious problem, which will require abstinence as well as a willingness to engage in the active process of change. The understanding of addiction as a disease and the knowledge that this disease can be brought into remission with appropriate treatment and support should be conveyed to addicts because it will serve to neutralize the addicts' self-denigration as well as the despondency associated with the consequences of their addiction. The stage will thus be set for the addicts to experience hope and a commitment to change.

A disease is a morbid process with characteristic identifying symptoms. The nature and severity of the disease is determined by the manner and intensity with which these symptoms are manifested. The DSM-IV (APA, 1994) distinguishes two levels of severity. The milder form is called substance abuse. It is defined as a pattern of use leading to significant impairment or distress, demonstrated by at least one of the following within twelve consecutive months:

1. Impairment of home, work, or school performance as a result of substance use
2. Hazardous behavior resulting from substance use

3. Legal problems resulting from substance use
4. Continued substance use despite significant resultant problems

The more severe form of the disease is called substance dependence. It is defined as a pattern of use leading to significant impairment or distress, demonstrated by at least three of the following within twelve consecutive months:

1. Tolerance—the diminished effect from the same amount of the substance, often leading to use of increased amounts to achieve the same effect
2. Withdrawal—onset of withdrawal syndrome if the substance is discontinued, often leading to continued use to avoid withdrawal symptoms
3. Substance taken more than intended
4. Persistent use despite efforts to cut down
5. Much effort expended to obtain or continue use of the substance, or recover from effects of use
6. Other important activities discontinued or reduced in order to continue substance use
7. Continued substance use despite knowledge that it is having harmful physical or psychological effects

As a disease of the body, chemical addiction involves neurophysiological changes as well as changes in the functioning of bodily organs. The most immediate and direct neurophysiological effect of consuming an addictive substance is intoxication. This refers to various neurochemical changes produced by ingestion of (or exposure to) the substance, which are manifested in varying degrees of an acutely altered mental state. The degree of intoxication experienced is a result of the amount of the substance ingested and the period of time it took to ingest it. Low or mild levels of intoxication are associated with a positive mental state of euphoria or pleasure. However, higher levels of intoxication are associated with increasing levels of impairment in cognitive, emotional, and behavioral functioning. Therefore, the greater the amount of substance consumed and the shorter the period of time taken to consume it, the greater will be the resulting impairment.

The most direct long-term effect of consuming the substance is the development of tolerance and withdrawal. When the pattern of use is extensive and chronic, the resulting tolerance is invariably accompanied by withdrawal symptoms. In other words, when one's pattern of consumption produces the need to use increasing amounts to achieve the same effect (i.e., tolerance), this will be accompanied by an altered neurophysiological state of withdrawal produced by the cessation or reduced consumption of the substance. This state will cause significant impairment in functioning. Moreover, the nature of withdrawal symptoms from any given substance tends to be the opposite of the symptoms of intoxication because the chronic presence of the substance in the brain leads to cellular adaptation. When the substance is removed, a neurophysiological "rebound" effect produces withdrawal symptoms that are opposite of intoxication effects (Leonard, 1993).

In order to understand how the disease unfolds, the focus must be on why people are inclined to consume addictive substances in the first place. The answer is simple: the substance makes the person feel good. Addictive substances possess inherent reinforcing properties so that their consumption becomes a self-reinforcing process. According to Gold and Miller (1992), addictive substances act directly on the reinforcing functions of the central nervous system through neurotransmitter-mediated responses of reward and pleasure. The reward and pleasure system in the brain was accidentally discovered by James Olds in 1954. He mistakenly placed electrodes in a part of the limbic system of rats' brains and discovered that these rats would self-stimulate this area as many as 5,000 times an hour. It is now understood that all addictive substances possess the capacity to activate this reward system. It has been recently argued that some individuals have a deficiency in this reward system that predisposes them to addictive, impulsive, and compulsive disorders, including alcoholism, attention-deficit disorder, drug abuse, and food bingeing (Blum et al., 1996). This reward deficiency syndrome can also emerge solely as a function of excessive substance use. It "involves a form of sensory deprivation of the brain's pleasure mechanisms. It can be manifested in relatively mild or severe forms that follow as a consequence of an individual's biochemical inability to derive reward from ordinary, everyday activities" (Blum et al., 1996, p. 132).

Addiction as a disease of the mind involves psychological, emotional, and behavioral adaptations to the positive and negative reinforcement properties of addictive substances. Most theories of motivation recognize humanity's hedonistic nature. Humans seek pleasure and avoid pain. In seeking pleasure, we respond to the positive reinforcement properties of a stimulus (the extent to which that stimulus can produce pleasure). In avoiding pain, we respond to the negative reinforcement properties of a stimulus (the extent to which that stimulus can make the pain go away). I have observed that my patients' addiction becomes more severe as they progress from using the substance as a positive reinforcer to using it as a negative reinforcer. The self-medication hypothesis suggests that individuals with a preexisting psychiatric disorder will make this transition more rapidly because they are more receptive to the tension reduction or negative reinforcement provided by the substance. Individuals with no preexisting psychiatric disorder become receptive to negative reinforcement because of the progressively negative biopsychosocial consequences of their addiction.

In human efforts to optimize pleasure and reward, sometimes addictive substances are ingested to experience the pleasure of mild intoxication. Continued consumption teaches that the procurement and ingestion of the substance can become a path of least resistance to the activation of pleasure. This can disrupt the normal process of reward procurement through the application of one's abilities and problem-solving skills to create rewarding circumstances. We work hard and reap the benefits of our efforts. We also learn to appreciate the rewarding properties of a variety of recreational/leisure activities. Progressive reliance on a substance for positive reinforcement has two serious consequences. First, the individual's problem-solving skills will atrophy through lack of use. Very little skill and effort is required to procure the drug as compared to the effort and skill necessary to create rewarding psychosocial circumstances. A vicious cycle is created whereby problem-solving skills atrophy because of reliance on the drug. These diminished skills increase reliance on the drug further, which results in further atrophy of skills, and so on. This vicious cycle can culminate in a complete and total reliance on the drug for reinforcement with an accompanying inability to engage in any other reinforcing activities.

Second, progressive reliance on the drug for reinforcement will diminish one's ability to appreciate, and eventually experience, the pleasure derived from previously rewarding recreational activities. The reward deficiency syndrome suggests a more general neurophysiological inability to experience pleasure from normally rewarding events. The chronic reliance on addictive substances for the artificial activation of one's reward center has essentially increased the activation threshold so that progressively higher levels of positive stimulation are required before one can experience the actual "feeling" of pleasure. A condition of anhedonia is produced that can be alleviated only by the use of the substance alone or in combination with other rewarding activities. Moreover, without consumption of the drug, one's compromised reward center will require excessive levels of stimulation to become activated. This helps to explain why addicts who are in their active addiction or in early recovery tend to seek out activities that provide a "rush." They are not suffering from an addictive personality; rather, they are attempting to escape from an anhedonic state by seeking the excessive levels of stimulation required to activate their compromised reward centers.

This biochemical explanation does not, however, capture the complete nature of this degenerative process. Psychological mechanisms also come into play. Addicts learn to turn their pleasure over to the drug by successively pairing the consumption of the drug with the specific recreational activity. The time, effort, and attention devoted to the activity diminish and, instead, are given over to the procurement and consumption of the drug. Eventually the activity is abandoned altogether in favor of procuring and ingesting the drug.

For example, suppose Fred enjoys bowling and belongs to a bowling league. For a variety of reasons, he and his friends start to drink during this activity. At first they drink while they socialize prior to the start of the bowling activity. Fred finds this quite pleasurable and starts to drink while he is actually bowling. The amount of time Fred spends bowling diminishes and is replaced by drinking and socializing. He continues to make a token appearance at the bowling lanes, but he is primarily motivated to drink and socialize at the bar. He eventually starts to leave his bowling ball in the car, choosing instead to go directly to the bar. He has learned that bowling is not nearly as much fun as drinking! This replacement process extends to other rewarding activities as the addiction progresses. A clear indication that an addiction is unfolding occurs when you cannot imagine enjoying any given recreational activity without consuming the substance. Indeed, this anhedonic consequence of addiction helps to explain why the state of boredom tends to be such a powerful relapse trigger for addicts. A state of craving is created, which possesses the qualities of a drive similar to the state of hunger.

The avoidance of pain is just as motivating as the pursuit of pleasure. Physical and emotional pain/discomfort is an aversive state that motivates us to make it stop. Unfortunately, the random elements of human existence make the experience of pain unavoidable. Sometimes despite our best efforts to control the occurrence of aversive events, they happen anyway. However, this is not necessarily bad, because the ability to endure pain and to learn from it comprises the essential elements of coping skills. Humans become more resilient and adaptive as they successfully integrate the aversive consequences of their mistakes and miscalculations. The unavoidable random-based pain helps to strengthen coping skills and this helps people to better endure and learn from the painful consequences of their mistakes. To err is human, but to persist in committing the same errors is quite dysfunctional since the result is continued suffering. This certainly lends credence to the recovery slogan: Pain is necessary but suffering is optional!

The tendency to use an addictive substance for negative reinforcement represents the most destructive aspect of the addiction process. The addiction no longer involves only the compulsive and dysfunctional pursuit of pleasure; it now has progressed to being the primary means of coping with pain/dysphoria. The same replacement process discussed in the context of positive reinforcement takes place with negative reinforcement. Previously effective negatively reinforcing coping responses are gradually replaced by the procurement and consumption of the drug. In this manner, continued use of the drug ensures that it becomes a progressively more powerful negative reinforcer.

The continued reliance on the drug as a coping response has two serious consequences. First, the individual's capacity to endure pain/ dysphoria diminishes so that the addict experiences a dichotomous all-or-none reaction to lower and lower levels of pain. The ability to discriminate between gradations of pain is lost. Relatively minor aversive events begin to hurt just as much major ones, thus creating a heightened sense of urgency to make the pain go away, even though the pain is relatively minor. This activates an urge to use the drug as a negative reinforcer. The urge to use the drug as a positive reinforcer most likely represents a different motivational state, which is experienced as a craving. Second, the addict's coping mechanisms tend to atrophy through lack of use. Yet another vicious cycle emerges in which the atrophy of coping mechanisms results in an increased reliance on the substance, which increases the atrophy, which increases the reliance on the drug, and so on. This vicious cycle can culminate in an extremely low pain threshold whereby the addicts invariably overreact to minor levels of pain and where they are unable even to consider any way of coping with the pain other than using the drug.

M. S. Gold (1997) has argued that negative reinforcement theories do not adequately account for the addictive process. He states "drug use according to this model is thus maintained by the aversive symptoms associated with withdrawal and reversed by the drug" (p. 62). Gold argues for the primacy of withdrawal symptoms in explaining the power of an addictive substance as a negative reinforcer. However, showing that withdrawal symptoms have inadequate explanatory power does not necessarily indicate that the concept of negative reinforcement should have less theoretical salience than the concept of positive reinforcement. A complete understanding of the addictive process requires both concepts. Positive reinforcement is probably more applicable to the initiation of a chemical addiction as well as the mild form of the disease (substance abuse). Negative reinforcement becomes more salient in explaining the emergence of the more severe level of addiction (substance dependence). It becomes even more salient in understanding the interaction between addiction and anxiety disorders, which will be discussed later in the chapter.

The progressive nature of the disease of chemical addiction toward increasing biopsychosocial degeneration is best conceptualized as the transition from reliance on the drug for positive reinforcement to reliance on it for negative reinforcement. When the drug is both a positive and negative reinforcer the addiction becomes more virulent. This transition is a direct function of the negative biopsychosocial consequences of the emerging addiction. These consequences can be organized into the following general categories:

1. Damage to the tissue and organs that creates a serious medical condition
2. Cellular adaptation in the central nervous system resulting in a neurophysiogical "rebound" into a state of physical withdrawal

3. Progressive worsening of a deficiency in the brain's pleasure and reward system
4. Poor management of emotions reflected in problematic recognition, identification, expression, and articulation of feelings
5. Low self-esteem reflected in a fragile and unstable sense of one's value, efficacy, and identity, which most likely results from the self-denigration and social rejection that tends to accompany chronic and excessive substance use
6. Difficulty in establishing and maintaining healthy interpersonal relationships

Drug consumption rewards itself and, in doing so, strengthens its inherent rewarding properties. Similarly, the negative consequences of excessive and chronic drug consumption create the need to use the drug to escape the subjective pain of these consequences and, in doing so, strengthens the power of the drug as a negative reinforcer. The tragedy is that addicts simply cannot or will not recognize that the subjective pain that they are seeking to quell by taking the drug is in actuality the direct result of their excessive drug consumption. The trap of addiction has been set. The diminished capacity to experience pleasure and the atrophy of one's capacity to generate rewarding experiences from the environment produces compulsive drug seeking and consumption as well as other forms of compulsive pleasure and sensation seeking. The biopsychosocial consequences of this activity then produce a state of subjective pain or trauma, which can be temporarily abated by the drug. This establishes the negative reinforcement properties of the drug. As long as negative consequences continue, and continue they will, the drug will become a more powerful negative reinforcer. What starts as one of many ways of experiencing pleasure turns into a compulsive pursuit of pleasure and excitement and culminates in a frantic avoidance of pain. In this way one enters the subjective world of addiction in which nothing feels good and everything hurts.

ANXIETY AND ANXIETY DISORDERS

Anxiety disorders comprise a broad and rather heterogeneous group of psychiatric disorders. Recent epidemiological studies indicate that they are even more common in the general population than depression. Narrow et al. (1993) found that 12.6 percent of the population suffers from an anxiety disorder in a given twelve-month period and, more recently, Kessler et al. (1994) reported a twelve-month prevalence of 17.2 percent. Maxmen and Ward (1995) observed that the majority of people suffering from anxiety do not present themselves to mental health settings. Instead, they tend to seek out medical care settings with anxiety-related physical complaints or they present to addiction settings. In both instances, the anxiety disorder may not be the primary focus of attention. In the medical setting, somative complaints may obscure the importance of the anxiety itself, and in an addiction setting the anxiety may be seen as secondary to the addiction. Anxiety symptoms are complex and variable and frequently co-occur with a variety of medical conditions, with other psychiatric disorders, and with chemical addictions. This most certainly complicates the diagnosis and treatment of anxiety disorders.

Everybody experiences anxiety, but only some experience pathological levels, which impair functioning. Moreover, moderate levels of anxiety have been shown to be highly adaptive in that optimal learning and adjustment to threatening or stressful circumstances occur at moderate rather than either high or low levels (Janis, 1971). Pathological anxiety is ascertained when the physiological symptoms are distressing and disturbing to the person's normal functioning and/or when the psychological symptoms impede one's ability to cope effectively. Psychological symptoms may include:

1. Subjective sense of apprehension and tension without a known cause or out of proportion to the specific situation
2. Feelings of unreality or derealization
3. Hypervigilance, whereby one becomes excessively attentive to the point of distractibility, irritability, or insomnia
4. Impaired attention and concentration

Physiological symptoms may include:

1. Trembling, shakiness, restlessness, muscle tension
2. Shortness of breath, smothering sensation
3. Tachycardia or rapid heartbeat
4. Sweating and cold hands and feet
5. Lightheadedness and dizziness

6. Paresthesia or tingling of the skin
7. Diarrhea, frequent urination, or both
8. Initial insomnia or difficulty falling asleep
9. Nervousness, edginess, or tension

Chemical addiction reflects the dysfunction of an adaptive neuro-physiological process centered around the reward/pleasure mechanisms of the brain. Similarly, anxiety disorders reflect the dysfunction of a neurophysiological process that has ensured the survival of the human species and which assists the individual in adapting to the environment: the fight-or-flight response. Preston, O'Neal, and Talaga (1994) suggest that a complex network of nerve pathways, brain structures, and glands are responsible for this response, and that this response

> triggers a multilevel neurochemical and hormonal reaction designed to mobilize the body and mind during times of potential danger. Nonessential physiological processes shut down (such as digestion, reproduction), and energy is channeled into a host of bodily functions preparing the organism for rapid action. The nervous system also shifts in a state of hyperarousal and vigilance. (pp. 84-85)

The fight-or-flight response evolved to ensure survival in the face of dangerous situations. It involves a cascading downward of information from the cortex to lower brain areas to various glands. A situation is perceived as threatening at the level of the cortex. The limbic system is then put on alert. If the person concludes that danger is imminent, a cluster of nerve cell bodies called the locus coeruleus is activated, and this excitation activates the limbic system into a state of further arousal. The limbic system then activates the adjacent hypothalamus, which then activates the pituitary gland, the adrenal cortex, the thyroid gland, and the autonomic nervous system. The result of this downstream activation is the release of a variety of stress hormones, which render the brain and body quite ready for rapid action. The critical structure in this process is the locus coeruleus (LC). The LC nerve cells are mediated by the neurotransmitter norepinephrine.

The LC has been shown to play a major role in the manifestation of anxiety. When it is stimulated either electrically or by the drug yohimbine, anxiety increases, whereas the chemical inhibition of the

LC by adrenergic blockers such as clonidine and propranolol will diminish anxiety (Leonard, 1993). The LC is also postulated to play a major role in social phobias (Preston, O'Neal, and Talaga, 1994). Individuals with social phobia fear being scrutinized and judged or humiliated in public. Animal studies show that infants who are separated from their parents enter a state of high arousal and agitation, which results from extremely high levels of neuronal activity in the LC. With psychological development and neurologic maturation, the threshold for activation of the LC gradually increases, resulting in an increased ability to tolerate separation as infants mature. If one assumes that the fear of being embarrassed, humiliated, or rejected underlies social phobia, and if this is seen as equivalent to separation, then the role played by the LC becomes apparent. Patients who are sensitive to humiliation, separation, and rejection may possess a low threshold for activation of the LC.

LC functioning is also the most plausible explanation for the occurrence of panic attacks, which are quite brief and exceptionally intense surges of anxiety that often and suddenly "come out of the blue." The subjective experience is extremely aversive and can occasionally be traumatic. Fortunately, most attacks will subside within three to ten minutes and will rarely continue for more than thirty minutes. LC functioning can cause these intense attacks in two possible ways. First, neurons in the LC can become hypersensitive so that the activation threshold is lowered. Second, the natural braking mechanism in the LC nerve cells can become dysfunctional. The electrical impulse traveling through an activated nerve cell's axon will stimulate the release of its neurotransmitter norepinephrine to the excitatory receptors of the next nerve cell. However, the nerve cell's axon also impinges back on the nerve itself and the electrical impulse will also stimulate the release of norepinephrine to the inhibitory receptors located back on the cell body. This process is termed autoinhibition (Leonard, 1993). The stimulation of these autoreceptors acts to reduce the cell's excitability. In panic disorder the inhibitory autoreceptors are thought to be dysfunctional. Thus, the brakes (autoinhibition) will fail to stop the LC from continuing to activate the limbic system and the result will be a neurologically based state of subjective panic.

A second major aspect of the nervous system relevant to anxiety was identified with the discovery of benzodiazepine (BZD) receptors in the brain (Skolnick and Paul, 1983). The BZD receptor appears to be part of the gamma-amino butyric acid (GABA) receptor complex. GABA is one of the major inhibitory neurotransmitters, which plays a major role in reducing neuronal excitation and thus diminishing anxiety. When stimulated, the BZD receptor will augment the inhibitory effect of GABA, thus enabling GABA to produce a stronger inhibition of the postsynaptic neuron. Approximately 40 percent of the nerve cells in the brain possess tiny gateways on their surfaces. These gateways are called chloride ion channels. When the ion channel is activated, it opens and the slightly negatively charged chloride ions are drawn into the cell. As the cell is infused with these negative ions, its excitability is diminished and it relaxes. When GABA activates the GABA receptor, the ion channel will be activated or opened. Stimulation of the BZD receptor will further enhance the opening of the ion channel, and the nerve cell is relaxed. This process functions to dampen the limbic alert produced by the LC and in this way calm down the brain's overall excitation.

The discovery of the BZD receptor indicates the probable existence of a naturally occurring (endogenous) neurochemical similar to BZD, which has not yet been identified. Moreover, dysfunctional levels of anxiety may very well arise as a consequence of a deficiency of this BZD-like neurochemical and its action on the BZD-GABA receptor complex. This dysfunction has been postulated to account for the occurrence of generalized anxiety disorder (GAD) (Maxmen and Ward, 1995; Preston, O'Neal, and Talaga, 1994). Individuals who suffer from GAD tend to experience chronic low-grade levels of anxiety and to generally overreact to stressful situations. They are worry-warts who tend to engage in chronic worrying over a multitude of possible aversive or threatening events. As a consequence, the limbic system is placed in a state of perpetual alert. It is possible that such individuals do not possess an adequate neurochemical braking or inhibitory mechanism to dampen this limbic alert and that this may reflect a deficiency in an endogenous BZD-like neurochemical. Interestingly, LC dysfunction is believed to be linked to panic disorder and a BZD-receptor dysfunction is linked to GAD.

Mention should also be made of those anxiety disorders that are primarily psychogenic, involving the activation of a conditioned fear response, but which can and often do progress to neurophysiological dysfunction. Specific phobias involve irrational dread or fear of specific objects, situations, or activities with a compelling desire to avoid them. They represent a category of phobic stimuli not covered by agoraphobia or social phobia. According to Maxmen and Ward (1995), approximately 60 percent of phobic disorders seen in clinical practice involve agoraphobia, 10 percent involve social phobia, and the remaining 30 percent are specific phobias. Phobias can arise from age-appropriate fears, which usually subside with maturation, or they can develop as conditioned responses, which can be diminished by desensitization procedures. These are always anticipated and can induce mild to severe levels of anxiety upon exposure to phobic stimuli or at the anticipation of such exposure. Unlike panic attacks, phobias never occur spontaneously. Often a set of avoidance behaviors occur, which help reduce anticipatory anxiety. The level of anticipatory anxiety is a function of how confident the person feels in his or her ability to avoid the phobic stimulus. Phobic symptoms result in a diagnosis of a phobic disorder when they cause undue distress and impair functioning. These specific phobias most likely involve a classically conditioned activation of the fight-or-flight response.

Agoraphobia is the most severe of the phobic disorders and refers to an intense fear of being in places or situations from which escape might be difficult. Originally, it meant "fear of the marketplace," but the tendency for agoraphobia to mushroom or generalize necessitated a more general definition, encompassing fears of a variety of public places or open spaces such as experienced when driving a car, riding a bus, crossing bridges, standing in lines, passing through tunnels, walking through crowds, or shopping. Exposure to the feared stimulus can often trigger levels of anxiety severe enough to be defined as panic attacks, and agoraphobia is often comorbid with panic disorder. The intensity of this anxiety response may account for the extensive stimulus generalization seen in agoraphobia. An intense reaction will strengthen avoidance behaviors and will also increase the level of anticipatory anxiety. This anticipation ultimately accounts for increased stimulus generalization as well as an increased anxiety reaction to actual exposure. The actual exposure will induce a highly aversive subjective experience, which will later be recalled as a catastrophic event. As the individuals anticipate further exposure they recall a catastrophic level of subjective pain rather than the actual level, which itself was probably an overreaction. Thus, they actually believe that an experience of catastrophic proportions is being avoided and will go to great lengths to avoid the stimulus and then to avoid even the risk of exposure. This "you can never be too careful" mentality will dictate a person's avoidance strategies. This is how a fear of taking a bus can escalate to fear of going anywhere by any means.

Applying what is known about the LC and the BZD-GABA inhibitory system, we can postulate the following: An individual learns (most likely through principles of classical conditioning) to fear a given stimulus through experiencing discomfort upon exposure to this stimulus. The stimulus develops the ability to activate the LC and thereby induces limbic alert. However, anticipation of the stimulus may maintain this limbic alert in a manner similar to the chronic limbic alert experienced in GAD. This will require excessive activity of the BZD-GABA inhibitory mechanism to dampen this chronic level of limbic activation. The increasing severity of anticipatory anxiety will continue to overburden the inhibitory mechanism and may eventually compromise or even damage it, thus creating the same manner of neurological dysfunction that seems to underlie GAD. Without this braking mechanism, the autoinhibition or self-braking mechanism of the LC may become the primary way for the brain to reduce the elevated level of chronic limbic alert. Such heavy reliance on this braking mechanism may compromise or damage it so that eventually the threshold for activation of the LC-mediated flight-or-fight response may decrease and/or the intensity of the activation may become greater and perhaps of longer duration. This process may result in a dysfunction of the LC similar to that seen in panic disorder. In this manner, specific phobias and agoraphobia may kindle the kind of neurophysiological dysfunction seen in GAD and/or panic disorder.

A third adaptive neurophysiological mechanism has been postulated to account for the occurrence of obsessive-compulsive disorder (OCD). This is based on the observed effectiveness of antidepressants, which act on the neurotransmitter serotonin in the treatment of OCD patients. The main features of OCD are recurring obsessions (thoughts) and compulsions (behaviors). Obsessions are persistent, intrusive, and disturbing thoughts or impulses that the individual finds senseless (ego dystonic) yet irresistible. Compulsions represent the expression of obsessions in repetitive behaviors or rituals such as repeatedly "checking" to see if doors are locked or excessive hand washing, counting, arranging, or hoarding. Compulsions are linked to obsessions and are viewed as methods for reducing anxiety. For example, obsessions regarding dirtiness, contamination, and germs activate compulsive cleaning and hand washing; obsessive worry over the safety of self and others will fuel repetitive "checking" rituals; or excessive self-doubt with a sense of incompleteness and lack of order will be manifested in a variety of rituals with the purpose of making the environment "just right."

OCD is distinct from obsessive-compulsive personality disorder (OCP) in that OCD symptoms are experienced as ego dystonic (not part of oneself), whereas OCP traits of perfectionism, stinginess, emotional rigidity, and overdevotion to work are experienced as ego syntonic (part of oneself). Also, compulsions are distinguished from nonchemical addictions (e.g., compulsive pursuit of food, gambling, sex, etc.) in that the compulsions and accompanying obsessions are not pleasurable. Rather than being a source of pleasure, they are disturbing and, at best, seen as necessary to alleviate distress, although they are experienced as ego dystonic. In other words, they are viewed as a "necessary evil."

The naturally occurring adaptive neural pathway whose dysfunction underlies OCD involves other elements of the fight-or-flight response. Recall that activation of this response begins with the perception of danger by the cortex. More specifically, the frontal cortex perceives danger and then guides and sustains perceptual focus and attention. This alertness and vigilance is maintained through a feedback loop whereby the frontal cortex activates a brain structure called the caudate. The caudate, in turn, activates the thalamus, and the thalamus maintains activation of the frontal cortex. Apparently, the caudate contains many serotonin neurons. When it is activated it also activates inhibitory autoreceptors, which reduce activation of the caudate. Relaxation of the caudate will then shut down the frontal cortex-caudate-thalamus reverberating loop. In OCD this neural loop fails to inhibit itself. The frontal cortex continues to perceive (or worry about) danger, despite evidence to the contrary. As a result, the individual becomes trapped in a constant repetition of worry (obsessions) and will engage in behavioral rituals (compulsions) in an attempt to reduce the worry. Antidepressants affecting serotonin levels are effective presumably because they act upon the inhibitory serotonergic cells of the caudate.

This obsession-compulsion trap might take place as follows: The elevated levels of alertness and vigilance resulting from dysfunction of the caudate's ability to autoinhibit may have two important consequences. First, a more restricted perceptual filtering process may take place in which threat/danger cues are filtered in and safety cues filtered out. Second, this filtering may create the anticipation of an aversive event, which may in turn activate the LC-mediated fight-or-flight response. Herein lies the key to understanding the trap. Individuals suffering from OCD are extremely sensitive to these internal neurophysiological processes, as are most anxiety-disordered patients. Moreover, they actually use this neurophysiological activation as a signal or cue that something very bad is about to happen. As a result, the intensity of one's activated fight-or-flight response will determine the perceived severity of the anticipated event. The greater the level of activation, the more likely the individual is to anticipate the occurrence of an event of catastrophic proportions, and the greater will be the urgency to avoid this event at all costs. This will place enormous value on the anxiety-reducing properties of the various behaviors (compulsions) that one believes will facilitate the escape from the dreaded catastrophic event. Performance of the compulsive behavior will reduce the level of fight-or-flight activation perhaps through the LC autoinhibition and/or BZD-GABA braking mechanisms. However, the dysfunctional autoinhibition of the caudate will maintain hypervigilance and perceptual filtering so that the LC-mediated fight-or-flight response will eventually reach unacceptable levels again. Of course, this will trigger yet another urgent need to perform the compulsion and avoid a catastrophe. Unfortunately, the individuals have completely lost their understanding of exactly what event they are avoiding. Instead, the individuals become obsessed with avoiding unacceptable levels of an activated fight-or-flight response with the belief that they are avoiding a rather nebulous dreaded event. The irony is that the person suffering from OCD really has nothing to fear but fear itself.

One final anxiety disorder that merits discussion is post-traumatic stress disorder (PTSD). The DSM-IV (APA, 1994) includes it as an anxiety disorder because anxiety symptoms predominate. PTSD occurs after a person has been exposed to a traumatic event in which the person experienced, witnessed, or was confronted with an event or events that involved actual or threatened death or serious injury, or a threat of the physical integrity of self or others, and the person's response involved intense fear, helplessness, or horror. The DSM-IV delineates three categories of symptoms:

1. Reexperiencing (intrusion) where the traumatic event is persistently reexperienced as recurrent, intrusive, and distressing.
2. Avoidance (denial) where there is persistent avoidance of stimuli associated with the trauma and numbing of general responsiveness not present before the trauma.
3. Arousal, where there are persistent symptoms of arousal not present before the trauma.

Horowitz (1985) presented a model for understanding normal emotional reactions to significant stress, which is useful in understanding PTSD symptoms. It is called the stress response syndrome. Five distinct phases have been delineated. A stressful event evokes an *outcry,* which leads to *denial,* which will tend to oscillate with *intrusion.* Eventually *working through* occurs and the process culminates in *completion.* This process can be examined more closely with an eye toward the distinction between normal stress reactions versus pathological intensifications.

The immediate response to a stressful event will encompass sadness, fear, and anxiety. If the stress is unusually intense or prolonged, the individual may be overwhelmed, dazed, and/or confused. Soon thereafter the outcry will take place and the individual will experience guilt, shame, rage, protest, and anxiety. If the stress is unusually intense or prolonged, the individual may experience panic, exhaustion, dissociative symptoms, and/or psychosis. The person is in a state of shock, which can last for a few minutes, a few hours, or a few days. Hours or months after the stressor, individuals can waiver between denial (avoidance) and intrusion. Often denial comes first, although it can occur after a period of intrusion. It involves emotional numbness and avoidance and can be expressed as minimization, hypersomnia, anhedonia, dysthymia, obsessions, lethargy, and repression. Pathological intensification can be maladaptive avoidances, such as isolation, suicide, and substance abuse, as well as such psychiatric symptoms as amnesia, rigid thought, psychic numbing, severe repression, and a variety of psychophysiologic symptoms such as headaches, fatigue, and bowel cramps. Intrusion brings on intense emotions and a strong impulse to think about, imagine, or mentally relive the event and is reflected in such symptoms as anxiety, psychophysiologic reactions, decreased concentration and attention, insomnia, and dysphoria. Pathological intensifications can encompass flooded states, hypervigilance, startle responses, illusions, hallucinations, obsessions, impaired concentration and attention, sleep and dream disruptions, emotional lability, preoccupation with and confusion over the event, fight-or-flight readiness, and compulsive reenactments of the trauma. Working through takes place when the individual makes an effort to discover the meaning of the event, mourn subjective losses, and generate new plans for the future based on the meaning ascribed to the event. Completion designates a return to preevent functioning and renewed psychological growth. When working through is blocked and, hence, completion is not reached, the individual will exhibit varying degrees of pathological intensifications associated with avoidance (denial) and/or intrusion.

The experience of a traumatic event results in a highly intense activation of the fight-or-flight response, which results in a subjective experience that is indeed of catastrophic proportions. The more severe the trauma, the more intense the neurophysiological symptoms of the fight-or-flight response will be, resulting in a more aversive subjective experience. Some authors (e.g., Triffleman, 1997; Langley, 1997) have argued that an unusually intense, prolonged, and/or frequently occurring trauma may result in a *kindling* effect. Kindling refers to "the development of seizures after repeated delivery of a series of subthreshold stimuli to any region of the brain" (Leonard, 1993, p. 95). As applied to this discussion, kindling can generally refer to a situation in which repeated episodes of trauma actually result in a change in brain functioning, specifically dysregulation of those aspects of the fight-or-flight response that are particularly relevant to anxiety (e.g., the LC and the BZD-GABA inhibitory system). The result is a lowered threshold for activation of the extreme levels of anxiety seen in patients suffering from PTSD. These anxiety symptoms comprise the pathological intensifications of avoidance and intrusion.

A fascinating suggestion was made by van der Kolk (1987) regarding the "flashbacks" (intrusion symptoms) experienced by PTSD patients. He argued that this phenomenon could be traced to the intense activation of the limbic circuitry involved in memory functions (the hippocampus and possibly the amygdala) by the LC. The result could be a strongly embedded memory of the highly aversive, subjective experience of the traumatic event. When recalled, this memory can be quite vivid and may perhaps even retraumatize the individual, particularly if dysregulation of the LC and the BZD-GABA inhibitory mechanism has been kindled.

To summarize this review and discussion of the major anxiety disorders, three aspects of the adaptive fight-or-flight response have been identified as important etiologic factors. First is the locus coeruleus (LC) and its ability to activate the limbic system. When it becomes dysfunctional, the result can be the emergence of those anxiety symptoms associated with panic disorder, social and specific phobias, and PTSD. Second, dysregulation of the BZD-GABA inhibitory mechanism is particularly relevant to the etiology of GAD and possibly anticipatory anxiety. Finally, dysfunction of the frontal cortex-caudate-thalamus neural loop is important to the etiology of OCD.

A brief discussion of pathological anxiety as a disease of the mind and body follows. An essential component of anxiety disorders is dysregulation of the otherwise adaptive neurophysiological mechanisms involved in the individual's reaction to threatening circumstances. Three fundamental aspects of one's reaction to threat are identified: neurophysiological arousal, response strategy formulation, and behavioral performance. The level of arousal elicited by the threat reflects the extent to which the various neurophysiological elements of the fight-or-flight response have been activated. This activation will determine the degree of motivation, drive, or urgency the individual feels to either flee/avoid or fight/contend with the threat. From a cybernetic standpoint, this neurocircuitry may be viewed as the person's "hardware." In the case of anxiety, this hardware includes the LC, the BZD-GABA inhibitory mechanism, and the cortex-caudate-thalamus loop. The neurotransmitters responsible for activating these structures are norepinephrine (NE), GABA, serotonin (5HT), and an as yet unidentified chemical resembling BZD. Ideally, there should be a linear relationship between the severity of the threat and the degree of activation.

The cybernetic perspective also delineates the notion of "software." For our purposes, the person's software refers to the programs and metaprograms used to process and respond to incoming information (e.g., attitudes, beliefs, habits, knowledge base, cognitive structures, schematas, etc.). Obviously, this software comprises the two remaining aspects of one's reaction to a perceived threat. Response strategy formulation begins with the cognitive processing of one's activation in the context of the threatening circumstances (e.g., labeling what one is feeling) and incorporating this information into the formulation of a response strategy. Behavioral performance entails the actual implementation of the response strategy and the various cognitive activities involved in response guidance. Ideally, one's software will produce an optimal adaptive response to the threatening circumstances. Damaged hardware and/or faulty software will produce pathological anxiety and dysfunctional responses.

Anxiety disorders provide an excellent example of how the causal relationship between one's hardware and software can be bidirectional. Humans perceive, react neurophysiologically, interpret, and then behaviorally respond to any given situation. The process always begins with one's perception of the situation or the manner in which the individual has "filtered" incoming situational information. This perceptual filtering explains why different people behave differently in the same situation and why the same person may behave the same across different situations. People respond to the situation they perceive and this perception may or may not reflect the objective elements of the situation. The filtering process is what determines the perceived situation and the response strategy is a direct function of this perception. Different people bring different software packages and, hence, different perceptual filters into any given situation. This will produce their differing perceptions of the situation, which will dictate their different responses. In addition, the person's software package may be damaged so that certain aspects of the situation (e.g., threatening elements) are always given great perceptual salience, resulting in the emission of similar behaviors across different situations. If one's software and hardware are fully functional, the individual's level of activation will be linearly related to the amount of threat present in the situation, and this activation will facilitate an accurate interpretation of what is being felt and what to do about it. An adaptive response strategy will emerge as a result. The disease of pathological anxiety reflects a disruption of this process whereby the hardware (the body) and/or the software (the mind) are faulty, and in which their interaction produces pathology and dysfunction.

People suffering from pathological levels of anxiety are unusually sensitive to potentially threatening elements of their environment.

Their perceptual filtering is damaged such that threatening elements of incoming information is filtered in and nonthreatening (safety) elements are filtered out. Indeed, the programming can be so damaged that external stimuli are not necessary to produce a sense of threat or dread. One's programming can actually create internal stimuli, which can activate a pathological fight-or-flight response. This can happen in two ways. One can recall a past event and excessively ruminate over it, or one might anticipate a possible future event and excessively ruminate over it. The situation is even more problematic when the faulty hardware is considered.

Recall that damage to the relevant neurophysiological mechanisms (hardware) involved in anxiety can be manifested in two ways. There can be a lowered threshold for activation and/or there can be excessive and continuous "firing" because of faulty braking or auto-inhibition. The result is a sensitive trigger for an intense level of activation, which will be difficult to dissipate. This is analogous to a bear trap where a very sensitive trigger will activate a powerful and potentially catastrophic consequence. However, unlike the spent trap, activated anxiety will continue and may even become more intense. This highly aversive level of activation will have two consequences. First, the perceptual filter will become even more constricted making it difficult if not impossible to perceive any safety in the situation. Second, one's already faulty programs for formulating an adaptive response will be further compromised. Indeed, the more intense one's arousal is in any given situation, the more he or she becomes a reactor rather than a decider, where irrational processes supplant rational ones. There will be a restriction in the range of possible response strategies with an inevitable reliance on more primitive learned behaviors, which can at times resemble the fixed action patterns seen in lower animals. The individuals are no longer trying to adapt or adjust to a threatening set of circumstances. Rather, they are trying to survive a subjectively experienced catastrophic event. It becomes easier to appreciate the hell that anxiety-disordered patients create for themselves.

The bidirectional relationship between one's hardware and software is also evident from a developmental perspective. One's total software package is formed and upgraded through the continual integration of knowledge learned from the person's transactions with the environment. In this manner, a continual upgrading of one's software occurs as more experience is accumulated. As a result, the accuracy of one's perceptions and the adaptiveness of one's reactions and behaviors will increase with experience, particularly if one's hardware is fully functional. Let us briefly explore how an individual might develop the faulty software and hardware seen in anxiety disorders.

It is possible that a person can be born with a severely damaged fight-or-flight response. However, this appears to be rare. Most individuals inherit a more or less sensitive neurophysiological hardware rather than a damaged one. The result could be a tendency to experience higher levels of activation to relatively low levels of stimulation. This can increase the chances of subjectively experiencing one's activation as aversive, which in turn may increase the urgency one feels in making this aversive state go away. If the developing infant's family unit is nurturing, the amount of objective situational threat will probably be limited. This nurturing developmental environment will allow for the effective integration of the caregivers' efforts to instill adaptive programming into the infant's software. Moreover, the stage will be set for continued healthy upgrading of the individual's software through the various modes of learning from exposure and direct experience.

However, if the caregiving environment is dysfunctional, threat rather than nurturance may predominate and nonadaptive programming may be passed on to the children. As a result, the children will experience elevated levels of chronic distress/anxiety, which will overburden their already sensitive hardware and will further compromise their development of adaptive programming from the caregiver's faulty programs and dysfunctional efforts at instilling them. A vicious cycle will emerge in which the children's faulty perceptual and adaptive programming will make their threatening environment even more threatening subjectively, thus creating even more aversive levels of activation. The chronic experience of such heightened stress reactions will further compromise their efforts at adapting to the environment and what is learned from these efforts, resulting in further damage to their already damaged programming. The chronic state of subjective trauma will eventually damage the oversensitive hardware that was inherited. In this way, the mutually exacerbating effects of faulty hardware and software can result in the emergence of an anxiety disorder.

COMORBIDITY

Before examining the interaction between anxiety and addictive disorders, the existence of an empirical relationship between them should be established. At a basic level it must be determined whether these two classes of disorders tend to "hang together" or co-occur at a level greater than expected. The term used to reflect the co-occurrence between two or more disorders is comorbidity. The comorbidity between anxiety disorders and chemical addictions has been examined in three ways: (1) within a mental health setting by establishing the percentage of anxiety-disordered patients who also suffer from a chemical addiction; (2) within an addiction setting by establishing the percentage of addicted patients who also suffer from an anxiety disorder; and (3) within a community/nonclinical population.

Anxiety-Disordered Patients Seeking Treatment

Most of the research investigating the prevalence of substance problems within this clinical population has focused primarily on alcohol. Quitkin et al. (1972) were the first to point out a possible relationship between anxiety and chemical addictions when they presented ten case studies of patients with phobias who abused drugs and alcohol. Thyer et al. (1986) found that 36 percent of the patients who were in treatment for anxiety also had a concurrent alcohol abuse/dependence diagnosis. Interestingly, Tilley (1987) showed that apart from the subgroup of anxiety-disordered patients who drank heavily, the remaining patients consumed moderate amounts of alcohol. They drank the same or less than their counterparts in the general population.

Reich and Chaudry (1987) estimated that 28 percent of the panic-disordered patients in their study had a history of alcoholism, with males being more likely than females to be alcoholic. Markowitz et al. (1989) found that the risk of someone with a panic disorder having a substance disorder is 2.4 times higher than in the general population. Brier, Charney, and Heninger (1986) reported that 17 percent of their patients who suffered from agoraphobia with panic also suffered from alcoholism. Boyd et al. (1984) found that the risk of alcoholism in persons with phobias of any type is approximately 2.5 times higher than in the general population. This risk was greater than fourfold in persons with panic disorder. Bibb and Chambless (1986) reported that 13 percent of a sample of agoraphobic outpatients were diagnosed as having alcohol problems. Finally, Stockwell and Bolderston (1987) found that 20 percent of their phobic patients reported problematic drinking.

In both inpatient and outpatient populations of patients suffering from PTSD, substance abuse disorders are the most commonly co-occurring psychiatric problems (Rundell et al., 1989). The prevalence rates for alcohol abuse/dependence are both elevated and variable among veterans with PTSD. They are as follows, depending on the study: 41 percent (Davidson et al., 1985); 45 percent (Behar, 1984); 54 percent (Faustman and White, 1989); 64 percent (Sierles et al., 1983); and 80 percent (Escobar et al., 1983). The same is true for abuse/dependence of all drugs other than alcohol among veterans with PTSD. They are as follows: 16 percent (Davidson et al., 1985); 20 percent (Sierles et al., 1983); 23 percent (Behar, 1984); 36 percent (Faustman and White, 1989); and 50 percent (Escobar et al., 1983).

Chemically Addicted Patients Seeking Treatment

More research has also been conducted with alcohol than drugs in this population. However, the discrepancy is not as great as is seen with anxiety disorder clinical populations. Regarding all anxiety disorders, Weiss and Rosenberg (1985) found a 23 percent lifetime prevalence and Bowen et al. (1984) reported a 44 percent prevalence in alcoholic inpatients. Brown, Irwin, and Schuckit (1991) reported 50 to 67 percent of alcohol-dependent males have high scores on state anxiety measures. The percentage of inpatient alcoholics suffering from any type of phobic disorder has ranged from 18 percent (Smail et al., 1984) to 27 percent (Hesselbrock, Meyer, and Keener, 1985) to 29 percent (Bowen et al., 1984). Mullaney and Trippett (1979) found that 17 percent of their inpatient alcoholics also had agoraphobia and 24 percent also had social phobia. Weiss and Rosenberg (1985) found that 12 percent of their alcoholic inpatients had a phobic disorder; 10 percent had a panic disorder; and 6 percent had GAD. Eisen and Rasmussen (1989) found that 6 percent of their fifty inpatient alcoholics were diagnosed with OCD using DSM-III-R criteria.

Nunes, Quitkin, and Klein (1989) found that 31 percent of their twenty-nine cocaine-dependent outpatients had a coexisting anxiety disorder. Myrick and Brady (1997) report a 13.9 percent lifetime prevalence of social phobia in a cocaine-dependent population. Washton and Gold (1984) estimate the prevalence of panic attacks in chronic cocaine users to be as high as 64 percent. Rosen and Kosten (1992) report that 13 percent of 141 methadone-maintained patients also had a panic disorder. Finally, in treatment-seeking substance users, 20 to 65 percent report a history of sexual and physical assault (Triffleman, Marmer, and Delvechi, 1993; Simpson et al., 1994; Grice et al., 1995). The lifetime prevalence of PTSD in this clinical population ranges from 36 percent to 50 percent (Grice et al., 1995; Triffleman, Marmer, and Delvechi, 1993; Dansky et al., 1995).

The generally high levels of comorbidity found in clinical populations has been questioned on several methodological grounds. Berkson (1946) pointed out that the identification of multiple conditions in patients is statistically likely. That is, people who are distressed enough to seek treatment are more likely to suffer from multiple disorders. The confounding effect of this treatment-seeking bias (also called Berkson's bias) is absent with epidemiological studies focusing on nonclinical populations. Other problems that may account for exaggerated rates of comorbidity are the differing criteria used for diagnosing disorders and the timing of the diagnostic interview relative to the active consumption of, as well as detoxification and prolonged abstinence from, substances (Brady and Lydiard, 1993; Bolo, 1996; Deas-Nesmith, Brady, and Myrick, 1997; Schuckit and Hesselbrock, 1994; Sajiv and Miller, 1997). Large-scale epidemiological studies can also control for these methodological contaminants with the use of standardized diagnostic instruments and procedures and with the assessment of lifetime prevalence rates.

Several epidemiological studies with nonclinical populations indicate a higher than expected level of comorbidity between anxiety disorders and chemical addiction. The Epidemiological Catchment Area study (Regier et al., 1990) reported a 16.7 percent lifetime prevalence for any substance use disorder, a 13.7 percent rate for alcohol abuse/ dependence, and 5.9 percent for drug abuse/dependence. They also reported a lifetime prevalence of 14.6 percent for any anxiety disorder. Regarding specific anxiety disorders, they reported 12.8 percent for any phobia, 10.1 percent for simple phobia, 2.8 percent for social phobia, 5.2 percent for agoraphobia, 2.5 percent for OCD, and 1.5 percent for panic disorder. Using a subsample from the larger

ECA study, Cottler et al. (1992) reported a 1.35 percent lifetime prevalence for PTSD.

Regarding comorbidity, Regier et al. (1990) reported that among those individuals with an anxiety disorder, 19.4 percent also had an alcohol problem and 28.3 percent had a drug problem. They reported that 24 percent of those with OCD also had an alcohol disorder. More recently, Ross (1995) reported similar findings in a community-based sample. Crum and Anthony (1993) found that the risk of developing OCD was 5.6 times higher for individuals reporting the use of both cocaine and marijuana than for those using no illicit drugs. This estimated risk for developing OCD was 2.1 times higher in those using marijuana alone, 0.8 times higher in those using marijuana and another drug other than cocaine, and 3.2 times higher for those using cocaine, marijuana, and at least one other drug.

Regier et al. (1990) reported that 36 percent of their respondents who had panic disorder had a comorbid substance disorder. Anthony, Tien, and Petronis (1989) also found a substantial comorbidity between panic disorder and cocaine abuse/dependence, with the highest relative risk in cocaine users who reported no marijuana use during the study interval. Massion, Warshaw, and Keller (1993) found that 18 percent (sixty-four) of their 357 respondents could be diagnosed with GAD, and of these sixty-four, 11 percent had a history of substance abuse or dependence, excluding alcohol. Finally, Helzer, Robins, and McEvoy (1987) reported that males with PTSD were five times as likely to have drug abuse/dependence as those without PTSD. Females were 1.4 times as likely. Cottler et al. (1992) found that 13 percent of their comparison group without a substance disorder reported a PTSD-qualifying traumatic event, compared to 43 percent of cocaine/opiate users, 23 percent of pill/hallucinogen users, 18 percent of marijuana users, and 16 percent of heavy alcohol users. Moreover, substance users were 2.63 times as likely to meet criteria for PTSD as comparison subjects, with cocaine/opiate users being 10.75 and pill/hallucinogen users being 3.68 times as likely.

THE INTERACTION

Pincus and Ramirez (1997) have argued that the best way to view comorbidity for the purpose of adequate treatment is to focus on the interaction between addictive and psychiatric disorders. This view places an emphasis on the notion of bidirectional rather than unidirectional causality, which in turn underlies the three elements of their suggested treatment approach for patients suffering from both disorders:

1. integration of relevant services;
2. simultaneous treatment of both disorders; and
3. the synthesis of treatment techniques reflected in the recovery versus mental health models, thus enabling the therapist to develop a truly individualized treatment plan.

Moreover, from this perspective, the question becomes one of establishing how the various biopsychosocial processes in addictive disorders both affect and are affected by those biopsychosocial processes involved in anxiety disorders. There are four fundamental ways in which they can mutually affect one another:

1. etiology—the way they mutually affect one another's emergence and progression;
2. presentation—the way in which they mutually determine the configuration of presenting symptoms;
3. treatment—the way they mutually affect the patient's response to treatment; and
4. maintenance—the way they mutually affect the patient's efforts at maintaining the gains garnered from successful treatment so as to avoid relapses and decompensations.

The present discussion will be limited to etiology and presentation.

The most widely held explanation for the high rates of comorbidity between anxiety and addiction, particularly alcoholism, is the self-medication hypothesis (Khantzian, 1985; Capell, 1975). The subjective experience of anxiety is assumed to motivate the individual to self-medicate this aversive state with alcohol, because alcohol is capable of reducing or eliminating dysphoric emotional states. This hypothesis has been investigated by determining the relative onset of each disorder (anxiety should precede the addiction) or by testing the anxiolytic properties of alcohol.

Research on relative onset indicates that the self-medication hypothesis may be appropriate for phobias. Researchers have found that the phobia generally began before the alcohol problem. Mullaney and Trippett (1979) found that 75 percent (thirty-three) of their forty-four patients with agoraphobia/simple phobia reported that the phobia preceded the alcohol problem. Stockwell et al. (1984) found that the median onset for social phobia or agoraphobia in their patients was two years before that of the alcohol problems. Bibb and Chambless (1986) reported that 41 percent (nine) of their twenty-two agoraphobics developed the disorder prior to alcohol abuse. In addition, 91 percent described using alcohol to control their phobic fears; a majority stated that the best thing about alcohol was its anxiolytic effect, and almost half noted that their reason for drinking alcohol was more to feel normal than to have fun or become intoxicated. Smail et al. (1984) found that all their agoraphobic or socially phobic patients attributed tension-reducing properties to alcohol and reported that alcohol helped them cope with feared situations. Schneier et al. (1989) found that sixteen (16.3 percent) of their ninety-eight socially phobic patients had a history of alcoholism and that social phobia preceded alcoholism in fifteen of them. Most of them also reported using alcohol to self-medicate symptoms. Finally, Hesselbrock, Meyer, and Keener (1985) and Chambless et al. (1987) showed that the chronology described by patients with simple phobias is one of the phobias preceding the alcoholism.

Research investigating the relative order of onset regarding anxiety disorders other than phobias has generally not supported the self-medication hypothesis. Ross, Glazer, and Germanson (1988) found that GAD began after substance abuse in 51 percent, began at the same time in 10 percent, and began before alcohol abuse in 35 percent of their patients. Regarding panic disorder and OCD, research shows more variability, suggesting that these two anxiety disorders can begin before, after, or at the same time as the alcohol problems (Ross, Glazer, and Germanson, 1988; Hesselbrock, Meyer, and Keener, 1985; Chambless et al., 1987; Powell et al., 1982; and Karno et al., 1988). Several authors have argued that virtually all of this research is flawed because of problems with the use of retrospective reporting in addicted and other clinical populations, as well as the presence of symptoms of both acute and protracted withdrawal syndromes (e.g., Schuckit and Hesselbrock, 1994; Allen 1995; Romach and Doumani, 1997). The denial and minimization seen in addicted populations as well as the debilitating effects of addictive and psychiatric symptoms on cognitive functioning certainly call into question the veracity and accuracy of retrospective reports. As discussed later, there is considerable symptom overlap between chronic intoxication, withdrawal, and anxiety disorders. Such confounding factors are not present when examining the anxiolytic properties of alcohol in laboratory settings.

Several reviews of the literature suggest that animal studies tend to consistently demonstrate the anxiolytic properties of alcohol (Romach and Doumani, 1997; Wilson, 1988; Young, Oei, and Knight, 1990). However, extrapolating to humans is rather problematic. These same reviews report that research with nonclinical human populations has produced mainly contradictory findings, which most likely reflect the complexity of the relationship between alcohol consumption and anxiety. These reviewers also argue that this complexity can be unraveled and contradiction can be reconciled by examining other mediating factors, such as the amount of alcohol consumed, individual physiological differences that influence response to alcohol, previous experience with alcohol, expectations about the effects of alcohol, cognitive set, gender, and how anxiety is operationalized. These reviews provide particularly comprehensive presentations of the conditions under which alcohol has and has not demonstrated anxiolytic effects within nonclinical populations.

More germane to this discussion is research on the anxiolytic properties of alcohol in clinical populations. Contrary to expectations based on the self-medication hypothesis, several studies suggest that alcohol consumption may actually increase anxiety. Freed (1978) notes that an increase in anxiety has been described in association with the consumption of large amounts of alcohol. Mendelson and Mello (1979) found that alcoholics become progressively more anxious, agitated, and dysphoric during chronic intoxication. Stockwell and Bolderston (1987) provide evidence that drinking increases rather than decreases psychological distress in alcoholic patients suffering from phobias.

Two studies merit particular attention. Kushner et al. (1996) found that panic-disordered patients who consumed alcohol and then underwent a panic challenge with carbon dioxide reported less state anxiety before and after the challenge and experienced fewer panic attacks than did similar patients who received a placebo. They conclude that alcohol acts acutely to reduce both panic and the anxiety surrounding panic and suggest that drinking behavior among those with panic disorder is reinforced by this effect. Stockwell, Hodgson, and Rankin (1982) described an increase in anxiety resulting from prolonged drinking. They monitored physiological and self-report indices of anxiety in alcoholic men as they drank over a two-day period. Diminished anxiety was reported shortly after these men started to drink. However, an increase in anxiety and dysphoria was reported as they continued to drink. Interestingly, despite this increase, they reported expecting to feel worse if they stopped drinking. Stockwell and colleagues suggest that patients may continue to attribute anxiolytic properties to alcohol in spite of an actual increase in clinical anxiety because they fear that stopping drinking will result in even more distress. Thus the initial anxiolytic affect of alcohol may be a more potent reinforcer of continued drinking despite the anxiogenic effects emerging over time. This provides support for Stockwell's (1980) earlier suggestion that alcohol reduces anxiety acutely, but its long-term effect is to exacerbate anxiety.

The earlier explanation of the disease of addiction can help us to better understand Stockwell's suggestion regarding the short-term versus the long-term effects of consuming alcohol on anxiety. The short-term intoxicating effects of alcohol include both euphoric and sedating (anxiolytic) elements, but the chronic consumption of alcohol may exacerbate an existing anxiety disorder or precipitate a new one due to the processes underlying tolerance and withdrawal. As argued earlier, the addictive use of substances will compromise one's reward center, which will result in an increased threshold for activating the experience of pleasure/euphoria. Moreover, this addictive degree of consumption will also result in a decreased threshold for activating pain/dysphoria as well as the atrophy of problem-solving skills and coping mechanisms. In this manner the chronic abuse of addictive substances for their immediate positive and negative reinforcement properties may, in fact, induce an intense state of anxiety, exacerbate an existing anxiety disorder, and/or precipitate a new one. The literature on chronic intoxication and withdrawal substantiates this notion.

Moran (1986) described six case studies of agoraphobia in which all six patients associated their panic symptoms with marijuana intoxication. Roy-Byrne and Uhde (1988) also showed that the use of marijuana can precipitate panic attacks. Aronson and Crain (1986) found that cocaine use can precipitate panic attacks in patients without a previous panic disorder. They described several patients whose panic disorder began during chronic use of cocaine and continued for up to three years of abstinence. They speculated that chronic cocaine use causes increased central noradrenergic activity possibly by depleting biogenic amines, which may result in receptor hypersensitivity. Price and Giannini (1987) found that panic attacks also can be induced by the use of intranasal phencyclidine in addition to cocaine. Finally, Louie, Lannon, and Ketter (1989) described ten patients who developed panic disorder after one to six years of cocaine use. These patients had persistent panic attacks for up to seven years after abstinence. They also found that these patients with cocaine-induced panic disorder had substantial symptom improvement with carbamazepine or clonazepam, thus suggesting that chronic cocaine use may have kindled increased limbic neuronal activity. The immediate intoxicating effects of marijuana, phencyclidine, and especially cocaine may include the activation or exacerbation of a state of anxiety and the chronic experience of intoxication with these drugs can actually precipitate an anxiety disorder.

Several authors have argued that symptoms of withdrawal from alcohol and other depressants are indistinguishable from those of major anxiety disorders (Blankfield, 1986; Griffin et al., 1987; Miller, 1995). Peyser (1982) showed that the abrupt reduction or discontinuation of alcohol intake after a period of chronic drinking can result in autonomic nervous system arousal, which is manifested in symptoms of tremulousness, tachycardia, insomnia, irritability, nervousness, sweating, hyperventilation, and gastrointestinal upset. All of these symptoms also occur in anxiety states. This degree of symptom overlap suggests that it may be quite difficult to distinguish between states of withdrawal and anxiety. Chambliss et al. (1987) found that alcoholics with GAD symptoms were unable to distinguish between these and symptoms of alcohol withdrawal. George et al. (1988) found that alcoholics with panic disorder could not discriminate withdrawal from panic symptoms. Tremor was the only withdrawal symptom from a list of twenty-nine physical and cognitive symptoms that subjects felt discriminated panic attack from alcohol withdrawal. A study by Johannessen et al. (1989) indicated another consequence of this symptom overlap. Not only are patients unable to distinguish between these symptom complexes, but apparently so are clinicians.

They found that only two (9 percent) of twenty-two alcoholic in-patients with clear-cut spontaneous panic attacks were actually diagnosed with panic disorder. They concluded that panic states may be overlooked in the treatment of alcoholics.

A possible etiologic connection between alcoholism and panic disorder is implied by the finding that a difference exists between panic-disordered patients with or without a history of alcoholism (George et al., 1989). This study used intravenous lactate infusion, which generally induces panic attacks. Panic-disordered patients with a history of alcoholism tended not to panic with lactate infusion, whereas those without such a history did panic. Also, in those panic-disordered patients with alcoholism who did panic, the panic disorder predated the onset of alcohol abuse. Three explanations were postulated:

1. repeated withdrawal desensitized these patients to the peripheral symptoms that elicit panic;
2. they were desensitized to lactate because they have elevated baseline plasma lactate concentrations; and
3. withdrawal kindles limbic structures to heightened excitability that could promote panic through increased norepinephrine and cortical release.

These authors settled upon the third explanation in a later paper (George et al., 1990). They speculate that the overlapping symptoms result from a common neurochemical dysfunction and that repeated episodes of withdrawal may result in the induction of panic attacks through a kindling process in vulnerable individuals. More recently, Romach and Doumani (1997) postulated that the common neurochemical disturbance that may underlie alcohol withdrawal and panic attacks is dysregulation and overactivity in the locus coeruleus.

To summarize, anxiety-disordered patients are more likely to suffer from chemical addictions than are individuals with no anxiety disorder. Likewise, chemically addicted patients are more likely to suffer from anxiety than are individuals with no addiction. However, these findings may be due to Berkson's bias, which would predict elevated rates of comorbidity in treatment-seeking patients. Epidemiological studies with nonclinical populations eliminate this source of contamination. These studies also show elevated levels of comorbidity between chemical addictions and anxiety disorders, although they are not as high as are seen in clinical populations. Regarding etiology, only the phobias seem to emerge consistently prior to the onset of addiction, whereas other anxiety disorders tend to begin before, during, or after the onset of addiction. The anxiolytic properties of alcohol have been demonstrated with animals in laboratory settings. Laboratory studies with nonclinical human populations show that alcohol may or may not demonstrate anxiolytic effects depending on a variety of mediating factors. In clinical populations, alcohol reduces anxiety acutely, but its long-term effect is to exacerbate anxiety. The immediate intoxicating effects of marijuana, phencyclidine, and especially cocaine may include the activation of intense anxiety or the exacerbation of an already elevated level of anxiety. Their chronic use may aggravate an existing anxiety disorder or precipitate a new one. Finally, withdrawal symptoms from alcohol and other CNS depressants are indistinguishable from symptoms of GAD and panic disorder, suggesting that repeated episodes of withdrawal may kindle a neurochemical dysfunction similar to that seen in GAD and panic disorder.

DIAGNOSTIC CONSIDERATIONS

Clinicians seldom, if ever, have the capacity to disentangle the exact manner in which a patient's comorbid anxiety and addiction disorders mutually affected each other's etiology. People tend to wait until their level of distress is severe enough to seek treatment due to myriad psychosocial factors that serve to inhibit treatment seeking. Therefore, by the time patients actually present for diagnosis they have reached the etiologic end point in the interaction between their comorbid disorders. Unfortunately, this etiologic end point is the clinician's diagnostic and treatment starting point. The previous discussion suggests that the clinician will have to sort out whether and to what degree the configuration of presenting symptoms reflects acute intoxication, acute withdrawal, or the long-term effects of chronic intoxication and withdrawal. This has enormous treatment implications because the acute and chronic effects of the addictive consumption of drugs will abate with continued abstinence, thus requiring an appropriate adjustment to the overall treatment plan. This is why one must place considerable importance on the differential diagnosis of comorbid anxiety and addictive disorders in the formulation of an effective individualized treatment plan.

It has been suggested that differential diagnosis should emphasize a primary/secondary distinction based on the chronological order of onset (e.g., Schuckit, 1985). Remember that retrospective recall is problematic so that the accuracy of information collected in this way may be compromised. The use of collateral sources of information can help. However, the clinical utility of this distinction is questionable. I have found this distinction to be useful for the sole purpose of satisfying the need for managed care to determine which stream of funding will pay for the patient's treatment: chemical addiction versus mental health benefits. As discussed, the treatment of the dually diagnosed patient has been hampered by the existence of two separate systems for the funding, managing, and treatment of addictive (recovery model) and psychiatric (mental health model) disorders (Pincus and Ramirez, 1997). A much more useful strategy is to combine the stabilization of a patient suffering with comorbid disorders with the process of differential diagnosis. In my experience, this approach invariably leads to addressing the addictive symptoms first. Eliminating the consumption of an addictive substance is a much less complicated endeavor than is the determination of whether, what kinds, and what dosage of medications may be required. Moreover, very little, if anything, can be done to stabilize, diagnose, and treat any patient who is actively abusing addictive substances.

The DSM-IV provides excellent descriptions of symptoms of intoxication and withdrawal associated with a variety of addictive substances. When combined with the American Society of Addictive Medicine (ASAM) patient criteria (Hoffman et al., 1991), the clinician is provided with clear decision-making strategies for appropriate stabilization and continued differential diagnosis. The best way to differentiate intoxication/withdrawal-induced transient symptoms from nonsubstance-induced anxiety symptoms is through observation during a period of abstinence from addictive substances. The severity of the presenting symptoms will determine whether this observation will take place in a hospital-based medically managed setting, a residential medically monitored inpatient setting, or on an outpatient basis entailing varying frequency and duration of clinical contact. An important issue is the minimal duration of abstinence in order to conduct an accurate rule out. Withdrawal symptoms may be protracted and several weeks of abstinence may be required for long half-life substances such as methadone or some benzodiazepines (BZDs). For shorter-action substances, such as cocaine and short-life BZDs, the acute intoxication and the withdrawal duration will be briefer. A good rule of thumb is that acute intoxication and withdrawal symptoms will generally cease within two weeks of abstinence.

Damage to the hardware resulting from chronic episodes of intoxication and withdrawal will take longer to return to normal functioning. The DSM-IV has recognized this and has introduced the category of substance-induced psychiatric disorders. They are delirium, persisting dementia, persisting amnestic disorder, psychotic disorder, mood disorder, anxiety disorder, sexual dysfunction, sleep disorder, and hallucinogen persisting perception disorder (flashbacks). Symptoms of a substance-induced anxiety disorder must appear during or within one month of intoxication or withdrawal from the substance. However, evidence for an independent anxiety disorder is indicated when the symptoms precede the onset of substance use, the symptoms persist for a substantial period of time (e.g., about a month) after the cessation of acute withdrawal or severe intoxication, or are substantially in excess of what would be expected given the type and amount of the substance used or the duration of use. I tend to be more cautious in ruling out a substance-induced anxiety disorder. In my experience these symptoms can abate within one month of abstinence but can continue for up to three months. A serious complication is the tendency for the addict to minimize, rationalize, and deny substance use, thus requiring the clinician to discern whether the patient is being truthful about self-reported abstinence. The following practices are helpful in addressing this problem:

1. the use of random urine screens;
2. placing an early emphasis on building a strong therapeutic alliance;
3. regularly using family and/or roommates as collateral sources of information;
4. incorporating family and/or roommates into the treatment plan as positive sources of change in the patient's recovery environment through joint sessions and collateral contact; and
5. refraining from immediate discharge if the patient relapses, provided that he or she voluntarily reports any relapse.

In addition to observation of the patient during a period of abstinence, several aspects of a comprehensive psychosocial history can be helpful in differential diagnosis of comorbid anxiety and addictive disorders. When assessing an anxiety-disordered patient, one should consider a chemical addiction if there is a history of heavy substance use, a pattern of consuming the substance to relieve anxiety, a history of dependence on BZDs, a family history of substance problems, poor treatment compliance, and/or poor treatment results for the anxiety disorder. Conversely, in evaluating a chemically addicted patient, one should consider an anxiety disorder when there has been poor compliance with addiction treatment, when there has been previous positive response to treatment of anxiety symptoms, when there are high unremitting levels of anxiety, when there are physical complaints that are difficult to diagnose, when there is a family history of anxiety disorders, and/or if the patient requests BZDs. Finally, one should also identify any over-the-counter medications (addictive and nonaddictive) as well as any medical conditions that can induce anxiety symptoms.

CONCLUSION

The conclusion will integrate previously discussed notions of etiologic "main effects" regarding chemical addictions and anxiety disorders into an interactive (bidirectional) etiologic model. This model will address the possible ways in which a condition of comorbid addictive and anxiety disorders may have emerged. There are three general classes of factors in this model: (1) dispositional factors, representing the individual's hardware and software; (2) situational factors, comprising the various objective stimuli present in any given situation which impinge upon the individual and to which he or she may or may not choose to respond; and (3) transactional factors, which refer to the bidirectional "give and take" that occurs between the person and the situation and how this process unfolds into a steady stream of actions, reactions, and responses.

The infant and its caregiving environment is a good place to start. One can assume that the main dispositional factors will reflect the infant's inherited hardware since there has not been enough time for software to develop. One's software develops as a result of myriad transactions with the environment and the integration of the consequences of these transactions into one's software/programming through the various learning processes (classical and operant conditioning, modeling, and direct instruction) and combinations of these processes. The brain's reward and pleasure center (R/PC) is of etiologic significance to addictive disorders. Infants are born with R/PCs possessing varying degrees of sensitivity. Those with insensitive R/PCs will require higher levels of positive stimulation in order to activate the experience of pleasure. However, it is also possible that one can inherit an oversensitive R/PC, requiring lower levels of stimulation to activate pleasurable feelings. Future research should focus on this, particularly as a possible inoculant against the development of addictions.

The neurocircuitry comprising the infant's fight-or-flight response (F/FR) is of etiologic significance to the development of anxiety disorders. Infants with an overly sensitive F/FR will experience higher levels of F/FR activation to relatively low levels of objective threat (sensitive locus coeruleus), will experience this activation for a longer period of time (insensitive locus coeruleus autoinhibition and/or BZD/GABA braking mechanism), and may remain hypervigilant to threat for a longer period of time (insensitive autoinhibition of the caudate). However, it is also possible to inherit an insensitive F/FR, whereby the individual will require higher levels of threat to activate the F/FR, will rapidly dissipate this activation, and will be relatively ignorant of threatening situational cues. This dispositional factor may be relevant to the etiology of an antisocial personality disorder. Another important issue is the other element of the F/FR: the experience of anger (versus fear) and the willingness to fight (versus flee). It is entirely possible that there is another category of individuals who possess an oversensitive F/FR and who remain hypersensitive to threat. However, they will experience anger rather than fear, and this anger will dissipate slowly leading to fight and approach strategies rather than fear-induced flight and avoidance strategies. I suspect that many of these individuals find their way into our jails and prisons as violent offenders. What accounts for this differentiation of an oversensitive F/FR into those who are fearful and develop anxiety disorders versus those who are angry and become violent? Is this a function of one's learning history, or are there different neurochemical factors involved in the LC activation of the limbic system? These are important and fascinating issues for future research.

One final dispositional factor involves the absence of a predisposition in the form of an R/RC and F/FR that are in the "normal" range of functioning. How can an otherwise normal nervous system become compromised to the point of independent and/or comorbid addictive and anxiety disorders? One part of the answer lies in the effects that one's initiation and continued need for the addictive consumption of drugs/alcohol and the avoidance of fear/threat have on the individual's hardware and software. The other part of the answer lies in the self-reinforcing properties of these two classes of behaviors. All of this happens as a result of frequent transactions with a dysfunctional social environment, which may result in damage to one's hardware and/or the development of dysfunctional programming. The developmental milieu (the family of origin) is critical. Elements of the family environment that are conducive to the development of addictive and anxiety disorders are delineated. Four basic aspects of the family environment are postulated to be important in the development of an addictive disorder:

1. the pleasure-seeking climate, which refers to the extent to which pleasure-seeking activities (which may possess compulsive qualities) are displayed by family members, thus providing opportunities for modeling;
2. the value placed on consuming addictive substances, which is reflected in the behaviors and spontaneous verbalizations of family members;
3. caretakers' efforts to instill the value of consuming addictive substances through instruction; and
4. the amount of behavioral dysfunction reflected in the frequency, intensity, and duration of harmful behaviors such as neglect and/or verbal, physical, and sexual abuse.

Likewise, four aspects of the family can be postulated to be important in the development of anxiety disorders:

1. the avoidance climate, which refers to the extent to which fear-induced avoidance behaviors are displayed by family members, thus providing opportunities for modeling;
2. the value placed on the avoidance of danger and the salience given to the notion of a dangerous world, both of which are re-

flected in the behaviors and spontaneous verbalizations of family members;

3. caretakers' efforts to instill the value of fear-induced avoidance strategies through instruction; and
4. the amount of behavioral dysfunction reflected in the frequency, intensity, and duration of harmful behaviors such as neglect and/or verbal, physical, and sexual abuse.

Remember that the delineation of dispositional and situational factors is primarily a conceptual enterprise. The real world of emotions, thoughts, and behaviors is reflected in the actual transaction between the person, the specific situation, and how it proceeds. Various combinations of dispositional and situational factors can produce intense and highly problematic transactions with enormous consequences for the individual's hardware and software. The more heavily loaded a situation is for anxiety and addiction and the more heavily laden the individual's disposition for addiction and anxiety, the more intense and problematic will be transactions spawned by this configuration, and the more serious the effect of these transactions on the individual's hardware and software. In the early stages of development the degree to which the family environment is loaded for addiction and anxiety will be paramount in affecting the individual's disposition in the form of dysfunctional programming and damaged hardware. Later in development, dispositional factors will become much more important in determining the nature of one's transaction with a specific situation so that the unfolding transaction will more likely manifest the baggage (dispositional factors) that the individual brought into the situation.

The most heavily loaded developmental configuration of dispositional and family factors for the emergence of addiction/anxiety comorbidity is when an infant is born with an undersensitive R/PC and an oversensitive F/FR, and is reared in a family environment heavily loaded with addiction and anxiety factors. This individual will be dually diagnosed from the onset. Seven more combinations of dispositional and situational factors can be derived. They are

1. an oversensitive F/FR and an anxiety-loaded family milieu,
2. an oversensitive F/FR and an addiction-loaded family milieu,
3. an undersensitive R/PC and an addiction-loaded family milieu,
4. an undersensitive R/PC and an anxiety-loaded family milieu,

5. normal hardware and an anxiety- and addiction-loaded family milieu,
6. normal hardware and an anxiety-loaded family milieu, and
7. normal hardware and an addiction-loaded family milieu.

Let me conclude by highlighting how a person with an anxiety disorder (perhaps resulting from the previous list's 1, 4, or 6) can develop a chemical addiction and how a person with an addiction (perhaps resulting from 2, 3, or 7) can develop an anxiety disorder.

Anxiety-disordered individuals are acutely sensitive to threatening/dangerous situational cues as well as their own neurophysiological reactions to these cues. Once their neurophysiology is activated they experience an urgent need to reduce this subjective state of anxiety and have learned a variety of avoidance strategies that have developed strong negative reinforcement properties. Imagine this individual's delight upon discovering that this dreaded state of subjective anxiety can be eliminated (avoided) by the simple act of consuming an addictive substance. The neurophysiologically based anxiolytic effects coupled with the ease of procuring the substance may rapidly elevate the value of consuming it. The procurement and consumption of the substance may eventually become the most frequently used avoidance strategy in the person's behavioral repertoire. Unfortunately, when used excessively this strategy will have its own consequences. The inevitable tolerance and withdrawal as well as the damage that chronic intoxication/withdrawal will produce in one's hardware may exacerbate the anxiety disorder. This will place even greater negative reinforcement value on procuring and consuming the substance. Furthermore, another unforeseen consequence is the compromise of one's R/PC. I have found anxiety-disordered patients to be relatively insensitive to pleasure. They experience the activation of their R/PC, but they are so preoccupied with avoiding a catastrophe that they ignore the internal feelings of pleasure. Sadly, the addictive use of drugs/alcohol will compromise what little ability they have to experience pleasure.

The chemically addicted individual takes a longer time to discover and become preoccupied with the negative reinforcement properties of addictive substances. This happens through the natural progression of the disease of addiction from using the substance as a positive reinforcer to using it as a negative reinforcer. Damage to one's R/PC leads to the compulsive pursuit of pleasure and excitement, which will, in turn, create a variety of biopsychosocial consequences. The F/FR can be damaged by chronic intoxication with stimulants and/or withdrawal from central nervous system depressants. This creates a built-in negative reinforcement tied to the direct neurophysiological effects of the drug. More important is the gradual erosion of one's adaptive programming so that the late-stage addict begins to view consumption of the drug in the same way that the anxiety-disordered person views it: as a very effective strategy for avoiding or eliminating a highly aversive internal state of anxiety/dysphoria. However, unlike the anxious person, the addict has experienced pleasure and become rather preoccupied with it. As a result, no matter how severe the substance-induced anxiety symptoms or disorder become, the extremely high pleasure threshold will continue to affect the addicts' transactions with their environment. In fact, the preoccupation with pleasure and excitement may once again take on compulsive qualities when withdrawal has abated, substance-induced neurophysiological damage to the F/FR has normalized, or the addiction-precipitated anxiety disorder has been remitted by successful treatment. Indeed, the clinician should not be fooled by the successful treatment of the addict's preoccupation with the drug's negative reinforcement properties and decide to discharge the patient positively. This would be quite premature, because the addict's compromised ability to experience pleasure will lead back to a preoccupation with the drug's negative reinforcement value unless the compromised ability to experience pleasure is addressed.

The diagnosis and treatment of dually diagnosed patients is a complicated endeavor because of the way in which addictive and psychiatric disorders interact with each other in their etiology, presentation, treatment, and maintenance. The approach taken in this chapter to organize the general knowledge base comprising chemical addictions and anxiety disorders was derived from the ANOVA statistical procedure. Hopefully, it has facilitated the understanding of the interaction between them, because effective treatment of comorbid anxiety and addictive disorders requires such an understanding. Rudimentary elements of an interactive etiologic model have also been presented. Perhaps a conceptual framework (versus model) might be a better description of what has been presented. I hope that the contents of this chapter will help the readers organize their thoughts about addictions and anxiety and how to treat their comorbidity.

REFERENCES

Allen CA. Alcohol problems and anxiety disorders—A critical review. *Alcohol and Alcoholism,* 1995; 30(2): 145-151.

American Psychiatric Association (APA). *Diagnostic and Statistical Manual of Mental Disorders,* Fourth edition. Washington, DC: American Psychiatric Association, 1994.

Anthony JC, Tien AY, and Petronis KR. Epidemiologic evidence on cocaine use and panic attacks. *American Journal of Epidemiology,* 1989; 129: 543-549.

Aronson TA and Crain TJ. Cocaine precipitation of panic disorder. *Americal Journal of Psychiatry,* 1986; 143: 643-645.

Behar D. Conformation of concurrent illnesses in post-traumatic stress disorder. *American Journal of Psychiatry,* 1984; 141: 1310.

Berkson J. Limitations of the application of four-fold tables to hospital data. *Biometric Bulletin,* 1946; 2: 47-53.

Bibb DL and Chambless DL. Alcohol use and abuse among diagnosed agoraphobics. *Behaviour Research and Therapy,* 1986; 24: 49-58.

Blankfield A. Psychiatric symptoms in alcohol dependence: Diagnostic and treatment implications. *Journal of Substance Abuse Treatment,* 1986; 3: 275-278.

Blum K, Cull JG, Braverman ER, and Comings DE. Reward deficiency syndrome. Addictive, impulsive and compulsive disorders—including alcoholism, attention-deficit disorder, drug abuse and food bingeing—may have a common genetic basis. *American Scientist,* 1996; 84: 132-145.

Bolo PM. Substance abuse and anxiety disorders. In Gold MS and Slaby AE (Eds.), *Dual diagnosis in substance abuse,* (pp. 45-56). New York: Marcel Dekker Inc., 1996.

Bowen RC, Cipywnyk MD, D'Arcy C, and Keegan D. Alcoholism, anxiety disorders, and agoraphobia. *Alcoholism: Clinical and Experimental Research,* 1984; 8: 48-50.

Boyd JH, Burke JD, Greenberg E, et al. Exclusion criteria of DSM-III: A study of co-occurrence of hierarchy-free syndromes. *Archives of General Psychiatry,* 1984; 41: 983-989.

Brady KT and Lydiard RB. The association of alcoholism and anxiety. *Psychiatric Quarterly,* 1993; 64: 135-148.

Brier A, Charney DS, and Heninger GR. Agoraphobia with panic attacks: Development, diagnostic stability, and course of illness. *Archives of General Psychiatry,* 1986; 43: 1029-1036.

Brown SA, Irwin M, and Schuckit MA. Changes in anxiety among abstinent male alcoholics. *Journal of Studies on Alcohol,* 1991; 52: 55-61.

Capell H. An evaluation of tension models of alcohol consumption. In Gibbins RJ et al. (Eds.), *Research advances in alcohol and drug problems,* Volume 2. New York: John Wiley, 1975.

Chambless DL, Cherney J, Caputo GC, and Rheinstein BJ. Anxiety disorders and alcoholism: A study with inpatient alcoholics. *Journal of Anxiety Disorders,* 1987; 1(1): 29-40.

Cottler LB, Compton WM, Mager D, et al. Posttraumatic stress disorder among substance users from the general population. *American Journal of Psychiatry,* 1992; 149(5): 664-670.

Crum RM and Anthony JC. Cocaine use and other suspected risk factors for obsessive compulsive disorder: A prospective study with data from the Epidemiologic Catchment Area surveys. *Drug and Alcohol Dependence,* 1993; 31: 281-295.

Dansky BS, Saladin M, Brady KT, Killeen T, Becker S, and Roitzsch JC. Prevalence of victimization and PTSD among women with substance use disorders: Comparison of telephone and in-person assessment samples. *International Journal of Addictions,* 1995; 30(9): 1079-1099.

Davidson J, Swartz M, Storck M, Krishman RR, and Hammett E. A diagnostic and family study of post traumatic stress disorder. *American Journal of Psychiatry,* 1985; 142: 90-93.

Deas-Nesmith D, Brady KT, and Myrick H. Drug abuse and anxiety disorders. In Kranzler HR and Rounsaville BJ (Eds.), *Dual diagnosis and treatment: Substance abuse and comorbid medical and psychiatric disorders* (pp. 203-221). New York: Marcel Dekker Inc, 1997.

Eisen JL and Rasmussen SA. Coexisting obsessive compulsive disorder and alcoholism. *Journal of Clinical Psychiatry,* 1989; 50: 96-99.

Escobar JI, Randolph ET, Puente G, Spiwak F, Asamer JK, Hill M, and Hough RL. Post-traumatic stress disorder in Hispanic Vietnam veterans. *Journal of Nervous and Mental Disease,* 1983; 171: 585-596.

Faustman WO and White PA. Diagnostic and psychopharmacological treatment characteristics of 536 inpatients with posttraumatic stress disorder. *Journal of Nervous and Mental Disease,* 1989; 177: 154-159.

Freed EX. Alcohol and mood: An updated review. *International Journal of Addiction,* 1978; 13:173-200.

George DT, Nutt DJ, Dwyer BA, and Linnoila M. Alcoholism and panic disorder: Is the comorbidity more than coincidence? *Acta Psychiatrica Scandinavica,* 1990; 81: 97-107.

George DT, Nutt DJ, Waxman RP, and Linnoila M. Panic response to lactate administration in alcoholic and nonalcoholic patients with panic disorders. *American Journal of Psychiatry,* 1989; 146: 1161-1165.

George DT, Zerby A, Noble S, and Nutt DJ. Panic attacks and alcohol withdrawal: Can subjects differentiate the symptoms? *Biological Psychiatry,* 1988; 24: 240-243.

Gold MS. The neurobiology of addictive disorders: The role of dopamine, endorphin, and serotonin. In NS Miller (Ed.), *The principles and practice of addictions in psychiatry*. Philadelphia, PA: WB Saunders Co., 1997.

Gold MS and Miller NS. Seeking drugs/alcohol and avoiding withdrawal: The neuroanatomy of drive states and withdrawal. *Psychiatric Annals*, 1992; 22: 433-435.

Grice DE, Brady KT, Dustan LR, Malcolm R, and Kilpatrick DG. Sexual and physical assault history and posttraumatic stress disorder in substance-dependent individuals. *American Journal of Addictions*, 1995; 4: 297-305.

Griffin ML, Weiss RD, et al. The use of the Diagnostic Interview Schedule in drug dependent patients. *American Journal of Drug and Alcohol Abuse*, 1987; 13: 281-291.

Helzer JE, Robins LN, McEvoy L. Post-traumatic stress disorder in the general population: Findings from the Epidemiological Catchment Area survey. *New England Journal of Medicine*, 1987; 387: 1630-1634.

Hesselbrock MN, Meyer RE, and Keener JJ. Psychopathology in hospitalized alcoholics. *Archives of General Psychiatry*, 1985; 42: 1050-1055.

Hoffman NG, Halikas JA, Mee-Lee D, and Weedman, RD. Patient placement criteria for the treatment of psychoactive substance use disorders. American Society of Addictive Medicine, Washington, DC, 1991.

Horowitz MJ. Disasters and psychological responses to stress. *Psychiatric Annals*, 1985; 15: 161-167.

Janis IL. *Stress and frustration.* New York: H. Hold and Co., 1971.

Johannessen DJ, Coulee DS, Walker RD, Jensen CF, and Parker L. Prevalence, onset, and clinical recognition of panic states in hospitalized male alcoholics. *American Journal of Psychiatry*, 1989; 146: 1201-1203.

Karno M, Golfing JM, Sorenson SB, and Burnam MA. The epidemiology of obsessive compulsive disorder in five US communities. *Archives of General Psychiatry*, 1988; 45: 1094-1099.

Kessler RC, McGonagle KA, Zhao S, Nelson CB, Hughes M, Eshleman S, Wittchen HU, and Kendler KS. Lifetime and 12-month prevalence of DSM-III-R psychiatric disorders in the United States. Results from the National Comorbidity Survey. *Archives of General Psychiatry*, 1994; 51(1): 8-19.

Khantzian EJ. The self-medication hypothesis of addictive disorders: Focus on heroin and cocaine dependence. *American Journal of Psychiatry*, 1985; 142: 1259-1264.

Kushner MG, Mackenzie TB, Fiszdon J, Valentines DP, Foa E, Anderson N, and Wangensteen D. The effects of alcohol consumption on laboratory-induced panic and state anxiety. *Archives of General Psychiatry*, 1996; 53: 264-270.

Langley M. Posttraumatic stress disorder and addiction: What are the links? In NS Miller (Ed.), *The principles and practice of addictions in psychiatry* (pp. 279-296). Philadelphia, PA: WB Saunders Co., 1997.

Leonard NE. *Fundamentals of psychopharmacology.* New York: John Wiley and Sons, 1993.

Louie AK, Lannon RA, and Ketter TA. Treatment of cocaine-induced panic disor-der. *American Journal of Psychiatry*, 1989; 146: 40-44.

Markowitz JS, Weissman MM, Ouellette R, et al. Quality of life in panic disorder. *Archives of General Psychiatry*, 1989; 46(11): 984-992.

Massion AO, Warshaw MG, and Keller MB. Quality of life and psychiatric morbid-ity in panic disorder and generalized anxiety disorder. *American Journal of Psychiatry*, 1993; 150(4): 600-607.

Maxmen JS and Ward NG. *Essential psychopathology and its treatment*, Second edition. New York: W.W. Norton and Company, 1995.

Mendelson JH and Mello NK. One unanswered question about alcoholism. *British Journal of Addiction*, 1979; 74: 11-14.

Miller NS. Psychiatric diagnosis in drugs and alcohol addiction. *Alcohol Treatment Quarterly*, 1995; 12(2): 75-92.

Moran, C. Depersonalization and agoraphobia associated with marijuana use. *British Journal of Medical Psychology*, 1986; 59: 187-196.

Mullaney JA and Trippett CJ. Alcohol dependence and phobias: Clinical descrip-tion and relevance. *British Journal of Psychiatry*, 1979; 135: 565-573.

Myrick H and Brady K. Comorbid social phobia and cocaine dependence. *American Psychiatric Association New Research Abstracts*, 1997; 471.

Narrow WE, Regier DA, Rae DS, Marderscheid RW, and Locke AM. Use of ser-vices by persons with mental and addictive disorders. *Archives of General Psychiatry*, 1993; 50(2): 95-107.

Nunes EV, Quitkin FM, and Klein DE. Psychiatric diagnosis in cocaine abuse. *Psychiatry Research*, 1989; 28: 105-114.

Peace K and Mellsop G. Alcoholism and psychiatric disorder. *Australian and New Zealand Journal of Psychiatry*, 1987; 21: 94-101.

Peyser H. Stress and alcohol. In Goldberger L and Breznotz S (Eds.), *Handbook of Stress*. New York: Free Press, 1982.

Pincus J and Ramirez J. Dual diagnosis: Issues in the treatment of comorbid mental health and substance abuse disorders. In VandeCreek L, Knapp S, and Jackson TL (Eds.), *Innovations in clinical practice: A source book;* 15 (pp. 71-81). Sarasota, FL: Professional Resource Press, 1997.

Powell BJ, Penick EC, Othmer E, Bingham SF, and Rice AS. Prevalence of addi-tional psychiatric syndromes among male alcoholics. *Journal of Clinical Psychiatry*, 1982; 43: 404-407.

Preston J, O'Neal JH, and Talaga MC. *Handbook of clinical psychopharmacology for therapists*. Oakland, CA: New Harbinger Pub Inc., 1994.

Price WA and Giannini AJ. Phencyclidine and "crack"-precipitated panic disorder. *American Journal of Psychiatry*, 1987; 144(5): 686-687.

Quitkin FM, Rifkin A, Kaplan J, and Klein DF. Phobic anxiety syndrome compli-cated by drug dependence and addiction: A treatable form of drug abuse. *Archives of General Psychiatry*, 1972; 27: 159-162.

Regier DA, Farmer ME, Rae DS, Locke BZ, Keith S, Judd L, and Goodwin F. Comorbidity of mental disorders with alcohol and other drug abuse: Results from the Epidemiologic Catchment Area (ECA) study. *JAMA,* 1990; 264: 2511-2518.

Reich J and Chaudry D. Personality of panic disorder alcohol abusers. *Journal of Nervous Mental Disease,* 1987; 175: 224-227.

Romach MK and Doumani S. Alcoholism and anxiety disorders. In Kranzler HR and Rounsaville BJ (Eds.), *Dual diagnosis and treatment: Substance abuse and comorbid medical and psychiatric disorders* (pp. 137-175). New York: Marcel Dekker Inc, 1997.

Rosen MI and Kosten T. Cocaine associated panic attacks in methadone maintained patients. *American Journal of Drug and Alcohol Abuse,* 1992; 18(1): 57-62.

Ross H. DSM-III-R alcohol abuse and dependence and psychiatric comorbidity in Ontario: Results from the Mental Health Supplement to the Ontario Health Survey. *Drug and Alcohol Dependence,* 1995; 39: 111-128.

Ross H, Glazer FB, and Germanson T. The prevalence of psychiatric disorders in patients with alcohol and other drug problems. *Archives of General Psychiatry,* 1988; 44: 1023-1031.

Roy-Byrne PP and Uhde TW. Exogenous factors in panic disorder: Clinical and research implications. *Journal of Clinical Psychiatry,* 1988; 49: 56-61.

Rundell JR, Ursano RJ, Holloway HC, and Silberman BK. Psychiatric responses to trauma. *Hospital and Community Psychiatry,* 1989; 40: 68-74.

Sajiv J and Miller NS. Anxiety disorders and addictions. In Miller NS (Ed.), *The principles and practice of addictions in psychiatry* (pp. 249-254). Philadelphia, PA: SB Saunders Co, 1997.

Schneier FR, Martin LY, Liebowitz MR, Gorman JM, and Fyer AJ. Alcohol abuse in social phobia. *Journal of Anxiety Disorders,* 1989; 3: 15-23.

Schuckit MA. The clinical implications of primary diagnostic groups among alcoholics. *Archives of General Psychiatry,* 1985; 42: 1043-1049.

Schuckit MA and Hesselbrock VM. Alcohol dependence and anxiety disorders: What is the relationship? *American Journal of Psychiatry,* 1994; 151(12): 1723-1734.

Sierles FS, Chen JJ, McFarland RE, and Taylor MA. Posttraumatic stress disorder and concurrent psychiatric illness: A preliminary report. *American Journal of Psychiatry,* 1983; 140: 1177-1179.

Simpson TL, Westerberg VS, et al. Screening for childhood physical and sexual abuse among outpatient substance abusers. *Journal of Substance Abuse Treatment,* 1994; 11(4): 347-358.

Skolnick P and Paul SM. New concepts in the neurobiology of anxiety. *Journal of Clinical Psychiatry,* 1983; 44: 12-19.

Smail P, Stockwell T, Canter S, and Hodgson R. Alcohol dependence and phobic anxiety states. I. A prevalence study. *British Journal of Psychiatry,* 1984; 144: 53-57.

Stockwell T. Relativity and the consequences of drinking. *British Journal of Addiction,* 1980; 75: 214-216.

Stockwell T and Bolderston H. Alcohol and phobias. *British Journal of Addiction,* 1987; 32: 971-979.

Stockwell T, Hodgson R, and Rankin H. Tension reduction and the effects of prolonged alcohol consumption. *British Journal of Addiction,* 1982; 77: 65-73.

Stockwell T, Smail P, Hodgson R, and Canter S. Alcohol dependence and phobic anxiety states II: A retrospective study. *British Journal of Psychiatry,* 1984; 144: 58-63.

Thyer B, Parrish RT, Himle J, Cameron OG, Curtis GC, and Nesse RM. Alcohol abuse among clinically anxious patients. *Behavior Research and Therapy,* 1986; 24: 357-359.

Tilley S. Alcohol, other drugs and tobacco use and anxiolytic effectiveness—A comparison of anxious patients and psychiatric nurses. *British Journal of Psychiatry,* 1987; 151: 389-392.

Triffleman, E. An overview of trauma exposure, posttraumatic stress disorder, and addictions. In Kranzler HR and Rounsaville BJ (Eds.), *Dual diagnosis and treatment: Substance abuse and comorbid medical and psychiatric disorder* (pp. 263-316). New York: Marcel Dekker Inc., 1997.

Triffleman E, Marmer C, and Delvechi K. Childhood trauma and PTSD in substance abuse inpatients. *Proceedings of annual college on problems of drug dependence.* New York: Elsevier, 1993: 89.

van der Kolk BA. *Psychological trauma.* Washington, DC: American Psychiatric Press, 1987.

Washton AM and Gold MS. Chronic cocaine abuse: Evidence for adverse effects on health and functioning. *Psychiatric Annals* 1984; 14: 733-743.

Weiss KJ and Rosenberg DJ. Prevalence of anxiety disorder among alcoholics. *Journal of Clinical Psychiatry,* 1985; 46: 3-5.

Wilson GT. Alcohol and anxiety. *Behaviour Research and Therapy,* 1988; 26: 369-381.

Young R, Oei TP, and Knight R. The tension reduction hypothesis revisited: An alcohol expectancy perspective. *British Journal of Addiction,* 1990; 85: 31-40.

Chapter 9

Schizophrenia and Substance Abuse

George S. Layne

INTRODUCTION

The patient with coexistent schizophrenia and substance use disorder represents the epitome of the dual-diagnosis problem. Not only do the two forms of disability interact in specific ways that exacerbate each other, they are traditionally treated by schools of professionals with such widely divergent philosophies that patients with one problem are typically excluded from treatment by programs that specialize in the other. Thus the patients who need the best of both worlds get the least of each.

The tragedy that this represents to the individual patient is compounded by the effect on the community. While schizophrenia is relatively rare, affecting about 1 percent of the population (APA, 1997), substance abuse among schizophrenic patients runs 50 percent or more in many studies (Dixon et al., 1991; McLellan and Druley, 1977; Richardson, Craig, and Haugland, 1985). Also, since schizophrenia is essentially an incurable brain disease, patients in given areas tend to accumulate if not treated effectively. In years past, this accumulation occurred in state hospitals. This resulted in the paradox that a disease affecting 1 percent of the population typically filled more hospital beds than any other medical diagnosis, especially when younger age groups were considered. The advent of de-institutionalization led to the closing of many chronic beds, and this population has become more and more visible. Community treatment programs have not been able to replace the caretaker function of the state hospital, and substance abuse has increased as many schizophrenic patients have had to cope with their illness on their own.

The picture is not hopeless, however. Studies in the 1980s showed that the schizophrenic substance abuser can be effectively treated and returned to a reasonable life (Hellerstein and Meehan, 1987; Kofoed et al., 1986; McBride, 1988). These studies are addressed later in this chapter. The answer is the same wherever success has occurred. If the best principles of psychiatric care for schizophrenia can be combined with the classically effective programs for substance abuse, recovery from substance abuse and relief of psychotic symptoms can be accomplished. The goal of most recent writings in this field, and of this chapter, is to encourage the development and enhancement of such interdisciplinary programs. This is not different from the situation with other psychiatric diagnoses combined with substance abuse; however, due to the higher degree of disability in schizophrenia, such combined programs are more critical to the care of the schizophrenic patient.

PREVALENCE OF COMBINED SCHIZOPHRENIA AND SUBSTANCE ABUSE

Substance abuse is seen far more often by individuals treating schizophrenics than schizophrenia is seen by those in the substance abuse field. The reason for this has to do with the development of the community mental health systems, which have traditionally treated the mentally ill, regardless of complications. Substance abuse programs have tended to be based on treatment philosophies that excluded the most severely mentally ill patients. Although dually diagnosed schizophrenic patients may not have received definitive care for their substance abuse, they have generally crossed paths with the mental health system on a regular basis.

Mclellan and Druley (1977) studied patients at the Department of Veterans Affairs Medical Center in Coatesville, Pennsylvania, and found that out of a randomly selected group of psychiatric inpatients, none of whom were in primary substance abuse treatment, 50 percent of 279 patients had a substance abuse problem. About 60 percent of the sample of 279 were schizophrenic.

Richardson, Craig, and Haugland (1985) studied fifty-six schizophrenic inpatients at the Rockland Psychiatric Center in New York, evaluating their treatment experiences over an average of a five-year period from the time of first treatment. This was a group of post-deinstitutionalization period chronic patients aged nineteen through forty-four (average age of twenty-seven). About 55 percent were substance abusers. Richardson and colleagues argued that their methods underestimated the degree of substance abuse and quoted other studies of similar groups with rates as high as 74 percent.

In the late 1980s, the prevalence of substance abuse and mental illness was assessed in the largest such study ever attempted. The National Institute of Mental Health sponsored the Epidemiological Catchment Area (ECA) Study, involving interviews with over 20,000 adults at several sites in the United States. The annual prevalence of mental illness and substance abuse combined was 28 percent. Over a one-year period, almost 15 percent of Americans used mental health or substance abuse services.

Use of services varied by disorder from a high of 60 percent of somatizing, schizophrenic, and bipolar patients to less than 25 percent for simply addicted individuals (Regier et al., 1993). ECA data also showed that the rate of alcoholism among schizophrenic individuals was ten times the general population with a 47 percent lifetime prevalence. The addition of cocaine raised the lifetime prevalence of substance abuse in schizophrenia to more than 50 percent (Dixon et al., 1991). The ECA survey was of households, not just identified patients, and probably gave a more accurate picture than clinic surveys. The American Psychiatric Association has warned that denial and delusional thinking make it prudent to use multiple sources for history taking in psychotic substance abusers, and the ECA survey went far in expanding sources for epidemiologic evaluation of dual-diagnosis issues (APA, 1997).

Comorbidity in schizophrenia is the rule, and the term "dual diagnosis" is a misnomer in this population. ECA data show lifetime prevalence rates for mental illness in general as high as 22 percent, for alcoholism 13 percent, and for other substance abuse 6 percent in the general population. Among the mentally ill, the substance abuse rate rose to almost 30 percent. Among alcoholics, the rate of comorbid mental illness was 37 percent, and other substance abuse diagnoses brought the rate of mental illness to more than half. The rate increases still further in certain settings (e.g., prisons). Among the specific mental illnesses, schizophrenia shared high rates of comorbid substance abuse with bipolar disorder and antisocial personality. None of these data are new to the dual-diagnosis practitioner, but the data are far more solid, being based on a general population survey (Regier et al., 1990).

It is difficult to document how frequently the substance abuse problems of the schizophrenic who is in treatment are not addressed adequately, but a good example was given by Alterman et al. (1980), who reported on schizophrenic patients hospitalized at the previously mentioned Coatesville VA hospital. The charts of 1,063 patients on nonsubstance abuse wards were reviewed. One hundred and one (9.5 percent) could be identified and categorized as schizophrenics with a secondary diagnosis of alcoholism. Of these patients, 45 percent were identified as having become intoxicated while in the hospital. Two-thirds of the drinking patients were intoxicated three times weekly, yet only 20 percent of the drinking group were receiving specialized treatment for their alcohol abuse problem.

Although it was hoped two decades would improve the problem of separation of attention to the different problems of the dual-diagnosis patient, this remains a problem. These descriptions remain typical. Programs still exist that do not integrate treatment (Buckley, 1998). The average schizophrenic patients seen in mental health clinics today probably drink, smoke marijuana and cigarettes to excess, and are not having their substance abuse issues dealt with adequately.

SCHIZOPHRENIA

What is schizophrenia, and what makes the patient with this illness different from any other substance abuser and significantly different, even, from other dual-diagnosis patients? Schizophrenia is a brain disease. It is a hereditary illness caused by genetic events set in motion before birth. The schizophrenic patient suffers from an imbalance of the chemicals that cause electrical impulses to pass from nerve to nerve in critical parts of the brain.

This definition is controversial. Some psychiatrists still believe that schizophrenia is a psychological illness caused by environmental factors in childhood. A very well-known psychiatrist has stated publicly in *The New York Times* that schizophrenia is not an illness at all, but akin to a problem of not learning to live well enough (Szasz, 1982). According to this psychiatrist, just as one must learn to play tennis, one must learn to live. This particular psychiatric professor believes that a "schizophrenic" street person who froze to death on the streets of New York simply had not learned well enough. Such attitudes fly in the face of scientific evidence. They are mentioned here only because resistance to the psychiatric approach is one of the major impediments to good treatment for schizophrenic substance abusers. Certainly, life skills must be taught to such patients as they must be taught to any severely disabled person, but schizophrenic patients can be differentiated from well people through chemicals in their spinal fluid, by the degree of premature atrophy of the brain shown by many on CAT scans, and by the neurological "soft signs" found in a large percentage of cases. Fortunately, medications can help alleviate the symptoms of schizophrenia, but to use them properly one must understand the underlying medical reality of the illness. Psychotherapy can help schizophrenics cope with their illness better, or help them abstain from substance use, but it cannot make the hallucinations stop. Treatment of the substance-abusing schizophrenic requires an enlightened and liberal attitude toward psychiatric medication, or the patient simply will not be "there" to treat.

Schizophrenia is characterized by symptoms that interfere with verbal forms of treatment to such a degree that they must be controlled before such treatment can begin. This differs from the depressed patient or the patient with a personality disorder who can participate in treatment without much change in his or her underlying mental state being required first. More than any other condition, schizophrenia attacks the ego, and the ego is the part of the mind conceptualized as being responsible for reasonable interpersonal transactions. The acute schizophrenic is in a state of ego dissolution. The result of this process is a series of changes in the patient's behavior and stated feelings that form the basis for diagnostic evaluation.

An oversimplified but adequate description of schizophrenia may be based on Linn's seven categories of psychiatric illness (1975). The schizophrenic may show significant symptoms in the areas of *affect, motor behavior, thinking,* and *perception. Consciousness* is usually not affected. *Memory* and *intelligence* are at least impeded by other symptoms. Following is a description of those four of Linn's categories most specifically applicable to schizophrenia.

Affect (emotional feeling tone). The schizophrenic patient may show inappropriate affect, whereby the expressed feeling is out of proportion or contrary to the actual events precipitating the affect. Affect is often described as flat in this illness but, in fact, the schizophrenic can at different times show great degrees of affect, mood swings, depression, elation, or panic.

Motor behavior. Schizophrenic patients may show unusual movement responses to requests or suggestions. Catatonia, a classic sign of schizophrenia, is rarely seen except in severe, untreated cases. What are seen, all too frequently, are the so-called negative symptoms, which include lassitude, lack of motivation, inertia, and difficulty following through on plans. Although not strictly a motor problem, these are particularly troublesome problems since they do not respond as well to traditional medications.

Thinking. Schizophrenia is said to be a thought disorder since, with affect limited or inappropriate and behavior not obviously related to reality, it is apparent that the schizophrenic is not thinking the same way as others. This occurs even when affect tone is not great, as opposed to the affectively disordered patient who may act strangely, but usually when obviously greatly disturbed or depressed. The expressions of thought in schizophrenia are unusual and may indicate delusional ideas that may be quite bizarre. The thought process as indicated by speech may appear to be random with associations that do not make sense. The problem may appear to the outsider to be one of intact thought processes with a delusional idea at the core, or a more disturbed condition in which the processes themselves do not connect in any rational way.

Perception. Schizophrenia is characterized most specifically by disturbances in perception, usually hallucinations, defined as false sensory perceptions not associated with real external stimuli. These may occur in any of the senses, but schizophrenics commonly have auditory hallucinations, often hearing voices when no one is speaking. Visual hallucinations are often seen in drug-induced psychosis, and olfactory hallucinations sometimes indicate brain tumors, but schizophrenics can have any type of hallucination.

The effect these symptoms have on the person suffering from them can be understood from the concept of ego functions. Freud spoke of reality testing, judgment, thinking, impulse control, and psychological defense as the work of the ego. The schizophrenic has profound difficulty in precisely these functions, as can be imagined from the type of basic malfunctions of thinking and feeling noted previously. Belak, Hurvich, and Gediman (1973), in their classic work *Ego Functions in Schizophrenics, Neurotics and Normals,* quantified these issues with the help of specific psychological tests. They found schizophrenics to be significantly impaired in all twelve of the areas tested including reality testing, judgment, impulse control, and thinking. More important, they found neurotic subjects to be closer to normals than to schizophrenics. To some extent it is appropriate to characterize the neurotic subjects as more like the typical substance abuse patient. The difference between the typical substance abuse patient and the schizophrenic then becomes very clear from Belak, Hurvich, and Gediman's data.

Those who will quibble about the difference between the neurotic patients in Belak, Hurvich, and Gediman's (1973) study and the typical personality-disordered substance abuse patient may prefer to look at the problem from the point of view of psychological defenses. The schizophrenic, at least when untreated, suffers from ego regression, which may be very severe and is characterized by the most primitive forms of defenses, including denial and projection, which reach unbelievable degrees of concrete literalness. Denial of reality makes hallucinations possible, while projection is the psychodynamic basis for paranoia. The regressed schizophrenic has great difficulty making abstract interpretations in conversations. When asked, "What brought you to the hospital?" the patient responds, "A taxi." Pitifully, this is neither a joke nor a hostile sarcastic response, but rather the natural response of a severely ego-impaired psychotic patient.

Johnson (1984) has described the defenses seen under the regressive tendency of alcoholics in an inpatient rehabilitation setting. Although he describes a severely impaired population, the denial he speaks of does not reach the level characterized by bizarre delusions and hallucinations that characterize schizophrenia. Furthermore, many of the defenses noted by Johnson, such as isolation, intellectualization, and rationalization through which the typical alcoholic manifests his regression, are actually too mature to be available to the schizophrenic in the midst of an acute episode.

Schizophrenia is a spectrum disorder and there are milder cases than those described here to illustrate the illness. For the sake of the dual-diagnosis issue, the more typical classic presentation should be kept in mind. In the individual case, a patient's strengths help him or her rise above the expectations presented by the illness, but programs must be based on the more usual cases. It should be clear that the schizophrenic patient represents a different sort of substance abuser, requiring a special approach.

The key to that approach is the use of medication. Although an adequate antipsychotic medication regimen will be listed later as part of every successful program, the issue is raised here since the need for medication is pivotal to understanding the schizophrenic patient. Since the medications needed are more mind altering than those used in the other major psychiatric illnesses (depression and mania), resistance to their use may be more of a problem in the schizophrenic population treated in a substance abuse program.

Running counter to the classic AA philosophy requiring abstinence from all mind-altering substances, the use of medication is a lifesaving measure for many schizophrenics. Since the discovery of the antipsychotic effect of chlorpromazine in the 1950s, the treatment of schizophrenia has moved from the arena of protective custody to one of community treatment and return to productive life.

Although the effect of antipsychotic medication is unfortunately not the same for all, most patients get tremendous relief of the more onerous disturbing symptoms. Delusional thinking and hallucinations, the so-called "positive" symptoms, simply stop for many patients and decrease significantly for many more. The "negative" symptoms, having to do with poor motivation and lack of energy, may not respond as well. Many schizophrenic patients have found relief from the voices, but still seem to be unable to find motivation to get on with their lives. This is probably a specific ego deficit that takes the form of the patient remaining regressed and emotionally dependent on others to an inappropriate degree. This may be as disabling as the "positive" signs of hallucinations and delusions. At any rate, the first step in treatment for the schizophrenic patient, substance abuser or not, is a good trial of antipsychotic medication. A review of the effectiveness of newer antipsychotic agents will be presented toward the end of this chapter.

Abstinence is a necessity for good treatment of the psychotic symptoms since, according to Bellack and Gearon (1998), all substances of abuse increase the activity of dopamine in the brain. Dopamine is an important neurotransmitter or mediator of brain function, and it is believed that increased dopamine activity is responsible for the symptoms of schizophrenia regardless of substance abuse. Antipsychotic medications all decrease dopamine activity and, obviously, the abstinent patient will see a better outcome from medication. As will be noted later, this is a complicated issue. Although abstinence is an important part of any treatment program, the ability of the schizo-phrenic to achieve being and remain abstinent is more difficult be-cause of the noted ego deficits. Thus the dual-diagnosis program must be more tolerant of the patient who cannot stop abuse, even as the greater need for abstinence in this group, to enhance the effects of medications, is realized.

THE EFFECT OF SCHIZOPHRENIA IN THE SUBSTANCE ABUSE PROGRAM

Not all treatment programs are alike, but most successful programs share certain characteristics. These include an abstinence orientation that excludes medications, has strict rules, a strong focus on responsi-bility for one's own actions, and a social milieu approach (Alcoholics Anonymous, Narcotics Anonymous, etc.). This is all mixed in a con-text of confrontation. One is confronted with one's own addictive lifestyle and asked, with some degree of pressure, to change. Those who can, do. Those who cannot, generally, are invited to try again some other time. Legal pressure may be used to help a person make an initial decision, but the kind of work needed in a typical substance abuse rehabilitation program does not come easily when one is in "to beat a rap."

The schizophrenic patient in need of substance abuse treatment challenges all of the above ideas. Typical patients must be on medica-tions, cannot tolerate abstinence in the face of truly terrifying delu-sions of persecution that may be dampened by alcohol, cannot organize their thinking well enough to comprehend the rules, may not be willing to come to treatment voluntarily because of fear, and are often phobic of large groups of people, making attendance at self-help meetings impossible.

All too often, the result of these conflicts is the invitation men-tioned above, to continue one's treatment at a later time and at a dif-ferent place. It need not be this way. Programs can be designed to be more flexible and to convey the understanding that treatment of re-gression by support and gradual institution of responsibility does not have to represent an enabling of addictive dependency. Such programs can help the schizophrenic substance abuser reach a stage of development at which the traditional treatments will work. In other words, the initial introduction and orientation to the program may need to be drawn out and expectations relaxed. Patients will become more trusting as they feel safe; then substance abuse treatment can begin.

As pointed out by Bellack and Gearon (1998) the schizophrenic substance abuser suffers from greater obstacles in the way of change than those experienced by others. These include specific deficits in motivation, cognitive ability, and social skills needed for treatment. These problems are based on documented neuropsychological deficits in the brain disease itself, as well as special cumulative effects of social isolation and the cognitive and negative motivational side effects of antipsychotic medication.

THE EFFECT OF SUBSTANCE ABUSE
ON SCHIZOPHRENIA

The effects substance abuse has on the schizophrenic patient's illness are important for two reasons. The first is the problem of the management of psychosis in a psychotic person taking a psychotogenic drug. When used to excess, all drugs of abuse have the potential to cause a psychotic reaction at some stage of use, either acute or chronic, or as a withdrawal effect. Obviously, then, these drugs, especially the psychotomimetic or hallucinogenic drugs, will cause psychotic symptoms to worsen in schizophrenic patients. They also create diagnostic confusion, which will be discussed later.

The second reason is the issue of drug of choice. Is there such a thing? Or is drug abuse so individualized that nothing can be learned from drug-of-choice studies? There are, in fact, patterns, and it is valuable to look at this question, but the ultimate answer in each case must come from the individual patient.

A person uses drugs either to feel a sought-after direct effect (such as euphoria or excitement) or because of the drug's moderating effect on a preexisting feeling. Abusers who use drugs to alleviate depression or to bring sleep after stimulant use are said to be "self-medicating." This is a hypothesis that changes the focus on the user from one of "thrill seeker," who might be viewed with disdain, to that of "unfortunate victim," who simply did not find help for the underlying problem. However, the self-medication model is disproven by reviewing drug-of-choice studies.

Is the patient choosing a drug for a recreational purpose? If so, abstinence is an issue of saying no to oneself, of avoiding a sought-after but damaging experience. If the patient is self-medicating dysphoria, abstinence may turn out to be a negative feeling state to be avoided. Another issue is peer pressure. If it is true, as suggested by Minkoff (1988), that some young adult chronic patients use drugs because their peers do, to become one of the group or to gain an identity, then that use cannot be challenged without addressing the identity issue. Self-help groups can be useful in this regard, but the issue is to determine just what the drug means to the patient. Issues of self-medication and identity may be interesting side notes for an adult personality-disordered alcoholic, but they are life itself to a twenty-two-year-old schizophrenic.

Most drug-of-choice studies have focused on general issues in drug use patterns or psychoanalytic considerations. However, because these are powerful drugs with strong effects, the pharmacological effects should be looked at first. These are the effects that will lead to psychological conditioning and true dependence.

Richardson, Craig, and Haugland (1985) found that the Rockland substance-abusing schizophrenics referred to previously used a variety of drugs. Seventy-nine percent used marijuana; 36 percent LSD; 29 percent stimulants; 14 percent used cocaine. Heroin, PCP, and barbiturates were each used by 11 percent. Fifty percent used alcohol and 38 percent used three or more substances. This is clearly a pattern of poly-substance abuse, a typical pattern in young schizophrenics who are engaged in drug use for all the reasons mentioned. Marijuana and alcohol are almost universally reported to be the primary drugs of abuse for schizophrenics, but this may simply be secondary to ease of obtaining the drugs.

Schneir and Siris (1987) looked at specific choices, reviewing eighteen studies that reported drug of abuse choice in schizophrenia. The following discussion summarizes these studies and their clinical significance.

Stimulants. Schizophrenics are reported to use more amphetamines and cocaine than controls. (Controls may be other diagnoses or normals.) Why would a schizophrenic person use speed? To get high, of course, in the same way as any other young sensation-seeking drug abuser. Prolonged amphetamine use can result in a toxic psychosis and therefore, the following questions must be asked: Why would a psychotic person seek to become more psychotic? Is the patient on medication? Is he or she taking a stimulant to counteract the sedation of chlorpromazine? Or is he or she depressed, with the depression being worse for the patient than the voices, which he or she may have become used to? If so, the euphoria of the amphetamines may be worth the worsening auditory hallucinations to the schizophrenic person on the street.

Marijuana. Schizophrenics are reported to use cannabis more frequently than other diagnostic groups. Marijuana may have many different effects, from sedation to paranoia production. First ask, "What does it do to you?" Then ask, "Why do you want that to happen?" The answers should be useful in treatment.

Hallucinogens. Here, too, more use by schizophrenics was reported. Why does a schizophrenic want to cause more reality diffusion? Perhaps to gain control over the process, although the idea of a schizophrenic taking a street hallucinogen must also be seen as a self-destructive issue. Loss of control is often reported by nonpsychotic people as what they fear most about "going crazy." Psychotic patients, horrified by the idea of psychotic symptoms they cannot control, may feel some relief at being able to worsen those symptoms by taking a drug. For other patients, the obvious risk of adding hallucinogenics to an underlying psychosis may in fact represent a self-destructive act, similar to cutting oneself, or it may be a suicidal act.

PCP. Phencyclidine causes psychotic states and, as with LSD, the diagnosis of schizophrenia made in the face of hallucinogen intoxication begs for more history. Young schizophrenics do take this drug, evidence that schizophrenic symptoms may not be the primary issue when the choice to take this drug is made.

Alcohol. Surprisingly, in the studies reviewed by Schneir and Siris (1987), schizophrenics were less likely to use alcohol than other psychiatric diagnostic groups. Of course, all diagnostic groups combined abuse alcohol at a higher rate than the general population, and this is true for schizophrenics as well. Alcohol may function as an antidepressant (while the blood level is rising) or, more likely, as an antianxiety agent.

Despite this apparent lower use of alcohol, schizophrenics who drink suffer a higher risk of worsening symptoms. In a 1999 report of a retrospective study of readmission rates for clients with schizophrenia and substance abuse, Gerding et al. (1999) showed that 46 percent of schizophrenic patients readmitted for treatment showed concomitant substance abuse. Alcohol dependence predicted a larger number of admissions and longer lengths of stay than nonsubstance-abusing patients. Moreover, this relationship was not shown with marijuana or cocaine abuse. Alcohol dependence is an important factor in the exacerbation of schizophrenic symptoms.

Opiates. The self-medication hypothesis would indicate heavy use here, since opiates are effective antipsychotics and can mask schizophrenia. Yet schizophrenics are relatively lower in use of these drugs. There may be an underestimation of the prevalence of opiate use, since opiate users might be underdiagnosed for schizophrenia.

Nicotine. In the past decade, the importance of nicotine as a substance of abuse has led to research into the specific problems of the cigarette-smoking schizophrenic patient. This problem has rightly been placed in the arena of the addictions professional, now being sought out for expertise in dealing with patients who may not have other forms of addictions. Smoking is more prevalent in schizophrenia than in other mental disorders and is at least three times higher than in the general population (Diwan et al., 1998). The schizophrenic shares all the health hazards of smoking in common with others but also has special risks. Nicotine increases the incidence of side effects of antipsychotic medication including dyskinesia. Furthermore, other substances (aromatic hydrocarbons or "tars") in cigarettes induce the cytochrome P450 enzyme system in the liver, leading to faster metabolism of medications and greater difficulty controlling psychotic symptoms (Dalack, Healey, and Meador-Woodruff, 1998; Nemeroff, DeVane, and Pollack, 1996).

The increased use of nicotine in schizophrenia may be due to a form of self-medication. Antipsychotic medications have many side effects, and from 5 percent to 40 percent of patients have reported "neuroleptic dysphoria," which creates major issues of noncompliance (Weiden et al., 1989). Nicotine has been shown to reverse some of these symptoms including haloperidol-induced cognitive impairment (Levin et al., 1996). Nicotine also affects direct clinical signs of schizophrenia, reversing the p50 auditory evoked response seen in the EEGs of schizophrenic patients.

The results of many of these drug-effect studies are counter-intuitive if only the self-medication model is considered. A more open mind is necessary in assessing why each patient uses certain drugs. Schizophrenics whose positive symptoms are controllable with medication may choose stimulants to counteract the negative ones or to counteract side effects of medication.

Millman (1988) suggested that what alcohol, marijuana, and stimulants have in common is a psychological distancing effect. As problems are separated from here and now effect, existential dysphoria is dampened. A study of schizophrenic patients' reports of why they use the drugs they do in the context of their subjective reports of their illness is clearly needed. Meanwhile, schizophrenic patients must be counseled that all drugs and alcohol are known to exacerbate their symptoms.

DIAGNOSTIC ISSUES

The key to treatment of schizophrenia with or without substance abuse complications is diagnosis. This is not a clear-cut issue. In the young adult age group, for example, three conditions commonly cause the psychotic ego disruption under discussion here. Schizophrenia is one, of course. Bipolar affective disorder, or manic-depressive illness, is another. Third is substance abuse. If substance abuse is so prevalent in this age group, and if bipolar disorder is as prevalent as schizophrenia, how can we make the diagnosis? The answer is: slowly and carefully.

Bipolar illness is characterized, classically, by alternating cycles of euphoria and depression. Either can be psychotic in degree. Euphoria or mania, in particular, can look exactly like agitated schizophrenia. The diagnosis can be made by taking a look at the long-term history, or by following patients for several months to see how they function. A return to complete normality suggests bipolar illness. Schizophrenia tends to have a steady, if slow, downhill course throughout life, at least through ages twenty to forty. In the absence of a life history, looking at a single slice of time, with the patient agitated, illogical, hallucinating, and with paranoid delusions, how can one differentiate schizophrenia from bipolar illness? It is nearly impossible. Many clinicians think they can, and many patients get the wrong diagnosis.

Be sure that the patients and their families know that the diagnosis is not clear so that proper follow-up must be done. This is an important point, since the treatment for both illnesses is the same for the acute episode (major tranquilizer-type antipsychotic medication). For long-term treatment, however, there are less toxic specific drugs for bipolar illness (lithium, valproic acid, carbamazepine, and others), and the proper diagnosis can save a young person from a lifetime of trouble with the side effects of major tranquilizers.

If psychotogenic drugs are known to be in the patient's blood or urine, or are suspected to have been used in the recent past, and there is no prior history of psychosis when drug free, a diagnosis of schizophrenia or bipolar illness should not be made. Alcohol can cause hallucinations in extreme intoxication and withdrawal. Schuckit (1983) warns that one should wait before making a diagnosis of primary psychotic illness in the face of intoxication.

Alcoholic hallucinosis was often confused with schizophrenia in the past, with rates reported as high as 30 percent for schizophrenia in alcoholic populations. This, in turn, led to the suggestion that schizophrenia and alcoholism were genetically related. Numerous studies have since proven this wrong, including a study of fraternal and identical twins with schizophrenia by Kendler (1985).

Stimulants can cause psychosis, and amphetamine psychosis is perhaps the closest simulator of schizophrenia that is known. LSD and PCP cause a psychotic state as their acute effect. Marijuana can cause paranoia and acute psychosis in vulnerable people. It is not known whether those who become psychotic with cannabis are schizophrenic to begin with or suffering from a peculiar ego weakness that makes them vulnerable. Andreasson et al. (1987) studied military conscripts in Sweden and suggest a causative effect of marijuana for schizophrenia, but this is controversial.

Schizophrenia, in its classic form, at present cannot be cured. It may wax and wane, but it generally follows a downhill course. The intoxicated psychotic person should be treated symptomatically and monitored closely. If after two weeks of abstinence psychotic symptoms are still severe, schizophrenia is likely. After four weeks, the diagnosis is virtually certain. If psychotic symptoms abate, antipsychotic medication may be decreased gradually. If the patient remains without psychotic symptoms, the diagnosis of the original condition is likely substance-induced psychosis. A return of psychosis suggests schizophrenia.

Long-term use of street drugs may lead to an organic brain syndrome from a number of possible causes and, of course, alcohol can cause psychosis from chronic abuse, but permanent psychosis caused solely by substance abuse is rare. Schizophrenia exacerbated by drug use is relatively common. Persistent psychotic symptoms several weeks after cessation of drug use calls for reexamination of the history, and the diagnosis should then be made without considering substance abuse to be an issue.

TREATMENT OVERVIEW

Treatment of the substance-abusing schizophrenic patient is not strange or new. It is rather a return to an old idea, that if a patient has two illnesses, treat him or her for both and they will both get better. For a number of reasons, mostly political, the treatment of psychiatric illness and substance abuse became separated, performed by different people in different institutions. The problems of the schizophrenic substance abuser are so severe that intensive treatment on both fronts is needed from the beginning. Separate programs cannot provide the intensity of the psychiatric and substance abuse work needed. Therefore, political compromises must be made to bring the two treatment sides together.

Schizophrenia is not an impossible problem for the psychiatrist to treat; neither is substance abuse for traditional psychiatric programs. A combination of the successful elements of both programs can result in an appropriate treatment program for the substance-abusing schizophrenic. In a later section, three examples of programs that claim some success in the field will be reviewed. These programs were developed separately in different institutions but share a number of programmatic similarities, most notably the interdisciplinary approach.

Kofoed et al. (1986) summarized the controversies that contribute to treatment problems for schizophrenic substance abusers. The list came out of work setting up a dual-diagnosis outpatient program in Oregon.

1. Causal relationships between drugs and severe mental illness are not clear. We do not know, often, whether mental illness is the cause or the result of substance abuse.
2. Diagnosis is complicated and difficult.
3. The appropriateness of a sequential approach to treatment is not clear and the choice is often arbitrary. The patient in need of psychiatric and substance abuse treatment can get lost as the treating professionals argue about which treatment should be done first.
4. Little data are available about concurrent treatment programs.
5. Use of medication is controversial outside of psychiatry.
6. Use of disulfiram is controversial even within psychiatry.
7. Timing and degree of abstinence enforcement is not clear once the absolute standard is departed from. It is easy to say "all drugs are bad and should be avoided." If this rule is broken to allow some drugs, i.e., the "good" ones the psychiatrist prescribes, there is no clear consensus about where to draw the new line.
8. Psychiatric programs often exclude patients with substance abuse problems and substance abuse programs may exclude psychiatric patients as a matter of policy.

PSYCHOSOCIAL APPROACHES TO TREATMENT

Herbert McBride (1988), who helped to develop the MICA (Mentally Ill Chemical Abuser) program in New Jersey, worked with Alcoholics Anonymous to increase tolerance of the special needs of mentally ill substance abusers. This work began with MICA AA meetings on hospital grounds. In addition, meetings were held around the state, facilitated by mental health workers who were also recovering addicts. These psychiatrically oriented AA meetings are known as "Double Trouble" meetings.

AA tradition leads to problems for schizophrenic substance abusers for at least two reasons. First, the abstinence approach is often taken so literally that the use of medically necessary antipsychotic medications is not supported. Thus, if the patient is to make a successful entry into the AA system, it may be at the expense of medication. This leads, predictably, to relapse in both psychosis and substance abuse. Second, many AA members fear the stigmatization of mental illness in society and tend to shun psychiatric patients and programs to avoid being characterized as mentally ill.

These problems can be overcome by using educational methods to overcome psychiatric stigma. The approach is aimed at the local AA organization, leading to a self-help support system that welcomes the newly abstinent schizophrenic.

SAMPLE PROGRAMS FOR THE TREATMENT OF SCHIZOPHRENIC SUBSTANCE ABUSERS

The Beth Israel, New York City Program

Hellerstein and Meehan (1987) described the Beth Israel program in New York City. They showed that an outpatient group therapy program designed for schizophrenic substance abusers could decrease days of hospitalization. Beginning in 1984, they set their first goal as keeping the patient in treatment. Traditional expectations of psychiatric and substance abuse programs were relaxed.

Compliance with medication regimens and abstinence from illicit drugs and alcohol were goals to work on, not conditions for participation. Initial steps were as follows:

1. Engagement of the patient in the group process by identification and sharing of mutual problems, especially those involving psychosis and substance abuse
2. Interpersonal skill development, to help the patients become better able to utilize the group process for their own benefit
3. Problem solving, to help patients work on family, housing, and work issues
4. Education about medication and addictions issues
5. AA/NA attendance and participation encouraged

For those patients able to make a minimal commitment to abstinence, the program worked. Those who had organic impairment and those who came to group intoxicated did poorly. For the patients who entered the program, hospitalization days decreased from twenty-five per year to eight per year. This included the dropouts.

The New Jersey "Mentally Ill Chemical Abuser" Program

McBride (1988) described an approach to treating the schizophrenic substance abuser adopted by the state of New Jersey. The MICA (Mentally Ill Chemical Abuser) program was organized to help reduce bureaucracy in the treatment of the 50 percent of admissions to state hospitals that were substance-abuse related. MICA mixed traditionally separate treatment programs. The program worked at the state level by mandating closer ties between drug treatment and mental health treatment bureaucracies. Patients who were identified as meeting the need for intensive services from both sectors were treated in special MICA units in the state hospitals. These became, essentially, substance abuse units for schizophrenics. The essentials of McBride's MICA unit at Marlboro State Hospital were as follows:

1. Intensive twelve-step program
2. Peer-oriented milieu
3. Medication for psychosis
4. Mental health-oriented group therapy
5. Peer-oriented behavior modification program
6. Vocational rehabilitation program
7. Support groups for families
8. MICA-oriented halfway houses

The Oregon "Psychiatrically Impaired Substance Abuser" Program

MICA's counterpart on the West Coast is PISA (Psychiatrically Impaired Substance Abuser), the program reported by Kofoed et al. (1986) in Oregon. The PISA program follows:

1. Initial focus is on symptom control, abstinence, and psychiatric medication. This includes psychiatric or detoxification inpatient stays if needed.
2. Outpatient program begins with assessment group, which provides orientation and education on dual-diagnosis issues. This can begin in the inpatient setting. This initial group experience helped define the patients' roles and was felt to aid retention in the program.

3. Once psychiatrically stable, AA and unmonitored disulfiram use are begun.
4. Goals are developed for ongoing treatment. Entry into an ongoing treatment group occurs once the patient makes a commitment to the program.
5. Treatment groups meet weekly.
6. Medications are continued. Compliance is monitored with blood and urine tests and Breathalyzer for disulfiram.
7. Abstinence monitored by urine drug screens and Breathalyzer.
8. AA attendance and participation continues.
9. As needed, individual psychotherapy, family therapy, day treatment, etc. are utilized.

The PISA program started with thirty-two patients, sixteen of whom were schizophrenic. Of these thirty-two, eight lasted eleven or more months in the program. Five of these eight were schizophrenic. The nonschizophrenic patients suffered from other psychiatric illnesses in addition to various forms of substance abuse. Thus the schizophrenic patients were retained longer in this program compared to their nonschizophrenic peers.

Kofoed et al. (1986) pointed out that previous outpatient treatment was associated with retention in this program, even without prior abstinence. Also, no psychosis due to disulfiram therapy was noted, probably due to use of antipsychotic medications.

SUMMARY OF TREATMENT COMPONENTS

A composite program based on the literature and personal experience could embody these features:

1. *Early engagement.* The schizophrenic substance abuser should be identified and involved in an active treatment program as early as possible. Psychiatric inpatients and detoxification patients should be approached by outpatient program staff during their inpatient stay.
2. *Peer-oriented therapy program.* Group therapy, behavior modification programs, and milieu therapy should use peer pressure and identification with recovering peers.

3. *Life skill rehabilitation.* It is hard to learn how to get along in society while suffering from delusions. The time in the program while medicated may represent a rare symptom-free period for some patients, and the opportunity should be taken to do some effective life skills training. The education process should include medical and addiction issues as well.

4. *Self-help groups.* Alcoholics Anonymous and Narcotics Anonymous networks serve many purposes. The schizophrenic patient needs substance-free role models. Furthermore, since some substance abuse may represent attempts at socialization, self-help groups provide a healthy alternative. Twelve-step programs lend needed structure to the patient's life.

5. *Appropriate abstinence orientation.* Substance abuse patients who must take psychoactive medication should be encouraged to see the difference between taking appropriately prescribed antipsychotic medication and using street drugs. Medications do not represent a relaxation of the goal of abstinence. The medicated patient who remains free of illicit drugs and alcohol should be appreciated as abstinent.

6. *Family involvement.* Family therapy is a powerful treatment for many problems. Family issues are always present, even if the family is not. Family work can range from having the patient ventilate hostile feelings about a parent to having networks of dozens of people to help motivate a dispirited patient.

7. *Psychiatric involvement.* The psychiatrist should be an active, ongoing member of the treatment team. Appropriate psychotropic medication is used routinely.

8. *One-on-one psychotherapy.* Whether supportive, psychodynamic, or behavioral, the one-on-one relationship is important throughout the treatment process. Some aspects of this role may be assumed by the AA/NA sponsor.

NEW APPROACHES

Bellack and Gearon (1998) reviewed newly developed treatment modalities for the schizophrenic substance abuser. These were based on the typical cognitive and motivational problems of these patients.

Relapse prevention programs have been developed for the treatment of all substance abusers and can be adapted to the schizophrenic population. Employing traditional behavioral learning techniques, such as biofeedback and positive reinforcement, patients were taught to recognize the events in their daily lives that trigger motivation to use drugs. In the dual-diagnosis group, such strategies can be applied separately to the issues of psychiatric symptoms as well as to substance abuse behavior (Ziedonis and Fisher, 1994). An example of this might be to conceptualize medication noncompliance as a relapse issue for schizophrenia.

Drake et al. (1993) proposed a program of intensive case management for the dually diagnosed population. The Program for Assertive Community Treatment involves the use of a multidisciplinary team available to the patient twenty-four hours a day in the patient's own environment. Besides tailoring intensive treatment to the individual's specific stage of substance abuse, the program includes broad support in housing, vocational rehabilitation, and crisis intervention. This program addresses the special additional areas of vulnerability of the dually diagnosed patient.

Contingency management as proposed by Higgins, Budney, and Bickel (1994) uses operant conditioning to counteract the strong reinforcing effects of drugs. Alternative positive reinforcers are provided for program compliance, abstinence, etc. This can also easily be broadened to mental health treatment issues.

Miller and Rollnick (1991) applied principles of motivational psychology to increase the patient's internal drive to change substance abuse behaviors. As opposed to traditional programs' use of confrontation, this approach is based on empathy and helping the clients understand their resistance to change. Their approach, called motivational interviewing, involves work with patients regarding specific life issues and targeted needs. The patient is assisted to recognize the value of abstinence as well as the deleterious effects of continued substance abuse.

Bellack and Gearon (1998) have incorporated these treatments in a program developed with the ego and cognitive problems of schizophrenia in mind. Under the name Behavioral Treatment for Substance Abuse in Schizophrenia (BTSAS), the program involves four modules employed in sequential fashion:

1. *Social skills and problem-solving skills training.* The goal here is to increase positive nondrug social contact and to decrease peer pressure to use drugs.
2. *Drug education.* Psychoeducation takes into account the special cognitive deficits of the schizophrenic patient. Medication issues are routinely discussed.
3. *Motivational interviewing.* Bellack and Gearon (1998) have modified this approach in light of the schizophrenic patient's difficulty with such cognitive processes as introspection and abstraction. Their approach is more concrete and focuses on short-term issues.
4. *Behavioral skill and relapse prevention training.* This includes positive reinforcement for negative urine drug screens.

PSYCHOPHARMACOLOGY IN TREATMENT

Significant strides have been made in the past ten years in the development of new medications for schizophrenia and in understanding the effects of medications on substance abuse, both in blocking and augmenting craving for drugs. The use of new antipsychotic medications such as clozapine and risperidone has brought about positive effects for many schizophrenic patients previously considered treatment resistant.

Research has also shown that while older medications such as haloperidol may actually increase the reinforcing effects of certain drugs, some of the new drugs may have the opposite effect. Kosten reported in 1997 that the behavioral effects of cocaine involve dopamine brain pathways as do the effects of antipsychotic medications. A simplistic view of this is that more brain dopamine activity produces psychotic symptoms. Drugs that block dopamine activity, such as haloperidol, reduce such symptoms. Similarly, cocaine acts to enhance dopamine activity at certain sites in the brain, leading to euphoria, a reinforcing effect. Thus haloperidol would be expected to decrease the behavioral effects of cocaine. Indeed, this is the case for short-term haloperidol use.

Alas, the brain is not simple. Long-term treatment with drugs that mediate neurotransmitters can lead to changes in the actual function of specific neurons in the brain, with corresponding supersensitivity of some areas and decreased responsiveness of others. Kosten (1997) found that chronic administration of haloperidol in rats led to enhanced behavioral effects when those rats were given cocaine, the opposite of the effect from short-term haloperidol.

Furthermore, antipsychotic drugs differ in their effects on the brain. Dopamine does not act on the brain in a singular fashion. Rather, there are several different kinds of dopamine receptors in different areas of the brain. Thus Kosten (1997) suggests that clozapine, an atypical drug, may be expected to have the opposite effect of haloperidol and may actually decrease craving in cocaine abusers after long-term use of clozapine. Although the evidence is ambiguous, it is clear that the choice of antipsychotic medication for all schizophrenic substance abusers (not just the treatment-resistant ones) may become more rational in the near future, with the same medication decreasing both psychosis and cravings for street drugs.

Most of us do not treat rats; however, Buckley (1998) documented that treatment-refractory schizophrenic patients who were substance abusers benefited equally from clozapine as those who were not drug users. Furthermore, Buckley discusses sketchy but hopeful reports of clozapine-responsive patients showing clearly decreased cravings while on the drug. In some studies, clozapine has shown a 25 percent decrease in craving for cocaine.

Clozapine, quetiapine, and olanzapine are known as "atypical" antipsychotic drugs because they have significantly different chemical effects when compared to the older drugs such as haloperidol or chlorpromazine. They are characterized by not causing increases in the pituitary hormone prolactin. With older antipsychotics, such increases can cause production of breast milk and lack of ovulation and menses in women. These new drugs seem to be relatively free of muscular side effects including, possibly, the dreaded irreversible tardive dyskinesia. They are also superior in the treatment of the "negative" side effects of schizophrenia—lack of motivation and inertia. Thus these new medications improve compliance by decreasing side effects and improving motivation. Of greater interest is the possible direct effect on reducing craving.

Like clozapine, olanzapine has shown beneficial effects in early clinical and research experience. Meil and Schecter (1997) reported decreased use and blocked reinforcing effects of cocaine in olanzapine-treated rats similar to that reported by Kosten (1997) for clozapine. Conley, Kelly, and Gale (1998) reported that substance-abusing schizophrenic patients had fewer negative symptoms but more muscular problems than nonaddicted schizophrenic patients, a reflection on the self-medication process noted previously. After olanzepine, the substance-abusing group did as well as the others with a decrease in muscular side effects. Littrell (1998) reported on nine addicted schizophrenic patients taking olanzapine for six months. Seven achieved complete abstinence and two had a decrease in drug use. The patients reported that the positive change was due to less dysphoria and depression as well as fewer negative and positive symptoms.

Because atypical antipsychotics are effective for positive and negative symptoms, have fewer compliance-compromising side effects, and decrease craving for some abused substances, they "are excellent choices for dually diagnosed patients and should be considered first-line treatment" (Ziedonis et al., 2000, p. 70).

Other medications may be as directly helpful in treating the schizophrenic substance abuser as they are in patients without the "dual" label. Disulfiram (Antabuse) has a clear place in the treatment of alcoholism, but the schizophrenic patient may not be reliable enough to maintain abstinence and avoid a bad reaction. Naltrexone, which blocks opiate receptors, has been demonstrated to reduce relapse to alcohol in non-schizophrenic drinkers by reducing craving and blocking euphoria (Volpi-celli et al., 1992, 1995). It may have a place in the medicinal regimen of certain well-monitored schizophrenic patients. Use of antidepressants to augment antipsychotic medication is as necessary in the schizophrenic substance abuser as in the nondrug-using population with psychotic depression.

WOMEN AND OTHER SPECIAL POPULATIONS

The essence of dual-diagnosis treatment is the recognition by the treating professionals of the special needs of subgroups of patients. The psychiatrist must deal with substance abuse, and the drug clinic needs special programs for schizophrenia. However, there are groups within these groups, and this fact can be lost in the overwhelming work of helping multiply handicapped populations. Bellack and Gearon (1998) stress the special needs of women. Women who are suffering from schizophrenia and who abuse drugs are the highest risk group today for contracting HIV infection. They are also subject to sexual and aggressive victimization far more often than men are. These special issues must be looked for and addressed on a case-by-case basis as well as in planning a program. Women with schizophrenia who are in treatment are also more vulnerable to pregnancy today than ever before. New antipsychotic medications such as clozapine, quetiapine, and olanzapine have less of an effect on the pituitary-ovarian hormone system. Women who may have been anovulatory on older medications such as haloperidol now will need more reproductive education and counseling and can be expected to become pregnant more frequently. Child care will become an issue for this population.

Cultural competency has been more strongly recognized lately as an essential part of a clinician's ability to treat emotionally disturbed clients. This becomes increasingly important as the client's disability increases, as with the addition of substance abuse. A patient with the motivational and ego deficits characteristic of schizophrenia requires treatment by professionals knowledgeable of the cultural background involved, who are able to communicate with the patient easily.

RESEARCH ASSESSMENT OF INTEGRATED TREATMENT

Combined treatment of substance abuse and mental illness has been known by experienced clinicians to be the best hope for the more severely mentally ill for at least twenty years. Yet ten years ago, when this chapter was first written, the message was sufficiently novel to make it the main point of the article. Unfortunately, some programs still try to use old stereotypes as the basis for treatment.

Substance abuse programs that reqire immediate abstinence must carefully select patients and will exclude those with schizophrenia. That is not to say that highly motivated substance abusers with good ego function should have to be treated in programs designed for those without; not all AA meetings should be of the "Double Trouble" variety. However, schizophrenic patients need help to find appropriate programs that suit their needs, or a negative treatment experience is guaranteed. Buckley (1998) suggests that, as recently as 1997, some programs for schizophrenic substance abusers separate the two sides of the treatment.

Can it be proven that integrated treatment works better, or is this just an intuitive point? Drake et al. (1998) reviewed thirty-six research studies seeking to answer this question. The results were not overwhelming for many reasons. Some of the studies suffered from flawed design. The most disappointing results came from studies of programs that added substance abuse programs to traditional services, intensive integrated programs in controlled settings (inpatient, residential, etc.), and demonstration projects such as the National Institute of Mental Health's Community Support Program. The best results came from programs that added intensive community-based case management services to complete integrated dual-diagnosis treatment with maximum outreach, even with mobile treatment teams. The bottom line seems to be that integrated treatment is necessary but not sufficient for successful treatment of the schizophrenic substance abuser.

Cuffel and Chase (1994) studied the results of integrated treatment using the ECA data. This study looked at the treatment of schizophrenic substance abusers in specialized programs using the ECA to provide control groups for comparison. Prior studies of good results were difficult to assess because of lack of knowledge of underlying natural relapse and remission rates of the untreated disorders. Cuffel and Chase's (1994) analysis showed that without treatment, relapse and remission rates balanced over a year with a steady number of affected people. Remission rates from specialized treatment programs exceeded the ECA rates, supporting the efficacy of such programs.

CONCLUSION

Schizophrenic substance abusers are among the most difficult patients to treat for either of their two diagnoses. The nature of schizophrenia makes relaxation of usual substance abuse rules necessary to keep patients in treatment. Application of the usual program techniques for substance abuse treatment can work for schizophrenics. For this to occur, the work must be combined with knowledge of the ego limitations of the patients. Close interdisciplinary cooperation with appropriate psychiatric support and antipsychotic medications provides a treatment program that has been proven to work. Although outcome studies of the interdisciplinary approach have been equivocal to date, hopefully new approaches such as Bellack and Gearon's (1998) BTSAS program will prove to be effective and reproducible. The addition of new antipsychotic medications promises to make the work more effective. Schizophrenia and substance abuse represent two of the most difficult illnesses to treat, and the combination can seem overwhelming to the patients and families as well as clinicians. Research does provide encouragement; there is reason for optimism.

REFERENCES

Alterman, A.I., Erdlen, F.R., McLellan, A.T., and Mann, S.C. (1980). Problem drinking in hospitalized schizophrenic patients. *Addictive Behaviors, 5,* 273-276.

American Psychiatric Association (APA) (1997). *Practice Guideline for the Treatment of Patients with Schizophrenia.* Washington, DC: APA.

Andreasson, S., Allebeck, P., Engstrom, A., and Rydberg, U. (1987). Cannabis and schizophrenia: A longitudinal study of Swedish conscripts. *Lancet,* December 26, 1483-1486.

Belak, L., Hurvich, M., and Gediman, H.K. (1973). *Ego Functions in Schizophrenics, Neurotics and Normals.* New York: John Wiley and Sons.

Bellack, A.S. and Gearon, J.S. (1998). Substance abuse treatment for people with schizophrenia. *Addictive Behaviors, 23,* 749-766.

Buckley, P.F. (1998). Novel antipsychotic medications and the treatment of comorbid substance abuse in schizophrenia. *Journal of Substance Abuse Treatment, 15,* 113-116.

Conley, R.R., Kelly, D.L., and Gale, E.A. (1998). Olanzapine response in treatment of refractory schizophrenic patients with a history of substance abuse. *Schizophrenia Research, 33,* 95-101.

Cuffel, B.J. and Chase, P. (1994). Remission and relapse rates of substance abuse disorders in schizophrenia. *Journal of Nervous and Mental Diseases, 182,* 342-348.

Dalack, G.W., Healey, D.J., and Meador-Woodruff, J.H. (1998). Nicotine dependence in schizophrenia. *American Journal of Psychiatry, 155,* 1490-1501.

Diwan, A., Castine, M., Pomerleau, C.S., Meador-Woodruff, J.H., and Dalack, G.W. (1998). Differential prevalence of cigarette smoking in patients with schizophrenic versus mood disorders. *Schizophrenia Research, 33,* 113-118.

Dixon, L., Haas, G., Weiden, P.J., Sweeney, J., and Francis, A.J. (1991). Drug abuse in schizophrenic patients. *American Journal of Psychiatry, 142,* 224-230.

Drake, R.E., Bartels, S.J., Teague, G.B., Noordsy, D.L., and Clark, R.E. (1993). Treatment of substance abuse in severely mentally ill patients. *Journal of Nervous and Mental Disorders, 181,* 606-611.

Drake, R.E., Mercer-McFadden, C., Mueser, K.T., McHugo, G.J., and Bond, G.R. (1998). Review of integrated mental health and substance abuse treatment for patients with dual disorders. *Schizophrenia Bulletin, 24,* 589-608.

Gerding, L.B., Labbate, L.A., Measom, M.O., Santos, A.B., and Arana, G.W. (1999). Alcohol dependence and hospitalization in schizophrenia. *Schizophrenia Research, 38,* 71-75.

Hellerstein, D.J. and Meehan, B. (1987). Outpatient group therapy for schizophrenic substance abusers. *American Journal of Psychiatry, 144,* 1337-1339.

Higgins, S.T., Budney, A.J., and Bickel, W.K. (1994). Applying behavioral concepts and principles to the treatment of cocaine dependence. *Drug and Alcohol Dependence, 34,* 87-97.

Johnson, R. (1984). Ego deficits in the personality of the alcoholic. *The Psychiatric Hospital, 15,* 37-40.

Kendler, K.S. (1985). A twin study of individuals with both schizophrenia and alcoholism. *British Journal of Psychiatry, 147,* 48-53.

Kofoed, L., Kania, J., Walsh, T., and Atkinson, R.M. (1986). Outpatient treatment of patients with substance abuse and coexisting psychiatric disorders. *American Journal of Psychiatry, 143,* 867-872.

Kosten, T.A. (1997). Enhanced neurobehavioral effects of cocaine with chronic neuroleptic exposure in rats. *Schizophrenia Bulletin, 23,* 203-213.

Levin, E.D., Wilson, W., Rose, J.E., and McEvoy, J. (1996). Nicotine-haloperidol interactions and cognitive performance in schizophrenics. *Neuropsychopharmacology, 15,* 429-436.

Linn, L. (1975). Clinical manifestations of psychiatric disorders. In Freedman, A.M., Kaplan, H.I., and Sadock, B.J. (Eds.), *Comprehensive Textbook of Psychiatry,* Second Edition (pp. 822-824). Baltimore: Williams and Wilkins.

Littrell, K.H. (1998). *Schizophrenia and Comorbid Substance Abuse.* Symposium: Obstacles in the Treatment of Schizophrenia, American Psychiatric Nurses Association, Annual Meeting.

McBride, H. (1988). *Psychiatric Disorders in Substance Abuse: Pragmatic Treatment.* American Academy of Psychiatrists in Alcoholism and Addictions, Annual Meeting Prarie Village, KS.

McLellan, A.T. and Druley, K.A. (1977). Non-random relation between drugs of abuse and psychiatric diagnosis. *Journal of Psychiatric Research, 13,* 179-184.

Meil, W.M. and Schecter, M.D. (1997). Olanzapine attenuates the reinforcing effects of cocaine. *European Journal of Pharmacology, 340*(1), 17-26.

Miller, W.R. and Rollnick, S. (1991). *Motivational Interviewing: Preparing People to Change Addictive Behavior.* New York: The Guilford Press.

Millman, R.B. (1988). *The Abuse of Marijuana and Psychedelics by Psychiatric Patients.* American Academy of Psychiatrists in Alcoholism and Addictions, Annual Meeting.

Minkoff, K.M. (1988). *Dual Diagnosis of Psychosis and Addiction.* American Psychiatric Association, Annual Meeting, Course 46, Washington, DC.

Nemeroff, C.G., DeVane, C.L., and Pollack, B.G. (1996). Newer antidepressants and the cytochrome P450 system. *American Journal of Psychiatry, 153,* 311-320.

Regier, D.A., Farmer, M.E., Rae, D.S., Locke, B.Z., Keith, S.J., Judd, L.L., and Goodwin, F.K. (1990). Comorbidity of mental disorders with alcohol and other drug abuse. Results from the Epidemiologic Catchment Area (ECA) study. *Journal of the American Medical Association, 264,* 2511-2518.

Regier, D.A., Narrow, W.E., Manderscheid, R.W., Locke, B.Z., and Goodwin, F.K. (1993). The de facto U.S. mental and addictive disorders service system: Epidemiologic catchment area prospective 1 year prevalence rates of disorders and services. *Archives of General Psychiatry, 50,* 85-94.

Richardson, M.A., Craig, T.J., and Haugland, G. (1985). Treatment patterns of young chronic schizophrenic patients in the era of deinstitutionalization. *Psychiatric Quarterly, 57,* 104-110.

Schneir, F.R. and Siris, S.G. (1987). A review of psychoactive substance: Use and abuse in schizophrenia. *Journal of Nervous and Mental Disease, 175,* 641-652.

Schuckit, M.A. (1983). Alcoholism and other psychiatric disorders. *Hospital and Community Psychiatry, 34,* 1022-1027.

Szasz, T. (1982). "The Lady in the Box," *The New York Times,* February 16, p. A-19.

Volpicelli, J.R., Alterman, A.I., Hayashida, M., and O'Brien, C.P. (1992). Naltrexone in the treatment of alcohol dependence. *Archives of General Psychiatry, 49,* 876-880.

Volpicelli, J.R., Watson, N.T., King, A.C., Sherman, C.E., and O'Brien, C.P. (1995). Effect of naltrexone on alcohol "high" in alcoholics. *American Journal of Psychiatry, 152,* 613-615.

Weiden, P.J., Mann, J.J., Dixon, L., Haas, G., DeChillo, N., and Frances, A.J. (1989). Is neuroleptic dysphoria a healthy response? *Comprehensive Psychiatry, 30,* 546-552.

Ziedonis, D.M. and Fisher, W. (1994). Assessment and treatment of comorbid substance abuse in individuals with schizophrenia. *Psychiatric Annals, 24,* 447-493.

Ziedonis, D.M., Williams, J., Corrigan, P., and Smelson, D. (2000). Management of substance abuse in schizophrenia. *Psychiatric Annals, 30,* 67-75.

Chapter 10

Disorders of Personality and Substance Abuse: An Exploration of Empirical and Clinical Findings

Micah R. Sadigh

During the past two decades, over thirty published studies have explored the relationship between substance abuse and personality disorders (e.g., Craig, 1984; Donat, 1988; Lesswing and Dougherty, 1993; McMahon, Kelly, and Kouzekanani, 1993; Skodal, Oldham, and Gallaher, 1999). These studies suggest a prevalence of substance-abusing behavior among those with particular characterologic features. Although many investigators have been searching for a specific addictive personality, no group of attributes or particular form of psychopathology has been found to be specific for addiction. Verheul, van den Brink, and Hartgers (1998) investigated the comorbidity between Axis II (personality disorders) and the rate of relapse in their study of 187 alcoholics. They concluded that the presence of a personality disorder was a solid predictor of relapse after completing a rehabilitation program. They especially attributed this finding to the difficulty of developing a strong working alliance with patients who present with such comorbidities.

In a study of 200 inpatient and outpatients, Skodol, Oldham, and Gallaher (1999) found that nearly 60 percent of the subjects with drug and alcohol abuse also presented with a personality disorder. The researchers noted that the most common personality disorders in their sample of current alcohol, cannabis, and stimulant users were borderline, avoidant, and dependent. The antisocial personality was much more prevalent among lifelong substance users.

Thomas, Melchert, and Banken (1997) investigated the comorbidity between substance dependence and personality disorders by using a large sample of patients who were repeatedly admitted to an inpatient facility. A structured clinical interview based on the criteria of the DSM-III-R was administered for Axis II diagnoses. Over 50 percent of the participants in the study had one or more personality disorder diagnoses. The majority of the participants presented with Cluster B (antisocial, histrionic, etc.) or Cluster C (dependent, avoidant, etc.) disorders. The researchers emphasized the importance of recognizing the prevalence of Cluster C in the substance-abusing population, an important finding that requires further attention. Another important finding of the study relates to the rate of relapse after participating in a treatment program. The results suggested a strong positive correlation between the diagnosis of a personality disorder and a tendency toward an inability to remain abstinent.

In another study, Pettinati et al. (1999) explored the prevalence of Axis II disorders in patients with a substance abuse disorder. One of the most salient findings of the study clearly suggested that the presence of Axis II diagnoses, such as avoidant, paranoid, and antisocial, was a good predictor of posttreatment relapse, especially in the presence of other psychiatric disorders. The findings of the study also revealed that the prevalence of personality disorders was nearly 50 percent higher among cocaine users than among alcohol users.

Although the antisocial and borderline personalities have been known to show the strongest tendency toward substance use, the problem appears to be much more widespread and may affect those with other specific personality characteristics such as histrionic, schizoid, dependent, and avoidant. For example, Craig, Verinis, and Wexler (1985) used the Millon Clinical Multiaxial Inventory (MCMI) to investigate the prevalence of personality disorders among alcoholics and drug addicts at inpatient VA hospitals. Their data showed that alcohol abuse was especially common among those with avoidant, dependent, and passive-aggressive personality types. Drug abuse, on the other hand, was more prevalent among those with narcissistic and antisocial personalities.

Flynn and colleagues (1995) found that cocaine users who presented with strong avoidant and self-deprecating attributes also presented with interpersonal deficits. Such findings emphasize the need for improving rehabilitation programs to help therapists and staff to develop a greater sensitivity toward those who may require a greater investment in terms of more intensive psychotherapeutic interventions. In other words, certain dually diagnosed patients may require additional treatment considerations, especially because of the experience of high levels of social anxiety and depression that are seen, for example, among avoidant individuals.

A study by Fals-Stewart (1992) concluded that in terms of the treatment outcome and participating in a rehabilitation program, those individuals with avoidant and schizoid personalities were more likely to terminate treatment prematurely and were unable to remain abstinent when compared against other personality types as measured by the MCMI. The study suggested that perhaps due to the experience of high levels of social discomfort and limited interpersonal coping skills, avoidant and schizoid individuals may tend to leave treatment against clinical recommendations and are likely to experience a relapse much sooner than others. These are also the individuals who gravitate toward substance abuse because of the inability to cope effectively with social stressors and who tend to have disparaging attitudes about self and others. This finding is similar to Fenichel's (1945) thesis that addiction appears to be a temporary substitute for mature interpersonal relationships and a possible defense against the overwhelming experience of anxiety and emotional pain.

These reviews suggest that practitioners working with the substance-abusing population need to have a more extensive understanding of particular personality styles and disorders and the challenges they present in a therapeutic setting. By understanding how specific personalities perceive and interact with their inner and outer worlds, it is possible to gain enough knowledge to learn the basic "language" of the personality to facilitate the needed therapeutic dialogue. Knowledge of the attributes of each personality type promotes access to the phenomenologic world of the patient, which makes a more effective intervention possible.

PERSONALITY AND PERSONALITY DISORDERS

The relationship between specific personality types and behavioral tendencies has been a source of much exploration since the time of Hippocrates and Galen. The ancient Greeks believed that bodily humors predisposed individuals to relate to their world in certain ways. The cheerful person was said to have plenty of blood. Too much black bile resulted in a melancholic personality, while excessive yellow bile brought about the characteristic of a hot-tempered and angry person. Finally, too much phlegm was considered the cause of sluggishness and a lack of drive (Corsini, 1977). If the humors were balanced and in harmony, the individual was considered healthy. An imbalance, however, brought about the manifestation of physical and mental disease.

Personality and its disorders entered its most intensive, systematic explorations in the nineteenth century, especially with the advent of psychoanalysis. Perhaps one of the most important contributions of psychoanalysis was the way by which the understanding of personality dynamics allowed the analyst to gain access to the unconscious world of the patient, where the determinants of overt and covert behavior resided.

Freud (1931) distinguished four character types. The *erotic* character was dominated by the persistent apprehension of losing the love of others and, as a result, manifested itself in terms of dependency on others. This character type could predispose one to develop hysterical symptoms. The *obsessional* character, on the other hand, was dominated by a fear of the conscience, which resulted in internal dependence, almost to the exclusion of the outside world, and was ruled by conservatism and self-reliance. People with obsessional character could potentially develop neurotic symptoms. The *narcissistic* character embodied the drive for self-preservation, and manifested tendencies for aggressiveness and opposition to the established rules. This character type predisposed the person to psychotic disorders. Finally, the *oral dependent* was characterized by dependence on others for love, affirmation, and acceptance. It was noted that these individuals tended to become extremely anxious and behaved neurotically when their source of support was removed due to disapproval or separation. For Freud, the *normal/ideal* personality possessed an equal proportion of these characteristics.

Allport (1937) reviewed over fifty definitions of personality and concluded that "personality is the dynamic organization within the individual of those psychophysical systems that determine his unique adjustment to the world" (in Corsini, 1977, p. 2). One may add that this "adjustment to the world" needs to be viewed as responding and adapting both to the intrapsychic world and the interpersonal milieu. More recently, Millon (1996), who has contributed extensively to our understanding of personality disorders, proposed that personality consists of deeply ingrained psychological tendencies that are, for the most part, outside conscious awareness and which tend to manifest themselves "automatically" in every aspect of the person's life. He suggested that ultimately what is referred to as personality arises from a complex of genetic, developmental, and learning experiences that define the individual's unique ways of reasoning, feeling, and adjusting to the world.

Therefore, by definition, persons diagnosed with a personality disorder are those who manifest chronic signs of rigidity and maladaptive patterns of perceiving and thinking about their environment and themselves (APA, 1994). Such inflexibility can bring about impairment in functioning (e.g., cognitively, affectively, and interpersonally) and may result in the experience of significant levels of distress, which tend to compel the person to potentially resort to ineffectual coping strategies, such as substance abuse.

Many researchers have suggested that personality disorders develop early in life and may be recognized as early as adolescence, and tend to be stable for the duration of the person's life. The diathesis-stress model, however, suggests that the underlying, hereditary, and environmental propensities for particular personality traits may surface under stressful circumstances. That is, there may be a inclination for a particular personality disorder that is manifested when the individual's coping and adaptive resources are depleted under stress. Due to diminished coping resources, the once dormant personality traits result in rigidity and inflexibility in relating to oneself and the environment, hence the disorder of the personality.

Based on this model, I have proposed the Personality Continuum Index (see Figure 10.1), which depicts the relationship between personality traits, coping resources, and exposure to prolonged stress and the emergence of personality disorders. For example, individuals with avoidant tendencies, when exposed to a variety of stressors (i.e., physical, psychological, environmental, etc.) may manifest certain tendencies in order to cope with their circumstances, such as by becoming more reclusive. However, as the stressors persist and the individuals' coping resources become more limited, more signs of rigidity and inflexibility may surface. It is under such circumstances that these people may seek behaviors such as substance abuse to cope and to survive. The replenishment of coping resources through therapeu-

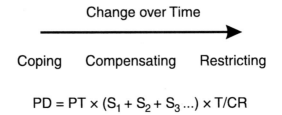

FIGURE 10.1. The Personality Continuum Index. (PD = personality disorder; PT = personality trait; S_1 = physical stress; S_2 = psychological stress; S_3 = environmental stress; T = time; CR = coping resources.)

tic means, hence, becomes a paramount focus of the process of rehabilitation and recovery.

THE CLASSIFICATION OF PERSONALITY DISORDERS ACCORDING TO THE DSM-IV

The fourth edition of the *Diagnostic and Statistical Manual of Mental Disorders* (APA, 1994) has proposed ten personality disorders placed under three distinct clusters. The clusters are based on configuration of defenses, interpersonal tendencies, and the core conflicts that are experienced by specific disorders.

1. *Cluster A:* This cluster includes "odd and eccentric" personality disorders such as paranoid, schizoid, and schizotypal. Individuals in this cluster often present with a restricted range of affect and may have a greater propensity for developing a thought disorder. They tend to be guarded and vigilant.
2. *Cluster B:* This cluster includes "dramatic and emotional" personality disorders such as antisocial, borderline, histrionic, and narcissistic. A large number of substance abusers tend to fall within this cluster. Emotionality and impulsivity are some of the most salient characteristics of these individuals. They also tend to be self-involved and exploitative in social situations.
3. *Cluster C:* This cluster includes "anxious and fearful" personality disorders such as avoidant, dependent, and obsessive-compulsive. People in this cluster tend to become easily overwhelmed under

stress. When in distress, they tend to manifest psychosomatic symptoms and may be particularly inclined to substance abuse.

Two additional personality disorders—that are not listed in these clusters due to a lack of sufficient empirical data, but appear in the Appendix B of the DSM-IV—are the depressive personality disorder and the passive-aggressive or negativistic personality, which fall under the anxious/fearful cluster in DSM-III-R (APA, 1987). Finally, the diagnosis of personality disorders not otherwise specified (personality disorder NOS) is reserved for those disorders that do not match the specifications of a particular personality disorder.

Many of the current studies that have explored the relationship between personality disorders and substance abuse suggest that in addition to Axis II disorders of antisocial, borderline, and histrionic, several other personality disorders such as dependent and avoidant may require attention, especially in terms of initial assessment and treatment protocols. These will be discussed in some detail in the next section although, because of the scope of the topic, the reader is encouraged to examine some of the source literature and suggested reading that appear in this section.

ANTISOCIAL PERSONALITY DISORDER

The term "antisocial" is often mistakenly used to describe a person with avoidant tendencies. In reality, people with antisocial personality disorder have very little, if anything, in common with those diagnosed with avoidant personality disorder. The antisocial personality tends to infringe upon the rights of others (APA, 1994). They usually fail to sustain good job performance over a period of several years, especially if they have to work alongside others. It has been observed that by the time they reach puberty they begin to show signs of aggressive sexual behavior. People with the antisocial personality almost always have difficulties with authority figures, a proclivity that follows them through life. Typical early childhood signs include fighting, chronic truancy, impulsive stealing, and excessive lying. In addition, at an early age, they begin abusing alcohol and other drugs (Millon, 1981). By the time they reach age thirty, it is not uncommon for these people to have compiled an extensive police record. A history of conduct disorder, starting about the age of fifteen, is essential to this diagnosis (APA, 1994). The inability to appropriately interact with authority figures often becomes a hallmark of this disorder and persists for a lifetime. Millon (1996) points out the strong overlap between substance abuse and the antisocial personality. He, however, emphasizes that this may be due more to social and economic pressures than to "intrapsychic" struggles.

At a drug and alcohol rehabilitation center, these individuals are commonly dismissed because of lack of compliance and a persistent reluctance to follow simple rules and facility regulations. Quay (1965) postulated that due to a much higher "threat-threshold," these patients sought "stimulating" and "exciting" activities, regardless of the consequences. You may often hear them say, "After you take care of my needs, I may entertain yours."

Individuals with the diagnosis of antisocial personality disorder tend to manifest the following features (also see DSM-IV diagnostic criteria, APA, 1994; Barley, 1986; Hare, 1991; Millon, 1981):

- Tend to become easily bored
- A need for constant stimulation
- Tendency to use charm to exploit others
- Inability to make or keep long-term plans
- Refusal to accept responsibility
- Poor behavioral controls
- Rarely experience guilt or remorse
- Inability to empathize with others

Treatment Suggestions

Persons with this diagnosis have difficulty comprehending the "interpersonal world." Secondary gain may be an important issue to consider when evaluating these individuals in a rehabilitation program. Finding a history of repeated recklessness, dangerousness, and criminality should give a strong indication as to the diagnosis of antisocial personality disorder.

Remember that when their needs are fulfilled, they can be very pleasant and even briefly compliant. Because of their impulsive nature, if instincts tell you that you are in danger, do not second-guess yourself. Ask for help from colleagues or be ready to contact the crisis center, especially if they use intimidation or threats. It is imperative that you do not reinforce their negative or destructive behavior by trying to engage them in an argument. A calm attitude will make a significant difference, especially in a crisis.

The literature on the treatment of antisocial personality disorder clearly suggests that behavior management is the best possible approach for working with these patients (e.g., Barley, 1986). Arguments and discourses about moral and ethical values rarely make a difference in terms of improving compliance. The therapist needs to be firm but not punitive. Define realistic limits clearly and enforce them without fail. Give the message that if they continue certain behaviors, you will not treat them. Be very clear, straightforward, and very concrete in stating your requirements. Honoring one exception means honoring a thousand. Therefore, adhere to your rules. Show interest in the patients, especially when they are following the rules. In time, they will find it difficult to act out because they do not want to lose the attention that they receive from you. Confront their behavior, actions, impulsiveness, but not their persons.

Your primary mode of relating to them should be reality based and not insight based. In therapy, it is best to deal with the here and now and not the past. As always, one of the most powerful methods of treating patients with difficult personality disorders is to be consistent. Consistency will reduce their anxiety and eventually reduces the chance of acting out behavior.

BORDERLINE PERSONALITY DISORDER

Freud (1931) first used the term "borderline" while trying to describe patients who did not respond to analysis and who seemed to develop psychotic tendencies when exposed to stress. Some have suggested that the term also describes a person who walks a tightrope between neurosis and psychosis (Grinker, Werble, and Drye, 1968). Although this at times is a possible presentation by the patient, a more current conceptualization of this disorder suggests a persistent pattern of experiencing instability in relationships, mood and emotional states, and a strong proclivity for acting impulsively (APA, 1994). Masterson (1981) suggested that in this disorder the person has internalized both accepting and rejecting parental objects, with the ego split between these introjects. This split ultimately prevents the self from becoming fully integrated, which results in the inability to control anxiety and to fend against impulsive, reactionary responses. In addition to splitting, some of the other ego defense mechanisms used by these individuals are the more primitive type such as denial and projection. Hence, when in a regressed state, it is difficult to rely on rational thinking as a method of active intervention. Chronic suicidality is one of the persistent features of this disorder. Rosenbluth and Silver (1992) pointed out that nearly ten percent of borderline patients succeed in committing suicide, and over 75 percent of them make numerous attempts at self-destruction.

Perhaps the word that best captures the very essence of the diagnosis of borderline personality disorder is *instability.* These patients manifest signs of instability and volatility, especially in their relationships. They are also plagued by impulsive and unpredictable responses to situations that may hint at any kind of demand or stress. Substance abuse may be a means of coping with such demands, especially when the individual's coping resources are diminished. A persistent fear of abandonment, which is often imagined, propels them to challenge furiously other people's promise of trust and support. Fear of abandonment may also cause them to become violent or physically self-damaging. When in crisis, they may develop uncertainty about self-image, gender identity, and values, and may find simple decision making almost impossible. Often individuals with the diagnosis of borderline personality disorder cannot tolerate being alone and tend to experience feelings of emptiness or boredom.

Patients with the diagnosis of borderline personality disorder often present with the following characteristics (also see DSM-IV diagnostic criteria, APA, 1994; Kernberg, 1975, 1984; Masterson, 1981; McWilliams, 1994):

- A diverse array of difficulties and symptoms, which may shift from week to week
- Impulsive and at times unpredictable behavior
- Intense, inappropriate reactions that are out of proportion to the situation
- Transient psychosis
- Tendency to confuse intimacy and sexuality
- Persistent suicidal ideations and attempts
- Strong ambivalence on many issues

- Significant difficulties with trust issues
- Rapid and often inappropriate shifts in mood and affect
- Strong tendency to idealize and devalue those who attempt to get close to them

Treatment Suggestions

The treatment of the patient with the borderline personality disorder in any setting is quite challenging and at times exhausting. Millon (1996) stated that these patients tend to be extremely dependent and require constant reassurance and support. Any thought of rejection is so terrifying to them that they prefer to end their life than to cope with the thought of being left alone. Ironically, it appears that they often go out of their way to make people reject them. It is this sort of "testing" that the therapist needs to acknowledge and confront.

To contain the extraordinary levels of anxiety experienced by these individuals, it is imperative that they are provided with structure and the utmost consistency. Make requirements for the treatment as clear as possible. Define goals as implicitly as possible so that there is no room for "guess work" on the part of the patients, which can invite manipulative behavior. The more predictable the sessions, the less anxiety they experience, and the more manageable they are. Do not hesitate to have them sign a contract if you see any hint of self-injurious behavior. In order to avoid acting-out and regressive behavior, the therapist must remain focused and confront defenses such as idealization, projection, and splitting (McWilliams, 1994). Use empathic interpretation, gentle confrontation, and clarification of their sources of distress in such situations.

In a rehabilitation setting, working with the borderline patient requires the combined team effort of clinicians and staff. Because of the importance of the issue of consistency, particularly with this population, it is imperative to make sure that everyone "speaks" the same language when it comes to enforcing rules and expectation. Otherwise, you may inadvertently invite manipulative behavior. I highly recommend discussing these cases during peer supervision sessions in order to regroup and get a different perspective of the patient and the treatment process.

HISTRIONIC PERSONALITY DISORDER

This is a disorder with the most visible manifestations. Patients with the histrionic personality disorder tend to be overly theatrical and flamboyant in terms of mannerism and speech (McWilliams, 1994). At the same time, these individuals tend to be overreactive and are perceived by others as extremely shallow, superficial, and insincere. The *Diagnostic and Statistical Manual of Mental Disorders* (DSM-IV) describes the essential features of the histrionic personality disorder as a persistent and excessive tendency to seek the attention of other people with an overly dramatic emotional presentation. Such tendencies become more noticeable by early adulthood (APA, 1994). These individuals usually have disturbed and often turbulent interpersonal relationships. While they tend to be seductive, they have poor sexual adjustment. Their spouses usually refer to them as sexually frigid or frustrating. Marital difficulties are quite common with these patients. These individuals draw attention to themselves by exaggerating feelings and emotions to the point that they cannot go unnoticed. Although they have a dramatic presentation with an excessive play with words, the essence of their message tends to lack substance and often is vague and devoid of any facts. Often they try to obtain admiration and find a way to gain the attention of their audience.

People with this diagnosis demand reassurance, approval, or praise from others. Ultimately, they will do anything to be loved. According to Mueller and Aniskiewicz (1986), deep down these individuals constantly grapple with the craving to be dependent, while at the same time they struggle with the fear of being viewed as vulnerable and needy. This is a major issue that can cause much frustration and confusion in their relationships. Struggles such as these compel them toward substance abuse. Millon (1996) also suggested that the histrionic person may use alcohol and drugs as a way of acting out certain impulses without the experience of remorse that may ensue.

Patients with the diagnosis of histrionic personality disorder often manifest the following features and characteristics (also see DSM-IV diagnostic criteria, APA, 1994; McWilliams, 1994; Mueller and Aniskowitz, 1986; Slavney, 1978):

- A persistent desire to be the center of attention
- People often label them as "actors" and do not take them seriously

- Often preoccupied with physical attractiveness
- May have frequent temper tantrums
- Tend become extremely angry if their "genuineness" is questioned
- Often driven by dependency needs
- Tend to act out sexually
- Live in a fantasy world where they can avoid the real issues

Treatment Suggestions

The histrionic patient is constantly trying to conceal tremendous sources of intrapsychic and interpersonal anxieties. They can talk for hours without allowing you to express a single thought. It is interesting to note that they may end up blaming their therapist for tiring them and "wasting the session." Hence, it is crucial that you structure your sessions and work on defined but not rigid goals. Be careful of their manipulative proclivity and a very real tendency to "punish" you if you do not pay enough attention to them. You need to be gently firm with them and reiterate goals from time to time. Do not reinforce their acting-out behaviors, especially in a group setting. In group therapy, it may be necessary to have very defined rules for the sessions, so as to avoid unnecessary interpersonal tension and monopolization of the time.

Because of their natural tendency to exaggerate feelings, sometimes it is difficult to readily determine whether the histrionic patient is in a true crisis state. Hence, it is crucial to spend an adequate amount of time with the patient in order to explore the cause of the distress. The first step in this process is to take whatever steps are necessary to bring the patient's anxiety under some control. Use statements such as, "I want to find out what is going on, but first you have to calm down." "I can see that you are very upset. Please stay focused; I want to help you. Explain to me what is upsetting you right now." When a reassuring tone of voice and demeanor make a discernible difference in the patient's physical and emotional presentation, it is likely that the situation is not critical. The main focus should be on anxiety reduction. Use active modes of distraction, but be attentive and show them that you are interested and listening.

Patient education is perhaps the most effective method of long-term treatment of a histrionic patient who is a substance abuser. This requires a well-defined plan of action. Be aware of the multitudes of distractions that the patient may introduce as you proceed with educational information. Whenever the patients beg for help, be very careful not to be seduced into the role of the savior, but guide the patients to become more directly involved in understanding the role of anxiety in the exacerbation of their symptoms. Remember, beneath an excited, animated mask lives a lonely and frightened person.

AVOIDANT PERSONALITY DISORDER

The diagnosis of avoidant personality disorder was first coined by Millon (1969) to describe a person who actively and persistently avoided engagement in social interactions. Patients with this diagnosis tend to be quite shy and withdrawn. Elsewhere, Millon (1996) has pointed out that avoidant personalities can be distinguished from schizoid personalities in their volitional drive to resist social involvement. A patient with this disorder is hypersensitive to criticism, which is perceived as a prelude to rejection. As a result, they tend to avoid relationships to safeguard themselves from the overwhelming pain of rejection (APA, 1994). Ironically, these individuals are "starved" for attention and human contact, although it appears that they literally go out of their way to avoid relationships.

People with the diagnosis of avoidant personality avoid entering into relationships unless they are given strong guarantees of uncritical acceptance (Millon, 1981). Hence, they are inclined to repeatedly test those who attempt to get close to them. In a therapeutic setting, they tend to appear vigilant and extremely guarded. Because of their persistent fear of rejection and their need for affection, these individuals live in a rich fantasy world that is often filled with images of tenderness, affection, intimacy, and attachment to others. From time to time, in a supportive and accepting therapeutic atmosphere, these individuals may allow their therapist to enter their elaborately constructed world of fantasy.

Patients with the diagnosis of avoidant personality disorder have a tendency to present with the following features (also see DSM-IV diagnostic criteria, APA, 1994; Millon, 1969; Widiger, 1992):

• Inability to tolerate anything that hints of criticism
• Constant fear of rejection

- Tendency to be very self-critical and self-deprecating
- Tendency to become overwhelmed in social situations
- Tendency to view themselves as socially inept and interpersonally incompetent
- Often live in a fantasy world where they are loved
- Appear to be constantly distracted
- May develop anxiety disorders, especially agoraphobia

Treatment Suggestions

In working with patients with avoidant personality disorder, it is important to realize that they expect to be rejected. Therefore, you must maintain a supportive and reassuring attitude. It is best to avoid criticism at all costs, even if it is meant for educational purposes. Instead, try to focus on their positive qualities with supportive coaching (Benjamin, 1996). Because of their self-deprecating and vigilant tendency, they may be especially sensitive to being physically approached. Respect their social space and instruct other staff to do the same.

As it was mentioned, people with avoidant personality often live in a fantasy world. This active fantasy life often helps them survive prolonged periods of social isolation. That is why they often appear distracted and disinterested in maintaining a dialogue. Hence, it is important to gain their attention before sharing new information with them. This may be gently accomplished by repeating their name as you talk to them.

In a rehabilitation setting, it is critical that they are not exposed to too much social stimulation at one time. The literature on substance abuse and the avoidant personality clearly suggests that they tend to prematurely terminate their treatment because of social discomfort (Fals-Stewart, 1992). It is best to expose them to social situations, such as treatment groups, in small doses. Meanwhile, structured and goal-focused individual therapy sessions can be most helpful in addressing issues of substance abuse. Focus on their positive qualities. Again, remember that they are starved for affection and your gentle, reassuring demeanor means a great deal to them. Finally, it may come as no surprise that these individuals often can interact better with animals than with people. Their pets are their best friends—often their only friends.

DEPENDENT PERSONALITY DISORDER

Many of the psychoanalytic theorists dedicated considerable writing to describing the dependent personality. Both Freud (1931) and Abraham (1924) viewed this disorder as relating to overindulgence or deprivation in the oral stage of development. Levy (1966) noted that children with a fixation in the oral stage of development showed manipulative tendencies, lacked initiative and drive, and tended to be demanding when the fulfillment of their needs were concerned.

The essential features of this disorder are getting others to assume responsibility for major areas of their lives and expecting others to attend to their needs. These individuals often tend to lack self-confidence, have a poor self-image, and exhibit intense discomfort when alone for brief periods (APA, 1994). Drug and alcohol use may be their desperate attempt at soothing themselves and to avoid facing some of their worst fears.

People with this diagnosis appear oversubmissive and show a strong fear of separation. It is as if they have never resolved the separation anxiety stage of development. These individuals may even endure all forms of abuse and humiliation to remain attached to someone who can take care of them. Similar to patients with the diagnosis of borderline personality disorder, these individuals show an overwhelming fear of abandonment. From a psychosomatic standpoint, they may develop medical conditions that require significant involvement by others in their daily care. Much like those with the avoidant personality, these individuals experience tremendous levels of anxiety, which may be the reason they gravitate toward substance abuse as a way of subduing their fears and trepidations. Because of a proneness toward the development of psychosomatic disorders, it is not uncommon for people with the dependent personality disorder to develop dependency on pharmaceutical agents, especially painkillers and anxiolytic agents.

Millon (1981) has noted that agoraphobia is often one of the more persistent presenting features of dependent persons. They are also prone to affective disorders, especially major depressive illness, which stems from the experience of overwhelming levels of helplessness and vulnerability.

Patients with the diagnosis of dependent personality disorder often present with the following characteristics (also see DSM-IV diagnostic criteria, APA, 1994; Millon, 1981, 1996; Benjamin, 1996):

- Tendency for strong depressive features
- Often suffer from adjustment disorder with anxiety and depression
- New responsibilities may cause anxiety or panic attacks
- Tend to belittle themselves
- A persistent engrossment with the fear of rejection
- Tend to easily agree with others
- Independence is synonymous with annihilation
- They can readily develop various medical symptoms in order to get attention
- Tendency to idealize their therapists

Treatment Suggestions

Anxiety management is perhaps the most important initial step that must be taken in the treatment of persons with the diagnosis of dependent personality. This can be best accomplished with a combination of psychotropic medications and anxiety-reduction techniques, as well as supportive forms of psychotherapy. By working on smaller goals, you can create the needed structure to contain apprehensive tendencies. Because of their poor self-confidence, it is best to engage them in activities that promote an increased sense of self-mastery. Make every attempt to focus on empowering them versus enabling them.

In working with patients with dependent personality disorder, you may note that, from time to time, they tend to exhibit regressive, childlike behavior. In such situations, it is prudent to remain supportive but avoid reinforcing such tendencies at all costs. The prolonged use of passive forms of therapy can be detrimental to the treatment process because of these individuals' insatiable desire to have things done for them instead of assuming responsibility for their needs and learning to take care of themselves.

Because "independence" is synonymous with "annihilation" to these individuals, it is crucial that you emphasize the need for improving their autonomy. Through active modeling, show them that gaining a sense of freedom can be exciting and very rewarding. You must hold their hands as you teach them to walk, so to speak. If it is up to them, they prefer to "use a wheelchair than to learn to walk alone" (Sadigh, 1998, p. 5).

Working with the dependent personality can be slow, arduous, and often quite frustrating. You need to remain patient and slowly work on specific goals. Again, be watchful of childlike, manipulative tendencies and encourage more responsible and mature behaviors. Improving the patient's social support network is an important task that requires much attention and planning.

CONCLUSION

A preponderance of literature suggests a significant relationship between personality disorders and a strong tendency for substance abuse. Contrary to some previous formulations, current studies have especially pointed out that substance abuse is not limited to the antisocial personality and may be seen in other disorders of personality. By gaining a better knowledge of the various personality styles, traits, and disorders, the clinician can more expediently move toward developing the appropriate therapeutic ambiance in order to address the patients' intrapsychic and interpersonal needs and concerns. Although the purpose of this chapter was not to provide a comprehensive examination of the different personality disorders, those personalities that tend to be most common in the substance-abusing population were examined in terms of their most salient features and treatment recommendations that may prove to be useful in a therapeutic, rehabilitation setting.

As it was pointed out, understanding people's personality characteristics is very much akin to learning to comprehend their intrapsychic and interpersonal "language" or mode of communication. When the therapist has a better understanding of this language, the task of conveying and achieving treatment expectations is more expediently realized. It is hoped that the reader will use this chapter as a stepping-stone toward gaining greater knowledge about personality disorders and their treatment.

REFERENCES

Abraham, K. (1924). *The influence of oral erotism on character formation: Selected papers on psychoanalysis.* London: Hogarth Press.

Allport, G.W. (1937). *Personality: A psychological interpretation.* New York: Holt, Rinehart and Winston.

American Psychiatric Association (APA) (1987). *Diagnostic and statistical manual of mental disorders* (DSM-III-R). Washington, DC: American Psychiatric Association.

American Psychiatric Association (APA) (1994). *Diagnostic and statistical manual of mental disorders* (DSM-IV). American Psychiatric Association. Washington, DC: American Psychiatric Association.

Barley, W. (1986). Behavioral and cognitive treatment of criminal and delinquent behavior. In W. Reid, D. Dorr, J. Walker, and J. Bonner (Eds.), *Unmasking the psychopath* (pp. 126-138). New York: Norton.

Benjamin, L.S. (1996). *Interpersonal diagnosis and treatment of personality disorders.* New York: The Guilford Press.

Corsini, R.J. (1977). *Current personality theories.* Itacsa, IL: F. E. Peacock.

Craig, R.J. (1984). Can personality tests predict treatment dropouts? *International Journal of the Addictions, 23,* 115-124.

Craig, R.J., Verinis, J.S., and Wexler, S. (1985). Personality characteristics of drug addicts and alcoholics on the Millon Clinical Multiaxial Inventory. *Journal of Personality Assessment, 49,* 156-160.

Donat, D.C. (1988). Millon Clinical Multiaxial Inventory (MCMI) clusters for alcohol abusers: Further evidence of validity and implications for medical psychotherapy. *Medical Psychotherapy, 1,* 41-50.

Fals-Stewart, W. (1992). Personality characteristics of substance abusers: An MCMI cluster typology of recreational drug users treated in a therapeutic community and its relationship to length of stay and outcome. *Journal of Personality Assessment, 59,* 515-527.

Fenichel, O.M. (1945). *The psychoanalytic theory of neurosis.* New York: W.W. Norton and Co.

Flynn, P., Luckey, J., Brown, B., Hoffman, J., Dunterman, G., Theisen, A., Hubbard, R., Needle, R., Schneider, S., Koman, J., Atef-Vahid, M., Karson, S., Palsgrove, G., and Yates, B. (1995). Relationship between drug preference and indicators of psychiatric impairment. *American Journal of Drug and Alcohol Abuse, 21,* 153-166.

Freud, S. (1931). *Libidinal types,* Standard edition (Volume 21). London: Hogarth Press.

Grinker, R.R., Werble, B., and Drye, R.C. (1968). *The borderline syndrome: A behavioral study of ego functions.* New York: Basic Books.

Hare, R. (1991). The Hare Psychopathy Checklist (Revised). Toronto: Multihealth Systems.

Kernberg, O.F. (1975). *Borderline conditions and pathological narcissism.* New York: Jason Aronson.

Kernberg, O.F. (1984). *Severe personality disorders.* New Haven, CT: Yale University Press.

Lesswing, G.L. and Dougherty, R.J. (1993). Psychopathology in alcohol and cocaine dependent patients: A comparison of findings from psychological testing. *Journal of Substance Abuse Treatment, 10,* 53-57.

Levy, D. (1966). *Maternal overprotection.* New York: W. W. Norton.

Masterson, J.F. (1981). *Narcissistic and borderline disorders: An integrated developmental approach.* New York: Brunner/Mazel.

McMahon, R., Kelly, A., and Kouzekanani, K. (1993). Personality and coping styles in the prediction of dropout from treatment for cocaine abuse. *Journal of Personality Assessment, 61,* 147-155.

McWilliams, N. (1994). *Psychoanalytic diagnosis: Understanding personality structure in the clinical process.* New York: The Guilford Press.

Millon, T. (1969). *Modern psychopathology: A biosocial approach to maladaptive learning and functioning.* Philadelphia, PA: Saunders.

Millon, T. (1981). *Disorders of personality: DSM-III, Axis II.* New York: Wiley.

Millon, T. (1996). *Disorders of personality: DSM-IV and beyond.* New York: Wiley.

Mueller, W.J. and Aniskiewicz, A.S. (1986). *Therapeutic intervention in hysterical disorders.* Northvale, NJ: Jason Aronson.

Pettinati, H.M., Pierce, J.D., Belden, P.P., and Meyers, K. (1999). The relationship of Axis II personality disorders to other known predictors of addiction treatment outcome. *The American Journal of Addictions, 8,* 136-147.

Quay, H.C. (1965). Psychopathic personality as pathological stimulation seeking. *American Journal of Psychiatry, 122,* 180-183.

Rosenbluth, M. and Silver, D. (1992). *Handbook of borderline disorders.* Madison, CT: International University Press.

Sadigh, M.R. (1998). Chronic pain and personality disorders: Implications for rehabilitation practice. *The Journal of Rehabilitation, 64,* 4-8.

Skodol, A.E., Oldham, J.M., and Gallaher, P.E. (1999). Axis II comorbidity of substance use disorders among patients referred for treatment of personality disorders. *American Journal of Psychiatry, 156,* 733-738.

Slavney, P.R. (1978). The diagnosis of histrionic personality disorder: A study of attitudes. *Comprehensive Psychiatry, 19,* 510-507.

Thomas, V.H., Melchert, T.P., and Banken, J.A. (1997). Substance dependence and personality disorders: Comorbidity and treatment outcome in an inpatient treatment population. *Journal of Studies of Alcohol, 60,* 271-277.

Verheul, R., van den Brink, W., and Hartgers, C. (1998). Personality disorders predict relapse in alcoholic patients. *Addictive Behaviors, 23,* 869-882.

Widiger, T.A. (1992). Generalized social phobia versus avoidant personality disorder: A commentary on three studies. *Journal of Abnormal Psychology, 101,* 340-343.

Index

Page numbers followed by the letter "b" indicate boxed material; those followed by the letter "i" indicate illustrations.

Order a copy of this book with this form or online at:
http://www.haworthpressinc.com/store/product.asp?sku=4597

MANAGING THE DUALLY DIAGNOSED PATIENT
Current Issues and Clinical Approaches

_____in hardbound at $49.95 (ISBN: 0-7890-0876-9)

_____in softbound at $27.95 (ISBN: 0-7890-0877-7)

COST OF BOOKS_____

OUTSIDE USA/CANADA/
MEXICO: ADD 20%____

POSTAGE & HANDLING_____
(US: $4.00 for first book & $1.50
for each additional book)
Outside US: $5.00 for first book
& $2.00 for each additional book)

SUBTOTAL_____

in Canada: add 7% GST____

STATE TAX____
(NY, OH & MIN residents, please
add appropriate local sales tax)

FINAL TOTAL____
(If paying in Canadian funds,
convert using the current
exchange rate, UNESCO
coupons welcome.)

☐ **BILL ME LATER:** ($5 service charge will be added)
(Bill-me option is good on US/Canada/Mexico orders only;
not good to jobbers, wholesalers, or subscription agencies.)

☐ Check here if billing address is different from
shipping address and attach purchase order and
billing address information.

☐ Signature_____

☐ **PAYMENT ENCLOSED: $_____**

☐ **PLEASE CHARGE TO MY CREDIT CARD.**

☐ Visa ☐ MasterCard ☐ AmEx ☐ Discover
☐ Diner's Club ☐ Eurocard ☐ JCB

Account # _____

Exp. Date_____

Signature_____

Prices in US dollars and subject to change without notice.

NAME_____

INSTITUTION_____

ADDRESS_____

CITY_____

STATE/ZIP_____

COUNTRY_____ COUNTY (NY residents only)_____

TEL_____ FAX_____

E-MAIL_____

May we use your e-mail address for confirmations and other types of information? ☐ Yes ☐ No
We appreciate receiving your e-mail address and fax number. Haworth would like to e-mail or fax special
discount offers to you, as a preferred customer. **We will never share, rent, or exchange your e-mail address
or fax number.** We regard such actions as an invasion of your privacy.

Order From Your Local Bookstore or Directly From
The Haworth Press, Inc.
10 Alice Street, Binghamton, New York 13904-1580 • USA
TELEPHONE: 1-800-HAWORTH (1-800-429-6784) / Outside US/Canada: (607) 722-5857
FAX: 1-800-895-0582 / Outside US/Canada: (607) 722-6362
E-mail: getinfo@haworthpressinc.com
PLEASE PHOTOCOPY THIS FORM FOR YOUR PERSONAL USE.
www.HaworthPress.com

BOF02